THE ADMINISTRATION OF JUSTICE IN THE COURTS

Book Two: The Administration of Criminal Justice in the Courts

A Selected Annotated Bibliography
Compiled and Annotated
by Fannie J. Klein, LL.B., LL.M.
Associate Professor of Law, Emerita.
Updating and Expanding
Klein, Judicial Administration
and the Legal Profession (1963).

Published for the

Institute of Judicial Administration and
National Center for State Courts

by

OCEANA PUBLICATIONS
Dobbs Ferry, New York

1976.

This project was supported by Grant Number 73 DF 99-0002 awarded by the Law Enforcement Assistance Administration, U.S. Department of Justice, under the Omnibus Crime Control and Safe Streets Act of 1968, as amended. Points of view or opinions stated in this document are those of the contracting agency and do not necessarily represent the official position or policies of the U.S Department of Justice.

Library of Congress Cataloging in Publication Data

Klein, Fannie J
    The administration of justice in the courts.

    Includes indexes.
    CONTENTS: book 1. The courts.--book 2. The administration of criminal justice in the courts.
    1. Justice, Administration of--United States--Bibliography. 2. Courts--United States--Bibliography. I. Title
KF8700.A1K39   016.347'73'1   76-2627
ISBN 0-379-10137-8 (v. 1)
ISBN 0-379-10138-6 (v. 2)

Manufactured in the United States of America

TABLE OF CONTENTS

BOOK ONE

THE COURTS

BOOK TWO

THE ADMINISTRATION OF

CRIMINAL JUSTICE IN THE COURTS

BOOK TWO

THE ADMINISTRATION OF CRIMINAL

JUSTICE IN THE COURTS

VI.   THE CRIMINAL JUSTICE SYSTEM

A. The Administration of Criminal Justice - General

   1. This section is an amalgam of items cover-
       ing more than one area of the entire spec-
       trum of the administration of criminal jus-
       tice and reform; also included are selected
       items on the administration of juvenile jus-
       tice, police administration, the incidence
       of crime generally, and other areas related
       to but not within the subject content of
       this bibliography; i.e., juvenile justice,
       the police, the penal system, probation
       and parole, criminology, and corrections
       are subjects not within the orbit of this
       bibliography.

ABA Minimum Standards for Criminal Justice -- a student symposium.
La L Rev 33:541-612 (1973).
                    Why the ABA Standards, by Justice Tom Clark, discusses
                    the implementation of the Standards throughout the
                    nation; students discuss the Standards generally, with
                    particular reference to implementation in Louisiana.
                                                                    3197

ALLEN, F.A.   The borderland of criminal justice: essays in law and
criminology. Chicago, Univ Chicago press, 1964. 139 p.
                    Seven of the author's essays with a common theme:
                    delineation of the scope of the criminal law in light
                    of our experience with criminal sanctions and the
                    development of social sciences. Contents: Legal
                    values and the rehabilitative ideal--Juvenile court
                    and the limits of juvenile justice--Garofalo's crim-
                    inology and some modern problems--Reflections on
                    hanging--Criminal responsibility and the Model Penal
                    Code--Criminal law and the future.   3198

AMERICAN Academy of Political and Social Science. Combating crime;
ed. by L.E. Ohlin and H.S. Ruth, Jr. Annals 374:1-169 (1967).
                    Selected contents: McIntyre, J. Public attitudes to-
                    ward crime and law enforcement.--Reiss, A.J. Jr.,
                    Black, D.D. Interrogation and the criminal process.--
                    Terris, B.J. The role of the police.--Rosett, A. The

negotiated guilty plea.--Blumstein, A. Systems analysis and the criminal justice system.--Gardiner, J.A.
Public attitudes toward gambling and corruption. <u>3199</u>

AMERICAN Academy of Political and Social Science, Philadelphia. The
future of corrections, ed. by J.P. Conrad. Annals 381:1-171 (1969).
<u>Contents</u>: Conrad, J.P. Introduction.--McGee, R.A.
What's past is prologue.--Platt, A. The rise of the
child-saving movement: a study in social policy and
correctional reform. I. Programs: Turner, M. The
lessons of Norman House.--Warren, M.Q. The case for
differential treatment of delinquents.--Luger, M.
Innovations in the treatment of juvenile offenders.--
Burdman, M. Realism in community-based correctional
services. II. New administrative forms: Moeller, H.G.
The continuum of corrections.--Bradley, H.B. Designing
for change: problems of planned innovation in corrections.--O'Leary, V. Some directions for citizen
involvement in corrections. III. Special problems:
Mattick, H.W., Aikman, A.B. The cloacal region of
American corrections.--Wolfgang, M.E. Corrections and
the violent offender. IV. Research: Wilkins, L.T.,
Gitchoff, T. Trends and projections in social control
systems.--Morris, N., Zimring, F. Deterrence and corrections.--Crowther, C. Crimes, penalties, and legislatures.   <u>3200</u>

AMERICAN Assembly. Ombudsman for American Government? ed. by S.V.
Anderson. Englewood Cliffs, N.J., Prentice-Hall, 1968. 188 p.
<u>Contents</u>: Anderson, S.V. Introduction.--Rowat, D.C.
The spread of the ombudsman idea.--Gwyn, W.B. Trans-
ferring the ombudsman.--Moore, J.E. State government
and the ombudsman.--Angus, W.H., Kaplan, M. The ombudsman and local government.--Anderson, S.V. Proposals and politics.--Gellhorn, W. Annotated model
ombudsman statute. 8-p. bibliography.   <u>3201</u>

AMERICAN Bar Association Project on Standards for Criminal Justice.
Standards relating to the administration of criminal justice; compilation with index. N.Y., IJA, 1974. 641 p.
R.A.Green, proj. dir. Text of each of the 17 Standards,
as approved and published in its original separate
edition [see items <u>3203a</u> to <u>3203r</u>], including introductions, but without commentary and supporting material. Newly added are: cross-references to related
sections of the other Standards; citations, limited
to "a few Supreme Court decisions of constitutional
dimension" that might affect a Standard; and the comprehensive, 152-p. index. Appendices on the committees
involved give history and personnel of the project.
                                                     <u>3202</u>

AMERICAN Bar Association. Project on Standards for Criminal Justice. [Originally called Project on Minimum Standards for Criminal
Justice] Institute of Judicial Administration, Secretariat. J.E.
Lumbard, chair., 1967-68, W.E. Burger, 1968-69, W.J. Jameson thereafter. R.A. Green, proj. dir. N.Y., IJA, 1966-73. 17 v.   **3203**

Standards are (grouped by author-committee):

Advisory Committee on the Criminal Trial. W.V. Schaefer, chair.;
W.R. LaFave, reptr.

Standards relating to joinder and severance. Tent. draft,
Nov. 1967. 68 p. Amendments Sep. 1968. 5 p. App'd Aug. 1968.
3203a

Standards relating to pleas of guilty. Tent. draft, Feb. 1967.
78 p. Prop'd rev., Dec. 1967. 5 p. (Reprinted as Supp., Mar.
1968). App'd Feb. 1968. (see item **3601**)   **3203b**

Standards relating to speedy trial. Tent. draft, May 1967.
56 p. App'd Feb. 1968. (see item **4157**)   **3203c**

Standards relating to trial by jury. Tent. draft, May 1968.
180 p. Amendments, Supp. Sep. 1968. 5 p. App'd Aug. 1968.
(see item **2512**)   **3203d**

Advisory Committee on Fair Trial and Free Press. P.C. Reardon,
chair.; D.L. Shapiro, reptr.

Standards relating to fair trial and free press. Tent. draft,
Dec. 1966. 265 p. Rev. of tent. draft, July 1967. 36 p. Prop'd
final draft, Dec. 1967. 36 p. App'd draft, Mar. 1968. 36 p.
App'd Feb. 1968. (see item **4066**)   **3203e**

Advisory Committee on Judge's Function. F.J. Murray, chair.;
T.J. O'Toole, reptr.

Standards relating to the judge's role in dealing with trial
disruptions (an advance report of part of Standards relating
to the function of the trial judge). May 1971. 22 p. App'd
July 1971, with revisions. (see item **3960**)   **3203f**

Standards relating to the function of the trial judge. Tent
draft, June 1972. 103 p. App'd Aug. 1972. [Includes Standards
relating to the judge's role in dealing with trial disruptions, as approved] (see item **3959**)   **3203g**

Advisory Committee on the Police Function. R.B. Austin, chair.;
G.R. Blakey, reptr.

Standards relating to electronic surveillance. Tent. draft,
June 1968. 250 p. Prop'd final draft, Feb. 1971. 27 p. App'd

Feb. 8, 1971. Supp., app'd draft, Mar. 1971. 30 p. (see item 4537)   3203h

Standards relating to the police function. Tent. draft, Mar. 1972. 303 p.[App'd with amendments, Feb. 1973] (see item 3416)   3203i

Advisory Committee on Pretrial Proceedings. A.P. Murrah, chair.

Standards relating to discovery and procedure before trial. D.G. Gibbens, reptr. Tent. draft, May 1969. 167 p. Supp. Oct. 1970. 8 p. App'd Aug. 1970. (see item 3641)   3203j

Standards relating to pretrial release. C.E Ares, reptr. Tent. draft, Mar. 1968. 88 p. Amendments, Supp. Sep. 1968. 5 p. App'd Aug. 1968. (see item 3531)   3203k

Advisory Committee on the Prosecution and Defense Function. W.E. Burger, chair., 1964-69, W.F. Rogosheske, thereafter; L.J. Mazor, reptr.

Standards relating to the prosecution function and the defense function. Tent. draft, Mar. 1970. 327 p. Supp. Mar. 1971. 21 p. App'd Feb. 1971. (see item 3692)   3203L

Standards relating to providing defense services. Tent. draft, June 1967. 85 p. App'd Feb. 1968. (see item 3786)   3203m

Advisory Committee on Sentencing and Review. S.E. Sobeloff, chair.

Standards relating to appellate review of sentences. P.W. Low, reptr. Tent. draft, Apr. 1967. 160 p. Amendments Dec. 1967. 5 p. Amendments, Supp., Mar. 1968, 5 p. App'd Feb. 1968. (see item 4478)   3203n

Standards relating to criminal appeals. C.R. Reitz, reptr. Tent. draft, Mar. 1969. 109 p. Amendments, Supp. Oct. 1970. 7 p. App'd Aug. 1970. (see item 4537)   3203o

Standards relating to post-conviction remedies. C.R. Reitz, reptr. Tent. draft, Jan. 1967. 123 p. App'd Feb. 1968. (see item 4564)   3203p

Standards relating to probation. H.S. Miller, reptr. Tent. draft, Feb. 1970. 110 p. App'd Aug. 1970.

3203q

Standards relating to sentencing alternatives and procedures. P.W. Low, reptr. Tent. draft., Dec. 1967. 345 p. Amendments, Sep. 1968. 9 p. App'd Aug. 1968. (see item 4319)   3203r

AMERICAN Bar Association Section of Criminal Justice. Comparative analysis of standards and goals of the National Advisory Commission on Criminal Justice Standards and Goals with standards for criminal justice of the American Bar Association. Washington, 1973. 594 p.
> Consists of black letter texts arranged side by side with comment, usually confined to "Consistent in principle," or "Inconsistent..." Preface by J.G. Day, Section chair., reviews both projects.   3204

AMERICAN Bar Association Section of Criminal Law. Criminal case in England: from arrest through appeal. Am Crim L Rev 10:261-331 (1971).
> Section chair: S. Dash. Edited transcript of proceedings and panel discussion involving American and English participants that took place during the annual meeting of the ABA in London, 1971.   3205

AMERICAN Bar Association Section of Criminal Law. Report of Pilot Study Committee on Minimum Standards for Criminal Justice. Chicago, 1964. 13 p.
> The scope and purpose of the project to formulate minimum standards are described and methods of operation, organization and budget are recommended.   3206

AMERICAN Bar Association Section of Criminal Law Committee to Implement Standards of Criminal Justice.

> Following are some of the comparisons of the Standards with individual state law, prepared as part of the Project's implementation phase. They are arranged alphabetically by state.

COMPARATIVE analysis of American Bar Association Standards for criminal justice with Alabama law, rules and legal practice. Birmingham, 1975. 348 p.   3207

CRIMINAL procedure: a survey of Arkansas law and the American Bar Association's Standards. Ark L Rev 26:169-208 (1972).   3208

COMPARATIVE analysis of American Bar Association Minimum standards for criminal justice with California law, prep. for the Judicial Council of Calif. by its special Advisory Committee, M. M. Marcus, chair. Sacramento, 1974. 459 p.   3209

COMPARATIVE analysis of American Bar Association Standards for criminal justice with Connecticut law, rules, and practice, prep. by Junior Bar Section, Conn. Bar Assn. Hartford, 1973. 1 v., var. pag.   3210

COMPARATIVE analysis of nine approved American Bar Association Standards for the administration of criminal justice with Florida statutory law, court rules, and legal practice, by the Spessard L. Holland Law Center (U. of Fla.) and the State Committee for

Implementation of the Standards for Criminal Justice. Jackson,
1970. 136 p.   3211

AMERICAN Bar Association Standards for the administration of
criminal justice: <u>Illinois</u> compliance, by S.A. Schiller.
Chicago, Chi B Assn, 1974. 444 p.   3212

COMPARATIVE study of ABA Standards of criminal justice with
present <u>Indiana</u> law and the proposed code of criminal procedure,
by C.A. Thompson and B.J. Small. Indianapolis, 1972. 745 p.
                                                                 3213

COMPARATIVE analysis of American Bar Association Standards for
criminal justice with <u>Kansas</u> law, rules, and legal practice,
by A. Hotchkiss ₍and others₎ . Topeka, 1972. 1 v., var. pag.
                                                                 3214

_____. 1974 supp. Topeka, 1975.
           (Consists of index, replacement pages)   3214a

COMPARATIVE analysis of American Bar Association Standards for
criminal justice with <u>Kentucky</u> laws, rules, and legal practice,
by P.M. Hopkins ₍and others₎. Frankfort, 1974. 255 p.   3215

REPORT and recommendations to implement the American Bar Association Standards for criminal justice, by the joint committees
of <u>Maryland</u> Judicial Conference and Maryland State Bar Association. Annapolis, 1974. 1 v., var. pag.   3216

COMPARATIVE analysis of American Bar Association Standards for
criminal justice with <u>Michigan</u> laws, rules, and legal practice,
by B.J. George ₍and others₎. Lansing, 1972. 1 v., var. pag.
                                                                 3217

COMPARATIVE analysis of American Bar Association standards for
criminal justice with <u>Minnesota</u> laws, rules, and legal practice,
by J.M. Livermore, D.L. Graven, and W. Danforth. St. Paul, 1971.
207 p.   3218

COMPARATIVE analysis of American Bar Association Standards for
the administration of criminal justice with <u>Mississippi</u> law, by
M. Featherstone, D. Raines. Jackson, 1973. 310 p.   3219

COMPARATIVE analysis of American Bar Association Standards for
criminal justice with <u>Missouri</u> laws, rules, and legal practice,
by R. Popper, J. Scurlock ₍and others₎. Kansas City, 1971.
209 p.   3220

COMPARATIVE analysis of sixteen approved American Bar Association Standards for the administration of criminal justice with
<u>New Jersey</u> statutory law, court rules, and case law, by R. Knowl-
ton. Trenton, 1972. 1 v., var. pag.   3221

COMPARATIVE analysis of American Bar Association Standards for
criminal justice with New York state law, rules, and legal
practice, by B.C. Agata. N.Y., 1972. 219 p.   3222

COMPARATIVE analysis of American Bar Association Standards for
criminal justice with North Dakota law, rules, and practice, by
L. Kraft [and others]. Bismarck, 1973. 1 v., var. pag.   3223

COMPARATIVE analysis of American Bar Association Standards for
criminal justice with South Carolina law, rules, and practice,
and with the proposed Code for South Carolina Criminal Procedure,
R.C. McCollough, II [and others]; J. Thames, reptr. Columbia,
U of S.C. Law Center, 1974. 667 p.   3224

COMPARATIVE analysis of American Bar Association Standards for
criminal justice with Tennessee laws, rules, and legal practice.
J.A. Moore, proj. dir. Memphis, Memphis State U School of Law,
1974. 1 v., var. pag.   3225

COMPARATIVE analysis of American Bar Association Standards for
criminal justice with Virginia laws, rules, and legal practice,
by R.E. Walck, T.A. Collins, and T.J. Sullivan. Richmond, 1973.
1 v., var. pag.   3226

COMPARATIVE analysis of ABA Standards for criminal justice with
Washington law, rules, and legal practice, by D.L. Chisum, J.M.
Junker, and F. Smith. Seattle, 1972. 516 p.   3227

AMERICAN Bar Association Section of Judicial Administration Special
Committee on Crime Prevention and Control. Citizens against crime;
a crime prevention program for state and local bar associations.
Chicago, 1968. 23 p.
          Booklet outlining organization of citizens groups; de-
          scribing first project; lists future projects.   3228

AMERICAN Bar Association's impact on the Organized Crime Control Act
of 1970. Am Crim L Q 9:1-184 (1970).
          With an introduction by Samuel Dash, chair., almost
          the entire issue is devoted to data regarding the ABA's
          impact upon the Act as finally passed, including ABA
          report and testimony of its representatives. Act itself
          is presented.   3229

AMERICAN Bar Foundation Administration of criminal justice series.
     DAWSON, R.O. Sentencing: the decision as to type, length, and
     conditions of sentence. 1969. (item 4346)

     LAFAVE, W.R. Arrest: the decision to take a suspect into cus-
     tody. 1965. (item 3438)

     MILLER, F.W. Prosecution: the decision to charge a suspect with
     a crime. 1969 (item 3715)

NEWMAN, D.J. Conviction: the determination of guilt or innocence without trial. 1966. (item 3622)

TIFFANY, L.P. Detection of crime: stopping and questioning,
search and seizure, encouragement and entrapment. 1967. 3230

AMERICAN Bar Foundation. Law enforcement in the metropolis; a working paper on the criminal law system in Detroit, ed. by D.M. McIntyre, Jr. Chicago, A B Found, 1967. 234 p.
          A description covering detection and identification,
          arrest, charging, adjudication, disposition, proba-
          tion, parole, pardon, and commutation of sentence,
          and the supervision and revocation of parole. The re-
          search material consisted of accounts of observations
          and supplemental interviews by ten field researchers;
          data were then reviewed and categorized by a super-
          visory staff with the objective of presenting a com-
          plete picture of law enforcement in one locale. (For
          five reports based on this and further research mater-
          ial, see item 3230.)   3231

AMERICAN Enterprise Institute for Public Policy Research. The economics of crime and punishment. Washington, Amer Enterprise Inst.,
1973. 232 p.
          A collection of essays expressing an economic approach
          to criminal behavior by a panel primarily composed of
          economists. Economic tools and methods are applied to
          determine criminal motives, deterrence of punishment,
          and viability of organized crime. Gives an overview of
          English and Continental criminal systems with analyses
          through economist's perspective.   3232

AMERICAN Friends Service Committee. Struggle for justice, a report
on crime and punishment in America. N.Y., Hill & Wang, 1971. 179 p.
          1. The nature of the problem. 2. Crime and punishment.
          3. Fallacy of individualized treatment model. 4. Gen-
          eral pertinence. 5. Crime prevention. 6. Crime of
          treatment. 7. Repressive functions of the criminal jus-
          tice system. 8. Discretion. 9. Proper role of criminal
          law. Bibliography.   3233

ASHFORD, H.A. and RISINGER, D.M. Presumptions, assumptions, and due
process in criminal cases: a theoretical overview. Yale L J 79:165-
208 (1969).
          Constitutional tests used to evaluate presumptive
          language contain serious flaws in both civil and crim-
          inal cases; leading cases examined to demonstrate how
          legal devices based on presumptions infringe on con-
          stitutional rights of criminal defendents. Suggests
          standards for presumptions that insure constitutionality
          of guilt-determining process and due process; ALI Model

Penal Code presumptions analyzed; problems of wording
in criminal statutes demonstrated; assumptions defined
and distinguished.   3234

AUERBACH, Associates, Inc. Criminal justice glossary. Draft II.
Philadelphia, 1973. 367 p.
Definitions of criminal justice terms commonly used
in criminal courts; App. A: courts by name in each
state; bibliography. Work done under LEAA grant; objective is to unify criminal justice terms - first
step in collection of uniform statistics.   3235

BARRETT, E., Jr. Criminal justice; the problem of mass production.
In American Assembly. The courts, the public, and the law explosion,
H. Jones, ed. Englewood Cliffs, N.J., Prentice-Hall, 1965. p. 85-
123.
Realities of criminal justice in lower trial courts;
in presenting a rundown of the system, Dean Barrett
stresses workload of each component of the system and
how it is processed (mass production) using California
courts as example. Suggests basic reforms to upgrade
these courts, improve their financing, and reduce
workload through civil penalties.   3236

BAZELON, D.L. Adversary process; who needs it? 12th James Madison
lecture delivered at New York University, April 21, 1971.
Published under various titles: New gods for old; efficient courts in a democratic society. NYU L Rev 46:
653-74 (1971) (see item 3238); excerpts as: Benefits
of judicial efficiency may have been oversold. Crim.
Justice Newsletter 2:66, 72 (1971); Speed-up in courts
is no cure-all for crime. Cong. Rec. 117:13398-9 (1971).
                                                         3237

BAZELON, D.L. New gods for old: efficient courts in a democratic
society. NYU L Rev 46:653-74 (1971). (James Madison lect. 12)
Judge Bazelon criticizes "speedy conviction of criminals" as an end-all. If "increased judicial efficiency"
means courts giving cursory examination of responses
to problems generated by criminal behavior, Judge
Bazelon does not approve. He enlarges on his ideas as
to the "judicial function" stressing the need to "force
into high public visibility the actions that are taken
by all official and unofficial participants in the
criminal process, and the justification of those actions." He describes the progress of courts in attempting to devise a scientific test for the insanity defense to illustrate that more time is needed today rather than less. "The way towards efficiency in the
courts is not to short-cut judicial procedures in order to dispose of more cases in less time...the way
to make courts more efficient is to deal with the

factors that cause people to commit their crimes."
He then proceeds to attack ABA proposals based on English criminal practices that deprive rather than protect criminal defendant's rights particularly in appellate procedure, and discusses shortcomings of the
criminal justice system in many areas, including plea
bargaining. In conclusion, he remarks that the judicial process is at its core fundamentally inefficient.
There are problems the courts cannot solve, but they
can take a close look to bring out hidden factors to
assure that responsible agencies are dealing with the
problem. He cautions against eliminating this judicial
function of bringing out hidden factors "on the altar
of the Great God Efficiency." (see also item 3237)
3238

BAZELON, D.L. The future of reform in the administration of justice. FRD 35:99-114 (1964). (Edward D. White lectures in law)
Thesis is that the criminal law should "abandon myth
of total individual responsibility and adapt to realities of scientific and psychiatric knowledge"; discusses standards for the insanity defense and social
causation of crimes of violence and theories of deterrence. The common law is flexible and can provide
tools to adapt itself to new scientific and psychiatric
knowledge.   3239

BEDAU, H.A., ed. The death penalty in America: an anthology. Garden City, N.Y., Doubleday, 1964. 598 p.
A comprehensive collection of information surrounding
capital punishment by a philosophy professor beginning
with an examination of capital crimes. Some topics
covered are arguments for and against the death penalty,
a survey of public reaction to the problem, and several
case histories. 11-p bibliography.   3240

BELL, D.A., Jr. Racism in American courts: cause for black disruption or despair? Calif L Rev 61:165-203 (1973).
Law professor cites, among others, study by President's
Crime Commission on conditions in the criminal courts
as supportive of his charge of racism. He discusses
the effect of racism on black people in general, and
black lawyers or law students, in particular.   3241

BILEK, A.J. America's criminal justice system - a diagnosis and
prognosis. In Change process in criminal justice...papers presented
at 4th National Symposium on Law Enforcement Science and Technology,
1972. Washington, USGPO, 1973. (Crim. Jus. Monographs) p. 85-110.
Discusses the limitations of the criminal justice system as to its deterrent effect and impact on causes of
crime; suggests the proper role for an effective criminal justice system and why the present system is not
fulfilling its role, including lack of coordination

> between branches of government, fragmentation of re-
> sponsibilities, and misplaced priorities leading to
> overcriminalization; offers suggestions for planning,
> improving law enforcement, correctional priorities,
> the prosecutorial function, and the courts.   3242

BOTEIN, B. Our cities burn while we play cops and robbers. N.Y.,
Simon & Schuster, 1972. 192 p.
> After commenting on dearth of information as to causes
> of crime and lack of action to remedy, former presid-
> ing judge presents short-range program to cope with
> crime in the streets. Makes recommendations to strength-
> en police, the courts, correction.   3243

BRATTON, H.C. Standards for the administration of criminal justice.
Natural Resources J 10:127-36 (1970).
> History and current status of the ABA Project on Stan-
> dards for Administration of Criminal Justice discussed
> by U.S. District Court judge; comments on judicial
> attention to Standards, citing cases.   3244

BREITEL, C.D. Criminal law and equal justice. Utah L Rev 1966: 1-19.
> Judge Breitel considers the question of equality of
> treatment of the poor and rich before the criminal
> law, particularly with respect to police power to stop
> and frisk and to conduct interrogations.   3245

BROWNELL, H. Crime and the courts, speech at Appellate Judges Conference, San Francisco, Aug. 11, 1972. N.Y., 1972. 18 p.
> Former United States Attorney General asserts that in
> order for the criminal justice system to function
> effectively, it must be coordinated and well-financed.
> He discusses two programs for court administrative im-
> provement: the establishment of the Institute for
> Court Management to train court administrators and the
> development of court rules and security arrangements
> for dealing with disruptive criminal trials.   3246

BURGER, W.E. For whom the bell tolls; remarks...Association of the
Bar of the City of New York, Feb. 17, 1970. Washington, 1970. 17 p.
> Chief Justice Burger reminds his audience that the pur-
> poses of any system of justice are to protect society
> and correct the wrongdoer, and he criticizes us for
> having failed to develop an effective system of correc-
> tion and rehabilitation. He deplores prison conditions
> and stresses the need for change.   3247

BURGER, W.E. New Chief Justice's philosophy of law in America.
NYSB J 41:454-79 (1969).
> Included because this address categorically defines
> author's criticism of our system of criminal justice;
> it is suggested these ideas "weighed heavily" in his

selection as Chief Justice.   3248

BURGER, W.E. Proposal: a national conference on correctional problems.
[Speech] Aug. 11, 1969, Dallas, Tex. Washington, 1969. 8 p.
        Calls for the ABA to initiate an examination of the
        penal-correctional system similar in scope to the
        ABA's criminal justice project.   3249

BURGER, W.E. Remarks ... at the prayer breakfast, ABA meeting, St.
Louis, Aug. 9, 1970. Washington, 1970. 4 p.
        Discusses the responsibility of the bench and bar to
        strengthen the judicial system and reform our correc-
        tional institutions.   3250

CASPER, J.D. American criminal justice, the defendant's perspective.
Englewood Cliffs, N.J., Prentice-Hall, 1972. 178 p.
        Interviews of seventy-one Connecticut defendants; their
        attitudes toward arrest, police, plea bargaining, pro-
        secutors, judges and defense counsel; discussion of
        the causes of crime.   3251

CASPER, J.D. Criminal justice: the consumer's perspective. Washington, USGPO, 1972. 62 p.
        The following areas in the American criminal justice
        system are examined from the viewpoint of the defen-
        dant: 1) arrest and plea-bargaining; 2) his perception
        of his attorney, the prosecutor, the judge, and his
        sentence; 3) his notions of the law and the causes of
        deviate behavior. Based on interviews with 71 accused
        felons in Connecticut, author concludes that defendant's
        perception of the judge as indifferent is a major fail-
        ure of the system.   3252

CHRISTIE, G.C. and PYE, K.A. Presumptions and assumptions in the
criminal law: another view. Duke L J 1970:919-42.
        High standards of proof imposed by U.S. Supreme Court,
        together with expanded notions of congressional power,
        have considerably reduced importance of presumption
        in state courts. Examines, among other areas of crim-
        inal justice, cases regarding presumptions involved
        in acceptance by court of guilty plea where defendant
        believes he is innocent. ABA Standards discussed.
        Attacks Ashford and Risinger's theory (see item 3234)
        as ignoring realities and dynamics of criminal process,
        leading to misguided trial tactics. "Meaningful reform
        will not be accomplished, however, by excessive pre-
        occupation with formal requirements divorced from the
        concrete realities of the legal process." Article is
        extensive analysis of presumptions, statutory and
        other, in many areas of criminal justice.   3253

CLARK, R. Crime in America: observations on its causes, prevention, and control. N.Y., Simon & Schuster, 1970.
Part 2, Criminal Justice deals with system from police to courts to prison, attacking each phase of the process. The entire book is an indictment of attitudes toward the accused, particularly poor ones, by former Attorney General.   3254

CLARK, T.C. The American Bar Association Standards for Criminal Justice: prescription for an ailing system. Notre Dame Law 47: 429-41 (1972).
History, discussion of various standards; describes implementation program to push adoption by legislation and courts.   3255

CLARK, T.C. Implementation story: where we must go. Judicature 55: 383-88 (1972).
Former U.S. Supreme Court justice relates the efforts of the ABA's Committee to Implement Standards for the Administration of Criminal Justice (which he chaired), to make the Standards become a living part of the criminal justice system in every jurisdiction.   3256

COHN, A.W. Training in the criminal justice nonsystem. Fed Prob 38:32-37 (June 1974).
Author contends that a criminal justice system really does not exist and although there are dangers in a true system, systematizing the network of criminal justice services is preferable. He tells of the importance of training programs in changing the nonsystem into a genuine system, by promoting dialogue and developing positive interrelationships among criminal justice workers.   3257

COMMITTEE for Economic Development. Reducing crime and assuring justice; a statement on national policy by the Research and Policy Committee of the Committee for Economic Development. N.Y., 1972. 86 p.
Businessmen examine problems concerning court congestion, the quality of prosecutors, police management and the correctional system; offer proposals for changes and reform in these areas. The establishment of an independent national agency, "Federal Authority to Ensure Justice" is urged.   3258

CONFERENCE on legal manpower needs of criminal law, at Airlie House, Va., June 24-26, 1966. FRD 41:389-418 (1967).
Sponsored by President's Commission on Law Enforcement and the Administration of Justice, ABA Project on Standards for Criminal Justice, and the National Legal Aid and Defender Project; chaired by Judge J.E. Lumbard. Background papers discussed in this report are: Silver-

stein, L., Manpower requirements on the administration
of criminal justice.--Hostetler, Z., Relationship between civil and criminal legal aid programs.--Connolly,
J.J., Law school programs to meet criminal manpower
needs.--Caplan, G.M., Career inhibiting factors, problems of public prosecutor and public defender.   3259

CONRAD, J.P. Crime and its correction: an international survey of
attitudes and practices. Berkeley, U. of Calif., 1965. 312 p.
Study of theory and practice of punishment, in the
United States, United Kingdom, Netherlands, Scandinavia,
France, Soviet Union, intended to foster development
of a rational system.   3260

CONTEMPORARY studies project: perspectives on the administration of
criminal justice in Iowa. Ia L Rev 57:598-813 (1972).
Presents intensive study originated to provide an accurate and complete description and analysis of the administration of criminal justice in Iowa's district courts,
and to recommend proposals for better and more efficient
procedural and substantive justice. Includes: scope
and methodology; the role, structure and working of the
prosecution, the defense and the courts; data tables,
appendix of right to appointed counsel in the states.
                                                   3261

COOK, J.G. Constitutional rights of the accused: pretrial rights.
Rochester, N.Y., Lawyers Co-op; San Francisco, Bancroft-Whitney,
1972. 572 p.
Provides extensive coverage, with annotations to all
jurisdictions, on adjudication in both state and federal courts, of federal constitutional rights of persons accused of crime. Covers arrest, search and seizure, trial, appeal; nature and cause of accusation,
grand jury indictment, speedy trial, guilty pleas; two
additional volumes to be published: Trial Rights (see
item 3263) and Post Trial Rights. To be kept up to date
by pocket parts.   3262

COOK, J.G. Constitutional rights of the accused: trial rights.
Rochester, N.Y., Lawyers Co-op: San Francisco, Bancroft-Whitney, 1974.
426 p.
Bibliographical references throughout.   3263

COUNCIL of State Governments. The states and criminal justice. Lexington, Ky., 1971. 30 p.
A survey of state programs in law enforcement, criminal
justice and corrections, developed with grants made
available under the 1968 Omnibus Crime Control and Safe
Streets Act.   3264

CRIMINAL justice in extremis: administration of justice during the
April 1968 Chicago disorder. U Chi L Rev 36:455-613 (1969).
(For annotation see item 652)   3265

CROCKETT, G.W. A black judge speaks. Judicature 53:360-65 (1970).
Detroit judge explains his release of 142 people, who
had been arrested in a church after a police officer
had been shot, because they had been denied their constitutional rights of warning and counsel. He uses this
as an example of a racist criminal system that denies
blacks their constitutional rights when the judicial
system remains unwilling to step in.   3266

CROCKETT, G.W. Commentary: black judges and the black judicial experience. Wayne L Rev 19:61-71 (1972).
Judge discusses how the past non-existent and present
limited representation of blacks in all phases of the
judicial system has caused a racially segregated system
in which it is still difficult for non-whites to find
justice and equality in the courts. The author urges
that black judges work together in making the court system work for blacks as well as whites.   3267

CROCKETT, G.W. Racism in the courts. J Pub L 20:385-89 (1971).
Arguments and statistics to support statement that
largest number of criminal court defendants are black.
Judge advocates more black judges, describing the role
they can play to secure more even-handed justice. Illustrated with examples from author's Detroit court.
                                                   3268

CURRENT History. American justice at work. Curr Hist 61:1-51 (Its
July, 1971, issue).
Partial contents: Goldman, S. American judges: their selection, tenure, variety and quality.--Landinsky, J.
Lawyer manpower in the criminal justice system.--Tif-
fany, L.P. Judicial attempts to control the police.--
Pious, R.M. Pretrial and nontrial in the lower criminal
courts.--Gillmor, D.M. Crime reporting: from delirium
to dialogue.--England, R.W., Jr. Is the prison becoming
obsolete? Bibliography, Pt. 2 (Pt. 1 in June, 1971,
issue).   3269

_____. American system of justice. Curr Hist 60:321-370 (Its June,
1971, issue).
Partial contents: Allen, F.A. Freedom, order, and justice.--Peterson, V.W. Development of local and state
law enforcement in America.--Glick, H.R. The system
of state and local courts.--Beaney, W.M. The federal
courts.--Remington, F. The role of the Supreme Court.--
Bloomstein, M.J. The American jury system.--Bibliography,
Pt. 1 (Pt. 2 in July, 1971, issue).   3269a

_____. Improving justice in America. Curr Hist 61:65-116 (Its Aug.
1971 issue).
> Partial contents: Nagel, S.S. The need for judicial re-
> form.--Lofton, J. Pretrial crime news: to curb or not
> to curb?--Gannon, E.J. Military justice.--Downie, L. Jr.
> Criminal court logjam.--Conrad, J.P. The need for prison
> reform.--Nanes, A.S. Jury system reform.--Canon, B.C.
> British, French, and American systems of justice com-
> pared.   3269b

DAMAŠKA, M. Evidentiary barriers to conviction and two models of
criminal procedure: a comparative study. U Pa L Rev 121:507-89 (1973).
> Law professor's comparative study contrasting difficul-
> ties that arise under the evidentiary rules of the com-
> mon law and civil law systems in proving guilt. Con-
> cluding that common law presents greater barriers in
> this area, author considers the possible nexus between
> the adversary and non-adversary procedures of the two
> systems. Discussed are evidentiary procedures of the
> systems, essential characteristics of adversary and non-
> adversary systems, and the historic commitment to truth
> of the two systems.   3270

DAVIS K.C. Discretionary justice; a preliminary inquiry. Baton
Rouge, La S U press, 1969. 233 p.
> Detailed treatment on unnecessary discretionary powers
> in regulatory agencies; included here because thesis
> is that there is a concentration of unnecessary dis-
> cretionary powers in police, prosecutors, judges, and
> others involved in criminal prosecutions. Suggests
> attention be concentrated on properly checking and
> structuring such powers to help courts.   3271

DAY, J.G. The quiet revolution in the criminal law: a foreword. Clev
State L Rev 23:1-7 (1974).
> Judge Day examines some of the reforms in the criminal
> law field and their effects, including the ABA Stan-
> dards and revised federal and state criminal codes.
>   3272

DOWNIE, L., Jr. Justice denied; the case for reform of the courts.
N.Y., Praeger, 1971. 224 p.; Penguin, 1971. 224 p.
> Journalist's picture of criminal trial court procedure
> based on personal observation and secondary research:
> the delay, incompetent lawyers and judges, and the
> bureaucracy. Bibliography.   3273

ERICKSON, W.H. The Standards of criminal justice in a nutshell. La
L Rev 32:369-407 (1972); Pa B A Q 43:454-83 (1972): condensed ver-
sion: Judicature 55:369-76 (1972).
> Based on address to the National Judicial Conference

on Standards for the Administration of Criminal Justice
held at Baton Rouge, La. in 1972; author covers briefly
background, preparation, methodology, personnel, and
impact of each of the standards; liberally footnoted
with pertinent cases and references to literature.
                                                    3274

FEDERAL act to extablish the Roscoe Pound Academy of Criminal Justice
(draft of a proposed law). Harv J Legis 2:131-45 (1965).
          Includes provisions of the proposed law with comments.
          Academy would be at Harvard Law School and would edu-
          cate and train those interested in the administration
          of criminal justice.   3275

FEELEY, M.M. Two models of the criminal justice system: an organizational perspective. Law & Soc Rev 7:407-25 (1973).
          Author presents and attacks the "rational goal model"
          for reform in criminal justice which emphasizes goals,
          ideals, and rules. He says that all steps proposed
          would not naturally make the actors in the system
          assume strong commitments to these goals. He suggests
          that the present "compliance mechanisms" (profession-
          alism and appellate procedure) are not enough to effect
          the needed reform.   3276

FELLMAN, D. The defendant's rights under English law. Madison, U.
of Wisconsin press, 1966. 147 p.
          Author's purpose is to describe rules of criminal law
          which in the United States would be constitutional
          rights of an accused. Topics covered are overview of
          English criminal court system, arrest, role of the po-
          lice, right to fair trial, and conduct of the trial.
                                                    3277

FINKELSTEIN, M.M. and KRANTZ, S. Perspectives on prison legal services: needs, impact, and the potential for law school involvement.
Washington, Nat Inst of Law Enforcement and Crim Just, 1972. 19 p.
          A summary report of a project carried out by the Center
          for Criminal Justice, Boston University School of Law;
          includes the need for prison legal services, the effect
          on frivolous petitions, the correlation between socio-
          demographic characteristics and attitudes toward law,
          and the effect of prison legal service on inmate atti-
          tude, rehabilitation and internal prison order. 3278

FRIENDLY, H.J. The Bill of Rights as a code of criminal procedure.
Cal L Rev 53:929-56 (1965).
          Judge, U.S. Court of Appeals (2d Cir), considers to
          what extent the Bill of Rights should be incorporated
          by the 14th Amendment into state criminal procedure. He
          criticizes Supreme Court decisions which establish in-
          flexible rules for situations in which the states should

be permitted experimental latitude or where a legislature might fashion a more adaptable procedural
standard. Discussing in particular the extension of
the right to counsel in every pretrial stage, he recommends a cautious judicial approach with reliance on
the due process clause rather than on specific inferences drawn from the broad provisions of the Bill of
Rights.   3279

GELLHORN, W. Ombudsmen and others; citizens' protectors in nine
countries. Cambridge, Harvard U press, 1966. 464 p.
Law professor examines the creation, duties, and effectiveness of the ombudsman in Denmark, Finland,
Norway, Sweden, and New Zealand. Included are analyses
of other methods which cope with official impropriety
by Yugoslavia, Poland, U.S.S.R., and Japan.   3280

GERMANN, A.C., DAY, F.D., and GALLATI, R.J. Introduction to law enforcement and criminal justice. Springfield, Ill., Thomas, 1973.
495 p.
A primer for students of criminal justice, presenting
basic principles regarding criminal justice processes
in the courts: philosophical background, constitutional
limitations, criminal justice agencies discussed.
Bibliography.   3281

GLUECK, S. Roscoe Pound and criminal justice. Dobbs Ferry, N.Y.,
Oceana, 1965. 262 p.
Professor has collected some of Pound's famous writings
dealing with the administration of criminal justice --
an invaluable reference aid. In memoir in appreciation
of Pound, Prof. Glueck applauds the Dean's work, sum-
ming up his many accomplishments to advance the administration of criminal justice, including justice in the
juvenile courts.   3282

GOVERNORS' Mutual Assistance Program for Criminal Justice. Where we
stand in the fight against crime. Washington, Nat Governors' Conf,
1973. 178 p.
Report on progress in states and cities after passage
of Safe Streets Act (1968). Surveys criminal justice
system totally; action by state legislatures, police
services, courts, corrections; includes statistical
and financial data; what sould be done in all these
areas.   3283

GRAHAM, F.P. The self-inflicted wound. N.Y., Macmillan, 1970.
377 p.
Analysis of U.S. Supreme Court's decisions in selected
criminal cases. Whether the Court's decisions merited
public rejection, what the rulings actually did, and
why they were made is the subject matter of the book.
                                                     3284

GREATER Philadelphia Movement Special Committee on Criminal Justice.
An information paper on criminal justice in Philadelphia. Philadelphia, 1971. 28 p.
> Paper contains factual data and list of questions of
> major community policy in effort to encourage candi-
> dates to focus on these issues. Topics include: bail
> and pretrial detention, court backlog, financial needs,
> probation problems, police abuse, police manpower de-
> velopment, juvenile gangs, drug problems, and the
> prison system.   3285

GRISWOLD, E.N. The long view. Speech ... at annual dinner in honor
of judiciary under auspices of the ABA Section of Judicial Administration ... Miami Beach. ABA J 51:1017-22 (1965).
> Law school dean argues that the recent Supreme Court
> decisions in the area of criminal justice will ulti-
> mately be viewed as protection of individuals from
> oppressive government. He outlines problems remaining
> to be solved, including pre-arraignment and pretrial
> conduct of enforcement agencies, prejudicial publicity
> at and before trial, bail practices, pretrial discovery,
> admissibility at trial of prior criminal conviction,
> and post-conviction remedies.   3286

HARRIS, R. Justice: the crisis of law, order, and freedom in America.
N.Y., Avon, 1969, 1970. 252 p.
> Contrasting administrative approaches of Attorneys
> General Ramsey Clark and John Mitchell, author describes
> unhappy situation resulting when politics rather than
> professionalism becomes the driving force in the Jus-
> tice Department. Subjects of particular interest are
> the differing policies on preventive detention, wire-
> tapping, and the protection of civil and constitutional
> rights.   3287

HUFSTEDLER, Shirley M. The directions and misdirections of a constitutional right of privacy. N.Y., Assn of the Bar of the City of N.Y.,
1971. 31 p.   (Benjamin N. Cardozo lect. 28)
> U.S. Court of Appeals judge examines the right of
> privacy secured by the Fourth Amendment: historical
> treatment by the Court; its failure to formulate a
> definition or to sketch parameters of the constitutional
> right to privacy; and recent cases. Author suggests
> that the individual's fundamental right of privacy
> should be given priority in all cases unless there is
> strong justification in favor of governmental intrusion.
>   3288

INSTITUTE of Defense Analyses. A national program of research, development, test, and evaluation on law enforcement and criminal justice. Washington, USGPO, 1968. 183 p.
> A. Blumstein, study director. Report proposes a com-

prehensive research program for the field of criminal
justice, to consist of four areas of goals: reducing
the need and desire to commit crimes increasing the
risk and difficulty in committing crimes, improving
the management of the criminal justice system, and
developing technical support for each of these areas;
evaluates existing programs and details management of
this program as to organization, staff, and implementation of research results.   3289

INSTITUTE of Judicial Administration. Anglo-American Interchange
on Criminal Justice. Working papers. 1964. 16 pts. (unpublished)
        Contents: Karlen, D. The machinery of criminal justice
        in the United States and England.--Niles, E.H. Criminal
        trial procedures.--Edwards, G. The role of the police
        in England and the United States.--Niles, E.H. Atmos-
        phere: fair trial and free press.--Traynor, R. Ground
        lost and found in criminal discovery.--Botein, B. Bail
        procedures in England and the United States.--Botein,
        B. Social services in the courts.--Williams, E.B. Un-
        popular clients and causes.--Decker, C.L. Defense of
        the indigent.--Hogan, F.S. The role of the prosecutor
        in the administration of criminal justice.--McIlvaine,
        J.W. Sentencing: grave responsibility; stimulating
        challenge.--Decker, C.L. Streamlining the administration
        of criminal justice.--Brennan, W.J., Jr. Post-convic-
        tion remedies.--Desmond, C.S. Methods of accusing a
        person of crime (information, presentment, indictment).--
        Courts having jurisdiction in criminal cases [English].--
        Napley, D. Judicial exchange: criminal law. (see also
        3297)   3290

INSTITUTE of Judicial Administration. Conference on New York City
juvenile justice resources, Mar. 7-8, 1974. ed. by B. Flicker. N.Y.,
IJA, 1974. 235 p.
        Speakers' outlines and articles for advance reading
        covers following topics: Arrest; Detention; Disposition;
        Roles of participants and providers of service. Appen-
        dix includes selected standards, review of recent
        reports.   3291

JACKSON, R.M. Enforcing the law. London, Macmillan; N.Y., St. Martin's press, 1967. 278 p.
        Author addresses himself to the administration of crim-
        inal law covering prosecution, defense, and sentencing.
        Mental disorder as it relates to criminal proceeding
        is examined. Separate attention is given to juvenile
        courts. Appendix includes Judges' Rules, procedure for
        making complaint against police, magistrates' associa-
        tion and consistency of penalties, and compensation for
        crime victims.   3292

JACOB, H. Urban justice: law and order in American cities. Englewood Cliffs, N.J., Prentice-Hall, 1973. 145 p.
Role of courts in city political system, describes
"intersections between justice and city politics,"
and police, bar, prosecutors, defenders, structure of
urban courts, and case disposition. Concludes that
courts play a fundamentally conservative role, they
"contain and suppress" disorder without fostering the
related underlying social change. 3293

JAMESON, W.J. The background and development of the Standards.
Judicature 55:366-68 (1972).
Chairman of the ABA Special Committee on Standards for
the Administration of Criminal Justice describes initiation by the IJA of the Standards project, giving
early history, preparation of standards, when and how
each standard was approved; forthcoming one-volume edition. (see item 3202) 3294

KAMISAR, Y. On the tactics of police-prosecution oriented critics
of the courts. Cornell L Q 49:436-77 (1964).
Law professor presents arguments to counter critics
who blame the courts for increasing crime, who believe
that rules of evidence have impaired law enforcement
efficiency. He particularly defends the decisions of
Mapp v. Ohio, 367 US 643 (1961), and McNabb v. U.S.,
318 US 332 (1943) as reaffirmed by Mallory v. U.S.,
354 US 449 (1957). 3295

KAMISAR, Y., INBAU, F.E., and ARNOLD, T. Criminal justice in our
time, ed. by A.E.D. Howard. Charlottesville, University press of
Virginia, 1965. 161 p.
Includes the following essays: Kamisar, Y. Equal justice in the gatehouses and mansions of American criminal procedure: from Powell to Gideon, from Escobedo
to ... (Discussion of right-to-counsel requirements and
the stage at which counsel must be provided to an indigent).--Inbau, F. Law enforcement, the courts and
individual civil liberties (Concerned with the unreasonable restrictions imposed on police interrogations, detention, arrest and search and seizure, rendering the
police practically powerless to prevent crime in order
to preserve individual civil liberties).--Arnold, T. The
criminal trial as a symbol of public morality (Examines
moral values in the administration of criminal law and
standards of insanity). 3296

KARLEN, D. Anglo-American criminal justice, by Karlen in collabora-
tion with G. Sawer and E. Wise. N.Y., Oxford, 1967. 223 p.
Compares and contrasts English and American criminal
justice. Part 1 is the machinery of the criminal justice system; role of the police; prosecution and de-

fense, including quality of representation; the criminal courts, including selection, tenure and training
of judges; penal institutions, reform, juvenile offenders. Part 2 details the stages of criminal prosecution
as to the power of the police, including judicial and
statutory limitations of powers of arrest, interrogation, search and seizure; pretrial proceedings including bail, preventive detention, preliminary hearings,
choice of court and mode of trial, conduct of the
trial, appeals and post-conviction remedies including
the right to appeal, appellate tribunals and appeal
procedures. Distillation of Anglo-American Exchange
of 1964. (see item 3290)   3297

KENNEDY, R.F.   The pursuit of justice, ed. by T.J. Lowi. N.Y., Harper & Row, 1964. 142 p.
Former attorney general discusses the challenge of
public service in protecting justice and integrity for
all and sets forth positions he took as attorney general and the remedies he feels to be most appropriate
for the major problems of the time, including local
poverty, juvenile delinquency, immigration problems,
organized crime, white collar crime, extremism, the
crisis of finding qualified lawyers, inequality in the
law.   3298

KERPER, H.B.   Introduction to the criminal justice system. St. Paul,
West, 1972. 569 p.
Overview of processes, procedures, and personnel involved in the American criminal justice system: foundation of law; steps of criminal process from appre-
hension and adjudication to sentencing and correction;
education, training and role of system professionals.
Includes some statutory law of New York, Delaware, California, and Texas. Appendices: Selected parts of Constitution; glossary of common legal terms; selected
bibliography.   3299

KIRSHEN, A.H. Appellate court implementation of the standards for
the administration of criminal justice. Am Crim L Q 8:105-17 (1969/70).
Report on how the ABA Standards for Administration of
Criminal Justice have been cited by the courts; chronology of the Standards is appended.   3300

KUTAK, R.J.   The Criminal Justice Act of 1964. Neb L Rev 44:703-50
(1965).
Practising lawyer points out that the passage of the
Act was an important clarification of national policy
on the accused's right to counsel. Explains the plan
for implementing the policies of the Act in Nebraska,
including text of plan.   3301

LANDES, W.M.   Economic analysis of the courts.   J L & Econ 14:61-107
(1971).

Using standard tools of economic theory and statistics,
a theoretical and empirical analysis of the criminal
justice system is presented, the purpose of which is
to determine why most cases are disposed of before
trial, the factors relevant to the choice between
settlement and trial, and the effects of the bail system and court delay on settlements. Several proposals
for improving the bail system and reducing delay are
considered and the argument that criminal justice system discriminates against poor defendants is evaluated.
Data on disposition of cases in state and federal criminal courts is analyzed.   3302

LAW and disorder: state planning under the Safe Streets Act: an interim report on Title I - The Omnibus Crime Control and Safe Streets
Act of 1968, by the Urban Coalition. Washington, 1969. 27 p. 3303

LAW and disorder II: state planning and programming under Title I
of the Omnibus Crime Control and Safe Streets Act of 1968, by the
National Urban Coalition. Washington, 1970. 43 p.   3303a

LAW and disorder III: state and federal performance under Title I
of the Omnibus Crime Control and Safe Streets Act of 1968, prepared
by the Lawyers' Committee for Civil Rights Under Law. Washington,
1972. 144 p.   3303b

The reports find the Dept. of Justice's Law Enforcement Assistance Administration failing to do what the
Safe Streets Act created it to do: lead the states in
improving their criminal justice systems. First report
finds LEAA planning agencies in 12 sample states consist almost entirely of those already administering
the system in need of reform; also that the LEAA agencies preserve traditional fragmentation contributing
to inefficiency, and that funds are rapidly dissipated
without producing appropriate programs and goals.
2nd report, one year later, finds many state programs
still in the condition described in first report, also
that most of action funds are spent on police equipment, hardly any on courts, corrections, juvenile or
narcotics treatment. 3rd report examines 5 states selected for variety of crime problems and programs:
Calif., Mass., Ohio, Pa., S.C.; cites LEAA for still
failing, after 4 years: to lead in developing effective programs, setting minimum standards, and filling
gaps of state programs with own; to use or make available own research so that poor programs would not be
duplicated but effective ones could be tried in various
settings and applications. Also critical of neglect
of civil rights and impact of crime on the poor.

LAWLESS, W.B. Machinery of criminal justice in England and the United
States. Syracuse L Rev 21:1061-93 (1970).
          Notre Dame Law School Dean examines and compares
          criminal law machinery here and in England under four
          major topics: police; proceedings prior to trial; the
          trial; and appeals and post-conviction remedies. Tech-
          niques for strengthening our process are suggested.
                                                                3304

LAWYERS' Review Committee to Study the Department of Justice. Report
... Washington, 1972. 76 p.
          The Department under Attorney General John Mitchell is
          examined and criticized for having failed to enforce
          school desegregation. It is charged with politicized law
          enforcement; other areas in which it has failed are
          briefly discussed.   3305

LEVI, E.H. The crisis in the nature of law. Record 25:121-41 (1970).
(Benjamin N. Cardozo lect. 26)
          Author addresses himself to the burden of balancing
          organized formalism of law with individual liberty.
          He focuses on standards in criminal trials as a barome-
          ter for the quality in government leadership.   3306

LEVINE, F.J. and TAPP, J.L. The psychology of criminal identification:
the gap from Wade to Kirby. U Pa L Rev 121:1079-1131 (1973); reprint.
A B Found research contributions 1973,4.
          An analysis of the inherent inequities in eyewitness
          pretrial identification through psychological theories
          and research; includes human limitations on identifi-
          cation and the social psychological theories of iden-
          tification; suggests various procedural reforms to im-
          prove the reliability and fairness of criminal identi-
          fication and discusses the legal implications as set
          forth in Supreme Court decisions.   3307

LEWIS, A. Gideon's trumpet. N.Y., Random House, 1964. 262 p.
          Complete narrative of the background, the events, and
          persons involved in Gideon v Wainwright; legal prin-
          ciples discussed.   3308

LEWIS, A. Talk with Warren on crime, the court, the country. N.Y.
Times (magazine) Oct. 19, 1969. p. 34+ (13 p.)
          Journalist interviews former Chief Justice regarding
          the constitutional decisions of his Court on race,
          reapportionment, and criminal law.   3309

LIEBERMAN, J.K. How the government breaks the law. N.Y., Stein &
Day, 1972. 309 p.
          Thesis is that the citizenry's general contempt for the
          law breeds constant official lawlessness for which there
          is very little remedy. Extensive description, and focus-

ing on particular categories, including illegal prosecution, sentencing, "cover-ups," crimes affecting
groups, everyone, and no one. Discusses causes and
effects.   3310

LOGAN, A.B. Justice in jeopardy. Springfield, Ill., C.C. Thomas,
1973. 260 p.
Covers penal reform, criminal procedure reform, inte-
grated court systems, professionalism of the bench,
appellate courts. Mass disorders, courtroom chaos reviewed. Fixes responsibility and gives agenda for
action. Bibliography.   3311

LUMBARD, J.E. Minimum standards for administration of criminal justice ... the roles of the bench, bar, press, and public. Mo B J
21:45-52 (1965).
Judge discusses project recently authorized by the ABA
and suggests some standards such as for providing
counsel to indigent defendants and bail reform. He
points out the roles which the bench, bar, press and
public should play in formulating such standards.3312

MCCLEAN, J.D.   Informers and agents provocateurs. Crim L R 1969:
527-37
English law professor examines the issue of how far
officials should be allowed to take steps to provoke
the actual commission of a suspected crime to ensure
that offenders will be caught. Discussed are: court
interpretation of entrapment; English development of
the law in this area; mitigation of sentence based on
entrapment; and judicial and administrative control.
Author suggests that some specific guidelines are necessary.   3313

MALTZ, M.D. Evaluation of crime control programs. Washington,
USGPO, 1972. 58 p.
A discussion of the problems of evaluating crime control programs including evaluation considerations in
program planning, problems with crime data, measures
of effectiveness and conduct of the evaluation; appendix: sources of data in police departments.   3314

MARGOLIS, L.S. Some answers to your criminal law problems: the
American Bar Association criminal justice standards. D C B J 39:23-
28 (Oct/Feb 1973)
U.S. Magistrate lists questions raised in the course
of a criminal trial and the answers as set forth in
the ABA Standards. Included are areas of control and
direction of the case, conditions of release and the
prosecutorial function.   3315

MEADOR, D.J.   Preludes to Gideon: notes on appellate advocacy, habeas
corpus, and constitutional litigation ...   Charlottesville, Va.,
Michie, 1967.   344 p.
    Law professor tells story of the litigation in the
    Holly, Jones, Chewning, and Hobbs cases, involving
    right to counsel issue. He focuses on the strategy of
    appellate litigation of constitutional questions, using
    as sources unreported court orders, correspondence,
    memoranda, and briefs. He also includes material on
    in forma pauperis litigation, habeas corpus, and the
    problem of recidivism.   3316

MECKLENBURG Criminal Justice Pilot Project.   Interim report, by D.
R. Gill. Oct. 11, 1971.   Chapel Hill, Univ. of N.C., 1971.   31 p.
    Discusses purposes of Project, which is focused on
    studying the feasibility of incorporating systems plan-
    ning into the criminal justice system; also specific
    activities of the Pilot Project and progress reports
    on original tasks; appendix is a separate volume in-
    cluding forms, charts and materials for various aspects
    of the Project, including a report: Strategies for cop-
    ing with drug abuse.   3317

MECKLENBURG Criminal Justice Pilot Project.   Relative seriousness of
criminal justice problems as seen by various groups in Charlotte-
Mecklenburg. May 25, 1972.   Chapel Hill, Inst. of Govt., U. of N.C.,
1972.   6 p.
    A background paper prepared for the Pilot Project as-
    sessing the seriousness of crimes as seen by profes-
    sional criminal justice organizations and citizens'
    organizations.   3318

MENNINGER, K.   The crime of punishment. N.Y., Viking, 1968.   317 p.
    Author's concern is with long range revision of societal
    approach to its deviants. Revenge is to be excised from
    punishment as predicated upon violence, a breeding
    ground for more violence. Rehabilitation should be the
    guiding principle in dealing with crime.   3319

MITCHELL, J.N.   Not will, but judgment. ABA J 57:1185-87 (1971).
    Judges should not impose their own ideologies when
    exercising judicial function but should sit in judgment
    on legal issues before them. Young persons should not
    attempt to make the courts into a "third house of Con-
    gress." Opportunity to change government is in the
    legislative and executive branches, says Nixon's
    Attorney General.   3320

MOSSMAN, K.   Prescription for criminal justice: the standards go to
the people.   Judicature 57:204-10 (1973).
    Former chairman of the ABA Section of Criminal Justice
    urges the joint implementation of the ABA Standards for

Criminal Justice and the standards issued by National
Advisory Commission on Criminal Justice Standards and
Goals; describes the process of implementation of the
ABA Standards including a comparative analysis for
each state's laws, the preparation of model court rules
based on the Standards, citizen involvement and law
school support.   3321

MUELLER, G.O.W. and LE POOLE-GRIFFITH, F. Comparative criminal procedure ... with contributions by J.L.J. Edwards, G. Williams, and
J. Chi-Chung Wang. N.Y., NYU press, 1969. 252 p.
Authors compare judicial supervision of pretrial procedures of the U.S. Commissioner with that of the European investigating magistrate, also investigation by
magistrates in Great Britain and Canada. They discuss
non-punitive detention, and briefly, French, German,
Scandinavian, and Japanese systems of training, appointment, and promotion of judges. Finally they evaluate
"judicial fitness" of the continental European judiciary.
                                                   3322

NAGEL, S.S. Disparities in criminal procedure. UCLA L Rev 14:1273-
1305 (1967).
Political science professor analyzes data relevant to
disparity at all stages of the administration of criminal justice, based on nationwide sampling of state
and federal assault and larceny cases, considering
the causes and proposing remedies. Explaining each procedural stage from preliminary hearing through sentencing, author relates desparities to the characteristics
of the defendant: age, sex, race, economics, education,
and other elements; he then proceeds to examine disparities relating to the characteristics of the courts,
state, federal, urban, rural. Major findings are summarized in tables.   3323

NAGEL, S.S. Judicial backgrounds and criminal cases. J Crim L 53:
333-39 (1962).
Research analyzes 313 state and federal judges listed
in 1955 Directory of American Judges, through examination of full court criminal cases heard by them in 1955.
Cases involved both appeals and habeas corpus and cen-
tered around guilt, punishment, or procedure. Scored
for times judge voted for defense, out of all times he
voted in criminal cases, each judge was analyzed on
several bases, including political party, education,
age, religion, region, nationality, and outside attitudes and occupations.   3324

NAGEL, S.S. The tipped scales of American justice. Transaction 3:
3-9 (May/June 1966).
Points up disparity in criminal procedure treatment

in federal and state courts; describes discrimination:
at preliminary hearing, setting of bail, in regard to
defense counsel, attitude of grand jury; delay, trial
by jury, conviction and sentencing; race, sex, economic class, urban-rural, north-south, all considered.
Article based on data gathered by American Bar Foundation for state courts in 1962, and for federal courts
by the Administrative Office of the U.S. Courts, 1963.
Bringing facts to light may expedite change, says
author.   3325

NAGEL, S.S. ed. The rights of the accused in law and action. Beverly Hills, Calif., Sage, 1972. 320 p. (Sage criminal justice system annuals, v. 1)

Inaugurates series dealing with significant problems;
the book is a compilation of ten essays that discuss
the most significant classes of rights of accused. Contributions by lawyers, law professors, political scientists begin with arrest, proceeding to post-conviction
remedy stage. Contents: Nagle, S.S. Rights of the accused.--Landynski, J.W. Search and seizure.--Rogge, O.J.
Confessions and self incrimination.--Karlen, D. and
Schultz, J.L. Justice in the accusation.--Beaney, W.M.
The right to counsel.--Wald, P.M. The right to bail
revisited.--Simon, R.J. and Marshall, P. The jury system.--Marshall, J. Trial, testimony, and truth.--Dawson,
R.O. The sentence and correctional process.--Sigler,
J.A. The new broom: the federalization of double jeopardy.   3326

NATIONAL Center for State Courts. Federal funding assistance for
state courts, by J.C.Ruhnka [and others]. Denver, 1973. 1 v., var.
pag.   3327

NATIONAL Conference of Commissioners on Uniform State Laws. Uniform
rules of criminal procedure (1974); approved draft, with prefatory
note and comments. [St. Paul, West, 1974] 407 p.   3327a

NATIONAL Conference on Criminal Justice, Jan. 23-26, 1973. (Working
papers) Washington, U.S. Dept. of Justice, LEAA, 1973. 1 v., var.
pag.

Papers contain standards for guidance and priorities
for action which have been developed by the National
Advisory Committee on Criminal Justice Standards and
Goals. Includes separate sections on the role of police,
the courts, correction, and the community in the criminal system. (For final report and standards, see item
3377)   3328

NATIONAL Institute of Law Enforcement and Criminal Justice. The
nature, impact and prosecution of white-collar crime, by H. Edelhertz.
Washington, LEAA, 1970. 77 p.

An intensive investigation and report on type of crime
and criminals which receives "scant national attention."
3329

NATIONAL Judicial Conference on Standards for the Administration of
Criminal Justice, Louisiana State Univ Law School, Feb. 10-14, 1972.
Chicago, 1972. 1 v., looseleaf.
Advance reading includes text of all Standards (without
commentary) and writings about them by T.C. Clark, L.B.
Nichols, A.H. Kirshen, H.C. Bratton, R.M. Ervin, H.S.
Miller, W.E. Burger, S. Dash, and H.I. Pollack. 3330

NATIONAL Judicial Conference on Standards for the Administration of
Criminal Justice, proceedings Feb. 10-14, 1972. Baton Rouge, La.,
FRD 57:229-474 (1973).
Partial contents: Jameson, W.J. Background and develop-
ment of the ABA Standards.--Erickson, W.H. Overview of
the ABA Standards and their implementation.--Jaworski,
L. The challenge and the response.--Gibbons, J.J. Stan-
dards relating to fair trial and free press.--Mossman,
K. Standards relating to the police function.--George,
B.J., Jr. Standards relating to the pretrial release.--
Van Hoomissedn, G.A. Standards relating to providing
defense services from the prosecution standpoint.--
Day, J.G. Standards relating to providing defense services from the defense standpoint.--Dash, S. Standards
relating to speedy trial.--Spears, A.A. Standards relating to discovery and pretrial procedure.--Harrison,
R.L., Jr. Standards relating to discovery and pretrial
procedure.--Gillespie, J.R. Standards relating to discovery and pretrial procedure.--Mock Omnibus hearing.--
Murray, F.J. Standards relating to the judge's function.--Pugh, G.W. Standards relating to pleas of
guilty.--Erickson, W.H. Standards relating to joinder
and severance.--Clark, T.C. Our opportunity.--Bennett,
D.E. Standards relating to probation.--Low, P.W. Standards relating to appellate review of sentences.--
Compton, L.D. Standards relating to appellate review
of sentences.--Low, P.W. Standards relating to sentencing alternatives and procedures.--Christian, W. Standards relating to trial by jury.--Onion, J.F. Standards
relating to post-conviction remedies.--Rogosheske, W.F.
Standards relating to ... the defense function.--Price,
J.M. Standards relating to ... the prosecution function.--Ervin, R.W. applying the rules.--Datz, A.J. Or
ganizing the bar.--Erickson, W.H. Writing the opinions.--
Murrah, A.P. Finalizing the job.--Lamont, N. LEAA and
the courts.--List of articles on standards.   3331

NATIONAL Symposium on Law Enforcement Science and Technology, 4th,
Washington, D.C., 1972 ... papers. Washington, USGPO, 1973. 9 v.
(U.S. Nat Inst of Law Enforcement and Crim Just. Crim just monographs)

Symposium conducted by University of Maryland's Institute of Criminal Justice and Criminology. Papers presented in nine volumes, as listed below: Deterrence
of crime in and around residences; Research on street
crime control (item 3335); Reducing court delay (item
4199); Prevention of violence in correctional institutions (item 3334); Reintegration of the offender into
the community; New approaches to diversion and treatment of juvenile offenders (item 4281): Change process
in criminal justice (item 3333); Innovations in law
enforcement; Progress report of the National Advisory
Commission on Criminal Justice Standards and Goals,
May 1972 (item 3377).   3332

NATIONAL Symposium on Law Enforcement Science and Technology, 4th,
Washington, D.C., 1972. The change process in criminal justice ...
papers. Washington, USGPO, 1973. 186 p. (U.S. Nat Inst of Law Enforcement and Crim Just. Crim just monograph)
Papers on the following topics: Mythology and the management of change: Inconsistencies in the behavior of
staff; Management of change in LEAA's impact program;
Pilot Cities Experience; Quantitative assessment of
improvement needs: The Albuquerque Pilot Cities experience; America's criminal justice system: A diagnosis
and prognosis; Hope and despair make the scene in crime
prevention; Research process as a factor in implementation of design for criminal justice changes; Correctional system: A rationale for determining program alternatives; Application of Magnitude-Estimation Scaling
to the establishment of priorities for criminal justice
programs; Political obstacles to change in criminal
justice agencies: An interorganizational perspective.
                                                        3333

NATIONAL Symposium on Law Enforcement Science and Technology, 4th,
Washington, D.C., 1972. Prevention of violence in correctional institutions ... papers. Washington, USGPO, 1973. 74 p. (U.S. Nat
Inst of Law Enforcement and Crim Just. Crim just monograph)
Papers describe and evaluate the sources and allevia-
tion of conditions that generate collective disorders
in correctional institutions, and the management of
tensions that arise. Ongoing research is also discussed.   3334

NATIONAL Symposiun on Law Enforcement Science and Technology, 4th,
Washington, D.C., 1972. Research on street crime control ... papers.
Washington, USGPO, 1973. 75 p. (U.S. Nat Inst of Law Enforcement
and Crim Just. Crim just monograph)
Papers cover research on the effectiveness of police
strategies to control street crime. In particular, manpower allocations, closed circuit television-equipped
patrol vehicles are considered. Also discussed is a

treatment effort to reduce drug-related crime.   <u>3335</u>

NATIONAL Symposium on Science and Criminal Justice, Washington,
June 22-23, 1966. Washington, USGPO, 1967. 196 p.
>Sponsored by the President's Commission on Law Enforce-
ment and Administration of Justice, the President's
Office of Science and Technology, and the Department
of Justice's Office of Law Enforcement Assistance, this
report includes papers on the criminal justice system
in general and on opportunities for the use of scientific techniques in prevention, enforcement, adjudication and corrections.   <u>3336</u>

NEJELSKI, P. Social policy and the administration of justice. Criminology 8:295-300 (1970).
>Acting Chief, Law and Justice Center of U.S. Dept. of
Justice, points out problems his organization faces in
trying to measure the effectiveness of the criminal justice system, since many individuals affect the administration of justice and make social policy in their
daily operations.   <u>3337</u>

NEJELSKI, P. and LERMAN, L.M. Researcher-subject testimonial privilege; what to do before the subpoena arrives. Wis L Rev 1971:1085-
1148.
>This article argues for the judicial or legislative
protection of researchers on the grounds of freedom
of expression, the right of privacy, and the rights of
criminal defendants.   <u>3338</u>

NEUBAUER, D.W. Criminal justice in middle America. Morristown, N.
J., General Learning press, 1974. 304 p.
>Study of unidentified Illinois industrial city's par-
ticipants in criminal process, especially prosecutors,
defense counsel, trial judges, and their exercise of
discretion (plea bargaining, jury selection, sentencing,
whether to prosecute), seen as expedients that reduce
disparity and move cases, but leave defendants' rights
also up to official discretion.   <u>3339</u>

NEW YORK (State) Commission of Investigation. The criminal justice
system in the city of New York: an overview. Nov. 18, 1974. N.Y.,
1974. 141 p.
>(For annotation see item <u>934</u>)   <u>3340</u>

NEW YORK (State) Governor's Special Committee on Criminal Offenders.
Preliminary report ... June 1968. N.Y., 1968. 328 p.
>Committee examines the theory, organization, and meth-
odology of the post adjudicatory treatment system in
an effort to find better ways to rehabilitate offenders
and to combat recidivism. Report based primarily upon
the laws, resources, procedures and services available

in New York in 1967. Changes are suggested, but no over-
all plan is given. Table of recommendations with corres-
ponding pages of report included.   **3341**

NEW YORK (State) Legislature Senate Committee on Crime and Correction.
The Tombs disturbances; a report. Albany, 1970. 55 p.
(For annotation see item 943)   **3342**

NEW YORK (State) Office of Crime Control Planning. Comprehensive
crime control plan, 1971- N.Y., 1971-
(For annotation see item 946)   **3343**

NEW YORK (State) Temporary State Commission on the Constitutional
Convention. Individual liberties; the administration of criminal
justice. March 16, 1967. N.Y., 1967. 211 p. (Study no. 7)
S.N. Corbin, Chair. Report discusses every aspect
of confessions, giving historical background; also
preliminary examination, bail under the federal constitution and New York statutes; searches, wire tap-
ping and privacy; the grand jury; public officials;
and immunity from prosecution.   **3344**

O'NEAL, H.T., Jr. Courts are not guilty. Ga SB J 1:413-18 (1965).
Lawyer argues against current criticism that courts are
creating imbalance in favor of the accused. He holds
view that courts are merely protecting constitutional
rights embodied in the Fourth, Fifth, Sixth, and Fourteenth Amendments.   **3345**

PACKER, H.L. Two models of the criminal process. U Pa L Rev 113:1-68
(1964).
The two are "the due process model" and the "crime control model." Describes basic aims and operation of
each at different stages of criminal process, and corre-
lates with present practice. Thesis is that operation
of the system has a great impact on the substantive
criminal law.   **3346**

PEAT, MARWICK, MITCHELL & CO. Program planning techniques, prep.
for the Law Enforcement Assistance Administration. Oct. 17, 1972.
Washington, USGPO, 1973. 1 v., var. pag.
Guide to techniques of planning and management organization for new and on-going programs under LEAA; included are the areas of program definition and analysis
and program planning, execution and evaluation, accom-
panied by diagrams and charts.   **3347**

PROCEEDINGS at the 1969 Judicial Conference, United States Court of
Appeals, Tenth Circuit, July 1-3, 1969, Jackson Lake Lodge, Wyo.;
Minimum standards for criminal justice, ed. by W.L. Whittaker. FRD
49:347-612 (1970).
Participants: Burger, W.E.; Murrah, A.P.; Ares, C.E.;

Arraj, A.A.; Bratton, H.C.; Breitenbach, H.E.; Carrigan,
J.R.; Clark, T.C.; Dash, S.; Erickson, W.H.; Flynn, J.J.;
Gerstein, R.E.; Gillispie, J.; Green, R.A.; Harris, C.C.;
Harrison, R., Jr.; Hathaway, S.K.; Hrysjam, R.L.; Kandt,
W.C.; Kleindienst, R.G.; LaFave, W.R.; Low, P.W.; McDon-
ald, D.P.; Murray, F.J.; Nichols, L.B.; Price, J.M.;
Pringle, E.E.; Rampton, C.R.; Spears, A.A.; Wilson, P.E.;
Yegge, R.B. Contents: (ABA) Standards relating to: pro-
viding defense services; pretrial release; speedy trial;
discovery and procedure before trial; pleas of guilty;
appellate review of sentences; sentencing alternatives
and procedures; post-conviction remedies.   3348

RADZINOWICZ, L. and WOLFGANG, M.E. Crime and justice. N.Y., Basic
Books, 1971. 3 v.
A collection of materials culled from the works of experts in the field, with analytical introductions. V.
1. The Criminal in society: scope of criminal law,
trends of crime, and social disharmonies, stressing juvenile delinquency. V. 2. The Criminal in the arms of
the law: enforcement, shortcomings of police performance,
class discrimination, threat to civil liberties; the
need for fundamental reappraisal of police. V. 3. The
Criminal in confinement: explores the correctional systems in terms of effects and effectiveness; the uninten-
ded consequences of imprisonment; oversimplified assumptions about probation or parole supervision; examines
outstanding recent correctional experiments; criticizes
experimental methods and statistical tools of criminology.   3349

REICH, R.B. Operations research and criminal justice. J Pub Law 22:
357-87 (1973).
Explores the use of operations research and systems analysis in the criminal justice field; pinpoints several
basic assumptions made in this approach such as the goals
of productivity, standardization and scientific neutral-
ity; describes various models used in systems analysis
of criminal justice and suggests a new model to eliminate the biases of assumptions.   3350

REID, H.O., Sr. The administration of criminal justice in the minority communities. How L J 17:275-95 (1972).
Law professor, speaking at National Bar Association meeting, discusses importance of lawyers' responsibility to
the community in the field of criminal justice, his role
on the Commission of Inquiry into the Black Panther Party
and Law Enforcement, the application of pretrial non-judicial punishment against blacks and other minorities,
and the great need for further study in these areas.
                                                  3351

ROSENBLATT, S. Justice denied. Los Angeles, Nash, 1971. 324 p.
    One attorney's opinions on hypocrisy and maladministra-
    tion in the American criminal justice system. Chapters
    include: American sex laws are a crime against nature,
    Judge the judges, and Police: society's patsies. 3352

ROSENGART, O.A. Busted; a handbook for lawyers and their clients.
N.Y., St. Martin's press, 1972. 191 p.
    Criminal law attorney and teacher offers down-to-earth
    advice on handling every stage of a confrontation with
    the criminal justice system in New York city from arrest
    to appeal; geared for the attention of underprivileged.
                                                        3353

SCURLOCK, J. Basic principles of the administration of criminal justice with particular reference to Missouri law. UMKC L Rev 38:172-
339 (1970).
    Sets out a detailed outline of criminal procedure based
    on federal and Missouri case law and statutory require-
    ments including interpretations of the principles of
    arrests, searches and seizures, self-incrimination, un-
    due harassment and essentials of a fair trial.   3354

_____. Basic principles ... revised. UMKC L Rev 41:165-291 (1972).
    Revision covers: Outline 1. Freedom from unreasonable
    deprivation of liberty. Outline 2, Freedom from unrea-
    sonable interference with privacy, as of Apr. 1, 1973.
    (Revision of Outlines 3 and 4 to appear in a subsequent
    review.)   3354a

SHERRILL, R. Justice in a torn nation. Nation 211:587-91 (Dec. 7,
1970).
    Author recounts conversation with former U.S. Attorney
    General Ramsey Clark about aspects of crime discussed
    in Clark's book, Crime in America. (see item 3254)
                                                        3355

STOCKDALE, E. The court and the offender. London, Gollancz, 1967.
208 p.
    Barrister critically examines the criminal courts in
    England and records some misgivings such as the iso-
    lation of the legal process from the penal system. He
    describes visits to the advanced penal systems of Holl-
    and, Denmark and Sweden and compares them with Eng-
    land, illustrating with three case histories. His sug-
    gested reforms include establishing an Institute which
    would combine the skills of psychiatrist, administrator,
    lawyer, and social worker to consider all aspects of
    the criminal process from arrest to the end of after-
    care, with the additional task of devising methods for
    the prevention of crime.   3356

SYMPOSIUM: Court and prison reform. Suffolk U L Rev 6:775-864 (1972).
Contents: Burger, W.E. Report on the state of the federal judiciary.--Clark, R.X. Prisons: a perspective from
within.--Berg, J.S. Assumptions of administrative responsibility by the judiciary: R for reform.--Cady, F.
C. Court modernization: retrospective, prospective, and
perspective.--Gallagher, O. Reforming the district court
system in Massachusetts.--Rothstein, L.E. Criteria for
the appointment of counsel in Massachusetts criminal
cases.   3357

SYMPOSIUM: The criminal and society. Harv J Legis 4:3-147 (1966).
Contents: Dickerson, R. Model defense of needy persons
act.--Swire, J.B. Eavesdropping and electronic surveillance: an approach for a state legislature.--Hamann, C.
M. The confinement and release of persons acquitted by
reason of insanity.--A state statute to liberalize criminal discovery.--A state statute to provide compensation
for innocent victims of violent crimes.   3358

SYMPOSIUM: Metropolitan courts conference. Judicature 53:227-57
(1970).
Contents: I. Computers and other aids for multi-judge
courts (Eldridge, W.B., Adams, E., Friesen, E.C.). II.
Are courts too soft on criminals? (Morris, N., Davis,
E.M.) III. Streamlining criminal procedures (Hudson,
E.A., Ellenbogen, H.).   IV. The public defender and
other suggested systems for the defense of indigents
(Anderson, L.L., Warner, V.O., Foster, D.).   V. Judges
and wardens: teammates for rehabilitation (Boldt, G.H.).
VI. The Canadian courts (Wilson, J.O.).   3359

SYMPOSIUM: New federal criminal code. Trial 9:11-33 (Oct. 1973).
Contents: McClellan, J.L. A landmark plan for criminal
law.--Brown, E.G. Unraveling a tangled skein.--Stein-
berg, R.A. New approach and treatment.--Burgess, J.A.
Progress or retreat.--Liebman, G.W. A dangerous explosion.--Downey, R.M. Privileged crime.--Nesson, C. A step
toward an autocratic state.--Hruska, R.L. A time for
humane sentencing.--Miller, H.S. Sentencing: the new
wave.   3360

SYMPOSIUM on crime and punishment in minority communities. Howard L
J 17:758-866 (1973).
Burns, H. Political uses of the law.--Tollett, K.S.
Bugs in the driving dream: the technocratic war against
privacy.--Bailey, D'A. Inequities of the parole system
in California.--Quintana, M.A. The erosion of the Fourth
Amendment exclusionary rule.--Singer, L.R. Enforcing the
constitutional rights of prisoners.--Moore, H., Jr. and
Moore, J.B. Some reflections on the criminal justice
system, prisons, and repressions.--Just, B. Bail and

pretrial detention in the District of Columbia: an empirical analysis.--Drew, J. Judicial discretion and the sentencing process.--Reid, H.O., Sr. Comments on the anti-crime legislation: a political and sociological analysis.   3361

SYMPOSIUM: Perspectives on innovation and reform in criminal justice. J Crim L 64:139-217 (1973).
Contents: Wolfgang, M.E. Foreword.--Miller, W.B. Ideology and criminal justice policy: some current issues.--Thompson, J.R., Starkwan, G.L. The citizen informant doctrine.--Campbell, W.J. Eliminate the grand jury.--Hamilton, W.A., Work, C.R. The prosecutor and the urban court system: the case for management consciousness.--Wilkins, L.T. Information overload: peace or war with the computor?--Blumstein,A. and Cohen, J. A theory of punishment stability.--Conrad, J.P. Corrections and simple justice.   3362

TENNEY, C.W., Jr. Higher education programs in law enforcement and criminal justice. June 1971. Washington, USGPO, 1972. 95 p.
Former Dean conducts survey to develop guidelines for schools initiating or expanding educational programs in criminal justice as well as to provide information for leaders of criminal justice agencies. Part I reviews and analyzes curriculum development projects and Part II sets forth results of other surveys and reevaluates criminal justice higher education.   3363

TRAYNOR, R.J. The devils of due process in criminal detection, detention, and trial. N.Y., Assn of the Bar of the City of New York, 1966. 32 p. (Benjamin N. Cardozo lect. 23); Record 21:357-84 (1966); Cath U L Rev 16:1-22 (1966).
California judge reviews recent decisions relating to criminal procedure and demonstrates that they may be too imprecise or impractical to apply in many situations. Considering the exclusionary rule, the right to counsel, and the privilege against self-incrimination, the author seeks to show how decisions concerning those rights may be interpreted so as to protect both the constitutional rights of the accused and the rights of the public to a reasonable protection from crime. Bibliography.   3364

TREBACH, A.S. The rationing of justice, constitutional rights and the criminal process. New Brunswick, N.J., Rutgers U press, 1964. 350 p.
Documents the infringement of constitutional rights via step-by-step analysis of criminal prosecution from arrest to imprisonment, based on personal observations and interviews with bench, bar and prisoners; a mixture of individual examples, statistics and policy considerations.   3365

TWO trial system in capital cases. NYU L Rev 39:49-77 (1964).
Note analyzes the concept of a two-trial system recently
introduced in New York, in which, after determination
that defendant is guilty of a crime punishable by death,
a second proceeding to determine whether the sentence
shall be life imprisonment or death is held before the
same jury without customary evidentiary rules. System
was designed to achieve a rational determination of who
shall suffer the death penalty. Discusses jury determination, voir dire, comparison of two-trial statutes, evidentiary rules in the second proceeding, and effects of
appellate modification of sentence; tables.   3366

U.S. ADMINISTRATIVE Office of the Courts. Report of the Judicial Conference of the United States on the Criminal Justice Act of 1964.
Jan. 13, 1965. FRD 36:277-390 (1965).
Contents: Report of the proceedings of a special session of the Judicial Conference of the United States;
Report of the committee to implement the Criminal Justice Act of 1964; Appendix 1, vouchers and other forms;
Appendix 2, six suggested district court plans; Appendix
3, Criminal Justice Act of 1964; Committee to implement
the Criminal Justice Act of 1964; Minutes of meeting of
October 17, 1964; Report of the Ad Hoc Committee to develop rules, procedures, and guidelines for an assigned
counsel system.   3367

U.S. ADVISORY Commission on Intergovernmental Relations. For a more
perfect union - court reform. Washington, USGPO, 1971. 22 p.
Summary of those findings and recommendations, relating
just to courts, contained in the Commission's report:
State-local relations in the criminal justice system
(see item 3370). Also presented is the following draft
legislation: "Judicial Constitutional Article" and
"Omnibus Judicial Act."   3368

U.S. ADVISORY Commission on Intergovernmental Relations. New proposals for 1972: ACIR state legislative program. Washington, USGPO,
1971. 98 p.
Legislative proposals are made to implement recommendations in the Commission's report (see item 3370).
They include, "Judicial Constitutional Article," "Omnibus Judicial Act," and "Omnibus Prosecution Act."3369

U.S. ADVISORY Commission on Intergovernmental Relations. State-local
relations in the criminal justice system. Washington, USGPO, 1971.
308 p.
Commission examines operation and problems of the country's fifty state-local criminal justice systems with
special reference to the need for a more expeditious
and coordinated criminal justice process. Many elusive
facts and statistics are included relating to different

areas of criminal justice systems starting with police
and prosecution functions. Special issues are examined
beginning with judicial selection, financing of courts,
and representation of accused. Forty-four recommendations are made respecting the judicial process, law enforcement and corrections. Special attention to lower
courts.   3370

U.S. LAW Enforcement Assistance Administration, and U.S. BUREAU of the
Census. Expenditure and employment data for the criminal justice sys-
tem, 1968/69-1972/73. Washington, USGPO, 1970-1975. 5 v.
(For annotation see item 2368)   3371

U.S. CONGRESS. House Select Committee on Crime. Crime in America:
aspects of organized crime, court delay, and juvenile justice; hearings. Washington, USGPO, 1970. 496 p. (91st Cong., 1st Sess.)
    Hearings, conducted across the U.S., include statements,
    discussions, letters, text of authorities, and articles
    of records concentrating largely on the drug problem and
    its impact on crime. Topics discussed include: narcotic-
    related deaths, the role of customs officials, use of
    airline pre-clearance procedures, health services avail-
    able to the drug user, public education programs, juven-
    ile crime, drug traffic, infiltration of organized crime
    into legitimate businesses, court observation programs,
    release without bail, needs of criminal courts, and
    court aid programs.   3372

U.S. CONGRESS. House Select Committee on Crime. Improvement and reform of law enforcement and criminal justice in the United States;
hearings. Washington, USGPO, 1969. 845 p. (91st Cong., 1st Sess.)
    Statements and letters presented and dialogue which
    took place at House hearings on various aspects of
    crime and crime control and its causes and effects.
                                                          3373

U.S. CONGRESS. Senate Committee on the Judiciary. Obstruction of
criminal investigations; report to accompany S. 2188. Aug. 24, 1966.
Washington, USGPO, 1966. 10 p. (89th Cong., 2d Sess.; S Rep 1499)
    Report sets forth amendments to a proposed bill prohib-
    iting the obstruction of justice by interfering with
    federal criminal investigations. Included are purpose
    and analysis of the bill, its legislative history, and
    statements by Deputy Att. Gen. R. Clark and Att. Gen.
    Katzenbach.   3374

U.S. LAW Enforcement Assistance Administration. Grants for comprehen-
sive law enforcement planning; a guide for State Planning Agency
Grants under the Omnibus Crime Control and Safe Streets Act of 1968 ...
Washington, USGPO, 1968. 1 v., looseleaf.

Detailed instructions for grant application. Supps.
or new editions issued as needed.   3375

U.S. LAW Enforcement Assistance Administration. Volunteers in law
enforcement programs; staff study, by LEAA, Off. of Operations Support, Program and Management Evaluation Div. Washington, 1972. 66 p.
    Study summarizes way LEAA volunteers are being utilized
    by law enforcement agencies throughout the country:
    projects involving police, courts, and probation; delin-
    quency prevention and court diversion; and YMCA projects.
                                                      3376

U.S. NATIONAL Advisory Commission on Criminal Justice Standards and
Goals. R.W. Peterson, chair.; T.J. Madden, exec. dir.

    Final report: A national strategy to reduce crime. Washington,
    USGPO, 1973. 195 p. (see item 3379)

    Task force reports: all published by USGPO, 1973. Community
    crime prevention. J. Michie, chair. 364 p.
        Corrections. J.F. Brown, chair. 636 p.
        Courts. D.J. Meador, chair. 358 p. (see item 3378)
        Criminal justice system. J.R. Plants, chair. 286 p.
        Police. E.M. Davis, chair. 668 p.

    Other reports of the Commission:
        Proceedings of the National Conference on Criminal Justice,
        Jan. 23-26, 1973. [to be published]
        Working papers for National Conference on Criminal Justice,
        Jan. 23-26, 1973. 1 v., looseleaf. (see item 3328)
        Progress report of the National Advisory Commission ... May,
        1972, in National Symposium on Law Enforcement Science and
        Technology, 4th, 1972. (see item 3332)   3377

U.S. NATIONAL Advisory Commission on Criminal Justice Standards and
Goals. Courts (by Task Force on Courts, D.J. Meador, chair.). Washington, USGPO, 1973. 358 p. Bibliography: p. 323-37.
    One of five Task Force reports on which Commission based
    final report, National Strategy to Reduce Crime (see
    item 3379). Standards in Courts are on: screening; di-
    version; negotiated pleas; the litigated case; senten-
    cing; appellate review; the judiciary: selection, com-
    pensation, discipline, education; lower courts: unifica-
    tion and administrative alternatives; court admininstra-
    tion; court-community relations; computers; prosecution;
    defense; juvenile justice; mass disorders. A treasury of
    elusive information; for instance, ch. 10 discusses poor
    treatment often given jurors and witnesses; see Standard
    10:6:Production of witnesses, p. 208-12; and 10:7:Compen-
    sation of witnesses, p. 213-14.   3378

U.S. NATIONAL Advisory Commission on Criminal Justice Standards and
Goals. A national strategy to reduce crime. Washington, USGPO. 1973.
195 p. N.Y., Avon, 1975. 678 p.
>   Russell W. Peterson, chair. Final report of Commission
>   appointed Oct. 20, 1971, by LEAA to develop standards
>   for state and local governments in crime prevention,
>   criminal court processing, corrections. Standards and
>   detailed recommendations are presented in five reports
>   (see item 3377); digested in this volume. See particu-
>   larly digest of The Courts, p. 93-129.   3379

U.S. NATIONAL Bureau of Standards. Studying criminal court processes:
some tools and techniques by E. Nilsson [and others]. Washington,
U.S. Dept of Commerce, 1970. 108 p. + app.
>   Guidelines for the design and implementation of studies
>   of criminal court systems are presented. Included are
>   a description of the structure and function of the court
>   system, a discussion of problem formulation and statement,
>   data collection, data analysis, and a summary of neces-
>   sary statistics and fundamentals. App. A: Data categor-
>   ies. App. B: suggested forms and coding manual. 3380

U.S. NATIONAL Commission on the Causes and Prevention of Violence.
To establish justice, to insure domestic tranquility; final report of
the National Commission on the Causes and Prevention of Violence.
Washington, USGPO, 1969. 338 p.
>   M.S. Eisenhower, chair. The basic causes of violence are
>   analyzed in this report. Recommends increasing expendi-
>   tures in the criminal justice process, establishing
>   central offices of criminal justice at the metropolitan
>   level, and expanding legal services programs.   3381

U.S. NATIONAL Commission on the Causes and Prevention of Violence.
Supporting reports:

>   Violence in America; report of the Task Force on Historical and
>   Comparative Perspectives, H.D. Graham, T.R. Gurr, co-directors.
>   1969. 2 v.   3381a

>   The politics of protest; report of the Task Force on Violent As-
>   pects of Protest and Confrontation, J.H. Skolnick, dirctor. 1969.
>   276 p.   3381b

>   Firearms and violence in American life; report of the Task Force
>   on Firearms, G.B. Newton, Jr., director. 1969 268 p.   3381c

>   Law and order reconsidered; report of the Task Force on Law and
>   Law Enforcement, J.S. Campbell, J.S. Sahid, D.P. Stang, co-direc-
>   tors. 1969. 606 p.   3381d

>   Assassination and political violence; report of the Task Force on
>   Assassination, J.F. Kirkham, S.G. Levy, W.J. Crotty, co-directors.
>   1969, 752 p.   3381e

Mass media and violence; report of the Task Force on mass media and violence, R.K. Baker, S.J. Ball, co-directors. 1969. 614 p.
3381f

Crimes of violence; report of Task Force on Individual Acts of Violence, D.J. Mulvihill, N. Tumin, co-directors. 1969. 3 v.
3381g

U.S. NATIONAL Criminal Justice Information Statistics Service. Crime in the nation's five largest cities; National Crime Panel surveys of Chicago, Detroit, Los Angeles, New York, and Philadelphia. Advance report, April 1974. Washington, USGPO, 1974. 29 p.
> Continuing surveys by National Crime Panel will analyze victims' (individual, households, commercial establishments) characteristics, relationship to offender, time and place of crime, injury or loss, and whether reported. Advance report finds unreported crime to be about twice that reported (confirming, through scientific sampling, what test studies have estimated). Methodology explained; to be covered more fully in next report.
3382

U.S NATIONAL Criminal Justice Information and Statistics Service. Sourcebook of criminal justice statistics by M. Hindelang [and others], Criminal Justice Research Center, Albany, and School of Criminal Justice, State Univ of N.Y., Albany. Aug. 1973. Washington, USGPO, 1974. 505 p.
> Brings together in one volume tables from many sources on: criminal justice system, including courts and judges; public attitudes on crime; nature, distribution of known offenses; arrests; judicial statistics; corrections. Dates vary; most tables are from 1970 or later. Limited to United States, with emphasis on state and local data. Analytic appendices interpreting selected data planned.
3383

_____. _____. 1974 ed. 252 p.   3383a

U.S. NATIONAL Institute of Law Enforcement and Criminal Justice. Evaluation in criminal justice programs: guidelines and examples, by E. Albright [and others]. Washington, USGPO, 1973. 165 p.
> Based on documents prepared by MITRE Corp. to aid federal High Impact Anti-Crime Program (est. Jan. 1972); includes general manual, and city project evaluators' manual, also, for eight specific types of project, a model of each is described with: purpose, budget/scope, general methodology, and specifics on data collection and analysis, results anticipated, measures of effectiveness. Projects are: Community-based rehabilitation; Automated court calendaring system; Police command and

control; Methadone maintenance; Youth services; Intervention center; Third party custody; Job development
for youthful offenders.   3384

U.S. NATIONAL Institute of Law Enforcement and Criminal Justice.
Evaluation of crime control programs, by M.D. Maltz. Washington,
USGPO, 1972. 64 p.
          Advice includes: define focus of program, then evaluate
          early, before expansion; geographical areas should in-
          clude one with similar crime rate, conditions, to use
          as control; watch out for crime displacement and in-
          crease in citizen reporting. Evaluation should include
          both crime reduction and efficiency of program. 3385

U.S. NATIONAL Institute of Law Enforcement and Criminal Justice. Ex-
emplary programs. Washington, 1974. 8 p.
          The Exemplary Projects Program is explained by G.M. Cap-
          lan, director of the National Institute. To focus na-
          tional attention on outstanding working criminal justice
          programs suitable for adoption by other communities,
          approximately 12 projects per year are designated as
          exemplary, and manuals are prepared, distributed through
          LEAA's National Criminal Justice Reference Service, giv-
          ing all specifics of the selected projects. Projects
          designated thus far: 1) Prosecutor Management Informa-
          tion System, D.C.; 2) Community-based Corrections Pro-
          gram, Polk County (Des Moines, Iowa); 3) Citizen Dispute
          Settlement Program (Night Prosecutor) Columbus, Ohio;
          4) 601 Juvenile Diversion Project, Sacramento, Calif.;
          5) Providence Educational Center, St. Louis, Mo.; 6)
          Neighborhood Youth Resources Center, Philadelphia, Pa.;
          7) The Public Defender Service (P.D.S.) of the District
          of Columbia.   3386

U.S. NATIONAL Institute of Law Enforcement and Criminal Justice. An
inventory of surveys of the public on crime, justice, and related
topics, by A.D. Biderman [and others] Bureau of Social Science Research, Inc. Washington, USGPO, 1973. 1 v., var. pag.
          Report explains inventory procedure and presents poll
          questions. Appendix includes index of originators, in-
          dex of key works and phrases, statistical profile of
          survey, inventory of other surveys, and bibliography.
                                                       3387

U.S. OFFICE of Law Enforcement Assistance. Program summary and guid-
lines on the Law Enforcement Assistance Act of 1965; List of approved
projects, fiscal year 1966. Washington, U.S. Dept. of Justice, 1966.
18 p.
          Covered in this summary are objectives and administra-
          tion of LEAA as well as complete information on grants.
          Included is a list of approved projects.   3388

U.S. PRESIDENT'S Commission on Crime in the District of Columbia.
Washington, USGPO, 1966.   2 v.
> Based on studies by and for the Commission, its public
> hearings, interviews with officials and residents, and
> review of existing studies. Vol 1 describes nature and
> extent of D.C. crime, the police dept., the prosecutors,
> the courts, and criminal process after conviction, in-
> cluding sentencing, probation and parole; also discusses
> special problems such as gun control, drug abuse, police
> interrogation, pretrial release, handling of mentally
> ill or alcoholic defendants, D.C's unsatisfactory crim-
> inal code. Juvenile justice and delinquency prevention
> efforts and proposals for Youth Commission are given
> considerable attention, followed by examination of
> social and economic conditions correlated with the Dis-
> trict's high crime rate. Recommendations are made
> throughout report; summarized at end of each chapter.
> Vol. 2 consists of the following reports: Survey of
> the Metropolitan Police Department, by the International
> Association of Chiefs of Police, April 1966, 452 p.;
> Description of active juvenile defenders and convicted
> adult felons in the District of Columbia, by Stanford
> Research Institute, July 1966, p. 453-644; Organization
> and effectiveness of correctional agencies, by American
> Correctional Association, June 1966, p. 645-748; The
> social order and delinquency, by Eli Ginzberg, Aug.
> 1966, p. 749-777.   3389

U.S. PRESIDENT'S Commission on Law Enforcement and Administration of
Justice. The challenge of crime in a free society. Washington,
USGPO, 1967. 340 p.
> Final report, based on Task Force reports and consul-
> tants' papers, all published in 1967. Task Force Re-
> ports are: Crime and its impact -- an assessment. 220 p.;
> The courts. 178 p. (see item 3391); Corrections. 222 p.;
> Drunkenness. 131 p.; Juvenile delinquency and youth
> crime. 428 p.; Narcotics and drug abuse. 158 p.; Organ-
> ized crime. 126 p.; The police. 239 p.: Science and
> technology.... [Prepared by the Institute for Defense
> Analyses] 228 p.   3390

U.S. PRESIDENT'S Commission on Law Enforcement and the Administration
of Justice. Task force report: the courts. Washington, USGPO, 1967.
178 p.
> N. deB. Katzenbach, chair. Partial contents: Recommen-
> dations. ch. 1: Disposition without trial (Decision to
> bring charges; Negotiated plea of guilty). ch. 2: Sen-
> tencing (Statutory sentencing framework; Information
> for sentencing: presentence investigation, disclosure,
> hearing, defense counsel; Exercise of court sentencing
> authority: disparity, sentencing councils, appellate
> review, jury sentencing; Capital punishment). ch. 3: The

lower courts (Urban; J.P.; U.S. Commissioners). ch. 4:
Court proceedings (Bail; Early discovery, Habeas corpus and finality; Appeals by prosecution; News media
and the administration of justice: court control, statements by police, prosecutors, defense counsel; discrimination and poverty). ch. 5: Counsel for accused (Legal manpower and financial needs for defense, civil
legal aid; Counsel for defendants: appointed counsel,
supervision for counsel, compensation, eligibility).
ch. 6: Officers of Justice (Judges: selection, obstacles to effective prosecution, training; Coordination
of state prosecutorial functions and local prosecution).
ch. 7: Administration of the Courts (Structural and
organizational reform of courts, clear and centralized
administration and rulemaking authority; Model timetable for processing of criminal cases; Case monitoring
and scheduling; Treatment of jurors and witnesses; ABA
Model Judicial Article; National Conference of Commissioners on Uniform State Laws, Model Act for State
Court Administrators). ch. 8: Substantive law reform
and the limits of effective law enforcement (examination of conduct now criminal that should receive examination, e.g. drunkenness, gambling, narcotics, va-
grancy, sexual behavior, abortion, etc.). Appendices
include essays on plea bargaining, lower court studies,
poverty and criminal justice, manpower requirements and
modernized court administration, by A. Enker, P. Wald,
L. Silverstein, N. Halloran.   3391

U.S. PRESIDENT'S Commission on Law Enforcement and Administration of
Justice. Field surveys. The following studies and surveys deal with
such subjects as how people feel about police, why they do or do not
report crime, which crimes are more likely to be reported; organized
crime, corruption, related areas.

BUREAU of Social Science Research. Report on a pilot study in the
District of Columbia on victimization and attitudes toward law enforcement, by A.D. Biderman [and others]   Washington, USGPO, 1967.
1 v., var. pag. (Field Survey 1)   3392

NATIONAL Opinion Research Center. Criminal victimization in the
United States; a report of a national survey by P.H. Ennis. Washington, USGPO, 1967. 1 v., var. pag. (F. S. 2)   3393

REISS, A.J., Jr. Studies in crime and law enforcement in major
metropolitan areas. Washington, USGPO, 1967. 2 v. (F.S. 3)3394

LOHMAN, J.D. and MISNER, G.E. The police and the community; ... in
changing society. Washington, USGPO, 1967. 2 v. (F. S. 4) 3395

NATIONAL Center on Police and Community Relations. National survey
of police and community relations. Washington, USGPO, 1967. 386 p.
(Field Survey 5)   3396

THE UNITED STATES Courts of Appeals, 1972-1973 term: Criminal law and procedure (preface by H.J. Friendly). Georgetown L J 62:401-777 (1973).
A comprehensive analysis of federal court cases (including U.S. Supreme Court) in all areas of criminal law and procedure from arrest to post-conviction procedures and other specific areas including juvenile.   3397

WARREN, E. All men are created equal. N.Y., Assn of the Bar of the City of New York, 1970. 22 p.
Chief Justice catalogues inequalities and indignities still suffered in the courts by minorities, particularly in criminal courts.   3398

WESTCHESTER Community Service Council. Crime and service study of Westchester County .. under a grant from the New York State Div. of Criminal Justice Services. White Plains, N.Y., 1973. 2 v.
(For annotation see item 2200)   3399

WESTON, P.B. and WELLS, K.R. Administration of justice. Englewood Cliffs, N.J., Prentice-Hall, 1967. 251 p.
Uses the California Penal Code and Evidence Code as a reference point for analyzing all aspects of the criminal justice system from incident through trial to final disposition; selected references for each aspect of the system.   3400

2. The items in this section are limited to incidents of civil disorders and the administration of justice during such periods. For items on disorder in the courtroom and contempt powers of the court, see Section VII A, The Criminal Trial Judge.

AMERICAN Bar Association. Section of Criminal Law. Bar leadership and civil disorders. Chicago, 1968. 32 p.
Legal powers, duties, and services of lawyers during civil disorders. Appendices include ABA House of Delegates resolutions; Michigan Emergency Powers Statute and a proposed amendment; 4-p. bibliography.   3401

BALBUS, I.D. The dialectics of legal repression; black rebels before the American criminal courts. N.Y., Russell Sage Found., 1973. 269 p.
Political scientist applies Marxian critical theory to study of ghetto riots in Chicago, Detroit, Los Angeles, ascribing relatively easy ending of them to establishment's (especially bar's) willingness to overlook occasionally illegal arrest and detention of blacks, and to blacks' own as yet undeveloped consciousness of causes and uses of revolution. Still concerned with struggle for equal justice, they settled for treatment as ordinary criminals, negotiating for minimal sanctions instead of risking severe ones for long-term political gains.

664   ADMINISTRATION OF CRIMINAL JUSTICE

Description and analysis for each city attempts to relate severity of sanctions to violence of riot and to
variations in courts' relationship to local political
system.   3402

BECKER, T. ed. Political trials. N.Y., Bobbs-Merrill, 1971. 255 p.
Profiles of eleven political trials from various countries, divided into categories by whether there was a
true trial, and whether the crime was really political.
Includes the Chicago conspiracy trial, the prosecution
of Jimmy Hoffa, the Der Spiegel trial and the Ghana trea-
son trial.   3403

BOTEIN, B. and STERN, G. Civil liberties and civil disorders: are
they reconcilable? N Y L F 14:763-79 (1968).
Former presiding justice and court director of administration review the cases involving violation of civil
rights and abuses of criminal justice during and immediately following the 1967 and 1968 civil disorders, naming a number of recent studies and reports; administrative problems are reviewed.   3403a

CRIMINAL justice in extremis; administration of justice during the
April, 1968, Chicago disorder. Research project of the Univ of Chi-
cago Law Review. U Chi L Rev 36:455-613 (1969). Reprint by ABA, 1970.
(For annotation see item 652)   3404

DISTRICT of Columbia Committee on the Administration of Justice under
Emergency Conditions. Justice in time of crisis. A staff report ...
prep. by W.A. Dobrovir. Washington, USGPO, 1969. 180 p.
Analysis of setting of bail by D.C. Court of General
Sessions and charging policy of U.S. Attorney's office
during and after civil disorders following the assassination of Dr. Martin Luther King, Jr. in 1968. Finds
bail procedure fair, considering the circumstances and
also approves charging process on the whole, but states
that there were too many felony indictments brought.
Recommends passage of looting statute and reformation
of plea bargaining guidelines for mass arrest situations.
                                               3405

DISTRICT of Columbia Judicial Council. Report of the Committee to
study the operation of the Bail Reform Act in the District of Columbia. Washington, 1968. 57 p.
Report says Act of 1966 has not been administered with
maximum effectiveness; examines bail from procedures
prior to setting bail to bail during civil disorders
and makes recommendations for imporvement in each area.
                                               3406

JANOWITZ, M. Social control of escalated riots. Chicago, U of Chicago, Center for Policy Study, 1968. 44 p.

A sociologist examines urban racial violence, its origins, and steps which need to be taken by law enforcement agencies to cope with it, such as the constabulary
approach wherein use of force would be at a minimum. He
also explores the impact of the mass media on the rioters, potential rioters and public opinion.   3407

LINCOLN, J.H. The anatomy of a riot: a Detroit judge's report. N.Y.,
McGraw-Hill, 1968. 208 p.
Based upon first-hand observation, Judge addresses himself to the causes of and participants in the Detroit
riot. He particularly describes the role of juveniles
and their judicial and custodial handling during the
riot. He focuses upon long range objectives, the achievements of which will obviate future unrest. Appendix includes detailed reports from various sources. See also
The administration of justice in the wake of the Detroit
civil disorder of July, 1967, Mich L Rev 66:1544-1630
(1968).   3408

ONE year later; an assessment of the nation's response to the crisis
described by the National Advisory Commission on Civil Disorders.
Washington, Urban America, Inc., and Urban Coalition, 1969. 122 p.
Finds that little progress has been made in the effort
to lessen the disparities between the lifestyle of the
poor and that of the rest of society, this inequality
having been identified as the major cause of civil disorders and riots in the cities.   3409

SYMPOSIUM: Anatomy of a riot: symposium of the causes and effects
of riots. J Urban L 45:499-901 (1968).
Contents: Harbrecht, P.P. Introduction.--Smith, J.,
Smith, L. First Amendment freedoms and the politics of
mass participation.--Freilich, R.H. The emerging general
theory of civil disobedience within the legal order.--
Komisaruk, R., Pearson, C. Children of the Detroit riots.--Corsi, J.R. Detroit 1967: racial violence or class
warfare.--Sengstock, M.C. The corporation and the ghetto:
an analysis of the effects of corporate retail grocery
sales on ghetto life.--Glicksman, E.B., Jones, V.M. Consumer legislation and the ghetto.--Ducharme, G.D. State
riot laws: a proposal.--Solomon, K., Yates, S. Riots,
Congress, and interstate commerce: the history of the
commerce clause and its relation to the Cramer Amendment.--Rinella, V., Jr. Police brutality and racial prejudice: a first close look.--Locke, H.G. Riot response:
the police and the courts.--Colista, F.P., Domonkos, M.
Bail and civil disorder.--Crockett, G.W., Jr. Recorder's
court and the 1967 civil disturbance.--Sultan, A., Howard, R. The efficient use of military forces to control
riots: some proposals for Congressional action.--Crum,
L.J. The national guard and riot control: the need for

revision.--Gartland, R., Chikota, R. When will the
troops come marching in?: a comment on the historical
use of federal troops to quell domestic violence.<u>3410</u>

SYMPOSIUM: [Civil disorder] Brooklyn L Rev 35:349-550 (1969).
<u>Selected contents</u>: Lindsay, J.V. Introduction.--Dodds,
R.H., Dempsey, R.R. Civil disorders ... .--Mackell, T.J.,
Ludwig, F.J. Orderly federal-state court relations v.
civil disorder.--Lefkowitz, L.J. Municipal liability
for damage caused by riot.--Bail and preventive deten-
tion ... .--Effect of federal firearms control ... .--
Insurance in riot-prone areas; Legislation and riots
... .--Scope of university discipline.--Bibliography.
<u>3411</u>

SYMPOSIUM: Proper handling of mass arrests: the experience of two
cities, Denver L J 46:26-129 (1969).
Contents: Jones, F. Chicago:1968.--Mackoff, B.S. Response.--Harper, A.R. Detroit:1967.--Brennan, V.J. Response.--Jones, N.R. Getting at the causes of riots
through legal services.--Griffen, B. Public morale a-
gainst the public peace.--Clark, L.D., Clark, C.P. Denial of rights to black citizens - speculation on the
relation to violence and civil disorders.--Toll, M.J.,
Allison, J.L. Advocates for the poor.--Merson, A. Closing the confidence gap: legal education's role.--Sykes,
G.M. Riots and the police.   <u>3411a</u>

U.S. NATIONAL Advisory Commission on Civil Disorders. Report. Washington, USGPO, 1968. 425 p.; N.Y., Bantam, 1968. 608 p.
O. Kerner, chair. Report on racial disorders in summer
of 1967; inadequacy of administration of criminal justice under emergency conditions; suggests measures to
improve criminal justice particularly at lower court
level; every aspect, including detention facilities,
studied.   <u>3412</u>

U.S. NATIONAL Institute of Mental Health Center for Studies of Crime
and Delinquency. Youth in turmoil; America's changing youth cultures
and student protest movements, by J.D. Douglas. Washington, USGPO,
1970. 250 p.
Deals mainly with American student protests and disruptive activities; includes chronology of events at
Berkeley, Columbia, S.F. State College, Cornell, U. of
Chicago, and Harvard.   <u>3413</u>

WESTIN, A.F. Freedom now: the civil rights struggle in America. N.Y.,
Basic Books, 1964. 361 p.
Author's purpose is to probe the moral dimension and the
processes of the civil rights struggle. Covered are the
sources of protest such as school segregation, discrimination in employment, housing, and law enforcement. An

extensive bibliography is included.   <u>3414</u>

ZINN, H. Disobedience and democracy; nine fallacies on law and order.
N.Y., Vintage Books (Random House), 1968. 124 p.
          The author points out nine fallacies in U.S. Supreme
          Court Justice Fortas's book, Concerning dissent and civil
          disobedience (N.Y., New American Libraries, 1968),
          in which law and order are upheld. He defends civil
          disobedience and protest beyond the law, and formulates
          a guide for civil disobedience.   <u>3415</u>

   B. Procedures Preliminary to Trial

      1. Arrest

          Selected items cover arrest, search and
          seizure, pretrial identification proce-
          dures, arraignment, preliminary hearing,
          confessions, right to counsel.

AMERICAN Bar Association Advisory Committee on the Police Function.
Standards relating to the urban police function, recommended by the
Advisory Committee on the Police Function. F.J. Remington, chair.;
H. Goldstein, S. Krantz, reptrs. Tent. draft, Mar. 1972. N.Y., IJA, 1972.
303 p. Approved draft, June 1973. 35 p. Approved, Feb. 1973.
          Standards cover police objectives and priorities, police
          methods, policy-making, control over police authority,
          police unions and political activity, adequate police
          resources, police performance in the criminal justice
          system, and the public view of police; appendix is a
          selected bibliography. (For other Standards, see item
          <u>3203</u>)   <u>3416</u>

AMERICAN Judicature Society. The English common law confession rule
and early cases decided by the United States Supreme Court, by W.
Gangi. Chicago, 1973. 27 p.
          Political scientist analyzes common law confession rule;
          gives demonstrative old and recent cases.   <u>3417</u>

AMERICAN Law Institute. Model code of pre-arraignment procedure.
Tent. draft no. 1. Mar. 1, 1966. 250 p. Study draft no. 1. Apr. 25,
1968. 169 p. Tent. draft no. 2. Apr. 15, 1969. 169 p. Tent. draft
no. 3. Apr. 24, 1970. 115 p. Tent. draft no. 4. Apr. 30, 1971. 47 p.
Tent. draft no. 5. Apr. 25, 1972. 113 p. Proposed official draft no.
1. Apr. 10, 1972. 239 p. Tent. draft no. 5A. Mar. 28, 1973. 21 p.
Tent. draft no. 6. Apr. 1, 1974. 329 p.   <u>3418</u>

ANDERSON, G.L. Preliminary hearing - better alternatives or more of
the same? Mo L Rev 35:281-325 (1970).
          Law professor analyzes preliminary hearing as working
          institution and evaluates proposals for improving the
          hearing. Examines function, development and current prac-

tices of preliminary hearing; benefits to accused and
prosecutor; prospects for improving existing hearing;
and various reform alternatives in which trial court
conducts hearing, which author feels to be necessary if
hearing is to be useful.   3419

CONSTITUTIONAL right to counsel at the preliminary hearing. Dick L
Rev 75:143-68 (1970).
> Note examines Coleman v. Alabama, 90 SCt 1999 (1970),
> in which the court held that a defendant has a right to
> counsel at the preliminary hearing, a critical stage in
> the proceedings; considers earlier related decisions.
> 3420

DIAMOND, H. Readings in arrest, search & seizure. Los Angeles, L. A.
State College, Dept. of Poli Sci and Admin., 1963. 236 p.
> Includes papers, presented at institutes sponsored by
> the Political Science Dept., on probable cause to arrest,
> search and seizure; the authority of the law enforcement
> officer; citizens' rights; police procedures; and the
> exclusionary rule. Includes chronological listing with
> comments of relevant U.S. Supreme Court cases and se-
> lected penal statutes.   3421

EASLEY, R.J. Preliminary arraignment. Penn BA Q 44:520-24 (1973).
> A justice of the peace contends that the practice of
> calling upon a JP to perform an immediate preliminary
> arraignment of a person arrested without a warrant
> after regular court hours is not needed in order to
> comply with the "unnecessary delay" requirement. He
> notes other states which do not have such a procedure.
> (For reply, see item 3478)   3422

ENKER, A.N. and ELSEN, S.H. Counsel for the suspect: Massiah v. United States and Escobedo v. Illinois. Minn L Rev 49:47-91 (1964).
> Authors review right to counsel before Massiah and Es-
> cobedo, take up impact and ramification of these de-
> cisions, criticize undesirable results, suggest alter-
> nate solutions and opine that the future may see the
> Supreme Court withdraw considerably from the broad
> language and implications of these decisions.   3423

FEENEY, F.F. Citation in lieu of arrest: the new California law.
Vand L Rev 25:367-394 (1970).
> Review of statute requiring investigation of possible
> use of citation in each misdemeanor arrest. Gives back-
> ground of citation procedure and compares with other
> plans.   3424

FEENEY, F.F. and WOODS, J.R. A comparative description of the New
York and California criminal justice systems: arrest through arraignment. Vand L Rev 26:973-1033 (1973).

Compares arrest and related processes for handling misdemeanor and felony defendants in New York City and Oakland; stresses problems in each, suggesting ways of
alleviating. Authors, Director of Center for Criminal
justice at Davis and attorney, give step-by-step procedures chronologically, including some statistics and
estimates on numbers and time; describe the Bronx Experiment (Pre-arraignment Processing Project) and conclude that at every stage the New York system is more
time-consuming: takes ten hours as opposed to three
in Oakland. (Comparative table)   3425

FORUM on the interrogation of the accused. Cornell L Q 49:382-435
(1964).
Panelists: Anolik, I., Fraenkel, O.K., Gaffney, G.H.,
Inbau, F.E., Kuh, R., McClellan, G.B., Moore, L.P.,
Murphy, M., Roulston, R.E., Stakel, W.J., Sutherland,
A.E. Article consists of comments and discussions of
panelists examining the problem of criminal interrogation. Discusses the viewpoint of the police, the importance of interrogation, the "Judges Rules" on interrogation in use in Canada, use of scientific techniques in interrogation, and the present and future
status of the law.   3426

FUNCTION of the preliminary hearing in federal pretrial procedure.
Yale L J 83:771-805 (1974).
Proposes reform of the federal preliminary hearing to
effect speedier trials; suggests alternative models:
backward-looking model concerning the legality of arrest
and detention, and forward-looking model concerning
probability of conviction at trial; discusses objections to forward-looking model and urges limited adoption of it in the federal system.   3427

GRAHAM, G. and LEWIN, L. Preliminary hearing in Los Angeles. UCLA
L Rev 18:636-757, 916-961 (1971).
Studies and records 200 preliminary hearings; includes
library and statistical research; analysis based on interviews and examination of court records. First part
examines collateral functions as discovery, substitute
for trial, determining legality of detention; also forum
for constitutional adjudication and opportunity for plea
bargaining; screening out cases not worthy of full
felony prosecution is explored.   3428

HERMAN, L. The Supreme Court and restrictions on police interrogation. Ohio S L J 25:449-500 (1964).
Law professor examines the scope and effect of constitutional restrictions, especially Escobedo, on police
interrogations. Discusses the nature of interrogation,
and the history and present status of: the coerced con-

fessions rule; 4th amendment restrictions; the privilege against self-incrimination; and right to counsel.
Author feels that effective police interrogaion is necessary and that the legislature should take steps, such
as assuring the presence of a third person at interrogation, so that rights can be protected while effective interrogation is maintained.   3429

HISTORICAL argument for the right to counsel during police interrogation. Yale L J 73:1000-57 (1964).
          Discussion of cases dealing with the right to counsel
          includes Powell v. Alabama, Gideon v. Wainwright and
          Betts v. Brady; describes the history of the common law
          right to counsel referring to the state's investigative
          process and interest in interrogation; analyzes the bal-
          ance between individual rights and the interest of the
          state; appendix is colonial provisions on counsel to
          1800.   3430

HUNVALD, E.H. The right to counsel at the preliminary hearing. Mo
L Rev 31:109-26 (1966).
          Law professor examines case history of right to counsel
          and discusses Missouri's interpretation of what consti-
          tutes a "critical stage" in the criminal process, call-
          for appointment of counsel for indigents. Author pre-
          sents his view that preliminary hearing is such a
          "critical stage" and asks that the courts use their
          rule-making power to provide for appointed counsel for
          indigents at preliminary hearings.   3431

INSTITUTE for Court Management. Pre-trial criminal procedures at the
Supreme Bench of the City of Baltimore, Maryland, by G.G. Kershaw.
Denver, 1972. 38 p.
          New procedures regarding arraignments, trials and re-
          lated actions in criminal cases examined to determine
          their efficacy in speeding criminal cases to trial. Con-
          cludes that new procedures were invoked without provid-
          ing supplemental services needed. Makes recommendations.
                                                       3432

INSTITUTE of Continuing Legal Education. A new look at confessions;
Escobedo -- the second round, ed. by B.J. George, Jr. Ann Arbor, 1967.
304 p.
          Editor presents lectures and discussions of seminar pro-
          grams following Miranda.Subjects include scope and sig-
          nificance; impact on police practices; new guidelines;
          procedural revolution; and the new role and obligation
          of counsel from custody to courtroom. Contributors in-
          clude: Cohen, H.B.; Edwards, G.; Finley, R.C.; Fuchs-
          berg, J.D.; George, J.B., Jr.; Gilmore, H.W.; Israel,
          J.H.; Kamisar, Y.; Kavanagh, T.M.; Lynch, T.C.; Nedrud,
          D.R.; Piersante, V.W.; Pringle, E.E.; Reed, J.W.; Sha-

piro, E.D.; Van Voorhees, J.; Wright, J.S.   3433

INSTITUTE of Criminal Law and Procedure. The pre-arraignment project; a preliminary report on the impact of Miranda in the District of Columbia. Washington, Georgetown U Law Center, 1967. 25 p.

> Report, with statistical data, is based on the first six months of a project which provides attorneys to defendants at the stationhouse interrogation, if requested by the defendants.   3434

INTERROGATIONS in New Haven: the impact of Miranda. Yale L J 76:1519-1648 (1967).

> Study of the implementation and effect of Miranda, researched through observation at New Haven Police Department for an 11-week period and interviews with various participants in the criminal process. Study examines the interrogatory process, the impact of Miranda on the suspect's willingness to cooperate, the importance of interrogation in solving crimes, and the impact of lawyers in the stationhouse. Finds little change since Miranda due to the secondary importance of interrogations to convictions and the slight impact it has had on the suspects. Appendices include questionnaires, methodology, interviews, factors relating to suspects, and a comparison of New Haven to other urban areas of similar size. Data tables.   3435

KAMISAR, Y. Some reflections on criticizing the courts and "policing the police." J Crim L 53:453-62 (1962).

> Law professor answers article of Prof. Inbau which emphasized the need for efficiency rather than the human element of the criminal system. Author criticizes Inbau's contentions that the Supreme Court has no authority to police the police in enforcing constitutional guarantees and asks for better documentation of Inbau's statements that new rulings involving confessions and admissions allow criminals to remain at large. This is a concluding article by Kamisar concerning Inbau's Public safety v individual liberties: the prosecutor's stand, J Crim L 53:85-89 (1962); Kamisar replied to the Inbau article: J Crim L 53:171-93 (1962); Inbau's rebuttal appeared in J Crim L 53:329-32 (1962).   3436

KOLBRECK, L. and PORTER, G.W. The law of arrest, search, and seizure. Los Angeles, Legal book store, 1965. 463 p.

> Authors discuss the law of arrest, search and seizure in a definitive effort to set out basic principles for the peace officer. Author provides guidelines including: background material, definitions, specific cases and procedures, statutes and examples.   3437

LAFAVE, W.R. Arrest: the decision to take a suspect into custody.
Boston, Little Brown, 1965. 540 p. (A B Found. Admin. of criminal
justice series)
> One of the first reports of the series (for others see
> item 3230) which focuses upon police policies and prac-
> tices relating to arrest. The role of police, of the
> law, and of the lawyer in respect to the arrest de-
> cision; their functions and activities are probed. Ob-
> jective descriptions rather than value judgements are
> presented. Practices in Kansas, Michigan and Wisconsin
> in 1956 and 1957 are the basis. Summary of contents:
> 1) decision to arrest 2) decision not to invoke criminal
> process 3) whether to take into immediate custody (al-
> ternatives and delays) 4) arrest to prosecute 5) arrest
> for other purposes. Conclusion: there are important
> unsolved issues; includes problems and role of various
> criminal justice agencies, trial and appellate judges
> and the legislature.   3438

LAFAVE, W.R. Detention for investigation by the police; an analysis
of current practices. Wash U L Q 1962:331-99 (1962).
> Law professor analyzes data on current detention prac-
> tices in Michigan and Wisconsin to explore the problem
> of detention for investigation. Discussed are: current
> police investigatory procedures, including opportuni-
> ties for release; charging suspect; and issues presen-
> ted by data, including when it is desirable to detain
> suspect who cannot be charged with, or arrested for,
> a specific crime and what safeguards are necessary to
> guard against police impropriety.   3439

LAFAVE, W.R. and REMINGTON, F.J. Controlling the police: the judge's
role in making and reviewing law enforcement decisions. Mich L Rev
63:987-1012 (1965).
> Law professors discuss the judicial role in law enforce-
> ment, focusing on involvement in determining whether
> arrest and search warrants should issue and judges'
> review of such decisions after warrants have been exe-
> cuted by the police; reexamines the exclusionary rule.
> Current practices and consequences are discussed. Author
> feels that none of these techniques prevent unconsti-
> tutional arrests and searches; better communication be-
> tween public and courts and sufficient judicial manpower
> are needed.   3440

LAW of citizen's arrest. Colum L Rev 65:502-13 (1965).
> Note discusses the inadequacy of existing laws of citi-
> zen arrest and the lack of protection afforded the
> citizen who voluntarily participates in law enforcement.
> The nature, rationale, and current procedure of citizen's
> arrest is examined. Author suggests revision of the law,
> allowing citizen arrest for conduct that presents a

danger to society and presents several principles that
would be workable for this revision.   3441

LEVINE, F.J. and TAPP, J.L. The psychology of criminal identification: the gap from Wade to Kirby. U Pa L Rev 121:1079-1131 (1973);
reprint, A B Found. research contrib. 1973,4.
          Sociologist and professor of psychology review and
          assess the empirical evidence related to errors in line-
          up identification and suggest the possible use and limi-
          tations of this evidence for remedying the problems of
          pretrial confrontations.   3442

LOHMAN, J.D. and MISNER, G.E. The police and the community: the dy-
namics of their relationships in a changing society. Washington,
USGPO, 1967. 2 v. (U.S. President's Commission on Law Enforcement
and the Administration of Justice; field survey 4)
          Study focuses on examining formal and informal social
          systems which seem to be central to the police-community
          relations field. Includes: social and governmental set-
          ting, including population, political system, and courts;
          police department goals and resources; public and police
          view of police community relations; activities of police
          with ethnic and juvenile groups; problems attendant on
          due process; effect of structural forms on police com-
          munity relations; and police control.   3443

MCGOWAN, C. Rule-making and the police. Mich L Rev 70:659-94 (1972).
          Federal appellate judge, in Oliver Wendell Holmes lec-
          ture, suggests that recent developments have generated
          many limitations upon police conduct, constituting, in
          effect, rules; compares impact to English Judges' Rules,
          which are advisory rather than mandatory; speaks also
          to legislative rules regulating police conduct during
          period of presentment in court; discusses ALI Modal
          Code of Pre-Arraignment Procedure; explores potential
          of self-regulation by police; suggests the future of
          police rule-making is interwoven with the future of
          the exclusionary rule. Many cases analyzed.   3444

MCINTYRE, D.M. A study of judicial dominance of the charging process.
J Crim L 59:463-90 (1968).
          Discusses lower court judges' procedures in reviewing
          felony accusations for purpose of charging in Cook
          County (Chicago).   3445

MEDALIE, R.J., ZIETZ, L., and ALEXANDER, P. Custodial police interrogation in our nation's capital: the attempt to implement Miranda.
Mich L Rev 66:1347-1422 (1968).
          Authors use empirical study to examine the Miranda de-
          cision and conclude that the three basic premises of
          Miranda, that police would give adequate and effective
          warning, that suspects would understand this, and that

the presence of an attorney would protect the accused's
Fifth Amendment privileges, do not hold. The warnings
are not given until they are basically ineffective,
many defendants do not understand or appreciate the
significance of the warnings, and counsel arrives too
late to be of significant help. Authors recommend an
educational campaign, that police should not question
suspect until actual interrogation begins, and that
paid attorneys be stationed at the police headquarters
so that they can effectively aid their clients. Appendices of questionnaires, forms, interviews, and data
tables.   **3446**

MILNER, N.A.   The court and local law enforcement: the impact of
Miranda.   Beverly Hills, Calif., Sage, 1971.   268 p.
        Study of police adjustment to Miranda in four Wisconsin
        cities finds that greater police professionalization
        and interaction with outside groups produces more favor-
        able police attitudes towards the Miranda decision, and
        more successful implementation. Includes chapter on
        the impact on interrogation behavior. 9-p. bibliography.
                                                     3447

MUELLER, G.O.W.   Position of the criminal defendant; an anthropocen-
tric survey of American criminal procedure.   N.Y., NYU School of Law,
1965.   146 p.
        "[A] journey along felony road in the United States,
        with the focus on the person labeled a felon," explains
        criminal law professor about the title and emphasis
        of the work: "Only few of those arrested will ultimately
        have to face a jury. Hence, mass justice must occur at
        the police station and before the magistrate." Descrip-
        tion of modern practices accordingly gives more atten-
        tion to pretrial stages; includes some historical back-
        ground to show development and reasons for present pro-
        cedures.   **3448**

MUNICIPAL court misdemeanor arraignment procedure of Hamilton County,
Ohio: an empirical study.   U Cin L Rev 41:623-68 (1972).
        Based on docket records and extensive interviews, con-
        cludes that the plan introduced in 1970, whereby not
        guilty pleas produce automatic continuances in order
        to set a definite trial date, does not substantially
        help witnesses or improve scheduling, but does allow
        judge shopping and unnecessary continuances and induces
        guilty pleas from fear of pretrial incarceration.**3449**

MURPHY, M.J.   Report ... on Manhattan Summons Project, National Conference on Bail and Criminal Justice on May 28, 1964, Washington, D.C.
N.Y., 1964.   15 p.
        Police commissioner reports on pilot summons program
        in New York City used in lieu of formal arrest and

detention, attempting to improve arrest procedures by
bringing the offending individual before a judicial
officer in a way which will reduce expense, free police
manpower, and safeguard the individual's rights. Defendant is brought in for interview by the arresting officer; whether detention or summons occurs depends on
the recommendation of trained interviewer. Offenses
for which summons may be issued, results of project to
date, and advantages of this method are discussed.3450

NEW YORK (City) Criminal Justice Coordinating Council and VERA Institute of Justice. Manhattan summons project. N.Y., 1969. 10 p.
(For annotation see item 994) 3451

NEW YORK City-Rand Institute. Analysis of the night and weekend
arraignment parts in the Bronx and Queens criminal courts, by J.B.
Jennings. April, 1973. N.Y., 1974. 68 p.
Results of analysis of procedure and its impact on the
City-wide arraignment system. Recommendations include:
a. continuting the new parts; b. better use of excess
capacity through longer hours and possibly use of the
Supreme Court building in the Bronx; c. discontinuing
use of Civil Court judges on weekends and holidays;
and d) extending legal aid to all defendants at arraignment. Appendices include original directive, detailed
findings, and observation forms. Data tables, glossary.
3452

NEW YORK (State) Attorney General. Your rights if arrested. Albany,
1966. 11 p.
Pamphlet for general public describes rights upon
arrest; what constitutes a lawful arrest, when a warrant
is necessary, citizen's arrest, detention without
arrest, right to remain silent, use of force by police,
search procedures and warrants, the record, notifying
family and lawyer, bail, court appearance, right to
be assigned attorney, and preliminary hearing. 3453

PRELIMINARY examination - evidence and due process. Kan L Rev 15:
374-87 (1967).
Historical development; changes necessary due to U.S.
Supreme Court decisions; due process and evidentiary
rules at hearing; right to counsel; illegally seized
evidence; leading cases discussed. 3454

PRELIMINARY hearing - an interest analysis. Iowa L Rev 51:164-83
(1965).
Note presents an historical perspective of judicial
proceeding held after arrest but prior to indictment;
interplay between rights of accused and society's interests; annotated with cases. 3455

PRETRIAL right to counsel. Stan L Rev 26:399-420 (1974).
Student examines U.S. Supreme Court's expansion of
pretrial right from 1932 to 1967, then proceeds to discuss recent cases dealing with right to counsel at pretrial identification. Summarizing Supreme Court opinions
and their implications; conclusion is that while Court's
reasoning is consistent "with the letter of their prior
precedent" recent cases, particularly Kirby v Illinois,
406 US 682 (1972) and US v Asch, 413 US 300 (1973) limit
the scope of the right and are inconsistent with prior
precedent.   3456

PYE, A.K. The Supreme Court and the police: fact and fiction. J Crim
L 57:404-18 (1966).
Law professor explores the nature and validity of police
objections to the Supreme Court cases dealing with pre-
arraignment procedure, concluding that the objections
are not that the Court has provided for new rights,
but that the Court has now held that the police must
actively protect these rights. Author proposes that
objective studies be undertaken to show whether the
new rulings have lessened police effectiveness and to
what extent, and suggests that guidelines for the police
are necessary.   3457

REGULATION and enforcement of pre-trial identification procedures.
Colum L Rev 69:1296-1306 (1969).
Discusses permissible identification procedures and
regulations which would lessen possibility of error and
abuse. Examines range of enforcement techniques that
may be utilized against defendant for failure to cooper-
ate, such as attempting to use refusal as evidence a-
gainst accused.   3457a

REISS, A.J. and BLACK, D.J. Interrogation and the criminal process.
Annals 374:47-57 (1967).
Authors focus on the courts' attempt to control behavior
of police through exclusionary rule as in Miranda, the
role of the police and the courts in the criminal system,
and the effect of Miranda. Data gathered through field
observation in Boston, Chicago and D.C. Authors find
interrogation, both pre- and post-Miranda, has little
impact on conviction, and that the effect of the decision is felt more strongly in the prosecution-orien-
tated detective department than by regular police.
                                                      3458

RIGHT to counsel at preliminary hearing. UMKC L Rev 39:237-51 (1970-
71).
An examination of Coleman v Alabama, 399 US 1 (1970),
in which it was held that defendant had right to counsel
at the preliminary hearing; earlier federal decisions

and Missouri's position in this are are also considered.   3459

THE RIGHT to counsel does not extend to a preindictment identification proceeding; Kirby v Illinois, 406 US 682 (1972). Syracuse L Rev
24:845-51 (1973).
          Author analyzes Kirby, where Court held that right to
          counsel does not attach until formal adversary judicial
          charges have been brought, and reviews Court's rationale
          in previous cases finding counsel needed at certain
          "critical stages." Author criticizes Kirby, stating that
          it allows for potential abuse of defendant's rights
          through prosecutorial delay in initiating charges.
                                                  3460

RIGHT to counsel in California. Santa Clara Law 5:75-80 (1964).
          Discusses People v Dorado, 394 P2d 952 (1964), and
          People v Anderson, 394 P2d 945 (1964), which held that
          the right to counsel arises once investigation has fo-
          cused on a particular suspect, that the suspect must
          be advised of his right to counsel or to remain silent,
          and that these rights can only be intelligently waived.
                                                  3461

RIGHT to counsel, preliminary hearing. Conn L Rev 3:366-71 (1970/71).
          Student questions Court's thinking in Coleman v Alabama,
          399 US 1 (1970), pointing out that it does not seem con-
          sistent with Court's other decisions concerning rights
          of accused persons.   3462

SCHAEFER, R.C. Patrolman perspectives on Miranda. L & Soc Order
1971:81-101.
          Government professor explores the impact of Miranda
          on the police: their feelings and how it affects their
          performance; interviewed rookie policemen in Minneapolis
          and found a general lack of understanding of Miranda
          guidelines. Suggests further research. Sample question-
          naires and data.   3463

SCHAEFER, W.V. Police interrogation and the privilege against self-
incrimination. Nw U L Rev 61:506-21 (1966).
          Justice examines the policy considerations advanced in
          support of the privilege against self-incrimination,
          suggests that subjects be interrogated before magis-
          trates, and proposes that comment upon the failure of
          a suspect to respond to orderly interrogation be allowed.
          Author advances view that whereas interests of accused
          are protected, interests of public are not.   3464

SCHAEFER, W.V. The suspect and society. Evanston, Ill., Northwestern
U press, 1967. 99 p. (Rosenthal lect., 1966)
          Lectures dealing with prevailing police practices in

interrogating suspects in police custody discuss constitutional doctrines bearing on privilege against self-
incrimination and right to counsel [precedes Miranda]
Includes legislative proposals.   3465

SEEBURGER, R.H. and WETTICK, R.S. Miranda in Pittsburgh; a statistical study. U Pitt L Rev 29:1-26 (1967)
        Law professors examine the extent that Miranda has im-
        paired custodial interrogation in Pittsburgh through data
        from the Detective Branch files. Discusses pre- and
        post-Miranda confession rates and the necessity of con-
        fessions for conviction. Authors find that the confes-
        sion rate has declined, but that Miranda has not sig-
        nificantly impaired law enforcement; there is still a
        sufficient rate of confession and conviction. Similar
        surveys are reviewed; data tables included.   3466

SKOLNICK, J.H. Justice without trial: law enforcement in democratic
society. N.Y., Wiley, 1966. 279 p.
        Law professor gives a descriptive analysis of police
        work, drawing data from a study of criminal law officials
        in the city of Westville, Calif. Chapters cover methods
        of arrest for various crimes, attitudes of the police
        toward criminal law, and the balancing of interests be-
        tween the judge as the guardian of constitutional prin-
        ciples and the policeman as the agent responsible for
        crime control.   3467

SOBEL, N.R. The new confession standards: Miranda v Arizona; a legal
perspective, a practical perspective. N.Y., Gould pub., 1966. 153 p.
        New York trial court judge examines older exclusionary
        rules with primary emphasis on their relationship to
        Miranda; the traditional involuntary rule, no longer
        relevant to future trials; the "defendant" and "accusa-
        tory" stage rules, the police custody stage rule, and
        problems likely to recur with greatest frequency in this
        area. Fourth Amendment primary taint exclusionary rule
        and procedural and practical problems are discussed.
                                                           3468

STEPHENS, O.H., FLANDERS, R.L., and CANNON, J.L. Law enforcement and
the Supreme Court: police perceptions of the Miranda requirements.
Tenn L Rev 39:407-31 (1972).
        Political scientists find a high level of adherence to
        the decision but limited compliance with its policy
        objectives.   3469

SYMPOSIUM: The Supreme Court and the police. J Crim L 57:237-317,
379-425 (1966).
        Contents. Pt. 1: Packer, H.L. The courts, the police and
        the rest of us.--Kuh, R.H. The "rest of us" in the "po-
        licing the police" controversy.--Souris, T. Stop and

frisk or arrest and search; the use and misuse of eu-
phemisms.--Inbau, F.E. Democratic restraints upon the
police.--Broderick, V.L. The Supreme Court and the police: a police viewpoint.--English, R.E. Lawyers in the
stationhouse?--Wilson, O.W. Crime, the courts, and the
police.--Desmond, C.S. Reflections of a state reviewing
court judge upon the Supreme Court's mandates in criminal cases.--Craig, D.W. To police the judges, not just
judge the police.--Wilkins, L.T. Persistent offenders
and preventive detention. Pt. 2: Finley, R.C. Who is on
trial: the police? the courts? or the criminally accused?--Pye, A.K. The Supreme Court and the police: fact
and fiction.--Thompson, J.R. The Supreme Court and the
police: 1968?   3470

TENNESSEE Law Revision Commission. Preliminary hearings and committing magistrates in Tennessee, by R. Brandt. Nashville, 1966. 46 p.
    Paper examines the law and actual practice of prelimin-
    ary hearings in Tennessee. Discussed are: the nature of
    a preliminary hearing; the right to a preliminary hear-
    ing; courts conducting hearings; procedure at hearing;
    time requirements and right to counsel. Author concludes
    that the system requires more coherency and uniformity
    and presents a proposed statute towards this end.3471

TIEGER, J.H. Police discretion and discriminatory enforcement. Duke
L J 1971:717-43.
    Categorizes situations where police exercise discretion
    in enforcement, and discusses the developing case law
    of alleged discrimination in enforcement.   3472

UNITED Nations. Study of the right to be free from arbitrary arrest,
detention, and exile. N.Y., 1964. 230 p.
    Commission on Human Rights presents the laws and prac-
    tices of arrest, detention, and exile of the several
    nations; fundamental principles, rights of the arrested
    or detained person, remedies available for violation of
    these rights or exile. Text of draft principles on
    freedom from arbitrary arrest and detention included.
                                                         3473

U. S. FEDERAL Bureau of Investigation. Due process in criminal interrogation. Washington, 1965. 54 p.
    Identification and discussion of the principles of fed-
    eral constitutional law which control the practice and
    procedure of criminal interrogation. History of due
    process, rights of accused, interrogation practices,
    actions against officers violating due process, and sug-
    gested police actions are examined. Appendix is synopsis
    of important Supreme Court decisions on this subject.
                                                         3474

U. S. FEDERAL Bureau of Investigation. Search of the person. Washington, 1966. 36 p.
Examines federal law, including: fundamental legal rights involved; search by warrant; search incidental to arrest; search of the person incidental to arrest; scope of reasonable seizure; frisk for dangerous weapons; search by consent; abandoned property; border searches; search of deceased persons; and search by military. Cases, statutes and procedures are discussed.   3475

UNIVERSAL pre-arraignment procedure. Hastings L J 18:633-42 (1967). Note discusses the effect of Miranda v Arizona, 384 US 436 (1966), on the procedural aspects of state and federal questioning of suspects and the possibility of a congressionally legislated Uniform Rule of Pre-Arraignment Procedures applicable to all states.   3476

WATTS, L.P.   In the wake of Miranda. Pop Govt 33:1-8 (1966)
Author considers problems facing law enforcement officials in view of the Miranda decision and makes some suggestions on how to overcome them. He observes that distrust of police is very old in Anglo-American society, and discusses decisions of the Supreme Court which demonstrate the Court's role in curbing law enforcement practices prior to Miranda.   3477

YOUNG, S.G.   Preliminary arraignment revisited; the necessity for continuously available justices of the peace to hold preliminary arraignments. Penn BA Q 45:83-7 (1974)
In reply to Easley's article, Preliminary arraignment (see item 3422), author argues that Judge Easley erred in his understanding of procedural and substantive law on "unnecessary delay"; maintains that the Pennsylvania practice of immediate preliminary arraignments is necessary to prevent abuses.   3478

2. Grand Jury

Items cover history, how selected, various functions and duties; witness immunity; right to counsel; arguments in support of and against the grand jury.

ANTELL, M.P.   Modern grand jury: benighted supergovernment. ABA J 51:153-56 (1965).
Indictment of grand jury by judge who demonstrates its archaic nature and that it no longer is guardian of liberty - or indeed ever was. (See also item 3527)
    3479

BARTLETT, J.W.   Defendant's right to an unbiased federal grand jury. BU L Rev 47:551-65 (1967).

Explores procedural safeguards and whether federal criminal defendant has right to curtail allowable quantum of
grand jury preconceptions concerning the case; examines
impact of Fifth Amendment and federal rules; quotes Justice Field's charge to the grand jury in US v Wells, 163
F 313,327,329 (D Idaho, 1908). Avows that if grand jury
objectivity were the fact, objections to grand jury
would diminish.   3480

BICKNER, M.K. The grand jury; a layman's assessment. Calif SB J 48:
661-66, 734-37 (1973).
A frustrating year's service as a grand juror leads
author, professor of administration, to review shortcomings in organization and functioning. Suggested improvements include limiting indictment function, careful
briefing of members, more pay. Empirical research on
grand juries should be promoted.   3481

BRAUN, R.L. The grand jury: spirit of the community? Ariz L Rev 15:
893-917 (1973).
Author presents historical development of grand jury
through recent lower court and Supreme Court decisions;
presents current standards relating to grand jury sub-
poenas and investigations, and suggests new approaches
including a bifurcated system separating the indicting
and investigative functions.   3482

BROWN, P.M. Ten reasons why the grand jury in New York should be retained and strengthened. Record 22:471-78 (1967).
Supports the grand jury as 1) a protection against un-
just prosecutions, 2) a buffer between the people and
the law, 3) nonpartisan, 4) secret, 5) a check on the
zealous prosecutor, 6) a strong weapon against organized crime, 7) a voice for the people's conscience as
shown by over 500 reports in New York County (1869-1960),
8) a Fifth Amendment protection, 9) a body having confidence of the public, and 10) abolition would give too
much power to prosecutors.   3483

CALIFORNIA Judicial Council. A report on the grand jury's criminal
law function. [prep. by E. Kaster] Its Ann rep 1974:23-65
Objective of study is to present complete picture of
grand jury indictment procedures, dealing only indirectly
with its watchdog or civil law functions. Taking up the
issues of the grand jury debate, the study sketches
briefly the grand jury's history; then gives details of
California's grand jury system - selection, orientation,
duties, staff, pay, procedures used for possible indictment, type of case presented. The evaluation discusses
advantages to prosecutor, disadvantages to defense counsel, and constitutionality of indictment procedures.
Recent reform proposals are explained, discussing various

recommendations made by ALI and National Advisory Commission on Criminal Justice Standards and Goals. 3484

CALKINS, R.M. Fading myth of grand jury secrecy. John Marshall L J
1:18-36 (1967).
Reviews the traditional reasoning against discovery of
grand jury minutes at various stages before and during
trial in light of the Dennis decision, and states that
Dennis has important implications on both grand jury
secrecy and pretrial discovery.   3485

CALKINS, R.M. Grand jury secrecy. Mich L Rev 63:455-90 (1965).
Discusses what author sees as movement to liberalize
outmoded rules of grand jury secrecy; reviews developing case law on permanent and temporary grand jury
secrecy, use of grand jury testimony for impeachment
purposes, and other topics. Argues the unconstitutionality of 1963 Illinois statute (now revised) which
vested the discretion to disclose such testimony solely
in the State's Attorney.   3486

CALKINS, R.M. and WILEY, R.E. Grand jury secrecy under the Illinois
criminal code - unconstitutional. Nw U L Rev 59:577-90 (1964).
Argues the unconstitutionality of the 1963 Illinois
statute which places discretion to disclose grand jury
testimony solely in the State's Attorney. In 1965 the
statute was revised to place the discretion in the
court.   3487

CAMPBELL, W.J. Eliminate the grand jury. J Crim L 64:174-82 (1973).
Federal district court judge calls attention to "leak
in the dike" surrounding support of grand jury expressed
in U.S. Supreme Court opinion US v Dionisis, 93 SCt 764
(1973). Concern over viability of grand jury expressed
by at least six members of U.S. Supreme Court. Author
presents details of evolution, functions and operations
of grand jury citing to cases and articles. He favors
an alternative: information, giving details of procedures. Article is part of Symposium: Perspectives on
Innovation and Reform in Criminal Justice. See also,
Hamilton, W.A. and Work, C.R. The prosecutor and the
urban court system; the case for management consciousness. J Crim L 64:183-89 (1973).   3488

CIVIL petitioner's right to representative grand juries and a statistical method of showing discrimination in jury selection cases generally. UCLA L Rev 20:581-654 (1973).
"Civil petitioner" refers to individuals or classes
challenging grand jury's watchdog powers over local
governments and composition of grand jury. Comment considers substantive and evidentiary issues involved
and proposes standardized method of presenting and an-

alizing relevant statistical data for jury discrimination cases generally. Data collected from a questionnaire survey of 191 former Alameda County (Calif.)
grand jurors.   3489

CLARK, L.D. The grand jury; the use and abuse of political power.
N.Y., Quadrangle, 1975. 163 p.
        Foreword by Sen. P.A. Hart; a publication of the Com-
        mittee for Public Justice. Law professor examines the
        institutional structure of the grand jury and its oper-
        ational abuses, especially under the Nixon administra-
        tion: its history and development; and the grand jury
        as a political weapon in utilizing illegal wiretaps,
        gathering intelligence on political activists, harass-
        ing and jailing of radical witnesses for "non-coopera-
        tion," depriving witnesses of Bill of Rights protections,
        and pressuring media, congress, and public officials.
        Author proposes solutions to abuses including possible
        abolishment and means of maintaining the grand jury
        within a system which would protect civil liberties.
                                                        3490

COMPULSORY immunity legislation; Title II of the Organized Crime Control Act of 1970. U Ill L F 1971:91-111.
        Discussion of the constitutionality of the "use immun-
        ity" before Grand Jury in Title II, as opposed to "trans-
        actional immunity" and the background, case law and
        policy connected with each method. Concludes that use
        immunity is unconstitutional. Appendix is table of
        Federal Witness Immunity Statutes.   3491

DEFENSE access to grand jury testimony: right in search of a standard.
Duke L J 1968:556-87.
        Discusses the issue of defense access to grand jury
        minutes as construed by Dennis and its progeny; concludes
        that the various and confused case law tests of "partic-
        ularized need" should be replaced with a uniform con-
        stitutional standard.   3492

DISCOVERY of a trial witness grand jury testimony. Rutgers Camden L J
1:93-103 (1969).
        Article discusses the problems the courts have faced
        in determining when discovery of grand jury testimony
        is appropriate; the reasons for secrecy, the develop-
        ment of new rules including the need for defendant to
        show a particular need that outweighs the need for
        secrecy, and pertinent cases. Authors conclude that
        none of the newly developed rules are adequate in sol-
        ving all of these problems.   3493

DUFF, B.B. and HARRISON, A.E. The grand jury in Illinois: to slaughter
a sacred cow. U Ill L F 1973:635-72.

Presents the arguments for and against the grand jury
system; analyzes the limitations through the dominance
of the prosecutor and details abuses of the system; presents alternatives for reform, including making the
grand jury adversary, abolition of the indictment, the
straight option allowing the prosecutor the choice of
proceeding by information or indictment, and limiting
the availability of the grand jury.   3494

EVALUATING the grand jury's role in a dual system of prosecution: a
case study.   Iowa L Rev 57:1354-75 (1972).
          Focus of the note is on grand jury in Iowa, with rele-
          vance to other states where the grand jury's role is
          similar to that in Iowa; writer reviews evolution and
          early criticism of grand jury; specifically describes
          Iowa grand jury, selection of its membership, its author-
          ity, and duties; its potential role and actual perfor-
          mance, which is found wanting because of its failure
          to initiate investigations charged to it under the
          statute. It has also not carried out its duty to review
          county attorney's discretionary decision to forego pro-
          secution or to prosecute. Various alternatives to the
          grand jury are discussed to ensure such review and pro-
          vide other improved criminal procedures. This evalua-
          tion of potential roles of the grand jury presents pro-
          posals in each area of interest to other states. 3495

EXAMINATION of the grand jury in New York. Colum J L & Soc Prob 2:88-
108 (1966).
          Discussion of role, composition and procedures of the
          New York grand jury. Disputes "rubber stamp" charges,
          reviews role of the preliminary hearing, use of the
          information in place of indictment, and the rights of
          the accused. Advises that secrecy after indictment be
          eliminated.   3496

GRAND Jury Association of New York County. The people's big stick:
a brief account of the roots, the achievements, and the present status
of the grand jury in New York state. N.Y., 1964. 30 p.
          Relates the accomplishments of grand juries in New York
          in making public reports, or presentments, on important
          issues. Also explains the origin of the Grand Jury
          Association and reviews its efforts toward grand jury
          improvement.   3497

GRAND jury -- future defendants entitled to witnesses' grand jury
testimony without showing of particularized need. Harv L Rev 81:712-
17 (1968).
          Article analyzes the court's opinion in US v Youngblood,
          379 F2d 365 (2d Cir., 1967), in which the court pro-
          spectively promulgated a new rule that defendant need
          not show particularized need in order to inspect grand

jury testimony of each trial witness relevant to the
subjects covered by witness's trial testimony. Author
concludes that defendant should have been given the
benefit of the new rule.   3498

GRAND jury -- secrecy of testimony -- protection afforded by traditional rule of secrecy is waived by a witness who seeks disclosure.
Fordham Urban L J 2:151-68 (1973).
        Note discusses In re Biaggi, 478 F2d 489 (2d Cir., 1973)
        in which the court denied limited review of unedited
        testimony and released edited testimony to the public
        holding that release of grand jury testimony without
        deletion of names violated the protection afforded by
        the secrecy rule. History of grand jury, justifications
        of secrecy, relevant cases, and future questions left
        unanswered are examined.   3499

GRAND jury secrecy: should witnesses have access to their grand jury
testimony as a matter of right? UCLA L Rev 20:804-26 (1973).
        Surveys development of grand jury, its veil of secrecy
        and modern trends to limit secrecy with regard to de-
        fendants; shows necessity to include witnesses when
        use immunity is granted; makes proposals, including man-
        datory recording and witness right to transcript. An-
        alyzes In re Russo (Pentagon Papers case).   3500

GRAND jury selection: voter registration as a cross section of the
community. Ore L Rev 52:482-98 (1973).
        This article describes the various grand jury selection
        systems and the constitutional standards articulated by
        the Supreme Court; analyzes the use of voter registra-
        tion lists and critizes the standards of the Federal
        Jury Selection Act; suggests new methods of compiling
        lists, including the use of supplemental lists and
        yearly census data.   3501

GRAND jury - transcript of minutes - court properly directed delivery
to Public Service Commission of transcript of minutes of grand jury
which found indictment against defendants for submitting rigged bills
to Con Edison Company of New York, Inc. Albany L Rev 35:403-410
(1971).
        Courts may grant inspection of grand jury minutes in
        aid of proceedings other than criminal to protect public.
        People v Denapoli, 35 AppDiv2d 28, 312 NYS2d 547 (1971).
        Note gives reasons for preserving grand jury secrecy
        and discusses cases providing exception to rules of
        secrecy in New York. Reviews federal court decisions
        in civil anti-trust cases having allowed inspection of
        grand jury minutes. Advocates limiting ban on disclo-
        sure of minutes.   3502

INDICTMENT sufficiency. Col L Rev 70:876-908 (1970).
        Grand jury secrecy means that the indictment is the only

proof of the grand jury's probable cause finding, and
must reflect consideration of each charge by a full
statement of the allegation. The note considers the
various case law tests, and suggest alternatives.
3503

JULIAN, A.S. The grand jury: necessary or decadent? Trial 8: 15
(Jan./Feb. 1972)
Chairman of the Board of Editors of American Trial Lawyers Association recommends abolition of the grand jury
as a tool of the prosecutor, anachronistic, and eco-
nomically wasteful. Points to absence of counsel for
witnesses as its worst aspect.   3504

JUROR selection - equal protection - deliberate inclusion of Negroes
on grand jury. NYU L R 42:364-370 (1967).
Comment analyzes Brooks v Beto, 366 F2d 1 (5th Cir.,
1966), in which the Court rejected appellant's claim
that the deliberate inclusion of Negro jurors violated
his right to equal protection of the laws, and discusses the use of deliberate inclusion. Because of
the possibility of discriminatory inclusion of minority jurors, the author suggests scrutiny of relevant
statistics before acceptance of deliberate inclusion
as a long term solution to fair representation, but
feels it is a useful short term solution.   3505

KUHNS, R.B. Limiting the criminal contempt power: new roles for
the prosecutor and the grand jury. Mich L R 73:484-536 (1975).
Limited to the criminal contempt sanction for refusal of a witness to testify. Law professor examines
substantive and procedural limitations, stressing
independence of judiciary, considers giving initiating
discretion to prosecutor instead, with right to grand
jury indictment in such cases. Analyzes cases under,
and suggests changes in, F R Crim P Rule 42 (b).
3506

MACCORKLE, S.A. The Texas grand jury. rev. ed. Austin, Inst of
Public Affairs, U of Texas, 1966. 28 p.
Author describes functions, powers and procedures;
juror's qualifications, duties and responsibilities.
3507

MAR, P. The California grand jury: vestige of aristocracy. Pacific
L J 1:36-64 (1970).
After detailing legislative efforts to reform, author
describes selection practices citing to cases and
studies regarding such practices; constitutional issues and court-made changes are discussed, with suggested legislation. Also deals with the civil law or
"watchdog" functions of the grand jury.   3508

MESHBESHER, R.I. Right of counsel before grand jury. FRD 41:189-
208 (1967).
Explores legality of procedure calling potential defendants before grand jury without counsel; asks: is
Escobedo to be finessed by proceeding against suspect
as witness rather than as arrestee? If so, this most
significant decision is an exercise in futility. Case
made for presence of counsel.   3509

NATIONAL Asbociation of Attorneys General. State investigative grand
juries. In its Organized crime control legislation. Raleigh, 1974.
p. 113-28.
Organized Crime Control Act has placed new responsibilities and reliance on the investigative grand jury. This
chapter explores origin and practices of the grand jury;
power of attorney general to call statewide investigative grand jury; opposition to certain powers of investigative grand jury. Discusses state grand jury legislation, where such investigative grand juries have been
established, and their powers.   3510

NEJELSKI, P. and FINSTERBUSCH, K. The prosecutor and the researcher;
present and prospective variations on the Supreme Court's Branzburg
decision. Social Problems 21:3-21 (1973).
Summarizes Branzburg: reporters are not protected ab-
solutely from summons of grand jury by First Amendment;
must answer relevant and material questions; explores
implications for social scientists; suggests specific
ways to claim confidentiality of data.   3511

OLSON, B.T. Ombudsman on the West Coast: an analysis and evaluation
of the California grand jury. Police 12:12-20 (Feb. 1968).
Author describes the organizational aspects of the grand
jury, its methods, processes, and achievements; concludes that the grand jury has the potential to function
as the prototype of an ombudsman within an American
context.   3512

OMNIBUS Crime Control Act of 1968--grand jury witness who has been
granted transactional immunity may refuse to answer questions which
are based upon information derived from unauthorized electronic surveillance. Vill L Rev 17:524-45 (1972).
Article analyzes In Re Egan, 450 F2d 199 (1971), in
which the court held that Egan, who had been granted
immunity, could properly refuse to answer grand jury
questions based upon illegally intercepted oral communications. History of the grand jury, Congressional
attempts to handle electronic surveillance problems,
cases relied on by the court, and the opinion are discussed. Author concludes that Egan has extended the
exclusionary rule at a time when the continued existence of the rule is being questioned by the Supreme

Court, and that, on appeal, the court may refuse to
permit the use of this rule by a witness before a grand
jury who has been granted immunity.   3513

RIGHTS of a witness before the grand jury. Duke L J 1967:97-135.
Right against self-incrimination often is difficult to
maintain without knowledge of the technical aspects of
avoiding contempt, waiver of the privilege, and perjury;
author discusses a witness's rights and hazards he faces;
recommends establishment of the right to counsel for
grand jury witnesses and greater use of immunity.3514

SAN DIEGO County Bar Association Grand Jury Committee. Report. San
Diego L Rev 9:145-89 (1972).
A detailed survey of the grand jury process in San Diego
County with comparative data from other counties. Find-
ings, recommendations.   3515

SCHWARTZ, H.E. Demythologizing the historic role of the grand jury.
Amer Crim L Rev 10:701-70 (1972).
Describes grand jury origin, its functioning during
periods of political stress, and recent abuses of its
function as a shield against political persecutions.
Includes a discussion of improper relationships of the
judge with the grand jury. Also points to specific examples of unrepresentative selection of grand jurors,
multiple grand juries, misdemeanor charges, change of
venue, indictments with insufficient evidence, and prejudicial presentments as abuses of the grand jury, but
does not recommend its abolition.   3516

SECRECY in grand jury proceedings: proposal for a new rule of criminal
procedure 6(e). Fordham L Rev 38:307-322 (1969).
Argues that R. 6(e) of FRCrimProc should be amended
to allow defendant to inspect grand jury minutes, as of
right, after indictment. Case analysis and historical
discussion, description of English procedure. 3517

SELTZER, C.Z. Pre-trial discovery of grand jury testimony in criminal cases. Dick L Rev 66:379-401 (1962).
History of traditional secrecy, court decisions in state
and federal courts; comparison with English system of
pretrial discovery; includes summary of discovery
methods in criminal cases. The trend is toward liberal-
ized criminal procedures affording accused equal opportunities with state for full disclosure of facts.3518

SHERRY, A.H. Unreasonable rule of secrecy of grand jury minutes. Va
L Rev 48:668-84 (1962).
The grand jury has remained largely unchanged since
Blackstone; author criticizes traditional secrecy, con-
trasting these procedures with statutory preliminary

hearing. Sound administration of criminal justice requires greater disclosure, says editor of American Bar
Foundation Survey of Administration of Criminal Justice;
discusses federal statutes, rules, cases.   3519

SPAIN, J. The grand jury, past and present: a survey. Am Crim L Q
2:119-42 (1964).
                Overview of typical grand jury requirements. Appendix
                is state-by-state summary of function, composition,
                number needed to indict, duties, in which cases needed
                to indict.   3520

STATE grand jury report chilling freedom of speech may be ordered
expunged by a federal district court as a violation of the Civil
Rights Act of 1871. Col L Rev 71:1090-1102 (1971).
                Case concerns the report on the Kent State killings,
                in which the grand jury sharply criticized statements
                of professors made before the shootings, and their
                teaching doctrines of dissent.   3521

STEELE, W.W.   Right to counsel at the grand jury stage of criminal
proceedings.   Mo L Rev 36:193-214 (1971).
                Argues for change permitting counsel at grand jury stage
                giving reasons; explains functions counsel can perform;
                gives rundown of state statutes permitting waiver of
                indictment.   3522

SYMPOSIUM: the grand jury. Am Crim L Rev 10:671-878 (1971).
                Weisman, P., Postel, A.D. The first amendment as a re-
                straint on the grand jury process.--Schwartz, H.E. De-
                mythologizing the historic role of the grand jury.--
                Kairys, D. Jury selection: the law, a mathematical
                method of analysis (refers to petit jury).--Dash, S.
                The indicting grand jury: a critical stage?--Rief, J.
                The grand jury witness and compulsory testimony liti-
                gation.--Bibliography.--Note, Fourth amendment protec-
                tion for grand jury witnesses. In the Dash article,
                at 812, n. 24, a footnote lists the states where an
                information of indictment is optional with the prose-
                cutor, starring states specifically requiring prelimin-
                ary hearing by information rather than grand jury in-
                dictment. (They are Calif., Kan., Mich., Minn., Mont.,
                Neb., Nev., New Mex., N. Dak., S. Dak., Utah, Wis.)
                                                                3523

TIGAR, M and LEVY, M.R. Grand jury as the new inquisition. Mich SB
J 50:693-700, 717 (1971).
                Law professors concerned with democratic values of Bill
                of Rights say political freedoms have been corroded be-
                cause of failure of grand jury to protect such freedoms;
                illustrates recent cases of repression of political
                rights by grand juries.   3524

UNCONSTITUTIONALLY obtained evidence before the grand jury as a basis
for dismissing the indictment. Md L Rev 27:168-182 (1967).
> Argues that an indictment presented by a grand jury,
> based in whole or in part on unconstitutionally gath-
> ered evidence, should be dismissed.   3525

U. S. ADVISORY Commission on Intergovernmental Relations. The grand
jury and the prosecutor. In its State-local relations in the criminal justice system. Washington, USGPO, 1971. p. 220-22.
> Discusses pros and cons, grand jury and information;
> gives rundown of use of grand jury in the fifty states.
> 3526

WICKERSHAM, C.W. The grand jury: a weapon against crime and corruption. ABA J 51:1157-61 (1965).
> Refutes Antell, Modern Grand Jury (item 3479), by de-
> monstrating exactly opposite facts and arguments.3527

YOUNGER, R.D. The people's panel; the grand jury in the United
States, 1634-1941. Providence, American History Research Center,
Brown U press, 1963. 263 p.
> A detailed account of the grand jury from colonial times
> showing traditions and reforms. A chapter entitled
> "Whither?" discusses threats to the institution, abuses
> claimed, and a defense of the grand jury.   3528

    3. Bail

        Items on bail setting, preventive de-
        tention, pretrial detention and release.

ADMINISTRATION of Illinois bail provisions: an empirical study of four
downstate counties. U Ill L F 1972:341-87
> Bail statute of 1963 prefers release on recognizance
> and threatened criminal sanctions rather than financial
> loss for insuring appearance at trial, but monetary
> bond is still used all too often. Authors recommend an
> interviewing and investigating system to implement the
> new statute.   3529

ALASKA Judicial Council. Bail in Anchorage: a description of the
process and summary of statistical data for 1973. Mar. 1975. Anchorage, 1975. 71 p. + app.
> Year-long study describes the legal procedures and sta-
> ted purposes of the bail process generally in Alaska
> and sets forth data and conclusions about the actual
> effects of the bail process during 1973. Examined are:
> data bases and demographic information; bail release
> rates, time frames, and release status by crime types;
> characteristics of defendants remanded to custody for
> new crimes, as accused recidivists, and for failure to
> appear at some stage of proceedings; defendants denied
> bail; data tables.   3530

AMERICAN Bar Association Advisory Committee on Pretrial Proceedings.
Standards relating to pretrial release, recommended by the Advisory
Committee on Pretrial Proceedings. A.P. Murrah, chair.; C.E. Ares,
reptr. Tent. draft, Mar. 1968. N.Y., IJA, 1968. 88 p. Amendments,
supp. Sept. 1968. 5 p. approved, Aug. 1968.
>Standards with commentary on the general principles
governing pretrial release and on release by law enforcement officers without an arrest warrant, the issuance of summons in lieu of an arrest warrant, release
at arraignment and the release decision; appendices
are Bail Reform Act forms and model provision setting
standards for preventive detention.   3531

ANSWER to the problem of bail: a proposal in need of empirical con-
firmation.   Colum J L & Soc Prob 9:394-441 (1973).
>"This article attempts to develop a new pre-trial re-
lease program which will accomodate the concerns and
social needs surrounding the problem of bail. An analysis is presented of the consequences to the individual
and society of present pre-trial release/detention programs and proposals are made toward the end of decreas-
ing nonappearance at trial and increasing the number of
appropriate pre-trial releases." [- editorial abstract]
3532

ARES, C., RANKIN, A. and STURZ, H.   The Manhattan Bail Project: an
interim report on the use of pre-trial parole.   NYU L Rev 38:67-95
(1963).
>Precursor of all other projects involving Release on
Recognizance (ROR) practices, this article presents
details of procedures, experiments, results. Findings
hold that with little or no risk more persons can be
released ROR upon proper testing of status in the community.   3533

ARES, C. and STURZ, H.   Bail and the indigent accused.   Crime and
Delin 8:12-20 (1962).
>The bail system in theory and in practice is discussed
and the origin and operation of the New York City bail
project is described. The project, which employs law
students, recommends for release on their own recognizance defendants who cannot afford bail and for whom
certain information can be verified.   3534

ASSOCIATION of the Bar of the City of New York.   Bail or jail.   Record
19:11-28 (1964).
>Report of the Bar Association's Committee on the Crimi-
nal Court examines weaknesses of the present system of
bail and offers suggestions for improvement. Discussed
are: the role of the bondsman; unnecessary detention;
excessive bail; kick-backs of attorneys to bondsmen;
use of high bail to give defendants "taste of jail";
and the operation of bail in a manner that favors or-

ganized crime. Suggestions include: use of the Office
of Probation to establish a pretrial release program;
mandatory judicial inquiry into the propriety of cash
bail; conditional release programs; compliance with
established court rules on bail; and legislation to
permit citizen sureties. Additional studies of use of
Office of Parole are suggested, toward eventual abolition of bondsmen.   3535

BAIL bondsman and the fugitive accused - the need for formal removal
procedures. Yale L J 73:1098-1111 (1964).
A run-down of laws giving bondsmen right to recapture
fugitive without complying with extradition safeguards.
                                                       3536

BAIL, preventive detention, and speedy trials. Colum J L & Soc Prob
8:1-32 (1971).
Speaker:H.R.Uviller, law professor. Moderator: Judge
J.D. Hopkins. Panel: P.D. Andreoli, New York Assistant
District Attorney, and New York Criminal Court Judges
I. Lang and H.J. Rothwax. Discussion of the criminal
process between arrest and trial, with questions from
the audience.   3537

BASES, N.C. and MCDONALD, W.F. Preventive detention in the District
of Columbia: the first ten months. Georgetown Inst Crim L and Proc,
and Vera Inst of Justice, 1972. 121 p.
Preventive detention under D.C. Crime Act of 1970
studied for first ten months shows it virtually unused:
invoked in only 20 of a total of 6,000 felonies entering D.C. criminal justice system in that period. Debate
pro and con issues arising, and many specifics are described with tables, cases and charts.   3538

BEELEY, A.L. The bail system in Chicago. Chicago, U of Chicago
press, 1927, 1966. 189 p.
Reprint of study which concluded that Chicago's bail
system had broken down. Analysis of the prisoners involved, and bail determination methods indicate that,
as the editors note, the problems have remained very
much the same.   3539

BOGOMOLNY, R.L. and GAUS, W. An evaluation of the Dallas pre-trial
project. SWLJ 26:510-37 (1972).
Concludes that this experimental release-on-recognizance
program is generally successful, though there is un-
usually slow release on non-monetary bail, and too many
categories of excluded offenses.   3540

BORMAN, P.D. Selling of preventive detention 1970. Nw U L Rev 65:
879-936 (1971).
Law professor discusses pretrial preventive detention
for noncapital crimes which was introduced in the Dis-

trict of Columbia Court Reform and Criminal Procedure
Act. He points out that in urging its enactment, the
Nixon Administration misstated its coverage; author
shows 1970 Justice Department Pretrial Recidivism Study
disputes statements made by the Administration. Constitutional issues where the Bill is likely to conflict
with existing law, existing legal detention procedures
and new alternatives to preventive detention are also
explored. Provisions of Bill appended.   3541

CALIFORNIA Law Revision Commission. A study relating to bail, by S.E.
Cohen. Oxnard, Calif., 1961. 222 p.
California statutes and cases relating to bail are ex-
amined. Proposed revisions in the law are suggested.
Useful for research involved.   3542

CONFERENCE on Bail and Indigency, University of Illinois College of
Law, April 1965. Proceedings. U Ill L F 1965:1-79.
Contents: McCree, W.H., Jr. Keynote address: bail and
the indigent defendant.--La Fave, W.R. Alternatives to
the present bail system.--Wright, F.E., McCullough, D.
H., Silverstein, L., Mann, C., Johnston, D.L. Panel
discussion: pretrial release problems.--Bowman, C.H.
The Illinois ten percent bail deposit provision.--Work-
shop: establishing bail projects.--Baron, R. The New
York projects.--Johnston, D.L. The Des Moines projects.--
Sparer, E.V. The new legal aid as an instrument of
social change.--Spangenberg,R.L. Legal services for the
poor: the Boston University Roxbury defender project.--
Wickland, R.F. Legal services for the poor: the Office
of Economic Opportunity.--Stiegler, M.H. Legal aid to
the indigent by law students. Includes forms.   3543

COSTS of preventive detention. Yale L J 79:926-40 (1970).
Many additional burdens on state and defendant are
described.   3544

DERSHOWITZ, A.M. Preventive confinement: a suggested framework for
constitutional analysis. Tex L Rev 51:1277-1324 (1973).
Professor presents a framework for analyzing procedural
and substantive constitutional problems raised by preventive confinement; confinement for past acts vs. confinement as future prevention of potential harm, actual
suspicion, duration of confinement, civil vs. criminal
confinement, judicial predictive determination, constitutional safeguards, developing approaches to the problem, and the need to strike a balance between the protection of society and individual liberty.   3545

DISTRICT of Columbia Bail Project. Bail reform in the nation's capital; final report of the D.C. Bail Project, by R. Molleur and the
staff. Washington, Georgetown U Law Center, 1966. 204 p.

The project under which certain defendants were released
on their own recognizance in lieu of bail is described
with results and statistical data substantiating the
success of the project. Appended: Report on the administration of bail in the District of Columbia by the
District of Columbia Bar Association, its conclusions
and recommendations; the Bail Reform Act of 1966, District of Columbia Bail Reform Act.   3546

DISTRICT of Columbia Bar Association Junior Bar Section. Bail system
of the District of Columbia. Washington, 1963. 105 p.
Experiences and results of D.C. Bail Project, a pretrial
release program, are reported. Examined are: present
bail system; role of bondsmen; origin and development
of project; procedures and criteria of pretrial release
program; results, listed by age, sex and other factors
and judged in terms of recidivism; and cost of detention.
Includes data charts and tables. Appendices: Report of
Bar Association Committee on the Administration of Bail;
Judicial Conference resolutions and program forms.
                                                    3547

DISTRICT of Columbia Judicial Council. Report of the committee to
study the operation of the bail reform act in the District of Columbia. Washington, 1968. 57 p.
(For annotation see item 3406)   3548

ERVIN, S.J. The legislative role in bail reform. Geo Wash L Rev 35:
429-54 (1967).
Senator gives first-hand account of legislative history
of the Bail Reform Act of 1966, identifying the experimental programs which influenced Congress, and the philosophy behind the Act.   3549

FOOTE, C. The coming constitutional crisis in bail. U Pa L Rev 113:
959-99, 1125-85 (1965); in his Studies on bail. U of Pa, 1966.
p. 179-283.
On the basis of the Eighth Amendment's historical background and application, with due regard to the anomalous
lack of an affirmative statement of the right to bail
in the Constitution, and present day inequitable bail
practices and related issues of due process and equal
protection, the author concludes that the Griffin rule
should be extended to cover bail, and that preventive
detention violates the Eighth Amendment.   3550

FOOTE, C. ed. Studies on bail. Philadelphia, U of Penn, 1966. 288 p.
Consists of articles from U. Pa. L. Rev.: Foote, C.,
Markle, J.P., Wooley, E.A. Compelling appearance in
court: administration of bail in Philadelphia.--Roberts,
J.W., Palermo, J.S. A study of the administration of
bail in New York City.--Symposium: Conditional release

pending trial.--Foote, C. The coming constitutional
crisis in bail. (see item 3550)   3551

FREED, D.J. and WALD, P.M. Bail in the United States: working paper
for the National Conference on Bail and Criminal Justice. Washington,
US Dept of Justice, 1964. 116 p.
> National survey finds financial bail system a failure:
> both ineffective protection against dangerous defendants
> and prejudicial to the poor. Authors recommend less
> reliance on money and bondsmen, and more fact-finding
> into defendants' community ties and likelihood of appear-
> ance at trial.   3552

FRIEDLAND, M.L. Detention before trial; a study of criminal cases
tried in the Toronto magistrates' courts. Toronto, Toronto press,
1965. 217 p.
> Author presents detailed study of pretrial custody cov-
> ering use of summons, detention of accused, initial
> court appearance, and complete bail setting practices.
> Extensive statistical data, collected without the use
> of sampling techniques, is included.   3553

GOLDFARB, R.L. A brief for preventive detention. N.Y. Times (Magazine), Mar. 1, 1970. p. 28, 73-76.
> Author relates why he favors pretrial detention for
> certain defendants and discusses proposed legislation
> which would provide for it.   3554

GOLDFARB, R.L. Ransom; a critique of the American bail system. N.Y.,
Harper & Row, 1965. 245 p.
> Graphic illustration of the bail system's malfunction-
> ing, with focus on discrimination against the poor.
> Bail as a political tool, experimental reform projects,
> pros and cons of preventive detention are discussed; a
> proposal for reform is advanced.   3555

GOLDMAN, H., BLOOM, D. and WORRELL, C. The pretrial release program.
Washington, Off of Economic Opportunity, Off of Planning, Research
and Evaluation, 1973. 47 p.
> Survey of 88 bail projects in progress; findings in-
> clude: wide variety in scope and funding; projects
> lacking in many large cities; majority of projects ex-
> clude felony defendants, use point system, and almost
> all make recommendations to court on whether to release
> on recognizance.   3556

HERMANN, D.H. Preventive detention, a scientific view of man, and
state power. U Ill L F 1973:673-99.
> Author examines the current practice of preventive de-
> tention following trial, before trial and in juvenile
> and insanity proceedings; analyzes scientific theories
> underlying the detection, definition and prediction of

dangerousness, and the treatment of the dangerous; explores the power of the state in preventive detention and concludes that it involves a high potential of abuse by the state.   3557

HESS, F.D. Pretrial detention and the 1970 District of Columbia Crime Act -- the next step in bail reform. Brooklyn L Rev 37:277-322 (1971).
The next reform is acknowledgment that danger to the community has always been an element in determining bail, says author, arguing that pretrial detention is constitutional. He indicates the anomaly of the Act in recognizing danger for release in capital cases, but not in non-capital cases.   3558

HINDELANG, M.J. On the methodological rigor of the Bellamy memorandum; a study of the effect of pretrial detention on the outcome of a criminal case. Crim L Bull 8:507-13 (1972).
Pointing out weaknesses of the study, Unconstitutional administration of bail: Bellamy v the judges of New York City, (item 3588); author believs that plaintiff's arguments are not destroyed but should be viewed more cautiously.   3559

HRUSKA, R.L. Preventive detention: the constitution, the congress. Creighton L Rev 3:36-87 (1969).
Senator reviews system of bail in U.S. and refers to various studies made; mentions Senatorial hearings and legislative sentiments on preventive detention; discusses constitutional protections and Eighth Amendment rights, with pertinent cases, referring to statutory exceptions to right of bail; proceeds to analyze Fifth Amendment protections, presumption of innocence, denial of fair trial, deprivation of liberty, footnoted to cases, reports, other writings. Refers to ABA Pretrial Release Standards, and Congressional action. Presents recommended preventive detention legislation. Appended: Pertinent substance of Senate recommended bills. 3560

JUST, B. Bail and pre-trial detention in the District of Columbia: an empirical analysis. Howard L J 17:844-57 (1973).
Describes problems and inequities in administration of bail and pretrial detention in D.C.; examines data on pretrial detention finding that there is a growing number of persons in jail pending trial and that purposes to diminish money bail have not been accomplished; recommendations by program secretary of Washington Pretrial Justice Program, American Friends Service Committee.   3561

JUVENILE'S right to bail in Oregon. Ore L Rev 47:194-204 (1968).
Included because right of juvenile to bail is rarely discussed in law review articles.   3562

KAMIN, A. Bail administration in Illinois. Ill B J 53:674-86 (1965).
Law professor analyzes state system and describes the
new bail procedures under the Code of Criminal Procedure,
such as a 10% bond system. He discusses his own survey
of bail administration in Cook County. The Manhattan
and other bail projects are considered. Experimentation
with similar release on recognizance program in Illinois
is one of his recommendations. Statistics are included.
                                                        3563

LACHEEN, S.R. A Philadelphia lawyer's view of English criminal justice: first impressions. Crim L Bull 11: 127-56 (1975).
A practicing lawyer of 17 years experience, the author
"hired on" as a solicitor's clerk for six weeks. He
recounts his experiences and observations of English
criminal justice, from arrest to trial. His views of
practically all procedures are harsh and surprisingly
condemnatory, indicating numerous abuses according to
American ideals of civil and constitutional rights. He
is particularly critical of bail practices, arrest procedures and many trial procedures. The solicitor-bar-
rister system leads to serious disadvantages for the
accused. He concludes with a quote from the Second Institute of Coke 48: "It is the worst oppression, that
it is done under the color of justice."   3563a

LAFAVE, W.R. Alternatives to the present bail system. U Ill L F
1965:8-19
Describes failure of police to use citations instead
of arrest due to lack of legislative attention as well
as to notion that arrest itself has punitive function.
                                                        3564

LANDES, W.M. The bail system: an economic approach. J Legal Studies
2:79-105 (1973).
Economic professor, through empirical research, demonstrates that not releasing defendants before trial increases cost to state, decreases guilty pleas, lessens
chance of defendants for successful defense, and making
bail is a function of wealth; pretrial imprisonment
falls most heavily on low-income defendants. Develops
alternative methods to select defendants for release:
first requires defendants to pay for their release
(based on algebraic formula devised by writer); second
compensates defendants for detention via a monetary
or other form of payment. Compares his model optimal
bail suggestions with current practices; includes bondsmen's role.   3565

LARKIN, T.J. Predicting defendant appearance: a statistical analysis
of bail procedures. Cleveland, Court Management Project, 1973. 38 p.
Attempt to identify characteristics common to good risks

for pretrial release fails to establish significance
of traits usually considered important, i.e. employment, family ties, length of residence, previous arrests;
only conclusion is that defendants with counsel (retained or assigned) probably will appear in court,
alias users probably will not. (See also item 3485)
3566

MCCARTHY, D.J. and WAHL, J.J. The District of Columbia Bail Project:
an illustration of experimentation and a brief for change. Geo L J
53:675-748 (1965).
Statistical analysis of pre-project bail system; interim report of project; organization, procedure; criteria for release; detention costs to municipality,
defendant. 3567

MELTSNER, M. Pre-trial detention, bail pending appeal, and jail time
credit: the constitutional problems and some suggested remedies.
Crim L Bull 3:618-24 (1967).
NAACP attorney discusses pretrial bail and bail pending appeal: when constitutionally required; discrimination against poor; what constitutes excessive bail;
relief available and steps to be taken by counsel when
bail is denied or is excessive; and an equal protection
argument for pretrial detention time to be credited
against sentence. 3568

MITCHELL, J.N. Bail reform and the constitutionality of pretrial
detention. Va L Rev 55:1223-42 (1969).
Former Attorney General gives historical argument for
constitutionality of preventive detention and outlines
the Nixon Administration's proposals for preventive
detention legislation. See also Tribe, L.H. An ounce
of detention: prevention justice in the world of John
Mitchell. Va L Rev 56:371-407 (1970), for rebuttal.
3570

MOLLEUR, R.R. Bail reform in the nation's capital; final report of
the D.C. bail project. Washington, Georgetown Law Center, 1966.
105 p.
Detailed account of federal bail reforms; includes
statistical charts and tables indicating various findings. 3571

NATIONAL Conference of Court Administrative Officers. Preliminary
materials on the Manhattan bail project. New York, N.Y., Judicial
Conference, 1964. 1 v., var. pag.
Includes: 1. The Manhattan Bail Report by the Vera
Foundation; 2. Address by Presiding Justice Bernard
Botein before the National Conference on Bail and Crimi-
nal Justice, May 27, 1964; 3. The Manhattan Bail Pro-

ject: an interim report on the use of pretrial parole,
by Ares, Rankin and Sturz, with forms. (see item 3533)
                                                    3572

NATIONAL Conference on Bail and Criminal Justice. Bail and summons:
1965: institute on the operation of pretrial release projects, New
York; proceedings of Oct. 14-15, 1965 [and] Justice conference on
bail and remands in custody, London; proceedings of Nov. 27, 1965.
Washington, 1966. 292 p.
          Two conferences, one in New York and one in London,
          presented by Justice (British Section of the Interna-
          tional Commission of Jurists), examine separately the
          systems of pretrial release in the United States and
          in England. Included are panel discussions on (1) legal
          issues involved in pretrial release projects, (2) prob-
          lems in pretrial release project operation, and (3) po-
          lice release of accused persons; which panels were at
          the New York conference.   3573

NATIONAL Conference on Bail and Criminal Justice. Proceedings of
May 27-29, 1964, and interim report, May 1964-April 1965. Washington,
1965. 429 p.
          The Conference explores the thesis that financial bail
          is often unnecessary to assure an accused person's
          appearance in court. Areas considered are release on
          recognizance programs, issuing summons in lieu of arrest,
          setting high bail to prevent pretrial release, pretrial
          release based on money or other conditions and pretrial
          release of juveniles. Appendix I is a report on pretrial
          release practices in Sweden, Denmark, England and Italy.
                                                            3574

NATIONAL Conference on the Extension of Legal Services to the Poor,
Oct. 1964. Status of bail reform in the U.S.: A report to the execu-
tive board of the National Conference on Bail and Criminal Justice.
Washington, 1964. 48 p.
          A state-by-state summary of bail reform developments
          compiled from the files of the Vera Foundation and the
          U.S. Department of Justice.   3575

NEW HAVEN Pretrial Services Council. The pretrial process in the
Sixth Circuit; a quantitative and legal analysis, by M.M. Feeley and
J. McNaughton. New Haven, 1974. 131 p.
          In addition to the diversion program of the Pretrial
          Services Council, others tried in the Circuit Court,
          which handles 95% of New Haven's criminal dispositions,
          are described: the Police Field Citation program, the
          Bail Commission, Redirection Center. Findings discussed
          and analyzed, including characteristics of defendants
          and cases; who is released, under what condition (own
          recognizance, bond, or citation); rearrest rate and
          failures to appear; pretrial diversion and police cita-

ation. Pretrial diversion was used by less than 1%
(partly due to restrictive requirements, more through
defendants' choice) so that program meant to save court
time and money not only fails, but adds own expense.
3576

NEW YORK (State) Judicial Conference. The case of the dangerous defendant: a study and proposal. Its ann rep 14:124-205 (1969).
Study based on research and personal interviews with
judges and district attorneys examines the desirability
and propriety of preventive detention by reviewing a
recent case in which this issue arose; examines history,
philosophy and purpose of bail, foreign systems of
release and detention. Study concludes that preventive
detention is a basic need, but should be circumscribed
to preserve the dignity of, and fairness to, the accused.
Appendix discusses interviews. Bibliography.   3577

PAULSEN, M.G. Pretrial release in the United States. Colum L Rev
66:109-25 (1966).
Professor examines some of the issues respecting the
operation of the bail system in the U.S.: status of
the law today; operation of the bail system, including
practical difficulties, abuses of the system in its use
for purposes other than the safe production of accused
at trial and role of the bondsman; the Manhattan Bail
Project and other reforms; poverty and bail; legislative
reform. Author concludes that the bail system has been
a costly failure, and that statutes in the next decade
will improve the administration of bail by providing
means of individualizing bail decisions and by providing release under systems other than bail.   3578

PREVENTIVE detention: a comparison of European and United States
measures. NYU J Int L & Politics 4:289-311 (1971).
Survey of French, German and British practices, all of
which allow more pretrial detention than American practice; comparison with the 1970 Bail Reform Act of the
District of Columbia.   3579

PREVENTIVE detention: an empirical analysis. Harv Civil Rights L
Rev 6:289-396 (1971).
Foreword by Sen S.J. Ervin. Analysis of Boston recidivism rate; D.C. type of pretrial detention would not
offer substantial protection to the community. The D.C.
Act's recidivism prediction criteria are insufficiently
precise to achieve their stated goal, and probably
violate due process.   3580

PREVENTIVE detention before trial. Harv L Rev 79:1489-1510 (1966).
Extensive discussion: limited provisions, carefully
hedged with adequate procedural safeguards, would sur-
vive constitutional attack.   3581

PREVENTIVE detention [proceedings of Conference on Preventive Detention, Oct. 28-30, 1969] Chicago, Urban research corp., 1971. 381 p.
Legal, professorial, and government experts examine
proposed preventive detention bills as a reaction to
and solution for increased crime; benefits of bail v.
benefits of preventive detention; the experiences of
a judge on the operation of the Bail Bond Act; preventive detention as a solution to problems of the habitual
offender and disorder; constitutional issues; and alternatives to detention. Includes appendices of legislative hearings and testimony on related subjects.
3582

RANKIN, A. The effect of pretrial detention. NYU L Rev 39:641-55
(1964).
Analyzing the factors of prior record, bail amount,
type of counsel, family integration and employment stability, the author finds support for a causal link between pretrial detention and unfavorable disposition
of defendant's case; statistical tables illustrating
findings in research for Manhattan Bail Project. 3583

RIGHT to bail and the pre-"trial" detention of juveniles accused of
crime. Van L Rev 18:2096-2112 (1965).
Note examines the bail and pretrial detention problems
facing the juvenile accused of "criminal" conduct:
right to bail prior to the Juvenile Court Act; right
to bail under Act; theoretical and practical problems;
and alternate solutions and recommendations. Author
suggests the establishment of screening centers to assist
the present juvenile court judges in making their de-
terminations.   3584

SCHAFFER, S.A. Bail and parole jumping in Manhattan in 1967. N.Y.,
Vera Inst of Justice, 1970. 107 p.
Examination of over 14,000 criminal court defendants
in early 1967 shows defaulting rate by those released
on recognizance (ROR) increased to 15% as compared to
the 1.6% of the Manhattan Bail Project period (1961-64),
but those who were recommended for ROR had considerably
lower non-appearance rate, 9.4% than those so released
with recommendation against ROR, 19.3% default rate,
or those with no report at all, 16.2%. Schaffer sees
above as demonstration of reliability of "roots in
community" point system used by Dept. of Probation in
its recommendations. Also finds, among other things,
that those on ROR for relatively minor charges default
most often, with little risk of punishment even when
arrested for other crimes; default rate is lowest of
all among defendants out on bond.   3585

SCHULTZ, L.G. Bail for the "have-nots"; the recognizance program
of the St. Louis Circuit Court. J MO B 20:8-15 (1964).

Probation and parole officer, after giving a brief
history of bail procedures, describes the use of recognizance in the United States and enumerates its advantages over pretrial detention. Considering the difficulty of fixing an appropriate bail figure and the
relative inefficacy of the possibility of bond for-
feiture as an incentive not to abscond, the author
suggests the abolition of bail and a broader use of
recognizance, pending a complete overhaul of pretrial
release laws.   3586

SILVERSTEIN, L. Bail in the state courts: a field study and report.
Minn L Rev 50:621-652 (1966).
              Analysis of the findings on bail practices in his study
              Defense of the poor [see item 3924] indicates wide dis-
              parities which may violate due process requirements
              and Eighth Amendment.   3587

UNCONSTITUTIONAL administration of bail: Bellamy v The Judges of New
York City. Crim L Bull 8:459-506 (1972).
              This is a detailed statistical study of the effect of
              detention on the outcome of a criminal case with a
              memorandum submitted to the court to substantiate that
              the present New York City bail system denies to plain-
              tiffs equal protection of the law. Study shows that
              whether accused is released or detained pending trial
              (above all other factors studied, like prior criminal
              record, seriousness of charge, family ties) determines
              the outcome of his case and the likelihood of his re-
              ceiving a prison sentence.   3588

U. S. ATTORNEY General's Committee on Poverty and the Administration
of Criminal Justice. Poverty and the administration of federal criminal justice. Feb, 25, 1963. Washington, 1963. 154 p.
              F.A Allen: chair. Survey of four federal district courts
              reveals among many things that only when bail is set
              low do a substantial number of defendants gain pretrial
              release.   3589

U. S. COMMITTEE on the District of Columbia. Crime in the national
capital; hearings before the Committee on the District of Columbia.
... on pretrial detention. Nov. 6-7, 1969. Pt 6 of 7 pts. Washington, USGPO, 1969. P. 1661-1757, A945-A1062. (91st Cong., 1st
sess.)
              Hearings on bill that would allow a judicial officer
              to jail, up to 30 days, a suspect accused of a serious
              crime if, after open hearings, the officer determines
              that the individual if released would commit further
              crimes before trial. Includes text of bill, reports
              of witnesses, prepared statements, data, an appendix
              including text of articles on related and relevant
              subjects, and final report of Judicial Council Cttee

to study the operation of the Bail Reform Act in D.C.
(May 1968).   3590

U. S. CONGRESS Senate Committee on the Judiciary. Federal bail procedures; hearings before the Subcommittee on Constitutional Rights
and the Subcommittee on Improvements in Judicial Machinery of the
Committee on the Judiciary, Aug. 4, 5 and 6, 1964. Washington, USGPO,
1965. 516 p. (88th Cong., 2d sess.)
    Texts of three proposals to modify federal bail proce-
    dures, together with statements made at the hearings,
    views submitted and publications pro and con.   3591

U. S. CONGRESS Senate Committee on the Judiciary. Fugitive bailees;
hearing before the Subcommittee on Constitutional Rights and the Subcommittee on Improvements in Judicial Machinery .. May 18, 1966.
Washington, USGPO, 1967. 121 p. (89th Cong., 2d sess.)
    Joint hearing on bill (S. 2855) providing procedure
    for return of fugitive bailees by bail bondsmen (text
    included), introduced out of concern for lack of due
    process in this area. Includes articles on subject,
    text of witnesses, statements, and discussions.   3592

U. S. NATIONAL Bureau of Standards. Compilation and use of criminal
court data in relation to pretrial release of defendants; pilot
study, by J.W. Locke [and others] Aug. 1970. Washington, USGPO, 1970.
236 p.
    Attempt to arrive at effective formula for predicting
    dangerousness, through analysis of sample of 712 D.C.
    defendants, finds that larger study and more data are
    needed. Prediction devices developed by others described,
    found inadequate. Bibliography.   3593

U. S. NATIONAL Institute of Law Enforcement and Criminal Justice.
Bail and its reform: a national survey by P.B. Wice. Washington,
USGPO, 1973. 70 p.
    On cover: Summary report. Describes 500-page report
    investigating pretrial release in the United States,
    based on interviews and observations conducted in 1970
    and 1971, and on questionnaires. The operation of the
    traditional bail systems in 11 large cities is described
    in Part 1. Part 2 evaluates bail reform projects in
    eight of the 11 cities and identifies key operational
    characteristics contributing to project effectiveness,
    and a Model Program is described. Part 3 reports results
    of a 72-city questionnaire mailed to judges, bail pro-
    ject directors, et al, on attitudes toward pretrial
    release. Statistics are included. Findings include the
    maximum effectiveness of certain bail reform programs.
                                                       3594

VERA Institute of Justice Pretrial Services Agency. Operations report for the Borough of Brooklyn, Sept. 23, 1974/Nov. 3, 1974- N.Y.,
1974-

Agency was established in June 1973 to provide court with background data on candidates for release on own recognizance (ROR) rather than money bail. This first-year report shows that while 7% of RORs ordinarily fail to appear in court, Agency-recommended RORs' skip-rate is just half of that (3.5%) and is being further reduced. Agency also aids in Supervised Release (briefly explained) for high-risk defendants who would otherwise remain in jail. Tables summarize various data available from program so far, pertaining to "straight" ROR, verified ROR, Supervised Release, and appearance rate for various degrees of felony and for misdemeanors and violations.   **3595**

WALD, P.M. Pretrial detention and ultimate freedom: a statistical study. NYU L Rev 39:631-655 (1964).
Reveals startling findings under Manhattan Bail Project research: for example, 49% of accused persons spend more time in jail before trial than after conviction and sentencing. Author, staff member of National Conference on Bail and Criminal Justice, reports on impact of jail confinement on outcome of trial and sentencing.   **3596**

WALD, P.M. and FREED, D.J. Bail Reform Act of 1966: a practitioner's primer. ABA J 52:940-45 (1966).
Changes explained, provisions of new act outlined: defense counsel's role in securing defendant's pretrial release.   **3597**

4. Plea Bargaining

Items on legitimacy of negotiated pleas, ethical considerations; waiver in pleas of guilty; prosecutors', defense lawyers', and judges' obligations; overcharging; withdrawal of pleas; appellate review of constitutional infirmities notwithstanding pleas of guilty.

ACCEPTING the indigent defendant's waiver of counsel and plea of guilty. U Fla L Rev 22:453-69 (1970).
Whether a defendant's plea or waiver is made voluntarily, with sufficient understanding and accuracy, is the problem treated in this note, through a consideration of federal decisions and Florida's Rules of Criminal Procedure.   **3598**

ALLEN, E.E. and STRICKLAND, J.R. Negotiating pleas in criminal cases. Prac Law 17:35-47 (Jan. 1971).
Oregon judge and attorney outline plea bargaining process from incentive to bargain through implementation

of the "deal". They provide a digest of federal cases
concerning the legitimacy of negotiated pleas and briefly
discuss ethical questions.   3599

ALSHULER, A.W. The prosecutor's role in plea bargaining. U Chi L
Rev 36:50-112 (1968).
            U.S. Justice Dept. attorney traces history of plea
            bargaining; justifies abolishing it in intensive ex-
            amination of prosecutor's motives as divergent from
            public's; discusses vices of overcharging; other basic
            shortcomings; cites cases and statutes.   3600

AMERICAN Bar Association Advisory Committee on the Criminal Trial.
Standards relating to pleas of guilty, recommended by the Advisory
Committee on the Criminal Trial. W.V. Schaefer, chair.; W.R. LaFave
reptr. Tent. draft, Feb. 1967. N.Y., IJA, 1967. 78 p. Proposed
revsn. Dec. 1967. 5 p. approved, Feb. 1968.
            Standards with commentary concerning receiving and act-
            ing upon the plea; withdrawal of the plea and plea
            discussions and agreements; the judge's role; aid of
            counsel. Bibliographical data.   3601

APPELLATE review of constitutional infirmities notwithstanding a plea
of guilty. Houston L Rev 9:305-28 (1971).
            Recommends statutory procedure for appellate review
            of convictions obtained by plea of guilty, citing the
            New York and California examples; asserts such a pro-
            cedure is necessary to adequately resolve defendants'
            claims, in the context of plea bargaining and guilty
            plea dispositions.   3602

BISHOP, A.N. Waivers in pleas of guilty. FRD 60:513-61 (1974).
            Detroit assistant prosecuting attorney describes just
            what the defendant surrenders and waives when he volun-
            tarily and knowingly pleads guilty. Questions of when
            such a plea is coerced or induced are considered and
            U.S. Supreme Court decisions re guilty pleas are sum-
            marized. The author offers guidelines and forms which
            he suggests should be used when a defendant desires to
            plead guilty so that the possibility of an appeal may be
            avioded.   3603

COGAN, N.H. Guilty pleas: weak links in the "broken chain". Crim L
Bull 10:149-59 (1974).
            Law professor analyzes and criticizes the decision in Tol-
            let v Henderson, 411 US 258 (1973), holding that a coun-
            seled guilty plea precluded a review of a claim of un-
            lawful indictment. Author disagrees with the Court's
            holding, finding that it operates in the interest of
            efficiency only, and unreasonably interferes with the vin-
            dication of important rights.   3604

CONSTITUTIONAL attacks on a guilty plea motivated by a coerced confession. Temp L Q 44:426-33 (1971).
> Note examines retroactive application of Jackson v Denno,
> 378 US 368 (1964), as limited in McMann v Richardson,
> 397 US 759 (1970).   3605

CONSTITUTIONALITY of reindicting successful plea-bargain appellants
on the original higher charges. Calif L Rev 62:258-93 (1974).
> The principles of due process, double jeopardy and
> equal protection as they apply to reprosecution are
> examined. The due process discussion centers on judicial
> and prosecutorial vindictiveness and contracts of ad-
> hesion. The double jeopardy section focuses on the
> reasoning of Mullreed v Kropp and implied acquittal.
> The equal protection tests of reasonableness, strict
> scrutiny, and intensified means scrutiny are explored.
> Concludes that the appellate safeguards available to
> plea-bargain convicts constitute the only appellate
> safeguards available to the great majority of the prison
> population.   3606

COOPER, H.H.A. Plea bargaining: a comparative analysis. NYU J Int'l
L and Pol 5:427-48 (1972).
> English and American practices, with some civil law
> examples, indicate that the American pattern of plea
> bargaining cannot be changed until the "bargaining mo-
> tive" - what the accused can offer to the system - is
> reduced.   3607

DAVIS, A. Sentences for sale: a new look at plea bargaining in England and America. Crim L R 1971:150-61;218-28.
> Author considers the guilty plea as a factor in senten-
> cing and the problems of voluntariness of the plea; he
> surveys the actual bargaining practices in use and the
> reasons behind their use, and evaluates the effect of
> guilty plea inducement and plea negotiation on the ad-
> ministration of justice in England and America. 3608

DAVIS, S.M. The guilty plea process: exploring the issues of voluntariness and accuracy. Valparaiso L Rev 6:111-34 (1972).
> Theme is standards of accuracy and voluntariness in ne-
> gotiated pleas; the author recommends a more visible
> bargaining process and more active participation by
> the judge, and discusses his recommendations with F.
> R. Crim. Proc. 11 and the American Bar Association
> Standards relating to pleas of guilty.   3609

EQUIVOCAL guilty pleas - should they be accepted? Dick L Rev 75:366-
76 (1971).
> Article discusses N.C. v Alfred, 91 SCt 160 (1970),
> which suggests that when an equivocal guilty plea is
> accepted, the court has the obligation to insure that

the plea is accurate by reviewing the facts. Author
examines characteristics and implications of the guilty
plea, policy considerations to be considered in determining acceptance of the plea, and concludes that examination of the facts should be required before acceptance of any guilty plea.   3610

ERICKSON, W.H.   The finality of a plea of guilty.   Notre Dame Law 48:
835-49 (1973).
Guilty plea case history is followed by discussion of
ABA Standards relating to pleas of guilty. Analyzed are
voluntariness, role of counsel and of prosecution; full
discovery is advocated for informed plea. ABA Standards
relating to criminal appeal provide for review of convictions based on guilty plea.   3611

FISCHER, D.A.   Beyond Santobello - remedies for reneged plea bargains.
U San Fernando Valley L Rev 2:121-43 (1973).
Discusses impact of Santobello v N.Y. holding plea bargaining to be essential component of administration of
justice. Author, public defender, discusses cases involving withdrawal of plea generally (bargain not
breached); bargain breached by prosecutor; bargain
breached by judge. He discusses also cases where defendant seeks specific performance. Sumarizes, in conclusion, present status in appellate courts.   3612

GENTILE, C.L.   Fair bargains and accurate pleas.   BU L Rev 49:514-51
(1969).
Extensive review of cases and literature involving
problems generated by plea bargaining with critique
and comment on ABA Standards relating to pleas of guilty.
                                                     3613

GUILTY plea and bargaining.   Loyola L Rev 17:703-18 (1970/71).
Comment focuses on the process of plea bargaining; its
constitutionality within the framework of recent Supreme
Court decisions; the use of the guilty plea as a procedural tool to clear overcrowded dockets; the necessity
that the defendant fully understand the impact of a
guilty plea; and F. R. Crim. Proc. 11, which sets
forth some minimum judicial guidelines in accepting
guilty pleas. Author concludes that given stricter constitutional guidelines, the use of the guilty plea can
lessen the court's burdens without impairing defendant's
constitutional rights.   3614

GUILTY plea bargaining: compromises by prosecutors to secure guilty
pleas.   U Pa L Rev 112:865-908 (1964).
In defense of charge reduction by prosecutor without
concurrence of the trial judge, discusses cases on
withdrawal of pleas; sets standards for acceptable plea

bargaining to make it visible and subject to control;
includes study of practices of 83 prosecutors in most
populous counties of 31 states; role of defense lawyer.
3615

HOFFMAN, W.E.   Plea bargaining and the role of the judge.   FRD 53:499-
507 (1972).
Chief Judge, federal district court, discusses role of
trial judge in plea bargaining in a system without direct judicial participation. He presents a recommendation for revision of F.R. Crim. Proc. 11.   3616

INSTITUTE for Court Management.   Plea negotiations in Denver, by S.A.
Knudson.   Denver, 1972.   72 p.
Discussion, analysis and other observations regarding
case processing, particularly pleas; close study of
results of formal plea negotiation procedure instituted
by DA's office Sept. 1971; charts, graphs and tables
included.   3617

JUDICIAL supervisor over California plea bargaining: regulating the
trade.   Cal L Rev 59:962-96 (1971).
Pt. 1: Factors that make plea bargaining the principal
form of criminal practice in California; Pt. 2: The
legal background of the guilty plea; insulating guilty
plea from attack on appeal; Pt. 3: Rules ensuring that
person will not plead in ignorance of rights; Pt 4:
Right to counsel in plea bargaining; Pt. 5: Threat to
judicial power in plea bargaining; how court can in-
dividualize justice.   3618

KUH, R.H.   Plea bargaining - guidelines for the Manhattan District
Attorney's office.   Crim L Bull 11:48-61 (1975).
New York County District Attorney spells out conduct
of plea bargaining to staff: general principles cover:
1. Plea negotiations (avoid over-indictment:covers non-
provable indictments, motion practice and bargaining
candor, sentencing, conferences with defendant's counsel,
deviations from policies herein); 2. Defendants charged
with multiple crimes; 3. Reduction of felonies in criminal court; 4. Plea bargaining generally: the pre-plead-
ing report; 5. Procedures in court; 6. Reduced pleas
concerning certain specific crimes.   3619

LAMBROS, T.D.   Plea bargaining and the sentencing process.   FRD 53:509-
24 (1972).
Federal trial judge recommends reform which would more
closely coordinate sentencing and rehabilitation goals
with guilty plea dispositions and place the judge at
the center of the negotiation process. He also describes
the experimental program in which he participated for
the early disposition of important criminal cases.
Bibliography.   3620

KANNENSOHN, M. and LYDAY, W. Legislators and criminal justice reform.
State Govt 48:122-27 (1975).
> Summary of results of a survey conducted for Council
> of State Governments of the attitudes of state legis-
> lators to recommendation made by National Advisory Com-
> mission on Criminal Justice Standards and Goals, 1973
> (see item 3377). Most controversial was Comission's
> recommendation that plea bargaining be abolished by
> 1978. Legislators were strongly in support of retention,
> regarding plea bargaining as a necessary part of crimi-
> nal justice.   3620a

MATHER, L.M. Some determinants of the method of case disposition:
decision-making by public defenders in Los Angeles. Law & Soc Rev 8:
187-216 (1974).
> Author examines plea bargaining function, the role of
> the defense attorney, and overview of felony disposi-
> tions, plea bargaining and case disposition, and plea
> bargaining determined by likelihood of conviction; con-
> cludes that the factors critical in determining whether
> a case will be settled by plea bargaining are the
> strength of the prosecution's case and the seriousness
> of the crime.   3621

NEWMAN, D.J. Conviction: the determination of guilt or innocence
without trial. Boston: Little, Brown, 1966. 259 p. (AB Found Administration of criminal justice series)
> One of five reports of the AB Found. survey of the
> Administration of criminal justice in the U.S., F.
> Remington, ed. (item 3230). Sociologist's field research
> in Michigan, Wisconsin and Kansas provides case history
> description of plea bargaining procedure, and an analy-
> sis, through detailed categorization of case dispo-
> sitions according to the motivations of the judges or
> prosecution: i.e., to meet the demands of the court
> calendar or leniency to white collar crime.   3622

NICHOLSON, F.B. A guilty plea dilemma: the recalcitrant pleader.
Judges' J 10:38-39 (1971).
> Following Standard 1.6 of ABA Standards relating to
> pleas of guilty and F.R. Crim. Proc. 11, trial judges
> receiving guilty pleas have increasingly instituted
> the practice of detailing the factual basis of the plea
> by having the defendant make, in effect, a judicial
> confession; cites to pertinent cases. Judge N. presents
> dilemma of a judge in the presence of conflicting pleas;
> gives illustrative cases and advice.   3623

PEOPLE v West. [(Cal) 477 P2d 409] recorded plea bargains. William-
ette L J 7:347-54 (1971).
> Note discusses cases in which California Supreme Court
> set up specific procedures for acceptance or rejection
> of a plea - under plea bargaining procedures.   3624

PLEA bargaining: proposed amendments to Federal Criminal Rule 11.
Minn L Rev 56:718-38 (1972).
> Critique of proposals by Advisory Committee on Criminal
> Rules of the Judicial Conference of the United States
> which render plea bargaining a recognized part of the
> criminal justice system. Note also recommends more
> liberal discovery rules to make bargaining more fair
> to defendants.   3625

PLEA of nolo contendere. Md L Rev 25:227-37 (1965).
> What it is, when accepted in federal and state courts,
> effects in the case, effects outside the case (defen-
> dant not stopped from denying facts in a civil suit),
> with a special section on the plea in Maryland. 3626

PLEA bargaining - the Supreme Court of Pennsylvania has held that
any participation by a trial judge in the plea bargaining process
prior to trial is forbidden. Duquesne L rev 8:461-70 (1970).
> An analysis of Commonwealth v Evans 434 Pa. 52 (1969)
> and earlier cases in the area.   3627

POLSTEIN, H. How to "settle" a criminal case. Prac Law 8:35-44 (Jan.
1962).
> Function of counsel for guilty defendant; timing and
> tactics respecting prosecutor and judge; lawyer's func-
> tion after guilty plea.   3628

PRE-SENTENCE withdrawal of guilty pleas in federal courts. NYU L Rev
40:759-70 (1965).
> Discusses Everett v U.S. where withdrawal was not per-
> mitted by U.S. Court of Appeals, D.C. Circuit. Reex-
> amines circumstances leading to granting or denial of
> motion for withdrawal and recommends various improve-
> ments for guilty plea system; among them limiting judge's
> discretion to refuse pre-sentence withdrawal.   3629

PROFILE of a guilty plea: a proposed trial court procedure for accepting guilty pleas. Wayne L Rev 17:1195-1239 (1971).
> Proposed guilty procedure presented with two proposed
> changes for Michigan statute and a study of 87 tran-
> scripts of guilty plea dispositions in Michigan courts.
>   3630

RESTRUCTURING the plea bargain. Yale L J 82:286-312 (1972).
> Note urges elimination of unregulated bargaining be-
> tween defendant and prosecutor; proposes changes to
> include advocacy proceeding permitting judge to exercise
> full responsibility for advantages defendant receives
> for plea; plea bargaining is important factor as a cause
> for sentence disparities; urges pre-plea conference.
>   3631

RIGHT to appeal - failure of counsel to advise defendant of his right
to appeal after a plea of guilty held insufficient ground to require
a Montgomery hearing. Fordham L Rev 40:949-57 (1972).
        The right to appeal rule enunciated in People v Mont-
        gomery 24 NY2d 130 (1969) and its application in sub-
        sequent New York decisions are examined.   3632

SUPREME Court's changed view of the guilty plea. Memphis St U L Rev
4:79-90 (1973).
        Note discusses recent trend in Supreme Court decisions
        to place judicial efficiency above individual rights
        in the area of plea bargaining and guilty pleas. Cases
        prior to 1970 are discussed and compared with more re-
        cent cases. Author suggests that closer scrutiny of
        all elements of the guilty plea by the trial judge is
        necessary in order that defendants' rights be protected.
                                                          3633

THOMAS, P. An exploration of plea bargaining. Crim L Rev 1969:69-79.
        Author is critical of the informal plea bargaining
        process in England (where there is no comparable figure
        to the D.A.), noting problems. He looks at its operation
        in the United States where plea bargaining is visible
        on the surface, but notes problems there as well.3634

THOMAS, P. Plea bargaining and the Turner case. Crim L Rev 1970:
559-66.
        An examination of an English Court of Appeal case which
        "seems to have recognized that a 'controlled' form of
        plea bargaining can play a useful part in dispensing
        justice," by setting rules for guidance in future ne-
        gotiated pleas and by involving the judge in the bar-
        gaining process.   3635

TRIAL judge's satisfaction as to voluntariness and understanding of
guilty pleas. Wash U L Q 1970:289-347.
        Interrelated presentation of case law, opinion and
        empirical data regarding taking of pleas in federal
        and state courts in St. Louis reveals that many federal
        and state trial court judges are not complying with
        U.S. Supreme Court mandates. Report combining empirical
        study of courts with questionnaires to judges, lawyers,
        law professors dealing with guilty plea procedure, and
        exhaustive examination of case law attempts to present
        model for judges to refer to during arraignment for
        plea. Questionnaire forms, tabulation of survey results
        are included. Study well-documented with cases. 3636

UNCONSTITUTIONALITY of plea bargaining. Harv L Rev 83:1387-1411 (1970).
        Note briefly describes institution of plea bargaining,
        analyzes present reforms recently proposed by the ABA
        (Standards relating to pleas of guilty), evaluates the

712 ADMINISTRATION OF CRIMINAL JUSTICE

constitutionality of curtailment of defendants' rights
in the interest of efficiency in administration of justice, and discusses the problem of enforcing a judicial
determiniation that plea bargaining is unconstitutional.
Author concludes that plea bargaining should be deemed
unconstitutional in order to restore defendant's fundamental trial rights to their traditional preeminence.
                                                    3637

UNDERWOOD, R.C. Let's put plea discussions - and agreements - on record. Loyola U L J (Chicago) 1:1-14 (1970).
          It is the opinion of the author, Chief Justice of Ill-
          inois Supreme Court, that record should be made of
          plea discussions and agreements, which would, in turn,
          avoid many appeals.   3638

USE of the nolo contendere plea in subsequent contexts. S Cal L Rev
44:737-67 (1971.
          Discusses reasons for use of the nolo plea and its ef-
          fect in later civil and criminal cases, for res judi-
          cata purposes, and for administrative rulings.   3639

WHITE. W.S. Proposal for reform of the plea bargaining process. U Pa
L Rev 119:439-65 (1971).
          Plea bargaining having been recognized as a valid prac-
          tice in Brady v U.S., 307 NY 742 (1970), Prof. White
          illustrates by describing the actual plea bargaining
          processes in Philadelphia and New York district attor-
          neys' offices, that they "are detrimental to society's
          interest" because of the wide discretion allowed in-
          dividual prosecutors. "It leads to disparate treatment
          and inevitably to disrespect for the law." Prosecutors'
          plea bargaining policies must be developed.   3640

     5. Pretrial Procedures

         Items include pretrial motions, pretrial dis-
         covery in criminal cases, pretrial conferen-
         ces, disclosure; omnibus hearings.

AMERICAN Bar Association Advisory Committee on Pretrial Proceedings.
Standards relating to discovery and procédure before trial, recomend-
ed by the Advisory Committee on Pretrial Proceedings. A.P. Murrah,
chair. D.G. Gibbens, reptr. Tent. draft, May 1969. N.Y., IJA, 1969.
167 p. Amendments, supp. Oct. 1970. 8 p. approved, Aug. 1970.
          Standards with commentary on general principles of
          pretrial procedure and discovery, disclosure to the
          accused and prosecution, regulation of discovery and
          procedure; appendices: additional views of Chief Jus-
          tice Taft; description, checklist and transcript of
          Omnibus Hearing Project in California; bibliography.
          (see item 3656a)   3641

BRENNAN, W.J., Jr. The Criminal prosecution: sporting event or quest
for truth? Wash U L Q 1963:279-95.
> Supreme Court Justice discusses whether civil pretrial
> discovery techniques that force both sides to "put all
> cards on the table" before trial should be extended
> to criminal cases as well: Procedural guarantees; the
> need for more interest in criminal law to be generated
> at the law school level; equal opportunity for discovery
> for all accused; developments in this area in California
> and other areas; how criminal pretrial discovery can
> better equalize the status of poor defendants and assist
> assigned counsel; arguments against criminal pretrial
> discovery and answers to these arguments; and how pre-
> trial discovery with appropriate safeguards can provide
> justice and truth in the criminal system.   3642

BROWER, H. Pre-trial procedure in criminal cases: a comparative view.
Portia L Rev 2:1-77 (1966).
> Examining the conflict between the adversary nature of
> criminal procedure and the growing body of procedural
> safeguards afforded the accused, the article compares
> United States procedure with that of Scotland, W. Ger-
> many, and India, discussing the right to silence, the
> right to counsel, and the "right to know," or discovery.
>   3643

CALKINS, R.M. Criminal justice for the indigent. U Det L J 42:305-42
(1965).
> The author examines the meaning of the constitutional
> mandate of the Gideon decision, that an indigent defen-
> dant must have effective representation. He demonstrates
> the importance of pretrial investigation and preparation,
> which is often not done by counsel for the indigent,
> and suggests that pretrial discovery rules be liberal-
> ized to overcome the absence of such investigations.
> This, he suggests will ensure that counsel for an indi-
> gent is properly prepared. Specific areas of pretrial
> discovery considered: (1) grand jury minutes (2) avail-
> able witnesses (3) statements given by the defendant,
> prosecution witnesses, et. al. (4) physical evidence
> and police reports.   3644

CLARK, T.C. The Omnibus hearing in state and federal courts. Cornell
L Rev 59:761-71 (1974).
> Introducing his subject with comments on the ABA Stan-
> dards for the Administration of Criminal Justice and
> how they have been cited and compared in some states,
> Justice Clark describes the Standards relating to dis-
> covery and procedure before trial, more specifically
> dwelling on the omnibus hearing procedure.   3645

COLLINS, J.G. Disclosure: an instrument of policy. Ore L Rev 47:
71-79 (1967).
>Examines changes in disclosure of information in fed-
>eral criminal cases resulting from the amendments to
>the Federal Rules of Criminal Procedure, effective
>July 1, 1966; describes disclosure practice in federal
>criminal cases in Oregon in particular.   3646

CRIMINAL discovery - comparison of federal discovery and the ABA
standards with the new statutory provisions in Wisconsin. Wis L Rev
1971:614-26.
>Note discusses procedures including historical back-
>ground; prosecutorial and defense discovery; modern
>trends; and a comparison of federal court procedure with
>ABA Standards and Wisconsin statutes. Author concludes
>that the Wisconsin statute still favors the prosecution,
>and that extra-legal cooperation between the parties
>is required.   3647

DEFENDANT'S right of discovery in criminal cases. Clev St L Rev 20:
31-42 (1971).
>Discusses absolute need for broad discovery rights in
>criminal cases if a trial is to be quest for truth rath-
>er than a joust; historical perspective of discovery
>and present Ohio law are reviewed. Author concludes
>that reform in Ohio's restrictive laws is necessary and
>presents several alternatives.   3648

DISCOVERY in criminal cases, a panel discussion before the Judicial
Conference of the Second Judicial Circuit, Sept. 8, 1967. FRD 44:481-
525 (1968).
>Presiding: McLean, E.C. Panelists: Kaufman, S.E.; Kos-
>telantz, B.; Newman, J.O.; Steinberg, H.   3649

DISCOVERY in New York: the effect of the new criminal procedure law.
Syracuse L Rev 23:89-112 (1972).
>Comment discusses various provisions of the statutory
>establishment of pretrial discovery procedure in New
>York's new Criminal Procedural Law (CPL): exemptions,
>discovery as a matter of right, duty to disclose, pro-
>cedure, discovery outside the CPL based on pre-CPL case
>law, and pretrial notice of the use of certain defenses.
>3650

DISCOVERY procedures under New York's new criminal procedure law.
Brooklyn L Rev 38:164-81 (1971).
>Article explains the specific criteria that judges are
>to follow in granting discovery as outlined in the new
>law, regarding scientific reports, examinations, and
>documents; other reports and property; statements by
>defendant and co-defendants; identity of witnesses and
>informers, exceptions to discovery, the prosecution's

right to discovery, and protective orders. Author concludes that the new law still provides for a great deal
of discretion, and the courts must remember the intent
of liberalization of the law.   3651

FAHRINGER, H.P. Brady rule: has anyone here seen Brady? John Marshall J 6:77-86 (1972); Has anyone here seen Brady?: discovery in
criminal cases. Crim L Bull 9:325-36 (1973).
        Although the decision in Brady v Maryland 373 US 83
        (1963) was viewed at the time as expanding discovery,
        the author observes how the authority of Brady has been
        since diluted. He suggests what lawyers may do to stave
        off Brady's further devaluation.   3652

FLORIDA University College of Law Criminal Law Seminar. Issue: the
desirability of the promulgation by the Supreme Court of Florida of
a rule regulating pre-trial conferences in criminal cases; affirmative
and negative arguments, prepared for the Supreme Court of Florida
by members of the Criminal Law Seminar, Prof. V.W. Clark, Supervisor.
Gainesville, 1962. 20 p.
        An objective presentation of the case for and against
        the promulgation of the rule.   3653

FONTANA, J. Discovery in criminal cases: a survey of the proposed
rule changes. Md L Rev 25:212-25 (1965).
        After commenting on past limitations and need for broad-
        er criminal discovery, attorney discusses present fed-
        eral criminal discovery rules, especially Rules 16,
        6(e), and 7(f) and recommends needed changes to limit
        restrictions and broaden bases of discovery; would give
        accused right to see: one's own written statement origi-
        nally made, lists of witnesses, and witnesses' state-
        ments, subject to certain procedures of the Jencks Act
        and under specified rules regarding books and documents.
        In addition, proposed change would give court power to
        decide whether a pretrial conference should be had; and
        make available recorded testimony of defendant before
        a grand jury for discovery purposes. The appendix pre-
        sents Rules 6, 7, and 17.1 with proposed changes.3654

GOLDSTEIN, A.S. The state and the accused: balance of advantage in
criminal procedure. Yale L J 69:1149-99 (1969).
        Yale law professor examines two major problems of crimi-
        nal trial: that of sufficiency of evidence to take case
        to the jury and that of disclosure by both prosecution
        and defense of issues and evidence to be produced at
        trial; gives development of law and case illustrations;
        discusses procedures from arrest through indictment by
        grand jury.   3655

GUZMAN, R. Arkansas' 1971 criminal discovery act. Ark L Rev 26;1-16
(1972).
        Law professor analyzes the new discovery act, calls

attention to possibilities for its use as well as problems it might present; evaluates criticisms of the
act; and compares the new rules with other current recommendations for criminal discovery reform.   3656

HIGGINS, G.V. Pretrial procedures in criminal cases: the ABA is wrong.
Mass L Q 55:53-57 (1970).
        Assistant U.S. Attorney, Massachusetts, states his ex-
        ceptions to conclusion of ABA Advisory Committee on Pre-
        trial Proceedings, in its standards on discovery (item
        3641); permitting pretrial discovery to criminal defen-
        dants as a right. Higgins feels that community's inter-
        est should be protected; that in some serious cases
        prosecution's advantage of surprise is necessary to
        conviction, also, that discovery in every case opens
        door to tampering with witnesses and other abuses.
                                                    3656a

JUDICIAL Conference of the United States. Pretrial Committee report
on recommended procedures in criminal trials. FRD 37:95-110 (1965).
        A.P. Murrah, chair. Part 2 of the report of the Subcom-
        mittee (J.M. Carter, chair.) recommends, among other
        things, who should suggest pretrial, in what type of
        cases, consent of defendant, presence of defendant at
        all times, binding effects of pretrial; whether pretrial
        judge should try case. Further discussion and recommen-
        dations cover discovery, bill of particulars, Jencks
        Act - disclosure of documents by government, waiver of
        self incrimination rights, assessment of cost against
        defendant; forms for stipulation and order for pretrial
        conference and pretrial stipulation and order recording
        the pretrial proceedings are appended.   3657

LOUISELL, D.W Criminal discovery and self-incrimination: Roger Traynor confronts the dilemma. Calif L Rev 53:89-102 (1965).
        Discusses Traynor theories on criminal discovery (item
        3686) and how he reconciles them with rule that a de-
        fendant in a criminal case may not be compelled to tes-
        tify or to produce documents in his possession. Author,
        commenting on the dilemma of criminal discovery versus
        no-self-incrimination, says candor compels admission
        that such discovery orders are an additional qualifi-
        cation of the no-self-incrimination principles. 3658

LOUISELL, D.W. Criminal discovery: dilemma real or apparent? Calif
L Rev 49:56-103 (1961); reprinted in substance in ch. 13 of his Modern California discovery (San Francisco, Berkeley press, 1963).
        History, common law background; arguments against; prac-
        tice in England; practice under FRCP; California pro-
        cedures; analysis of the dilemma; conclusion is that
        when discovery "promotes ascertainment of the facts,

it cannot be arbitrarily withheld in the name of protecting the balance between the state and the accused."
See decision of Judge J. Weinstein in US v Percevault
61 FRD 338 (N.Y.E.D. 1973)   3659

LOUISIANA and criminal discovery. La L Rev 33:596-612 (1973).
          Comment traces the history of criminal discovery and
          analyzes the arguments for and against its use; urges
          adoption of the ABA standards (item 3641) to provide
          for flexibility in the discovery proceedings.   3660

MACCARTHY, T.F. and FORDE, K.M. Discovery in criminal cases under
the new local rules of the federal court. Chi B Rec 52:41-50 (1970).
          Authors examine the innovation and impact of the new
          discovery rules included in the Ill., N.D., District
          Court's local rules of criminal procedure: automatic
          pretrial discovery, request and motion for additional
          disclosure, time considerations, reciprocal discovery,
          contested motions, and discovery of grand jury pro-
          ceedings. Appendix is text of rules.   3661

MILLER, E.L., Jr. The omnibus hearing: an experiment in federal criminal discovery. San Diego L Rev 5:293-326 (1968).
          U.S. Attorney gives detailed description of experimen-
          tal pretrial omnibus discovery hearings after one year's
          implementation in California's Southern District; con-
          cludes the experiment should be altered to be somewhat
          defense orientated. Cites advantages to eliminating
          written motion practice, encouraging stipulations, help-
          ing prepare the case, and maintaining communication.
          Sample pretrial order appended.   3662

MURPHY, J.W. Criminal discovery: what progress since US v Aaron Burr.
Crim L Bull 2:3-14 (no. 5, 1966)
          Finds very little progress: examines California cases
          on criminal discovery which shifted from very progres-
          sive approach in the late 1950's to almost full rever-
          sal.   3663

NAKELL, B. Criminal discovery for the defense and prosecution; the
developing constitutional considerations. NC L Rev 50:437-516 (1972).
          Predicts Supreme Court will uphold broad defense dis-
          covery by full disclosure and depositions on due process
          grounds, and rejects prosecution discovery as infring-
          ing on the Fifth Amendment and unnecessary in view of
          the prosecutor's investigatory arsenal. Examines prose-
          cutor's effective investigatory powers, new limitations
          on prosecution discovery, privilege against self-in-
          crimination and how these affect discovery.   3664

NAKELL, B. Effect of due process on criminal discovery. Ky L J 62:
58-90 (1973/74).
          The author examines two defense discovery devices, that

of file disclosure and depositions; the discovery principles established in Wardius v Oregon 93 SCt 2208
(1973) and Gagnon v Scarpell 93 SCT 1756 (1973); and
problems in exchanging evidence. He also considers the
nature of the preliminary hearing as required by due
process and notes that the hearing is not for discovery.
                                                      3665

NIMMER, R.T. The omnibus hearing, an experiment in relieving inefficiency, unfairness and judicial delay. Chicago, AB Found, 1971. 125 p.
           A study of omnibus hearing in the federal district court,
           S.D. Calif., in San Diego in 1967 offers intensive analy-
           sis of cases with negative conclusions as to efficiency;
           reasons suggested with lessons to be learned. Omnibus
           hearing procedure is suggested in ABA Standards relat-
           ing to discovery and procedure before trial. Bibliog-
           raphy on criminal court delay and discovery.   3666

NIMMER, R.T. A slightly movable object; a case study in judicial
reform in the criminal justice process: the omnibus hearing. Denver
L J 48:179-209 (1971/1972).
           Details of how and why the Omnibus Hearing procedure
           failed to achieve its ends in San Diego federal dis-
           trict court. Lesson to be learned is that criminal jus-
           tice reforms produce actual change only as they are
           filtered through the discretionary adjustment procedure
           under which the system functions. Hypothetical models
           do not always work because of discretionary difficulties
           they face.   3667

NINTH annual postgraduate conference of the Columbia Law School Association Alumni Association, Mar. 23, 1968. Changes ahead in pretrial
discovery. FRD 45:479-505 (1969).
           Contents: Rosenberg, M. Changes ahead in pretrial dis-
           covery.--Freund, F.A. Work product.--Doskow, A. Pro-
           cedural aspects of discovery.   3668

NORTON, J., JENNINGS, S.E. and TOWE, T.E. Truth and individual rights:
a comparison of United States and French pretrial procedures. Am
Crim L Q 2:159-77 (1964).
           Comparison leads to conclusion that U.S. procedures are
           uncompromising in guaranteeing constitutional protec-
           tion while the French system concentrates on the search
           for truth.   3669

OLIVER, J.W. Omnibus pretrial proceedings: a review of the experience
of the United States District Court for the Western District of Missouri. FRD 58:270-98 (1973).
           Reports the utility of maximum pretrial discovery and
           firm scheduling as means of maximizing the efficiency
           of the omnibus procedure. Gives statistics showing that
           the omnibus procedure reduces the time for disposition

of cases and does not hinder the obtaining of convictions.   3670

OMNIBUS hearing: a proposal for California criminal pretrial motion
procedure.   Pacific L J 4:861-79 (1973).
　　　　　Author assesses merits of omnibus hearings, in which
　　　　　all pretrial motions are made at one time, in light
　　　　　of California law. Discusses current California pre-
　　　　　trial procedure; history and nature of the omnibus hear-
　　　　　ing. Analysis concludes that omnibus hearings serve
　　　　　both justice and efficiency and should be established
　　　　　throughout state.   3671

THE OMNIBUS proceding: clarification of discovery in the federal
courts and other benefits.   St Mary's L J 6:386-406 (1974).
　　　　　Comment examines Omnibus Hearing Project, a formal pre-
　　　　　trial conference held in open court wherein issues
　　　　　normally raised in trial are fully explored prior to
　　　　　trial for more expeditious administration of criminal
　　　　　justice in federal courts. Authority for hiring, hearing
　　　　　and procedures are described; relevant cases are exam-
　　　　　ined. Author finds experiments successful and worth
　　　　　continuing.   3672

ORFIELD, L.B.   Discovery during trial in federal criminal cases: the
Jencks Act.   S W L J 18:212-35 (1964).
　　　　　Traces, in light of the limitation on pretrial discovery,
　　　　　case law on Act which allows the defendant a copy of
　　　　　government witness's out-of-court statement only if and
　　　　　when the witness testifies.   3673

ORFIELD, L.B.   Lists of witnesses and jurors in federal criminal
cases.   FRD 44:527-38 (1968).
　　　　　Prof. Orfield discusses 10 USC 3432, mandating that
　　　　　accused in certain crimes receive, among other data,
　　　　　a list of witnesses. He also discusses defendant's
　　　　　right to a list of the jurors. He annotates details and
　　　　　specifics by references to cases.   3674

PARLEY, L.I. and WHITE, F.   Expanding criminal discovery: law and
tactics under Public Act 680 of the Connecticut general statutes.
Conn B J 44:335-345 (1970).
　　　　　Authors analyze and interpret Act, which establishes
　　　　　the right of the criminal defendant to obtain state-
　　　　　ments of prosecution witnesses by does not define pro-
　　　　　cedural or technical aspects: scope of application,
　　　　　discoverable oral and written statements, making the
　　　　　motion, the meaning of "possession of the prosecution,"
　　　　　prosecution objections, and enforcement.   3675

PETERSON, D.L.   Omnibus hearings in criminal cases in North Dakota
federal district court.   ND L Rev 49:537-61 (1973).

> Assistant U.S. Attorney gives details of all-purpose
> hearing dealing with a wide variety of matters. Order
> of the court is appended.   <u>3676</u>

PRE-TRIAL discovery of conviction records of prosecution witnesses.
Ia L Rev 58:1194-220 (1973).
> Note examines how prior conviction records can provide
> an invaluable evidentiary function of impeaching pro-
> secution's witnesses, and how defendants need this in-
> formation, presently unavailable to them. Suggests that
> a specific discovery right be granted to defendants to
> obtain these records and that this right may be con-
> stitutionally required to satisfy due process standards.
> Author presents legislative and preferred judicial solu-
> tion.   <u>3677</u>

PRETRIAL identification confrontations. Miss L J 45:489-511 (1974).
> An examination of types of pretrial identification con-
> frontations and the possibilities of prejudice inherent
> in the conduct of such confrontations are presented.
> Suggestions are offered as to how the prejudice can be
> lessened.   <u>3678</u>

RIGHT to counsel at pretrial lineups. UMKC L Rev 42:251-57 (1973).
> Note analyzes <u>Arnold v State</u>, 484 SW2d 248 (Mo. 1972),
> in which the court held that evidence of a pretrial
> line-up, where the confrontation was after the initia-
> tion of adversary proceedings and without presence of
> counsel for accused, was inadmissible at trial. Examined
> are the facts of the case, previous Supreme Court de-
> cisions leading to this case, and the workability of
> this exclusionary rule.   <u>3679</u>

ROETHER, R.H. Criminal discovery in Michigan: the pursuit of justice.
J Urban L 50:753-67 (1973).
> Discussion of recent development of rules of criminal
> discovery, and operation under the Michigan statute.
>   <u>3680</u>

ROTHBLATT, H.B. and LEROY, D.H. The motion in liminie in criminal
trials: a technique for the pretrial exclusion of prejudicial evidence. KY L J 60:611-37 (1972).
> Motion to enjoin prosecutor from introducing evidence
> more inflammatory than probative and to prevent the
> posing of a question which could prejudice a jury with-
> out being answered. The authors give arguments for ju-
> dicial acceptance and tactical instruction for counsel.
>   <u>3681</u>

STRAYHORN, E.E. Full criminal discovery in Illinois: a judge's experience. Judicature 56:279-89 (1973).
> Chicago trial judge considers Illinois Supreme Court's

new criminal discovery rules, how they operate and how
they have helped to shorten pretrial preparation and
trial procedure.   3682

SYMPOSIUM: Criminal discovery. U San Francisco L Rev 7:203-15
(1973).
          Kane, R.F. Criminal discovery - the circuitous road to
          a two-way street.--Lapides, G.D. Cross currents in pro-
          secutorial discovery: a defense counsel's viewpoint.--
          Hewitt, J.F., Bell, F.O., Jr. Beyond rule 16: the in-
          herent power of the federal court to order pretrial dis-
          covery in criminal cases.--Depositions as a means of
          criminal discovery.--Prosecutorial discovery: how far
          may the prosecution go?--Governmental privileges: road-
          block to effective discovery.--Quasi-judicial adminis-
          tration hearings: is a dual system of discovery neces-
          sary?--Discovery rights in juvenile proceedings.--Sup-
          pression: the prosecution's failure to disclose evidence
          favorable to the defense; Bibliography: 369-89. 3683

SYMPOSIUM: Discovery in criminal cases, a panel discussion before the
Judicial Conference of the Second Judicial Circuit, Sept. 8, 1969.
FRD 44: 481-525 (1967).
          Prosecutors and defense lawyers debate usefulness of
          liberalizing federal criminal discovery rules and some
          of the general problems of motion practice. Presiding:
          McLean, E.C. Panelists: Kaufman, S.E., Kostelaneta, B.,
          Newman, J.O., Steinberg, H.   3684

SYMPOSIUM: Discovery in federal criminal cases. FRD 33:47-128 (1963).
          Partial contents: Brennan, W.J. Remarks on discovery.--
          Remington, F.J. Introduction: role of discovery in the
          adversary system; statement of issues facing the revi-
          sers of the criminal rules.--Flannery, T.A. The prose-
          cutor's case against liberal discovery.--Pye, A.K. The
          defendant's case for more liberal discovery.--Panel
          discussion.--Appendix: Conference papers on discovery
          in federal criminal cases prepared for the Judicial
          Conference, D.C. Circuit, by the Junior Bar Section of
          the Bar Association of the District of Columbia. 3685

TRAYNOR. R.J. Ground lost and found in criminal discovery. NYU L
Rev 39:228-50 (1964).
          Justice elucidates how there is little opportunity for
          pretrial discovery on defendant's part in the courts;
          discusses Supreme Court cases; cites to experiences in
          this area in California and other states in the hope
          that there will be wider acceptance of the principle
          that preoccupation with surprise tactics be abandoned.
          (see also item 3658)   3686

VAN SICKLE, B.M. Omnibus pretrial conference. N D L Rev 50:178-90
(1973).
> Judge discusses the benefits of the omnibus pretrial
> conference, which allows the defendant to go into court
> understanding the case which will be presented against
> him and the lawyer to defend the case at ease with court
> procedure. Includes appendices of proposed omnibus pre-
> trial forms on discovery, motion, and subpoena, and
> letter of explanation of procedure at an omnibus pre-
> trial conference.   3687

WHY the omnibus hearing project? A panel discussion. Judicature 55:
377-82 (1972).
> The comprehensive form of pretrial in which all issues
> to be raised are explored in advance by both prosecu-
> tion and defense lawyers has been in successful opera-
> tion in the Western District of Texas since 1967. The
> Chief Judge, A.A. Spears, Assistant U.S. Attorney, R.L.
> Harrison, and practicing attorney, J.R. Gillespie, all
> of San Antonio, discuss at the National Judicial Con-
> ference on the Standards (item 3331) how the project
> works, giving procedures, case histories and advantages
> such as eliminating written motions and achieving more
> guilty pleas. Same material covered, same panelists
> in Why the omnibus hearing project? panel, at Tenth
> Circuit Judicial Conference, Jackson Lake, Wyo. July 2,
> 1969. 25 p.   3688

WILDER, M.S. Prosecution discovery and the privilege against self-
incrimination. Am Crim L Q, 6:3-25 (1967).
> Examines the history of criminal discovery, policy and
> scope of the privilege against self-incrimination and
> rules of defendants' disclosure under alibi statutes.
> Concludes that prosecutorial discretion is of doubtful
> constitutionality, but if construed to be constitutional,
> scope should be limited to items specifically related
> to accused's proposed defense.   3689

C. Prosecutorial and Defense Functions

1. The Prosecutor

Items cover qualification, selection, re-
muneration; part-time prosecutors; screening and investigative methods; decision to
charge; ethics; forensic misconduct; role
in plea bargaining and in sentencing; suppression of evidence favorable to accused;
newspaper and television publicity. Data
on attorneys general are included.

ABRAMS, N.   Internal policy: guiding the exercise of prosecutorial
discretion.   UCLA L Rev 19:1-58 (1971).
Argues feasibility and desirability of developing comprehensive policy statements governing prosecutorial
discretion; discusses theories of prosecutorial discretion, possible methods of formulation and internal
and external review, and concludes that internal rules
and review should now be implemented.   3690

ALSHULER, A.W.   The prosecutor's role in plea bargaining.   U Chi L
Rev 36:50-112 (1968).
For annotation see item 3600)   3691

AMERICAN Bar Association Advisory Committee on the Prosecution and
Defense Functions.   Standards relating to the prosecution function
and defense function, recommended by the Advisory Committee on the
Prosecution and Defense Functions. Tent. draft, Mar. 1970. N.Y.,
IJA, 1970.   327 p.   Amendments, supp. Mar. 1971.   21 p.   approved,
Feb. 1971.
Standards with commentary on the role of the advocate
in a prosecution function cover Organization of the
prosecution function, Investigation for prosecution
decision, Plea discussions, The trial, and Sentencing.
Standards on defense function cover Access to counsel,
Lawyer-client relationship, Investigation and prepara-
tion, Control and direction of litigation, Disposition
without trial, Trial, and After conviction; appendix:
Professional standards of ethics and discipline of advocates in England. Bibliography.   3692

AMERICAN Judicature Society.   Selected readings in prosecution, defense and bail, by A. Ashman and T. Asperk.   Chicago, 1971.   119 p.
A compendium of articles covering selected powers and
operation of the prosecutor's office and his decision
to charge; other excerpts include pertinent protions
from various Presidential reports; there is a reprint
of the ABA Standards on the Defense Function (item 3692)
and the brief amicus curiae of the National Legal Aid
and Defender Assn in Argersinger v Hamlin.   3693

BRADY v Maryland and the prosecutor's duty to disclose. U Chi L Rev
40:112-40 (1972).
>Comment examines cases that have followed, interpreted,
and expanded the rule in Brady that a criminal defendant
has a constitutional right of access to certain of the
prosecution's information; discusses the rule, necessity of request, timing of disclosure, what constitutes
suppression, what constitutes necessary evidence, rationales for reversal, and the role of the prosecutor.
Author concludes that complete disclosure is desirable.
>3694

BURGER, W.E. Counsel for the prosecution and the defense; their role
under minimum standards. Am Crim L Q 8:2-9 (1969); Nat Judicial Conference on Standards for the Admin of Crim Justice, Baton Rouge, 1972.
p. 74-81.
>The Chief Justice, formerly chairman of the ABA Special
Committee on Minimum Standards for Criminal Justice,
relates the Committee's conclusions, resulting from
consultation with prominent criminal defense lawyers
and judges, with respect to the role of the defense
attorney in controlling the case, when ethical questions
arise, such as knowing that the defendant intends to
perjure himself, and conduct in the courtroom. 3695

CARTER, J.M. Suppression of evidence favorable to an accused. FRD
34:87-91 (1964).
>Brady v Maryland, 373 US 83 (1963), held that suppres-
sion violates due process where evidence is material,
irrespective of good or bad faith of the prosecution.
Judge lays down workable ground rules, in examining
pertinent cases dealing with evidence favorable to
accused and evidence material to punishment.   3696

CAVE, J.M. Professional responsibilty of the prosecuting attorney
to the indigent defendant in a criminal case. Mo L Rev 29:339-46
(1964).
>Article examines the duties and power of the prosecuting
attorney and the impact of Gideon on his job. The professional responsibility of a prosecuting attorney is
neither increased nor lessened by the nature of the
defendant; the rights of all people accused of crimes
are the same. A greater professional awareness of this
should lessen the problem of adequate representation
of the indigent defendant.   3697

CENTER for Criminal Justice, Boston University School of Law. Prosecution in the juvenile courts: guidelines for the future; S. Krantz,
director, M. Finkelstein, proj. dir. Boston, 1973. 368 p.
>Comprehensive examination of need for attorney prose-
cutors in juvenile delinquency proceedings as a result
of recent trend away from paternalistic attitude. Study

considers scope of the prosecutor's responsibilty. Prosecution procedure in Boston courts is outlined as well
as in other representative jurisdictions and guidelines
are proposed. Data appended.   3698

COLORADO Legislative Council. Compensation of district attorneys
and assistant and deputy district attorneys; report to the Colorado
General Assembly. Denver, 1970. 25 p.
        Report of findings and recommendations concerning com-
        pensation for district attorneys; included are: sug-
        gestion that all Colorado district attorneys serve
        full time; that staff be hired on a part-time basis;
        and that state finance all district attorneys' offices.
        Statistical data supports the report.   3699

DISCRETION exercised by Montana county attorneys in criminal prosecutions. Mont L Rev 28:41-93 (1966).
        Empirical study of the extent of prosecutor's discre-
        tion in decision to prosecute, plea bargain, and in
        other areas; the limits of his discretion; and the
        sanctions to which prosecutor may be subject. 3700

DUTY of the prosecutor to call witnesses whose testimony will help
the accused to establish his innocence. Wash U L Q 1966:68-101.
        The history and current scope of the affirmative duty
        to call witnesses is examined, reasons for its continu-
        ance or elimination are explored and recent attempts
        to establish it on constitutional grounds through ex-
        pansion of the right of confrontation and the due
        process limits on suppression of evidence are described.
                                                        3701

FREEDMAN, M.H. The professional responsibility of the prosecuting
attorney. Geo L J 55:1030-47 (1967).
        Discussion of six ethical questions faced by prosecutors
        including decision to prosecute, plea bargaining tactics,
        taking advantage of ineffective defense counsel. Author
        also discusses several propositions regarding ethical
        strictures - or lack of them - upon defense. (See item
        3752, reply by defense lawyer.)   3702

GIVELBER, D.J. The application of equal protection principles to
selective enforcement of the criminal law. U Ill L F 1973:88-112.
        Prosecutorial discretion to be lenient is also discre-
        tion not to be lenient, and this results in discrimina-
        tory law enforcement policies, or anomalous prosecutions.
        Author says present doctrine, that a discriminatory
        purpose must be proved by the defendant, is too pro-
        tective of prosecutors. He proposes that prosecutors
        should have to answer questions arising from statistics,
        similar to questions of discrimination raised by sta-
        tistics in jury selection cases.   3703

HARVARD Student District Attorney Project: a clinical experience in
prosecution of minor criminal cases by senior law students; first-
year final report submitted to Office of Law Enforcement Assistance.
Washington, USGPO, 1968. 94 p.
> Describes project; offers recommendations, including
> continuance of student prosecutor programs, increased
> encouragement by the federal government of such programs
> in law schools; appendices are project training material
> and project articles.   3704

HERRMANN, J. Rule of compulsory prosecution and the scope of prosecutorial discretion in Germany. U Chi L Rev 41:465-505 (1974).
> West German system allows much less discretion: prose-
> cutor failing to charge in felonies and serious mis-
> demeanors may face criminal liability, also victim may
> challenge insufficient evidence or prosecute privately.
> The greater discretion allowed in most misdemeanors,
> and beginning of trend to subtle plea bargains, is
> described.   3705

HOGAN, F.S. The role of the prosecutor in the administration of criminal justice. N.Y., 1964. 39 p.
> New York County District Attorney describes his office,
> its role in the administration of criminal justice,
> the grand jury system and treatment of youthful offend-
> ers. He also discusses current problems involving motions
> to suppress evidence, use of defendant's pretrial state-
> ments, wiretapping, writs of coram nobis, and denial of
> grand jury's right to make reports.   3706

INTERROGATION of criminal defendants: some views on Miranda v Arizona.
Fordham L Rev 35:169-262 (1966).
> Case and its implications discussed in articles by G.
> Edwards, B.J. George, Jr., A.K. Pye, T.C. Lynch, R.H.
> Kuh, M.W. Hogan, O.K. Fraenkel, E.J. Younger, following
> digest of the decision.   3707

JACOBY, J.E. Case evaluation: quantifying prosecutorial policy.
Judicature 58:486-93 (1975).
> Executive director of National Center for Prosecution
> Management discusses various bases for establishing
> caseload priorities by the prosecutors. Case evaluation
> systems used by prosecutors are described. The Bronx
> case evaluation system dealing with the evidentiary
> strength of a case is labelled satisfactory and is de-
> tailed. Forms used in extracting the necessary data
> in the Bronx project are reproduced. Annotated to other
> case evaluation systems.   3707a

KAPLAN, J. Prosecutorial discretion. Nw L Rev 60:174-93 (1965).
> Law professor, former assistant U.S. Attorney, describes
> standards used to determine whether to prosecute, cit-
> ing cases and examples.   3708

LEONARD, R.F. and GARBER, J. Screening of criminal cases. Chicago, Nat Dist Attys Assn, 1972. 80 p.
> Material, designed to aid prosecutors in determining whether to charge offender or use alternative method, examines: role and function of prosecutor; Michigan law on prosecutorial discretion and model citizen volunteer program; overview of present screening procedures and recommendations for improvement; and guidelines on preliminary hearings and issuance of warrants. 3709

LILES, W.T. and PATTERSON, J.C. Prosecutorial disclosure: in camera and beyond. Fla L Rev 22:491-514 (1970).
> History of prosecutorial disclosure; future development of Brady; problem of threshold showing by defendant, method of disclosure, standards for appeal, application of harmless error rule to failure of prosecutor to disclose. 3710

LIMITATIONS on prosecutor's discretionary power to initiate criminal suits: movement toward a new era. Ottawa L Rev 5:104-23 (1971).
> Student writes on traditional exercise of prosecutor's discretion, supported by cases and other writings; discussing the decision not to prosecute where evidence of guilt is clear, decision to prosecute when normal procedure is non-prosecution. Reports on dissatisfaction with current practice, examining closely the discretion element. Concludes by commenting on cases that demonstrate movement toward the review of prosecutor's discretionary power. 3711

LOS ANGELES County District Attorney. Prosecution of adult felony defendants in Los Angeles County: a policy perspective, prepared for the Los Angeles County district attorney's office, by P.W. Greenwood [and others] Santa Monica, Rand Corp, 1973. 156 p.
> Uses empirical analysis to examine the stages of the criminal justice system in Los Angeles County for adult felony defendants; offers statistical data, findings, conclusions and recommendations to remedy the variations found within the District Attorney's office in prosecuting offenses. Bibliography. 3712

MCINTYRE, D.M. and LIPPMAN, D. Prosecutors and early disposition of felony cases. ABA J 56:1154-59 (1970).
> An overview of early disposition of felony cases in different jurisdictions, whether at preliminary arraignment, or non-jury trial or by the judiciary or prosecutor's office. The methods are related to cities' political background, and the chances of reform are discussed. 3713

MATERIALITY and defense requests: aids in defining the prosecutor's duty of disclosure. Ia L Rev 59:433-51 (1973).

Article, focusing on <u>Davis v Heyd</u>, 479 F2d 446 (5th Cir., 1973), examines the duty of the prosecuting attorney to disclose favorable evidence to the accused; the case development of this duty, the standard by which he must decide, obligation to disclose, and the role of a defense request for disclosure and how it can aid the prosecuting attorney are discussed.   <u>3714</u>

MILLER, F.W. Prosecution; the decision to charge a suspect with a crime. Boston, Little, Brown, 1969. 366 p. (AB Found. administration of criminal justice series)
One of five "Reports of the Survey of criminal justice in the U.S."; F.J. Remington, ed. (See item <u>323</u> for others) Field data of three jurisdictions (Kan., Mich., Wis.) are analyzed to determine who shares in prosecutor's decision to charge, what bases are used in guiding or controlling the decision and what sanctions are available if proper guides are not applied. Also discussed are judicial involvement in and review of the decision to charge. One part is given over to analysis of discretion including reasons for decision not to charge.   <u>3715</u>

MILLER, F.W. and TIFFANY, L.P. Prosecutor dominance of the warrant decision: a study of current practices. Wash U L Q 1964:1-23.
Law professors examine the argument that there is a need for an impartial third party determination of the sufficiency of evidence to justify issuance of a warrant. Nature of the warrant, police participation in decision, divergence of law and practice, the role of the prosecutor, self-imposed controls, and other alternatives are discussed. Authors conclude that use of a magistrate is anomalous under the public prosecution system as it now exists.   <u>3716</u>

MILLS, J. The prosecutor. N.Y., Farrar, Straus & Giroux, 1969. 245 p.
Subject is Queens County, N.Y., Assistant District Attorney and his work in three murder cases. Bulk of book is investigation and trial of a gangland murder.   <u>3717</u>

MORGAN, R.B. and ALEXANDER, C.E. A survey of local prosecutors. State Govt 47:42-45 (1974).
Summary of a national survey conducted by the Committee on the Office of Attorney General; includes basic statistics of budgets, salaries, staffs, training and the relationship between the attorney general and local prosecutors.   <u>3718</u>

NATIONAL Association of Attorneys General Committee on the Office of Attorney General. Former attorneys general analyze the office. Raleigh, 1970. 32 p.

Analysis of responses of 115 former attorneys general
to questionnaire concerning various aspects of the office is set forth. They relate their powers and duties
and rank certain activities in terms of amount of time
they devoted to them in office. The appendix contains
the text of the questionnaire and the names of the
former attorneys general who responded.   3719

NATIONAL Association of Attorneys General Committee on the Office of
Attorney General. Prosecutor training and assistance programs.
Raleigh, 1974. 137 p.
        Summary for each state describes program for training
        at local level and improvement of prosecution function
        at state level; discussions follow of typical and need-
        ed programs, staff and budgets, national programs
        and publications. Sample publications appended. 3720

NATIONAL Association of Attorneys General Committee on the Office of
Attorney General. The office of attorney general: organization,
budget, salaries, staff and opinions. Raleigh, 1973. 50 p.
_____. Appendix: Additional data ... for Arkansas, Oklahoma,
Virgin Islands. Mar. 19, 1974. 6 p.
        Tables based on questionnaires list sections and divi-
        sions, with number of lawyers in each; appropriations;
        LEAA grants; limitations on private practice; attorney
        positions authorized; other positions authorized; sal-
        aries and average salaries, data on opinions.   3721

NATIONAL Association of Attorneys General Committee on the Office of
Attorney General. Organized crime control legislation. Raleigh, 1974.
147 p.
        Covers powers in prosecution, electronic surveillance,
        infiltration of legitimate business, loansharking, pro-
        fessional gambling, protection of witnesses, state in-
        vestigation of grand juries, witness immunity.   3722

NATIONAL Association of Attorneys General Committee of the Office of
Attorney General. Organized crime control units. Raleigh, 1974.
103 p.
        Describes establishment, budgets, funding, personnel,
        prosecution and investigation units, intelligence opera-
        tions, training programs, equipment of Crime Control
        Units in the states; appendices include position de-
        scriptions and program for organized crime workshops.
                                                       3723

NATIONAL Association of Attorneys General Committee on the Office of
Attorney General. Organized crime prevention councils. Raleigh, 1973.
46 p.
        Gives data regarding the councils as to purpose, status,
        membership and meetings, funding, functions and duties
        (LEAA Standards), relationship with other agencies, col-

lecting and disseminating information; this last includes surveys of state problems, public information,
and legislative programs.   3724

NATIONAL Association of Attorneys General Committee on the Office of
Attorney General. Report on the office of Attorney General. Raleigh,
1971. 616 p.
Result of two-year study of powers, duties, and operations of the office of Attorney General in the states
and territories; its recommendations outline program
of active involvement in improving a state's criminal
justice system, particularly through training systems,
vigorous prosecution of certain crimes, and cooperation
with and coordination of local law enforcement efforts.
                                                 3725

NATIONAL Association of Attorneys General Committee on the Office of
the Attorney General. Summary of proceedings: management institute,
Nov. 3-6, 1971, University of Denver Law Center. Raleigh, 1972.
90 p.
Remarks on legal management generally and on specific
aspects, such as workload management, computer applications, by law professors, management specialists, members of attorney general offices.   3726

NATIONAL Association of Attorneys General Committee on the Office of
Attorney General. Summary of proceedings: second management institute, May 30-Jun.1, 1973, Atlanta, Ga. Raleigh, 1973. 57 p.
Short papers on management of financing, personnel,
workload, by attorney generals, management and finance
specialists.   3727

NATIONAL Association of Attorneys General Committee on the Office of
Attorney General. Survey of local prosecutors: data concerning 1,000
local prosecutors. Raleigh, 1973. 1 v., var. pag.
This study presents the results of a nationwide survey
of local prosecutors; the questionnaire covered: length
of experience, budget, salary, staff, records and reports, training programs, caseloads and advisory functions and attitude toward and relationship with attorneys general; appendices include recommendations on
the prosecution function and charts analyzing the results of this study.   3728

NATIONAL Center for Prosecution Management. Minimum standards for
the design and use of a prosecutor's case jacket. Washington, 1973.
29 p.
Within the case jacket are the important papers reflect-
ing the history as well as the efforts and all procedures in the case. Standards are set down to form a
model case jacket for use by prosecutor. Information
can be easily retrieved and trial documents are organized to ensure that they appear in the order needed

THE CRIMINAL JUSTICE SYSTEM   731

by the prosecutor. The jacket and commentary are help-
ful to a prosecutor improving the filing system. 3729

NATIONAL District Attorneys Association. Managing case files in the
prosecutor's office. Chicago, 1973. 75 p.
Handbook designed to help the prosecutor increase the
efficiency of his operation with specific suggestions
for methods, equipment, and supplies. Recommends granting authority to a supervisor to oversee case management. Appendices contain a list of state agencies responsible for records disposition information, a list
of prosecutor training coordinators, and a model case
file jacket.   3730

NATIONAL District Attorneys Association. Prosecutor's deskbook, ed.
by P.F. Healy and J.P. Manak. Chicago, 1971. 693 p.
Collection of brief papers by judges, prosecutors, and
practicing lawyers on role of prosecutor, prosecutorial
discretion, other general subjects and many specifics
of pretrial and trial procedure, appeals and post-conviction proceedings and selected special problems;
papers by well-known authorities in each field. 3731

NATIONAL District Attorneys Association. Prosecutor's screening
function: case evaluation and control. Chicago, 1973. 92 p.
Manual provides introduction to the screening process
and develops practical guidelines for reducing number
of cases that proceed to trial. Stressing the high
priority of this process, the manual recommends staffing by senior trial personnel. Includes an office design, suggested records and information to be used,
evaluation techniques, and numerous forms now in use.
                                                        3732

NATIONAL District Attorneys Association. Report on proceedings, recommendations, and statistics of the NDAA Metropolitan Prosecutors'
Conference[s]. Chicago, 1971. 50 p.
Proceedings of committee workshops covering areas of
common concern, and recommendations resulting from a
series of metropolitan prosecutors' conferences held
in 1970, with statistical charts.   3733

NEW YORK County Criminal Courts Bar Association. Code of ethics and
principles for the prosecution and defense of criminal cases. N.Y.,
1941, repr. 1962. 12 p.   3734

PANEL discussion: Minimum standards on prosecution and defense functions. In Proceedings of the thirty-first annual judicial conference
of the District of Columbia Circuit. FRD 51:25-134 (1971), p. 36-76.
Panelists: Burger, W.E.; Pollock, H.I.; Green, R.A.;
Discussion.   3735

PROSECUTORIAL discretion on the initiation of criminal complaints.
SC L Rev 42:519-45 (1969).
Documents the discretion from personal observation:
legal and non-legal factors, variance of prosecution
by character of defendants and victims and other in-
fluences. Proposes elimination of limitless discretion
by rewriting substantive law to end over-criminaliza-
tion, and creation of a specific law enforcement policy
by the legislature.   3736

PROSECUTOR'S role in California sentencing: advocate or informant?
UCLA L Rev 20:1379-1407 (1973).
Comment explores role by analyzing possible principles
and objectives on which to predicate a sentencing and
correction system, discussing the effect of adversary
sentencing, and reviewing the impact the prosecution
may have under current California procedures. Finding
that the role of the prosecutor is inconsistent with
the rehabilitative goals of the system, the author provides several alternative approaches. Author concludes
that the prosecutor should take an informing, rather
than adversary, role.   3737

RABIN, R.L. Agency criminal referrals in the Federal system: an empirical study of prosecutorial discretion. Stan L Rev 24:1036-91
(1972).
Examination of the disposition of criminal referrals
from Federal agencies by the Justice Department and
U.S. Attorneys; factors entering into the decision to
prosecute and discretion in plea-bargaining. Also discusses possible guidelines and procedures for the exercise of discretion.   3738

REPORT on diagnostic visit to the state's attorney's office, Cook
County, Ill., Sept. 24-29, 1972, submitted by P. Trimble [and others]
Washington, Criminal Courts Technical Assistance Project, American U,
1972. 23 p.
A team of consultants view the office and make findings
and recommendations concerning its operation, administration, planning and program development. Among other
things, they stress the need for the office to develop
good paperwork procedures.   3739

SINGER, R.G. Forensic misconduct by federal prosecutors, and how it
grew. Ala L Rev 20:227-79 (1968).
Focuses on cases appealed because of prosecutor's inflammatory and prejudicial words and conduct. Quotes
Dean Pound's Criminal Justice in America (1930) on political reasons for such conduct; gives six doctrines
for affirmance in face of forensic misconduct; describes
the curative instruction by the trial judge and reviews
"harmless error" cases. Suggests ways to prevent such
misconduct. See Ann 40 L Ed 866 (1975).   3740

SYMPOSIUM: Discretion of the prosecutor in criminal procedure. Am J Comp L 18:483-548 (1970).
> Vouin, R. The role of the prosecutor in French criminal trials.--Grosman, B.A. The role of the prosecutor in Canada.--Jescheck, H.H. The discretionary powers of the prosecuting attorney in West Germany.--Dando, S. System of discretionary prosecution in Japan.--LaFave, W. The prosecutor's discretion in the United States.
> 3741

SYMPOSIUM: Standards of conduct for prosecution and defense personnel. Am Crim L Q 5:8-31 (1966).
> Series of comments on ethical questions of defending a hypothetical case involving a known guilty defendant, cross examination of a known truthful witness and other problems. Contributors are: Burger, W. Standards of conduct for prosecution and defense personnel: a judge's viewpoint.--Starrs, J.E. Professional responsibility - three basic propositions.--Bress, D.G. Standards of conduct of the prosecution and defense function: an attorney's viewpoint.--Bowman, A.M. Standards of conduct for prosecution and defense personnel: an attorney's viewpoint.
> 3742

U. S. NATIONAL Institute of Law Enforcement and Criminal Justice. Case screening and selected case processing in prosecutors' offices, by W.J. Merrill, M. Milks, and M. Sendrow. Washington, 1973. 53 p.
> Based on study of case screening and processing in five large prosecutors' offices, report tells how to screen and select efficiently. Alternate screening and special case-processing programs are offered, factors in selecting, steps in implementing a program; staffing.
> 3743

UVILLER, H.R. The virtuous prosecutor in quest of an ethical standard. Mich L Rev 71:1145-68 (1973).
> Former prosecutor, seeking to define the "ethical ingredient in the use of discretion" criticizes the unorthodox ideas of M. Freedman (item 3778) and discusses, also critically, the ABA Standards (item 3692). He offers his own ideas of prosecutorial motivation and suggests how he would recast the ABA Standards. 3743a

WILCOX, A.F. The decision to prosecute. London, Butterworth, 1972. 137 p.
> Former Chief Constable of Hertfordshire discusses English practice, comparing it with American and Scottish law. Describes the locus of decision to prosecute: by the police, by private persons, and by the Department of Public Prosecutions. Also discusses control of discretion. Bibliography. 3744

YOUNGER, E.J. Changing role of the district attorney. LAB Bull 45:
455-60 (1970).
>   District Attorney of Los Angeles County discusses pre-
>   sent and future programs of his office, such as the
>   creation of (1) a Special Investigations Division for
>   misconduct of public officials, and (2) an Advisory
>   Council which assists the office in its contacts with
>   the community.   3745

YOUNGER, E.J. Prosecution problems. ABA J 53:695-707 (1967).
>   Obstacles prosecuting attorneys meet: the exclusionary
>   rule, outdated criminal code provisions, police restric-
>   tions which stymie prosecutors, overworking "due pro-
>   cess," disruption due to defendant's right to represent
>   himself, imbalance against prosecution, restriction of
>   right of prosecution appeal.   3746

YOUNGER, E.J. Results of a survey conducted in the District Attorney's
office of Los Angeles County regarding the effect of the Miranda decision upon the prosecution of felony cases. Am Crim L Q 5:32-39
(1966).
>   Former district attorney shows that confessions are
>   essential to successful prosecution in only a small per-
>   centage of criminal cases.   3747

     2. The Defense Lawyer

>   Items cover defense strategy and tactics; re-
>   habilitation planned services for defense to
>   negotiate pretrial disposition; ethics; news-
>   paper and television publicity; counseling
>   prior to act; right to appear at various
>   stages of the prosecution; role in plea bar-
>   gaining; role after conviction. For items on
>   training and qualifications of lawyers, see
>   Section IV C, The Lawyers; for items on un-
>   ruly conduct of defense lawyers, see Section
>   VII A, The Criminal Trial Judge.

AMERICAN Bar Association Advisory Committee on the Prosecution and
Defense Functions. Standards relating to the prosecution function
and defense function, recommended by the Advisory Committee on the
Prosecution and Defense Functions. Tent. draft, Mar. 1970. N.Y., IJA.
1970. 327 p. Amendments, supp. Mar. 1971. 21 p. approved, Feb. 1971.
            (For annotation see item 3692)   3748

AMERICAN Judicature Society. Selected readings in prosecution, defense and bail, by A. Ashman and T. Asperk. Chicago, 1971. 119 p.
            (For annotation, see item 3693)   3749

AMSTERDAM, A.G., SEGAL, B.L. and MILLER, M.K. Entrance into the criminal case -- representing the client shortly after arrest. Prac Lawyer
14:19-33, 55-60 (1968).

A short "how-to" manual for defense counsel's job upon the arrest of a client. The article also offers a useful view of the criminal jsutice system at this stage of operation. (see item 4892) 3750

BAZELON, D.L. The defective assistance of counsel. U Cin L Rev 42: 1-46 (1973). (Robt S. Marx lect.)
Federal appellate judge's observations on both the general problems of inadequate counsel within the criminal justice system, i.e. understaffed public defenders, incompetent private counsel, and possible reforms, and remedies for counsel's performance in individual cases. Discusses the role of the courts; recommends judicial adoption of minimum standards of performance for counsel, and certification of criminal lawyers. 3751

BAILEY, F.L. and ROTHBLATT, H.B. Fundamentals of criminal advocacy. Rochester, N.Y., Lawyers Coop, 1974. 617 p.
Experienced criminal trial lawyers present detailed roadmap to experienced and inexperienced lawyers for preparation and trial of narcotic,. white collar, and crimes of violence cases. Authors take reader from arrest through sentencing, from opening to jury to closing summation. Methods of dealing with possible prejudices of the trial judge and inflammatory prosecutorial remarks are presented; all cited with authority. Along these same lines see Amsterdam, A.G., Segal, B.L. and Miller, M.K. Trial manual 3 for the defense of criminal cases. 3d ed. Philadelphia, ALI-ABA Committee on continuing professional education, 1974. 695 p. 3751a

BRAUN, R.L. Ethics in criminal cases: a response. Geo L J 55:1048-64 (1967).
Reply to item 3702 emphasizing ethics of defense lawyer. 3752

BURGER, W.E. Counsel for the prosecution and the defense; their role under minimum standards. Am Crim L Q 8:2-9 (1969); Nat Judicial Conference on Standards for the Admin of Crim Justice, Baton Rouge, 1972. p. 74-81.
(For annotation see item 3695) 3753

BURGER, W.E. The role of the advocates in criminal justice; remarks ... at second plenary session, American Bar Association, July 16, 1971, Grosvenor House, London, England. Washington, 1971. 17 p.
(For annotation see item 2732) 3754

CHRISTENSON, A.S. Courtroom decorum as an aid to proper judicial administration. FRD 27:445-66 (1961).
Tract from the judge's standpoint, respecting the conduct and deportment of the trial attorney, incisively looks into all the pertinent relationships of the trial

lawyer in court and lays down basic principles of conduct. Author is U.S. district court judge.   <u>3755</u>

CRIMINAL co-defendants and the Sixth Amendment: the case for separate
counsel. Crim L Bull 6:432-53 (1970).
          Note, focusing on <u>Glasser v U.S.</u>, 315 US 60 (1942),
          considers whether one attorney, representing two or
          more co-defendants being tried jointly, can provide
          constitutionally guaranteed effective counsel; examines
          concept of effective counsel, standards of ineffective-
          ness, conflict of interests, varying interpretations
          of <u>Glasser</u>, and waiver. Author proposes that the em-
          phasis in future decisions be the existence of a con-
          flict of interest between jointly represented defendants
          that has the potential of depriving an individual of
          effective assistance of counsel. Discusses possible pro-
          cedure for making this determination.   <u>3756</u>

DASH, S. The emerging role and function of the criminal defense lawyer. NCL Rev 47:598-632 (1969).
          Professor discusses availability of service, relations
          with the court and client, and ethical problems of the
          criminal defense lawyer.   <u>3757</u>

DASH, S. MEDALIE, R.J., and RHODEN, E.G., Jr. Demonstrating rehabilitative planning as a defense strategy. Cornell L Rev 54:408-36 (1969).
          Final report of demonstration project conducted by Inst
          of Criminal Law and Procedure of Georgetown U Law Center
          finds that rehabilitation services must be brought to
          bear as soon as possible after arrest; community-based
          rehabilitation programs are necessary. Illustrates re-
          lationship of rehabilitation to defense.   <u>3758</u>

EFFECTIVE assistance of counsel. Va L Rev 49:1531-62 (1963).
          To determine if right to effective counsel is protect-
          ed, note looks at court-developed standards, consid-
          ers also positions taken by federal courts in facing
          allegations of inadequate representation; fully case
          noted.   <u>3759</u>

EFFECTIVE assistance of counsel - appointed counsel must actually
and substantially assist his client in determining whether or not to
plead guilty. J Urban L 51:564-74 (1974).
          Note analyzes <u>Walker v Caldwell</u>, 476 F2d 213 (5th Cir.,
          1973), in which the court found effective assistance of
          counsel had been denied because of the questionable
          methods of public defenders in the Baldwin court. De-
          fendant's counsel, a resident attorney, who was appoint-
          ed to handle ten or more defendants at every Friday
          morning plea day, did not investigate the case and did
          not ask for the correct sentence before pleading guilty;
          also, defendant was illiterate and was not fully cogni-

zant of the meaning of a guilty plea. Other cases dealing with ineffective counsel are considered.   3760

EFFECTIVE assistance of counsel for the indigent defendant. Harv L
Rev 78:1434-51 (1965).
    Considers circumstances in which a defendant may charge
    that his counsel was inadequate and so denied him due
    process and also the problems facing the appointed
    attorney and the reviewing courts. Suggests standards
    and methods by which counsel and courts may be pro-
    tected from unwarranted attacks and frivolous claims,
    while preserving the accused's right to the effective
    assistance of counsel.   3761

"BEFORE sentence is pronounced ... " a guide to defense counsel in
the exercise of his post-conviction responsibilities. Crim L Bull
9:140-57 (1973).
    Attorney suggests steps to take and procedures for the
    practitioner to use in fulfilling his role in the sen-
    tencing process.   3762

FINER, J.J. Ineffective assistance of counsel. Cornell L Rev 58:
1078-1120 (1973).
    Gives standards defining or tests suggesting ineffec-
    tiveness bordering on malpractice; circumstances con-
    stituting ineffectiveness in advising defendant to
    plead guilty; counsel's ignorance of the law; failure
    to investigate facts; insufficient time to prepare for
    trial due to laxness in appointment; failure to con-
    duct trial properly in many specifics; conflict of
    interest of counsel; cites cases in all areas and con-
    cludes with suggestions, insuring more effective re-
    presentation.   3763

INSTITUTE of Criminal Law and Procedure, Georgetown University Law
Center. Rehabilitative planning services for the criminal defense:
an evaluation of the Offender Rehabilitation Project of the Legal
Aid Agency for the District of Columbia, conducted by the Institute ...
Washington, Nat Inst of Law Enforcement and Crim Just, 1970. 210 p.
    Experimental program, funded by Office of Economic
    Opportunity Legal Services Program, to provide defense
    counsel with information on indigent clients for use
    in rehabilitation projects. Counsel would then use
    this information, and the client's participation in
    the program, in negotiating a pretrial dispostion.
    Found successful for defendants, and also reduced re-
    cidivism.   3764

KAUFMAN, I.R. In defense of the advocate. UCLA L Rev 12:351-60
1965).
    Judge Kaufman demonstrates the vital role played by
    lawyers in the criminal process; some popular miscon-

ceptions; suggests law schools can act to aid in producing better advocates, and the bar can take a hand
in the training; he also suggests ways for a young lawyer to gather trial experience and encourages this interest. The judge is sanguine about new opportunities
for young lawyers.   <u>3765</u>

KAUFMAN, I. The trial lawyer: the legal profession's greatest asset.
ABA J 50:25-29 (1964).
> Judge Kaufman urges lawyers to become trial lawyers,
> explaining the need for and role of an advocate in
> court; he discusses the requirements of education and
> experience and suggests internship programs for trial
> lawyers in prosecutors' offices and law firms.   <u>3766</u>

LEWIS, A. American lawyers: Gideon's army? Address before ABA Committee on Legal Aid Work, and National Legal Aid and Defender Assn,
New York, Aug. 10, 1964. 12 p.
> The author of "Gideon's Trumpet" (N.Y., Random, 1964)
> relates that his love of the law led him to write book;
> he takes the American Bar to task, however, for its
> failure or delay in acting in several areas, including
> race relations and civil rights. He briefly compares
> the American and British legal systems of advocacy.
>   <u>3767</u>

LUMBARD, J.E. Better lawyers for our criminal courts. Atlantic
Monthly 213:86-90 (June 1964).
> Judge analyzes the kinds of lawyers who represent de-
> fendants and draws on New York's experience where 75%
> of accused are indigents represented by the Legal Aid
> Society. Noting inadequacies with the system of assign-
> ing counsel to represent indigents, he urges establish-
> ing the public defender type of office in every com-
> munity, with additional funding where needed. He calls
> for a change in attitude of the bar toward the criminal
> courts and the administration of criminal justice and
> makes some suggestions to achieve this.   <u>3768</u>

LYNCH, G.P. Pre-trial motion practice in state criminal cases. Chi
B Rec 51:273-78, 349-57 (Mar./April 1970).
> These articles are designed as working guides for the
> defense attorney and contain practical considerations
> to be weighed by the attorney as well as the law re-
> lating to the pretrial motions. Appendices include typi-
> cal motions.   <u>3768a</u>

MATHENY, M.D. Role of the court-appointed attorney. Tex B J 38:789-
93, 796 (1973).
> Author discusses the importance of providing indigent
> defendants with competent attorneys; suggests a step-
> by-step procedure for the defense of an indigent, es-

THE CRIMINAL JUSTICE SYSTEM 739

pecially for court-appointed attorneys who do not regu-
larly practice criminal law.   3769

MEDALIE, R.J.   The offender rehabilitation project: a new role for
defense counsel at pretrial and sentencing. Georgetown L J 56:2-16
(1967).
          Purpose of Legal Aid Agency project is to develop pro-
          grams to rehabilitate the accused not only after he
          pleads or is found guilty but also immediately after
          he is assigned a defense attorney. The significance
          of the project is highlighted by an examination of the
          precharge, plea negotiation and sentencing stages. The
          operations of the project and the evaluation being made
          to assess its impact on the administration of criminal
          justice are described.   3770

NAGEL, S.S.   Effects of alternative types of counsel on criminal procedure treatment.   Ind L J 48:404-26 (1973).
          Study compares different types of criminal procedure
          treatment between defendants having different types
          of counsel: (1) counsel vs no counsel, (2) hired coun-
          sel vs provided counsel, (3) public defender vs assigned
          counsel, and (4) early obtained counsel vs late obtain-
          ed counsel. Author concludes that increased provisions
          are necessary for providing attorneys to the poor,
          through either judicare or adequately financed and
          staffed public defenders. (Study is based on data in-
          cluded in item 3924)   3771

PANEL discussion: Minimum standards on prosecution and defense functions.   In Proceedings of the thirty-first annual judicial conference of the District of Columbia Circuit. FRD 51:25-134 (1971),
p. 36-76.
          (For annotation see item 3735)   3772

PORTMAN, S. Defense lawyer's new role in the sentencing process.
Fed Prob 34:3-8 (Mar. 1970).
          Discusses recent Supreme Court decisions which have ex-
          tended role of defense lawyer beyond the trial. 3773

RIGHT of a criminal defense attorney to withhold physical evidence
received from his client. Chi L Rev 38:211-29 (1970).
          The question is considered in the context of canons of
          ethics, attorney-client privilege, privilege against
          self incrimination, and other policy issues. Concludes
          that refusal to extend the present narrow right of non-
          disclosure would probably not create serious risk for
          the innocent defendant.   3774

ROSENGART, O.A. Busted; a handbook for lawyers and their clients with
reference to the new criminal procedure law. N.Y., St. Martin's press,
1972, 175 p.

Tactical guide for criminal defense in New York City,
from observing political demonstrations and police conduct
to trial techniques and "D.A. shopping;" emphasizes
defense tactics in representing political offenders.
                                                  3775

SINK, J.M. Political criminal trials: how to defend them. N.Y.,
Clark Boardman, 1974. 666 p.
        California lawyer with experience in such cases advises
        those without experience with details on strategy at
        every step: e.g. relations with clients, assembling
        and using evidence, discovery, preparation of witnesses,
        jury selection, opening statements, cross-examination,
        final argument. Sample forms, motions, and jury in-
        structions included.   3776

SYMPOSIUM: Criminal defense practice. J Crim L 62:139-93 (1971).
        MacCarthy, T.F. Introduction.--Cotsirilos, G.J. Meet-
        ing the prosecutor's case: tactics and strategies of
        cross-examination.--Sullivan, T.P. Presentation of the
        defense.--Magidson, S.C. Preparation and argument of
        the criminal appeal.   3777

SYMPOSIUM on professional ethics. Mich L Rev 64: 1469-98 (1966).
        Freedman, M.H. Professional responsibility of the
        criminal defense lawyer: the three hardest questions.--
        Noonan, J.T. The purposes of advocacy and the limits
        of confidentiality.--Bress, D.G. Professional ethics
        in criminal trials: a view of defense counsel's respon-
        sibility.   3778

SYMPOSIUM: Standards of conduct for prosecution and defense personnel. Am Crim L Q 5:8-31 (1966).
        (For annotation see item 3742)   3779

WALTZ, J.R. Inadequacy of trial defense representation as a ground
for post conviction relief in criminal cases. Nw U L Rev 59:289-
342 (1964).
        Discusses basis of right to assert inadequate defense,
        the degree of success achieved with such pleas, the
        grounds for asserting the right including the counsel's
        tactical errors, inexperience. Concludes that the so-
        lution lies in a system of providing better defense
        counsel.   3780

WRIGHT, J.S. The renaissance of the criminal law: the responsibility
of the trial lawyer. Duquesne U L Rev 4:213-23 (1965).
        Address given at International Academy of Trial Lawyers
        meeting, San Juan, Puerto Rico, Jan. 2, 1965.   3781

D. Available Legal Services for Indigents

Items cover primarily various types of
services available to indigents charged
with crime; include description, duties,
cost, evaluation; free and low cost community law offices, judicare, open and
closed panels, public defenders; services
prior, during and after criminal trial;
many items cover civil and criminal services; included also are items on costs
and attorneys' fees and a selection on
right to defend pro se; also problems of
right to legal services on the part of
persons of moderate means.

ALASKA   Judicial Council. The Alaska public defender agency in perspective; an analysis of the law, finances and administration, 1969-
74. Anchorage [1974] 134 p.
        Includes history of office and act creating office,
        including analysis of preceding assigned counsel sys-
        tem; appraises quality of representation under defender
        system; recommends various steps to improve service
        including better administration internally, legislative
        improvements, fuller cooperation by Alaska Bar, calen-
        daring changes by courts.   3782

ALLISON, J.L.   Introduction to an evaluation program. Chicago, Nat
Legal Aid and Defenders Assn, 1970. 20 p.
        Executive director of NLADA gives methods for evaluating
        a legal service; criteria, procedure; NLADA standards
        and practices for civil legal aid.   3783

AMERICAN Bar Association. Joint informational report: the corporation
for legal services, a study by American Bar Association Section of
Individual Rights and Responsibilities and the Standing Committee
on Legal Aid and Indigent Defendants. Chicago, 1971. 131 p.
        Report considers moving Legal Services Program from
        U.S. Office of Economic Opportunity, which has admin-
        istered funds since Program's creation in 1965, to:
        another federal agency or executive department; the
        Judicial Dept.; or a private non-profit corporation.
        Reasons for considering move, e.g.: conflicts of inter-
        est, use of federal funds to challenge law, other prob-
        lems, make private corporation best. Structure, duties,
        financing of proposed corporation and existing model
        (Corporation for Public Broadcasting) described. Append-
        ed studies include those of other independent govern-
        mental entities, such as National Science Foundation,
        and of other government-funded legal service programs.
        3-p. bibliography.   3784

AMERICAN Bar Association. The legal needs of the public, by B.A.
Curran and F.O. Spalding; preliminary report of a national survey
by the Special Committee to Survey Legal Needs. Chicago, 1974. 228 p.
(For annotation see item 2721)   3785

AMERICAN Bar Association Advisory Committee on the Prosecution and
Defense Functions. Standards relating to providing defense services,
recommended by the Advisory Committee on the Prosecution and Defense
Functions. W.E. Burger, chairman; L.J. Mazor, reptr. Tent. draft,
June, 1967. New York, IJA, 1967. 85 p. Approved, Feb. 1968.
          Standards with commentary on general principles of pro-
          viding defense services; assigned defense systems;
          types and stages of preceedings; prepaid legal costs
          (reports on Shreveport, Los Angeles programs). Includes
          model acts, Bernstein, J. Group legal services and the
          collective bargaining process: prospects and problems.
          Bibliography p.281-90.   3786

AMERICAN Bar Association Special Committee on Prepaid Legal Services.
Prepaid legal services; special report to the National Conference
on Prepaid Legal Services, Washington, April 27-29, 1972. St. Louis
B J 19:15-33 (1973).
          Summarizes pertinent ABA Canons of Ethics, activity
          of ABA and state and local bar associations in legal
          services; describes Shreveport plan and other private
          group legal service plans.   3787

AMERICAN Bar Foundation. Franchising justice: the Office of Economic
Opportunity legal services program and traditional legal aid, by K.P.
          Fisher and C.C. Ivie. Chicago, 1971. 18 p. (Its series
          on legal services for the poor)
          Authors offer an analysis of the legal services program
          funded by the Office of Economic Opportunity in Miami,
          San Francisco and St. Louis. Conducted by sociologists,
          the study presents an evaluation of various factors
          illustrated through tables and comment. Problems, in-
          cluding those of race, are discussed. Comparison is
          made between clientele reached by traditional legal aid
          and the OEO legal services program.   3788

AMERICAN Bar Foundation. Indigent accused persons project for the
state of Louisiana, prepared by H.F. Connick. Chicago, 1963. 45 p.
          Study examines criminal procedure as it affects indi-
          gents in felony and misdemeanor cases. Survey covers
          at what stage counsel should be provided and financing
          arrangements; results are opinions of judges, prosecu-
          tors and defense counsel. Includes charts and tables.
                                                             3789

ANALYSIS and comparison of the assigned counsel and public defender
systems. N C L Rev 49:705-19 (1971).
          Comparison of assigned counsel and experimental public

defender offices created in two North Carolina counties concludes that public defender proves more effective representation at lower cost to the state.   3790

ANDALMAN, E. and CHAMBERS, D.L. Effective counsel for persons facing civil commitment: a survey, a polemic, and a proposal. Miss L J 45: 43-91 (1974).
        Constitutional right to counsel in civil commitment cases; role of counsel; description of counsel systems in Phoenix, Arizona, Iowa, Austin , Texas, Memphis, Tennessee, Chicago, Cleveland, New York. Includes proposed statute creating a statewide Mental Health Advocacy Agency with a section on duties of attorneys.
                                                     3791

ANDERSON, L., WARNER, V.O. and FOSTER, D. Public defender and other suggested systems for the defense of indigents. Judicature 53:242-49 (1970).
        District Court judge Anderson describes defense services in Minneapolis, particularly in reference to the State Public Defender and scope of the right to counsel. Warner, Presiding Judge, Superior Court, San Diego, describes the operation of the assigned counsel system, the Defender Program of San Diego, and a special panel to serve those not quite indigent, but unable to pay the usual fee. Foster, Chief Judge, Supreme Bench of Baltimore City, describes the successful operation of assigned counsel there but recommends installation of a Public Defender.   3792

ASHMAN, A. The new private practice: a study of Piper & Marbury's neighborhood law office. Chicago, Nat Legal Aid and Defender Assn, 1972. 112 p.
        Foreword by Abe Fortas. Baltimore firm's branch office in low-income area appraised as to aims, operation, success in reaching community and working with agencies such as Legal Aid, existing black bar association, ACLU: briefer report on similar Philadelphia office. Based on observation and interviews in first 18 months (1969-1971); seen as good beginning.   3793

BARVICK, W.M. Legal services and the rural poor. U Kan L Rev 15: 537-51 (1967).
        A discussion of the adaptability of legal services to the rural environment; its importance and function, and factors involved in the actual implementation of a rural legal service program.   3794

BENJAMIN, R.W. and PEDELISKI, T.B. The Minnesota public defender system and the criminal law process; a comparative study of behavior at the judicial district level. Law & Soc Rev 4:279-320 (1969).
        Authors describe the effects of the introduction of the

public defender system upon the criminal law process
in Minnesota. Analyses of selected criminal process
variables (such as dsimissals and acquittals), financial support patterns, and reactions of key personnel
to the system are explained with statistics.   3795

BERRY, T.M. The national conference on law and poverty; The role of
the federal government. ABA J 51:746-50 (1965).
    Director of OEO Community Action Program outlines
    agency's plans for legal aid; administration, funding,
    community participation in creation, direction of in-
    dependent legal aid agencies; content of services and
    allied programs; indigency determination.   3796

BORRIE, G.J. and VARCOE, J.R. Legal aid in criminal proceedings; a
regional survey. Birmingham, Eng., Inst of Judicial Administration,
U of Birmingham. 1970. 102 p.
    An examination of English legal aid based on applica-
    tion of 1967 Criminal Justice Act, Part IV, covering
    all facets of legal aid system in West Midlands; of par-
    ticular interest is Ch. 5, The Contribution system.
                                                     3797

BOSTON University Center for Criminal Justice. The right to counsel;
the implementation of Argersinger v Hamlin: an unmet challenge.
Boston, 1974. 5 v.
    Dir. S Krantz. v. 1: Summary of findings and recom-
    mendations, by P. Froyd [and others]--v. 2: Review of
    practices and procedures in other jurisdictions, by
    J. Hoffman [and others] --v. 3: Implications for the
    legal process, by D. Rossman [and others]--v. 4: Impli-
    cations for the defense functions, by C. Smith [and
    others]--v. 5: Implications for the role of the crimi-
    nal law and its enforcement, by P. Froyd [and others]
                                                     3798

BOWLER, C.A. National legal services: the answer or the problem for
the legal profession. Chi-Kent L Rev 50:415-34 (1973).
    Author traces history and controversies of OEO legal
    services program and the proposed National Legal Ser-
    vices Corporation. It is found that OEO has greatly
    increased the demand for legal services, magnified the
    volume and range of litigation with an explosion of
    "rights" and "grievances." Three approaches offered are
    1) development of new "people's legal institutions,"
    2) return to tradition, leaving social and economic
    problems to political process and 3) expanding tradition-
    al legal services through new "delivery of services"
    mechanisms. Conclusion is that proposed NLSC would not
    provide solution of filling the demand for free or in-
    expensive legal services.   3799

BOWLER, C.A.   Prepaid legal services and the alternative practice
of law.   Chi-Kent L Rev 51:41-61 (1974).
> This article examines new developments in the private
> and quasi-private (government subsidized) practice of
> law. Explores Judicare, prepaid legal services (in
> theory and in reality), and Pro Bono Publico practice
> of law. ABA activities in the prepaid legal services
> arena are related.   3800

BOWMAN, C.   Indigent's right to an adequate defense: expert and
investigational assistance in criminal proceedings.   Crim L Bull
6:491-504 (1970).
> Author discusses inherent inequalities between in-
> digent and the prosecution, with its realm of scientific
> techniques, investigators, and experts at its disposal.
> Examined are: present statutory aids available to
> defendant in federal and state courts, constitutional
> considerations, and methods by which adequate services
> could be provided for defendants.   3801

BRAKEL, S.J.   The case for judicare.   ABA J 59:1407-11 (1973).
> ABA study described by its author, concludes that ju-
> dicare, using private lawyers to give legal service,
> should be primary system for national program. Prefer-
> ence for staffed office system is not well conceived
> or well founded.   3802

BRAKEL, S.J.   Free legal services for the poor: staffed office vs.
judicare: the client's evaluation.   Wisc L Rev 1973:532-33; repr.
AB Found research contributions, 1973, 3.
> Interview survey of clients in Wisconsin, Montana and
> Michigan plans reveals mixed opinion similar to pro-
> fessional criticism, but concludes that rural poor
> prefer the judicare system.   3803

BRAKEL, S.J.   Judicare: public funds, private lawyers, and poor
people.   Chicago, AB Found, 1974.   145 p.
> This study of how Judicare operates in areas of Wis-
> consin, Montana and Michigan explores reaching the
> poor; types of lawyers; types of cases; quality of
> service; and cost of service. The Judicare system of
> using private lawyers already practicing where the poor
> client lives is found to be preferable to the staffed-
> office approach.   3804

BRAKEL, S.J.   The trouble with judicare evaluations.   ABA J 59:
704-08 (1972).
> Takes to task article by H. Goodman and J. Feuillan,
> The trouble with Judicare (ABA J 58:476-81, 1971);
> points to errors in data and analysis. Concludes Judi-
> care is neither worse nor better and neither cheaper
> nor more costly than staff attorney programs; data are
> yet to be gathered and analyzed.   3805

BRAKEL, S.J.   Wisconsin judicare; a preliminary appraisal.   Chicago,
AB Found, 1972.   122 p.
> Report in process describing the judicare approach of
> making free legal services in civil matters available
> to the poor. Discussed are: Awareness of the program
> among eligible persons; Characteristics of the lawyers;
> Types of cases handled; Quality of services. Appendi-
> ces contain judicare programs in the U.S.; evaluations,
> pros and cons of judicare and methodology.   3806

CAHN, E.S. and CAHN, J.C.   War on poverty: a civilian perspective.
Yale L J 73:1317-52 (1964).
> Authors enumerate attacks on poverty and analyze failure
> of society to produce redress for certain segment of
> its population. They propose neighborhood law offices
> describing its relationships and functions.   3807

CAHN, E.S. and CAHN, J.C.   What price justice: the civilian perspective revisited.   Notre Dame Law 41:927-60 (1966).
> A basic report on why and how neighborhood law offices
> are falling into the existing pattern of failing to
> provide systemic redress to persons who do not respond
> to institutional assistance. (see also item 3807)3808

CALIFORNIA Legislature Assembly Committee on Criminal Procedure.   Defense of indigents in criminal proceedings; hearings, San Francisco,
July 21, 1964.   Sacramento, 1964.   89 p.
> Testimony and discussion concerns the effect of recent
> court decisions on the defense of indigents in criminal
> proceedings and problems surrounding their defense in
> California. Appendix 1: report by the Committee on Le-
> gal Service, Criminal Defense Division, to the Cali-
> fornia State Bar. Appendix 2: report on the Contra Costa
> County Public Defender office.   3809

CARLIN, J.E. and HOWARD, J.   Legal representation and class justice.
UCLA L Rev 12:381-437 (1965).
> Part 1 summarizes available data on class differences
> in the use of lawyers and in the quality of the legal
> representation provided. Part 2 discusses the problems
> of the poor and how differences in quality of legal
> representation result in a denial of justice to the
> poor, as neither private bar nor substitutes have
> effectively dealt with these problems. Part 3 considers
> factors leading to this inequality of legal representa-
> tion, including attitudes of society and attorneys to-
> wards the poor. Part 4 suggests how legal services can
> meet the needs of the poor and reviews the two new
> proposals of the neighborhood law office and group le-
> gal service. The authors conclude that there is an ur-
> gent need for an "advocacy explosion" if the needs of
> the poor are to be met.   3810

CHARGING costs of prosecution to the defendant. Geo L J 59:991-1006
(1971).
> A discussion of cost assessment, the rationales for it,
> such as compensation, punishment, and restraint, and
> the potential effects of cost assessment for those who
> cannot pay. Legislative and judicial scrutiny are
> needed to develop a coherent system of criminal cost
> assessment.   3811

CHEATHAM, E.E. A lawyer when needed. N.Y., Columbia U press, 1963.
139 p.
> Law professor examines practical and ethical factors
> in making counsel available to a hated defendant and
> to the poor. He discusses methods of bringing legal
> services to the middle class, specialized legal services,
> and need for public representation in controversies
> which are private in form.   3812

CHRISTENSEN, B.F. Lawyers for people of moderate means; some problems
of availability of legal services. Chicago, AB Found, 1970. 313 p.
> Discusses types of legal services, needs of people in
> $5,000-$15,000 income bracket, costs and quality of
> legal services, specialization, bringing lawyers and
> clients together, lawyer referral services, special
> offices for people of moderate means, group legal ser-
> vices.   3813

CHRISTENSEN, B.F. Professionalism, justice and availability of legal
services. Harv L Bull 22:1-6 (1971); repr. AB Found research contributions, 1971, 5.
> Author recounts the inequalities in the legal system
> in resolving the problems, both outside and within the
> courts, of those of moderate means; suggests that the
> legal profession must seek ways of achieving greater
> legal equality for parties.   3814

CITIZEN'S Governmental Research Bureau. ... a public defender to
provide legal services to the indigent merits consideration. CGRB
Bull 56:1-10 (May 22, 1968).
> Milwaukee research group reports the findings of its
> survey of public defender systems in 14 urban areas
> in the United States, undertaken to help evaluate the
> feasility of establishing a defender system in Mil-
> waukee.   3815

CLIENT service in a defender organization: the Philadelphia experience.
U Pa L Rev 117:448-69 (1969).
> Study focusing on the amount of professional time re-
> ceived by the average client of the Philadelphia De-
> fenders Association in a given type of case examines
> methodology of study; representation procedures in a
> zone defense (lawyer assigned to cover particular

748   ADMINISTRATION OF CRIMINAL JUSTICE

courtroom and in a man-to-man defense (lawyer assigned
to particular client); and specific resources provided
at pre-trial, trial, and post trial stages. Author concludes that client receives a better defense in the
man-to-man method of assignment.   3816

COLE, G.F. and GREENBERGER, H.L.   Staff attorneys vs. judicare: a
cost analysis. J Urban L 50:705-16 (1973).
          Analysis of data collected in evaluation of the Meriden
          (Conn.) Legal Services Project (see item 3843) an ex-
          perimental program to compare judicare and staff legal
          services, finds costs similar, but the staff system
          has the potential to be more economical at full opera-
          tion; judicare appears preferred by clients.   3817

CONFERENCE on Extension of Legal Services to the Poor. Proceedings
... November 12, 13, 14, 1964, Washington. Washington, USGPO, 1965.
213 p.
          Lawyers, social workers, and social scientists explore
          legal needs of the poor; new legal services programs
          for low-income communities in New York, Boston and
          New Haven; the canons of professional ethics relating
          to those who render legal aid to the poor; education
          of the poor on legal matters; the roles and relation-
          ships of lawyers and social workers; and the role of
          the law schools in the extension of legal services.
          3818

COOKE, B. View of the contribution aspect of the criminal legal aid
scheme. Crim L R 1970:485-95.
          Author evaluates English legal aid system whereby le-
          gally aided persons contribute toward the cost of ser-
          vices supplied to them. He assesses figures for 1969
          on the number of legal aid applications, orders and
          contributions, and suggests changes to simplify the
          scheme and make it more economical.   3819

CRIMINAL costs assessment in Missouri; without rhyme or reason. Wash
U L Q 1962:76-118.
          An analysis of the statute dealing with liability for
          costs of criminal cases and methods of defendant's dis-
          charging liability when it accrues; discusses the dis-
          parities and inconsistencies in the law and urges re-
          writing of the statutory provisions.   3820

CURRAN, B. Legal services for special groups; reprinted from Encyclo-
pedia of Social Work, 1971 ed. Chicago, AB Found, 1972. 8 p. (Its
research contributions 1972, 1).
          Author examines the legal services available to indiv-
          iduals who cannot afford private bar; court appointed
          counsel, in forma pauperis petitions, public defenders,
          legal aid and OEO Legal Services Program. All of the

programs suffer financial malnutrition, and there is
still a problem of costs for persons of moderate means.
Author feels that, given time and proper financing,
the OEO can be successful.   3821

DAY, J.G. Coming: the right to have assistance of counsel at all
appellate stages. ABA J 52:135-38 (1966).
    Criminal lawyer, now a judge, justifies this right on
    constitutional bases, yet reserves the right to intelli-
    gent, informed waiver of counsel. Well footnoted.3822

DEFENSE pro se. U Miami L Rev 23:550-67 (1969).
    Comment on the nature of the right; qualifications of
    the right (time of election and the orderly conduct of
    the trial); advisory counsel, and the Florida position.
    Concludes that employment of advisory council would
    solve many problems arising; pertinent cases are dis-
    cussed.   3823

DORSEN, N. The role of the lawyer in America's ghetto society. Tex
L Rev 49:50-67 (1970).
    General counsel, A.C.L.U., discusses lawyers' tradition-
    al services to the privileged of America's "gilded
    ghettoes" and present methods of public service: the
    public interest law firms, radical lawyers, civil lib-
    erty lawyers, poverty lawyers, the ethical and profes-
    sional problems of these practices and the general in-
    fluence of the public interest on private practice.
                    3824

DOWLING, D.C. Escobedo and beyond: the need for a fourteenth amendment code of criminal procedure. J Crim L 56:143-57 (1965).
    Author analyzes Escobedo, 378 US 478 (1964), where the
    court barred the use in evidence of a statement taken
    from a man under arrest and in custody who was denied
    request to consult with attorney and not warned of his
    right to remain silent: the judicial evolution leading
    up to this decision; facts of the case and decision
    rendered; its effect on the general concept of due pro-
    cess of the law; and future issues raised.   3825

DUNIWAY, B.C. The poor man in the federal courts. Stan L Rev 18:
1270-87 (1966).
    Federal judge discusses history and amendments of the
    federal in forma pauperis statute since 1892, the lim-
    ited problems it covers, and the restrictive interpre-
    tation given it by the judges. Sees ultimate solution
    in government legal aid operations.   3826

FENDLER, O. Utilization of legal manpower to assist the poor. Ark
L Rev 25:203-33 (1971).
    Attack on OEO social action law reform philosophy by

proponent of judicare and emphasis on the individual
client. Summary of Arkansas legal aid.   3826a

FINMAN, T. OEO legal service programs and the pursuit of social
change: the relationship between program ideology and program performance. Wisc L Rev 1971:1001-84; repr. AB Found series on legal
services for the poor.
> Evaluation of five city OEO legal service programs in-
> dicates that OEO often gauges the social reform capa-
> city of particular programs on the basis of form, not
> substance.   3827

FISHER, K.P. and IVIE, C.C. Franchising justice: the Office of Economic Opportunity legal services program and traditional legal aid.
Chicago, AB Found, 1971. 18 p. (Its series on legal services
for the poor).
> Based on the ABA's study of utilization by the poor
> of legal services, comparisons are made between tra-
> ditional legal aid and the OEO legal service program.
> Study shows similiarities in clients and legal prob-
> lems, but the OEO neighborhood office attracted less
> educated clients. Only time will tell if the OEO is
> an actual improvement over others.   3828

FRANKEL, M. Experiments in serving the indigent. ABA J 51:460-64
(1965).
> The thesis of this article is the expansion of services
> to the poor and the need to change traditional legal
> aid techniques and forms in experimenting with new
> approaches. Author enumerates experimental possibilities
> on such service by the private lawyer under a prototype
> of England's Legal Aid and Advice Act, or by a public
> counsel, or by establishment of an Ombudsman.   3829

FREE transcripts - indigent misdemeanants. Gonzaga L Rev 8:321-31
(1973).
> An analysis of Mayer, 404 US 189 (1971), in which the
> Court found that under the 14th Amendment individual
> defendants cannot be denied an adequate appeal because
> of inability to pay for transcripts and that this right
> cannot be limited by differentiation in sentences.
> Analysis includes discussion of other relevant cases.
>   3830

GRAHAM-GREEN, G.J. Criminal costs and legal aid. In consultation
with E.J.T. Matthews. London, Butterworth, 1965. 249 p.
> Power of individual tiers of courts to award costs in
> criminal cases; grant of legal aid; remuneration to
> solicitors and counsel; includes table of statistics,
> rules and cases; book is combined effort of Master of
> Supreme Court of Judicature and secretary of Law Society
> for Contentious Business.   3831

GRANO, J.D. The right to counsel: collateral issues affecting due
process. Minn L Rev 54:1175-1264 (1970).
　　　　　An examination of the defendant's right to conduct the
　　　　　entire defense, defense waiver of objections to uncon-
　　　　　stitutional government action, and the claim of inef-
　　　　　fective assistance of counsel; includes an analysis
　　　　　of the right to proceed pro se and analogizes with the
　　　　　right to waive jury trial; discusses the difference
　　　　　in defense waiver by accused or counsel and suggests
　　　　　the abolishment of waiver in the context of unconstitu-
　　　　　tional government conduct; also offers tests for in-
　　　　　effective assistance of counsel in managing the trial
　　　　　decisions.   3832

GREENE, W.M. Prepaid legal services: more than an open and closed
case. Cleveland State L Rev 22:425-38 (1973).
　　　　　Review of history of prepaid legal services, critique
　　　　　of open and closed panel plans and analysis of plans
　　　　　as related to their ability to serve needs of middle
　　　　　class and poor clients. Makes cautionary note about
　　　　　insufficient research for decisions at time of writing.
　　　　　 3833

GROSS, M.P. Reckoning for legal services: a case study of legal
assistance in Indian education. Notre Dame Lawyer 49:78-104 (1973).
　　　　　By former legal services lawyer, a critique of public
　　　　　interest lawyers' methods making policy decisions for
　　　　　the clients they serve. Argues that this is the same
　　　　　as traditional patronizing charity, and that resources
　　　　　must be placed in the hands of the poor, so that they
　　　　　can subordinate experts in decision-making.   3834

GROUP and prepaid legal services. Miss L J 45:208-223 (1974).
　　　　　Reviews need of middle income people for legal services,
　　　　　the role of the bar, and various proposed systems.
　　　　　 3835

HALLAUER, R.P. Low-income laborers as legal clients: use patterns
and attitudes toward lawyers. Denver L J 49:169-232 (1972).
　　　　　Study of low-income black laborers, later to be included
　　　　　in the Shreveport prepaid legal services program. Con-
　　　　　cludes that bulk of interviewees trust lawyers very
　　　　　little, feel overcharged by them, and have no rational
　　　　　system for selecting lawyers.   3836

HALLAUER, R.P. The Shreveport experiment in prepaid legal services.
J Legal Studies 2:223-42 (1973); Chicago, AB Found, 1972. (Its research contributions, 1973, 2.)
　　　　　Plan developed by the Shreveport Bar Association pro-
　　　　　vides prepaid legal services, i.e. legal insurance, to
　　　　　a group of unskilled, low-income construction workers
　　　　　who are union members. Their use of lawyers and atti-

tudes about lawyers under pre-plan and plan conditions
are examined and compared. Finds that 75% would pay
for such a plan on their own.   3837

HAZARD, G.C., Jr. Law reforming in the anti-poverty effort. U Chi
L Rev 37:242-55 (1970); Chicago, AB Found, 1971. (Its series on legal
services for the poor.)
          Although law reforms made on behalf of the poor are
          extensive, their accessibility is limited by unorgan-
          ized aspect and diverse characteristics of the poor.
          He discusses reform through the judiciary and the role
          of the Legal Services Program in promoting legislation.
                                                  3838

HAZARD, G.C., Jr. Legal problems peculiar to the poor. J Social
Issues 26:47-58 (1970); Chicago, AB Found, 1971. (Its series on legal services for the poor.)
          Professor examines formal content of the law as it re-
          lates to the poor and how it can be changed: the in-
          equality of the law in sanctioning of activity that
          results in acquisition of unequal amounts of property
          and the need for a policy of income redistribution;
          how social programs for the poor actually benefit others
          and necessary changes; and provisions of the law ad-
          verse to cultural subgroups of the poor and how to
          reduce this conflict.   3839

HAZARD, G.C., Jr. Social justice through civil justice. U Chi L
Rev 36:699-712 (1969); Chicago, AB Found, 1969. (Its series on legal
services for the poor.)
          Disputes the assumption that providing free legal assist-
          ance to the poor through the OEO Legal Services Pro-
          gram, for example, will significantly improve their
          situation; he discusses concepts of Legal Services Pro-
          gram and describes problems engendered; in speaking of
          the relationship of civil justice to social jsutice,
          he suggests the contribution of the former to the latter
          is "diffuse, microcosmic and dull." The Legal Services
          Program would better serve the needs of the poor if it
          confined itself to civil justice formulated as appeal
          to community conscience.   3840

INDIANA Criminal Law Study Commission. Report ... Proposed public
defender system: Indianapolis, 1970. 45 p.
          Following the principles of achieving effective repre-
          sentation of indigent defendants and an equitable con-
          cept of eligibility and distribution of the economic
          burden for defense services, this report sets forth
          proposed legislation with commentary.   3841

INSTITUTE of Judicial Administration. Law officer project in the
Family Court of New York City: an evaluation. Oct. 1973. New York,

1973. 103 p. (+ appendices)
Problems caused by introduction of "attorney-prosecutor" in juvenile courts generally and in New York City particularly. Recommendations, guidelines, questionnaire survey of law officers' (attorneys for juveniles) background, performance, attitudes. 3842

INSTITUTE of Judicial Administration. Legal service demonstration ... Meriden, Connecticut; final report to Conn State Welfare Dept. H.L. Greenberger, research dir.; G.F. Cole, principal investigator. Sept. 1, 1972. N.Y., 1972. 1 v., var. pag.
Evaluation of project to test specific hypotheses regarding costs and effectiveness of the competing neighborhood law offices' legal services with Judicare, and to test the "family lawyer" concept whereby client is encouraged to discuss legal problems other than the immediate one. The final report describes organization, techniques, problems, evaluating both services as to cost, quality and satisfaction of clients. 1st six month report - Nov. 1, 1970. 2nd progress report - Apr.- Sept. 30, 1970. 3rd progress report - Nov. 1, 1970 - Mar. 31, 1971. 4th report - Apr.-Sept. 1971. Appendix A: Research and evaluation. (see item 3817) 3843

INSTITUTE of Judicial Administration. Report to the Mayor of the City of New York on the cost of providing defense for indigents in criminal cases. N.Y., 1965. 19 p.
Study of the Legal Aid Society Criminal Branch indicates an assigned counsel service would cost between four and ten times as much to operate as legal aid. 3844

IRVING, J.F. and GETTY, L.M. The Rockland County (New York) survey of the need for an organized defense system for indigents. Chicago, ABA, 1965. 36 p.
Recommendations include establishment of an organized legal defense and how it should operate. Reports results of a survey of attorneys practicing in the county; and discusses the structure of the court and present methods of assigning attorneys. 3845

JACOB, B.R. and SHARMA, K.M. Justice after trial: prisoners' need for legal services in the criminal-correctional process. Kan L Rev 18:493-628 (1970).
Report on when, where and how needed, present practices and programs, suggestions for law school programs; recommendations include call for statewide appellate and post-conviction defender's office, also a similar federal institution. 3846

JAIL fees and court costs for the indigent criminal defendant: an examination of the Tennesses procedure. Tenn L Rev 35:74-99 (1967).

Comment examines whether it is constitutionally permissible to 1) charge a room and board fee to an indigent awaiting trial or 2) charge an indigent fees
accrued pretrial and court costs and have him "work
it out." Discussed are statutory provisions, state
and federal interpretations, and constitutional arguments against such action. Author suggests both judicial
and legislative solutions to these problems.   <u>3847</u>

JARMEL, E. Legal representation of the poor: a guide for New Jersey's
Legal Services Project attorneys.   Newark, Inst for Continuing Legal Education, 1968. 419 p.
Director of the Institute has prepared this book from
a series of lectures by various experts. Material covered relates to: social workers and the law; welfare
problems; consumer problems; landlord and tenant problems; challenging arbitrary official conduct. Included
are discussions of relevant cases and statutes. <u>3848</u>

JUDICIAL problems in administering court appointment of counsel
for indigents. Wash & Lee L Rev 28:120-34 (1971).
Note discusses how the lack of uniform criteria for
determining indigency, and adequate inquiry into financial status, and of obligation of defendant to pay
court costs has led to problems of criminal justice
administration in the area of court-appointed counsel.
Cases illustrating this problem are examined. Author
finds that a better examination of defendant's financial abilities can solve much confusion.   <u>3849</u>

JUSTICE Department and other views on prepaid legal services get an
airing before the Tunney Subcommittee. ABA J 60:791-96 (1974).
Excerpts from testimony on prepaid legal services plans
before the Senate Subcommittee on Representation of
Citizen Interests, May 14-15, 1974, of which Sen. J.V.
Tunney is chair. The discussion revolves around amendments to the Code of Professional Responsibility (Feb.
1974) which appear to be discriminatory as between open
and closed panel plans, raising anti-trust problems
for any bar association that adopts them. Bar associations should limit their role in prepaid plans to development, organization and promotion of the concept.
<u>3850</u>

KARABIAN, W. Legal services for the poor: some political observations.
U San Francisco L Rev 6:253-65 (1972).
Author examines the growth of legal services for the
indigent, the OEO's success in legal reforms providing
for equal treatment of the poor, and the increasing
political opposition from the "establishment" caused
by this success. Author suggests that legal services
be removed from the political arena and that poverty

lawyers work with legislators as well as the courts
and lobby for appropriate new laws and resources.3851

KARLEN, D. Legal aid for the criminal accused in England and the
United States: a comparative study. Legal Aid Rev 63:26-33 (1965).
        Law professor compares the uniform statutory British
        system with the diverse public and private American
        systems, showing that in spite of their important dif-
        ferences, they share common problems of setting stand-
        ards for eligibility, defendants' waiver of the right
        to counsel, and provision of counsel immediately after
        arrest and on appeal.   3852

KATZ, L.R. Gideon's trumpet: mournful and muffled. Crim L Bull 6:
529-76 (1970).
        Law professor describes principal methods used to pro-
        vide legal assistance to the indigent criminal defend-
        ant; discusses at what stages legal assistance is re-
        quired and the quality of that assistance. Pointing
        out the weaknesses in the system of assigning private
        attorneys, he proposes the adoption of a public defend-
        er system and suggests creating urban Departments of
        Justice which would include the offices of Public Prose-
        cutor, Public Defender, Court Administrator, Police,
        and Probation and Parole.   3853

KETTEL, N.G. Defense of the poor: a study in public parsimony and
private poverty. Ind L J 45:90-112 (1969).
        Government professor presents statistical study of two
        midwestern counties' legal services for the poor, and
        attempts to determine why one provides services equal
        to private services and the other provides inferior ser-
        vices. Court structure, procedures and resources, and
        comparison of representation provided by public defend-
        ers and private counsel are discussed. Factors account-
        ing for differences include time devoted to case, qual-
        ity of attorneys, resources allocated attorney, inde-
        pendence of counsel, speed of court system, and bail
        bond requirements.   3854

KLEIN, J. Law school legal aid programs: a survey. Chicago, National
Legal Aid and Defender, 1969. 50 p. (NLADA Monograph series 1)
        Questionnaire survey: types of cases law school pro-
        grams handle, their funding, relationships with the
        bar, clients' attitudes.   3855

LAMKIN, C.F. Compensation of appointed counsel in criminal cases.
J Mo B 19:412-18 (1963).
        Describes the Missouri provision for no compensation
        for counsel to indigent defendants and alternative pro-
        posals including the public defender system and legal
        aid societies where compensation is set by statute;

argues for the present Missouri system, with added provision for the attorney's expenses.   3856

LASSOW, D. The Legal Services Corporation Act: a guide to the legislative history. NLADA Briefcase, 32:37-68 (1974).
    Chronology, with citations and excerpts, of passage
    of act in 1974 transferring funding of legal aid in
    civil cases from federal Office of Economic Opportunity
    to a private non-profit corporation.   3857

LEGAL Aid Society of New York. Community law offices: a volunteer
legal services program serving the community of East Harlem. N.Y.,
1968. 1 v., var. pag.
    Describes the organization, purposes and operations
    of the program which is run by volunteer attorneys in
    practice with private firms.   3858

LEGAL problems of the rural poor. Duke L J 1969:495-621; Chicago,
AB Found, 1969. (Its series on legal services for the poor.)
    Detailed study of North Carolina poor rural area to
    determine the types of legal problems typical of this
    enviornment, the individual's response to his legal
    problems, and whether the population is aware of avail-
    able services. Appendix includes description of federal
    programs and the questionnaire used as a basis of the
    study.   3859

THE LEGAL services corporation: curtailing political interference.
Yale L J 81:231-286 (1972).
    Argues that clear policies and responsive administra-
    tion are necessary to curtail political obstructions
    to a legal services corporation's goals, and offers
    proposals to provide these elements.   3860

LEGAL services - past and present. Cornell L Rev 59:960-88 (1974).
    Note reviews the development, achievments and contro-
    versies of all the legal services programs 1965-1971.
    The origin, funding; goals, ethical problems are de-
    tailed. The National Legal Services Corporation to
    replace the current legal services program is separately
    described with comment on congressional action to June,
    1974.   3861

LOVELL, R.E., II. The case for reimbursing court costs and a reasonable attorney fee to the non-indigent defendant upon acquittal. Neb
L Rev 49:515-35 (1970).
    Referring to United States v McLeod, 385 F2d 734 (5th
    Cir., 1967), which awarded costs, including reasonable
    attorney's fees, to those who were illegally prosecuted,
    the article discusses present cost systems in the United
    States; drawbacks of the tort remedy of malicious pro-
    secution; the English costs system; and the possibility

of improving on the latter by the adoption of the
Scottish form of verdict.   3862

MCLAUGHLIN, G.T. The recovery of attorney's fees: a new method of
financing legal services. Fordham L Rev 40:757-88 (1972).
    Analyzes precedent for awarding legal aid attorney's
    fees on successful litigation, and argues for a rule
    of award in all cases for more effective legal repre-
    sentation and access to courts.   3863

MAKING the indigent pay to obtain out-of-state witnesses. U San
Francisco L Rev 1:326-31 (1967).
    Author feels that the defendant has been kept outside
    the protection of the Uniform Act to Secure the Attend-
    ance of Witnesses from Without A State in Criminal Pro-
    ceedings, which provides that material witnesses can
    be compelled to appear by court order and will be
    paid expenses, by interpretation of most courts that
    the defendant must pay the witness. Legislature should
    spell out that the intent of the Act is to provide ma-
    terial witnesses, paid by the defendant only if defend-
    and is able.   3864

MANSON, P.C. Virginia [report on criminal courts in Virginia] prepared with the assistance and under the supervision of the ABA Associates Committee ... Richmond, 1964. 22 p.
    (For annotation see item 1231)   3865

MARKS, F.R., HALLAUER, R.P. and CLIFTON, R.R. The Shreveport plan;
an experiment in the delivery of legal services. Chicago, 1974.
106 p.
    Examination of first year of legal insurance plan using
    open panel of lawyers developed on a relatively small
    scale for a union. Study focuses on whether potential
    client was enabled to use needed services more effect-
    ively. Discussed are: methodology of study; use and
    non-use of lawyers before plan; pre-plan attitudes to-
    wards use of legal services; and use of lawyers, econ-
    omics, members' reactions, lawyer reaction, and pattern
    of services under plan after one year. Study concludes
    that plan was a success.   3866

MATTIS, T. Financial inability. Neb L Rev 49:37-69 (1969).
    Author, stating that the need for counsel at all stages
    of a criminal proceeding is undisputed, focuses on the
    duties of the court to appoint counsel and the duty of
    taxpayers to pay for the defense; he discusses what
    are the financial circumstances of the defendant in
    which counsel should be appointed, the broad criteria,
    specific factors to be considered, and the redetermina-
    tion of ability to pay for all or part of the defense.
                                                             3867

MAZOR, L.J. The right to be provided counsel: variation on a familiar theme. Utah L Rev 9:50-89 (1964).
Law professor examines a Utah survey of representation of the accused, case development since the survey and application of new constitutional principles to Utah, and the prospect that long discussed proposals may now be implemented. Discusses scope of obligation to provide counsel: at what point and for which defendants, and methods of providing counsel, costs and waiver.
3868

MILLS J. "I have nothing to do with justice." Life, March 12, 1971, 57-68.
Interview with Martin Erdmann,Legal Aid attorney, who discusses his experiences in and attitudes toward the criminal justice system in New York City and his defendant-clients. Mr. Erdmann was censured by the Appellate Division, First Department for some of his comments reported in this article. The New York Court of Appeals reversed the censure order. 3869

MINIMUM standards for group and prepaid legal service plans, [and] Growth continues for group and prepaid legal services. Wis B Bull 46:18-23 (Dec. 1973).
Standards adopted by Wisconsin State Bar mandate that plans be in writing, and specify benefits, extent of undertaking, and protection of attorneys' independence. Article following explains,emphasizing **rules** flexibility, with some local plans modeled after Shreveport and another in cooperation with an insurance company.3870

MORRISON, W.A. Recent decisions requiring the appointment of counsel at trial and on appeal. Tex B J 28:23-24, 69-72 (1965).
A review of U.S. Supreme Court requiring counsel at trial and pretrial, and upon appeal; second part discusses Texas cases dealing with the appointment of counsel at trial and Gideon applied retroactively.
3871

NAGEL, S.S. Effects of alternative types of counsel on criminal procedure treatment. Ind L J 48:404-26 (1973).
Compares: counsel vs no counsel; hired counsel vs provided counsel; public defender vs assigned counsel; and early obtained counsel vs late obtained counsel, using nationwide sample of 1,101 grand larceny cases, controlling for urban setting and economic class. Isolates effects at preliminary hearing, bail conviction, sentencing. Concludes that the public defender is the best compromise for effectiveness and economy. 3872

NATIONAL Center for State Courts. Implementation of Argersinger v Hamlin: a prescriptive program package. Jan. 1974. Denver, 1974. 78 p.

Guidebook to help states and localities meet Supreme
Court's extension of right to counsel in all cases
with possible jail sentence; based on study of nine
states providing such service prior to decision; examines problems of determining indigency and eligibility, use of law students and paraprofessionals, policy-
related issues in expanding defender for assigned counsel systems. Example given, with budgets, caseloads,
of public defender system for a small urban state and
for a rural county. Appendices: Fees for private assigned counsel; ABA model student practice rule; Model defense of needy persons act; DC eligibility questionnaire
and work sheet.   3873

NATIONAL Conference of Commissioners on Uniform State Laws. Model
defense of needy persons act. Chicago, 1966. 19 p. App'd 1966.
Act with comments, covering the indigent's right to
competent counsel. 1st tent. draft, Aug. 6, 1964. 7 p.;
2d tent. draft, 1965. 17 p.; 3d tent. draft, 1965.
12 p.; 4th tent. draft, 1966. 13 p.   3874

NATIONAL Conference of Commissioners on Uniform State Laws. Model
public defender act, with prefatory note and comments. Chicago,
1970. 19 p. App'd 1970.
Modification of 1966 Model Defense of Needy Persons
Act updates Act in light of subsequent Supreme Court
decisions. The proposed Model Public Defender Act provides greater procedural safeguards and suggests a
statewide defender system rather than the previous
county option plan. Flexible definition of adequate
defense allows for change with future Court decisions.
Text of Act and commentary.   3875

NATIONAL Conference on prepaid legal services, Washington, 1972.
Transcript of proceedings. Chicago, ABA, 1972. 439 p.
Thirty-seven speakers and panelists; areas are: services
to moderate income clients, group and prepaid legal
services, closed and open panel plans, role of legal
profession, insurance industry, consumers' demands.
                                                        3876

NATIONAL Legal Aid and Defender Association. Clinical training programs in law schools. Washington, Georgetown Law Center, 1968. 5 p.
Association emphasizes the need for quality criminal
attorneys and proposes that law schools establish clinical undergraduate courses as a means of fulfilling
this need. Programs should combine classroom instruction with the professional learning process, and could
be funded under Title XI of the Higher Education Amendments of 1968.   3877

NATIONAL Legal Aid and Defender Association. Institutionalization
of defender services. Washington, Georgetown Law Center, 1969. 10 p.

Discusses following reforms in criminal justice system
to assist the individual criminal defendant regardless
of his financial position: A United States Defender
General, a Defender General for each state, a nationwide computerized brief bank, and a defender crime laboratory and expert witness agency.   3878

NATIONAL Legal Aid and Defender Association. 1971 statistics of legal
aid and defender work in the United States and Canada. M. Steigler,
ed. Chicago, 1971. 53 p.
        Statistical information in chart form on the actual ex-
        perience for 1971 of 355 of the 420 legal assistance
        offices. The compilation is of civil statistical data.
                                               3879

NATIONAL Legal Aid and Defender Association. The other side of justice. Chicago, 1973. 164 p.
        Nation-wide survey of defense services in state court
        systems includes defender systems, assigned counsel
        systems and various legal views comparing the two, anal-
        yzed in light of standards proposed by various legal
        organizations; appendices are the type of indigent de-
        fense system by county, expenditures for assigned coun-
        sel systems, selected data for counties using each sys-
        tem, the National Advisory Commission on Criminal Jus-
        tice Standards and Goals' Standards 13.1 to 13.16 (see
        item 3378) and ABA Standards Relating to Providing De-
        fense Services (item 3786); also National Legal Aid
        and Defenders Association 1965 Handbook of standards
        for legal aid and defender offices.   3880

NATIONAL Legal Aid and Defender Association. Report to the National
Defender Conference, May 14-16, 1969. Chicago, 1969. 118 p.
        Report prepared by National Defender Projects of NLADA
        for Washington, D.C. conference presents survey of im-
        provements in the establishment of organized defender
        systems representing the financially disadvantaged.
        Examined are: types of systems; historical background;
        when counsel should be provided; guaranteeing effective
        representation; and proposal for restructuring the
        system of criminal jsutice. Appendices include state-
        by-state table of defender statutes, ABA criminal jus-
        tice standards, recommendations of President's Cmssn
        on Law Enforcement, and Model Law School Clinic Programs
        grams.   3881

NATIONAL Legal Aid and Defender Association. Study and recommendations for Kentucky statewide public defender system, by R. Rogers
and S. Singer. Washington, Criminal Courts Technical Assistance Project, American U, 1973. 64 p.
        (For annotation see item 735)   3882

NEIGHBORHOOD law offices: the new wave in legal services for the poor. Harv L Rev 80:805-50 (1967).

Using mainly personal interviews, authors present overview of legal services available to the poor, with emphasis on neighborhood law office. They explore both the service function and the law reform function of legal services, and review the advantages and disadvantages of the different methods used, their success or failure, and alternatives. Conclusion is that an adequately funded and staffed neighborhood law office can best fulfill both functions of legal services, also make legal system really available to the poor. <u>3883</u>

NEW ENGLAND Defender Conference. J Am Jud Soc 47:159-200 (1964).

<u>Contents</u>: Reardon, P.C., Vorenberg, J. Summary Report.--Sutherland, A.E. Constitutional obligation to provide counsel for the indigent.--Seymour, W.N. Methods of providing defense.--Trebach, A.S. New England defender systems, basic problems and questions.--Lumbard, J.E. The adequacy of lawyers now in criminal practice.--Kennedy, R.F. The Department of Justice and the indigent accused.--Implementation - a discussion of how to improve defense systems.--Participants, program, Resolution of the Conference, standards for defender services. <u>3884</u>

THE NEW JERSEY public defender. Columbia J L & Soc Prob 5:153-63 (1969).

Article examines New Jersey's experience: history of system, administrative structure, benefits of new system over assigned counsel, and weaknesses of the system. <u>3885</u>

NEW YORK (City) Criminal Justice Coordinating Council. A comparative analysis of the legal aid society all-purpose part (Part IC, Queens Criminal Court), by S.H. Clarke. N.Y., 1970. 42 p.

Report on case handling all-purpose Part IC; examines its performance to date as compared with other Parts: output; efficiency of disposal; workload; efficiency with heavier workload; justice of case disposals; and implications for citywide court management. Report found efficiency declining as workload increased, and concludes that if this Part functioned with the same workload as other comparable Parts its output efficiency would approach theirs. Report does not support citywide adoption of all-purpose Parts. Includes description of methodology; measurement of workload, output and efficiency; data tables; text of Legal Aid Society's memo approving all-purpose Parts, and its response to this NYC CJCC report. <u>3886</u>

NEW YORK (State) Supreme Court Appellate Division 1st and 2d Depts. Subcommittee on Legal Representation of Indigent and Limited Income

Groups. Report on the legal representation of the indigent in criminal cases. N.Y., 1971. 33 p.

> Finds determination of who is eligible for assignment
> of free legal counsel in criminal cases is not based
> on well-defined standards; recommends specifics; sees
> need for adjunct social services as part of free legal
> aid system; recommends type of services needed; recom-
> mends use of paraprofessionals from law schools and
> social work schools. Other needs include establishing
> maximum case level, better training, supervision and
> evaluation of legal aid lawyers, and involvement of
> community.   3887

NEW YORK (State) Supreme Court Appellate Division 1st and 2d Depts.
Subcommittee on Legal Representation of Indigent and Limited Income
Groups. Representation of the indigent before administrative agen-
cies. N.Y., 1973. 44 p.

> Report finds the poor underrepresented before adminis-
> trative agencies and sets forth recommendations in the
> areas of public assistance, school suspension hearings,
> housing matters and unemployment insurance.   3888

NEW YORK (State) Supreme Court Appellate Division 1st and 2d Depts.
Subcommittee on Legal Representation of Indigent and Limited Income
Groups. Representation of the indigent in landlord-tenant matters.
O. Marden, chair. Mar. 1973. N.Y., 1973. 30 p.

> This report examines the types of cases in which in-
> digents are represented in New York City Civil Court
> concluding that in agencies representing such indigents,
> cases are heavily weighted in landlord-tenant matters;
> assesses the quality of such services and makes recom-
> mendations to increase and improve.   3888a

New York (State) Supreme Court Appellate Division 1st and 2d Depts.
Subcommittee on Legal Representation of Indigent and Limited Income
Groups. Representation of the indigent in uncontested matrimonial
matters. O. Marden, chair. Mar. 1973. N.Y., 1973. 16 p.

> After reviewing the increasing need for plaintiff as-
> sistance in undefended matrimonials, committee recom-
> mends expanded use of paraprofessionals and more help
> from bar associations and other legal services organi-
> zations. Sees little use for Conciliation Bureau and
> recommends abolition. Suggests changes in court rules
> to facilitate such actions and recommends that legis-
> lature abolish certain publication requirements. 3888b

OAKS, D.H. and LEHMAN, W.A. Criminal justice system and the indigent;
a study of Chicago and Cook County. Chicago, U of Chicago press,
1968. 203 p.

> Survey of criminal prosecution from arrest through ap-
> peal to examine treatment of the indigent defendant.
> Includes statistical analysis at each level; recommen-
> dations for reform.   3889

OLIPHANT, R.E. Reflections on the lower court system; the development of a unique clinical misdemeanor and a public defender program.
Minn L Rev 57:545-58 (1973).
>Describes a three-year-old program which a law school
clinical misdemeanor course combines with providing
legal assistance to indigent defendants. Recommends
similar programs.   3890

OREGON State Bar Committee on Legal Aid. Statewide legal aid feasibility study. Portland, 1971. 78 p.
>Study on need for statewide legal services program in
Oregon outlines a unified statewide program incorpor-
ating current government-assisted legal services programs. Poverty in Oregon, legal problems of the poor,
and the extent to which they are handled are discussed.
Includes the views of attorneys, the poor, and social
services agencies operating in the field on the effectiveness of current legal aid assistance. Maps and
tables.   3891

PALMER, K.T. Indigent defender systems in New York: a preliminary
report. NYSBJ 40:7-18 (1968).
>Government professor examines the adoption and imple-
mentation of recent indigent defender systems in New
York state: statutory plan options afforded the counties, such as public defender, assigned counsel, legal
aid, or a combination; which counties chose which plans
and why; implementation of plans; and initial results.
                                                     3892

PAULSEN, M.G. Equal justice for the poor man. N.Y., Pub Affairs
Cttee, 1964. 20 p.
>Professor describes the constitutional right to coun-
sel, the scope of that right, the systems of assigning
lawyers and public defenders, and problems of providing
legal assistance in civil cases. He also discusses the
English Legal Aid and Advice Act and prepaid legal services.   3893

PAULSEN, M.G. Expanding horizons of legal services. W Va L Rev 67:
179-200, 267-89 (1965).
>Extensive examination of programs offering legal ser-
vices, i.e. services for indigent defendants, legal
services as an attack on poverty, services in the juvenile court, new ways of serving the middle classes
(neighborhood law office models), and the English system. Recommends group legal services.   3894

PIOUS, R. Congress, the organized bar, and the legal services program. Wisc L Rev 1972:418-46.
>Describes hammering out of legislation for federally
funded legal services in the Johnson and Nixon adminis-

tration and efforts of the bar, the OEO, and the legislators to determine the program's purposes, administration and budget.   3895

PIOUS, R. Policy and public administration: the legal services program in the war on poverty. Pol & Society 1:365-91 (1971).
    Political scientist presents history and development
    of civil legal services for indigents and the various
    philosophies and endeavors of individuals who made the
    planning models. He covers the local political settings
    of projects, the continuing conflicts.   3896

PLATT, A., SCHECTER, H. and TIFFANY, P. In defense of youth: a case
of the public defender in juvenile court. Ind L J 43:619-40 (1967/
1968).
    Based on data from observations of public defender of-
    fice in a sample city, researchers from University of
    Chicago Center for Studies in Criminal Justice analyze
    the role of the lawyer in juvenile court in light of
    In re Gairey, 387 US 1 (1967), in which the Supreme
    Court held, inter alia, that juveniles have a right to
    counsel. Examined are: characteristics of juvenile
    clients; the lawyer as officer of the court, advocate,
    and "social worker;" plea bargaining; and clients' per-
    ception of the defender.   3897

PORTMAN, S. Public defender office administration. Legal Aid Briefcase 29:107-18 (Mar. 1971).
    Public defender of Santa Clara County (San Jose, Calif.)
    draws on his experience as administrator in this dis-
    cussion of how to achieve an effective defender organi-
    zation. He emphasizes the importance of obtaining a
    sufficient number of qualified personnel and of proper
    training of personnel. Some statistical data is given.
                                                      3898

PORTMAN, S. State defender's office: boon or boondoggle? Calif SB
J 47:92-97, 143-48 (1972).
    Public Defender of Santa Clara County discusses the
    background behind the proposal to establish a State
    Public Defender's Office to provide indigents with
    representation in criminal appeals; includes provisions
    of two bills, which were vetoed, and two proposed pro-
    jects designed to demonstrate the advantages of differ-
    ent systems of criminal appellate representation for
    the indigent.   3899

PRESIDENT signs National Legal Services Corporation Act. ABA J 60:
1050-52 (1974).
    Brief summary of history and provisions of Act, which
    removed legal services in civil cases from federal Of-
    fice of Economic Opportunity to private, non-profit

corporation empowered to receive funds from public and
private sources, to administer the funds to state and
local qualified programs, and to engage in research
and training and technical assistance.   3900

PROBLEM of adequate representation of indigent and other defendants
in criminal cases; a panel discussion at the Judicial Conference of
the Second Judicial Circuit.   June 26, 1974, Manchester, Vermont.
FRD 36:129-73 (1965).
           Members of the panel: Lumbard, J.E.; Marden, O.S.; An-
           derson, R.P., Morganthau, R.; Moldow, B., Polsky, L.,
           Gelb, S.   3901

PYE, A.K.   The administration of criminal justice.   Col L Rev 66:286-
304 (1966).
           Discusses such indigent defense reforms as: methods of
           providing counsel, release from custody, alternatives
           to bail. Gives statistics on defendants unable to make
           bail, findings of D.C. and Manhattan Bail Projects,
           Manhattan Summons Project; rehabilitation, D.C. Legal
           Aid Agency experience; also discusses auxiliary legal
           services; investigations; expert witnesses; compulsory
           process; general reforms for benefit of poor.   3902

RANDOLPH, G.F.   What bars should consider in prepaid legal services
plans.   ABA J 60:797-801 (1974).
           Points out pitfalls to be watched by bar associations
           interested in prepared legal services plans; tax, anti-
           trust and insurance considerations are foremost. Author
           says best plan is one approved by the bar association
           but marketed and operated by an insurer; discusses tax
           and anti-trust pertinent rules and cases; gives the
           Feb. 1974 amendments to the Code of Professional Respon-
           sibility relating to legal organization. The National
           Insurance Commissioner's Committee report and poll are
           discussed and recommendations to bar associations are
           made. On p. 799 is an insert of the report: "Legal care"
           in New York, by Sen. J.R. Dunne, Chair., N.Y. Select
           Cttee on Insurance.   3903

REARDON, P.C. and VORENBERG, J.   New England defender conference: a
brief report.   BU L Rev 44:1-9 (1964).
           Massachusetts Supreme Court justice and law professor
           report on discussions including: scope of legal obli-
           gation to provide counsel and reach of recent Supreme
           Court decisions; when counsel should be provided; types
           of systems that can be used in providing counsel; need
           for a sufficient number of qualified defense lawyers;
           need for expansion of resources in the defense of the
           indigent; and conclusion of conference, calling on legis-
           lature, bar, and judiciary to work together in meeting
           the urgent need to provide fair representation.   3904

REIMBURSEMENT of defense costs as a condition of probation for indigents. Mich L Rev 67:1404-20 (1969).
>Comment examines the constitutional validity and prac-
tical wisdom of imposing a condition of repayment of
defense costs as part of probation. The article reviews the scopes of state and federal responsibility
to provide free services to the indigent, the amount
of discretion allowed a judge in setting conditions
of probation, the potential chilling effect of this
type of condition, and the lack of rehabilitative effect of the condition and finds that it is an unwise,
if not unconstitutional, use of probation.   3905

REPORT of the conference on legal manpower needs of criminal law.
FRD 41:389-418 (1966).
>Covers needs of prosecution and defense system in terms
of lawyers and costs; discussion of eligibility for
aid; adequacy of representation; supporting services;
related civil proceedings; methods of providing lawyers,
full-time defenders, and assigned counsel; operating
efficiency; recruitment and training of attorneys;
state and federal funding.   3906

REPRESENTATION of indigent criminal defendants in federal district
courts. Harv L Rev 76:579-618 (1963).
>Questionnaire and interview survey of federal district
judges and U.S. attorneys. Analyzes present system:
assigned counsel and methods of assignment; guilty pleas;
waiver of right to counsel; assigned counsel's case
preparation, expenses, willingness to serve; determination of indigency; defender organizations and their
funding and availability for federal cases; alternative
systems; payment of assigned counsel, public defenders,
and public funding of private **defender** organizations;
judges' and prosecutors' views; analysis of proposed
federal statutes for legal aid.   3907

RIGHT of an accused to proceed without counsel. Minn L Rev 49:133-
53 (1965).
>Right to waive counsel, limitations; standards for
competent waiver; role of trial court: explanation and
inquiry as to defendant's understanding; appointment
of counsel and advisory counsel.   3908

RIGHT of self-representation. Washburn L J 12:257-61 (1973).
>Article discusses whether there is a constitutional
right to defend pro se in Kansas, exploring Sixth Amendment guarantees. In order to assure that defendant has
due process, the right to defend pro se in Kansas is
conditioned on the trial judge's discretion. Author
feels this satisfies the Sixth Amendment.   3909

RIGHT of the indigent misdemeanant to appointed counsel. SD L Rev
16:400-12 (1971).
> Note refers to six-month rule (indigent faces incarcer-
> ation for more than six months) and the ninety-day rule
> as determinative of the right to counsel; pertinent
> cases are discussed including problems arising, as
> where petty offense carries serious offense implica-
> tions, where misdemeanant is accused of multiple counts
> carrying nominal penalties. Also discusses imprison-
> ment in lieu of fine, unrealized potential sentences,
> status of South Dakota law.   3910

RIGHT to aid in addition to counsel for indigent defendants. Minn
L Rev 47:1054-78 (1963).
> Discusses right to investigation and psychiatric wit-
> nesses; equal protection; due process; right to counsel
> supportive of right to auxiliary legal aid.   3911

RIGHT to an interpreter. Rutgers L Rev 25:145-71 (1970).
> Article examines the use of an interpreter at trial
> when required for the benefit of a non-English-speaking
> accused: statutory and constitutional basis purporting
> to grant the right to interpretation; case law; trial
> court discretion in applying this right; scope of re-
> view; and problems of incompetent or biased interpreters.
> Author concludes that too much of this right is left
> to trial court discretion and adequate standards have
> not been provided. Text of model act for appointment
> and use of interpreters is included.   3912

RIGHT to appear pro se: the constitution and the courts. J Crim L
64:240-49 (1973).
> An exploration of the controversy as to whether there
> is a constitutional right for a defendant to proceed
> without counsel. Contrasts the U.S. Court of Appeals,
> 2d Circuit, position that there is an absolute, primary
> right to appear pro se with the California Supreme
> Court decision sanctioning a state constitutional amend-
> ment taking away the right to appear pro se; appendix
> gives results of a survey of Illinois trial judges con-
> cerning pro se defendants.   3913

RIGHT to counsel - sixth amendment does not grant accused the right
to counsel at pretrial photographic display. Vand L Rev 26:1323-30
(1973).
> Note focuses on United States v Ash, 93 SCt 2568 (1973),
> examining the stage in proceedings against an accused
> when assistance of counsel is required, as set forth
> in earlier Supreme Court decisions.   3914

RIGHT to defend pro se. NC L Rev 48:678-87 (1970).
> Discusses limits of the right and nature of the waiver.

Argues that the existence of judge's discretion to refuse to allow a defense pro se when requested during
trial is irreconcilable with recognition of an absolute
right to defense pro se before trial.   3915

RIGHT to defend pro se in criminal proceedings. Wash U L Q 1973:679-
707.
Aspects of self-representation considered include the
question of whether there is a constitutional right
to defend pro se, the importance of the time when the
right is asserted, and whether the waiver of counsel
is knowingly made and valid.   3916

ROSENTHAL, D.E., KAGAN, R.A. and QUATRONE, E. Volunteer attorneys
and legal services for the poor: New York's CLO program. N.Y.,
Russell Sage Found, 1971. 221 p.
Research report on Community Legal Offices gives specifics on the operation of the first autonomous poverty
law program in the U.S. The nine sections cover, in
addition to research methods, the formation and growth
of CLO, its program, and evaluation of the performance
of its volunteer attorneys; the representation of group
clients, the relationship of CLO with its volunteers
and their training and with the private bar. The support obtained and needed is described as is the relationship of CLO with the East Harlem community. 3917

ROTHSTEIN, L.E. The myth of Sisyphus: legal services efforts on be-
half of the poor. U Mich J L Ref 7:493-515 (1974).
The poor as litigants in the legal system are at a
disadvantage. After enumerating categorically the types
of disadvantages, professor examines the legal profession's role and the confrontation between lawyers for
the poor and the legal system since early times; criticizes past and present programs: legal aid, OEO, neigh-
borhood-controlled legal services, NAACP, War on Poverty, and others.   3918

SAN FRANCISCO Committee on Crime. Report on the San Francisco Public
Defender's Office. San Francisco, 1970. 25 p.
Concludes that the office has performed reasonably well,
but a history of "dull leadership," heavy caseload
burden and inadequate staffing has caused the Public
Defender to be held in low esteem by its minority group
clients. Discusses the plea bargaining process, "in-
sensitivity of the Public Defender to the duties, pur-
pöses and proprieties of his office," problems of representing felony, misdemeanor and juvenile cases, and
broad recommendations for upgrading the office. Appendix
is: "An analysis of plea bargaining and trials in felony cases in the San Francisco Public Defender's office."
Recommendations include appointment rather than election
of Public Defenders.   3919

SARGANT, T. Legal aid in criminal appeals. New L J 117:1067-69
(1967).
          Author examines British Criminal Justice Act of 1967,
          which provides for every circumstance in which legal
          assistance in making an application for appeal may
          be required: background of act, and past experience
          and practices of legal aid; provisions of new act; and
          the need for all concerned to work for a fair and just
          trial to lessen the need for appeals.   3920

SEARLE, H.R. An argument for the public defender system. Santa
Clara Law 5:48-59 (1964).
          Former public defender summarizes the arguments favor-
          ing the public defender system as opposed to the assign-
          ed counsel system of providing representation for in-
          digent defendants in criminal cases in California.
                                                         3921

SELF-REPRESENTATION in criminal trials: the dilemma of the pro se
defendant. Cal L Rev 59:1479-1513 (1971).
          Note considers legal problems of self-representation
          and defendants' motivation for self-representation.
          An argument is made for an alternative approach, that
          of appointing advisory counsel to assist the defendant.
                                                         3922

SELF-REPRESENTATION in criminal trials - the pro se defendant. Wake
Forest L Rev 9:265-73 (1973).
          Analysis of Mems, 190 SE2d 164 (1972), holding that
          defendant has a right to handle his own case without
          interference by, or assistance of, counsel forced up-
          on him against his wishes, and discussion of the ram-
          ifications of the decision. Author finds that the right
          to defend pro se has been found to be a constitutional
          right; therefore the courts will have to clarify what
          discretionary powers the trial judge has on this issue.
                                                         3923

SILVERSTEIN, L. Defense of the poor in criminal cases in American
state courts; a field study and report. Chicago, AB Found, 1965.
3 v.
          Contents: V. 1: National report (bibliography, p. 269-
          276); V. 2: State reports Alabama-Mississippi ; V. 3:
          State reports Missouri-Wyoming . One-year audit of
          criminal cases in state courts. Describes the various
          assigned-counsel systems and defender systems in opera-
          tion, and compares them as to cost and effectiveness
          (by case dispositions). Discusses present practices
          and opinions concerning time of appointment. Offer
          and waiver of counsel, methods to determine eligibility,
          counsel for misdemeanors, counsel for post-trial pro-
          ceedings, minimum standards of operation and financing.

Volumes 2 and 3 include state reports: docket studies
of how procedure affects the poor, opinions of judges
and attorneys, and recommendations.   3924

SILVERSTEIN, L. Defense of the poor in criminal cases in American
state courts - a preliminary summary. Chicago, AB Found, 1964. 78 p.
Based on data collected for item 3924, describes the
different systems in use, major problems; summarizes
state statutes.   3925

SILVERSTEIN, L. Eligibility for free legal services in civil cases.
U Det Urban L J 44:549-84 (1967); repr. AB Found series on legal services for the poor.
Survey of financial and subject-matter eligibilty standards in 275 legal aid offices finds liberalization
trend, but over-restriction as measured by accepted minimum income standards.   3926

SIMEONE, J.J. and RICHARDSON, O. The indigent and his right to legal
assistance in criminal cases. St Lous U L J 8:15-58 (1963).
Analysis of state constitutions, statutes, and case
law concerning right to counsel; type of crime; stage
of proceeding; staff; investigation; discovery; methods
of assignment; voluntary defenders; public defenders.
                                             3927

SKOLNICK, J.H. Social control in the adversary system. J of Conflict
Resolution 11:52-70 (1967).
Examines prosecutor-defender relations, the limits of
adversary relationship, and institutionalized cooperation. Based upon study of a California county; shows
that differences in behavior between public defender
and the successful private defender have been exaggerated.   3928

SOLOMON, H.W. "This new fetish for indigency:" justice and poverty
in an affluent society. Colum L Rev 66:248-74 (1966).
Analysis of Report of the Attorney General's Committee
on Poverty and the Administration of Criminal Justice:
historical background; evaluation; adequate representation; detention of accused, bail, appellate review;
proposals for reform; role of legal education. 3929

STATE Bar of California. Report of the Standing Committee on Group
Legal Services: group legal services. J SB Calif 39:639-742 (1964).
Reporting that there is an unfulfilled public need for
legal services, Committee details several California
group legal service plans, proposed and existing, which
respond to this need. Legal status is considered, particularly as presented in NAACP v Button, 371 US 415
(1963), and Brotherhood of RR Trainmen v Virginia State
Bar, 377 US 1 (1964). Other methods of providing legal

services as well as the Committee's recommendations
are presented. Appendix B describes how group legal
plans could be certified.   3930

STIFLER, J.G. Determining the financial status of an accused. Ill
S B J 54:868-80 (1966).
          Statutory and case law criteria of eligibility for le-
          gal aid; statistics on percentage of felony defendants
          who require aid.   3931

STOLZ, P. Insurance for legal services: a preliminary study of feasibility. U Chi L Rev 35:417-76 (1968).
          Law professor explores the feasibility of an insurance
          scheme, similar to community health insurance, which
          would help the public pay the cost of legal services:
          problems of planning and underwriting; types of insur-
          ance for specific kinds of legal services; and a model
          plan, including benefits, coverage, costs, and potential
          commercial value.   3932

STOLZ, P. Legal needs of the public; a survey analysis. Chicago,
AB Found, 1968. 14 p. (Research contributions, 1968, 4.)
          (For annotation see item 2757f)   3933

STUDENT practice as a method of legal education and a means of providing legal assistance to indigents: an empirical study ... for the
American Bar Foundation. W&M L Rev 15:353-485 (1973).
          This documentary supplement presents research on legal
          education as it relates to trial practice; includes
          discussion and data on the educational impact, profes-
          sional responsibility, adequacy of student counsel,
          effects of student practice on the legal system and
          an analysis of the multiple relationships involved.
                                                       3934

STUMPF, H.P. Law and poverty: a political perspective. Wis L Rev
1968:694-733.
          Political science professor examines programs for le-
          gal services to the poor and Silverstein's Defense of
          the poor (see item 3924). Commenting on lack of issues
          raised by the inception of legal services as a com-
          ponent of the war on poverty; scant attention also has
          been given to the role of the judge in the war on pov-
          erty. The relationship of community and welfare agencies
          is also commented upon; "goal of this paper was to
          bring to the social sciences and the legal profession
          an awareness of the numerous research opportunities
          posed by the inception of the legal services program."
                                                       3935

STUMPF, H.P. and JANOWITZ, R.J. Judges and the poor. Stan L Rev
21:1058-76 (1969).

Political science professor and lawyer examine judicial
attitudes towards the philosophy and operation of the
OEO Legal Service Program in the Bay Area and find,
through interviews with local judges, that most judges
did not accept the use of legal reform to better the
economic and social situation of the poor; this negative attitude of the bench hindered legal service work.
3936

SULLIVAN, L.A. Law reform and the legal services crisis. Calif L
Rev 59:1-28 (1971).
Law professor gives details on OEO legal services programs; law reform activities; a case study of the
Housing and Economic Development Law project; evaluation from a professional perspective; legal services
under attack. Conclusion is that legal profession should
press for independence and freedom from efforts to reduce the commitment and quality of legal services leadership and administration.   3937

SYMPOSIUM: The American Bar Association and delivery of legal services. Penn B A Q 65:343-68 (1974).
Contents: Smith, C. A general overview.--Kadison, S.L.
The American Bar Association Committee on Delivery of
Legal Services.--Edley, C.F. Contributions of the organized bar.--Sutton, J.F. The code of professional
responsibility and delivery of legal services. 3938

SYMPOSIUM: The Denver public defender. Denver L J 50:1-136 (1973).
Based on study conducted at the Institute of Defense
Analyses, Arlington, Virginia for the National Institute of Law Enforcement and Criminal Justice, LEAA.
Complete study is published in IDA Study S-396 (item
3945). Articles include description of Denver Felony
Defense System, methodology, analysis and data resources;
detailed analysis of defense counsel in Denver County
and District Courts. Compares with retained counsel
in numbers and types of dispositions. Authors include
Taylor, J.G., Stanley, T.P., deFlorio, B.J. and Seekamp,
L.M. Also includes two Notes: The right to effective
counsel: a case study of the Denver Public Defender;
and Comparison of public defenders' and private attorneys' relationship with the prosecution in the city
of Denver.   3939

SYMPOSIUM: Group legal services and the availability of counsel.
UCLA L Rev 12:279-463 (1965).
Contents: Schwartz, M.L. Foreword.--Bodle, G.E. Group
legal services: the case for BRT.--Simpson, F., III.
Group legal services: the case for caution.--Christensen,
B.F. Lawyer referral service: an alternative to lay-
group legal services.--Kaufman, I.R. In defense of the

advocate.--Sparer, E.V. The role of the welfare client's
lawyer.--Carlin, J.E., Howard, J. Legal representation
and class justice.--Cheatham, E.E. Availability of
legal services: the responsibility of the individual
lawyer and the recognized bar. Bibliography.   3940

SYMPOSIUM: Justice and the poor. Notre Dame Law 41:843-960 (1966).
Partial contents: Marden, O.S. Introduction.--Bamberger,
E.C., Jr. The legal services program of the Office of
Economic Opportunity.--Bayh, B. Poverty and justice.--
Pye, A.K., Garraty, R.F., Jr. The involvement of the
bar in the war against poverty.--Pincus, W. Programs
to supplement law offices for the poor.--Broden, T.F.,
Jr. A role for law schools in OEO's Legal Services
Program.--Notre Dame Conference on Federal Civil Rights
Legislation and Administration: a report.--Cahn, E.S.,
Cahn, J.C. What price justice: the civilian perspective
revisited.--Notes: Ethical problems raised by the
neighborhood law office; Judicial safeguards on the
rights of indigent defendants; Federal Criminal Justice
Act of 1964: catalyst in the continuing formulation
of the rights of the criminal defendant.   3941

SYMPOSIUM: Right to counsel. Minn L Rev 45:691-896 (1961).
Contents: Douglas, W.O. Foreword.--Celler, E. Federal
legislative proposals to supply paid counsel to indigent persons accused of crime.--Cuff, E.E. Public defender system, Los Angeles.--Pollock, H.I. Equal justice in practice.--David, L.T. Institutional or private
counsel; judge's view of public defender system.--
Beaney, W.M. Right to consel before arraignment.--Bos-
key, B. Right to counsel in appellate proceedings.--
Kadish, S.H. The advocate and the expert: counsel in
the peno-correctional process.--McKesson, W.B. Right
to counsel in juvenile proceedings.--Rauh, J.R., Jr.,
Pollitt, D.H. Right to and nature of representation
before Congressional committees.--Gordon, C. Right
to counsel in immigration proceedings.   3942

TAXATION of court costs. Vand L Rev 17:1572-76 (1964).
Supports the proposition that the defendant found
guilty should be taxed with the costs of his trial,
but criticizes the practice of confining the defendant
who cannot pay his fines or costs, advocating instead
some kind of parole arrangement.   3943

TAYLOR, J.G., STANLEY, T.P., DEFLORIO, B.J. and SEEKAMP, L.M. Analysis of defense counsel in the processing of felony defendants in San
Diego, California. Den L J 49:233-75 (1972).
Statistical analysis of performance of appointed, retained, and "Defender, Inc." counsel in San Diego, and
interrelated factors which bear on the successful de-

fense rate concludes that only slight variations in
performance exist.   3944

TAYLOR, J.G., STANLEY, T.P., DEFLORIO, B.J. and SEEKAMP, L.M. Comparison of counsel for felony defendants, Arlington, Va., Institute
for Defense Analyses, 1972. 2 v. (Its study S-396)
        Comparative analyis of services of privately retained
        counsel, counsel appointed by bar and counsel from
        publicly supported defender agencies; felony courts
        in Denver, Colorado and San Diego, California were
        studied; disposition, sentencing and time lapse between
        arrest and final disposition were analyzed as well as
        appeal rates. Volume 1 presents major results in tabu-
        lar form with analysis; Volume 2 contains detailed re-
        ports for each city and the statistical methodology of
        the study.   3945

U. S. ATTORNEY General's Cttee on Poverty and the Administration of
Federal Criminal Justice. Poverty and the administration of federal
criminal justice. Washington, 1963. 154 p.
        Ch. 1: Scope of study and basic concepts; Ch. 2: Ade-
        quate representation [what constitutes]; Ch. 3: Bail
        and pretrial release [theory and practice in federal
        courts]; Ch. 4: Access to appellate review [federal
        practices in forma pauperis; this section reviews in
        forma pauperis procedures in Illinois, Texas, Califor-
        nia, Iowa, Missouri and under Uniform Code of Military
        Justice; also includes proposals to improve criminal
        appeals system in federal court, to insure full access
        and adequate representation] . App. 1: Report of the
        Four-District survey: California (San Francisco and
        Sacramento), Illinois, North Dakota, and Connecticut.
        App. 2: Criminal Justice Bill: text and commentary.
                                                        3946

U. S. COMPTROLLER General. The legal services program -- accomplishments of and problems face by its grantees; report to the Congress.
Washington, USGPO, 1973. 63 p.
        Analysis of the operations of seven standard grantees
        finds inadequate involvement in the goals of economic
        development and law reform, assays results in provid-
        ing quality legal services, educating target area resi-
        dents, advocacy (lobbying) for the poor. Makes recom-
        mendations for management, and discusses Wisconsin
        Judicare.   3947

U. S. CONGRESS Senate Cttee on the Judiciary Subcttee on Constitutional Rights. The Criminal Justice Act in the federal district courts,
by D.H. Oaks. Washington, USGPO, 1969. 300 p. (90th Cong., 2d sess.)
        In study commissioned by Justice Department and U.S.
        Judicial Conference law professor evaluates impact of
        the Criminal Justice Act of 1964, which provides that

financially deprived criminal defendants will be repre-
sented at every stage of federal criminal proceedings.
His findings and recommendations concerning the operation or content of the act pertain to: promulgation of
district court plans to furnish representation, defendants' eligibility, appointment and compensation of
attorneys and the public defender alternative. Appendix
contains a discussion of statistics relating to disburse-
ments and various categories of crimes in the district
courts. Index.   3948

U. S. OFFICE of Economic Opportunity. Guidelines for legal services
programs. Washington, 1967. 14 p.
Guideline examines relationship of a legal service program to community action programs: requirements for
legal services programs; characteristics and scope of
legal service programs.   3949

U. S. OFFICE of Economic Opportunity. Report ... of the Commission
on California Rural Legal Assistance. June 25, 1971. Washington,
USGPO, 1971. 88 p. + app.
Report, based on statewide hearings, of operation of
CRLA answers charges that it abuses its charter. Focuses
on CRLA priorities in taking cases, suits against the
government, relations with clients; discusses internal
administration, labor relations, and criminal work.
                                                       3950

U. S. WELFARE Administration. Neighborhood legal services: new dimensions in the law; report by J. Handler; L.W. Woods, ed. Washington,
1966. 79 p.
An examination of the philosophy, ethics, acceptance,
common problems, early achievements, and future goals
of legal service programs for the poor and a report on
the operation of four specific programs in New York,
Boston, New Haven, and Washington.   3951

VIRGINIA Advisory Legislative Council. Public defenders and related
matters; report. Richmond, 1965. 26 p.
Recommendations are aimed at improving the system of
court appointed attorneys for indigents, amending recidivist statutes, regulating professional bondsmen,
improving bail procedures including release on recognizance. Includes proposed amendments and revisions.
                                                       3952

WALD, P.M. Law and poverty, 1965, ed. by A. Chayes and R.L. Wald.
Washington, Nat Conf on Law and Poverty, 1965. 19 p.
Working paper for Conference gives overview of the legal
needs of the poor, role of the legal profession in the
War on Poverty, with recommendations for the original
OEO legal services program; includes Economic Opportun-
ity Act of 1964.   3953

WEXLER, D.B. Counseling convicts: the lawyer's role in uncovering
legitimate claims. Ariz L Rev 11:629-40 (1969).
> Legal clinics' services to prisoners are inadequate
> in uncovering bona fide legal claims; it is only by
> chance that prisoners will know of new decisions. A
> systematic approach to prisoner legal education and
> investigation of their claims is needed.   3954

WHAT costs or fees are contemplated by statutes authorizing proceedings in forma pauperis. ALR 2d:292-97 (1964).
> Annotation, confined to items normally expressed in
> money terms, such as fees, discusses in forma pauperis
> statutes and the application of these statutes in var-
> ious cases; how different provisions have had vary-
> ing results, and which items have been held not to be
> covered by statutes.   3955

WILKERSON, G. Public defenders as their clients see them. Am J Crim
L 1:141-55 (1972).
> Based on data obtained during a ten-week study of the
> public defender's office in Denver, author examines
> what the client thinks of the public defender and sug-
> gests ways to improve attorney-client relations; client
> criticisms, response of their lawyers, evaluation, and
> suggestions. Data tables.   3956

ZIEGLER, D.H. and HERMANN, M.G. The invisible litigant: an inside
view of pro se action in the federal courts. NYUL Rev 47:159-257
(1972).
> Having had five years of experience as law clerks deal-
> ing with pro se litigation, the authors give thorough
> presentation of its procedures and problems in both
> district and appellate federal court, with emphasis
> on the differences between actual practices and those
> contemplated in the rules and statutes. The authors
> discuss the general difficulties encountered by indi-
> gents in court and by habeas corpus petitioners, who
> constitute the vast majority of pro se litigants. They
> recommend fair and efficient screening of cases, a
> fair opportunity to present claims for review, and
> simplified and workable court procedures. The article
> is fully footnoted and gives numerous statistics. Ap-
> pendices provide statutes, court rules, and proposed
> forms for orders to show cause and for assignment of
> counsel.   3957

VII.   THE CRIMINAL TRIAL

    A.   The Criminal Trial Judge

        Selected items on the function of the crimi-
        nal trial judge; aspects of judicial control
        and conduct including basic duties; decorum
        in the courtroom, contempt powers; pretrial
        publicity. For trial judges' duties regard-
        ing pleas and waivers, see Section VI B, Sub-
        section 4, Plea Bargaining. For trial coverage
        by the press, see Section VII D, Fair Trial -
        Free Press. For the activist judge, see Sec-
        tion IV A, The Trial Judge.

ALSCHULER, A.W. Courtroom misconduct by prosecutors and trial judges.
Tex L Rev 50:629-735 (1972).
        Explores thoroughly and evaluates judicial, statutory
        and disciplinary remedies; gives examples of prosecu-
        torial misconduct; discusses harmless error doctrine;
        recommends remedies in trial court and on appeal against
        prosecutors and judges, supports punishment of prose-
        cutor for contempt, a remedy used more often against
        disruptive defense counsel and defendant; enumerates
        modern disciplinary procedures against judges and prob-
        lems of constitutionality in case of federal judges
        as demonstrated by Chandler; discusses also "Chicago 8"
        trial, and example of possible provocation by judge.
                                        3958

AMERICAN Bar Association Advisory Committee on the Judge's Function.
Standards relating to the function of the trial judge, recommended
by the Advisory Committee on the Judge's Function. F.J. Murray, chair.;
T.J. O'Toole, reptr. Tent. draft, June 1972. 103 p. approved, Aug.
1972. N.Y., IJA, 1972.
        Standards with commentary on aspects of judicial con-
        trol and conduct including basic duties, facilities
        and staff, pretrial duties, pleas and waivers, trial
        procedures, decorum in the courtroom, contempt power,
        sentencing and post-conviction remedies and procedures
        regarding judicial malfeasance, nonfeasance and disa-
        bility.   3959

AMERICAN Bar Association Advisory Committee on the Judge's Function.
Standards relating to the judge's role in dealing with trial disruptions [and advance report of part of Standards relating to the
function of the trial judge] recommended by the Advisory Committee
on the Judge's Function. May 1971. N.Y., IJA, 1971. 22 p. approved,
July 1971.
        Standards with commentary since integrated into report
        on Standards relating to the Function of the Trial
        Judge. N.Y., IJA, 1972.(item 3959)   3960

AMERICAN Bar Association Young Lawyers Section. A new challenge to
our court system: the spirited lawyer representing political defendants; a panel ... St. Louis, 1970. Jacksonville Beach, Fla., Thyra
D. Ellis & Assoc, 1970. 113 p.
>Transcript of panel proceedings with participants J.A.
>Ball, C.R. Garry, A.E. Jenner, W.M. Kunstler, S.H. Rif-
>kind, D.E. Santarelli and M.E. Tigar; An exchange of
>widely divergent views as to the role of the criminal
>defense lawyer vis à vis his client, the court, the
>judicial system and socity.   **3961**

AMERICAN College of Trial Lawyers Committee on Disruption of the Judicial Process. Report and recommendations on disruption of the judicial process. N.Y., IJA, 1970. 23 p.
>Principles to be applied, with commentary; standards
>affect the trial counsel (prosecutor and defense) and
>the court (defining contempt). Sanctions include termi-
>nation of attorney's right to continue as counsel, and
>suspension for six months. Admission pro hac vice to
>be carefully supervised.   **3962**

AMERICAN College of Trial Lawyers Report and recommendations on disruption of the judicial process. Catholic Law 16:242-56 (1970).
>Recommendations made by the College were meant to pre-
>vent the willful use of disruptive courtroom tactics,
>as these tactics demean the judicial system and obstruct
>justice. The authors point out the need for order so
>that all issues may be decided on their merits alone.
>   **3963**

AMERICAN Judicature Society. Mass trials: courtroom disruption and
the rights of defendants, by S.D. White. Chicago, 1971. 5 p.
>Summary of articles and cases which explore problems
>and suggest solutions.   **3964**

ASSOCIATION OF THE Bar of the City of New York Special Committee on
Courtroom Conduct. Disorder in the court, by N. Dorsen and L. Friedman. New York, Pantheon, 1973. 432 p.
>Comprehensive analysis of courtroom disruption in his-
>torical context finds no serious quantitative problem.
>Discusses scope of problem, history, recent examples
>in detail. Recommends remedies for regulating defendants,
>prosecutors, and defense counsel, discusses responsibil-
>ity of the judge, and the contempt power, recommends
>that summary contempt be abolished. Full statistical
>report on questionnaire surveys of trial judges, attor-
>neys general, bar association presidents, prosecutors.
>Table of state laws governing courtroom misconduct.
>Selected bibliography on courtroom disorder, p. 383-
>88.   **3965**

BELL D.A., Jr. Racism in American courts: cause for black disruption
or despair? Calif L Rev 61:165-203 (1973).

Examines motivation of defendant of the courts in
Illinois v Allen; thesis is that there are a limited
number of disruptive trials and that blacks constitute
a minute percentage of such defendants; gives statistics; reviews various studies of crime, race and racism to posit the disadvantages of blacks in and out
of the courts, throughout the entire court process.
Refers also to studies that dispute findings of racial
bias in courts; goes on to discuss effect of racism
on law students and lawyers; richly footnoted.   3966

BRAUTIGAM, R.C. Constitutional challenges to the contempt power.
Geo L J 60:1513-36 (1972).
Author examines the validity of the contempt power,
civil and criminal, pointing out that often it is used
although more moderate alternatives exist. He considers
statutes that create contempt power but are vague and
fail to define contemptuous conduct, making them possibly unconstitutional: he proposes a contempt statute
that would be constitutional.   3967

BRENNAN, W.J., Jr. The judge's supervisory role. Amer Crim L Q 2:
53-62 (1964).
Pointing to the reforms in the administration of civil
justice, Justice Brennan expresses the hope that similar attention will be given to reform of criminal procedure. He stresses the importance of judicial supervision of the administration of bail, the appointment
of counsel, parole conditions, and the protection of
federal constitutional rights, and gives criteria for
an adequate system of post-conviction review.   3968

BURGER, W.E. Address to the American Law Institute. Wash, D.C.
May 19, 1970. In ALI Ann proc 47:24-28 (1970).
Discusses, among other things, courtroom disruption.
                                                 3969

CHEVIGNY, P. Cops and rebels: a study of provocation. N.Y., Pantheon, 1972.
Trial of young Black Panthers for weapons possession
and conspiracy to armed robbery and murder involved
an agent provocateur. Author, counsel of one of defendants, describes events and politics behind the arrest
and trial, gives history of provocation. Makes recommendations for control of this practice and broadening
of defendant's discovery rights to remedy official un-
lawfulness.   3970

CLAVIR, J. and SPITZER, J. eds. The conspiracy trial. Indianapolis,
Bobbs-Merrill, 1970. 615 p.
Trial transcript of the Chicago conspiracy trial; fore-

word by L.I. Weinglass, intro. by W.M. Kunstler. Includes the indictment, legal cites and contempt proceedings.   3971

COHEN, N.M. The contempt power -- the lifeblood of the judiciary.
Loyola U L J 2:69-108 (1971).
          Judge uses cases, statutory law and common practices
          in an examination of the contempt power; its history,
          various types of contempt, sanctions available, rights
          of the person cited for contempt, and the need for the
          contempt power in an orderly system of law and justice.
                                                     3972

COHEN, N.P. Trial in absentia re-examined. Tenn L Rev 40:155-93
(1973).
          Law professor discusses federal and state rules and
          cases dealing with necessity of defendant's presence
          at criminal trial, with a comparison of procedures in
          England and France; the history and constitutional bases
          are detailed, followed by a presentation of argument
          for and against requiring the presence. Author suggests
          procedural safeguards for waiver, comment by counsel
          on absence, jury instructions as to absence.   3973

CONNER, L.L. The demeanor of a trial judge: its effect on justice.
Am Crim L Q 6:175-86 (1968); Case & Comment 76:13-24 (July/Aug. 1971).
          Discusses the importance of the image the trial judge
          creates by actions, general demeanor and remarks, so
          as not to prejudice the case, or lessen the average
          citizen's respect for the law.   3974

CONTEMPT powers of the Arizona courts. Ariz L Rev 8:141-48 (1966).
          Examines nature and extent of the contempt powers and
          the types of conduct to which it may be applied, based
          on a consideration of Arizona's statutes and case law.
                                                     3975

CONTEMPT, transcript of the contempt citations, sentences, and responses of the Chicago Conspiracy 10. Chicago, Swallow, 1970. 254 p.
          With a preface by R. Clark and introduction by H. Kalven,
          Jr., on Confrontation and contempt, this record includes
          the testimony of defendants.   3976

CONTROLLING lawyers by bar associations and courts. Harv Civil Rights
L Rev 6:301-42 (1970).
          1. Bar associations and radical lawyers: the politics
          of ethics. 2. The Bar as trade association: economics,
          ethics and the First Amendment. 3. The contempt weapon
          against lawyers in court.   3977

COURTROOM restraint of the criminal defendant. Baylor L Rev 25:147-
155 (1973).

Considers problems encountered in Texas in an appeal
on the grounds of improper restraint. Describes the
uncertainty about the meaning of "exceptional circumstances" which justify restraint, about what constitutes prejudice in the minds of the jury, and about
the burden and standard of proof. Recommends that the
court set guidelines on these matters.   3978

DISRUPTION, discipline and due process. Summary of Symposium [held
by American Bar Association, 1971] Human Rights (ABA, Section on
Individual Rights and Responsibilities) 1:132-58 (July 1971).
          Participants: Leonard B. Boudin and Judge Frank J.
          Murray ; commentators are Charles R. Garry, Charles
          Morgan Jr. and Sir Dennis Buckley. An exchange of views
          touching upon the trial of the Chicago Seven, the be-
          havior of trial judges, prosecutors and defense attor-
          neys, the American College of Trial Lawyers' statement
          on disruption of the judicial process, and the nature
          and purpose of a criminal trial. Bibliography.   3979

DISRUPTIVE defendants and prejudice-prone jurors: toward an implied
waiver of trial by jury? Dick L Rev 75:572-84 (1971).
          Comment examines the problem of coping with disruptive
          defendants, existing solutions, and new alternative
          of implied waiver approach to the right to trial by
          jury. Discussed are: defendant's constitutional right
          to be present at trial, right to a speedy trial, right
          to be free of double jeopardy, and right to a public
          trial; and the constitutionality of author's implied
          waiver approach.   3980

DOBBS, D.B. Contempt of court: a survey. Cornell L Rev 56:183-284
(1971).
          Discusses the acts and persons subject to contempt;
          civil and criminal contempt; intent requirements and
          sanctions. Notes the general confusion from unclear
          precedent and undefined offenses such as misconduct,
          and recommends reform for clarification, and attempt
          to use alternate remedies to narrow the scope of the
          contempt power.   3981

DORSEN, N. and FRIEDMAN, L. Civil courts, civilized justice. Trial
10;38-39, 42, 46-47 (July/Aug. 1974).
          Authors discuss the nature of disorderly political and
          criminal trials: types of disorderly conduct of defend-
          ants, lawyers, prosecutors, and judges, and appropriate
          preventive and remedial measures; the contempt power;
          and the integrity of the courtroom.   3982

DUNAHOO, K.L. The scope of judicial discretion in the Iowa criminal
trial process. Iowa L Rev 58:1023-1131 (1973).
          Prosecutor reviews and analyzes the use of judicial
          discretion in the conduct of a criminal case from pre-

trial through sentence and appeal. Every step in the
process of a case involving the trial judge's discretion is precisely examined. Author finds individualized justice has merit; that discretion is seldom
abused and elimination of discretionary power is un-
desirable.   3983

EPSTEIN, J. The Great conspiracy trial: an essay on law, liberty
and the constitution. N.Y., Random House, 1970. 433 p.
          Narrative and political commentary on the Chicago con-
          spiracy trial.   3984

EPTING, R.L. Dealing with unruly persons in the courtroom. Crim
L Bull 6:473-90 (1970).
          Author examines the history, statutes, and cases in
          which contemptuous courtroom conduct has been treated
          and finds that the methods used, such as physical re-
          straint, armed guards in the courtroom, removal of de-
          fendant or spectator from the courtroom, and criminal
          contempt, are sufficient to handle the problem. 3985

ERICKSON, W.H. How can trial disruptions be cured? Penn BA Q 40:
15-22 (1972).
          Colorado Supreme Court justice presents ABA Rules of
          Professional Responsibility and discusses ABA Standards
          relating to responsibility of judge, prosecutor, de-
          fense counsel. Recommendations of ABA in response to
          specific problems are noted. See author's How can trial
          disruption be curbed, in Judicature 56:75-77 (1972).
                                                        3986

EXCLUDING the unruly defendant. U Colo L Rev 42:485-94 (1971).
          Comment examines Illinois v Allen, 397 US 337 (1970),
          where the court denied defendant's writ of habeas cor-
          pus on the issue of whether the removal of a disruptive
          defendant from the courtroom violated his Sixth Amend-
          ment right to confront the witness. Discussed are: His-
          torical perspective of the right to confrontation and
          waiver; the need for standards of exclusion, warnings
          and readmission; the right to act as one's own counsel;
          and appellate review of the trial court's decision to
          exclude defendant.   3987

EXCLUSION from the trial as controlling defendant misbehavior: an
alternative approach. U Ill L F 1970:273-88.
          Comment considers the importance of an orderly trial,
          and the problem of the unruly defendant when the con-
          tempt power of the court is ineffective. Examined are:
          upholding of trial court's decision to remove defend-
          ant in Allen; the conflict between exclusion and de-
          fendant's right of confrontation; historical perspec-
          tives of this problem; and alternatives, such as hold-

ing a hearing apart from jury in which defendant is
advised of pending exclusion if he continues his disruptive behavior, postponement of trial, and removing
defendant to a special area where he can view the proceedings through use of electronic recording.   3988

FALCO, J.E. Federal criminal contempts and the proposed new federal
criminal code. Am Crim L Rev 11:429-65 (1973).
          U.S. Justice Dept. Attorney criticizes proposals of
          the National Commission on Reform of the Federal Crimi-
          nal Laws for revamping federal contempt laws. He finds
          that no reasons are given for vast removal of judicial
          discretion, confusing sentencing procedure and a large
          loophope for corporate defendants.   3989

FLAUM, J.M. and THOMPSON, J.R. The case of the disruptive defendant:
Illinois v Allen. J Crim L 61:327-38 (1970).
          Analysis of case and Supreme Court's holding; discusses
          former cases in point to prove "long recognized and
          respected precedent did exist."   3990

FORTAS, A. Concerning dissent and civil disobedience. N.Y., New
American library, 1968. 64 p.
          Former Supreme Court Justice defines and explains the
          basic principles and limits of lawful dissent and civil
          disobedience as an alternative to violence.   3991

FREUND, P. Contempt of court. Human Rights 1:4-9 (1970).
          Reflections on contempt, outbursts in court. Suggests
          that the judge's main weapon is his moral authority,
          and indicates the limits of other means of keeping
          order.   3992

FREUND, P. Contempt power: prevention, not retribution. Cong Rec
117:5395-96 (1971).
          Author criticizes those, both attorneys and clients,
          who would turn the nature of a trial from a reasoned
          search for truth into a trial of antics, and states that
          of the three types of contempt (that occurring outside
          of judge's presence, disobedience of an order, and mis-
          behavior in the courtroom) the need for the contempt
          power is greater in the last. The contempt power is
          to be used for prevention, not retribution. The best
          "cures" for the problem of courtroom disruption are
          expiation, mediation, and education.   3993

FRIEDMAN, L. Political power and legal legitimacy, a short history
of political trials. Antioch Rev 30:157-70 (1970).
          Describes types of trial that may come under rubric
          "political trials" and gives details of specific "pol-
          itical" trials; discusses tactics used in Chicago Con-
          spiracy and New York Black Panther trials.   3994

784   ADMINISTRATION OF CRIMINAL JUSTICE

FULD, S.H. The right to dissent: protest in the courtroom. St. John's L Rev 44:591-96 (1970).
> Chief Judge, New York state, finds dissent which violates the rules of law transcends the bounds of constitutionally protected rights, especially in a court of law guaranteeing a fair trial. To find an appropriate solution to the problem of courtroom disruption he is asking the presiding Justices of the Appellate Divisions to join with him in establishing guidelines assuring a fair trial and courtroom decorum.   3995

GOLDFARB, R.L. The contempt power. Garden City, N.Y., Anchor, 1971. 322 p.
> Analysis of the purposes and procedures of this amorphous set of summary sanctions for interference with the operations of the legislature, administrative agencies and the judiciary by examination of the history, varities and extension of the contempt power. Extensive discusssion of its limits, especially constitutional protections and proposals for reform. Bibliography.   3996

GOLDSTEIN, H. Trial judges and the police. Crime & Delin 14:14-25 (1968).
> Expounds on improving relationships with police yet safeguarding judicial neutrality; offers advice on what trial judge should do in scheduling court business, and controlling police practices under "exclusionary rule" and review of police policies. Suggests written comment to police.   3997

HAZARD, G.C., Jr. Securing courtroom decorum. Yale L J 80:433-50 (1971).
> Critique of American College of Trial Lawyers Report and recommendations on the disruption of the judicial process (item 3962), and the American Bar Association's Standards relating to the function of a trial judge. (Preliminary report)   (see item 3960)   3998

HELWIG, G.J. Coping with the unruly criminal defendant; options of the Allen case. Gonzaga L Rev 7:17-33 (1971).
> Author discusses the three constitutionally permissible methods for a judge to handle an unruly defendant as outlined in the Illinois v Allen case: (1) physical restraint, (2) removal of defendant from courtroom until he promises to behave, and (3) citing the defendant for contempt.   3999

HOMAN, F.J., Jr. Abuse of attorneys by judges. Cleve Mar L Rev 14; 79-93 (1965).
> Discusses cases in which judges abused lawyers, abuse as grounds for appeal, and the judge's power of con-

tempt; offers solutions for curbing judicial abuse including judicial power to discipline and the ABA Canons
of Ethics.   **4000**

HUGHES, G. In defense of disruption. Antioch Rev 30:171-76 (1970).
Presents a moral argument for selective courtroom disruption for those defendants who believe that the court
as an institution is discriminating against them.**4001**

ILLINOIS v Allen, 397 US 337 (1970). U Cin L Rev 39:350-56 (1970).
An accused who persists in disorderly, disruptive and
disrespectful conduct may be held, after due warning,
to have waived his right to be present in the courtroom; contempt powers of trial judge discussed. See
also Mayberry v Pennsylvania, 400 US 455 (1971) in
which the U.S. Supreme Court recommends contempt procedures to be employed by trial judge in face of disruption.   **4002**

ILLINOIS v Allen: expulsion and the disruptive defendant. Calif
Western L Rev 7:286-300 (1970).
Note examines Allen and discusses inadequacies of pre-
Allen discretionary powers in preserving court room
order; also the need for effective judicial guidelines
as disruptive behavior increased in the 1970's, and
the logical use of the expulsionary sanction. The right
of the defendant to be present at trial is a relative
right to the extent that it is a denial of due process
only if defendant's absence would prevent a fair and
just hearing.   **4003**

ILLINOIS v Allen: the unruly defendant's right to a fair trial. NYU
L Rev 46:120-63 (1971).
Posits that the history of confrontation leads inevi-
tably to the Allen opinions; critically analyzes the
Allen test for actionable misbehavior; discusses civil
and criminal contempt on part of party, also of lawyers,
codefendants, spectators.   **4004**

KALVEN, H. Jr. Confrontation comes to the courtroom. Human Rights
1:10-23 (1970).
Professor discusses the concept of the political trial,
compares Scope's defense plan of appealing to the public over the heads of jury and court, with the events
of the Chicago conspiracy trial. Finds that the Chicago
defense team did not coordinate strategy to the same
end. Discussion of conduct and political issues, and
tactics, in trials.   **4005**

KALVEN, H., Jr. "Please, Morris, don't make trouble;" two lessons
in courtroom confrontation. J Social Issues 27:219-30 (1971).
Law Professor explores current challenges to courtroom

decorum, looking in detail at the Scopes trial (1925)
and the Chicago Conspiracy trial before Judge Hoffman
(1970), and assesses the future of trial process in
the face of contemporary styles of protest.   4006

KARLEN, D.   Disorder in the courtroom.   S Cal L Rev 44:996-1035 (1971).
General discussion of courtroom disruption, possible
sanctions, and the duties of lawyers and judges. Appendix: "Principles as to disruption of the judicial
process of the American College of Trial Lawyers."
                                                   4007

KRAUSKOPF, J.M.   Physical restraint of the defendant in the courtroom.
St. Louis U L J 15:351-73 (1971).
Author explores early British and American history in
discussing the right of the prisoner to be unfettered
in the courtroom. The author feels that even light-
weight handcuffs can interfere with free communication
with counsel, prejudice the jury, and detract from the
dignity of the courtroom; the only justification for
the use of physical restraint is threat of either es-
cape or disruption, and it is the burden of the state
to prove that such threat exists.   4008

KUTNER, L.   Contempt power: the black robe; a proposal for due process.   Tenn L Rev 39:1-72 (1971).
General discussion of the contempt power, civil and
criminal, contempt by publication, and consistency with
civil liberties. Author discusses wide range of activities subject to contempt rulings, and concludes that
a study commission is necessary.   4009

LAFAVE, W.R. and REMINGTON, F.J.   Controlling the police: the judge's
role in making and reviewing law enforcement dicisions.   Mich L Rev
63:987-1012 (1965); summarized in Trial Judges' J 5: 14 (Oct. 1966).
What trial and appellate judges can do to more effectively control police decisions. On the appellate side,
courts should insist on maximum judicial participation
in the decision to issue process and on the exclusionary rule; on the trial level, court should make more
meaningful decisions in hearings to suppress evidence
which have an impact on police policies.   4010

LAUB, B.   The problem of the unrepresented, misrepresented and rebel-
lious defendant in criminal court.   Duquesne L Rev 2:245-59 (1964).
Discussion of trial judge's problems in presiding over
a trial disrupted by an unrepresented or misrepresented
defendant who is ignorant of the law, refuses to follow
the normal procedure, or chooses to disrupt the trial,
as in Dennis. Argues for limited appellate review of
trial judge's rulings.   4011

LUCAS, J. The barnyard epithet and other obscenities; notes on the
Chicago conspiracy trial. N.Y., Harper & Row, 1970. 107 p.
  A New York Times reporter's report, sometimes verbatim,
  of disruptive episodes on the part of parties, lawyers,
  the judges.   4012

MAINTENANCE of courtroom decorum. Harv L Rev 84:90-100 (1970).
  Criticizes the Supreme Court decision in Illinois v
  Allen for leaving too much to the discretion of the
  trial judge and not setting guidelines for the use of
  the sanctions it authorizes judges to use.   4013

MIDDLEBROOKS, D.M. Disruption in the courtroom. U Fla L Rev 23:560-
89 (1971).
  Note examines the legal and philoposhical issues involved in courtroom disruptions, criticizes present
  methods of dealing with the problem, and concludes that
  order and decorum in the courtroom cannot become an
  isolated goal; the damage done to the judicial system
  in loss of respect may be greater than the problem itself.   4014

MISCONDUCT of judges and attorneys during trial: informal sanctions.
Ia L Rev 49:531-51 (1964).
  All of the injunctions offered in this note apply in
  both civil and criminal cases. As to the lawyer, ob-
  jectionable conduct is defined, sanctions, including
  reprimand and contempt, are discusses. As to judges,
  unjudicial types of conduct are named and various sanctions as exercised in a number of states are reviewed.
  These are not removal procedures but are in effect
  "intermediary" discipline.   4015

MURRAY, D.E. Power to expel a criminal defendant from his own trial,
a comparative view. U Colo L Rev 36:171-86 (1964).
  Examines laws of U.S., England, South Africa, Spain,
  West Germany, Italy and France and finds all provide
  for the right to be present at trial and the power of
  the judge to remove a defendant for voluntary acts of
  disrupting misconduct.   4016

MURRAY, F.J. ABA Standards; the judges' function report. Penn BA Q
40:7-14 (1972).
  U.S.D.C., Massachusetts, judge, chair of ABA Advisory
  Committee on Judges' Function, discusses preliminary
  reports and details of final report. (see item 3959)
                                                         4017

NEW YORK (State) Supreme Court Appellate Div., First Dept. Special
rules concerning court decorum; Part 609, effective March 24, 1971.
N.Y., 1971. 15 p.

Rules 609.1-609.4 cover obligations of judges and attorneys, judicial exercise of contempt power, disqualifi-
cation of judge, disruptive conduct, restraint of defendant, discipline of attorneys, other sanctions.
                                                    4018

NEW YORK (State) Supreme Court Appellate Div., First and Second Judicial Depts. Departmental Committees for Court Administration Joint
Subcommittee on Court Decorum and Allied Problems. Report of the
subcommittee on security in the courts of New York City. July 15,
1971. N.Y., 1971. 29 + p.
          Text of special rules concerning court decorum empha-
          sizes the importance of decorum in the courtroom; de-
          fines disruptive conduct and the obligations of attorney
          and judge; and sets standards for the judicial exercise
          of contempt power, judges' disqualification, judicial
          handling of the disruptive criminal defendant, and
          discipline of attorneys.   4019

O'DONNELL, W.J. Common errors in criminal trials; rulings by trial
judge out of presence of jury. Annapolis, Admin Off of the Courts,
1972. 56 p.
          Discusses, through specific cases, erroneous rulings
          of judges out of the presence of jury regarding con-
          fessions, identifications, legality of search warrants
          and arrests.   4020

SCHWARTZ, H. Judges as tyrants. Crim L Bull 7:129-138 (1971).
          Law professor examines problem of dictatorial and biased
          trial judges who abuse their power, with special em-
          phasis given Judge Hoffman in the Chicago Conspiracy
          Trial; discusses the bar's indifference to judicial
          abuse in political trials and how judicial abuse and
          disruptive defendant behavior feed one another. 4021

SIXTH Amendment confrontation clause - right of defendant to be present at criminal trial. Ky L J 59:489-97 (1970/71).
          An examination of cases that consider the problem of
          a defendant's disruptive behavior in the courtroom,
          particularly Illinois v Allen 397 US 337 (1970) which
          held that a defendant's continued disruption of court
          proceedings constitutes a voluntary waiver of his right
          to be present at trial.   4022

SPECIAL Project: Judicial response to the disruptive defendant. Geo
L J 60:487-503 (1971).
          Suggests restriction of the contempt sanction to de-
          fendant conduct which actually obstructs trial, and
          series of other graduated remedies and sanctions, in-
          cluding warnings, presence of guards; incarceration
          and removal.   4023

Symposium: Disruption in our courts: why. Trial 7:12-34 (Jan./Feb. 1971).

> Freund, P. Contempt power: prevention, not retribution.--Littlejohn, B. Legal vandalism.--Rowland, H.H. The crucial code.--Garry, C.R. Who's an officer of the court?--Koskoff, T.I. Quest for a fair trial.--Rothblatt, H.B. Prejudicial conduct.--Newman, J.O. Is the problem simple?--American College of Trial Lawyers Principles concerning trial disruption.--Kodas, M.L. The American Trial Lawyers Association: its argument.
>
> 4024

TALES of Hoffman, edited from the original transcript by M.L. Levine, G.C. McNamee, and D. Greenberg. N.Y., Bantam, 1970. 312 p.

> Excerpts from the 22,000 page transcript of the Chicago 7 conspiracy trial in which defendants were charged with conspiring to encourage riots at the August 1968 Democratic National Convention.
>
> 4025

THOMPSON, J.R. and STARKMAN, G.L. Multiple petty contempts and the guarantee of trial by jury. Geo L J 61:621-54 (1973).

> Arguing from a basically anti-jury perspective, U.S. Attorney and Assistant U.S. Attorney state that aggregation of multiple petty offenses is contrary to the language and policy of the federal statute, and that trial by disinterested judge provides sufficient safeguard and insures the swift remedy necessary to effect courtroom control by the contempt power.
>
> 4026

THREE constitutionally permissible ways for trial judges to handle unruly defendants. U Kan L Rev 19:305-16 (1971).

> Note examines the Allen case, where unruly defendant after repeated warnings was expelled from the courtroom, gives history of appeals, culminating with the Supreme Court upholding the trial court's action; criticizes the three alternatives (expulsion, restraint, and criminal contempt) suggested by the Supreme Court in Allen. Author concludes that the best way to deal with the problem is through the use of civil contempt powers of the judge.
>
> 4027

VIOLENT misconduct in the courtroom--physical restraint and eviction of the criminal defendant. U of Pitt L Rev 28:443-457 (1967).

> Concludes that where the contempt power proves to be an insufficient remedy, eviction of a defendant from the courtroom, or restraint of a defendant are permissible under the present law; eviction is preferable to restriction in front of the jury.
>
> 4028

WRIGHT, E.A. Courtroom decorum and the trial process. Judicature 51:378-82 (1968).

> Former judge discusses the importance to decorum of a

respectful atmosphere in court, formal opening cere-
monies, judicial robes, the judge being abreast of
what is on the day's calendar, and an orderly trial.
4029

B. The Jury in the Criminal Trial

See Section IV B, The Petit Jury.

C. The Witness

Items are limited to protection of material
witnesses, government witnesses; immunity
statutes, privilege against self-incrimination, pretrial detention, spouse as witness; there is a small number of items on
care, comfort, compensation.

ASH, M. On witnesses: a radical critique of criminal court procedures. Notre Dame Law 48:386-425 (1972); condensed in National Symposium on Law Enforcement Science and Technology, 4th, 1972. Reducing court delay. Washington, USGPO, 1973. P. 1-34. (Title: Court
delay, crime, control, and neglect of the interests of witnesses)
        Author examines procedures for handling witnesses in
        criminal court and finds that they are still subjected
        to unnecessary discomfort, apprehension, frustration,
        and expense. Author finds subject still neglected de-
        spite alerting by A.T. Vanderbilt and F.J. Klein in
        1949, 1954; suggests that research be undertaken re-
        garding witness' appearances, costs, attitudes, disaf-
        fection, perspective, and public attitude, and also
        suggests some specific proposals for improvement.4030

AVINS, A. Right to be a witness and the fourteenth amendment. Mo
L Rev 31:471-504 (1966).
        Law professor, stating that the right to testify largely
        shaped the original conception of the Equal Protection
        Clause, examines that right; pre-14th Amendment ex-
        clusion of negro witnesses, denial of protection to
        slaves, statutory regulations granting the right to
        testify to negroes, and the effect of the 14th Amend-
        ment.   4031

BROOKS, A.D. Treatment of witnesses in the proposed rules of evidence for the United States district courts: article IV. Record 25:
632-47 (1970).
        Law professor examines various proposed rules of evi-
        dence pertaining to competence to testify and impeach-
        ment of witnesses.   4032

CARLSON, R.L. Jailing the innocent: the plight of the material witness. Ia L Rev 55:1-25 (1969); also Crim L Bull 6:115-141 (1970).

Law professor explores the current status of the "material witness" laws and confinement and analyzes the necessity for and constitutionality of such provisions. Author concludes that their constitutionality is doubtful. Appendix: relative statutes in the states. 4033

COMPETENCY of spouses to testify against each other in criminal trial -- compelling the spouse to testify. SC L Rev 16:615-33 (1964). Comment discusses whether a spouse can be compelled to testify against spouse, focusing on a recent case, State v Antin, 197 NE2d 548 (1964), holding that spouse can be compelled to do so. Comment examines the development of this area of law: the situation at common law; statutory changes; South Carolina and federal court practices; and cases which have compelled spouses to testify. Author concludes that there is no justification for holding otherwise. 4034

CONFINING material witnesses in criminal cases. Wash & Lee L Rev 20: 164-68 (1963). Comment discusses Quince v State, 179 A2d 485 (R.I. 1962), regarding the rights of material witnesses. In this case, two witnesses were confined at excessive bond for an excessive period of time, and later successfully filed suit against the state and received monetary damages. Comment examines the statutes under which petitioners were confined, the right to counsel in this instance, and the right to a judicial hearing to determine a witness' materiality and character before confinement. 4035

CONFRONTATION of witnesses: witness' repeated claim of fifth amendment privilege in presence of jury denied defendant's sixth amendment right to confront witness. Wash L Rev 44:474-80 (1969). Article analyzes State v Nelson, 72 Wash Dec2d 269 (1967), in which the court held that witness' continued refusal to answer gave rise to incriminating inferences not subject to cross-examination, thus abridging defendant's constitutional right to confrontation; historical perspective of the privilege against self-incrimination, prosecution misconduct, and a criticism of the opinion included. 4036

CONFRONTATION: prior testimony, confessions and the sixth amendment. Tenn L Rev 36:382-99 (1969). Comment analyzes new constitutional limitations upon the state's use of former testimony and confessions of a co-defendant witness as exemplified in Bruton v US, 88 SCt 1620 (1968), and Barber v Page, 88 SCt 1318 (1968), and evaluates their application in lower courts in subsequent cases. 4037

CONSTITUTIONAL rights of witnesses in federal grand jury proceedings: Bursey v United States (466 F2d 1059). U Pa L Rev 121:900-20 (1973). Analysis of opinion providing procedural and substantive constitutional safeguards for witnesses in federal grand jury proceedings; its probable effect on future proceedings.   4038

EXERCISE of the privilege against self-incrimination by witnesses and codefendants: the effect upon the accused. U Chi L Rev 33:151-65 (1965).
        Discussion of problems and effect of allowing a witness or a codefendant to refuse to answer questions and the cases, Namet v US, 373 US 179 (1963) and DeLuna v US, 308 F2d 140 (1962), rehearing denied 324 F2d 375 (1963).   4039

EXTENSION of the fifth amendment right against self-incrimination. BU L Rev 52:149-68 (1972).
        Case comment analyzes Bowles v US, 439 F2d 536 (D.C. Cir., 1970); the court's decision, permissibility of a jural inference based on a witness' invocation of his Fifth Amendment privilege, constitutional issues, probative value and dangers of inference, and the right to have a witness appear before the jury even if he has told the judge he plans to invoke this privilege. Author concludes that the decision has extended the rule that no inference may be drawn from invocation by a witness of his privilege.   4040

EXTENT of the government's informer privilege in federal and Florida criminal cases. U Fla L Rev 21:218-228 (1968).
        Note examines exceptions to the informer privilege in the federal and Florida courts, including: nature of the privilege; extent of privilege relative to the issue of guilt; and extent of privilege in establishing probable cause for search or arrest. Author concludes that the privilege is necessary for controlling crime, but must be closely supervised in order to protect the defendant; the burden of proving that the privilege should be invoked must be placed on the state.   4041

FEDERAL immunity statutes: problems and proposals. Geo Wash L Rev 37:1276-92 (1969).
        Editorial note examines the incongruities in the federal investigatory process caused by the numerous disuniform immunity statutes. Reviewed are: automatic and claim statutes; frustration of inter-agency functions; application and scope of immunity; and the advantages of a uniform statute. Appendix of statutes.   4042

FEDERAL witness immunity acts in theory and practice: treading the
Constitutional tightrope. Yale L J 72:1568-1612 (1963).
>Comment explores the conflict between the Act, grant-
ing power to compel residents to testify, and the privilege against self-incrimination; historical perspective,
and the role of immunity and how it can and has been
used. Author feels that immunity can serve a useful
function, but that value of the information that may
be received must be weighed against the value of the
sanction, whose use is likely to be foreclosed. Appendix of federal witness immunity acts.   4043

HUNTER, R.L.C. Imputations on the character of prosecution witnesses.
Jurid Rev 1968:238-53.
>Author looks at British statute providing that the
accused taking the stand as a witness should not be
required to answer questions impugning his character,
as applied in Scotland and in England following the
interpretation of that statute in Selvey v DPP 2 All ER
497 (1968). Discussed are the Selvey dicision, historical perspective, other interpretations of the Act,
and the need for further guidance as to its meaning.
                                                4044

INDIGENT'S right to pre-trial technical assistance - People v Watson
and the discretionary approach. Idaho L Rev 8:188-93 (1971).
>Article examines People v Watson, 36 Il12d 228 (1966),
in which Illinois Supreme Court held that in a non-
capital case (forgery) where an expert witness was necessary to enable court appointed counsel to establish a
defense, the state must provide the witness. Discussed
are: constitutionally required appointment of witnesses
and appeal to the trial judge's discretion where appointment of witnesses is not constitutionally required.
                                                4045

INFORMER privilege: What's in a name? J Crim L 64:56-66 (1973).
>Comment argues for rejection of absolute disclosure
and a return to the Roviaro v US, 353 US 53 (1957),
test that defendant is entitled to the identity and
contents of communication of an out-of-court informer
only when it is necessary to a fair determination of
the case. Included are: history of the privilege of
the government informer, examination of the development
and present status of the law, and competing interests
involved.   4046

MARSHALL, J., MARQUIS, K.H. and OSKAMP, S. Effects of kind of question and atmosphere of interrogation on accuracy and completeness of
testimony. Harv L Rev 84:1620-43 (1971).
>Lawyer, sociologist and psychologist present the re-
sults of an experiment measuring the effects of various

means of interrogation on the quality of courtroom
testimony; witness' bias shown, time lapse, stress,
supportive v. challenging atmosphere, changes in testimony, and the limitations of this experiment. Authors propose that the legal profession consider the
use of multiple interrogatories, given before trial,
as the most efficient form of interrogation. Tables.

4047

NEW YORK (State) Supreme Court, Appellate Division, 1st and 2d Depts.
Subcommittee on the Rights of the Complainant. The plight of the
complaining witness -- property in police custody. N.Y., 1973. 22 p.
Report explores problems in retrieving property after
final disposition of the case; recommendations include
creation of new uniform procedures to be promulgated
by the District Attorneys' Offices and by amendment to
the Administrative Code of New York City; appendices
include staff report on subject and recent court cases
relating to the power of the police property clerk.

4048

NEWARK, M. and SAMUELS, A. Let the judge call the witness. Crim L
R 1969:399-406 (1969).
English law lecturers examine the judge's power to call
a witness and the procedure that should be followed
when he does. Authors feel that this power should be
exercised with caution and discretion, but should be
used when necessary to the fair outcome of trial.4049

ORFIELD, L.B. Examination of witnesses in federal criminal cases.
Ariz L Rev 4:215-53 (1963).
Law professor examines the general rules and ethics of
examination of witnesses in federal criminal court
cases, and relevant cases including interviews before
trial; need to take oath; interpreters; sequestration;
presentation and seating of defendant; use of free
narrative; leading questions; calling and examination
of witnesses by the judge; recollection; cross and re-
direct examination; rebuttal evidence; recall of witnesses; and re-opening the case.   4050

PHILLIPS, J.J. Comparative study of the witness rules in the proposed federal rules of evidence and in Tennessee law. Tenn L Rev
39:379-406 (1972).
Law professor looks at Article 6 of the proposed federal Rules of Evidence, dealing with the competence,
qualification, and interrogation of witnesses, and
explains how it differs from common law practice, especially in Tennessee. Author concludes that the new
Rules are substantially more liberal than Tennessee
rules.   4051

POLICE coercion of witnesses. Wash U L Q 1973:865-88 (1973).
Note examines the conventional approach to the issue
of a defendant ability to assert the constitutional
rights of a coerced witness: standing and the exclusionary rules; third party standing and the Fourth
and Fifth Amendments; exclusion of witness' testimony
in joint trials; concept of denial of fair trial; relevant cases. To date, defendants have had little success
in excluding testimony of a coerced witness, despite
the fact that the exclusionary rule was intended to
prevent such injustice.   4052

PRE-TRIAL detention of witnesses. U Pa L Rev 117:700-34 (1969).
Comment considers the restriction on individual liberty
caused by pretrial detention of witnesses, finding this
procedure to be unneccessary, ineffective, unconstitutional and that there are other methods that better
strike the necessary balance between the rights of the
state, the defendant, and the witness. Examined are
duty to testify, federal and state statutes, constitutional questions, abuse of detention, and alternatives.   4053

RAFALKO, W.A. Duty of absent witness to return and testify in the
forum state. Washburn L. J 5:9-28 (1965).
Law professor examines federal, state, and international methods of imposing a duty upon unwilling witness
to return or be brought back in light of procedural
problems inherent in the territorial concept of sover-
eignty. Also discussed are possible sanctions for refusal.   4054

REQUIRING witnesses to repeat themselves. Tex L Rev 47:266-74 (1969).
Comment examines the right of a witness who gives incriminating evidence at one step of a criminal proceeding, and later asserts his privilege against self-incrimination. How can the individual's constitutional
rights be protected while still serving society's interest? Discussed are: current law, the need to preserve exclusionary rules, limited immunity, and means
for change.   4055

RIGHT of the criminal defendant to the compelled testimony of witnesses. Colum L Rev 67:953-77 (1967).
Article examines rights of defendant when witness asserts his Fifth Amendment privilege against self-incrimination; comparisons of prosecution's power to
offer immunity and defendant's impotence, due process,
interests and the role of the courts. Author concludes
that interests of the criminal defendant in having
access to the evidence necessary for his defense requires legislative support.   4056

SAMUELS, A. Attendance of Witnessess Act 1965. L J 115:539-40 (1965).
Article explains new British law making uniform the
procedure for securing the attendance of witnesses at
criminal trial, including power to arrest a reluctant
witness and the power of the court to impose sanctions
for failure to appear.   4057

SINGER, A.D. State grants of immunity, the problem of interstate
prosecution prevention. J Crim L 58:218-23 (1967).
Author examines two Supreme Court cases: Malloy v Hogan,
378 US 1 (1964), holding that federal standards must
be used to determine the extent and limitation of the
self-incrimination privilege, and Murphy v Waterfront
Commission of NY Harbor, 378 US 52 (1964), holding that
the self-incrimination privilege would be violated if
state compelled testimony could be used to convict a
witness in federal court, and that once a state granted
immunity, such testimony could not be used for federal
prosecution. Discussed are general procedural aspects
of granting immunity and the traditional extent of this
grant, immunity statutes, and the problem of conflict
between the various jurisdictions which will, of necessity, occur following these decisions. Author offers
some solutions.   4058

SPOUSE'S testimony in criminal cases. Wyo L J 19:35-42 (1965).
Article examines the rules regarding testimony by the
spouse of accused with emphasis on Wyoming; historical
development, present status, the concept of a "wrong"
against the spouse, and the need for legislative clarification in this area.   4059

STATE immunity statutes in constitutional perspective. Duke L J 1968:
311-42 (1968).
Comment considers the constitutionality of immunity
statutes in light of extension of Fifth Amendment to
the states, state and federal statutes, intra-and extra-
jurisdictional immunity, current constitutional standards and tests for judging the validity of immunity
statutes, and conditions for statutory grants of immunity. Author suggests the creation of a single, all-
inclusive immunity provision by the legislature. 4060

TITLE II of the omnibus crime control and safe streets act of 1968
as it affects the admissibility of confessions and eyewitness testimony. Miss L J 40:257-85 (1969).
Comment considers the new provisions of Title II and
how they will affect the rules laid down by recent
Supreme Court decisions, also the scope of Act's appli-
cability. Author feels that many parts of the Act, if
not its entirety, will be found to be unconstitutional
by the Supreme Court.   4061

THE CRIMINAL TRIAL 797

WEXLER, D.B. Automatic witness immunity statutes and the inadvertent frustration of criminal prosecutions: a call for congressional action. Geo L J 55:656-62 (1967).
Law professor examines automatic immunity statutes; the effect they have had in stifling criminal prosecution where, for example, a federal inquiry unintentionally precludes state prosecution, and recent cases in which these problems are illustrated. Author emphasizes the need for reform in this area. 4062

WISCONSIN Legislative Reference Bureau. Court witness fees and mileage allowances in the 50 states. April 1966. Madison, 1966. 4 p.
Bureau compiles tables of specifications of court witness fees and mileage allowance in each state. 4063

WITNESS immunity. In National Association of Attorneys General. Organized crime control legislation, 1974. p. 129-51.
Chapter reviews fundamental constitutional issues involved and gives state-by-state current legislation citing to cases. 4064

D. Fair Trial - Free Press

Selected items include various press-court-bar association standards proposed and adopted; court silence orders; courtroom photography; comments by counsel. Protection of newsman's sources of information is not within the subject coverage.

AINSWORTH, R.A., Jr. "Fair trial - free press." FRD 45:417-26 (1969).
Judge contrasts the ABA Standards relating to fair trial and free press (item 4066) with report of the U.S. Judicial Conference's Committee on the Operation of the Jury System and urges that a sensitive balance between these conflicting rights be studied, and reached, by the bar and press. 4065

AMERICAN Bar Association Advisory Committee on Fair Trial and Free Press. Standards relating to fair trial and free press, recommended by the Advisory Committee on Fair Trial and Free Press. P.C. Reardon, chair.; D.L. Shapiro, reptr. Tent. draft, Dec. 1966. N.Y., IJA, 1966. 265 p. Rev. tent. draft, July 1967. 36 p. Proposed final draft, Dec. 1967. Approved draft, Feb. 1968. 36 p.
Standards with commentary relative to the criminal trial conduct of attorneys, law enforcement officers, judges and judicial employee conduct of the proceedings, and the exercise of contempt power; appendices are statement of principles of the bench-bar-press of the state of Washington, guidelines issued by prosecuting attorney, St. Louis, Missouri and results of empirical research undertaken by the committee. 4066

AMERICAN Bar Association Legal Advisory Committee on Fair Trial and
Free Press. The rights of fair trial and free press; an information
manual for the bar, news media, law enforcement officials and courts.
Chicago, 1969. 62 p.
> Includes ABA Standards relating to fair trial and free
> press (text) and their origins, what they do and do
> not do, commentary on controversial points, similarity
> of the ABA and Federal standards. A summary of major
> Supreme Court decisions, court rule defining duties of
> lawyers and sample voluntary bar-media codes are also
> presented.   4067

AMERICAN Bar Association Project on Minimum Standards for Criminal
Justice. Selected readings on fair trial and free press, comp. by
F.J. Klein. N.Y., IJA, 1965. 78 p.
> Materials include various proposed fair trial-free press
> guidelines, bills and recommendations, as well as papers
> by E.N. Griswold, Z. Cowen and G. Blake.   4068

AMERICAN Bar Association. Standing Committee on Bill of Rights. Report ... August, 1964. Chicago, 1964. 50 p.
> Report deals with the fair trial-free press conflict
> and the status of constitutional liberties as reflected
> in United States Supreme Court decisions.   4069

AMERICAN Civil Liberties Union. Statement of Board of Directors on
fair trial and free press. N.Y., 1966. 9 p.
> Guidelines applying to the release of information to
> news media by law enforcement officials and prosecutors
> and appropriate sanctions directed against those re-
> sponsible for presenting a case to the press instead
> of to the court are suggested. Expanding the challenge
> for cause of jurors influenced by pretrial publicity
> is another measure proposed.   4070

AMERICAN Judicature Society. News media and the administration of
justice, by D. Grooses. Chicago, 1970. 33 p. (Rep. 4)
> Includes text of ABA canons and code of professional
> responsibility, Statement of principles of bar-newsmen
> associations, the status of state voluntary codes and
> of ABA Canon 35, and an annotated bibliography. 4071

AMERICAN Judicature Society. Selected readings: fair trial - free
press, ed. by G.R. Winters. Chicago, 1971. 204 p.
> Contents: Powell, L.S. The right to a fair trial.--
> Dale, F.L. First and Sixth Amendments: can they co-
> exist?--Tauro, G.J. Fair trial-free press revisited.--
> Wright, J.S. A judge's view: the news media in crimi-
> nal justice.--Royster, C.V. The free press and a fair
> trial.--Daly, J.C. Ensuring fair trial and a free
> press.--Younger, E.J. Fair trial, free press and the
> man in the middle.--LeWine, J.M. What constitutes pre-

judicial publicity in pending cases?--Wessel, M.R.
Controlling prejudicial publicity in criminal trials.--
Scripp, J. Controlling prejudicial publicity by the
contempt power.--Smith, W.R., Jr. Free press - fair
trial.--Helwig, G.J. Should special facilities be provided for courtroom photography and broadcasting?--
Monroe, W.B., Jr. The case for television in the courtroom.--Raichle, F.G. If there is to be abridgement of
pretrial communication, should it be coupled with expansion of radio and TV coverage?--Wright, D.R. Fair
trial and free press: practical ways to have both.--
Appendices: 1) ABA standards relating to fair trial
and free press. 2) State of Washington ex. rel. Supreme
Court of Snohomish County v Sam Sperry, et. al., Appellants; 3) Report of the U.S. Judicial Conference
Committee on the Operation of the Jury System on the
"Free Press - Fair Trial" Issue; 4) Guidelines for press
and police; Bibliography.   4072

AMERICAN Newspaper Publishers Association. Free press and fair trial.
N.Y., 1967. 154 p.
Conclusion is reached that the right to a free press
is a fundamental right which must not be controlled
or restricted. Appendices cover histories of the First
and Sixth Amendments and of contempt powers; the law
as enunciated by the Supreme Court, as to allegedly prejudicial news coverage of criminal cases before, during
and after trial; a review of representative proposed
codes and guidelines relating to news media and their
reporting of court trials.   4073

AMERICAN Society of Newspaper Editors Press-Bar Committee. Report
1964/65. N.Y., 1965. 14 p.
Following a year's study of the free press-fair trial
issue, newsmen find that their important role of keeping the public informed is not recognized and that
they receive the blame for prejudicing juries, a charge
that is not documented. Citing difficulties with regu-
latory codes, they would prefer more discussions between the press and bar.   4074

ANDERSON, B.B. Resolving a constitutional conflict. Trial Judges'
J 5:6-7 (Oct. 1966).
A discussion of the work of Washington State Bench-Bar
Press Committee, including the adoption of a state-
ment of principles and educational projects such as a
newsmen's seminar and a course in court reporting.
                                                    4075

ASSOCIATION of the Bar of the City of New York Special Committee on
Radio, Television, and the Administration of Justice. Freedom of the
press and fair trial; final report with recommendations. N.Y., Colum

U press, 1967. 115 p.
          H.R. Medina, chair. The committee presents its conclu-
          sions and recommendations for preserving both a free
          press and the principle of fair trial. It urges curbs
          on lawyers who try their cases in the press, regulations
          of law enforcement officers and rejects additional con-
          tempt powers to fine or imprison newsmen or police be-
          fore a case comes on for trial.   4076

ASSOCIATION of the Bar of the City of New York Special Committee on
Radio and Television. Radio, television, and the administration of
justice; a documented survey of materials. N.Y., Colum U press, 1965.
333 p.
          H.R. Medina, chair. Various types of broadcasts and
          telecasts that may affect the administration of justice
          in the criminal and civil courts are examined. Documents
          and materials presented include rules, regulations,
          cannons of ethics, statutes, etc., dealing with the use
          of radio and television throughout the country; the
          voluntary bar-press codes adopted in Massachusetts and
          Oregon; and court opinions and proposals on controlling
          conduct of attorneys, law enforecemnt officers and
          others.   4077

BADGER, R.K. The unsworn and unfettered witness in our courtrooms:
prejudicial publicity. Amer Crim L Q 4:5-19 (1965).
          Discusses specific examples of prejudicial publicity
          drawing on case examples, involving such problems as
          character assassination of a defendant, comments on
          the evidence, communication to the jury.   4078

BARIST, J.A. The first amendment and regulation of prejudicial publicity: an analysis. Fordham L Rev 36:425-52 (1968).
          Discusses the First Amendment conflict between fair
          trial and free press as it relates to the Supreme Court
          contempt cases and the effect of this constitutional
          standard on jury trials; suggests a new approach to
          the conflict based on the temporal framework of the
          trial, the bias of the publicity and content of the
          publication.   4079

BRAITHWAITE, W. T. Fair trial-free press; a memorandum on the problem and some solutions. Chicago, AB Found, 1966. 40 p. (Research
Memo 38)
          Studies news media and an impartial jury; kinds of in-
          formation that may be prejudice; outside-of-courtroom
          activities of the news media and arguments for Canon 35;
          solutions to problems of prejudicial publicity outside
          of courtroom during, before and after trial; five
          crucial cases discussed; appendix annotates additional
          cases and gives a rundown of activities in the states.
                                                             4080

BUSH, C.R., ed. Free press and fair trial; some dimensions of the
problem. Athens, U of Georgia, 1971. 133 p.
> Contents: Siebert, F.S. Trial judges' opinions on pre-
> judicial publicity.--Hough, G. III. Felonies, jury
> trials, and news reports.--Wilcox, W. The press, the
> jury, and the behavioral sciences.--Siebert, F.S. Access
> by newsmen to judicial proceedings.--Bush, C.R. What
> we have learned.--Appendices: Some press-bench-bar
> agreements.   4081

CALIFORNIA Judicial Council. Report on photography and broadcasting
of court proceedings, by the Court Management Committee. San Francisco, 1965. 7 p.
> Report on California experiments with photography and
> broadcasting in court rooms finds that there should be
> a rule, replacing the uneforceable canon of judicial
> ethics now existing, banning photography, recording
> and broadcasting for the following reasons: unfair in-
> fluence; unnecessary distraction and delay; not neces-
> sary for public trial; purpose of trial is justice, not
> entertainment. Text of proposed rule included.   4082

CALIFORNIA Legislature Assembly Interim Committee on Judiciary. Transcript of proceedings on fair trial - free press, El Dorado Hotel,
Sacramento, Sept. 22, 1965. Sacramento, 1965. 48 p.
> Representatives of the bar and media discuss and debate
> the proposed California rule to abolish TV and other
> cameras from the courtroom in order to preserve court-
> room dignity in light of the right of the public to
> know, the right of the media to publish opinions and
> to photograph and televise matters of public importance
> and interest, and the right of the trial participants
> to privacy.   4083

COLDSTREAM, G., Sir. Pre-trial publicity: an aspect of the English
practice. Trial Judges' J 9:4-6 (Jan. 1970).
> An analysis of the events requiring the passage of Sec-
> tion 3 of the Criminal Justice Bill, in July 1967, re-
> stricting news reports of committal proceedings before
> magistrates.   4084

COLE, J. and SPAK, M.I. Defense counsel and the first amendment: "a
time to keep silence and a time to speak." St Mary's L J 6:347-85
(1974).
> Mr. Cole and Prof. Spak argue persuasively that rules
> proscribing extrajudicial comments by counsel of record
> made during pending litigation and for public dissemina-
> tion are consistent with the First Amendment and that
> the clear and present danger test of Sebenck v US 249
> US 47 (1919) is not the measure of the constitutionality
> of such rules. Authors discuss cases since the Holmes
> opinion.   4085

COLLISION COURSE? Free press and the courts; a symposium of lawyers
and journalists at Osgoode Hall Law School ... April 15, 1966. Toronto, Ryerson Polytech Inst, 1967. 77 p.
    Discussion of the problems of free press and fair trial
    includes pro and con comments by Canadian judges, de-
    fense and prosecution counsel, and media members on
    the compatibility of free press and fair trial, consti-
    tutional issues, and a responsible press; bibliography.
                                                           4086

COLUMBIA Broadcasting System. CBS news guidelines for reporting pretrial and trial procedures. N.Y., 1965. 1 p.
    Demonstrates balance between free reporting and the
    rights of the accused, including some limits on report-
    ing confessions and prior records, and judicious choice
    of words. Covering memo from Fred W.Friendly, Pres.
    CBS.   4087

CONFERENCE of State Trial Judges. The Washington bench-bar-press
story; some philosophical and sociological observations. August 3,
1967. Honolulu, 1967. 10 p.
    Speaker praises the achievements of the Bench-Bar-Press
    Committee in improving bench-bar media relations in
    state of Washington. The culmination of the Committee's
    efforts has been the formulation of guidelines for
    proper reporting. Included are the Committee's State-
    ment of Principles and Guidelines for the Reporting of
    criminal proceedings, juvenile court proceedings, civil
    proceedings, and public records.   4088

DANIEL, C. Press outlines five ground rules for free press and fair
trial. Trial 1:38 (Oct. 1965).
    Newspaper editor details the press position on censor-
    ship and other abridgements of the press; proposes
    several courses of action to insure both a fair trial
    and a free press including discussions between the
    press, bench, and law enforcement officials, and draw-
    ing up newsmen's codes of etiquette and pooling criteria.
                                                           4089

DISTRICT of Columbia Bar Association. News media and the Washington,
D.C. courts: some suggestions for bridging the communications gap;
study report by Community Education Committee, Young Lawyer's Sect.
DCB J 39:18-53 (May/Sept. 1972).
    Study looks at how newsmen, judges and other court
    officials view the problems of news coverage of court
    activity. The Committee's recommendations include
    greater courts-media dialogue, employment of legally
    trained reporters, public information officers in the
    courts and increased use of television and radio. 4090

DOUBLES, M.R.   A camera in the courtroom.   Wash & Lee L Rev 22:1-16
(1965).
> Support for ABA judicial canon 35 which prohibits photo-
> graphs and telecasts in the courtroom, not because
> they lessen dignity and decorum of the trial, or dis-
> tort the events, but because such activity distracts
> witness. Urges redrafting.   4091

DUE process -- failure to insulate criminal trial from prejudicial
publicity deemed denial of due process. St John's L Rev 41:438-46
(1967).
> Analysis of Supreme Court's opinion in Sheppard v Max-
> well as emphasizing the inherent powers of the trial
> court in resolving the fair trial-free press conflict.
>   4092

FAIR TRIAL and free press: resolution of a conflict. W Va L Rev 69:
198-202 (1967).
> Examines powers of trial court in balancing fair trial
> with freedom of press as set out in Sheppard v Maxwell;
> suggests that while the Supreme Court has limited the
> contimpt power, the trial judge may still control the
> news media's sources of information which may prove
> to be an effective protection of the defendant's rights.
>   4093

FAIR TRIAL v. free press: the need to compromise. U Cinn L Rev 34:
503-24 (1965).
> Reviews American system and possible procedural reme-
> dies to assure impartiality of jury; describes English
> appraoch, emphasizing distinctions. Suggested revisions
> strike a compromise between courts and the press.4094

FELSHER, H. and ROSEN, M. The press in the jury box. N.Y., MacMillan, 1966. 239 p.
> Offers examples from newspaper articles and headlines
> to illustrate the basic theme that the press is often
> irresponsible in covering crimes and criminal trials
> and thereby endangers the fairness of the trial; dis-
> cusses this theme in relation to the power of the edi-
> tor, leaks to the press, subjective reporting, the de-
> fendant's rights. Compares the English system with that
> of U.S.; proposes statute which would mandate the de-
> lay in publication of some information.   4095

FRANCIS, J.J. The bar, the press and criminal justice. Trial Judges'
J 4:1, 15 (Apr. 1965).
> Assessment of trial judge's ability to deal with ex-
> tensive pretrial publicity through jury selection, re-
> course to local bar ethics committees, and pre- and
> post-trial motions.   4096

FREE PRESS - fair trial revisited: defendant-centered remedies as a
publicity policy. U Chi L Rev 33:521-30 (1966).
> Analysis of present treatment of the problem including
> pretrial remedies and grounds for appeal, recent pro-
> posals including Attorney General's 1965 Directive,
> Senator Morse's proposal, Massachusetts proposed legis-
> lation and Prof. Jaffee's proposal, and the possibili-
> ties for and details of automatic defendant-centered
> remedies by statute or judicial ruling.   4097

FREE PRESS v. fair trial: insulation against injustice. La L Rev 33:
547-59 (1973).
> Analyzes ABA standards concerning the conduct of attor-
> neys, law enforcement officials, conduct of the trial
> and contempt power, and the role of the news media; dis-
> cusses the Supreme Court opinion in Sheppard as it re-
> lates to the trial judge's power; suggests the exercise
> of caution on the part of the courts in dealing with
> the news media.   4098

FRIENDLY, A. and GOLDFARB, R.L. Crime and publicity; the impact of
news on the administration of justice. N.Y., Twentieth Century Fund,
1967. 335 p.
> Newspaper editor and trial lawyer report findings of
> their studies undertaken to obtain information about
> frequency of prejudicial publication, and point out that
> the real problem arises with the sensational crime.
> They examine procedures governing juries and the means
> courts use to filter out potentially prejudicial pub-
> licity. Various remedies are evaluated, including Brit-
> ish system; recommendations are made. Append. B: law
> governing press regulation is reviewed.   4099

GERALD, J.E. Press-bar relationships: progress since Sheppard and
Reardon. Journalism Q 47:223-32 (1970).
> Author discusses progress in resolving conflict between
> free press and fair trial. Major changes have been large-
> ly effected through voluntary committees.   4100

GILLMOR, D.M. Free press and fair trial. Washington, Public Affairs
press, 1966. 260 p.
> Journalism professor examines cases which illustrate
> the power and effect of publicity on their outcome, and
> reviews issues involved in the free press-fair trial
> controversy. Traces history of freedom of press and
> speech and trial by jury; discusses efforts by the bar
> and press to reconcile the First and Sixth Amendments,
> the English remedy, and proposals for resolving the
> conflict.   4101

GILLMOR, D.M. Free press and fair trial in English law. Wash & Lee
L Rev 22:17-42 (1965).

Review of English case law respecting rights of press
in trial process, impact of law on contempt.   4102

GILLMOR, D.M. The Reardon report: a journalist's assessment. Wisc
L Rev 1967:215-30.
    The report of the ABA's Advisory Committee on Fair Trial
    and Free Press is scrutinized by a journalism professor
    who strongly objects to its findings and conclusions.
    He feels that the Committee is proposing a "qualified
    English system in which the press would eventually ex-
    ist in a state of constant terror and uncertainty."
                                                   4103

GOODWIN, A.T. A judicial role in the bar-press dialogue. Trial
Judges' J 6:1, 20 (April, 1967).
    Discusses the role of the judge in the Washington and
    Oregon bar-press joint committees, finding that judges
    tend to be catalysts in the constructive dialogue be-
    tween newsmen and lawyers.   4104

GRACE, R.M. The courts v. the news media: is the conflict necessary?
Case & Comment 79:3-10 (1974).
    Reports on recent cases involving judge-issued gag
    orders and the resulting antagonism between the news
    media and the court; urges a reasonable dialogue be-
    tween judge and press to resolve this conflict. 4105

GUIDELINES for press and police. Judicature: 50:6-11 (1966).
    Analysis of Sheppard's standards for trial and appell-
    ate courts in protecting free trial rights in light of
    press publicity including such safeguards as insulating
    witnesses, limitations on newsmen in the courtroom and
    attempting to control news releases by participants
    in the trial. (Also examines Miranda's guidelines for
    police.)   4106

HAIMBAUGH, G.D., Jr. Free press versus fair trial: the contributions
of Mr. Justice Frankfurter. U Pitt L Rev 26:491-520 (1965).
    Frankfurter's views of the relationship between the
    communications media and state courts, as expressed in
    his dissents and concurrences in Supreme Court cases
    involving contempt by publication and trial by news-
    paper, are presented and contrasted with the views of
    the majority.   4107

HOCKENBERRY, S.H. Pennsylvania's courtroom ban on camera equipment.
Penn BA Q 36:76-83 (1964).
    Based upon a survey, author concludes that the court-
    room camera ban will remain. He attributes this find-
    ing to greater judicial unity in opposition to the
    camera than journalistic unity in support of it. Al-
    though the use of modern camera equipment would be un-

noticed by a subject, it is pointed out that knowledge
of the cameras could encourage dramatics. Urges well-
researched studies into the practical application of
courtroom photography.   4108

THE IMPARTIAL jury - twentieth century dilemma: some solutions to the
conflict between free press and fair trial. Cornell L Q 51:306-27
(1966).
           Proposes alternatives to restriction of press, viz.
           voluntary restraint and statutes punishing for speci-
           fied types of press articles. Discusses constitution-
           ality of preventive remedies, labeling them question-
           able. Offers other possible solutions such as regula-
           tion of disclosure to press, blue ribbon jury, notify-
           ing potential jurors.   4109

INFLAMMATORY publicity in state criminal cases. Neb L Rev 44:614-34
(1965).
           The problem of trial by newspaper and past approaches
           to its solution are considered. A comparative analysis
           is also presented of proposed new solutions such as an
           amendment of, or enforcement of, Canon 20 of the ABA
           Canons of Professional Ethics, adoption by the news
           media of rules for self-restraint, or adoption of crimi-
           nal legislation to punish divulgence or publication of
           prejudicial material.   4110

JAFFE, L.J. Trial by newspaper. NYU L Rev 40:504-24 (1965).
           Discusses the causes and consequences of pretrial and
           pending trial publicity through Supreme Court decisions,
           including cases dealing with contempt and publicity
           affecting voir dire; offers solutions based not on
           suppression of the press but on control over police,
           prosecutors and attorneys through canons of ethics and
           contempt power.   4111

JUDICIAL Canon 35 ... revise or retain? Fla B J 37:16-37 (1963).
           Sixteen opinions concerning the possible elimination
           of ABA canon prohibiting photography and broadcasting
           in the courtroom.   4112

JUDICIAL Conference of the United States Committee on the Operation
of the Jury System. "Free Press - Fair Trial" issue; report ...
Washington, 1968. 42 p.; FRD 45:391-415 (1968).
           I.R. Kaufman, chair. Report examines problem, discuss-
           ing Sheppard v Maxwell in particular. Recommendations
           including control of prejudicial information by attor-
           neys and courthouse personnel are suggested, and the
           adoption of rules in widely publicized cases is urged.
                                                           4113

JUDICIAL Conference of the United States Committee on the Operation of the Jury System. Supplemental report on the "Free press - fair trial" issue. FRD 51:135-38 (1971).
> I.R. Kaufman, chair. Amended recommendation for rules regarding attorney's dissemination of information on pending trials, grand jury investigations, or arrests.
> <u>4114</u>

KANDT, W.C. Courtroom photography. Trial Judges' J 4:11 (Oct. 1965).
> Judge defends ABA Judicial Canon 35 on theory that public does not have unlimited right to know and that individual right to privacy must not be sacrificed to the goal of public education.   4115

KAUFMAN, I.R. Dilemma in crime reporting. Los Angeles Times, Nov. 5-8, 1967. 4 pts. in 1.
> Federal judge discusses the conflict between First Amendment freedom of press and Sixth Amendment guarantees to a fair trial in newspaper series. Examined are: media interference in the courtroom; media influence outside the courtroom; dilution of publicity before trial; possible solutions; and guidelines for the press.
> <u>4116</u>

KAUFMAN, I.R. The judges and the jurors: recent developments in selection of jurors and fair trial-free press. U Colo L Rev 41:179-200 (1969).
> Chair of Committee on Operation of Jury System (see item <u>4113</u>) discusses two developments improving quality of federal juries: random selection of jurors from voter lists insures a representative body; special committee has drafted guidelines to ameliorate the conflict between press and bar. The most significant recommendation concerns public release of information likely to interfere with a fair trial.   <u>4117</u>

KAUFMAN, I.R. The press, the courts, and the law schools: towards justice and an informed public. Address ... at annual dinner of the Tulane Law Review Association (1965), New Orleans. N.Y., 1965. 28 p.
> Discussion of need for bar involvement in some of the pressing problems now facing the judicial system suggests that law schools provide better practical training in criminal advocacy; that lawyers work for important judicial reforms; and that the bar, courts, and media work together to make for an informed public with better understanding of the judicial system.   <u>4118</u>

KLINE, F.G. and JESS, P.H. Prejudicial publicity: its effect on law school mock juries. Journalism Q 43:113-16 (1966).
> To explore the effect pretrial publicity has on a jury, research fellow and journalism professor relate how they simulated the jury situation and found some of the jurors to have been influenced.   <u>4119</u>

LEWINE, J.M.   What constitutes prejudicial publicity in pending cases.
ABA J 51:942-48 (1965).
> Author examines control of the press in English and
> American courts and analyzes what types of publicity
> are prejudicial. He remarks on the need for some re-
> straints on the press and suggests that an effective
> deterrent is possible under the clear and present danger
> test, i.e. publication presents a clear and present
> danger to the orderly and impartial administration of
> justice.   4120

LOFTON, J.   Justice and the press. Boston, Beacon, 1966. 476 p.
> Author examines and illustrates, from early times to
> present, how newspapers flout rights of due process
> and how courts also abuse rights of due process and
> obstruct rights of a free press. He considers effects
> of press influence on law enforcement as well as other
> deleterious influences, such as public pressure. He
> reviews various remedies proposed by the press and bar
> and suggests under what circumstances and in what ways
> the individual right to due process should take pre-
> cedence over the collective public right to know and
> when right to know should come first.   4121

MCCULLOUGH, D.H.   Trial by newspaper; free press and fair trial. SD
L Rev 12:1-61 (1967).
> Gives background writings and discussions on Canon 35,
> discusses impact of newspaper publicity in notorious
> cases; comprehensive article graphically details battle
> by powerful interests for repeal of Canon 35; suggests
> guidelines for publicity in criminal cases. Author is
> member Fair Trial-Free Press Committee, Ohio State Bar
> Association. Appendix is "Guidelines on Publicity in
> Criminal Proceedings" adopted by Toledo, Ohio, news-
> papers.   4122

MCKAY, R.B.   An academic view. In Free press and fair trial symposium
(item 4146). Vill L Rev 11:726-36 (1966).
> Law professor asserts that although fair trial rights
> are not adequately protected against prejudicial pub-
> licity, they cannot be secured at the price of limita-
> tions on free expression. Professional self-discipline
> is urged, and if that fails to prevent prejudicial dis-
> closures, courts must apply present standards, even at
> the risk of releasing guilty defendants.   4123

MACKENZIE, J.P.   On clearing the courtroom; the public's right to a
public trial. Am U L Rev 18:769-88 (1969).
> Newspaper reporter deplores absence of guidelines for
> judges who may clear the court without regard to the
> right to a public trial. He draws on four actual pro-
> ceedings to illustrate the need for judicial standards
> and suggests minimum standards which should govern the

right to a public trial. Appends excerpts from the ABA
Standards for fair trial and free press, of which the
author is critical.   4124

MEYER, B.S. Free press v. fair trial: the judge's view. ND L Rev
41:14-23 (1964/65).
       Trial judge concludes that a statute prohibiting pub-
       lication of specified material regarding jury trials
       for a specified time would be the best way to balance
       the rights of a free press and a fair trial.   4125

MEYER, B.S. Justice and the news media: a reply and a challenge.
Trial 3:38-40 (Feb./Mar. 1967).
       Reply to Dr. Stanton's criticism (item 4143) of the
       ABA Standards on fair trial-free press citing the pur-
       poses of the recommendations, including the obtaining
       of opinions and gathering of information, and how those
       purposes were met.   4126

MEYER, B.S. Trial judge's guide to news reporting and fair trial.
J Crim L 60:287-98 (1969).
       Guide for trial judges during entire process from pre-
       arraignment and pretrial motions to and after ultimate
       conclusion, emphasizing problems that trial judge in
       publicized case encounters. Author suggests measures
       to assure prosecution and defendant fair trial with
       proper press coverage. Judge's orders must be specific
       and understood and made to fit each case; covers grand
       jury transcript, exhibits, names and addresses of pro-
       spective jurors, use of courtroom and facilities by
       public, press, sketch artists; cautioning and sequest-
       ering jurors and contempt powers for violation of court
       order. Offers ABA Standards and Cannons, recent case
       law as guides. Substantially same as Chapter 22 in
       State trial judges book. (item 2500)   4127

MILLS, J.E. Critique on the press coverage of trials; an address ...
delivered before the International Academy of Trial Lawyers, Feb. 17,
1967, Mexico City. N.Y., 1967. 19 p.
       Former newspaper editor opposes efforts to restrict
       the freedom of the press and comments on the importance
       of preserving this freedom.   4128

MORRIS, E.F. Justice and the news media. Ill B J 55:554-59 (1967).
       President-elect of American Bar Association responds to
       American Newspaper Publishers Association report oppos-
       ing restrictions on communication with the media by
       law enforcement officials. Contends that court regula-
       tion of disclosure to the press does not violate the
       separation of powers doctrine. Endorses ABA recommen-
       dation of voluntary press guidelines.   4129

MOSK, S. Free press and fair trial: placing responsibility. Santa
Clara Lawyer 5:107-20 (1965).
        California Supreme Court justice, reviewing recent cases
        on press coverage of trials, concludes that since legis-
        lative or Supreme Court restriction of the press is
        unlikely and a voluntary code of press behavior would
        be ineffective, restrictions on police and lawyer com-
        munication with the press are the best means of assur-
        ing a fair trial.   4130

NAGER, E. The argument against pretrial publicity in criminal cases.
Wis B Bull 39:60-65 (Apr. 1966).
        Assemblyman contends that the issue is not one of a
        free press but of whether public officials have the
        right to prejudice a defendant's case by using the news
        media to establish the idea of the defendant's guilt
        in the public consciousness prior to trial.   4131

NEW REFLECTIONS on fair trial-free press: Sheppard v Maxwell and the
ABA proposals. Ill L F 1966:1063-80 (1966).
        Note describes the problems of prejudice of criminal
        defendants' rights by the press in general; the Shep-
        pard case, and the ABA Standards on fair trial-free
        press, which fall short of the main purpose because
        they do not regulate pretrial publicity. Another stu-
        dent note in a similar vein: Ala L Rev 19:150-56 (1966).
                                                               4132

NATIONAL Conference of State Trial Judges. Report of Special Committee on News Reporting and Fair Trials. Chicago, 1964. 1 v., var.
pag.
        Committee explains its proposal to establish a research
        project to learn the effect of news reporting on trial
        jurors, and presents the project's design, methodology
        and cost, as determined in a pilot project prepared by
        Columbia University.   4133

NEW YORK County Lawyers Association. Television and the accused; a
report of the Committee on Civil Rights. N.Y., 1964. 20 p.
        Report discusses television's invasions of the accused's
        rights, corrective measures taken by the Appellate Divi-
        sion and the police department, and prospects of volun-
        tary restraint by the television industry; recommenda-
        tions include adoption of regulations by the Police
        Department and amendments to the Code of Criminal Pro-
        cedure and Canons of Ethics to guard the right to a
        fair trial.   4134

OREGON bar-press-broadcaster's joint statement of principles. Trial
Judges' J 6:4 (Apr. 1967).
        Attempt to keep the public informed without violating
        the rights of the individual by calling for accuracy,

objectivity, good taste, and the exercise of informed
judgement on the part of the media and the bar. <u>4135</u>

REARDON, P.C. and DANIEL, C. Fair trial and free press. Washington,
Am Enterprise Inst for Public Policy Research, 1968. 181 p.
     Massachusetts Supreme Court Justice debates with New
York Times managing editor in a sharp exchange with
rebuttals and three later discussions joined by other
lawyers and journalists. Reardon supports his ABA committee's recommendations (item <u>4066</u>) restricting the
communication of certain specific information to the
press by the bar or law enforcement officials between
arrest and trial. Mr. Daniel opposes any mandatory restraint which would tend to make trials more secret.
<u>4136</u>

RENDLEMAN, D. Free press-fair trial: review of silence orders. NC
L Rev 52:127-64 (1973).
     Discusses how to obtain appellate review of a silence
order issued to the media in a criminal proceeding.
Examines procedural routes into appellate court, ter-
minal review, interlocutory review, review by prerogative writ and review of contempt. Questions as to party
status of media, legal nature of the order and lack of
time for full-dress review are discussed. <u>4137</u>

ROYLSTON, R.N. Pretrial publicity enjoined. Trial Judges' J 5:6, 28
(Apr. 1966).
     Judge discusses various methods of preventing pretrial
publicity including injunctions against court officials,
law enforcement officials and the press. <u>4138</u>

SEYMOUR, W.N., Jr. The "public's right to know:" who decides what the
public should be told? Record 29:625-30 (1974).
     President of New York State Bar describes the New York
Fair Trial-Free Press Conference created to develop
mutual respect and understanding about the problems
of the Sixth Amendment vis-à-vis the First Amendment
when there is a conflict between them in newsworthy
criminal cases. Headed by the Chief Judge of New York,
the Conference includes editors, broadcasters and other
representatives of the press, district attorneys, chiefs
of police and others associated with the administration
of criminal justice. It has developed a set of voluntary guidelines as to information not to be released
to the press and what editors ought not to publish.
Author discusses continuing problems generated by the
public's right to know. <u>4139</u>

SHEPPARD v Maxwell, 384 US 333 (1966) -- duty of trial judge to protect accused from prejudice. Nw U L Rev 62:89-98 (1967).
     A discussion of the "totality of circumstances" approach

taken by the Supreme Court in determining jury prejudice, asserting that the standards set up in Sheppard
v Maxwell are inconsistent; argues that the standard
of "reasonable likelihood" that a fair trial will take
place and the standard of "reasonableness" to be employed by the trial judge in handling the news media
would detract from the trial judge's discretionary
powers.   4140

SIEBERT, F.S., WILCOX, W. and HOUGH, G. III. Free press and fair
trial: some dimensions of the problem. Athens, U Ga Press, 1970.
133 p.
          Contents: Siebert, F.S. Trial judges' opinion on pre-
          judicial publicity with appendices.--Hough, G. Felonies,
          jury trials and news reports (with demonstrative ta-
          bles).--Wilcox, W. The press, the jury and the behavior-
          al sciences (with demonstrative table, bibliography,
          and cases).--Siebert, F.S. Access by newsmen to judicial
          proceedings (tables).--What we have learned.   4141

STANGA, J.E. Judicial protection of the criminal defendant against
adverse press coverage. Wm & Mary L Rev 13:1-74 (1971).
          Review of case law on remedying adverse trial publicity
          through voir dire, change of venue, dismissal of charges,
          at various stages before and during trial.   4142

STANTON, F. Justice and the news media. Trial 13:40 (Dec./Jan.
1966/67).
          CBS President criticizes the ABA Standards (item 4066)
          on the grounds that the ABA report is based on assump-
          tion and superficially researched and documented. (For
          reply, see item 4126)   4143

SYMPOSIUM: Fair trial and a free press. NYSB J 41:7-58 (1969).
          Contents: Meyer, B.S. Introduction.--Addresses by Fuld,
          S.H., Finley, R.C., Cleavinger, H.C., Tondel, L.M., Jr.
          and Fichenberg, R.--U.S. District Court, N.Y.N.D. Order
          to regulate pretrial and trial conduct and disclosure
          of information in criminal cases.--Reynolds, H.J. Post-
          verdict interrogation of jurrors.--Keating, K.B. The
          nature of responsible dissent.   4144

SYMPOSIUM: News Media, fair trial. NDAA 1:36-45 (May/June 1965).
          Contents: Daniel, C. Free press v. fair trial.--Alex-
          ander, B. Publicity and the law.--Cedarquist, W.B. De-
          fendant's right to a fair trial.--Schmidt, R.M., Jr.
          Shall we have silence in court?   4145

SYMPOSIUM on a free press and a fair trial. Villanova L Rev 11:677
741 (1966).
          Dowd, D.W. Introduction.--Graham, F. A newspaperman's
          view.--Monroe, W.B. A radio and television newsman's

view.--Specter, A. A prosecutor's view.--Foreman, P.
A defense attorney's view.--Trescher, R.L. A bar associa-
tion view.--Smith, W.F. A judicial view.--McKay, R.B.
An academic view (item 4123).--McKay, R.B. and Graham,
F. Addendum: Comments on Sheppard v Maxwell.   4146

SYMPOSIUM: The recommendations of the ABA Advisory Committee on Fair
Trial and Free Press. Notre Dame Law 42:881-924 (1962).
        Contents: Cooper, G.B. The rationale for the ABA recom-
        mendations.--Shaffer, T.L. Direct restraint on the
        press.--Ragan, S. The ABA recommendations: a newspaper-
        man's critique.--Lower, E.W. The first amendment under
        attack: a defense of the people's right to know.--Smith,
        W.H.T. The implications of the ABA recommendations for
        police administration.--Reichle, W.G. If there is to be
        an abridgement of pretrial communication, should it be
        coupled with an expansion of trial coverage by radio
        and television.--Monroe, W.B. The case for television
        in the courtroom.--Burgess, J.A. The efficacy of a change
        in venue in protecting a defendant's right to an impar-
        tial jury.--Griffin, H.C. Prejudicial publicity: search
        for a civil remedy.--Scripp, J. Controlling judicial
        publicity by the contempt power: the British practice
        and its prospect in American law.   4147

TALTY, F.J. Court order: fair trial-free press. Trial Judges' J
6:19-20 (Jan. 1967).
        Judge Talty's court order, entered in State of Ohio v
        Sam H. Sheppard, Court of Common Pleas, Cuyahoga County,
        Ohio, upon retrial of the case on Oct. 19, 1966, regu-
        lating the conduct of the press and public.   4148

TANS, M.D. and CHAFFEE, S.H. Pretrial publicity and juror prejudice.
Journalism Q 43:647-54 (1966).
        Authors describe their test of the effects of crime
        stories on potential jurors who received questionnaire
        booklets. Despite admitted shortcomings in the experi-
        ment, authors find that it lends credence to the belief
        that pretrial publicity produces juror prejudice.4149

TWENTIETH Century Fund. A free and responsive press: Task force report for a national news council; background paper by Alfred Balk.
N.Y., 1973. 88 p.
        Recommends the establishment of a National Press Coun-
        cil whose primary focus would be to supply accurate
        news, preserving the freedom of the press. The task
        force offers specifics in establishing such a Council
        and the background paper presents information on exist-
        ing Councils in England, Ontario, Honolulu and Minnesota.
        Appended: Press Conference constitutions, bibliography.
                                                       4150

U. S. CONGRESS Senate Committee on the Judiciary Subcommittee on Improvements in Judicial Machinery. Free press and fair trial; hearings ... on S. 290 ... August 17-20, 1965. Washington, USGPO. 1966.
2 v., 762 p. (89th Cong.; 1st Sess.)
> S. Ervin, subcommittee chair. Statements, exhibits,
> articles, memoranda, reports, speeches proposed legis-
> lation.   4151

WILCOX, W. The press, the jury, and the behavioral sciences. Austin,
Assn for Education in Journalism, 1968. 56 p.
> Journalism professor shows that there is not much more
> than speculation to support the contention that juries
> are prejudiced by pretrial publicity of information
> concerning the defendant; 3-p. bibliography.   4152

WILSON, J. Justice in living color: the case for courtroom television.
ABA J 60:294-7 (1974).
> Former television political editor contends that the
> judicial system needs exposure by television; considers
> ABA's new Canon 3 (a) (7) of the Code of Judicial Con-
> duct too limiting. Problems can be solved by making
> firm but practical guidelines.   4153

WRIGHT, J.S. Fair trial - free press. FRD 38:435-39 (1966).
> Submits that in very few trials would full exercise of
> the press's First Amendment right prejudice the accused's
> right to a fair trial. Points out the important func-
> tion performed by press exposure of police and district
> attorney activities and the protection of the accused
> afforded by the possibility of dismissal for cause or
> peremptory challenge of prejudiced jurors. Calls for
> self-restraint both from attorneys and from the press.
>   4154

WYOMING Law Journal. Proposed statement of principles for the Wyoming
Bar Association and Wyoming Press Association. Wyo L J 1965:128-29.
> Text of statement between bar and press recognizes the
> importance of freedom of the press and open trials,
> subject to individual rights of the participants, and
> the responsibility of both organizations to ensure a
> fair and impartial trial.   4155

ZAGRI, S. Free press, fair trial. Chicago, Chas Hallberg, 1966.
117 p.
> Covers the Kennedy prosecution of Jimmy Hoffa and the
> attendant publicity, which author argues violated Hoffa's
> right to fair trial. The extensive appendix includes
> Life and Look articles, on Hoffa, U.S. Justice Dept.
> press release, and other examples of publicity in this
> case.   4156

E. Delay in Criminal Trials

   1. Items on speedy trial rules, items de-
       fining a speedy trial; consequences of
       denial of speedy trial; continuances;
       other recommendations to facilitate trial
       of criminal cases; comparative statistics
       on disposition time, mainly in felony
       cases.

AMERICAN Bar Association Advisory Committee on the Criminal Trial.
Standards relating to speedy trial, recommended by the Advisory Com-
mittee on the Criminal Trial. W.V. Schaefer, chair.; W. LaFave, reptr.
Tent. draft, May 1967. N.Y., IJA, 1967. 56 p. appd., Feb. 1968.
          Standards with commentary covering the trial calendar,
          determining what is a speedy trial, special procedures
          for persons imprisoned, and consequences of denial of
          speedy trial. App.: Uniform Mandatory Disposition of
          Detainers Act; suggested state legislation on Agree-
          ment on Detainers.   4157

BAIL, preventive detention and speedy trials; a panel. Colum J L
and Soc Prob 8:1-32 (1971).
          Participants: Moderator: J.D. Hopkins; Speaker: H.R.
          Uviller; Panel: P.D. Andreoli, I. Lang, and H.J. Roth-
          wax. Discussed are 1) Pretrial interval, 2) Bail or
          detention, 3) Plea bargaining. The comments give many
          enlightening specifics on the criminal justice system
          in New York and generally.   4158

BANFIELD, L. and ANDERSON, C.D. Continuances in Cook County criminal
courts. U Chi L Rev 35:256-316 (1968).
          Detailed study by law students of the role and impact
          of continuances in the administration of the Cook
          County Criminal Courts examines: background and dimen-
          sions of problem; discrepancies in law and practice;
          cost and abuse of continuance; varying treatment of
          racial and ethnic groups; and proposals for reform.
                                                               4159

BECKER, W.H. and STEWART, D.J. Prisoner petition processing in the
federal courts by use of pattern forms, parajudicial personnel, and
computers. Kan L Rev 20:579-629 (1972).
          Chief Judge, U.S. District Court, W.D. Missouri, and
          a lawyer have devised a system to process ordinary
          repetitive civil and criminal actions and prisoner
          petitions in particular, using form paragraphs in the
          memorandum and judgment of disposition, and a properly
          programmed computer.   4160

BERGAN, F. Old court and the new law. Record 27:13-22 (1972).
          Judge discusses the present impasse created by failure

to meet heavy caseload brought about by increase in
crime and improved protective measures in criminal
law. He recommends advance agreement on limitation of
the range of relevant proof, independent judicial fact
finding such as reliability of a witness' identification, loan of court facilities and personnel to relieve
congestion, and identical Federal and State statutes
of limitation on instituting habeas corpus proceedings.
4161

BOTEIN, B. A twenty-four hour arraignment court. Legal Aid Brief
Case 25:127-30 (1967).
(For annotation see item 971)   4162

BURGER, W.E. The image of justice. Judicature 55:200-202 (1971).
Address delivered at 1971 Judicial Conference of Second
Circuit, on criminal delay, recommends speedy trial
priority for: a. those denied bail, b. those accused
of serious violent crime, c. those out on bail with
records of violent crime.   4163

CALIFORNIA. Superior Court, Los Angeles Co. Special Committee on
Judicial Reforms. Report and recommendations. Los Angeles, 1971.
40 p.
Covers speedy trial concepts; App. 1: timetable for
felony cases.   4164

CAMPBELL, W.J. Delays in criminal cases; before Conference of Metropolitan Chief District Judges of the Federal Judicial Center. FRD
55:229-56 (1973).
Federal district judge asserts that the reason for increase in federal criminal case burden is the decisions
of the Supreme Court requiring multiple proceedings,
when only few cases require them. Provides suggestions
to speed cases, including specialized federal criminal
bar, extended use of computers, elimination of indictments of more than five counts, cutting pretrial detention, strict time limits for trial and appeal, expanded criminal discovery, upgraded plea bargaining,
repeal of the conspiracy statute.   :4165

CAMPBELL, W.J. Proposals for improvements in the administration of
criminal justice. Chi B Rec 54:75-81 (1972).
Suggests elimination of grand jury, repeal of conspiracy statute, diversion from criminal court of certain
cases (Brooklyn Plan), deciding criminal appeals per
curiam where possible, and tightening up of appellate
procedures.   4166

CASPER, G. and ZEISEL, H. Lay judges in the German criminal courts.
J Leg Studies 1:135-91 (1972).
How used and their effect on facilitating criminal cases.
4167

COHEN, M. Speedy trial for convicts: a re-examination of the demand
rule. Val U L Rev 3:197-205 (1969).
>   Historical retrospect of speedy trial and what consti-
>   tutes waiver; run-down of pertinent cases defining
>   speedy trial.   4168

COMISKY, M. Slow justice is preferable to speedy injustice. Pa B A Q
40:23-28 (1972).
>   Author enumerates dangers inherent in "speedy" justice;
>   and discusses recent U.S. Supreme Court decisions a-
>   bridging rights - a "return to yesterday;" suggests
>   alternatives other than to attack those seeking to pro-
>   tect certain rights.   4169

CONVICT'S right to a speedy trial. J Crim L 61:352-66 (1970).
>   Students consider the decision of Smith v Hooey, 393
>   US 374 (1969), in which convicts were assured their
>   right to a speedy trial. They also examine the convict's
>   right to a speedy trial before Hooey and explore the
>   ramifications of Hooey on penal administration, the
>   law concerning speedy trial, and relevant procedural
>   mechanics.   4170

CONVICTS - the right to speedy trial and the new detainer statutes.
Rutgers L Rev 18:828-74 (1964).
>   Review and analysis of cases dealing with right; impact
>   of detainer statutes; and applicability of constitu-
>   tional right to convicts; waiver and exceptions; im-
>   prisonment in another jurisdiction; remedies. Appendix:
>   Constitutional and statutory compilation of right to
>   speedy trial in all of the states.   4171

CURTISS, W.D. Achieving prompt criminal trials in New York. NYSB J
44:517-23 (1972).
>   Law professor examines judicial decisions, administra-
>   tive rules and legislative enactments which pertain
>   to the necessity for and the achievement of prompt crim-
>   inal trials; also discusses problems of funding prompt
>   trial plans.   4172

DONVITO, P.A. An experiment in the use of court statistics. Judicature 56:56-66 (1972).
>   Presents indicators to measure and compare amount of
>   time taken to dispose of criminal cases, extent to
>   which convicted had pleaded guilty, percent of jail
>   prisoners awaiting trial, backlog of criminal cases
>   relative to court's caseload, average number of cases
>   disposed of per judge and extent to which probation
>   is used as alternative to imprisonment. Courts selected
>   try felony cases in San Diego, Los Angeles, Philadel-
>   phia, New Jersey, San Francisco, Baltimore, and Wash-
>   ington, D.C.; tables with comment.   4173

ADMINISTRATION OF CRIMINAL JUSTICE

ECONOMIC Development Council of New York City. Cost/saving analysis
of administrative improvements in the New York City Criminal Courts.
N.Y., Peat, Marwick, Mitchell & Co., 1973. 1 v., var. pag.
    Various administrative improvements occurred in N.Y.C.
Criminal Court from Dec. 31 to June 30, 1972. (see item
4209) This study presents resulting cost savings prepared according to cost accounting practices. Annual
estimated net savings to city is found to be $6,774,000.
Time savings to court and defendants is also evaluated
in dollars.   4174

ELLENBOGEN, H. The administration and scheduling of criminal court
business; an address delivered ... at a National Symposium on Science
and Criminal Justice ... Washington, D.C., June 23, 1966. Pittsburgh,
1966. 9 p.
    Judge observes that criminal courts must be administer-
ed so as to have an adequate number of judges and facilities and must schedule quick trials to help deal with
crime and criminals. He notes that the Criminal Courts
of Allegheny County have been successful in eliminating backlog, and urges the use of automation to help
in handling criminal cases. The Judge also criticizes
the executive branch of government for failing in the
treatment and rehabilitation of criminals.   4175

ERICKSON, W.H. The right to a speedy trial: standards for its implementation. Houston L Rev 10:237-250 (1973).
    Colorado Supreme Court justice discusses the limits of
the U.S. Supreme Court's ad hoc balancing test for
speedy trials, and urges judicial or statutory adoption
of the ABA standards (item 4157) which he describes.
Author presents proposal for statutory reform and cites
sources of right to speedy trial in state constitutions,
statutes and court rules.   4176

ERVIN, S.J. Speedy trial: by legislation or court rule. Judges' J
13:16-18 (1974).
    After discussing Federal Judicial Center studies on
delay in federal cases, Senator comments on FRCrim P
50(b) and U.S. Second Circuit speedy trial rule, stressing shortcomings and deficiencies: claims that courts
are usurping legislative power, rules are proving ineffective. Only Congress can break logjam in courts,
by ordering courts, prosecutors, and defense lawyers
to seek speedy trial and by providing the wherewithal
to accomplish this; describes his legislative proposal,
S.754 (item 4231).   4177

FLEMING, M. The law's delay: the dragon slain Friday breathes fire
again on Monday. Public Interest 32:13-33 (1973).
    After analyzing why the litigant, the advocate, and
the judge may seek delay and so contribute to long

periods of waiting before the criminal trial, the author
gives specific examples in run-of-the-mill cases of
untoward delay, including appellate court. He then examines procedures initiated to expedite criminal cases,
with illustrative examples. He discusses effective calendar control by the court advocating control by the
judge over routine criminal cases. Author compares
cases: Lord Haw-Haw (English) with Tokyo Rose (American), where defenses were similar but chronologies
differed widely. He discusses special problems of the
extraordinary criminal case and speaks to the art of
the trial judge in controlling such proceedings and
the difficulties involved.   4178

FOSCHIO, L.G. Empirical research and the problem of court delay, in
Reducing Court delay, National Symposium on Law Enforcemnt Science
and Technology, 4th, 1972. Washington, USGPO, 1973. p. 35-44.
          Co-director summarizes methodology and major findings
          of University of Notre Dame's Systems study in court
          delay: LEADICS, joint Law and Engineering School ef-
          fort (see item 4240). Survey described here covers
          1963-1970, analyzes effect in two Indiana criminal
          courts of statutes, court rules, practices on criminal
          procedure at three stages: arrest to arraignment,
          arraignment to disposition, appellate stage. Findings
          include: law itself builds in delay; judges need to
          exercise greater individual control, especially in view
          of high volume of plea-negotiated dispositions; appel-
          late delay is excessive. Discusses benefits and limi-
          tations of empirical studies of delay.   4179

GAZELL, J.A. State trial courts: the increasing visibility of a
quagmire in criminal justice. Criminology 9:379-400 (1972).
          Delay in various procedures, dearth of competent trial
          attorneys, high bail, and inconsistent sentences are
          indigenous to state trial courts dispensing criminal
          justice, various efforts to stem the backlog in Cook
          County criminal courts are described. The author sug-
          gests methods to improve.   4180

GODBOLD, J.C. Speedy trial: major surgery for a national ill. Ala
L Rev 24:265-94 (1972).
          Circuit court judge delves into history behind the
          "speedy trial" clause; he analyzes U.S. Supreme Court
          cases involving this issue, discussing, among others,
          the essential element, prejudice. He then looks to all
          causes of delay both on the government and defendant
          sides. ABA Standards Relating to Speedy Trial (item
          4157) are analyzed as to 60-day limitation suggested
          by Chief Justice Burger; the author describes the com-
          prehensive efforts of the Supreme Court under the rule-
          making power to expedite criminal cases in the federal

disctict courts, mentioning the Second Circuit rules.
A summation of the significant points is made of <u>Barker
v Wingo</u> 407 US 514 (1972).   <u>4181</u>

GORMAN, T.O. Excessive delay in the courts: toward a continuance
policy relating to counsel and parties. Cleve St L Rev 21:118-140
(1972).
    Discusses grounds for granting continuances and court's
inherent power as decided by civil and criminal cases;
makes recommendations for court rules regarding ill-
ness, counsel withdrawal, absence of parties, docket
conflicts; sanctions, costs.   <u>4182</u>

GROSS, S.E. Denial of the right to a speedy trial: strict remedy
for an uncertain doctrine. J System J 1:73-83 (1974).
    Law assistant discusses particularly <u>Strunk v U.S.</u>,
412 US 434 (1973), involving issue raised that defendant had been denied his Sixth Amendment right to a
speedy trial. Seventh Circuit had held that relief less
drastic than dismissal could be granted under certain
circumstances. In that event, defendant could be credited with time equal to length of delay. Supreme Court
in Strunk unanimously reversed and held the only remedy
was dismissal. Author then proceeds to discuss the
essence of this right compared to other constitutional
guarantees, giving examples. Discussion broadens into
possible solutions and illustrations of experiments to
reduce court congestion in New York City's criminal
courts. The "speedy trial" balancing tests enumerated
in <u>Barko v Wingo</u>, 407 US 514 (1972), are analyzed.
                                                      <u>4183</u>

HAYNES, H.P. Reducing court delay, in <u>Reducing court delay</u>, National
Symposium on Law Enforcement Science and Technology, 4th, 1972.
Washington, USGPO, 1973. p. 45-65.
    After literary and legal references to delay, including
state speedy trial statutes, and after pointing out
that U.S. Supreme Court aviods specific limits, author
calls for studies in many courts to determine what is
normal in each, without which delay cannot be defined.
Cautions that delay is symptom of deeper trouble, so
resists the hitherto piecemeal solutions of many reports and studies. Court delay a misnomer: delay occurs
at every stage and involves many actors in criminal
process, so that only coordinated efforts can succeed.
Cites (but doesn't describe) one such effort in D.C.
Superior Court, where author is Asst. Court Executive.
                                                      <u>4184</u>

HENN, R.B. Speedy trial: no "mere ceremonial." Cleve St L Rev 21:
147-161 (1972).
    Evaluates Sixth Amendment cases guaranteeing speedy
trial; discusses waiver doctrine and demonstrates con-

stitutional weakness as applied to speedy trial clause;
doctrine needs clarification by U.S. Supreme Court.
4185

IMPLEMENTATION of the speedy trial guarantee in Louisiana. La L Rev
33:568-79 (1973).
Comment examines post-arrest delays under the Louisiana
Code of Criminal Procedure in terms of constitutional
limitations; suggests use of the ABA standards to provide guidelines in applying the procedural rules.4186

INSTITUTE For Court Management. A comparison of disposition times
in the felony level courts of Baltimore City and Montgomery County,
Maryland, by G.G. Kershaw. Denver, 1972. 25 p.
Nine tables, two appendices, and narrative report comparing disposition times in felony courts of a big
city and a suburban court.   4187

INTERNATIONAL Symposium on Criminal Justice Information and Statistics
Systems, 1972. Proceedings of the International Symposium on Criminal Justice and Statistics Systems, sponsored by Project SEARCH and
the Law Enforcement Assistance Administration, October 3-5, 1972,
New Orleans. Washington, LEAA, 1973. 633 p.
Developments in criminal justice technology; information and statistical systems; computer uses.   4188

JUSTICE British style -- lessons U.S. lawyers see [changes that might
speed trials and end disruptions]. U.S. News & World Rep 1971:36-37
(Aug. 2).
U.S. lawyers praise British system for maintaining high
professional standards for bar and bench. They contend
lack of court congestion is a result of: Limiting appeals by disallowing legal technicalitites as grounds
for reversal; broad police powers in arrest and questioning; admissibility of illegally obtained evidence.
4189

KATZ. L. Analysis of pretrial delay in felony cases: a summary report. Washington, USGPO, 1972. 14 p.
Author presents the conclusions and recommendations of
an empirical study of the Cuyahoga County Court (Cleveland, Ohio). Time-consuming pretrial procedures are
reviewed to show inordinate unnecessary delays. Author
offers twenty-five procedural changes regarding preliminary hearings, plea bargaining, motion practice
and bail.   4190

KATZ, L.R., LITWIN, L. and BAMBERGER, R. Justice is the crime - pretrial delay in felony cases. Cleveland, Case Western Reserve U, 1972.
386 p.
Prepared originally for the National Institute of Law
Enforcement and Criminal Justice, LEAA, the purpose of
book is to analyze pretrial criminal procedures and

show how these contribute to delay; authors examine
goal of each procedure, whether essential to due process, identifying problem areas; changes are recommended to alter drift toward greater delay; an extensive
examination is made into origins of our system and
delay in the courts. All processes before trial including bail are scrutinized, with case histories. The
judge's role is analyzed. App. A gives court statistics
of time lapses, Cuyahoga County Court of Common Pleas;
App. B is a state-by-state analysis of basic procedures
applicable in each state to the preliminary stages of
a criminal prosecution. Material includes statutes,
criminal rules, and judicial opinions. Bibliography
(367-375).   **4191**

KLEINDIENST, R.G. Toward speedy justice. Tex Police J (Feb. 1972);
Repr. Cong Rec 118:4899-4901 (1972).
U.S. Deputy Attorney General is concerned with the backlogs and delays in many federal district courts and
suggests not only increased workloads and manpower but
also revisions in the jurisdiction of the federal district courts, post-conviction remedies, pretrial motion
practice and reform of the jury system.   **4192**

LAMBROS, T.D. Plea bargaining and the sentencing process. FRD 509-
24 (1972).
(For annotation see item **3620**)   **4193**

LEGAL AID Society of New York. Memoranda for Justice Dudley and
Judge Massi ... on all-purpose part of the Criminal Court, Queens
County. N.Y., 1969, 1970. 20 p.
A series of four memoranda analyzing the effect of the
all-purpose part in the Queens Criminal Court; urges
the extension of all-purpose parts and cites the re-
education of case backlogs and the higher case loads
in this part.   **4194**

LOOK at the new second circuit rules for the prompt disposition of
criminal cases. Minn L Rev 56:73-94 (1971).
Evaluation of Second Circuit's six month ready rule
for swift case disposition. Concludes that the rules
are good, but more specific standards for implementation and reporting are needed at the district court
level.   **4195**

MARLOW, R.A. Proposed changes in the criminal court system. Advocate
(Bronx Co, N.Y., Bar Assn) 13:163-75 (1966).
Describes calendaring process and suggests changes for
New York City in the areas of drawing of complaint,
arraignment, post-arraignment and calendaring, and
assignment to trial; proposes that all calendaring be
done by the clerk.   **4196**

MILLER, J.N. New York group produces "instant" court reforms. Nat
Civic Rev 61:120-27 (1972).
(For annotation see item 988)   4197

NATIONAL Conference of Commissioners on Uniform State Laws. Uniform
Mandatory Disposition of Detainers Act 1958. Its Handbook 1968:262-
63.
Act, adopted in eight states as of 1972, provides for
request by prisoner for final disposition of any pending untried complaint, information, indictment. Includes responsibility of warden to notify prisoner
of such complaints of which he knows and of prisoner's
right to request disposition; requires court and prosecutor to act promptly, i.e. within 90 days.   4198

NATIONAL Symposium on Law Enforcement Science and Technology, 4th,
1972. Reducing court delay ... papers at National Symposium ...
conducted by Institute of Criminal Justice and Criminology, University of Maryland. Washington, USGPO, 1973. 116 p. (Criminal Justice Monograph)
Contents: Ash, M. Court delay, crime control, and neglect of the interests of witnesses (see item 4030).--
Foschio, L.G. Empirical research and the problem of
court delay (see item 4179).--Haynes, H.P. Reducing
court delay (see item 4184).--Nayar, R., Bleuel, W.H.
Simulation of a criminal court case processing system
(see item 4200).--Pabst, W.R., Jr. A study of juror
utilization (see item 2623).   4199

NAYAR, R. and BLEUEL, W.H. Simulation of a criminal court case processing system, in Reducing court delay, Fourth National symposium on Law Enforcement Science and Technology, 1972. Washington, USGPO, 1973. p. 66-90.
Description of authors' model of all agencies involved
in criminal process from arraignment to disposition in
Rochester and Monroe Co., New York (city and county
courts), constructed so that computer analysis can
pinpoint bottlenecks by length of "queues" of cases
at various stages. Lists parameters used for misdemeanors and felonies separately, describes validation method
briefly.   4200

NEW JERSEY Supreme Court. Report of the Joint New Jersey Supreme
Court and the New Jersey Bar Association Committees on Expedition
of the Criminal Calendars. March 9, 1971. Trenton, 1971. 31 p.
Series of recommendations, including: Six-member juries
in all but capital cases, limit of ten peremptory
challenges in capital cases, five in others; elimination of Municipal Courts and probable cause hearings
in indictable offenses; determination of motions to
suppress before the jury is sworn, automatic discovery,
expansion of the practice of disposing without con-

viction the cases of first offenders. Rejects the elimination of the grand jury, introduction of the omnibus
hearing, and other proposals.   4201

NEW YORK (City) Criminal Justice Coordinating Council. New York City
Criminal Court: case flow and congestion from 1959 to 1968; report
to the Mayor's Criminal Justice Coordinating Council by S.H. Clarke,
NYC Criminal Justice Information Bureau, Apr. 1970. N.Y., 1970.
38 p.
          This report analyzes developments in the Criminal Court
          on the basis of statistical data; refers to the increase
          in reported crimes, the resulting criminal court work-
          load, summonsed offenses and the flow of cases through
          the court; concludes that there is a need for revision
          of court operating procedures and development of a
          management information system; appendix is supportive
          tables and figures.   4202

NEW YORK (City) Criminal Justice Coordinating Council and VERA Institute of Justice. Manhattan summons project. N.Y., 1969. 10 p.
          (For annotation see item 994)   4203

NEW YORK (County) District Attorney. Proposals for reducing delays
in criminal justice in New York City; statement of the District
Attorney of New York [F.S. Hogan] N.Y., 1971. 43 p.
          Presents detailed findings and recommendations in the
          areas of the police department, the courts, the dis-
          trict attorney's office, legal aid, the corrections
          department, probation and other related institutions;
          proposals include the elimination of mass arrests of
          suspected drug addicts and prostitutes, elimination of
          the separate New York City Criminal Court, the com-
          puterization of court records and correction department
          records, the disciplining of attorneys for unexcused
          lateness or absence, allowing waiver of grand jury,
          and restrictions on right to appeal.   4204

NEW YORK courts seek to cut backlog. Judicature 54:262 (1971).
          Judicial Conference announces steps to alleviate the
          criminal case backlog in New York City courts, such
          as transferring judges from civil to criminal cases,
          increasing the number of trial parts and reviewing pend-
          ing cases to ascertain reasons for their not being
          tried.   4205

NEW YORK State Bar Association Committee on Administration of Criminal Justice. Memorandum from R.P. Patterson, Jr., chair, Feb. 23,
1972; subject: prompt trials budget. Albany, 1972. 1 v., var. pag.
          Memorandum consists of actual budgets for implementa-
          tion of recommendations to allow for prompt trials in-
          cluding: specified allocations to individual courts;
          means of relieving overcrowded detention facilities;

and the renovation of courthouses to provide adequate
space. Appendices of salaries and cost schedules of
New York City Grand Jury and Trial Part criminal-con-
verted civil parts.   4206

NEW YORK (State) Judicial Conference. Rules governing release from
custody and dismissal of prosecution, to be effective May 1, 1972.
N Y Jud Conf Rep 17:A18-A20 (1972).
            Rules require speedy trial and disposition of criminal
            cases, or release of defendant or dismissal of prosecu-
            tion. (see N.Y. Session Laws 1972, c. 184, sec. 30.20)
                                                       4207

NEW YORK (State) Judicial Conference Committee on Court Delay in New
York City. Achieving prompt trials in New York City: a report ...
Mar. 6, 1972. N.Y., 1972. 59 p.
            Committee, called by Judicial Conference and consisting
            of it plus the five District Attorneys of New York City,
            the Appellate Divs., 1st and 2d Depts., Legal Aid So-
            ciety, criminal justice planning agencies, and others,
            assesses capacity of Supreme Court in the city (where
            felony trials take place) to meet speedy trial stand-
            ards adopted by the Judicial Conference. Data is pre-
            sented on sample of 1,242 defendants throughout city,
            based upon which this report recommends additional
            grand jury sessions and Supreme Court parts, improved
            court management and case processing, uniform rules of
            procedure.   4208

NEW YORK (State) Supreme Court First Judicial District Criminal Branch.
Quarterly report to the administrative board of the Judicial Conference of the State of New York on the administrative reorganization of
the Criminal Branch, Supreme Court, First Judicial District. June 14,
1973. N.Y., 1973. 2 v., 65 p. Eight month report ... Jan. 10, 1974.
52 p.
            (For annotations see items 1001, 1001a)   4209

NORTH CAROLINA Administrative Office of the Courts. Delay in the
Superior Courts of North Carolina and an assessment of its causes,
by J.O. Williams and R.J. Richardson. Raleigh, 1973. 55 p.
            Two political science professors using scientific sam-
            pling procedures, with Administrative Office coopera-
            tion, examine extent of criminal delay. After defining
            "backlog," authors look at measure of conformity of
            North Carolina courts to speedy trial rules and ABA stand-
            ards. Procedures in misdemeanor and felony cases are
            analyzed to determine caseloads, extent of delay, rea-
            sons for delay; average time in felony and misdemeanor
            cases is determined. Numerous tables give criminal
            statistics as to numbers of cases and extent of delay
            in each stage. Comparison is made with other states,
            and rural and urban area delays receive comment. 4210

ADMINISTRATION OF CRIMINAL JUSTICE

PROVINCE, J.T. The defendant's dilemma: valid charge or speedy trial.
Crim L Bull 6:421-31 (1970).
> Author discusses statutory provisions implementing
> speedy trial constitutional guarantees and considers
> whether defendant's challenge to the validity of an
> indictment should constitute voluntary delay, thus dis-
> charging the statute. Cases pro and con are examined.
> Author concludes that defendant should not be forced
> to choose between his constitutional right to a speedy
> trial and challenging the validity of the charge against
> him.   4211

REED, J.C. Application of operations research to court delay. N.Y.,
Praeger, 1973. 300 p.
> How-to-do-it book in which business administration pro-
> fessor demonstrates problem solving through mathematical
> models as applied to criminal case-flow in U.S. District
> Court for D.C. Some preliminary definition and theory;
> 8-p. bibliography.   4212

RIGHT to a speedy trial: a case study of the St. Louis criminal docket.
St. Louis U L J 16:84-111 (1971).
> Comment examines extent to which the interest in speedy
> trial prevails in the St. Louis criminal court system,
> and problems preventing speedy trial, also nature and
> constitutional basis of the right to a speedy trial,
> the present situation, and possible solutions. Appen-
> dices: felony cases issued by year; elapsed time from
> arraignment to sentencing; numbers of and averaged
> elapsed time for cases nolle prossed.   4213

ROTHWAX, H.J. The Criminal court: problems and proposals; Memorandum
to New York City Criminal Justice Coordinating Council. Sep. 1970.
N.Y., 1971. 30 p.
> Law professor details his experiences in New York City
> Criminal Court, pointing out the fragmentation of sys-
> tem, lack of adequate counsel for defendants and lack
> of preparedness by prosecutors; offers practical sug-
> gestions covering negotiating pleas, calendaring, utili-
> zation of courtroom facilities, selection of judges,
> and setting standards for Legal Aid attorneys. Is also
> critical of the Court's judges.   4214

SAN FRANCISCO Committee on Crime. A report on the criminal courts
of San Francisco. San Francisco, 1970, 1971. 2 v.
> V.1: Superior court backlog: consequences and remedies.
> December 22, 1970. V. 2: Bail and O.R. release. Feb.
> 10, 1971. Part 1. Description, reasons for, and sta-
> tistics of backlog in superior court criminal cases,
> discussion of plea bargaining, and recommendations
> for its improvement, such as judicial involvement, use
> of presentence reports, and a comprehensive list of

recommendations to cut the backlog, directed to the
Courts, the legislature, the mayor and the board of
supervisors, the D.A. and Public Defender, including
changes in the substantive law, reassignment of judges,
use of civil courts for felony preliminary hearings
and pretrial motions. App. A: Processing of defendants ... in San Francisco. App. B: Disposition of felony cases by guilty pleas in San Francisco Superior
Court and San Francisco Municipal Court. Part 2: Description of San Francisco bail system, effects of bail
or detention on disposition of cases; operation of the
San Francisco O.R. Bail Project, operation of O.R.
(own recognizance) in misdemeanor cases. Recommends
continuing and expanding O.R. program. Also discusses
the state's mandatory assessment of 25% of bail as a
penalty, "ten percent bail," supervisory conditions on
release, and preventive detention.   4215

SCHINDLER, P.M. Interjurisdictional conflict and the right to a
speedy trial. U Cin L Rev 35:179-93 (1966).
        Author discusses prejudice to sentenced accused in de-
        laying prosecution and trial in another jurisdiction;
        illustrative cases.   4216

SEYMOUR, W.N., Jr. Speedy trial from the standpoint of the federal
prosecutor. Cong Rec 118:30404-05 (1972).
        Noting importance of speedy trials, U.S. Attorney, S.D.
        N.Y., describes successful experience of his office in
        expediting criminal prosecutions. He remarks on the
        benefits that have resulted from speedy trial rules,
        the net effect being increased rates of disposition
        and of conviction.   4217

SOLFISBURG, R.J., Jr. Judicial administration of criminal cases;
problems confronting our court system. Ill B J 57:624-31 (1969).
        Chief Justice poses problems of unresolved need for
        revenue, shortage of lawyers and personnel, and in-
        creased burden on the court system. He recommends "ne-
        gotiated" guilty pleas, limitation on retroactivity
        for new rights, and legislative aid to the judicial
        system.   4218

SPEEDY trial. Cal L Rev 60:900-12 (1972).
        Explores California courts' view of prearrest and pre-
        prosecution delay, particularly Jones v Superior Court,
        3 Cal3d 734 (1970), which held that an unjustified de-
        lay of 19 months between filing of a complaint and an
        arrest violated defendant's right to speedy trial.
                                                       4219

SPEEDY trial: a comparative analysis between the American Bar Association standards of criminal justice and Arkansas law. Ark L Rev 25:
234-49 (1971).

Student compares Arkansas criminal law with the ABA
Standards and notes that they differ in four major
areas: court control over its calendar, continuance,
specificity in the speedy trial statutes and exempted
periods of delay.   4220

SPEEDY trial: a constitutional right in search of a definition. Geo
L J 61:657-702 (1973).
Examination of U.S. Supreme Court and other federal
cases interpreting speedy trial right and factual report on criminal activities due to court delay. Author
examines four sets of speedy trial rules: New York
state's, ABA Standards, U.S. Second Circuit rules, and
S.895, the federal Speedy Trial Act of 1971. Concludes
that S.895 provides best approach because it integrates
judicial and legislative efforts to eliminate delay,
recognizes fiscal needs, and makes courts accountable.
                                                     4221

SPEEDY trial in Florida: Has the defendant's shield become his sword?
U Fla L Rev 24:517-40 (1972).
Description of Florida Supreme Court's new speedy trial,
in context of previous Florida law and other states'
practices. Discusses what constitutes a speedy trial,
who is entitled, and procedural rules, such as waiver
and good cause prejudice, which weaken the Florida
statute. Appendix includes tables of other states' rules,
and statistics on speedy trial in criminal cases.4222

SPEEDY trial protection for criminal defendants under Indiana's amended Criminal Rule 4. Val U L Rev 8:683-714 (1974).
Note explores amended rule in light of problems courts
have had in interpreting the rule's predecessors. Critically analyzes new rule: exceptions; time periods; its
application to defendants imprisoned on other offenses;
demand requirements; the burden of establishing cause
of delay; and possible future problems and solutions.
                                                     4223

SPEEDY trial schemes and criminal justice delay. Cornell L Rev 57:
794-826 (1972).
Note examines the likelihood of success of the recent
statutory and court rules setting specific time limits
within which an accused must be brought to trial. Analysis includes: the constitutional right to speedy trial;
redefinition of this guarantee in terms of unavoida-
bility; and general speedy trial schemes and their effect. Author concludes that a well-designed plan, back-
ed by adequate financing, could be effective in hasten-
ing trial and could ensure judicial efficiency and provide a fair trial for the accused.   4224

SPEEDY trial: the three term rule. W Va L Rev 73:184-90 (1971).
Article discusses historical perspective of right to
speedy trial, and rule that persons remanded for trial,
W Va Code ch 62 art 3821 (Michie, 1966), shall be dis-
charged if no trial results within three court terms,
in light of Farley v Kramer, 169 SE2d 106 (W. Va.,
(1969), in which the court held that the challenge to
indictments constituted a statutory exception to the
counting of terms. Analyzes opinion of the court and
effect of the holding, including the issue of bad faith
indictments.   4225

SPEEDY trials and the Second Circuit rules regarding prompt disposition of criminal cases. Colum L Rev 71:1059-76 (1971).
Note discusses the problem of congestion in the trial
courts and analyzes the setting for the U.S. Court of
Appeals Second Circuit rules. Details the rules, which
establish a priority for criminal cases, require biweekly reports from each U.S. Attorney listing persons
in pretrial custody, require the accused's release if
the government is not ready for trial within 90 days,
provide for a dismissal of charges if the prosecution
is not ready for trial within six months, allow for general exceptions to the six-month limit, and eliminate
the requirement that the defendant demand prompt trial
or be deemed to have waived it. Analyzes the constitutional requirements for speedy trial as set forth in
recent case law and evaluates the new rules as a stricter standard than previously required.   4226

[STATE protection of the right to a speedy trial in Kansas, Colorado,
Oklahoma and New York.] Cong Rec 109:11256-58 (1963).   4227

TRIAL delay indemnity - insuring our criminal justice machinery. Notre
Dame Law 42:936-65 (1973).
Historical background regarding indemnifying those un-
justly convicted and later declared innocent, gives
statistics, charts, and statutes regarding such delays,
including preliminary detention and erroneous conviction compensation statutes. Explains types of delay,
burden of proof procedures, standards of proof, type
of damages, measure of damages; Presents proposed model
bill on which to base trial delay indemnity law; case-
annotated.   4228

TUTTLE, J.B. Catch 2254: federal jurisdiction and interstate detainers. U Pitt L Rev 32:489-503 (1971).
Author explains the detainer system and cases which
consider right to speedy trial of prisoner held under
a detainer, in particular Smith v Hooey, 393 US 374
(1969). Author discusses lower courts' attempts to
establish guidelines for speedy trial-detainer cases

and notes that the issue of federal court jurisdiction
remains unresolved.   4229

U. S. COMPTROLLER General. Federally supported attempts to solve
state and local court problems: more needs to be done; report to the
Congress. May 8, 1974. Washington, U.S. Gen Accounting Off, 1974.
46 p.

General Accounting Office, perceiving delay in criminal
cases as area of greatest public and Congressional concern, reviewed LEAA grants in California, Colorado,
Illinois, Massachusetts, New York, and Pennsylvania;
finds that both LEAA and State Planning Agencies failed
to allocate sufficient work in criminal delay (only 17%
spent directly on court administration). Calls for
more specific goals and standards in state plans, and
evaluation of projects, more technical assistance from
LEAA, and development of state statistical systems to
measure any improvement achieved.   4230

U. S. CONGRESS. Senate S.754 to give effect to the Sixth Amendment
right to a speedy trial for persons charged with criminal offenses ...
[text, statement] Cong Rec 119:3263-68 (1973).

Statements by Sen. Ervin and other sponsors of the bill,
which provides for trials within 60 days or dismissal
of charges, and for the creation of demonstration pretrial services agencies to help reduce recidivism. Gives
text of bill and accompanying memorandum.   4231

U. S. CONGRESS. Senate S.1801, to effectuate the provision of
the Sixth Amendment of the U.S. Constitution requiring that defendants in criminal cases be given the right to a speedy trial;
text; statement. Cong Rec 109:11743, 11882-83 (1963).   4232

U. S. Congress. Senate S.3669, to amend the Omnibus Crime Control
and Safe Streets Act of 1968 to require the prompt trial of defendants in criminal cases and provide grants to state and local governments for improving the administration of criminal justice; statement;   Cong Rec 118:19691-96 (1972).

Jackson discusses the bill he is introducing which provides for prompt trials. Included in his statement are
two exhibits: (1) An article, "The War on Crime: The
First 5 Years" by James Vorenberg and (2) Excerpts from
recommendations of the ABA Special Committee on Crime
Prevention and Control.   4233

U. S CONGRESS Senate Committee on the Judiciary. Speedy trial; hearings before Subcommittee on Constitutional Rights. Washington, USGPO,
1971. 983 p. (91st Cong., 2d Sess.)

Bill requires trials for all federal defendants within
60 days of indictment of information. Witnesses include
Sen. Case, D. Freed, W. Rehnquist of the Office of Le-

gal Counsel. Contains statements, texts of bills, proposed amendments, existing and proposed court rules,
reports and studies relating to speedy trials, including the Administrative Office of the United States
Courts' Annual Report of the Director, 1970; Federal
Judicial Center Study on age of criminal cases at termination, fiscal year 1970-71.   4234

U. S. CONGRESS Senate Committee on the Judiciary. Speedy trial;
hearings before the Subcommittee on Constitutional Rights. Washington, USGPO, 1973. 467 p. (93rd Cong., 1st Sess.)
        Discussion of proposed bill (S.754) on 60-day rule in
        federal criminal trials. Witnesses include: G.G. Rosen-
        thal, for ABA Criminal Law Section; J.T. Sneed, Deputy
        Attorney General; C.S. Vance, Pres., National District
        Attorneys Association. Appendix includes: Administra-
        tive Office of the U.S. Courts, Average time lapse
        data supplied to the Constitutional Rights Subcommittee,
        June 1973; Rule 50 (b), model plan of U.S. Judicial
        Conference; and a speedy trial study done for the Ju-
        diciary Cttee by the Federal Judicial Center.   4235

U. S. DEPT. of Justice Office of the Attorney General [Analysis of
the problem of court delay; submitted to Senate Constitutional Rights
Subcommittee concerning proposed amendment to S.895, the speedy
trial act of 1972]. Cong Rec 118:35767-70 (1972).
        Analysis of court delay and comments on new federal
        rule requiring district courts to formulate plans to
        achieve prompt disposition of criminal cases. It op-
        poses such uniform and inflexible rules which fail to
        deal with the underlying causes of delay. Discusses
        experiences in the District of Columbia under the Court
        Reform and Criminal Procedure Act of 1970 where delay
        has been reduced without such rules.   4236

U. S. JUDICIAL Council of the Second Circuit Court of Appeals. Speedy
trials; not preventive detention. [Series of new speedy trial rules
for the federal courts of the second circuit; promulgated Jan. 5,
1971] Reprinted: Cong Rec 117:14711-27 (1971).
        Sen. Ervin addresses the President on S.895, a bill in
        favor of speedy trial and opposed to preventive deten-
        tion, discussing the need for the bill and constitu-
        tional defects of preventive detention. Exhibits in-
        clude text of cases, articles, and studies showing
        the need for, or supporting, this bill.   4237

U. S. LAWS, statutes, etc. Speedy trial act of 1974. P.L. 93-619;
88 Stat. 2076.
        Text of statute, passed Jan. 3, 1975, whose purpose
        is to assist in reducing crime and danger of recidi-
        vism by requiring speedy trials, deals with: time lim-
        it required; sanctions; requirements of district court

plans to assure speedy trial; reports to Congress on progress; advice of Federal Judicial Center; assemblage of information and data to facilitate planning and implementation; appropriations; recommendations where district court cannot comply with time limits because of backlog; and establishment of pretrial service agencies, including function and powers.   4238

U. S. NATIONAL Institute of Law Enforcement and Criminal Justice. Citizen dispute settlement, the night prosecutor program of Columbus, Ohio. Washington, 1974. 16 p.
            Brochure describes the program, created in 1971, in which minor criminal cases arising from neighborhood and family desputes are screened by the prosecutor's office and referred to law student hearing officers for mediation.   4239

UNIVERSITY of Notre Dame Law School and School of Engineering. Systems study in court delay; LEADICS: law-engineering analysis of delay in court systems. Notre Dame, 1971, 1972. 3 v.
            V. 1: Executive summary. V. 2: Legal analysis and recommendations. V. 3: Engineering section (methodology). Study of criminal courts in Indianapolis and South Bend attempts to find time and activity needed for each function of felony process from arrest to disposition (appeals included), by computer analysis of 2,500-case sample. Simulation model (described) permits testing of various solutions, as well as analysis of functions, without disruption of actual judicial system. Findings generally: outmoded legal procedures and admininistrative inertia in both courts and prosecutors' offices cause needless delay; some legislative correction desirable but much improvement possible through exercise of existing power. (For summary, see item 4179) 4240

WALTHER, D.L. Detainer warrants and the speedy trial provision. Marq L Rev 46:423-29 (1963).
            Considers decisions involving right to speedy trial in effort to resolve the problem area of detainer warrants when a prisoner's trial may be delayed.   4241

WILSON, C.H., Jr. Delay and congestion in the criminal courts; some proposals for reform. Fla B J 46:88-92 (1972).
            Author discusses the growing problem and burden of court congestion, leading to a crisis of confidence in the judicial system: the effect of delay; the threat of innocent people pleading guilty to avoid months of pretrial detention; and possible reforms such as restoring judicial control, fixed time limits, nodified court procedures, elimination of grand juries, accelerated appeals, and use of management techniques.   4242

WRIGHT, E.W. Some thought on judicially caused delay. Judges' J
11:38-40 (1972).
> Judge's lecture at National College for State Trial
> Judges deals with specific cases illustrating how judge
> adds to delays in trial of criminal cases; includes
> delays in starting trial, remarks causing mistrials and
> appeals, delay in issuing opinions or judgment, and in
> imposing sentence.   4243

2. Items on diversion of cases from the criminal justice system; this section includes
   juveniles; also covers intervention at all
   stages; description and evaluation of programs; some items give cost.

ADDICT diversion as alternative for the criminal justice system. Geo
L J 60:667-710 (1972).
> Note considers procedures currently used to divert drug
> addicts out of court process and into treatment before
> conviction. Examined are: various existing programs;
> fundamental characteristics of addict diversion programs;
> and constitutional problems. Author finds liberal eli-
> gibility, minimum punitive connotations, early treat-
> ment, and incentives essential to success of programs
> and advocates extended use of such programs.   4244

AMERICAN Bar Association National Pretrial Intervention Service Center. Descriptive profiles on selected pretrial criminal justice intervention programs; portfolio. Washington, ABA Cmssn on Correctional
Facilities and Services, 1974. 49 p.
> Describes ten pretrial intervention programs in Boston,
> Atlanta, Baltimore (2), California, Florida, D.C., Min-
> neapolis, Jersey City and New York; accents administra-
> tive and operational characteristics. Profiles include
> establishment, eligibility characteristics, program
> duration, termination, staff, participant screening,
> services, research and evaluation done, participant
> characteristics, and results. All projects start at pre-
> arraignment period, offer similar counseling, vocational
> training, job placement, and educational and social
> services. Five programs handle only youthful offenders
> with no serious prior record, five programs accept ap-
> plicants up to 45 years old with no serious prior record.
> All exclude those accused of serious crimes, although
> crimes excluded differ. See also the Center's Sourcebook
> in pretrial criminal justice intervention techniques
> (1974, 188 p.) which has descriptions of four projects,
> a list of most known projects as of May 1974, and
> samples of court rules, commission recommendations,
> legislation, evaluation research aids.   4245

AMERICAN Correctional Association Juvenile Services Project. Juvenile
diversion: a perspective. College Park, Md., 1972. 24 p.

The acute caseload pressure on juvenile correctional
facilities necessitates diversion, especially to handle
the estimated 40-50% of offenders held for offenses
for which adults would not be liable. A summary of
types of diversion programs and their common elements
is given. Bibliography: p. 21-24.   4246

AMERICAN Judicature Society. Statutory review of the use of volunteers in the court, by J.T. Duax. Chicago, 1971. 16 p. (Rep 32)
          The author urges the enactment of statutes which would
          authorize the use of volunteers to assist in the re-
          habilitation of criminals, including juveniles. Sug-
          gestions for a "model act" are set forth. App. 1: texts
          of laws in eight states that have statutory authori-
          zation.   4247

BAER, H. Recidivism, discretion and deferred prosecution. Record
29:141-48 (1974).
          Describes federal programs administered by Vera Insti-
          tute of Justice for deferred prosecution called "Brook-
          lyn Plan" and "Court Employment Project." "Brooklyn
          Plan" involves deferring prosecution against juveniles
          in Kings County while the "Court Employment Plan" re-
          fers to juveniles in the Southern District; narcotic
          and second offenders are not included; the plans in-
          volve counseling, placement, rehabilitation.   4248

BARON, R. and FEENEY, F. Preventing delinquency through diversion:
the Sacramento County Probation Department 601 Diversion Project: a
first year report. Davis, U of Cal Center of Admin on Crim Just,
1972. 58 p.
          Program handling Sec. 601 "pre-delinquent offenders"
          (truants, runaways), through short term family crisis
          therapy in lieu of juvenile court procedures, produces
          more diversion, reduction of detention and of repeat
          cases, and lowers operating costs.   4249

BORUCHOWITZ, R.C. Victimless crimes: a proposal to free the courts.
Judicature 57:69-78 (1973).
          Suggests diversion from criminal courts of vagrancy,
          gambling, drunkenness cases; also certain aspects of
          juvenile behavior: drug use, and sex offenses. Cites
          to state statutes.   4250

BRAKEL, S.J. Diversion from the criminal justice process: informal
discretion, motivation and formalization. Denver L J 48:211-38
(1971/1972).
          Explains concept of diversion; specific practices and
          their rationales include diversion of white collar
          crime, shoplifting, family disputes and first offense;
          suggests types of punishments including grace periods
          for restitution; fines for shoplifting; peace bonds for

family disputes and deferred sentences, court employment programs for first offenders.   4251

BRAKEL, S.J. and SOUTH, G.R. Diversion from the criminal process in
the rural community. Am Crim L Q 7:122-73 (1969); reprint AB Foundation research contributions, 1969, 6.
> Study of two areas in southern Illinois finds that in
> contrast with urban areas, arrest is not the initial
> step to disposition of a problem with a determination
> to be made later, but is a choice of disposition. In-
> formality dominates and authors found a serious lack
> of coordination with authorities on mental health,
> alcohol cases. Very little retention of local control
> of juvenile offenders is indicated.   4252

CALIFORNIA Judicial Council. Recommendation concerning a system for
classifying minor traffic violations as non-criminal traffic infractions. San Francisco, 1966. 41 p.
> This proposed reclassification would result in the
> elimination of time-consuming trial procedures such as
> right to a jury trial and right to appointed counsel.
> Includes proposed bill which contains the Council's
> recommendation and a listing of Vehicle Code violations
> to be classified as infractions.   4253

CARTER, R.M. The diversion of offenders. Fed Prob 36:31-36 (Dec.
1972).
> Explores origins of diversion and identifies major opera-
> tional and philosophical problems associated with move-
> ment. Demonstrates pressing need for guidelines, stand-
> ards, role of community and study of the long-range im-
> pact on criminal justice and society. Movemement needs
> planning and evaluation.   4254

COULSON, R. Justice behind bars: time to arbitrate. ABA J 59:612-
15 (1973).
> Suggests arbitration of conflicts between prisoners
> and prison administrators instead of resorting to
> courts. Gives specifics on how to create a collective
> bargaining system.   4255

COUNCIL of State Governments. Gambling: a source of state revenue,
by V.G. Cook. Lexington, Ky., 1973. 42 p.
> Report analyzes experiences in eight states having
> lotteries; examines off-track betting in New York City
> and gambling in Nevada; gives state-by-state report on
> the status of gambling. Presents arguments for and
> against legalized gambling with references to other
> studies on gambling.   4256

CRAWFORD, G.C. Rehabilitation of the alcohol addict by use of court
probation. Dicta (San Diego Co. B.A.) 12:3-7 (June 1965).

> Judge presents a progress report on a San Diego pro-
> gram which views the chronic inebrate as a community
> medical problem and attempts to solve the problem
> through the probationary power of the court and use of
> existing community facilities, referring for treatment
> rather than automatically imprisoning. The program has
> been successful in lowering the drunk arrest rate.
>   4257

CRESSY, D.R. and MCDERMOTT, R.A.   Diversion from the juvenile justice
system.   Ann Arbor, Nat Assessment of Juvenile Corrections, U of
Michigan, 1973.   63 p.; also: published by U.S. Nat Inst Of Law Enforcement and Crim Just, Washington, USGPO, 1974.   36 p.
> Exploratory study of diversion processes in juvenile
> justice in some communities in Michigan. Defining the
> term as used in the study, the researchers describe
> their project conducted in "Westlane," "Scottville"
> and "Van Dyke" located in the Mountain View metropoli-
> tan area.   4258

DANZIG, R.   Toward the creation of a complementary decentralized system of criminal justice.   Stanford L Rev 26:1-55 (1973).
> All about designing a neighborhood criminal justice
> system and increasing effectiveness of decentralizing
> some or all of the operations of existing systems; sets
> down working principles. Linking overcriminalization
> with overcentralization, author stresses that certain
> "crimes" do not call for isolation of offender but rath-
> er better integration into society. Community insti-
> tutions are designed to conciliate and keep disputants,
> deviants, delinquents.   4259

DITMAN, K.S., CRAWFORD, G.C., FORGY, E.W., MOSKOWITZ, H. and MACANDREW,
E.   A controlled experiment on the use of probation for drunk arrests.
AM J Psychiatry 124:160-63 (1967).
> Experiment involving court dispositions of chronic
> drunk offenders finds forced referrals to Alcoholics
> Anonymous and clinics did not reduce the likelihood of
> recidivism compared to no treatment.   4260

EMPEY, L.T.   Juvenile justice reform: diversion, due process, and
deinstitutionalization.   In American Assembly.   Prisoners in America,
ed. by L. Ohlin.   Englewood Cliffs, N.J., Prentice-Hall, 1973.   p. 13-
48.
> Review of development of juvenile courts.   4261

GEIS, G.   Not the law's business? an examination of homosexuality,
abortion, prostitution, narcotics, and gambling in the United States.
Washington, USGPO, 1973.   262 p. (National Inst. of Mental Health Center for Studies of Crime and Delin. Crime and delin. issues)
> Uses historical and recent materials from broad interdis-
> ciplinary range; recommends decriminalization of these
> "victimless" crimes. Extensive bibliography in note 15,
> p. 155.   4262

GOLDBERG, N.E. Pre-trial diversion: bilk or bargain. Brief Case
(NLADA) 31:490-93, 499-501 (1973).
> Defining pretrial diversion as involving a decision not
> to prosecute an arrestee on condition that he do some-
> ting in return, author, deputy director of Defender
> Services (NLADA) stresses the need to decide which
> agencies have the discretion, and who are the planners
> of the new system to take on the role of funneling in-
> dividuals into diversionary programs. She comments on
> the standards of the National Advisory Commission Crimi-
> nal Justice Standards and Goals and reports on ABA and
> other pretrial diversion programs, with some evalua-
> tions.   4263

KAPLAN, J. Non-victim criminal offenses. In American Bar Association. Quest for Justice. Chicago, 1973. p. 85-91.
> Describes aspects of gambling, drugs, abortion, sexual
> conduct, prostitution and drunkenness within the orbit.
>   4264

KIESTER, E., Jr. Crimes with no victims; how legislating morality
defeats the cause of justice. N.Y., Alliance for a Safer New York,
1972. 87 p.
> A report stemming from a 1971 statement of principles
> adopted by the Alliance's constituent organizations
> calling for removal of victimless crimes from the crim-
> inal justice system.   4265

KOLE, J. Arbitration as an alternative to the criminal warrant.
Judicature 56:295-97 (1973).
> Center for Dispute Settlement, auspices of American
> Arbitration Association, has succeeded in Philadelphia
> (case load of private criminal hearings in municipal
> court reduced 20%): provides informal handling of all
> but murder cases; if, after two years, arbitrator's
> award or remedy has been carried out, both parties
> still satisfied, charges expunged from court record.
>   4266

KORNBLUM, G.O. and BLINDER, M.G. The alcoholic driver: a proposal
for treatment as an alternative to punishment. Ins L J 1972:133-
50; Chicago, Am Jud Soc, 1972 (its Rep 35); also condensed in Judicature 56:24-28 (1972).
> Law professors discuss the nature of alcoholism and
> the inadequacy of the present system of dealing with
> this problem. They propose reform which emphasizes
> rehabilitation programs, advise on how to administer
> such a program, and offer a model statute. Annotated.
>   4267

LEONARD, R.F. Prosecutor's manual on screening and diversionary
programs. Chicago, Nat District Attorneys Assn, 1972. 291 p.

Manual presents three programs in operation (Michigan, Minneapolis, and Hawaii) which serve to divert selected offenders from the criminal justice processes. Michigan and Minneapolis programs are government funded, with initial screening information going to prosecutors who make determination. Hawaii's has a pretrial screening program involving unsupervised release on condition as part of a plea-bargaining process. Discusses how each program handles constitutional problems.   4268

MEDALIE, R.J.   The offender rehabilitation project: a new role for defense counsel at pre-trial and sentencing.   Georgetown L J 56:2-16 (1967).
        D.C. legal aid agency operates a rehabilitation project in the criminal courts emphasizing pretrial and presentence activity. Professor describes project's purposes and the role of counsel in diverting defendants from criminal process in each stage of prosecution.
        4269

MORRIS, J.A.   First offender, a volunteer program for youth in trouble with the law.   N.Y., Funk & Wagnalls, 1970.   214 p.
        Story of Judge Keith J. Leenhout's successful volunteer probation program for juveniles and misdemeanants in Royal Oak, Michigan, and the spread of these programs to more than 400 cities throughout the country. Chapter 9 provides statistics on the lower recidivism rates in the Royal Oak court compared with those of a control court in a similar community.   4270

MORRIS, N. and HAWKINS, G.   The honest politician's guide to crime control.   Chicago, U of Chicago press, 1970.   282 p.
        Law professor and criminologist contend that the criminal justice system should not be used to enforce private morality, particularly in regard to alcohol, gambling, drugs, and sex. They present a concrete program for coping with the crime problem based on the substantial fund of information now available, with constant attention to the financial costs of any change.
        4271

MUELLER, G.O.W.   Imprisonment and its alternatives.   In Program for prison reform; final report, Annual Chief Justice Earl Warren Conference on Advocacy in the United States, June 9-10, 1972, sponsored by the Roscoe Pound-American Trial Lawyers Foundation.   Cambridge, Mass., 1973.   p. 33-46.
        Brief descriptions of methods of post-conviction diversion used in Europe: work release, conditional supervised release, relocation (e.g. from slums) and "day-fines": units of day's pay, to equalize impact regardless of economic status.   4272

NATIONAL Committee for Children and Youth. A benefit-cost analysis
of Project Crossroads by J.F. Holahan. Washington, 1970. 71 p.
    Analysis of the Project, a manpower program for first
    offenders in D.C., includes: nature and rationale of
    Program; economic costs of crime; benefits from pro-
    jects and diversion, earnings and education; and bene-
    fits in recidivism reduction. Extensive data tables
    and charts.   **4273**

NATIONAL Committee for Children and Youth. Project Crossroads as
pre-trial intervention; a program evaluation. Washington, 1970. 39 p.
    Report describes recent experimental program in which
    Project worked with court and personnel, providing
    counseling and job training for youthful first time
    offenders. Discussed are: project's impact on court
    adjudication of participants; results in terms of re-
    cidivism and employment of participants; and character-
    istics of participants who were "successful." **4274**

NATIONAL Conference of Commissioners on Uniform State Laws. Uniform
State Laws. Uniform alcoholism and intoxication treatment act ...
approved and recommended ... Aug. 21, 1971, with prefatory note and
comments. Chicago, 1971. 32 p.
    Recognizing alcoholism and public intoxication as an
    illness and not a crime, Act provides for the estab-
    lishment of a division of alcoholism in the state de-
    partment of health. It also covers treatment programs
    and facilities and voluntary, involuntary and emergency
    commitments.   **4275**

NATIONAL Council on Crime and Delinquency. The DesMoines Community
Correction Project: an alternative to jailing. Hackensack, 1973.
12 p.
    Project consisted of closely supervised release (daily
    reporting, counseling, help with education, job, medi-
    cal needs) for selected defendants unable to meet
    Release on Recognizance requirements. Considered suc-
    cess; county adopted program after first year of NCCD
    sponsorship. Trial appearance rate about same as ROR
    and money bail defendants.   **4276**

NATIONAL Council on Crime and Delinquency. Board of Directors. The
nondangerous offender should not be imprisoned: a policy statement.
Crime & Delin 19:449-56 (1973).
    Argues that only dangerous offenders should be imprison-
    ed because prisons have proven to be a failure for
    correction and protection, and other means of correc-
    tions have not been adequately implemented. **4277**

NATIONAL Institute of Mental Health Center for Studies of Crime and
Delinquency. Diversion from the criminal justice system. Washington, USGPO, 1971. 33 p.

Authors review present diversion programs for drug addicts, chronic alcoholics, petty misdemeanants, and
juveniles and the legal problems resulting, pointing
up the lack of due process in civil commitments. Although the study suggests community-based programs,
the authors find that none of these offenders responds
very favorably to treatment either through the criminal justice system or through service agencies and conclude that a rational policy of diversion would ap-
parently require that society simply broaden its definition of tolerable behavior to include certain victimless crimes and non-dangerous deviant activities rather
than extend its efforts to cope with this behavior by
control or coercion. Bibliography, p. 27-33.   4278

NATIONAL Institute of Mental Health Center for Studies of Crime and
Delinquency.   Instead of court; diversion in juvenile justice, by
E.M. Lemert.   Washington, USGPO, 1972.   100 p.
A sociologist criticizes the juvenile courts as an ineffective and even harmful means of coping with the
problem of delinquency, citing their tendency to be
substandard, their bureaucracy, their lack of orientation toward psychiatric treatment and social work
methods, and their stigmatization of young people for
often minor deviant behavior. He proposes the use of
courts only as a last resort for serious and dangerous
offenses, with all other cases handled by social agencies
which will attempt control and treatment, rather than
prevention, of the problem.   4279

NATIONAL Institute of Mental Health Center for Studies of Crime and
Delinquency.   Legal sanctioning and social control, by A.T. Turk.
Washington, USGPO, 1972.   82 p.
Raises questions about desirability of increased legal control of behavior, showing that there is little
scientific evidence pointing to the effectiveness of
such efforts. Numerous statistics, bibliography. 4280

NATIONAL Symposium on Law Enforcement Science and Technology, 1972.
New approaches to diversion and treatment of juvenile offenders ...
papers presented at 4th National Symposium on Law Enforcement Science
and Technology, May 1-3, 1972, conducted by Institute of Criminal
Justice and Criminology, University of Maryland. Washington, USGPO,
1973.   202 p. (Criminal Justice Monographs)
Contents: Sargent, F.W. (Gov.) Community-based treatment for juveniles in Massachusetts.--Gemingami, R.J.
Diversion of juvenile offenders from the juvenile justice system.--Smith, R.L. Diversion: new label - old
practice.--Jameson, F.L., Lindheimer, J.H., Mayhugh,
S.L. New directions in diverting juvenile offenders.--
Nejelski, P. Diversion of juvenile offenders in the criminal justice system.--Bottoms, A.M. The workshop as a

device for developing juvenile justice programs.--Keve,
P.W. Juvenile detention without a building.--Warren,
M.Q. Action research as a change model for corrections.--Yaryan, R.B. The community role in juvenile
delinquency programs. Bibliography.   4281

NEW YORK (City) Criminal Justice Coordinating Council, and VERA Institute of Justice. Manhattan Bowery Project: treatment for home-
less alcoholics. N.Y., 1970. 9 p.
    Description of the Project which includes a detoxifica-
    tion center, an out-patient clinic and an emergency
    unit to serve homeless alcoholics; explains the rela-
    tionship of Project to various city agencies and the
    impact of the program.   4282

NEW YORK (City) Criminal Justice Coordinating Council, and VERA Institute of Justice. Manhattan Court Employment Project. N.Y., 1970.
12 p.
    Project offers selected defendants, at the time of
    arraignment, an opportunity to be trained and placed
    in a job; explains selection criteria, organization
    and staffing, the job-finding process and court review.
                                               4283

NEW YORK (City) Transportation Administration. Annual report, 1973.
N.Y., 1973. 36 p.
    Includes at p.31-36 report on the Parking Violations
    Bureau, from its creation in 1970 to relieve congestion
    in criminal court, where wholesale plea bargaining had
    become the only means of coping; describes Bureau's
    functions, including collection of fines, provision
    of hearings before lawyer-examiners for not-guilty pleas,
    coordination with State Motor Vehicle Dept. Adminis-
    trative Adjudication Bureau (item 4285) for moving
    violations. Contains a few statistics on caseload,
    finances.   4284

NEW YORK (State) Dept. of Motor Vehicles Administrative Adjudication
Bureau. Administrative adjudication of traffic violations in New
York City. Albany, 1971. 15 p.
    Brief promotional explanation of intent and procedures
    of removal of both moving and parking violations from
    criminal court in New York City. Emphasis is on edu-
    cation and reform rather than punishment. Includes text
    of enabling legislation.   4285

NEW YORK (State) Dept. of Motor Vehicles Administrative Adjudication
Bureau. Regulations: administrative adjudication of traffic violations. July 1, 1070. N.Y., 1970. 25 p.
    Procedures for handling moving violations (all but most
    serious) by mail payment of fines, lawyer-referee hear-
    ings of contested cases, with relaxed rules of evidence,

ADMINISTRATION OF CRIMINAL JUSTICE

right of appeal; schedule of fines, sample multi-copy
summons and complaint included, which also provides
for parking violations.   4286

NEW YORK (State) Library Legislative Research Service. Pre-trial
intervention for adults: a selected annotated bibliography, by I.M.
Hallowell and M. Gehr. Albany, 1975. 34 p.
        Partially annotated bibliography, eighty items, de-
        scribing programs in operation which intervene to
        "side-track the criminal justice offender from the
        criminal justice routine and provide the court with
        a middle ground alternative to discharge or trial."
        Preceded by an information introduction giving statis-
        tics and costs, the bibliography includes items of
        general coverage; items on operating programs; fund-
        ing; standards, guidelines and legislation with evalua-
        tion analysis and suggestions.   4287

NIMMER, R.T. Diversion, the search for alternate forms of prosecution. Chicago, A B Found, 1974. 133 p.
        Study defines and discusses "traditional" diversion
        and "new" diversion programs, outlining the rationale
        and practice of each type of diversion; describing
        selected programs. The final chapter summarizes the
        analysis of diversion practice. Notes refer to other
        pertinent writings and reports.   4288

NIMMER, R.T. The public drunk: formalizing the police role as a
social help agency. Geo L J 58:1089-1119 (1970); reprint: A B Found
research contributions, 1970, 6.
        A study of the police response to the formal redefini-
        tion of their role in the handling of drunks in Wash-
        ington, D.C., and, in particular, their response to
        the District of Columbia Rehabilitation Act. 4289

NIMMER, R.T. St. Louis diagnostic and detoxification center, an experiment on non-criminal processing of public intoxicants. Wash U
L Q 1970:1-27; reprint: A B Found research contributions, 1970, 4.
        Describes and analyzes the attitude of the police toward
        the center. Shows that the detoxification system is not
        a panacea, and that it must be set up with an eye to
        the particular characteristics of each jurisdiction in
        order to be a success.   4290

NIMMER, R.T. Two million unnecessary arrests; removing a social service concern from the criminal justice system. Chicago, A B Found,
1971. 202 p.
        Examination of traditional arrest and criminal court
        processing of derelicts in skid row areas in Chicago
        and New York, and alternative programs of St. Louis,
        the District of Columbia, and the Vera Institute in
        New York City.   4291

NON-TRIAL disposition of criminal offenders: a case study. J L Reform 5:453-84 (1972).
> Subject is the Citizens Probation Authority of Genessee
> County, Michigan, originally part of the prosecutor's
> office and now an autonomous county department. Select-
> ed offenders referred to it are placed on probation
> with counseling instead of being prosecuted. Various
> legal and constitutional problems of this method of
> diversion are discussed.   4292

OLIVIERI, A. and FINKELSTEIN, I. Report on "victimless crime" in
New York State. NY L Forum 18:77-120 (1972).
> Discusssion of crimes involving gambling, prostitution,
> public drunkenness, drugs, pornography, homosexuality
> as potentials to be removed from the courts, with
> specific advantages to courts and and society. Cases,
> other legislative reports and investigations are re-
> viewed.   4293

PARMAS, R.I. Judicial response to intrafamily violence. Minn L Rev
54:585-644 (1970).
> Based on observations of Chicago's Court of Domestic
> Relations, N.Y.C. Family Court and other courts in De-
> troit and Milwaukee, author gives description of various
> methods of case disposition in cases arising from family
> fights, such as probation, continuance, referral to
> agencies or outright dismissal. Focuses on reasons for
> use of each method.   4294

PETERSEN, T.K. Dade county pretrial intervention project: formalization of the diversion function and its impact upon the criminal justice system. U Miami L Rev 28:86-114 (1973).
> Project director discusses the use of pretrial diver-
> sion as a rehabilitative strategy of value to the crim-
> inal justice system and describes the project; his-
> torical perspective, eligibility, structure and methods,
> results, cost benefit analysis, and emerging issues.
> Author concludes that diversion offers a valuable and
> relatively effective resource to the criminal system.
> Statistics.   4295

POLOW, B. Reducing juvenile and domestic relations caseloads. Juvenile Justice 24:55-59 (Aug. 1973).
> Morris County (N.J.) court judge describes first eight
> months of experimental diversion of non-criminal juven-
> ile matters into more appropriate channels, operated
> under judicial supervision, but with a minimum of ju-
> dicial intervention. Intake procedures are described
> in detail. Author describes similar handling of family
> relations.   4296

PRETRIAL diversion from the criminal process. Yale L J 83:827-54
(1974).

Note analyzes pretrial diversion suspended prosecution,
and rehabilitation of nonaddict, adult accused offenders; describes the diverted population, the intake decision, the rehabilitation programs used and the termination decision; argues that the existing programs must
prove themselves before the system is expanded. 4297

RICHERT, J.P. The court employment project of New York. ABA J 61:
191-92, 194-95 (1975).
          Author examines diversion project in which criminal
          proceedings are dismissed on the condition that the
          accused participate in and successfully complete a pro-
          gram of counseling and job placement; includes pro-
          cedures followed by project screeners and applicants;
          discussion of need for early access to offenders; guide-
          lines for acceptance and exclusion; social services
          utilized; benefits and future of project. Data tables
          on characteristics of accepted applicants and employ-
          ment status and salary of participants.   4298

ROBERTSON, J.A. Pre-trial diversion of drug offenders: a statutory
approach. Boston U L Rev 52:235-71 (1972).
          The high cost of administration of drug offender laws
          makes diversion appealing. Author discusses Massachu-
          setts Comprehensive Drug Abuse and Rehabilitation and
          Treatment Act (eff. Jan 1, 1971) that diverts from court
          certain arrested drug related offenders to treatment
          facilities. Who is eligible, screening, examination,
          ruling of court, commitment, facilities and consequences
          of conversion are discussed. Problems encountered are
          detailed; future diversionary programs are offered.
          The experience points to need for centralized coordina-
          tion and increased facilities in every step of the pro-
          ceedings. Author concludes that if the statute effec-
          tively reorders value preference in criminal proceed-
          ings to be treatment, rehabilitation, non-stigmatiza-
          tions, attitudes in favor of non-criminal alternatives
          toward drug offenders will grow.   4299

RUBIN, T. Law as an agent of delinquency prevention. Washington,
Youth Development and Delinquency Prevention Administration, 1971.
70 p.
          Former juvenile court judge gives blueprint for reform,
          recommending extending diversion and using court pro-
          cedure for serious crimes only. He advocates litigation
          to develop juveniles' rights, legal education in schools,
          and revision of juvenile courts.   4300

SCHUR, E.M. Crimes without victims; deviant behavior and public policy. Englewood Cliffs, N.J., Prentice-Hall, 1965. 180 p.
          Three types of deviance discussed: abortion, homosexual-
          ity, drug addiction - from the standpoint of public

policy and social policy. The British experience with
narcotics problem is explained. Author recommends policy
changes.   4301

SCHUR, E.M. Radical non-intervention; rethinking the delinquency
problem. Englewood Cliffs, N.J., Prentice-Hall, 1973. 180 p.
    Attacks classification of the delinquent as "sick" or
    a product of social-economic forces, and the unsatis-
    factory policies these concepts produce; Proposes a
    focus on the delinquent-defining process itself; radi-
    cal non-intervention accommodates to diverse society
    and behavior rather than setting narrow norms based on
    confused "conventional wisdom."   4302

SCHUR, E.M. and BEDAU, H.A. Victimless crimes: two sides of a controversy. Englewood Cliffs, N.J., Prentice-Hall, 1974. 146 p.
    Two separate articles: sociologist Schur argues for
    decriminalization of certain consensual transactions
    because social demand persists despite legal penalties,
    and because of unintended results of criminalization
    such as cynicism toward law, revolving door justice,
    unconstitutional enforcement techniques, and control
    by organized crime. Bedau, the philosopher, points out
    inconsistency of laws that prohibit some harmful sub-
    stances or forms of gambling, for instance, while allow-
    ing others; also discusses legislation of morality as
    invasion of inviolable privacy. References throughout
    to leading works relating to problem; bibliographies.
                                                         4303

SPECTER, A. Diversion of persons from the criminal process to treatment alternatives. Penn BA Q 44:691-98 (1973).
    District Attorney discusses the Philadelphia Accelerated
    Rehabilitative Disposition Program, designed primarily
    for first offenders charged with non-violent crimes.
    The goals of this program are to cut court backlog and
    to divert persons from criminal processes to treatment
    alternatives by the incentive of a fresh start and the
    threat of prosecution if they do not take a new start.
    Procedure is informal hearings and community rehabili-
    tative services are utilized. The program has been suc-
    cessful in lessening backlog and rearrest rates. 4304

STEADMAN, H.J. and BRAFF, J. Crimes of violence and incompetency
diversion. J Crim L 66:73-78 (1975).
    The balance between individual rights and civil liber-
    ties of the accused and the protection of society is
    weighed. Statistical comparison is made of representa-
    tion in violent crimes in New York of incompetent as
    against similar crimes by competent persons. Findings
    indicate, among other things, inappropriate diversions.
    Study supported by funds from the Center for Studies of
    Crime and Delinquency, includes statistical tables.
                                                         4305

TATE, S.D. Youth and senior citizens in creative rural courts. Juvenile Court J 22:52-54 (1971).
>   Older volunteer probation officers have time to listen,
>   at length and without judging, to juvenile offenders
>   who in turn do chores for them to work out probation.
>   Success has led to other diversionary plans.   4306

U. S. MANPOWER Administration Pre-trial Intervention Program. Report on the operations of Baltimore Pre-trial Intervention project, Baltimore, Maryland, based on a visit conducted during the week of Jan. 3, 1972, by ABT Associates. Cambridge, Mass., ABT Assoc, 1972. 30 p.
>   A description of the development, operation and organization of the project which seeks to provide rehabilitative services to juvenile offenders during a period
>   where official court action is postponed.   4307

U. S. MANPOWER Administration Pre-trial Intervention Program. Report on the operations of Cleveland Offender Rehabilitation Project, Cleveland, Ohio, based on a visit conducted during the week of Nov. 29, 1971. Cambridge, Mass., ABT Assoc, 1971. 38 p.
>   A description of the development, operation and organization of the project which seeks to rehabilitate defendants who either enter no plea or a plea of no contest to certain classes of misdemeanors.   4308

U. S. MANPOWER Administration Pre-trial Intervention Program. Report on the operations of Operation de Novo, Minneapolis, Minnesota, based on a visit conducted during the week of Nov. 29, 1971, by ABT Associates. Cambridge, Mass., ABT Assoc, 1971. 40 p.
>   A description of the development, operation and organization of the project which diverts an accused offender from the court system prior to trial and places him in service programs. The requested continuance period is
>   six months.   4309

U. S. MANPOWER Administration Pre-trial Intervention Program. Report on the operations of Project Detour, San Antonio, Texas, based on a visit conducted during the week of Dec. 13, 1971. Cambridge, Mass., ABT Assoc, 1971. 44 p.
>   A description of the development, operation and organization of the project which seeks to divert selected defendants from the criminal prosecution system in order to provide rehabilitative services.   4310

U. S. NATIONAL Institute of Law Enforcement and Criminal Justice. Alcohol and the criminal justice system: challenge and response, by H. Erskine. Washington, 1972. 30 p.
>   Pamphlet presents information useful to criminal justice personnel in planning programs and research in alcohol abuse: alcohol use in America; historical basis for present attitudes; dimensions of problem within the criminal justice system; alternatives to the criminal process, including programs in St. Louis, D.C.,

THE CRIMINAL TRIAL

and New York; and treatment and control of alcohol problems.
4311

U. S. NATIONAL Institute of Law Enforcement and Criminal Justice.
Diversion of the public inebriate from the criminal justice system,
by C.W. Weis. Sept. 1973. Washington, USGPO, 1974. 64 p. (Its Prescriptive packages)
> Guidelines for transferring the inebriate from the law
> enforcement system to health and social services agen-
> cies, and for maintaining the program; five specific
> services are discussed: medical evaluation and treat-
> ment, shelter, intermediate care, community residential
> living facilities and aftercare. App. A: Program Guide:
> Public Inebriate Program.
> 4312

VERA Institute of Justice. Bronx Sentencing Project, an experiment
in the use of short form presentence reports for adult misdemeanants,
by J.B. Lieberman, S.A. Schaffer, and J.M. Martin for the National
Institute of Law Enforcement and Criminal Justice. Washington, USGPO,
1973. 53 p.
> How the short form was developed to help judges select
> good risks for probation or conditional release. Result:
> post-conviction diversion available to much wider group;
> probation office formerly limited by length and com-
> plexity of reports to doing them mainly for first of-
> fenders. No significant increase in recidivism. Short
> form subsequently adopted by N.Y. state law. Authors
> note by-product of study; finding that Legal Aid de-
> fendants and those in custody at sentencing time re-
> ceive prison sentences much more frequently than those
> represented by private counsel, not in custody. Includes
> Vera"s guidelines.
> 4313

VORENBERG, E.W. and VORENBERG, J. Early diversion from the criminal
justice system: practice in search of a theory. In American Assembly.
Prisoners in America, ed. by L.E. Ohlin. Englewood Cliffs, N.J.,
Prentice-Hall, 1973. p. 151-83.
> Examples, pros and cons of 1. diversion from arrest
> (police decision) 2. diversion from pretrial detention
> (release on recognizance or supervised release) 3. pre-
> trial diversion by prosecutorial discretion (plea bar-
> gaining, arbitration, dismissing charges on defendant's
> promise to get help, get job, make restitution) 4. Post-
> trial diversion (variations on probation). 4314

WEINSTEIN, D. and DEITCH L. The impact of legalized gambling: the
socio-economic consequences of lotteries and off-track betting. N.Y.,
Praeger, 1974. 208 p.
> Authors describe the entire operation of existing state
> lotteries and off-track betting and identify the social
> and economic consequences; they develop methodologies
> to determine future consequences, for the benefit of

those jurisdictions contemplating legalized gambling;
includes compilation of state lottery laws. Extensive
bibliography (p. 180-204) gives leading writings on
varieties of gambling and its impact on people and
government.   4315

WESTERBROOK, J.W. Crimes without plaintiffs; The challenging concept of "victimless crimes." Baylor L Rev 25:37-51 (1973).
    Former federal and state prosecutor relates personal
experiences in cases to support thesis that cases of
alcoholism, drunkenness, use of drugs, pronography,
gambling are crimes without victims, divert talent and
energy away from where desperately needed. Footnotes
with references to studies and reports.   4316

ZALOOM, J.G. Pretrial intervention under New Jersey court rule 3:28;
Proposed guidelines for operation. Crim Justice Q 2:178-209 (1974).
    Chief, Pretrial Service, N.J., traces the development
of pretrial intervention in New Jersey based on the
1970 pretrial intervention Supreme Court rule. Rule
outlines procedures for participation and termination.
The operation of the several county programs is described and ten guidelines are presented with commentary.   4316a

VIII.   SENTENCING PROCEDURES AND ALTERNATIVES

A.   Statutory and Judicial Discretion

Items cover informational bases for sentencing,
sentencing criteria, sentencing procedures;
items dealing with compulsory disclosure of
sentencing reports to convicted defendant;
Model Penal Code, provisions also of Model
Sentencing Act; disparity in sentencing; judges
visiting penal institutions; sentencing institutes; credit for institutional time served;
resentencing; selected state sentencing institutes and list of federal sentencing institutes,
giving programs and participants. See also Section
VIII B, Appellate Review of Sentences.

AGATA, B. C.   Time served under a reversed sentence or conviction - a
proposal and a basis for decision. Mont L Rev 25:3-74 (1963)
Law professor examines effect of time served pursuant
to a reversed proceeding as a limitation on another
sentence to be served by defendant in the case of
conviction after a new trial, resentencing, or con-
secutive sentences. He considers measure of credit
for time served; authority to grant credit; maximum
credit; credit where error in sentence; discretionary
problems which may arise; constitutional issues; and
good conduct and parole. Appendices: statutes dealing
with credit for time served; proposed Uniform
Act.   4317

ALEXANDER, M. E.   A hopeful view of the sentencing process. Am
Crim L Q 3:189-97 (1965).
Author attacks punitive legislation as ineffective,
particularly in drug cases; commends proposed federal
legislation that would permit courts flexibility and
discretion, away from mandatory sentences.   4318

AMERICAN Bar Association Advisory Committee on Sentencing and
Review. Standards relating to sentencing alternatives and procedures, recommended by the Advisory Committee on Sentencing
and Review. S. E. Sobeloff, chair.; P. W. Low, reptr. Tent.
draft, Dec. 1967. N.Y., IJA, 1967. 354 p. Amendments, supp.
Sept. 1968. 9 p. Approved, Aug. 1968.
Standards with commentary covering sentencing authority,
statutory structure, judicial discretion, informational
basis for sentencing, sentencing procedures, further
judicial action and development of sentencing criteria; appendices are Judge Stanley's view as to
compulsory disclosure of presentence reports, Model
Penal Code sentencing provisions, Model Sentencing
Act, and selected bibliography.   4319

AMERICAN Bar Association Resource Center on Correctional Law
and Legal Services. Sentencing computation laws and practice: a
preliminary survey, by R. C. Hand and R. G. Singer. Washington,
1974. 178 p.
>Survey of 50 states, D.C., and federal system examines
>disparity and diversity in sentencing procedures:
>issued surrounding indeterminate and determinate sen-
>tence; habitual offender laws; credit for institutional
>time, street time, and "good" time; each jurisdiction's
>sentencing computation practices; and statutory authority.
>Includes detailed chart summarizing individual state
>data.   4320

AMERICAN Friends Service Committee. Struggle for justice; a
report on crime and punishment in America. N.Y., Hill & Wang,
1971. 179 p.
>(For annotation see item 3233).   4321

AMERICAN Judicature Society. Sentencing patterns and problems;
an annotated bibliography, by W. S. Carr and V. J. Connelly.
Chicago, 1973. 97 p.
>Supplements Am Jud Soc Rep. no. 28 (1969). Books,
>model statutes, comments on sentencing institutes,
>all types of sentences, appellate review, and other
>specifics of sentencing including presentence reports,
>work release programs, dangerous offenders, juveniles,
>fines, and sentencing for specific crimes. Miscellaneous
>section covers specific state laws, multiple sen-
>tences, right to address court, delay in sentencing.
>Also covers increase in sentence on retrial and credit
>for time served.   4322

ASSOCIATION of the Bar of the City of New York Committee on the
Federal Courts. Report on sentencing practices in federal courts
in New York City. June 11, 1973. New York, 1973. 32 p.
>After reviewing present practices evidencing great
>disparity, the committee recommends 1) Three-judge
>advisory procedure now used in Eastern District;
>2) Informal presentence conferences between judges and
>lawyers; 3) Judge to give his reasons; 4) Judge to
>advise Bureau of Prisons and Parole Board; 5) Develop-
>ment of a data bank of relevant factors involved in
>each sentence available to all judges; 6) Frequent
>sentencing seminars. A. Hellerstein, chair.   4323

BAER, H., Jr. Recidivism, discretion, and deferred prosecution.
Record 29:141-48 (1974).
>Author explores the high rate of recidivism and the
>judge's discretion in sentencing; presents the
>results of a study of federal judges in New York as
>to the judges' considerations in sentencing; ana-
>lyzes the sentencing of juvenile offenders and suggests
>a program of deferred prosecution for such cases.4324

BARKIN, E. N. Impact of recent legislation and rule changes upon
sentencing. FRD 41:494-506 (1966).
>Examines effect of changes in the Federal Rules of
Criminal Procedure on federal sentencing; impact
of Bail Reform Act on juveniles committed under
Federal Juvenile Delinquency Act or Youth Corrections
Act; and the Narcotic Rehabilitation Act and its
effect on sentencing.   4325

BIFURCATED trial procedure and first degree murder. Suffolk U L
Rev 3:628-40 (1969).
>Notes the additional evidence a sentencing jury
could receive which would be prejudicial at trial;
discusses N.Y. and Calif. procedure and argues for
bifurcation.   4326

CALIFORNIA Center for Judicial Education and Research. Maximum
and minimum sentences for common misdemeanors and infractions, prep.
by P. M. Saeta and S. Sloan, sponsored by Judicial Council of
Calif. and Conference of Calif. Judges. Mar. 1974. Berkeley, 1974.
2 p.
>Checklist for judges summarizes sentences and fines,
lists exceptions, gives Penal Code citation, for
quick bench reference.   4327

CALIFORNIA Judicial Council. Proceedings of the first sentencing
institute for Superior Court judges ... Santa Barbara, Mar. 5-6,
1965. St. Paul, West, 1965. 119 p.
>Proceedings include panel discussions on (1) sen-
tencing standards for granting probation, committing
the offender to local correctional facilities; (2)
sentencing standards for committing the offender to
state correctional institutions; (3) state rehabilitative and correctional facilities; and (4) adult
authority term setting and parole revocation policies.   4328

CALIFORNIA Judicial Council. Proceedings of the 1966 sentencing
institute for Superior Court Judges ... Santa Barbara, Apr. 1-2,
St. Paul, West, 1966. 116 p.
>Proceedings include panel discussions on (1) sen-
tencing the offender: standards and significant
factors; (2) questions about negotiating pleas;
(3) recent appellate decisions: their impact on
criminal procedures; and (4) the sex offender.   4329

CALIFORNIA Judicial Council. Proceedings of the 1967 Sentencing
Institute for Superior Court judges sponsored by the Judicial Council of Calif., Santa Barbara, Mar. 17-18, 1967. St. Paul, West,
1967. 128 p.
>Discussion involves sentencing standards and signifi-
cant factors; the narcotic offender; the female criminal offender; the work furlough; and probation
subsidy programs.   4330

CARTER, J. M. and KUNZEL, F.   Forms of adjudication for use in
sentencing.   FRD 44:197-224 (1968).
> Suggested forms of sentencing for 20 different types
> of situations in which sentencing judge may be
> placed.   4331

CENTER for Judicial Education.   Sentencing alternatives for
Indiana judges, by R. A. Willis.   Indianapolis, 1973.   58 p.
> Designed to assist the new Indiana judge with the
> sentencing function, booklet presents statutory
> material and case law on, for example, the sentencing
> of certain types of offenders, and creative sen-
> tences.   4332

CHICAGO Seven (Dellinger, In re, 461 F 2d 389) contempts: the
decision on sentencing.   Crim L Bull 10:239-45 (1974).
> Article provides background to and transcript of
> the sentencing in the contempt proceedings growing
> out of the trial of the Chicago Seven.   4333

CLARK, T. C.   Sentencing and corrections.   U San Francisco L Rev
5:1-9 (1970).
> Former U.S. Supreme Court justice discusses the
> problem of recidivism, new commissions and standards
> recently established to solve this problem; needed
> reform in the areas of sentencing, prisons, and
> parole.   4334

COHEN, F., Sentencing, probation, and the rehabilitative ideal;
the view from Mempa v. Rhay.   Tex L Rev 47:1-59 (1968).
> Sees Mempa as indication of increased judicial
> scrutiny over the penocorrectional process, and that
> a due process hearing is required in parole revocation
> and sentencing. App: table of state sentencing
> procedures: statutory and common law provisions. 4335

COLORADO Legislative Council.   Criminal laws and indeterminate
sentencing.   Denver, 1966.   70 p.
> The Legislative Council considers three existing
> criminal laws: attempt, theft, and sanity testing
> procedures, and submits three bills incorporating
> recommended changes. It reviews other state and
> federal approaches to sentencing with comparison
> tables, and suggests three approaches to sentencing
> changes in Colorado: Indeterminate sentencing for
> certain crimes, a full time parole board and a
> diagnostic and treatment center. Stresses elimination
> of sentencing disparities, and need for additional
> study.   4336

COLORADO Legislative Council.   Indefinite sentencing and the
Colorado correctional system.   Denver, 1968.   108 p.

Recommends such changes as indefinite sentencing,
the establishment of a reception and diagnostic
center, a procedure for the disposition of detainers,
a full-time parole board, and a procedure for pleas
of guilty to certain crimes. Two bills that incor-
porate these changes are proposed; previous Legislative Council studies are discussed.   4337

COOK, B. B. Sentencing behavior of federal judges: draft cases,
1972. U Cin L Rev 42:597-633 (1973).
Political science professor, examining draft sentences
in 1972, seeks an explanation of judicial discretionary
behavior on the basis of judicial character and
background. Discussed are: the sentence as a depen-
dent variable, public opinion, economic-social and
demographic explanations, and the effect of court
structure. Generalizations from the study are
presented.   4338

COUNCIL of Europe. Suspended sentence, probation, and other
alternatives to prison sentences; replies to a questionnaire on
current practice in member countries prepared by an ad hoc committee of the European Committee on Crime Problems. [Strasbourg]
Council of Europe, 1966. 128 p.
Part I presents resolution on suspended sentence,
probation, and alternatives to prison sentences;
Part II outlines the systems in fifteen member states
of the Council of Europe.   4339

CRAIG, W. E. Sentencing in federal tax fraud cases. FRD 49:97-115
(1970).
A district judge concludes that there is no easily
formulated policy to apply, that the factors of
rehabilitation and deterrence to the individual
violator are de minimis, but that short sentences are
desirable as a deterrent to the public. Specifies
relevant factors to consider in determining an
appropriate sentence.   4340

CREDIT for time served between arrest and sentencing. U Pa
Rev 121:1148-56 (1973).
Comment deals with the rights of an accused jailed
for a non-bailable offense, contending that, when a
prisoner is sentenced to a maximum term, a constitutional right ot receive credit for presentence
incarceration does exist. Examined are: double
jeopardy, unconstitutional conditions, cruel and
unusual punishment, and some recent cases.   4341

CRIME Commission of Philadelphia. Fourth judicial sentencing
institute: violence today - a judicial concern. June 20-21, 1968.
Bedford, FRD 46:497-604 (1969).

<u>Contents</u>: Crawford, J.M., Introduction.--Gomberg, E.R., Sentencing
institute: substance and process.--Bazelon, D.L.,
Responsibility and mental competence.--Wechsler, H.,
Sentencing innovations.--Wolfgang, M.E., Violence
and its relation to sentencing.--Toch, H.H., The
violent criminal.--Heller, M.S., Dangerousness, diagnosis, and disposition.--Wolfgang, Toch, Heller.
Panel summary.   <u>4342</u>

CRIMINAL sentencing: an overview of procedures and alternatives.
Miss L J 45:782-99 (1974).
Speaking harshly of disparity in federal sentencing,
student note examines state practices that seek to
bring about more uniformity. After discussing the
objectives of sentencing, five identifiable categories of state programs are discussed. Among them
are the New Jersey experiment; states permitting
appellate review statutorily by an appellate court;
the Alaskan review procedures; the extra-judicial
sentencing boards; states permitting affirming,
modifying, and reversing judgments. The note then
offers new proposals such as the Model Sentencing
Act, the Model Penal Code, and categorization of
felonies. Further described are the ABA proposal and
proposed revision in Mississippi.   <u>4343</u>

CROSS, R. The English sentencing system. London, Butterworth,
1971. 184 p.
Law professor describes the law and practice of
sentencing in England and Wales. How the Courts fix
the length of a prison sentence and theories of punishment which influence it are also treated. Questions
about the present sentencing system are raised
and tables of criminal statistics are included. <u>4344</u>

CRUEL or unusual punishment: indeterminate sentence with no maximum term for a second offense of indecent exposure is so disproportionate to the crime as to violate the cruel or unusual
punishment provision of the California constitution. Loyola U L
Rev (LA) 6:416-28 (1973).
Author analyzes <u>In re Lynch</u>, 503 P 2d, 921 (1972),
in which the court held the statutory penalty unconstitutional on grounds that it was disproportionate
to the crime so as to shock the conscience. Article
examines the tests applied by the court and suggests
other arguments that might have been applied. <u>4345</u>

DAWSON, R. O. Sentencing; the decision as to type, length, and
conditions of sentence. Boston, Little, Brown, 1969. 428 p.
(AB Found. Administration of criminal justice series)
One of series ed. by F. Remington. (For others see
item 3230). Professor explores wide range of sentencing procedure possibilities, including statutory

proposals, ALI Model Penal Code and NCCD's Model
Sentencing Act. P 1. Presentence information, P 2.
Probation system, P 3. Determining the length of
incarceration, P 4. The Correctional process and the
legal system.   4346

DEFENDANT'S right to access to presentence reports. Crim L Bull 4:
160-170 (1968).
          Student's winning essay argues for disclosure of
          report on the grounds of fair play, the possibility
          of prejudicial errors in the report, and constitutinal
          rights. Counters claims that disclosure would dry
          up sources, delay sentencing, or harm the defendant;
          names states giving right to access.   4347

DEVITT, E. J.   How can we effectively minimize unjustified disparity in federal criminal sentences? FRD 41:249-56 (1967).
          Discusses specific defects in sentencing authority
          of judge under federal statutes and recommends
          changes in the light of the NCCD Model Sentencing Act.
          Suggests divesting judges of some wide discretionary
          power in favor of limitations confining them by
          safeguards and guidelines, as is proposed in the
          Dangerous Offender Bill.   4348

DISCLOSURE of presentence reports: a constitutional right to
rebut adverse information by cross-examination. Rutgers-Camden
L J 3:111-28 (1971).
          Article examines the case of State v Kunz, 250 A 2d
          137 (N.J. 1969), in which court held that defendant
          has the right to participate in post-conviction hear-
          ing where the defendant challenges information in
          the presentence report that is crucial to the
          sentencing judge's determination; and considers the
          application of due process to the rights guaranteed
          by this case, including disclosure, cross examin-
          ation, and competing state interests.   4349

DISCRETION in felony sentencing; a study of influencing factors.
Wash L Rev 48:857-89 (1973).
          A detailed analysis of data and methodology of
          study conducted by the Washington State Superior
          Court Judges in 1971. This analysis isolates
          factors used in judicial sentencing, demonstrating
          their relative importance. "The date ... challenge
          the constitutionality and public policy underlying
          discretionary sentencing and indicate that discretion-
          ary sentencing embodies systematic and racial biases
          in no way dependent upon culpability of the of-
          fender, his background, and circumstances of the
          crime."   4350

EICHMAN, C. J. The impact of the Gideon decision upon crime and
sentencing in Florida: a study of recidivism and sociocultural
change. Tallahassee, Fla. Div. of Corrections, 1966. 84 p.
> More than 1000 inmates serving felony sentences in
> Florida were released following the Gideon v
> Wainwright decision of March 18, 1963. In this
> master's thesis, author reports his study of the im-
> pact of that decision on those prematurely released,
> on those remaining in custody and on trends in
> criminal sentencing. Includes research procedures
> and analyses together with statistics.   4351

EQUAL protection: disparate statutory sentencing schemes for
males and females declared unconstitutional. Catholic U L Rev
23:389-94 (1973).
> Article examines State v Chambers, 307 A 2d 78
> (1973), where statutory indeterminate sentencing
> for females and minimum-maximum terms for males was
> examined and found to be unconstitutional; historical
> analysis of this and similar statutes, and the
> constitutional analysis used by the court.   4352

FAHRINGER, H. P. Sentencing; making the best of a bad situation.
NYSB J 46:279-89 (1974).
> Author presents proposal to aid the public defender
> and the judiciary in sentencing indigent defendants
> who may plead guilty in order to avoid the costs
> and time of trial. The sentencing judge should be
> provided with a presentence memorandum, demanding
> a copy of the probation report and providing him
> with information as to defendant's background, family,
> medical history, criminal record, mitigating cir-
> cumstances, comparative sentences, and character
> references. Counsel should stress the need for
> leniency and the judge should present a statement of
> reasons for the sentence given.   4353

FAILURE to pay a fine after conviction under a statute providing
for a fine as the only punishment, cannot be automatically con-
verted to a term of imprisonment for an indigent person. J Urban L
49:602-612 (1972).
> Article examines Tate v Short, in which the court
> held that where a fine is the only punishment for
> a crime, the sentence cannot be automatically con-
> verted to a term of imprisonment for failure to
> pay the fine by an indigent defendant. Article dis-
> cusses history, nature and purposes of fines, and
> relevant cases as well as presenting several
> alternatives to imprisonment.   4354

FEDERAL due process of judicial sentencing for felony. Harv L
Rev 81:821-46 (1968).
>   Student study of development of sentencing theory,
>   sentencing under due process clause, plea bargaining,
>   rights of representation personally and by counsel,
>   right of allocation; presentence report dis-
>   closure.   4355

FEDERAL Judicial Center. The Second Circuit sentencing study; a
report to the judges of the Second Circuit, prep. by A. Partridge
and W. B. Eldridge. Washington, 1974. 54 p.
>   All active Second Circuit federal district judges
>   participated in this sentencing disparity study,
>   unique in that all used the same cases. Results showed
>   large differences in length of prison term "imposed",
>   disagreement on whether to incarcerate. Further analy-
>   sis includes whether test situation approximates
>   actual courtroom conditions; judges' consistency;
>   disparity within districts; effect of certain charac-
>   teristics (probation recommendations, narcotics use,
>   prior record) in producing different sentences.
>   Tables, some explanation of methodology.   4356

FOOTE, M. W. Some further observations on sentencing. Trial
Judges' J 5:10, 25, 29 (April 1966).
>   Focusing on the problems facing the trial judge when
>   sentencing offenders, judge funds more questions
>   than answers. Defferent approaches to resolving the
>   problem of sentencing disparity are noted and author
>   points out that in most of the solutions, the
>   judge is called upon to justify his decision,
>   placing him on the defensive.   4357

FORTAS, A. Criminal justice "without pity." Trial Lawyers Q 9:9-14
(Summer 1973).
>   An indictment of the 1973 "Criminal Reform Act"
>   proposed by President Nixon; the bill reflects
>   a return to punitive criminal jurisprudence--
>   official homicide, longer sentences, bigger jails,
>   more and more severe punishment.   4358

FRANKEL, M. E. Comments of an independent variable sentencer.
U Cin L Rev 42:667-71 (1973).
>   Judge commends Prof. Cook's article (item 4338) for
>   its contribution in adding to the evidence that
>   trial judges have far too much discretion in
>   sentencing.   4359

FRANKEL, M. E. Criminal sentences; law without order. N.Y. Hill
and Wang, 1973. 124 p.
>   Author's 1971 Marx lectures (see item 4361) edited
>   for general audience, footnotes omitted.   4360

FRANKEL, M. E. Lawlessness in sentencing. U Cin L Rev 41:1-54
(1972). (Marx lect. 1971)
>   U. S. imposes harshest sentences in the world;
>   federal district court judge argues, giving specifics,
>   regarding the "deeply flawed status quo"; criticizes
>   current evils, difficulties involving personnel,
>   lack of communication. In mulling over existing
>   devices for improvement, author demonstrates short-
>   comings of sentencing institutes, sentencing councils,
>   mixed sentencing tribunals, appellate review of
>   sentences, indeterminate sentences. Chapter on
>   Suggestions for reform, covering legislative pro-
>   posals (substantive and procedural), and a pro-
>   posed Commission For Sentencing Studies and Law
>   Revision.   4361

GILMORE, H. W. Responsibility in sentencing. Trial Judges' J
5:1,17 (Jan. 1966).
>   Judge remarks on the problem of disparity in sen-
>   tencing, describes how the sentencing council in
>   the U. S. District Court, E. D. Mich., works and
>   comments on how the Model Penal Code deals with
>   the problem.   4362

GUZMAN, R. Defendant's access to presentence reports in federal
criminal courts. Iowa L Rev 52:161-85 (1966).
>   Proposed statute authorizes full disclosure of the
>   presentence report to the defendant, but defendant
>   would have no right to cross examine or confront the
>   sources; judge would have discretion to withhold
>   names of sources or items of information if he
>   concludes that identification would lead to
>   harm.   4363

HALL, J. The purposes of a system for the administration of
criminal justice. Washington, Georgetown U., 1963. 20 p.
(Edward Douglas White lect. 1.)
>   Law professor argues with those who would abolish
>   retributive punishment and replace it with rehabili-
>   tation alone. He supports the practice in some
>   institutions of combining punishment with non-punitive
>   treatment.   4364

HARRIES, K. D. and LURA R. P. The geography of justice; sentencing variations in U. S. Judicial districts. Judicature 57:
392-401 (1974).
>   Dealing only with federal offenses, this study
>   examines significant regional variations; seeks to
>   develop a model, explaining in a statistical
>   sense observed variations in sentencing patterns;
>   comment illustrated by maps.   4365

HERLANDS, W. B. When and how should a sentencing judge use probation? FRD 35:487-509 (1964).
> Southern District Court judge balances values, including costs, of keeping condemned persons in jail as against placing them under probation and finds in favor of the latter. He cites to statistics, statutes and cases in support of his arguments and names specific factors to be considered in ordering probation. He discusses mixed or "combination sentences"; appends bibliography. 4365a

HIGGINS, J. P. Confidentiality of presentence reports. Albany L Rev 28:12-44 (1964).
> Critique of proposed change in Federal Rules of Criminal Procedure to make disclosure of a summary of the presentence report mandatory. Author argues in support, but states that "summary" needs to be more specifically defined. Includes a poll of practices and attitudes concerning discretionary disclosure in the federal system. 4366

HOFFMAN, W. E. Sentencing philosophy. In Smith, M. E. As a matter of fact, an introduction to federal probation. Washington, Federal Judicial Center, 1973. p. F1-F44.
> Chief Judge U.S. District Court, E. D. Va., covers whole spectrum of sentencing; of special help to new judges. 4367

HOGARTH, J. Sentencing as a human process. Toronto, U of Toronto press, in assn. with Centre of Criminology, U of Toronto, 1971. 434 p. (Canadian studies in criminology, No. 1)
> Professor presents interdisciplinary study of decision making in the area of sentencing. While the research and investigation transpired in the Toronto area, the report, analyses, problems, and materials apply to any jurisdiction. Author and aids have thoroughly examined background and motivation of sentencing judges, their legal and social constraints and information accessible to them. Predictable sentencing behavior is identified and model sentencing behavior is ventured. Summary of principal findings and extensive bibliography complete the book. 4368

HOLT, I. L., Jr. The judge's attitude and manner at sentencing. Crime & Delin 10:231-34 (1964).
> Judge enumerates four essentials of attitude and manner in delivering sentence in open court: confidence, dignity, understanding of self and offender, impartiality. 4369

HOOD, R. Sentencing in magistrates' courts; a study in variations of policy. London, Stevens, 1962. 168 p.

Fact finding inquiry into the inconsistent use of
prison sentences; author compares characteristics
of offenders and examines community characteristics
to determine effect on sentencing. Appendices contain trends in use of imprisonment, note on
statistical methods, and form for recording data
on offenders; English system.   4370

HOSNER, C. T. Group procedures in sentencing: a decade of practice.
Fed Prob 34:18-25 (Dec 1970).
          Chief Probation Officer of the U.S. District Court,
          Detroit, reviews the formation and operation of the
          Sentencing Council, created in 1960 to eliminate
          inequities in sentences, and notes its effectiveness.
          He also focuses on the benefits which have accrued
          to the probation office through its close relation-
          ship with the court in the sentencing process. 4371

IMPRISONMENT of indigent defendants for non-payment of fines.
U Richmond L Rev 5:373-91 (1971).
          Comments discuss the constitutionality of default
          statutes used as a means of coercion or as an
          alternative punishment to fines, examines recent
          Supreme Court cases involving this issue, and presents
          several alternatives to imprisonment for de-
          fault.   4372

JAFFARY, S. K. Sentencing of adults in Canada. Toronto, U. of
Toronto press, 1963. 122 p.
          Author examines the structure of criminal justice
          in Canada: its background, aims, and practice, with
          emphasis on the sentencing process. Studies role
          of the magistrate with attention to the training
          of the magistracy in the sentencing process. Des-
          cribes some English and American experiences in
          penal reform. Charts and statistical tables pre-
          senting a picture of the incidence of crime in
          Canada and showing variations in sentencing are
          studied.   4373

JUDGMENT and sentence. Suffolk U L Rev 6:1087-96 (1972).
          Comment on Mann v Commonwealth,271 NE 2d 331 (1971),
          which held that defendant could receive greater
          sentence on appeal than he had received in trial court.
          Criticizes the court's refusal to extend to a de novo
          trial the rule of N.C. v Pearce 395 US 711 (1969),
          which requires a showing where a greater sentences
          is imposed, of justifying conduct by the defendant
          and no vindictiveness on the part of the appellate
          judge.   4374

KANSAS state reception and diagnostic center; an empirical
study.   Kan L Rev 19:821-45 (1971).
>After describing the inadequacy of presentence
report and referring to states in which presentence
diagnostic centers or similar procedures are established, student authors give details of central
receiving prison (Kansas Reception and Diagnostic
Center), describing personnel, procedures, and who
is sent to KRDC. This empirical study concludes
there are problems in differences among judges in
sentencing who should be sent to KRDC, due mainly to
lack of standards. Table gives figures on disposition
of KRDC recommendations.   4375

KAUFMAN, I. R.   Enlightened sentences through improved technique.
Fed Prob 26:3-10 (Sept. 1962).
>Judge Kaufman discusses the purpose of sentencing,
emphasizes the significance of supervised release,
and summarizes recently enacted federal sentencing
statutes which contain provisions for observation
and study prior to sentence, indeterminate sentences,
split sentence and dealing with the young offender.
He also comments on appellate review of sentences.   4376

KAUFMAN, I. R.   The sentencing process.   St John's L Rev 49:
215-22 (1975).
>Chief Judge in a foreword to a Second Circuit note,
discusses the sentencing study released by the Cttee
on Sentencing Practices appointed by him in 1973
(see item 4356). He suggests that the problem of
disparity "stems in a large measure from an uncertainty over the relevance and importance of
the myriad characteristics which combine to make
each offender a special case." He elaborates on
further analysis needed.   4377

KNOWLES, M. F.   Lawlessness in our criminal law: criminal sentences and the need for appellate review.   Ala Law 35:450-69
(1974).
>Law professor examines Judge Frankel's Criminal sen-
tences: law without order, (item 4360), which presents the problem of sentencing disparity and suggests the establishment of a commission on sentencing and discusses the desirability of instituting
appellate review of sentencing, presently proposed
in Alabama. Includes excerpts from book and appendix of Alabama criminal statutes providing for imprisonment in which the defference between minimum
and maximum sentence is more than 400 %.   4378

KUH, R. H. Sentencing: guidelines for the Manhattan district
attorney's office. Crim L Bull 11:61-66 (1975).
> Presents strong view that prosecutor's role is
> minimal in sentencing. Exceptions to prosecutorial
> nonparticipation are spelled out, quoting the ABA
> Standards on Sentencing, Prosecution Function, and
> the Function of the Trial Judge. Mr. Kuh then
> gives specifics as to limitations on the D.A., yet
> stating what he or she may freely do to aid the
> trial judge. Appended sample form for Report on
> Sentences.   4379

LEHRICH, R. S. The use and disclosure of presentence reports in
the United States. FRD 47:225-52 (1970).
> Since 80-90% of all criminal cases are disposed of
> through guilty pleas, the crucial determination is
> the sentence to be imposed by the judge. Author
> describes the current practice in federal courts as
> to presentence investigation and report made,
> neither of which is available as of right to the
> defendant or his counsel, but is discretionary with
> the judge. The author analyzes cases and discusses
> the constitutional dimensions of non-disclosure de-
> claring that non-disclosure is an anomaly of the
> law; the article includes also a run-down and dis-
> cussion of cases on state practices in this regard;
> much footnoted with cases and reports.   4380

LEVIN, M. A. Impact of criminal court sentencing decisions and
structural characteristics. Springfield, Va., Nat Tech Info Svc
1973. 67 p.
> Brandeis professor describes studies that have tried
> to relate sentencing practices with recidivism rate.
> Feels that there is some pattern, despite many
> variables: Pittsburgh and Minéapolis court studies
> showed lower recidivism for parolees than for
> those imprisoned.   4381

LEVIN, T. Toward a more enlightened sentencing procedure. Neb
L Rev 45:499-509 (1966).
> Chief Judge, U.S. Dist. Ct. E.D. Mich., describes
> new sentencing procedures instituted by judges of
> his court in 1960; enumerates tools used by judges
> for more effective sentencing and discusses the
> developments in the various district and circuit courts
> to improve sentencing. Through process of refinement,
> plan instituted five years ago is working well and
> has been adopted in other districts. Appendices demon-
> strate this.   4382

LIEBERMAN, J. B., SCHAFFER, S. A., and MARTIN, J. M. The Bronx
sentencing project; an experiment in the use of short-form presentence reports for adult misdemeanants. Washington, USGPO, 1973.
53 p.; N.Y., Vera Inst., 1970. 87 p.

Vera Inst. of Justice experiment conducted in the
Bronx criminal court used short presentence reports
to inform the court of relevant characteristics of
defendants. The operation and implications of the
project are discussed. Appendices include forms,
questionnaires and guidelines used in the experiment.   4383

LORENSON, W. D.   The disclosure to defense of presentence reports
in West Virginia. W. Va L Rev 69:159-66 (1967).
        Discussion of federal and state statute law on
        disclosure; also judicial practices; details of
        W. Va. practice, favoring disclosure.   4384

MCELROY, P. R.   Sentencing -- denial of credit for time served
or longer sentence imposed on retrial. NC L Rev 46:407-18 (1968).
        Discusses cases that involve harsher sentences in
        retrial, particularly Patton v North Carolina, 381
        F2d 636 (4th Cir. 1967) where increased sentence
        was reversed because of a denial of due process and
        equal rights; also double jeopardy. See also
        Phillips, C. A., Increased sentence upon retrial,
        Wash & Lee L Rev 25:60-69 (1968), a discussion of
        this case.   4385

MCGEE, R. A.   New look at sentencing. Fed Prob 38:3-8 (June 1974).
        Author discusses the complex interests involved in
        sentencing; briefly reviews the purposes of criminal
        law (retribution, deterrence, incapacitation, rehabili-
        tation, and respect for the law); stresses the need
        for changes; and suggests use of the California
        system as a model.   4386

MCKAY, R. B.   Ten commandments of sentencing for prison reform.
Reno, Nat. Coll. State Judiciary, 1973. 14 p. (Robert H. Jackson
memorial lect.).
        Law school dean who, as NYC Board of Correction
        chairman investigated Attica prison revolt, sug-
        gests guidelines for sentencing as evenhandedly and
        justly under present conditions as possible: 1.
        Ascertain purposes of sentencing--2. Consider
        alternatives--3. Know yourself--4. Visit institutions
        to which you may sentence offenders.   4387

MARYLAND Governor's Commission to Study Sentencing in Criminal
Cases. Report. Dec. 17, 1965. Annapolis, 1965. 40 p.
        A. Kaufman, Chair. After noting other jurisdictions'
        systems of sentencing review, Commission recommends
        adopting system of review of criminal sentences in
        Maryland by a panel of trial judges, patterned upon
        the Massachusetts and Connecticut experiences. A
        proposed statute, and rule of the Court of Appeals,
        are appended.   4388

MATTINA, J. S. Sentencing: a judge's inherent responsibility.
Judicature 57:105-10 (1973).
Judge maintains that "judging" is the responsibility
of the judge and his most important function. He
offers an appraisal of the Model Sentencing Act,
giving excerpts.   4389

METH, T. S. Sentencing the recidivist; an ethical dilemma. Ky L J
51:711-19 (1963).
Limiting discussion to repeated acts of civil disobedience (refusal to be drafted), author lists
perplexing sentencing alternatives and ethical
dilemmas of the judge.   4390

MILLER, H. S. The new wave. In Symposium; a new Federal criminal
code. Trial 9:11-33, at 31-33 (Sept./Oct. 1973).
Acting Director, Institute of Criminal Law and Procedure, Georgetown University Law Center, "highlights
the basic differences in sentencing approaches and
practices among four major proposals promulgated in
the last six years." They are recommendations in ABA
Criminal Justice Standards, the Report of the National
Commission on Reform of Federal Criminal Law, 1971,
the McClelland bill, S.1, and the Administration
bill, S.1400, both introduced 1973. Discussion includes a comparison of provisions regarding appellate review of sentences at p. 33.   4391

MITFORD, J. Kind and usual punishment; the prison business. N.Y.,
Knopf, 1974. 340 p.
A thorough and shocking indictment of how things work
behind the walls, based on the author's fieldwork;
describes for example how the discretion of California's Adult Authority in indeterminate sentencing
is abused, how parole is granted, how work furlough
harms prisoners, how order is maintained. Also
describes the profits from prison industries, new
"Clockwork Orange" methods of "behavior modification",
the extensive experimentation on prisoners done by
drug companies, the economics of the business and
the cocoon of secrecy maintained by the prison
officials to protect their domain.   4392

MORRIS, N. Future of imprisonment: toward a punitive philosophy.
Mich L Rev 72:1161-80 (1974).
Law professor examines the scope and use of imprisonment as a penal sanction and offers a new model of
imprisonment recognizing justice as well as society's
power over the individual. Author discusses whether
imprisonment is needed and when. The idea of keeping
an individual imprisoned until "cured" is ex-
amined.   4393

MOTLEY, C. B. "Law and order" and the criminal justice system.
J Crim L 64:259-69 (1973).
> Judge Motley examines the various stages in the
> criminal justice system with a view towards eluci-
> dating the problem of lack of adequate standards to
> guide the exercise of discretion by officials,
> and presents her view as to how this can be changed
> in the sentencing phase through use of mandatory,
> graduated, relatively short sentences, with longer
> sentences for repeat offenders as prescribed by the
> legislature. Purpose of imprisonment discussed. <u>4394</u>

MUELLER, G. O. W., and COOPER, H. H. A. The Criminal, society, and
the victim. Washington, Nat Crim Justice Ref Service, 1972. 19 p.
(Selected Topic Digest #2)
> Renewed awareness of primary interest of victim
> dictates civil remedies. Authors describe com-
> pensation, portion of fine to victim, day-work system,
> attachment of prison and non-institutional earnings,
> combining civil and criminal proceedings, private
> and public insurance. Bibliography. <u>4395</u>

MURRAH, A. P. Dangerous offender under the Model Sentencing Act.
Fed Prob 32:3-9 (Jun. 1968).
> Model Sentencing Act defines dangerous offender and
> suggests procedures. <u>4396</u>

NARROWING the Pearce doctrine: increased sentence on a trial
de novo. St. Louis U L J 18:426-39 (1974).
> Comment analyzes doctrine prohibiting vindictive
> sentencing on retrial, and its subsequent narrowing
> as construed by <u>Colton v Kentucky</u>, 407 US 104 (1972)
> in light of subsequent Supreme Ct. decisions that also
> narrow the effect of <u>Pearce</u>. Discussed are: double
> jeopardy; the Pearce Doctrine; equal protection and
> due process considerations; subsequent interpre-
> tations of <u>Pearce</u>; and its applicability to jury
> sentencing. <u>4397</u>

NATIONAL College of the State Judiciary. Sentencing and probation; by G. H. Revelle. Reno, 1973. 397 p.
> Areas covered are: philosophy of sentencing and
> probation; selecting the disposition; sentencing
> alternatives and procedures (includes Model Sen-
> tencing Act and ABA Standards for Criminal Justice);
> the sentencing, probation and revocation hearing.
> App A: annotated bibliography on sentencing pat-
> terns and problems. <u>4398</u>

NATIONAL Conference of judges on sentencing, Toronto, 1964. Proceedings ... May 27-29, 1964, Convened by Centre of Criminology,
Univ. of Toronto. Toronto, 1964. 70 p.

Chair: J. R. Cartwright. Conference deals with the
great disparity in sentencing presently existing in
Canada. Discussions explore: the responsibility of
sentencing judges, recent development in the penal
system, functions of the parole board, the problem
of habitual criminals, and presentence reports.
Appendices include: selected bibliography, statement
from the Lord Chief Justice on sentencing conferences
in England, and remarks by a U.S. federal judge on
sentencing.   4399

NATIONAL Council on Crime and Delinquency. Model Sentencing Act.
2d ed. Hackensack, N.J., 1972. 32 p.
Revises 1963 edition; prepared by Council of Judges
under chairmanship of Hon. A. P. Murrah, this model
act proposes individualized sentencing, appropriate
clinical diagnoses, rehabilitation, treatment of
dangerous offender. Imprisonment is virtually abol-
ished for persons eligible for non-institutional
sentences in favor of probation, suspended sentences,
fines, restitution. Guidelines offered for presentence
investigation, sentences for different types or
classes; discusses bases for criminal responsibility;
other areas are sentence hearing, sentence modification, merger of sentence and parole board authority.
                                                     4400

NEW JERSEY   Administrative Office of the Courts. Sentencing
manual for judges.   Trenton, 1971.   117 p.
Ready reference for judges in courts of general
jurisdiction of the New Jersey law. Contents include
role of the judge, counts and indictments, presentence reports, right to counsel, statement of
reasons for sentence, plea of guilty, habitual offenders; sex offenders, capital cases, narcotic offenses,
sentencing alternatives, post-sentence procedure.
Replaces 1969 ed. and 1970 Supp.   4401

NEW YORK (State) Legislature Select Committee on Crime, its
Causes, Control, and Effect on Society.   Study of illegal narcotics sentences in New York County ... by R. J. Marino, chair.
Sept. 27, 1974.   N.Y., 1974.   54 p.
Sixty-seven specific examples of conditional or
unconditional discharges in violation of Penal Law
of 1967, which prohibited such discharges for
felony narcotics convictions. Suggests controls to
prevent future occurrences.   4402

ORLAND, L.   Justice, punishment, treatment; the correctional
process.   N.Y., Free press, 1973.   579 p.
Casebook materials, relevant statutes, judicial
decisions covering such aspects of the correctional
process as presentence investigation, alternatives

to judicial incarceration, differential sentencing.
The entire rationale of coercive penal treatment is
reviewed. It is crucial that the present system
of punishment and incarceration treatment be re-
examined; training the federal and state judge is
one aspect.   4403

PALMER, L. I.   A model of criminal dispositions; an alternative to
official discretion in sentencing. Geo L J 62:1-59 (1973).
Proposal for restructuring criminal dispositions
by replacing the present broad discretion which
purports to tailor sanctions and treatment to individual cases with judicially created standards. The
standards would be based upon an"interest analysis"
of society's reasons for various dispositions. Would
also outline the role of the judiciary, administrative
agencies and the legislature.   4404

PAROLE release decision making and the sentencing process.   Yale
L J 84:810-902 (1975).
Project provides valuable information concerning
the operation of the parole system administered by
the United States Board of Parole. Authors allege
that only by understanding how the system works can
judges rationally determine appropriate length of
sentence. The investigation includes Section IV
Implications of the Guidelines for the Criminal
Justice System which dwells on sentencing practices.
                                                              4404a

PARSONS, J. B.   The presentence investigation report must be
preserved as a confidential document. Fed Prob 28:3-7 (1964).
A judge of the U.S. District Court, N.D. Ill., emphasizes the need to retain the discretionary power
of the court to determine in each instance whether
disclosure of the presentence report should be
made. He asserts that changing this rule to make
disclosure mandatory would limit essential sources
of information, result in fewer probation grants and
would be damaging to the defendant.   4405

THE PRESENTENCE report; an empirical study of its use in the
federal criminal process. Geo L J 58:451-86 (1970).
Financed by the Federal Judicial Center, study
examines whether advance presentence investigation
increases judicial efficiency. It discusses the mechanics of the investigation, the reason for its
implementation, legal and pragmatic problems and
recommendations. The role of the probation officer
is also studied and suggestions for expanded use
of his services are made.   4406

PRE-SENTENCE reports: utility or futility? Fordham Urban L J
2:27-53 (1973).
>Author examines use, benefits, and detriments of
the pre-sentence report: the N.Y. experience; presentence reports where there is a plea of guilty;
the problem of delay of sentencing; and long range
and interim solutions. Appendices: table of judges'
evaluation of probation report data; effect of
use of Vera report on disposition patterns by
type of legal counsel; and sample short form presentence report.   4407

PRETTYMAN, E. B.   The indeterminate sentence and the right to
treatment. Am Crim L Rev 11:7-37 (1972).
>Evaluation of indeterminate sentence theory based
on study of a Maryland institution and its inmates
and personnel; history of indeterminate sentencing,
arguments for; analysis of shortcomings from
inmates' view; inadequacy of treatment and rehabilitation; author condemns as self-defeating.   4408

PROCEDURAL due process at judicial sentencing for felony. Harv
L Rev 81:821-46 (1968).
>Background, sentencing under due process clause,
plea bargaining, right to be personally present,
right to allocution, right to counsel, presentence
report, mitigating evidence, justifiable sentencing
standards.   4409

PROCEEDINGS of the 1966 Sentencing Institute for Superior Court
Judges. Cal Rptr 52:app. 9-76 (1966).
>Subjects cover standards and significant factors
in sentencing, recent appellate decisions - their
impact on criminal procedure, judicial isolation and
other aspects of sentencing including sentencing
the sex offender.   4410

PUBLIC Research Institute. Deterrent effectiveness of criminal
justice sanction strategies; a summary, by S. Kobrin and S.
Lubeck. Washington, Nat. Crim. Justice Reference Service, 1972.
38 p.
>It is hypothesized that the greatest contributions
by criminal justice agencies to crime control come
from sanctions at the police and sentencing stages.
                                                       4411

PUGH, G. W. and CARVER, M. H. Due process and sentencing: from
Mapp to Mempa to McGautha. Tex L Rev 49:25-49 (1970).
>Authors point to shifting emphasis in protection of
defendant's rights from law enforcement to sentencing
and corrections. Discusses the wide discretion of
the trial judge and the need for advice of counsel
at sentencing. Argues for access of defendant to presentence report and present constitutional arguments
in favor of reliable sentencing standards.   4412

RECTOR, M. G.   Sentencing reform and litigation.   Judicature
53:58-62 (1969).
Director, National Council on Crime and Delinquency,
discusses that organization's Model Sentencing Act,
published in 1963, and the relation of the bar to
sentencing reform.   4413

RECTOR, M. G.   Sentencing the racketeer.   Crime & Delin 8:385-89
(1962).
Syndicate members are not adequately dealt with
under traditional sentencing laws. National Council
on Crime and Delinquency provides extended terms
for persons deemed dangerous under the Model Sentencing Act.   4414

RESENTENCING jury may impose a harsher sentence on retrial.   Vand
L Rev 23:859-67 (1969).
Discussing Pinkard v Henderson, 452 SW2d 908 (Tenn
Cr App, 1969), in which defendant received harsher
sentence on retrial, after original conviction set
aside, student states threat of harsh sentence
frustrates those seeking post-conviction remedies.
                                                            4415

RESENTENCING: the procedural due process protections established
in North Carolina v Pearce to guard against the possibility of
vindictiveness when a judge imposes a harsher sentence upon
retrial are to be applied only prospectively and are inapplicable
to those cases in which the jury performs the resentencing
function.   Brooklyn L Rev 40:786-802 (1974).
Examination of U.S. Supreme Court decisions involving
the question of whether harsher sentences on retrial
are constitutional.   4416

REVELL, G. H. and HAYDEN, R. F. C.   Sentencing and probation.   Reno,
Nat Coll of State Trial Judges, 1970.   257 p.
Unpublished teaching material, mostly case histories
with discussion of various aspects of sentencing;
i.e. philosophy of sentencing, selecting the disposition, responsibility of the judge after sentencing. Bibliography, p. 155, is reprint from Am
Jud Soc, Sentencing problems and patterns [item 4322]
                                                            4417

ROCHE, A. W.   The position for confidentiality of the presentence
investigation report.   Albany L Rev 29:206-24 (1965).
Reviews nature of presentence report, how information
is obtained; presents views of probation officer;
discusses practices in federal and New York courts
and various studies and survey findings on opinions
of judges and counsel; arguments against disclosure
are specifically outlined; they include drying up of
sources. Author asserts that convicted defendant has no
constitutional right to disclosure and disclosure may
interfere with rehabilitation.   4418

ROSETT, A. Discretion, severity, and legality in criminal justice.
So Cal.L Rev 46:12-50 (1972).
> Deals with the impact of discretion on the criminal
> justice system as presently exercised by those in
> the bureaucratic setting within which discretion
> typically operates. How this dilemma can be approached,
> other than through "judicialization", is discussed.
> Analyzing the causes and effects of discretion, the
> author offers procedural and organizational reforms
> to relieve offensive aspects of discretion.   4419

RUBIN, S. Allocation of authority in the sentencing-correction
decision. Tex L Rev 45:455-69 (1967).
> Counsel to National Council on Crime and Delinquency
> discusses various plans for sentencing by jury,
> board, judge, and combinations of the above. He
> concludes by recommending increased judicial authority
> for sentencing, more flexible methods including no
> minimum time for parole eligibility.   4420

RUBIN, S. Developments in correctional law. Crime & Delin 15:283-94
(1969).
> Author, in analysis of case law, synthesizes senten-
> cing with probation and prison administration; cruel
> and inhuman punishment cases are discussed.   4421

RUBIN, S. Disparity and equality of sentences; a constitutional
challenge. FRD 40:55-78 (1966).
> Author gives examples of shocking disparities in
> sentencing, with possible remedies including appel-
> late review. Reviews cases on constitutional ques-
> tions, and individualized sentences; demonstrates
> that statutes themselves foster discrimination;
> suggests that Model Sentencing Act meets require-
> ments of statute that makes valid distinctions be-
> tween defendant sentenced to long and short terms
> based not on view of the judge but on criteria and
> findings.   4422

RUBIN, S. Federal sentencing problems and the Model Sentencing
Act. FRD 41:506-17 (1967).
> Discusses details of NCCD Model Sentencing Act;
> demonstrates how provisions will achieve better
> sentencing practices.   4423

RUBIN, S. Model Sentencing Act. NYU L Rev 39:251-62 (1964).
> Highlights, implications of Act examined section
> by section, by counsel to NCCD.   4424

SCHREIBER, A. M. Indeterminate therapeutic incarceration of dangerous criminals; perspectives and problems. Va L Rev 56:602-34
(1970).

Discusses, among other things, experiment at Patuxent
Institution of Maryland, combining indeterminate sentences with therapeutic treatment for recidivists;
article focuses on drawbacks of system exemplified
by Patuxent, but it assumes that indeterminate sentences may be used as a means of protecting public
safety; constitutionality of this approach discussed.
4425

SENTENCE crediting for the state criminal defendant, a constitutional
requirement.   Ohio S L J 34:586-98 (1973).
Note examines whether the state criminal defendant
charged with a criminal offense and unable to make
bail is constitutionally entitled to have his
pretrial jail time credited against the sentence later
incurred, and concludes that such a right exists.
Discussed are: historical perspective, the possible
conflict between this right and trial judge discretion, and constitutional arguments of Equal
Protection, Eighth Amendment, excessive bail, Sixth
Amendment right to trial, and Fifth Amendment guarantee against double jeopardy.   4426

SENTENCING indigents: the validity of imprisonment in lieu of
payment of a fine.   Ohio S L J 32:175-81 (1971).
The application of the equal protection clause in
Williams v Illinois 399 US 235 (1970), is considered.
4427

SENTENCING Institute, New York University, 1963. Sentencing
institute for justices and judges charged with the judicial administration of the criminal law in the First, Second, and Eleventh
Judicial Districts, Sponsored by the Administrative Board of the
Judicial Conference of the State of New York, Mar 29-30, 1963.
N.Y., 1963. 1 v., var. pagings.
Five pre-sentence probation reports are presented
which are to be the subject of panel discussions.
4428

SENTENCING practices, problems, and remedies.   Judicature 53:74-78
(1967).
W. S. Carr, developing bibliograpny for American
Judicature Society (see item 4322) reviews literature since 1952; he covers the history and decries
what it reveals in this area. He discusses various
attempts to improve and innovations, and expresses
his ideas as to what can be done.   4429

SENTENCING selective service violators: a judicial wheel of
fortune.   Colum J Law & Social Prob 5:164-93 (1969).
An examination of the widespread disparity and
inequity in sentencing selective service violators,
based on the Journal's questionnaire and other

statistics, is presented. Policies underlying these
sentencing patterns are analyzed. Reforms such as
sentencing panels or compulsory work programs as
an alternative to prison are suggested.   4430

SEX discrimination--disparate sentencing of male and female
offenders violates equal protection. Suffolk U L Rev 8:830-42
(1974).
          Case comment analyzes State v Chambers, 63 NJ 277
          (1973) holding that where males were given a
          statutory minimum-maximum sentence and females an
          indeterminate sentence for the same crime, there was
          an unconstitutional denial of equal protection.
          Author examines the history of disparate sentences
          and previous cases dealing with the subject.   4431

SEYMOUR, W. N. Jr. Major surgery for criminal courts. Bklyn
L Rev 38:571-85 (1972).
          U.S. Attorney, S.D.N.Y., proposes for discussion
          these changes in trial judges' options as to sen-
          tencing: judicial censure, monetary penalty, injunc-
          tion; he discusses white collar crimes
          and when jail sentences should or should not be
          imposed; also proposes classifications of offenses
          to decide under which category thay belong: 1. crimi-
          nal sanctions only 2. criminal/or civil sanctions
          3. civil sanctions only. Only this type of major
          surgery will eliminate from the purely criminal
          process a large block of cases where rigid criminal
          procedures are unsuitable. Such innovations will
          reduce the burden on the criminal courts, reduce
          delay in criminal cases.   4432

SEYMOUR, W. N., Jr. 1972 sentencing study for the Southern District of N.Y. NYSB J 45:163-71 (1973).
          Detailed study, case by case, by US Attorney's
          office, S.D.N.Y. of all sentences imposed in the
          court over six-month period (May 1, 1972 to October
          1, 1972) covers sentencing of 645 individual defen-
          dants. Indicates discrimination in treatment of
          offenders for different classes or violations, white
          collar defendants (mostly white) being more leniently
          treated while common criminals (mostly black) are
          more likely to be sent to prison; poor persons
          therefore are often more harshly treated. Specifics
          are presented; covers disparity in sentencing between
          individual judges in Southern District, illustrating
          that defendants in Selective Service violations (cases
          of similar nature) are variously sentenced; further
          testing, a five-year study of sentences imposed on
          postal employees charged with postal theft showed
          similar variances in sentences given. Also demon-

strates disparity in sentencing between the districts,
with illustrative cases. Recommendations give short-
range and long-range goals. Various exhibits are
attached.   4433

SEYMOUR, W. N. Jr. Social and ethical considerations in assessing
white-collar crime. Am Crim L Rev 11:821-34 (1973).
          Former United States Attorney is critical of dis-
          parities in sentencing common criminals and white-
          collar criminals, as shown in a 1972 Sentencing
          Study of the Southern District of New York (item 4433),
          in the Appendix (including recommendations and some
          statistics). He calls upon law enforcement officials
          to give top priority to prosecuting white-collar
          crimes and suggests what businessmen can do to
          thwart such crimes.   4434

SIGNORELLI, E. L. Judicial analysis and critique of the new
drug and sentencing laws. NYSB J 46:9-19 (1974).
          Judge describes the changes in the New York State
          law relating to drug and drug related offenses and
          their sentencing. He objects to provisions which
          have, in his opinion, placed the judge in a strait
          jacket.   4435

SINGER, R. G. and HAND, R. C. Sentencing computation: laws and
practices. Crim L Bull 10:318-47 (1974).
          Report surveys disparities in sentencing computation
          practices in all 50 states, D.C., and the federal
          system. Examined are: indeterminate and determinate
          sentencing; habitual offender laws; pretrial deten-
          tion and constitutional issues raised; use of community
          correctional facilities and credit for "street time";
          and reduction of sentence for "good behavior." Aut-
          hors consider it imperative that issues discussed
          be clarified to prevent the inequalities and in-
          justices they found while doing their study.   4436

SKOLER, D. L. There's more to crime control than the "get tough"
approach. Annals 397:28-39 (1971).
          Balancing results, staff director of ABA Commission on
          Correctional Facility and Services finds that train-
          ing, education, placement, counseling, and community
          acceptance offer more than tough, punitive sentences.
                                                              4437

SMITH, T. The Sentencing Council and the problem of disproportionate sentences. Fed Prob 27:5-9 (Jun. 1963).
          Federal judge in Eastern District of Michigan reports
          new sentencing procedure which attempts to correlate
          each disposition with the needs of the individual
          offender. Describes the use of a presentence report;
          the individual judge's summary of the report in a

study sheet; and the panel meeting of three judges
as a salutary method of determining the final disposition. For an earlier description of a sentencing
council, see Doyle, A Sentencing council in operation.
Fed Prob 25:27-30 (Sep. 1961).   4438

STANTON, N. Sentencing provisions in proposals for a new federal
criminal code. Ind L Rev 7:348-60 (1973).
Author analyzes and compares several changes regarding sentencing proposed by bills S.1 and S.1400,
which attempt to reform the federal criminal law
and Title 18. Examined are: classification of
crimes; length of prison terms; mandatory minimum
terms; appellate review of sentencing; and resentencing to longer terms. Author concludes that both of
these bills, although valuable, should be brought
into more conformity with the ABA Minimum Standards
for Criminal Justice. Relevant portions of the ABA
standards are in footnotes.   4439

STUDY of the California penalty jury in first-degree murder cases.
Stan L Rev 21:1297-1497 (1969).
Empirical inquiry into the operation of the jury and
the death penalty, establishing determinants of jury
decisions for or against capital punishment in
California where there is a separate trial on penalty after guilt is established. The methodology,
universe of the study, and analyses of findings are
presented in the preface by Professor Harry Kalven,
Jr. Death penalty given in less than half the
cases where jury had power to give it.   4440

SUSPENDED sentence: what has gone wrong? New L J 120:1144-1146
(1970).
Note analyzes the use of suspended sentences in
England: activation of suspended sentences on second
offense within the sentence period has placed many
in jail for minor offenses for which there is
usually no imprisonment; the use of suspended
sentences as a substitute for other punishment and
as a "way out" for judges; and the unexpectedly low
success rate of the suspended sentence. Date tables
included.   4441

SYMPOSIUM on sentencing. Judicature 53:51-78 (1969).
Keve, P. W. Sentencing; the need for alternatives--
Rector, M. G. Sentencing reform and litigation--
Kirby, B. C., Doubts about the indeterminate sentence.--Tydings, J. D., Ensuring rational sentence;
the case for appellate review.--Note: Sentencing
practices, problems, and remedies.   4442

TEXAS sentencing practice; a statistical study. Tex L Rev 45:
471-564 (1967).
>   Comment examines Texas criminal process to define
>   factors influencing sentencing; examines charac-
>   teristics common to offenders; seeks predictable im-
>   pact of these sentencing factors on severity of dis-
>   position to determine where disparity exists and
>   recommends possible changes to eliminate disparity;
>   differences from court to court and from jury to
>   court are scrutinized.   4443

THOMAS, D. A. Current developments in sentencing: the Criminal
Justice Act in practice. Crim L Rev 1969:235-49.
>   Suspended sentences; future trends in England.   4444

THOMAS, D. A. Establishing a factual basis for sentencing. Crim
L Rev 1970:80-90.
>   Law lecturer, London School of Economics, emphasizes
>   the importance of establishing an accurate version
>   of the facts for the purpose of sentencing. This
>   may even include extraneous facts not involving the
>   accused. One suggestion the author makes is to hold
>   a separate hearing after conviction of any issue
>   relevant to sentence which remains in dispute and
>   has not been determined by the conviction.   4445

THOMAS, D. A. Sentencing: the basic principles, Parts I and II.
Crim L Rev 1967:455-65, 503-25.
>   Analyzes England's dual system of sentencing, using
>   both individualized measures related to the offender's
>   needs, and fixed sentences based on possible need
>   for deterrence; unusual conditions in a particular
>   locality, or the concept of retribution. Part II
>   discusses methods of calculating the proper length
>   of sentence; the effect of mitigating circumstances,
>   using sexual offense cases as illustrations; and the
>   use of fines.   4446

THOMAS, D. A. Theories of punishment in the Court of Criminal
Appeal. Modern L Rev 27:546-67 (1964).
>   Examines the relative roles in England of the con-
>   cepts of retribution, deterrence, prevention, and
>   rehabilitation in sentencing; concludes that
>   modern ideas of rehabilitation may eventually in-
>   fluence even sentencing for serious crimes.   4447

THORESBY, R. British briefs; how sentencing works in England.
ABA J 60:479-81 (1974).
>   Outline of the system, with historical background.
>   English courts rely on "sentencing tariffs",
>   schedules of time to be served for various offenses,
>   overlaid with reform considerations of the personal

background of the defendant, under a statute which
sets maximum sentences only and leaves wide discretion to the judges. Discusses the review of sentences by the new Court of Appeal, Criminal Division,
and criticizes insufficient reporting of sentence
decisions, the lack of the right to appeal by the
prosecution, and judges without criminal practice
experience sitting on appeal.   4448

TOWARD lawfulness in sentencing: thank you, Professor Dworkin.
Rutgers Camden L J 5:80-106 (1973).
Note examines the dispositional stage of the criminal
process by expanding on Prof. Dworkin's model of
the adjudication process. Arrives at a theoretical
model of sentencing principles which the author
feels will solve sentencing problems. Note explains
Dworkin's model and examines basic principles of
sentencing. See Dworkin, R. M. Symposium: Philosophy
of law: judicial discretion. J Philosophy 60:624
(1963).   4449

U. S. ADMINISTRATIVE Office of the United States Courts. Div. of
Probation. The presentence investigation report. Washington,
1965. 46 p.
To achieve greater uniformity in presentence reports, the outline, content and format of the report to be used by the probation officer are presented with suggestions.   4450

U. S. CONGRESS Senate District of Columbia Committee. Court
Reform Act impact on correctional systems; hearings before
Subcommittee on Business, Commerce, and the Judiciary, on impact
of Court Reform and Criminal Procedure Act of 1970. Washington,
USGPO, 1971. 491 p. (92d Cong., 1st sess.)
Includes information on impact of Act on sentencing
diversion from criminal justice system in District
of Columbia.   4451

U. S. PRESIDENT'S Commission on Law Enforcement and Administration
of Justice. Sentencing, chap. 2 in its Task force report: the
courts. Washington, USGPO, 1967. p. 14-26.
Discusses, with recommendations, the following:
Statutory framework of sentencing (number of punishment categories, imprisonment, probation, fines); Information for sentencing (the presentence investigation
and report, duties of defense counsel, disclosure,
hearing, diagnostic commitments, critical analyses
of sentencing information); Exercise of court
sentencing authority (improvement of judicial sentencing councils, appellate review of sentences and
jury sentencing).   4452

U. S. WELFARE Administration. The sentencing and parole process, by D. Glaser, F. Cohen and V. O'Leary for the National Parole Institutes. Washington, USGPO, 1966. 26 p.
Authors consider the interrelationships of legislatures, courts and parole boards in the sentence-fixing process and the power of the parole boards to alter length of confinement; also discuss the Model Penal Code and the Model Sentencing Act.   4453

VANN, C. R. Pretrial determination and judicial decision-making; an analysis of the use of psychiatric information in the administration of criminal justice. U Detroit L J 43:13-33 (1965).
Examines issue of the influence of psychiatric evaluation of criminal offenders on length and type of sentence.   4454

WHITE, S. Suspended sentences reviewed. New L J 120:1117-18 (1970).
Author discusses several recent British Court of Appeal decisions and their impact on suspended sentences: suspended sentences and fines; activation of suspended sentences; immediate and suspended sentences; and judicial discretion in fixing the length of suspended sentences.   4455

WOODS, G. D. Criminology and sentencing in the New South Wales Court of criminal appeal. Crim L R 1974:409-14 (Jul. 1974).
Law lecturer discusses the emphasis on sentencing in Australian courts of appeal; the traditional method of looking at the facts of the particular case and the more recent broad delineation of policy. Author concludes that judges should be familiar with criminological studies to aid them in sentencing.4456

YOUNGDAHL, L. W. Development and accomplishments of sentencing institutes in the federal system. Neb L Rev 45:513-19 (1966).
How the sentencing institutes were created under H.R.J. Res. 424, P.L. 85-752, Sec 1, 72 Anat. 845 (1958); the agenda of the institutes, a chronological presentation and progress made; describes establishment of the committee on the Administration of the Probation System in 1963. (For examples, see items 4462 to 4474).   4457

ZASTROW, W. G. Disclosure of the presentence investigation report, Fed Prob 35:20-2 (1971).
Following his review of the arguments for and against disclosure, chief probation officer, U. S. District Court, Milwaukee, describes the practice of disclosure in his district, begun five years ago, and notes its many advantages   4458

878   ADMINISTRATION OF CRIMINAL JUSTICE

ZAVATT, J. C. Sentencing procedure in the United States District
Court for the Eastern District of New York. FRD 41:469-93 (1966).
Judge Zavatt describes the sentencing council procedure in which three judges, including the sentencing judge, confer. Statistics for the first
three years of this procedure, 1962-64, are set
forth and analyzed.   4459

ZEISEL, H. Methodological studies in sentencing. Law & Soc
Rev 3:621-31 (1969).
A review of various studies made to explore reasons
behind judicial and jury sentences.   4460

ZUMWALT, W. J. The anarchy of sentencing in the federal courts.
Judicature 57:96-104 (1973).
Director, Federal Defenders, Inc., describes brief
docket study indicating wide federal intercircuit
sentencing disparities. Reviews scope of federal
judge's sentencing discretion, lack of appellate
review, rules on disclosure of sentencing information and present bases used for sentencing review.
Recommends reform through guidelines for the exercise of discretion. Uses U.S. Bureau of Prisons
statistics. See letter in Judicature 57:459 (1974)
taking issue with author's use of statistics as
comparing apples with oranges.   4461

Federal Sentencing Institutes:

INSTITUTE on sentencing for U. S. District Judges, [sponsored by]
Judicial Conf. of the U. S., Cttee on Administration of the Probation System, Lompoc, Calif., Oct. 1964; papers ... FRD 37:
111-90 (1965).

> Contents: Youngdahl, L. W., opening remarks--Westover,
> H. C., Basic sentencing philosophies--Herlands, W. B.,
> Guttmacher, W. S., MD, & Rappaport, W., MD, Panel
> on treatment of the mentally ill defendant--Lacovara,
> D. J., MD, Workshop on mental illness--Oliver, J. W.;
> Kunzel, F., Panel on mental competency to stand
> trial: insanity as a defense--Evjen, V. H., Guide-
> lines in preparing presentence reports--Wright,
> R. L., Jail sentences in anti-trust cases--Summary,
> recommendations.   4462

INSTITUTE on sentencing for United States District Judges,
[sponsored by] Judicial Conference of U. S., Committee on Administration of the Probation System. Lewisburg, Pa., Nov. 1964.
FRD 37:191-214 (1965).

> Contents: Barkin, E. N. Comments on various senten-
> cing situations.--Roche, P. Q., MD, and Smith, C. E.,
> MD, Mental Health and criminal behavior.--Chappell,
> R. A., Federal parole.--Summary, recommendations.
> 4463

PAPERS delivered at the institute on sentencing for United States
District Judges, Denver, Colorado, Feb. 1964. FRD 35:381-509
(1964).

> Contents: Youngdahl, L. W., Opening remarks-- Dusen,
> F. L., Trends in sentencing since 1957--Summary
> list of sentencing alternatives--Carter, J. M.,
> Forms of adjudication for use in sentencing--Parsons,
> J. B., Aids in sentencing--Oliver, J. W., Application
> of psychiatry to study, observation, and treatment
> of the federal offender--Settle, R. O., Medical
> center for federal prisoners--Herlands, W. B.,
> When and how should sentencing judge use probation?
> 4464

PAPERS delivered at the institute on sentencing for U. S. judges
of the Eighth and Tenth Judicial Circuits, Denver, Colo., Jul.
11-13, 1966; papers ... FRD 42:175-233 (1968).

> Contents: Murrah, A. P., Foreword--Rome, H. P.,
> MD, Identification of the dangerous offender--
> McGee, R. A., Objectivity in predicting criminal
> behavior--Smith, M. A., Treatment of the nondangerous
> offender--Rubin, S., Sentences must be rationally
> explained--Devitt, E. J., How can we effectively mini-
> mize unjustified disparity in federal criminal
> sentences?--Rubin, S., Constitutional aspects of
> the Model Sentencing Act.   4465

SEMINAR and institute on disparity of sentences for Sixth, Seventh, and Eighth Judicial Circuits, under the auspices of the Judicial Conference of the United States, Highland Park, Illinois, Oct. 12-13, 1961. FRD 30:401-505 (1962).

Partial contents: 1. Introduction: Origin; Legal background; Purpose; Scope of problem; and Format of Institute; Background reference date--II. The Conference: Summaries of addresses [see Appendix for addresses in full]; Address of U. S. Att Gen R. F. Kennedy--III. Workshops: A. Presentence reports, with issues, balloting results, for: Dyer Act violator and Income tax violator (chair, E. J. DeVitt)--for Bank Robbery Act violator (chair, G. S. Register)-- for forgery violator (chair, T. P. Thornton)-- for Bank embezzlement violator (chair, K. P. Grubb)-- B. Presentence information, particularly 4208(b) commitments for diagnosis--C. Probation or incarceration--D. Personality and background characteristics of offender--E. Ability to make restitution-- F. Effect of guilty plea--G. Effect of ill health of defendant--H. Incarceration decision--1. Analysis of "Before and after Institute" sentencing poll--IV. Summation: areas of agreement; Consensus, significant trends, areas on which no consensus was reached, by E. A. Robson----V. Preliminary evaluation--VI. Appendix. (addresses given at conference, full text): Robson, E. A., Objectives of Institute; Celler, E., Legislative views on importance of Sentencing Institute; DeLoach, D. C., Relationship of criminal sentences to law enforcement; Sharp, L. J., Presentence investigations and reports;--New sentencing procedures available to federal courts, J. V. Bennett; Parole, R. A. Chappell; Methods of dealing with young offenders, G. E. Murch; Tables: before and after sentencing polls.   4466

SENTENCING institute and joint council for the Fifth Circuit, New Orleans, La., May 9-10, 1961. FRD 30:185-328 (1962).

Contents: I. Tuttle, E. P., Welcome--II. Clayton, C. F., Objectives of Institute--III. Clinical presentation of actual cases, imposition of sentences, comparison of results: Gourley, W. S., presiding, Many, M. H., Boyle, E. J., Bennett, J. V., Levin, T., Chappell, R. A., Celler, E., participants-- IV. Celler, E., Legislative views, value of the Institute--V. Presentence process: Sharp, L. J., The presentence report--Simpson, B., Utilization of the presentence report-- VI. What can a judge do?: Lynne, S. H. ... with an adult defendant--Johnson, F. M., Jr., ... with juvenile delinquent, youth offender, young adult defender--VII. Deloach, C. D., How the FBI feels about the relationship of sentences

and law enforcement--VIII. The automobile thief:
Hoffman, W. E., the basic problem--Dawkins, B. C.
Jr., Probation or prison? Youth or adult?--Estes,
J. E., Setting the maximum or minimum--IX. The
fraudulent offender: Bootle, W. A., The basic
problem--Hunter, E. F., Jr., Offender who violates
both federal and state law--Hannay, A. B., Probation
or prison?--X. The income tax violator: Wright,
J. S., The basic problem--Grooms, H. H., Violation
related to other crimes--Miller, W. E., Violations
not related to other crimes--Thomas, D. H.,
Misdemeanants--XI. Goodman, L. W. Would a system
where sentences are fixed by a board of experts be
preferable?XII. Connally, B. C., Summary and evaluation.   4467

SENTENCING Institute for the First and Second U. S. Judicial
Circuits, Crotonville, N.Y., 1973. Justice in sentencing: papers and
proceedings ... ed. by L. Orland, H. R. Tyler, Jr. Mineola, N.Y.,
Foundation press, 1974. 353 p.
          Co-chair: H. R. Tyler, Jr., and F. J. Murray,
          Institute proceedings: Panels on Sentencing ob-
          jectives; Prison or probation; If prison, how much?;
          Collegial sentencing or sentence review; Plea
          bargaining; Courts and the parole board. Papers
          include: Nat Inst Law Enforcement & Crim Justice,
          Variations in prison and probation sentencing--U.S.
          Att'y Off., N.Y. So Dist, 1972 sentencing study--
          U.S. Admin. Off. of Courts, Sentencing alternatives--
          Selected excerpts from Commission reports and from
          ABA Criminal Justice Standards.   4468

Sentencing institute of Ninth Circuit, MacNeil Island, and Lakewood
Center (Tacoma), Washington, September 1965. FRD 39:523-66 (1966)
          Contents: Barkin, E.N. Sentencing problems.--Oliver,
          J.W. Judicial hearings to determine mental competency
          to stand trial--Smith. C.E. Psychiatric approaches to
          the mentally ill federal offender.   4469

SENTENCING institute, United States Court of Appeals for the
Second Circuit. N.Y. Nov. 11, 1966. FRD 41:467-517 (1967).
          Contents: Tyler, H. R., Jr., Introductory statement--
          Zavatt, J. C., Sentencing procedures in the U. S.
          District of N.Y.--Barkin, E. N., Impact of recent
          legislation and rule changes upon sentencing--
          Rubin, S., Federal sentencing problems and the
          model sentencing act.   4470

SYMPOSIUM: Excerpts from the proceedings of the institute on
sentencing for United States Judges of the District of Columbia
Circuit. Nov., 1968. FRD 54:285-357 (1972).
          Contents: Bazelon, D. L., Opening remarks--Barkin,
          E. N., Legal problems in sentencing--Lanham, D. A.

Psychiatric diagnostic services--Shuman, A. M.,
Institutional study of youth offenders--Dash, S.,
The defense lawyer's role at the sentencing stage
of a criminal case--Zavatt, J. C., Sentencing procedure in the United States District Court for
the Eastern District of New York--Redkey, H., What
is NARA?--Ferell, H. A., Impact of sentencing on
parole decision making--Judicial Conference, Model
parole hearing--Alexander, M. E. The trend of
corrections.   4471

SYMPOSIUM: Pilot institute on sentencing under the auspices of
the Judicial Conference of the United States; proceedings ...
Boulder, Colo., Jul. 16-17, 1959.   FRD 26:231-383 (1960).
Contents: I. The opening of the institute: Campbell,
W. J., Introductory remarks--II. Background and ob-
jectives of the institute program: Celler, E.,
An expression of congressional interest in the
Federal Sentencing Institute--Willis, E. E.,
Statement--Brickfield, C. F., Statement--Walsh,
L. E., An expression of interest on the part of the
Dept. of Justice--Olney, W. Objectives of pilot in-
stitute--III. Legal framework of sentencing: Campbell, W. J., Introductory remarks--Connor, R. G.,
Legal framework for sentencing--IV. Sentencing
the income tax violator: Campbell, W. J., Scope of
the session--Boldt, G. H., Statement of basic
problems--Weber, R. H., Sentencing income tax
violator when violation is incident to other
crimes--McIlvaine, J. W., Sentencing income tax violator when violation is unrelated to other crime--
Gignoux, E. T., Sentencing the income tax violator-
misdemeanant--V. Sentencing the auto thief: Campbell, W. J., Scope of session--Hoffman, W. E.,
Statement of basic problems--Youngdahl, L. W., Sentencing the auto thief to probation or prison, as
youth or adult--Devitt, E. J., Setting the maximum
and minimum term-- VI. Resources in the disposition
of the offender: Campbell, W. J., Scope of session--
Goodman, L. E., Utilization of presentence resources--
Sharp, L. J., Objectives of the presentence report--
Bennett, J. V., Evaluation of the offender by the
Bureau of Prisons--Reed, G. J., The role of the
United States Board of Parole--VII. Sentencing the
fraudulent offender: Campbell, W. J., Scope of
session--Kaufman, I. R., Statement of basic problems--
Carter, J. M., Offender who violates both federal
and state law--Thomsen, R. C., Choice between pro-
bation and prison--Smith, W. F., Setting the maximum and minimum--VIII. Summary: Bryan, A. V.,
Sheehy, J. W., Principal areas of consensus and
disagreement; Discussion.   4472

SYMPOSIUM: Sentencing institute, the circuit conference of the
Ninth Judicial Circuit, held at Pebble Beach, Calif., Jul. 8,
1960. FRD 27:287-391 (1961).
  Contents: Goodman, L. E., Introductory remarks--
  McCord, W. M., Juvenile delinquency--Boldt, G. H.,
  Use of Sec 4208(a), eligibility for parole--Carter,
  O., Use of Sec 4208(b) and (c), commitment for study--
  Wahl, A., The new sentencing statutes from the pro-
  bation officer's standpoint--Bennett, J. V., The
  viewpoint of the Bureau of Prisons on the evaluation
  of prisoners--Reed, G. J., Policies of the parole
  board--Goodman, L. E. Must an adult prisoner committed
  for study be returned to court for final sentencing?--
  Jameson, W. J., Effect of Rule 35 with respect to
  Sec 5010(e)--Solomon, G. J., Effect of Rule 35
  with respect to Sec 4208(b)-- Appendices.   4473

UNITED States Court of Appeals for the Fourth and Fifth Circuits,
institute on sentencing, Atlanta, Ga., Oct. 30-31, 1967. FRD 45:
149-98 (1969).
  Contents: Hoffman, W. E., Rule 11 and the plea of
  guilty--Stanley, E. M., Requirements of Rules 11 and
  44, Federal Rules of Crim Procedure--Murrah, A. P.,
  The dangerous offender under the Model Sentencing
  Act--Thomsen, R. C., Sentencing the dangerous offender
  --Dusen, F. L., Some aspects of federal probation
  with emphasis on the work of probation officers and
  discussions between sentencing judge and probation
  officer prior to sentencing--Morris, N., Politics and
  pragmatism in crime control--Recommendations and
  concluding remarks.   4474

B. Appellate Review of Sentences
    Items cover review of criminal sentences;
    review by courts, review boards, parole boards;
    alteration of sentences upon review of sentences.
    See also Section VIII A, Statutory and Judicial
    Discretion.

ADVISORY Council on Appellate Justice. Expediting review of felony
convictions after trial, a report of the Committee on Criminal
Appeals. Aug. 1973. Washington, Federal Judicial Center, and
Nat. Center for State Courts, 1973. 18 p. (FSC Research ser. no.
73-1)

> W. Feinberg, Cttee chair. Focus of work is direct review
> of trial court proceedings in felony cases in which
> there has been an adversary trial and conviction.
> Committee recommends that 1) procedures may and
> should differ from civil appeals; 2) such appeals
> should be monitored by appellate court to prevent
> unnecessary delay; 3) central staff of lawyers
> should assist judges in ways specified; 4) there
> be continuity of representation of appellants for
> trial and appeal; 5) transcript be made available
> to appellate court within 30 days from sentence.
> Based on the recommendations, specific procedures
> are described. Unresolved problems are mentioned.
> Appended is a form to be used at time of sentencing,
> to be transmitted to chief judge of court of appeals;
> also appended is explanatory statement of cost
> involved in implementing recommendations.   4475

AGATA, B. C. Time served under a reversed sentence or conviction:
a proposal and a basis for decision. Mont L Rev 25:3-74 (1963).

> Law professor shows that there is no consistent
> framework within which to decide the issues raised
> by the problem of time served under a reversed
> conviction or sentence. App 1: statutes from four-
> teen jurisdictions and Model Penal Code proposed
> official draft; App 2: statute proposed by author.
> 4476

ALASKA Judicial Council. Alaska sentencing conference, Dec. 12,
1968, Sitka. Anchorage, 1968. 1 v., looseleaf.

> Typewritten, verbatim report of speakers testifying
> before the Statewide Committee on Sentencing and
> Appellate Review of Sentencing. Discussion among
> experts, judges, and legislators ranges over entire
> field of sentencing, including probation and review
> of sentences. (see also item 4478)   4477

ALASKA Judicial Council. Statewide Committee on Sentencing and
Appellate Review of Sentences; Conference, Juneau, Feb. 19, 1969.
Anchorage, 1969. 80 p.

This typewritten report presents a verbatim discussion limited to appellate review of sentences,
following a broader exchange by this group on
sentencing some months previous (see item 4477).
It is of interest because it reveals the ideas of
the experts and the hesitations of the judges themselves and makes numerous comparative references to
review of sentences in the appellate courts in those
states that so provide. These conferences were held
in order to enable the committee to make recommendations to the Judicial Council on revision of
the Alaska Criminal Code. Effective Jan. 1, 1970,
the Alaska Supreme Court is expressly authorized to
review criminal sentences (Alas. Stat. S. 22:05:010
(19B)) and defendant may appeal from a sentence he
claims is excessive, while state may appeal from a
sentence it says is too lenient (Alas. Stat. S.
12:55:120(1973)).   4477a

AMERICAN Bar Association Advisory Committee on Sentencing and
Review. Standards relating to appellate review of sentences,
recommended by the Advisory Committee on Sentencing and Review.
S. E. Sobeloff, chair.; P. W. Low, rep. Tent. draft, Apr. 1967.
N.Y., IJA, 1967. 160 p. Amendments supp. Dec. 1967. 5 p. Reprinted Mar. 1968. Approved, Feb. 1968.
Standards with commentary covering general principles
of appellate review of sentences, the availability
and scope of review; appendices are selected state
review statutes, federal and state proposals,
Dean D. Meador's report on the Review of criminal
sentences in England, and selected bibliography
of early and recent materials.   4478

APPEALABILITY of a criminal sentence -- sentence modified on
appeal. Rutgers L Rev 16:186-91 (1961).
The New Jersey Supreme Court held in State v Johnson,
170 A2d 830 (1961) that although appellate court
does not have the power to modify a sentence imposed
by the trial court, it may do so even though the
sentence is within the statutory limits where
sentence is manifestly excessive. The student note
briefly discusses common law background and gives
state statutes permitting appellate review of sentences. Discusses arguments favoring, and those
against; discusses proposals made to permit review
by others than appellate court. Appellate review
to the state is rejected, giving reasons.   4479

APPELLATE review -- federal appellate court may remand criminal
sentence based on unverified information. Vand L Rev 25:252-57
(1972).
Ninth Circuit in U.S. v Western, 448 F2d 626
(9th Cir. 1971) vacated sentence and remanded where

maximum sentence was based on unverified statements
in presentence report. The note discusses cases
justifying this holding.   4480

APPELLATE review of criminal sentencing -- limiting the scope of
the nonreview doctrine. U Pitt L Rev 33:917-28 (1972).
            In duscussing U.S. v Daniels, 446 F2d 967 (6th Cir.
            1971), this note examines the limited area of appel-
            late review of sentences to determine whether the
            Sixth Circuit had the power to impose a reduced
            sentence in this case. If such power existed, the
            note further discusses whether it was applicable in
            Daniels and whether by this case a workable standard
            for aid in future sentencing has been established.
            The case involves a Jehovah's witness who was
            convicted of willfully disobeying a selective
            service order; the trial court had imposed penal
            service, ignoring a suggestion by the appellate court
            for solution other than imprisonment. Writer con-
            cludes modern penological prospectives provide
            adequate justification for Daniels, which established
            among other things that the "individualized model
            must be used as a basis for all criminal sentencing."
            See other student notes on this case: Case W Rev
            L Rev 23:430-36 (1972); U Cin L Rev 41:195-205 (1972).
                                                       4481

APPELLATE review of primary sentencing decisions; Connecticut case
study. Yale L J 69:1453-78 (1960).
            Eleven states permit appellate review of sentences,
            nine vesting power to affirm or reduce in existing
            appellate courts. Massachusetts and Connecticut
            created special tribunals; this study evaluates
            Connecticut's Sentence Review Division. Failures
            are discussed. Unfavorable results, lack of interest
            of bench, bar, and public in the work of the
            Division point to ultimate ineffectiveness of the
            effort.   4482

APPELLATE review of sentence imposed by trial court. J Urban L
48:536-49 (1971).
            Note discusses Scott v U. S. 419 F2d 264 (CA D. C.
            1969) where the trial judge expressed his disbelief
            of defendant's testimony in open court and gave a
            harsh but legal sentence upon conviction because
            defendant insisted on his innocence and was not
            contrite. The Court of Appeals for the District of
            Columbia remanded the case for resentencing.
            Similar cases, similar findings in other circuits are
            discussed.   4483

APPELLATE review of sentences. In Arizona Supreme Court 1971-72, Ariz L Rev 14:409-625 (1972) at 477-87.
The Supreme Court of Arizona had virtually renounced its statutory authority to reduce sentences, says the writer, documenting the statement by reference to and analyses of cases; the last term, however, saw a new trend toward more vigorous use of the statutory power and a "concomitant change in the attitudes of the state judiciary toward purposes of criminal punishment." There appears to be a redirectment from restraint and deterrence toward rehabilitation. Arguments for trend against view are restated, with discussion of leading cases. See item 4500

4484

APPELLATE review of sentences; a survey. St. Louis ULJ 17:221-62 (1972).
Cites numerous state and federal cases indicating that review of sentences passed by trial judge is sorely needed; cites also articles and reports indicating similar need; student note then discusses sentence review cases in the federal court system, characterizing the attitude toward such review as "federal judiciary schizophrenia on sentence modification by appellate review" citing particularly to Smith v U.S. 273 F2d 462 (10th Cir. 1959), Judge Murrah dissenting. This extensive note proceeds to examine case law and case statutes giving power to appellate courts to review sentences, distinguishing between the various types of statutes. Arguments for and against are made and the next section deals with other methods of sentence review--executive clemency, administrative tribunal and indeterminate sentencing, sentencing councils, a single judge to sentence all similar offenses. App A: chart indicates availability of appellate review and type of disposition in the states, App B: state-by-state rundown citing to statutes with cases interpreting them.   4485

APPELLATE review of sentences and the need for a reviewable record. Duke L J 1973:1357-76.
There is statutory authority for sentence review of various kinds in 15 states. This extensively foot-noted note covers history of the rule against review of sentences. Discusses cases demonstrating avoidance of the rule by U.S. courts of appeals (to ensure due process, to protect defendant's privilege against self-incrimination, to enforce sentencing statutes, to exercise supervisory control, to review abuse of discretion). Author then discusses prospects for the rule, concludes reviewing court must have a review-able record (with the presentence report) and a

statement of reasons for the sentence. Author
suggests that sentencing judge's discretion should not
be unlimited.   4486

APPELLATE review of sentences in Florida; a proposal. U Fla L Rev
23:736-53 (1971).
Proposal to eliminate "almost unlimited discretion"
in trial judges, suggests 1) appellate review by
right for sentences over one year, 2) statement of
reasons by sentencing judge, 3) complete record and
presentence report sent to appellate court, 4) power
in appellate court to modify or remand sentence,
5) statement of reasons by appellate court.   4487

APPELLATE review of sentences in Wisconsin. Wis L Rev 1971:1190-
1208.
Note speaks first to the common law concept that
sentencing is within the sole discretion of the trial
court and of the reluctance of appellate courts to
review sentences. Sentences that violate statutory
or constitutional norms have always been reversible
but lawfully imposed sentences were not scrutinized.
Today at least 13 states provide for appellate
review of legal or excessive sentences. In Wisconsin,
Arkansas, Idaho, Oklahoma, Pennsylvania, and New
Jersey, courts have held general review statutes
to provide for appellate review of sentences (cases
in these states are cited). The note proceeds to
examine the role of Wisconsin Supreme Court in exer-
cising appellate control over sentencing. Discussed
are the legal theories involved in review, and the
problem of developing criteria by which to judge
the appropriateness of the sentence. Concludes that
the Wisconsin Supreme Court has failed to develop
explicit standards by which to judge whether a
sentence is illegal.   4488

APPELLATE review of sentencing. La L Rev 33:559-68 (1973).
Current problems of sentence disparity, trial judge
discretion, and excessive sentencing are described;
writer suggests that Louisiana judges promulgate
guidelines for sentencing.   4489

APPELLATE review of sentencing: a new dialogue? U Colo L Rev
45:209-28 (1973).
Note deals with the decision of McGee v U.S., 462
F2d 243 (2d Cir. 1972), involving an appeal from
a motion to reduce sentence, where appellate court
remanded to trial court for a justification of the
sentence. Note examines Supreme Court cases dealing
with sentencing and the McGee opinion to show the
manner in which the opinion departs from precedent.
Author feels that McGee requirement of an explanation
from the sentencing judge is a rational one. Text of
trial court response included.   4490

APPELLATE review of sentencing procedure. Yale L J 74:379-89
(1964).
> To avoid the rule that a federal appellate court
> will not review a criminal sentence, the Court of
> Appeals for the District of Columbia set aside a
> sentence in Leach v U.S., 344 F2d 945 (1964) because
> the trial court refused to refer the prisoner for a
> mental examination as directed. This was an abuse of
> discretion in failing to use resources provided by
> Congress in such cases. This note reviews the
> leading cases refusing review of sentences, referring
> to Judge Frank's opinion in U.S. v Rosenberg 195 F2d
> 583, 604 (2d Cir. 1952). Author also discusses
> cases in which courts review defects in sentencing
> procedure as distinguished from general review
> of the merits of sentence. The note also discusses
> constitutional, statutory, and supervisory bases
> for the power to review sentencing procedure. Favoring
> review of sentences, the writer discusses reasons
> against invalidating each one with persuasive argu-
> ments.   4491

BRANDON, B. In Van Alstyne's wake: North Carolina v Pierce.
U of Pitt L Rev 31:101-17 (1969).
> It is suggested that the Van Alstyne article (item
> 4534) influenced Supreme Court's decision to set
> aside two sentences where a heavier sentence was
> imposed on defendants, attacking their first con-
> victions. Concludes post-conviction relief must not
> result in possibility of harsher sentencing.   4492

BREWSTER, L. Appellate review of sentences. FRD 40:79-88 (1966).
> Federal district court judge demonstrates that review
> of trial judge's sentence is not in the interest of
> accused or society; is not a matter of right but
> ot grace; would not achieve uniformity, or eliminate
> disparity or unjust sentences. In summary, an ap-
> pellate judge could not get a true picture of de-
> fendant by mere reading of record.   4493

BURR, C. B., II. Appellate review as a means of controlling
discretion; a workable alternative? U Pitt L Rev 33:1-27 (1971).
> Inordinate discretionary sentencing power has led
> to gross inequalities. Appellate review provides
> needed control of judicial sentencing. Author offers
> proposed statute to implement appellate review of
> criminal sentences, after describing selected state
> statutes, suggests also review by administrative
> tribunal.   4494

COBURN, D. Disparity in sentences and appellate review of sentencing. Rutgers L Rev 25:207-26 (1971).

Public Defender of New Jersey demonstrates the
fallibility of judicial sentencing; he appraises
appellate review of sentencing under the present system and suggests alternate methods such as the
creation of a Permanent Court of Sentence Appeals
such as first appeared in England in 1907, or the
creation of a Rotating Court of Sentence Appeals which
he describes. He suggests utilization of a system of
judicial sentencing councils and discusses administrative sentencing tribunals. All of these sections
are annotated to reports, cases, and writings. In
discussing proposed reforms, the author speaks to
shorter terms and psychiatric treatment; in the
light of these goals, he submits a proposed statute
(within the present N.J. system) to establish a
separate court of sentencing review.   4495

COUNCIL of State Governments. Review of sentences in criminal
cases. In its Suggested state legislation. 21:61-64 (1962):
repr. 22:176-79 (1963).
Lists and discusses Massachusetts and Connecticut
statutes providing for appellate review; based on
them, suggests state legislation entitled: Act
permitting review of sentencing in criminal cases.
4496

DECORE, J. V. Criminal sentencing: the role of the Canadian
Courts of Appeal and the concept of uniformity. Crim L Q 6:324-80
(1964).
The author examines the right of appeal of criminal
sentences under the federal Criminal Code, which
should be applied uniformly but is not. He deplores
the inconsistent attitudes of the appeal courts
toward sentencing and use of precedent. He discusses the purpose of sentencing and factors considered by the courts of appeal in imposing sentence;
exploring extent and application of the sentence
review powers of the courts, and calling for code
revisions to make these powers clearer.   4497

DECOSTA, F. A., Jr. Disparity and inequality of criminal sentences:
constitutional and legislative approaches to appellate review and
reallocation of the sentencing function. How L J 14:29-59 (1969).
Assistant Attorney General of Maryland reviews
present cases and trends within the judiciary to
create standards of sentencing review that may limit
the exercise of judicial discretion in sentencing. He
seeks to evaluate policy questions that may decide
where the Supreme Court may finally be prepared to
go in this area absent legislative action. In three
parts: 1. Traditional approach to sentencing review.
2. Recent judicial trends toward a more enlightened
approach to sentencing review (disparity, credit,

longer second sentences) 3. Legislative and judicial
trends toward a reallocation of the sentencing
function (appellate review, a single sentencing
judge, expert administrative sentencing board). 4498

DEVINE, M. J.   Solution to an "incredible dilemma": the original
sentence as a ceiling. SD L Rev 13:130-45 (1968).
Author posits that the original sentence should be
the absolute ceiling that appellate court can give in
resentencing defendant. In his due process, equal
protection, and double jeopardy arguments, the
author looks into the reasoning behind the imposition
of more severe sentencing, with disapproval.   4499

DIX, G. E.   Judicial review of sentences: implications for
individual disposition. L & Soc Order 1969:369-418.
Law professor examines thirty years of appellate
review in Arizona and concludes that it has had
little effect on trial court sentencing; gives
arguments for and against judicial review of sentences, then describes review of criminal sentences
by the Arizona Supreme Court. Author discusses wisdom of individual disposition in criminal cases.
There are numerous illustrative charts and statistics.
4500

DUE process and the harsher penalty after appeal: an unwarranted
extension of Pearce. U Richmond L Rev 5:401-409 (1971).
Article examines Wood v Ross, 434 F2d 297 (4th Cir.
1970) in which the court found that due process
prevented the augmenting of punishment on appeal
beyond the original penalty. Author feels that the
court placed improper reliance on N.C. v Pearce,
395 US 711 (1969), and came to an irrational result.
4501

FEDERAL appellate review of sentences. Suffolk U L Rev 1128-36
(1973).
Student note discusses U.S. v McKinney 466 F2d 1403
(6th Cir. 1972) and cites to other cases in point.
Posits that McKinney will be primary authority cited
for existance of power to directly review sentences
on appeal until a uniform rule for the entire
federal judiciary is promulgated.   4502

FEINBERG, W.   Expediting review of felony convictions. ABA J
59:1025-28 (1973).
Chairman of Committee on Criminal Appeals of the
Advisory Council on Justice explains recommendations
of Advisory Council, limited to appeal from felony
convictions after trial. Judge Feinberg enumerates
the recommendations (see item 4475:Advisory Council's
Expediting review of felony convictions) with comment

explaining also that cost of implementing recommendations would not be substantial, and that increased cost should be balanced against expenditures for other comparable criminal justice purposes.   4503

FRANKEL, M. E. Lawlessness in sentencing. U Cin L Rev 41:1-54
(1972). (Marx lectures, 1971)
            (For annotation see item 4361)   4504

FRANKEL, S. The sentencing morass, and a suggestion for reform.
Crim L Bull 3:365-83 (1967).
            Author gives numerous examples of differing sen-
            tences by judges in the same courts in similar cases;
            indicates these differences depend upon the person-
            ality, mood, and circumstances surrounding the
            trial judge; refers to 17 states providing for ap-
            pellate review because of the severity of sentence,
            although within the statutory maxima. He proceeds to
            discuss, with examples and suggestions, how appel-
            late review may be significantly improved.   4505

GEORGE, B. J., Jr. Unsolved problem: comparative sentencing
techniques. ABA J 45:250-54 (1959).
            Professor writes that U.S. is the only country in
            the free world where a single judge may sentence
            without being subject to a review of his sentence.
            He remarks that U.S. sentences are the longest in
            the world and proceeds to show how sentences are
            imposed and reviewed in Italy, Germany, and in
            England. Calls for reform in sentencing, emphasizing
            need to review sentences.   4506

HALL, L. Reduction of criminal sentences on appeal: I and II.
Colum L Rev 37:521-56, 762-82 (1937).
            A classic, often cited, and included because it is
            a basic study embodying the law as to the legal
            bases of the appellate court's power to reduce sen-
            tenced and the theories regarding purposes of crimi-
            nal law prompting appellate courts to exercise the
            power. The professor also enlightens on statewide
            sentencing policies, influence of other agencies on
            the court in sentencing, the correction of pro-
            cedural errors by sentence reduction on appeal, and
            procedural problems in the appellate court.   4507

HALPERIN, D. J. Appellate review of sentence in Illinois: reality
or illusion? Ill B J 55:300-14 (1966).
            The Illinois Code of Criminal Procedure of 1963 con-
            ferred on the appellate courts power to reduce sen-
            tence on appeal. Viewing this power as giving op-
            portunity to achieve improved uniform sentencing
            policies, the author examines, by analysis and dis-

cussing appellate cases dealing with reduction of
sentence, the extent to which this potential has been
realized. He also treats cases where reduction was
refused, examining the reasoning in each case. Encourages Illinois appellate tribunals to exercise
the power, while mentioning the important role of
defense counsel in the sentencing process in making
a complete record for sentencing.   4508

HALPERIN, D. J. Sentence review in Maine: comparison and
comments. Maine L Rev 18:133-54 (1966).
          As of Dec. 1, 1965, Maine has an appellate division
          of the Supreme Judicial Court to review sentences
          to the state prison. Professor describes the Maine
          provisions (similar to Connecticut and Massachusetts)
          discussing eligibility for appeal, time, and mode
          of seeking review, and disposition. He writes on
          alternatives taken by other states, as, for example,
          authorizing sentence modification, then proceeds to
          make predictions and suggestions for the new Maine
          system.   4509

HRUSKA, R. L. Appellate review of sentences. Am Crim L Q
8:10-15 (1969).
          U.S. Senator discusses S.1561, providing for ap-
          pellate review of federal court sentences. Cites
          to ABA Standards on Appellate Review (item 4478)
          approving such review; balances arguments for
          and against, favoring former. Gives history of ap-
          pellate review of sentences and of the act in
          question.   4510

HRUSKA, R. L. A time for humane sentencing. In Symposium: a
new federal criminal code. Trial 9:11-33, 29, 33 (Sep./Oct. 1973).
          Reviews legislative concern for sentence disparities;
          discusses recent initiatives that include his S.716
          to provide for appellate review of sentences in
          criminal cases in U.S. District Courts. Says it
          is identical to S.2228 and S.1501 introduced in
          92d and 91st Congress respectively and to S.1540
          passed unanimously by Senate in 90th Congress.
          Refers to Final Report of the National Commission on
          Reform of Federal Criminal Laws which embraced the
          concept of appellate review of sentences. Sen.
          Hruska quotes the suggested amendment by the Commis-
          sion to 18 U.S.C. 1291 giving appellate courts power
          to review, modify, or set aside a sentence. He then
          suggests certain possible modifications of his bill
          based on extensive hearings of the Subcommittee
          on Criminal Law and Procedures.   4511

IN RE LYNCH and beyond to judicial review of sentences. San
Diego L Rev 10:793-813 (1973).
          Discusses the limited judicial review of sentencing
          in California, against the background of other
          jurisdictions, the role of California's Adult
          Authority, and sentences of unlimited duration. 4512

KARLEN, D. Sentencing (Chap. 9); Appeals and post-conviction
remedies (Chap. 10). In his Anglo-American criminal justice.
N.Y., Oxford, 1967. p. 194-208; 209-28.
          Professor presents a comparative picture of sen-
          tencing in England and the United States; dwelling
          on the distinction in sentencing responsibilities
          he covers sentencing institutes, and pre-sentence
          investigation and reports. Appeals by the prosecution
          and by the defendant receive comment as does the
          difference in treatment of more serious cases in
          the two countries. The author emphasizes the dis-
          tinctions between availability of appeal, con-
          trasting the few English cases reviewed even
          once as compared to the successive stages of appeal
          in the United States. He explains use of collateral
          attack in the U.S., non-existent in England, and
          the differences in the appellate powers and the
          discretion of the respective courts, mentioning
          the English courts' right to review sentences as
          distinguished from the federal practices generally
          not to review sentences.   4513

KUTAK, R. J. and GOTTSCHALK, J. M. In search of a rational sentence: a return to the concept of appellate review. Neb L Rev
53:463-520 (1974).
          Authors explore the historical background, devel-
          opment and future of the doctrine of appellate non-
          review of sentencing: early judicial construction;
          the anomaly between legislative authorization of
          review and the judicially created non-review doc-
          trine; sources for a review doctrine; existing and
          pending statutory exceptions; and arguments for and
          against review. Authors conclude that appellate
          review does exist, but the form it should take must
          still be considered. Postscript deals with recent
          decision Dorszynski v US, 94 S Ct 3042 (1974) in
          which the court served notice that there was not
          authority for the power of appellate review of sen-
          tencing. Authors feel that this will encourage
          congress to pass legislation providing for such
          review. App. proposed statute.   4514

MEADOR, D. J. The review of criminal sentences in England; report. In ABA Advisory Committee on Sentencing and Review.
Standards relating to appellate review of sentences. N.Y., IJA,
1967. (App. C, p. 94-157).

Professor spans the judicial machinery for administering criminal justice commencing with criminal procedures in the trial courts, to sentencing at trial
level. He then covers judicial review of sentencing,
describing specifics from initial procedure to the
bases of the decision and the sentencing policy.
Author elucidates regarding procedures for non-judicial
review of sentences and the royal prerogative of
mercy. Appended, among other items, are English statutes, memorandum on power to increase sentences,
statute prohibiting sentence increase, and bibliography
of predominantly English source material.   4515

MUELLER, G. O. W. Penology on appeal; appellate review of legal
but excessive sentences. Vand L Rev 15:671-97 (1962).
"Mr. Mueller traces the development of the technique
of sentence appeals in relation to the evolution of
penological theory and examines the practices of representative American jurisdictions in this area. In
evaluating the status of the law, the author's reasoned
judgment is that too few appellate courts have the
power to review excessive sentences, and even these
courts do not exercise the power in terms of functional
penology." [editors' intro.] Appended: chart indicating
the availability of this recourse to the appellate
court and the types of dispositions in the fifty states
and the D.C.; state-by-state statutory source report
with selected pertinent cases.   4516

MUELLER, G. O. W. and LE POOLE, F. Appellate review of legal but
excessive sentences; a comparative study. Vand L Rev 21:411-22
(1968).
This article follows up a study made by the authors
as advisors to the Senate Committee on the Judiciary.
Commenting on the lack of criteria for the trial judge
in sentencing and the largely unavailable right of
judicial review of sentences in the United States, the
authors examine the Continental system in which the
criminal codes generally provide guidelines for sentencing, thus enabling sentence review as a matter of
law. Guidelines for sentencing are discussed, and it
is demonstrated that most Continental countries do not
distinguish between appellate review of convictions and
sentences. The conclusion is that specific guidelines
for sentencing are imperatively needed. Norway, Germany,
and France are mentioned. App. B: guidelines for sentencing in Greece, Italy, Poland, USSR, Yugoslavia,
Germany, and Switzerland. App. C: examples of provisions solely stating the various goals of punishment. See also Mueller, G., Penology on appeal.
Vand L Rev 15:671 (1962). (item 4516)   4517

NORRIS, H. Appellate review of sentencing: an argument in its favor
and a proposed Michigan statute. Mich SB J 53:344-50 (1974). __4518__

PLEA for appellate review of sentences. Ohio S L J 32:410-25
(1971).
> The first part of this note reviews disparity in
> sentencing by illustrative cases and statistics;
> student then gives criticisms of appellate review
> based on unworkability, unattainability of goals,
> undesirability of sentence review; discusses
> alternatives to sentence review, followed by sug-
> gested provisions to be included in an appellate re-
> view of sentences statute; one footnote cites to 13
> state statutes. Limitation on the right to review,
> the proper court to review sentences, and the need
> to articulate reasons for sentence are discussed.__4519__

PRESENT limitations on appellate review of sentencing -- McGee v
U.S. (462 F2d 243 (1972)).
> Comment on McGee where the Second Circuit questioned
> the validity of the sentence and remanded with in-
> structions to reduce it or explain why not. The
> district judge did not reduce the sentence, giving
> his reasons why not. The two issues raised by the
> dissent, a)the correctness of the decision and b)
> its practical value to the defendant, are examined.
> Judge Friendly's views (the writer of the opinion)
> are also presented. Leading cases focussing on
> review of sentences are discussed with final ap-
> proval for McGee.   4520

REHBOCK, E. Z. Sentence appeals in perspective: the Alaska way.
Judicature 54:156-61 (1970).
> Pointing out that sentencing disparities existsin
> Alaska as they do elsewhere, the author discusses
> that state's efforts to improve criminal sentencing
> and review, with its new sentence appeal procedure.
> The proceedings of a two day seminar on sentencing
> held in Sitka in Dec. 1968 are noted (item 4477).__4521__

REVIEW of legal but excessive sentences in federal courts. De
Paul L Rev 10:104-16 (1960).
> A footnote lists cases, during past 70 years, where
> each circuit court has held that it is not within its
> power to review sentences within the statutory limits
> prescribed by Congress. Rationale of the doctrine
> disallowing sentence is explained while U.S.C. Sec
> 2106 is cited in opposition; author describes cases
> leading up to U.S. v Wiley, 278 F2d 500 (7th Cir.
> 1960) where, upon a second appeal, the appellate court
> suspended the trial judge's sentence in the exercise of
> its supervisory control over the district court. Ques-
> tion--does this case herald a departure from the 70
> years of stare decisis?   __4522__

SCOPE of appellate review of sentences in capital cases. U Pa L
Rev 108:434-49 (1960).
> This student report on review of sentences in capital
> cases takes up several cases to show variations in
> sentencing, explaining why in some cases sentences
> were remanded, in others not. All the variables con-
> sidered are mentioned.   4523

SEVERITY of sentence as well as sentencing procedure, is subject
to appellate review in the eighth circuit. Drake L Rev 23:191-6
(1973).
> Note analyzes the decision in Wooseley v U.S., 478
> F 2d (8th Cir. 1973), holding that an appellate court
> has the power to review sentence severity where a
> judge has grossly abused his discretion, and the
> present need for the abrogation of the non-review
> doctrine, with the resultant assurance of individual
> sentencing.   4524

SMITH, G. P., II. Title 28, Section 2255 of the United States
Code: motion to vacate, set aside or correct sentence: effective
or ineffective aid to a federal prisoner? Notre Dame Law 40:
171-90 (1964-1965).
> Law professor examines effectiveness of section 2255
> and obstacles that have arisen as a result of poor
> administration; historical background and evolution
> of statute; current procedure and administration; and
> proposed solutions. Author concludes that despite some
> inefficiencies the section is workable and should be
> maintained.   4525

SOBELOFF, S. A recommendation for appellate review of criminal sentences. Brooklyn L Rev 21:2-11 (1954).
> The author reviews the history of appellate review
> of sentences from the earliest Iowa statute in 1860,
> explaining the two approaches adopted by the states.
> He then discusses the English system and previous
> and current activity in Congress. He suggests that
> the courts, by rule, can spell out mechanics of the
> practice. He enumerates and explains reasons favoring
> this type of legislation.   4526

SOBELOFF, S. The sentence of the court - should there be appellate
review? ABA J 41:13-24 (1955).
> Judge is concerned that the sentencing power is
> limited to one man, leaving the convicted defendant
> with little protection. There is strict insistence
> on the rights of accused during trial and opportunity
> for reversal of technical errors of the judge, but
> sentencing by one man may bring overseverity in sen-
> tencing or inadequacy. It should comfort the judge
> to know that "any error he may have committed in this
> most crucial step ... is subject to correction on
> appeal." Included, albeit spoken in 1955, because of
> its impact.   4527

SYMPOSIUM: Appellate review of sentences, at the Judicial Conference of the United States Court of Appeals for the Second Circuit,
Sept. 24, 1962, Manchester, Vermont. FRD 32:249-321 (1963).
     Contents: Remarks by Kaufman, I. R.; Sobeloff, S. E.,
     Walsh, L. E.; Wechsler, H.; Broderick, V. L.--Hyde,
     G. M., Canadian law on appellate review of sentences--
     Celler, E., Checks and balances on sentencing dis-
     cretion--Bennett, J. V., Letter.   4528

SYMPOSIUM: Modern trends in sentencing. ABA Section of Criminal
Law, Proceedings 1962:45-81.
     Moderator: B. White; speakers: G. H. Boldt, J. S.
     Palmore, H. E. Parker, G. C. Doub, R. L. Hruska.
     After an exchange of ideas regarding necessary changes
     in bases of sentencing, the Hruska bill S.2873 is
     explained by Mr. Doub. Discussion ensues with a
     question and answer period regarding appellate review
     of sentences. At pp. 76-81 appears an article by
     Senator Hruska on his bill that gives reasoning and
     authority in its favor.   4529

THOMAS, D. A. Appellate review of sentences and the development
of sentencing policy: the English experience. Ala L Rev 20:193-
226 (1968).
     Visiting English professor argues in favor of the
     English system of appellate review of sentences that
     has led to the development of a coherent body of
     sentencing principles significantly influencing
     sentencing at trial level. The English system is des-
     cribed; the procedures and areas of judicial policy
     making, as well as the bases of the sentencing poli-
     cies, are fully laid out and specific offenses are
     used to demonstrate; author proceeds to give argu-
     ments favoring appellate review of sentences with
     illustrative English cases and writings; concludes
     appellate court can develop a meaningful case law
     of sentencing, provided it discards normal approach
     of "seeking only errors and abuses." English prac-
     tices prove that, if properly administered, it can
     be effective, and arguments against appellate review
     fail.   4530

TYDINGS, J. D. Ensuing rational sentences; the case for appellate
review. Judicature 53:68-73 (1969).
     Commenting on the shocking disparity in some senten-
     ces, Senator cites examples given by Judge Sobeloff
     in his testimony before the Senate Subcommittee on
     Improvements in Judicial Machinery during the 89th
     Congress. He also points to the Federal Bureau of
     Prisons Statistical Report for 1967 and 1968, inci-
     cating continuing patterns of wide disparity in
     sentencing among the federal district courts, quot-
     ing specific fugures. He then explains S.B. 1520
     (Hruska), giving arguments to support it, and dis-
     cusses sentencing by council.   4531

U. S. CONGRESS Senate Committee on the judiciary. Appellate review
of sentences; hearings before the Subcommittee on Improvements in
Judicial Machinery ... Mar. 1-2, 1966. Washington, USGPO, 1966.
196 p. (89th Cong.; 1st sess.)
>Statements by law professors, judges; report excerpts;
>symposia, references to foreign writings, biblio-
>graphy (p. 146-49).   4532

U. S. v ROSENBERG, 195 F2d 583 (2d Cir. 1952).
>Departing from a rule not to include cases, per se,
>attention is called to pp. 604-609 of this opinion
>of Judge J. Frank because it presents a full review
>of statutes, literature, and cases supporting federal
>criminal practice denying control of the appellate
>court over the sentence of the trial court.   4533

VAN ALSTYNE, W. W. In Gideon's wake: harsher penalties and the
"successful" criminal appellant. Yale L J 74:606-39 (1965).
>The article contends that harsher sentences imposed
>on retrial are unconstitutional whether imposed by
>federal or state courts, showing that the risk of
>a harsher sentence renders worthless defendants'
>right to a second, constitutionally fair trial. Also
>argues that states should protect defendants on
>retrial for nonconstitutional error. After dis-
>cussing Green v U.S. 355 US 184 (1957) and People v
>Henderson 386 P 2d 677 (1963), the author con-
>cludes that the imposition of a harsher sentence
>on retrial is arguably prohibited by the double
>jeopardy clause. Finally, applying an equal protec-
>tion argument, suggests that imposing the risk only
>on those who appeal a conviction constitutes an ar-
>bitrary discrimination. (See also item 4492)   4534

WEIGEL, S. A. Appellate revision of sentencing: to make the
punishment fit the crime. Stan L Rev 20:405-22 (1968).
>Federal district court judge gives brief summary
>of sentence choices available to federal judges;
>he then discusses present means available for cor-
>recting sentencing errors in the federal system
>including appellate and non-appellate remedies which
>include indeterminate sentencing; appellate review
>procedures recommended are examined with some ap-
>proval.   4535

WHAT is the proper scope of appellate review of sentencing. Harv
L Rev 75:416-18 (1961).
>Note involves U.S. v Wiley, 278 F 2d 500 (7th Circ.
>1960) where defendant Wiley was convicted and sen-
>tenced to three years while co-defendants with prior
>felony convictions, upon pleading guilty, received
>only one or two years. Relying on its "supervisory"
>power the court of appeals finally suspended the

sentence. Other pertinent cases are discusses, See
another student note about this case entitled Federal
court of appeals vacates sentence on grounds
severity and remands for sentencing. U Pa L Rev
109:422-28 (1-61).   4536

IX. CRIMINAL APPEALS

> Items dealing with frivolous criminal appeals,
> prosecutor's right to appeal, limitation on
> number of criminal appeals, appeals in forma
> pauperis, right to counsel; federal review
> of state convictions. See also Section V,
> The Appellate Process and Section X, Post
> Conviction Remedies.

AMERICAN Bar Association Advisory Committee on Sentencing and
Review. Standards relating to criminal appeals, recommended by
the Advisory Committee on Sentencing and Review. S. E. Soboloff,
chair.; C. R. Reitz, reptr. Tent draft, Mar. 1969. New York,
IJA, 1969. 109 p. Amendments, supp. Oct. 1970. 7 p. Approved
Aug. 1970.

> Standards concerning structure of and access to ap-
> pellate system and its internal operation include:
> possibility of appeal should exist in but not be
> necessary part of every criminal conviction (i.e.,
> defendant must initiate appeal); prosecution has right
> to appeal if certain issues (such as double jeopardy,
> speedy trial) terminate case; other standards deal
> with time limits, duties of counsel, inducements
> and deterrents, frivolous appeals, transcripts for
> indigent defendants. 9-p. bibliography. Supplement
> covers prosecution appeals, release pending appeal,
> bail pending appeal, processing appeal and record
> on appeal; numerous comparisons with system of
> criminal appeal in England. App A: A second circuit
> rule on trial counsel's duty with regard to appeal.
> App B: D.C. Circuit form for appointed counsel.
> App C: D.C. Circuit form for indigent appellant. 4537

BELL, G. B. Appellate court opinions and the remand process. Ga
L Rev 2:526-37 (1968).

> Judge examines selected federal cases to demonstrate
> methods used by the courts in the exercise of the
> remand power, methods which are both settled or new,
> workable or unworkable.   4538

BLACKMUN, H. A. Allowance of in forma pauperis appeals in Sec.
2255 and habeas corpus cases. FRD 43:343-61 (1968).

> Author, then Eighth Circuit Judge, examines four
> statutes relating to proceedings and appeals in
> forma pauperis and cost-free transcripts. He dis-

cusses the standards required under sections 1915,
2253 and 2255 to grant such appeals. The United
States Supreme Court holding in Nowakowski v Maroney,
that once a district judge issues a certificate of
probable cause in a state prisoner's federal
habeas case, he binds his appellate court to accept
the appeal, whether paid or in forma pauperis, is
discussed; the author cautions that the certificate
should not be issued routinely.   4539

BRYAN, A. V. For a swifter criminal appeal: to protect the
public as well as the accused. Wash & Lee L Rev 25:175-86 (1968).
Judge submits proposal to limit readying of a federal criminal appeal to 25 days in the interests of
the accused as well as the public. He offers suggestions to cure the paramount delays in preparing
the transcript and brief.   4540

CALIFORNIA Judicial Council. Proposed system for limiting un-
meritorious criminal appeals. July 1, 1968, rev. San Francisco,
1968. 22 p.
Study points to increasing number of appeals in
California and notes limitations on bringing them
used by other states. Essentially the proposed system would eliminate the right to appeal and substitute a petition for leave to appeal. Appendices:
the recommended bill and proposed amendments to
Court Rules, to implement the bill.   4541

COOPER, A. M. Procedure on appeals by stated case. Crim L Q
7:155-69 (1964).
Author discusses the Canadian procedure governing
appeals by stated case in summary conviction proceedings. He enumerates the necessary steps to
arrive at an order of the superior court. Appendix
includes examples of forms used in these proceedings.
                                                   4542

DOWLING, D. C. Extending the state's right to appeal criminal
cases in Illinois. Chi B Rec 42:361-67 (1961).
Author discusses generally the People's right to
appeal, then speaks specifically of a proposed
Illinois Criminal Code section that would extend
the right to appeal in matters preliminary to the
trial, including appeal from holdings in various
motions.   4543

FRIVILOUS appeals and the minimum standards project; solution or
surrender. U Miami L Rev 24:95-111 (1969).
Critical examination of the proposed ABA Standards
for the Administration of Criminal Justice. Discussed
are: the scope and functioning of the appellate pro-

cess; pre-appeal notice, counsel, and screening;
and supervision and procedures of appeal. Author
feels the fundamental idea of the Standards as
regards defendants' right to appeal are sound, but
that endorsement of change in the implementation of
these ideas is a necessary part of the new Standards.
Some innovative alternatives presented.   4544

GERARD, J. B.   Right to counsel on appeal in Missouri: a limited
inquiry into the factual and theoretical underpinnings of Douglas
v California.   Wash U L Q 1965:463-85.
Law professor gives the results of a study of the
three types of criminal appeals used in Missouri
before a state rule change occasioned by Douglas v
California, 372 US 353 (1963). Concludes that the
motion for a new trial appeal, even when filed by
an attorney, does not satisfy the Douglas requirements, and that the percentages of affirmances of
various types of appeals show that there is a possibility that full argument by an attorney made
a difference in the result. Concludes that Douglas
may require the state to compensate lawyers for indigents or to create a public defender to handle
appeals.   4545

HERMANN, R.   Frivolous criminal appeals.   NYU L Rev 47:701-21 (1972).
Committee chairman of New York Legal Aid Society
discusses the problem posed by frivolous appeals.
Includes a consideration of the dilemma they create
for assigned counsel, of the method of handling a
frivolous appeal, and of the problem created by
unqualified or otherwise inadequate counsel. Points
out the need for judicial clarification of the dis-
tinction between frivolous and meritless appeals
and for specification of proper court procedures.
Suggests that routine review of sentences would obviate
some problems caused by frivolous appeals.   4546

HOPKINS, J. D.   Small sparks from a low fire: some reflections on
appellate process.   Brooklyn L Rev 38:551-69 (1972).
(For annotation see item 3157)   4547

INDIGENT defendant's rights on appeal in New York.   Brooklyn L Rev
29:261-85 (April 1963).
Examines how the New York courts have interpreted
and extended Griffin v Illinois in which the Supreme
Court held that defendants may not be denied appellate review solely because they are indigent. Whether
the courts may inquire into the merits of the claim
before the indigent is granted the right to appeal
is considered.   4548

INDIGENT'S right to a transcript of record. Kan L Rev 20:745-67
(1972).
> "Paupers need not be afforded the same review offered
> to affluent defendants; it is only necessary that
> they be given equivalent and fundamentally fair
> treatment." Latest U. S. Supreme Court cases are
> offered in support; student reviews direct appeals
> in state cases, state collateral proceedings, federal
> habeas corpus for state prisoners and original
> federal proceedings. Appellants who cannot afford
> transcripts of trial must be given free records of
> sufficient completeness to permit adequate review.
> This is applicable to both state and federal pro-
> ceedings.   4549

JUSTICE (British Section of the International Commission of Jurists).
Criminal appeals. London, Stevens, 1964. 92 p.
> Report traces the history of the English criminal
> appeal system and examines the statutory provisions
> which govern it as well as the powers of the Court
> of Criminal Appeal, legal aid in connection with crim-
> inal appeals, and procedure of the court; makes
> recommendations.   4550

KARLEN, D. Frivolous appeals. Legal Aid Brief Case 22:205-08
(Apr. 1965).
> Director of Institute of Judicial Administration dis-
> cusses two ways to deal with frivolous criminal ap-
> peals: by limiting the right to appeal and by summary
> disposition of such appeals.   4551

KIMBALL, E. L. Criminal cases in a state appellate court; Wisconsin
1839-1959. Am J Lég Hist 9:95-117. (1965).
> Analyzes docket to indicate the relative place of
> criminal matters in the courts' work, the state's
> and individuals' interests involved and changes
> in criminal justice administration. Finds little
> direct reflection of social and economic changes in
> the appellate court docket.   4552

KIRSHEN, A. H. Appellate court implementation of the standards
for the administration of criminal justice. Am Crim L Q 8:105-17
(1970).
> Author presents results of study of appellate court
> response to ABA's Standards of Criminal Justice,
> based on citation to standards in cases and use by
> legislative and administrative bodies. Data pre-
> sented classified by title of Standards. In two
> years, almost 100 cases have cited the Standards,
> and they are being used as guidelines by groups
> dealing with similar problems.   4553

LEVY, H. M. Justice - after trial. N.Y.L.F. 11:240-313,
369-457 (1965).
>The conditions necessary for the granting of new
>trials on the basis of newly discovered evidence
>and how five test judicial systems - the federal
>courts, New York, California, Illinois and Louisiana -
>apply them are examined. The author recounts the
>various proceedings of a Utah case in which a seem-
>ingly innocent man was convicted and denied a new
>trial despite new evidence, and suggests how
>other jurisdictions might have acted. The granting
>of executive clemency when judicial relief is denied
>is considered and responses to the author's ques-
>tionnaire (Appendix B) sent to all state governors
>are discussed. Remedies to insure judicial and
>executive relief to the innocent are recommended.
>Appendix A is a chart of a state-by-state statutory
>survey of the main factors in granting or denying
>a new trial.   4554

MARGOLIS, E. Criminal appeals in motion. Conn B J 45:114-45
(1971).
>Pointing out that a successful criminal appeal begins
>the day the accused enters his attorney's office,
>the author discusses important pre-plea and pre-
>trial motions which can preserve the record on
>appeal.   4555

MAYERS, L. Federal review of state convictions: the need for
procedural reappraisal. Geo Wash L Rev 34:615-65 (1966).
>The author discusses the following proposals to
>improve the federal review of state convictions: (1)
>the enactment by Congress of uniform procedural rules
>for the assertion and determination of federal
>rights in state criminal proceedings; (2) provision
>for a federal post-conviction proceeding, to be
>instituted and determined in the state court, based
>on claimed denial of federal right not reflected in
>the record of the proceedings leading to conviction;
>(3) provision for proper presentation of claims of
>federal right for federal review; and (4) final
>review of state court records by a single nation-
>wide federal tribunal.   4556

MEADOR, D. J. Criminal appeals; English practice and American
reform. Charlottesville, Univ. press of Virginia, 1973. 305 p.
>Law professor's overview of English criminal appel-
>late courts describes practice and procedures,
>administrative staff, screening to "deterrence" of
>appeals. He comments on judicial attitudes and
>decisional flexibility, discusses time lapses in
>each successive stage, and refers to the English
>court's annual productivity, giving comparative

statistics for the U. S. Court of Appeals. He describes a unique experiment where three American
judges were asked to write separate opinions in
the same case on the same papers presented to the
appellate court; their approaches, different from
each other and from the English courts, are reported.
The major recommendation is innovation; the last
chapter is devoted to innovation in the U.S. The
ideas on unified review in Chap. 10 are similar
to those in Standard 6 of the U. S. National Advisory Cmssn on Criminal Justice Standards and
Goals, Courts. (Wash., USGPO, 1973.) p. 116-55
(see item 3378); report authored by Prof. Meador.<u>4557</u>

NATIONAL Conference on Appellate Justice, 1975. Appellate justice,
1975: materials for a national conference, San Diego, Jan. 23-25.
Denver, National Center for State Courts, 1974. 4 v.
(For annotation see item 3088) <u>4558</u>

NOKES, G. D. Fresh evidence in criminal appeals. Crim L Rev
1963:669-78.
Law professor discusses introduction of new evidence
on the hearing of an appeal. The appropriate English
statute is included and its ambiguity is noted. In
contested cases the conditions recognized to admit
new evidence include unavailability at trial,
relevance to an issue, credibility, and such material
as might have caused doubt in the minds of the jury.
<u>4559</u>

ROBINSON, P. H. Proposal and analysis of a unitary system for
review of criminal judgments. BU L Rev 54:485-514 (1974); Denver, Nat
Center for State Courts, 1974. 30 p.
"By providing each defendant with an evidentiary
hearing immediately subsequent to trial, the proposed system offers a means of integrating direct
and collateral claims into a single 'unitary' review
procedure." After commenting on the repetitiveness
and disarray of the criminal judgment review system,
the author submits his design, with diagrams, of the
current avenues open for repeated appeals. He
compares this to his proposed system for unitary review which substantially reduces the likelihood that
the federal courts will continue to entertain so
freely claims for appeal. He evaluates both existing
and proposed systems. <u>4560</u>

SOKOL, R. P. In forma pauperis appeals: the University of Virginia experiment with a neglected asset. J Legal Ed 18:96-100
(1965).
Author, director of the Appellate Legal Aid project,
describes the involvement of students and faculty
members in handling in forma pauperis litigation as
part of a two-credit Appellate Litigation seminar
offered at the Law School. A table of cases handled
by the project is included. <u>4561</u>

STRAZZELLA, J. Review of criminal convictions: Michigan and
the ABA Standards relating to criminal appeals and post-conviction
remedies. Mich S B J 50:748-60 (1971).
> Law professor discusses the ABA Standards for
> Criminal Justice and their possible use in Michigan.
> Examined are the positive aspects of allowing appeal
> for every criminal conviction, including those
> based on pleas of guilty; and post conviction reme-
> dies, including habeas corpus proceedings and waiver
> or forfeiture of rights and remedies. Author believes
> the Standards offer a viable context with which
> Michigan courts can devise a more efficient criminal
> justice system.   4562

TIMELY Appeals and federal criminal procedure. Va L Rev 49:971-95
(1963).
> The application of Rule 37(a)(2), Crim Proc, which
> provides that notice of appeal must be filed within
> a prescribed period, is reviewed to determine what
> direct or collateral relief is available from an
> untimely filing. The factors which support or
> oppose a change in the rule to permit discretionary
> extension of the period are examined.   4563

X. Post Conviction Remedies

Items concerning principles of post-
conviction remedies and scope of remedy;
finality of judgment; right to counsel
right to bail; stay of execution; federal
and state habeas corpus.

AMERICAN Bar Association Advisory Committee on Sentencing and Review.
Standards relating to post-conviction remedies, recommended by
the Advisory Committee on Sentencing and Review. S. E. Sobeloff,
chair; C. R. Reitz, reporter. Tent draft, Jan. 1967. N.Y., IJA, 1967.
123 p. approved, Feb. 1968.
Standards with commentary covering general principles
of post-conviction remedies, scope of remedy, the application, processing applications, appellate review
and finality of judgments; appendices are model form
of application, Second Revised Uniform Post-conviction
Procedure Act with comparison to Standards, table of
post-conviction acts, and a selected 12-p. bibliography of articles, notes, ALR and ALR 2d annotations.
4564

ANDERSON, G. L. Post-conviction relief in Missouri; five years
under amended rule 27.26. Mo L Rev 38:1-46 (1973).
Law professor discusses 1967 post-conviction rule,
designed to adjudicate all claims for refief in one
application: nature and grounds of appeal; the limited
relief that has been granted by the courts despite
full consideration of federal constitutional questions
on their merits; and the increase in post-conviction
caseload.
4565

APPLICATIONS for writs of habeas corpus and post conviction review
of sentences in the United States courts. FRD 33:363-505 (1964).
Contents: Phillips, O. L. Letter--Report of the Judicial Conference Committee on Habeas Corpus--Pope,
W. L. Suggestions for lessening the burden of frivolous
applications.--Pope, W. L. Further developments in the
field of frivolous applications; is proliferation
possible--Breitenstein, J. S. Remarks on recent post-
conviction decisions--Caffrey, A. A. The impact of
the Townsend and Noia cases on federal district
judges--Becker, W. H. Text of speech ... analyzing
recent Supreme Court opinions--O'Sullivan, C. Remarks on post-conviction remedies.
4566

BADGER, R. K. A judicial cul-de-sac: federal habeas corpus for
state prisoners. ABA J 50:629-34 (1964).
Winning constitutional law essay traces federal habeas
corpus since Act of Feb. 5, 1967, giving federal
courts habeas corpus jurisdiction over state prisoners; argues that Fay v Noia may mean nullification

of all state criminal judgments; suggests return of
concept of the remedy as a collateral remedy, lying
only to test jurisdiction of the state.   4567

BAILEY, F. L. Federal habeas corpus--old writ, new role: an
overhaul for state criminal justice. BU L Rev 45:161-215 (1965).
Author focuses on federal habeas corpus used to correct state convictions: brief history of the writ of
habeas corpus; analysis of Fay v Noia, 372 US 391
(1963), and Townsend v Sain, 372 US 293 (1963), and
their impact on habeas corpus; doctrine of exhaustion
of state remedies; mechanics and procedures of a
suit in habeas corpus; elements of "federal constitutional violations"; and the future of habeas
corpus.   4568

BATOR, P. M. Finality in criminal law and federal habeas corpus
for state prisoners. Harv L Rev 76:441-528 (1963).
The circumstances under which the habeas corpus
jurisdiction of the federal courts should be used
to redetermine the merits of federal questions in
state criminal proceedings are examined. The author
also analyzes the development of the habeas corpus
jurisdiction from 1789-1952 and the doctrine of
Brown v Allen, that all federal constitutional questions decided in state criminal cases may be deter-
mined on the merits of federal habeas corpus.   4569

BAUDE, P. L. Grounds for relief under 28 USC 2255: a suggested
standard. Am Crim L Q 5:112-24 (1967).
Author dissects sec. 2255, showing how each provision
permitting trial court to vacate, set aside, or
correct the sentence is subject to several interpretations making it difficult for the trial court
to act. Thus the writ of habeas corpus is overemployed;
he demonstrates by cases how the U. S. Supreme Court
has contributed to this problem. He suggests that
sec. 2255 be distinguished from habeas corpus and that
the procedures for post-conviction remedies be improved.   4570

BEYOND the ken of the courts: a critique of judicial refusal to
review the complaints of convicts. Yale L J 72:506-58 (1963).
The note examines: traditional "hands-off" doctrine
of courts and its effect on legal remedies of prisoners, the rationales advanced to support it, and
possible implications of abandoning it. Among the
available remedies discussed is the writ of habeas
corpus. Guidelines are given for judicial review of
the prison system naming specific causes for complaint.   4571

BRENNAN, W. J., Jr. Federal habeas corpus and state prisoners, an
exercise in federalism. Utah L Rev 7:423-42 (1961).
> Associate Justice, U.S. Supreme Court, explaining
> and justifying extension of remedies to state
> prisoners, explains how state laws have it within
> their power to substantially reduce the occasion
> for resort by state prisoners to federal habeas
> corpus by permitting certain claims to be raised
> in state on direct appeal from conviction.   4572

BURGER, W. E. State criminal cases in federal courts; some proposals for self-help and mutual aid; remarks to National Association
of Attorneys General, Washington, D.C., Friday, February 6, 1970.
Washington, 1970. 13 p.
> The Chief Justice is concerned with deluge in federal
> courts of habeas corpus cases from state prisoners.
> He discusses ABA standards to provide trained coun-
> seling to prisoners to assist in the preparation
> of habeas corpus applications and European alter-
> natives to habeas corpus; he suggests prison reform
> and alternatives to habeas for prison grievances.4573

CARTER, J. D. The Use of federal habeas corpus by state prisoners,
Am Crim L Q 4:20-35 (1965).
> Judge examines delay caused by the use of habeas
> corpus by prisoners, respective jurisdiction of
> state and federal courts in respect to rights arising
> under the constitution, historical development of
> the writ, and recent bills introduced in Congress
> to remedy delay problems. Author concludes that the
> present procedure is unnecessary to protect the
> rights of the accused and causes substantial impair-
> ment to prompt and effective administration of
> justice.   4574

CARTER, J. M. Pre-trial suggestions for sec. 2255 cases under
Title 28 USC. FRD 32:393-408 (1963).
> Author says that sec. 2255 has destroyed the finality
> of a criminal judgment citing as the usual grounds
> for invoking it alleged incompetence or insanity
> of the defendant, lack of effective counsel, use of
> perjured testimony or suppression of exculpatory
> evidence, or an involuntary guilty plea. Suggests
> a full pretrial hearing in order to lessen the prob-
> ability of another petition from the same prisoner.
> Appends a pretrial order, findings of fact, con-
> clusions of law, and judgment from a sample case.4575

CIVIL discovery in habeas corpus. Colum L Rev 67:1296-1312 (1967).
> Note considers whether pre-trial discovery contem-
> plated by the Federal Rules of Civil Procedure should
> be made available in habeas. Examined are: civil rules

in habeas corpus, cases allowing civil discovery,
pre-Rule procedure and its effect, potential uses of
civil discovery in habeas, and objections to the
use of civil discovery in habeas.   <u>4576</u>

COFER, J. D. Observations on habeas corpus and post-conviction
relief in state and federal courts. Tex B J 28:947-48, 996-999
(1965).

> Author examines various court's jurisdiction to
> issue writs of habeas corpus in Texas, including
> statutory and constitutional authority and relevant
> decisions and concludes that the Legislature has no
> power to limit these habeas corpus powers provided
> for in the Constitution either substantively or
> procedurally. After discussing complex post convic-
> tion procedures in Texas, author suggests that motion
> for new trial based on new evidence be allowable;
> that the trial court retain jurisdiction to grant
> probation upon application after conviction; and
> that an adequate statute restoring remedy in the
> nature of the writ of error coram nobis be passed.
> <u>4577</u>

CONFERENCE of Chief Justices. Report of Committee on post-conviction remedies. Chicago, 1966. 6 p.

> Committee disapproves of habeas corpus legislation
> recommended by United States Judicial Conference as
> being too diluted, encourages the Conference to
> recommend to the states the development of sound
> post-conviction proceedings to the end that all
> federal constitutional issues shall be fully heard
> and determined within the state courts, and recommends
> approval of the revised Uniform Post-Conviction Act,
> with several reservations.   <u>4578</u>

DESMOND, C. Federal and state habeas corpus: how to make two
parallel judicial lines meet. ABA J 49:1166-68 (1968).

> Chief judge, N. Y. Court of Appeals, suggests prac-
> tical approach to avoid two full-fledged reviews
> for state prisoners. He restates L. Mayer's sug-
> gestions for the enactment of federal legislation
> imposing on states precise requirements as to
> procedure and post-conviction remedies. [See item
> 4604].   <u>4579</u>

DOUB, G. C. The case against modern federal habeas corpus. ABA J
59:323-28 (1971).

> Former U.S. Attorney traces history of expansion
> of federal habeas corpus litigation and finds it
> an unjustified burden on the courts. He recommends
> statutory modifications to require defendants to
> raise federal claims in earlier state proceedings
> and to apply a stronger standard of res judicata
> to state criminal judgments.   <u>4580</u>

EISENBERG, H. B. Post-conviction remedies in the 1970's.
Marq L Rev 56:69-86 (1973).
Author examines 1969 revision of Wisconsin Criminal
Procedures Code establishing a post-conviction
motion and virtually abolishing habeas corpus proceedings; discusses various remedies available to
defendant after conviction, including extraordinary
remedies, and recent case law in this area. Author
concludes that counsel should be aware of all remedies and choose the remedy that best fits the
crime.   4581

FAIRCHILD, T. E. Post conviction rights and remedies in Wisconsin.
Wis L Rev 1965:52-7.
Wisconsin Supreme Court justice presents some of
the important problems faced by an appellate court
in dealing with post-conviction rights: challenges
to conviction and sentence by appeal and by habeas
corpus; procedures for handling habeas corpus;
right to counsel on appeal; possibility of post-
conviction remedy by trial court; and challenges to
valid sentence for denial of parole or conditional
release with respect to treatment received in prison.
4582

FEDERAL habeas corpus. Harv L R 83:1038-1280 (1970).
Habeas corpus is reviewed historically and at present,
exploring relevance of alternate proceedings of exhaustion and waiver; the scope of the factual inquiry,
including whether to hold a federal evidentiary
hearing and burden and standard of proof; the
habeas corpus procedure; extra-judicial detentions,
i.e. review of courts-martial and review of administrative restraints in military administrative
decisions, conscription and deportation and exclusion
of aliens; and the suspension clause.   4583

FEDERAL habeas corpus for state prisoners: the isolation principle.
NYU L Rev 39:78-135 (1964).
Note examines the current scope of habeas review
in light of recent Supreme Court decisions and the
development of the concept of the "isolation principle" permitting constitutional claims to be
considered free from the effect of prejudicial state
procedural rules. Discusses devices in the abortive
state procedure (waiver, independent state grounds);
granting a hearing; and criticism of the widespread growth of habeas corpus cases.   4584

FEDERAL habeas corpus treatment of state fact-finding: a suggested approach. Harv L Rev 76:1254-72 (1963).

Note discusses proper treatment of problems of
state findings of fact that have caused wide controversy. Reviews Brown v Allen, 344 US 443 (1953)
and other cases involving a record with full hearing
and where this does not exist. The note suggests
standards to channel the discretion of the district
judge so that cases may be uniformly and fairly
decided yet perform the functions established for
it by the Supreme Court in Brown v Allen.   4585

FEDERAL jurisdiction: habeas corpus; a state prisoner may petition
for a writ of habeas corpus in the federal district court within
the state, issuing a detainer warrant against him based on his
claim that he is being denied his constitutional right to a
speedy trial. Brooklyn L Rev 40:475-89 (1973).
          Note examines recent decision explained in title of
          Braden v Thirtieth Judicial Circuit Court of Ky.
          Prior relevant cases are discussed. This case
          broadened the Court's interpretation of the right
          to speedy trial and resolved the habeas corpus
          jurisdictional issue by holding that federal courts
          may step in to protect constitutional rights being
          flagrantly violated.   4586

FINAN, T. B. The Uniform post-conviction procedure act: one
state's experience. Harv J Legis 2:185-188; 189-211 (1965).
          Maryland Attorney General discusses the inadequacies
          of the Uniform Post-Conviction Act as applied by the
          courts of that state and suggests new legislation
          as the only appropriate remedy. Appended proposed
          legislation with comment as drafted by the Harvard
          Student Legislative Research Bureau.   4587

FLANNERY, J. Habeas corpus bores a hole in prisoners' civil rights
actions - an analysis of Preiser v Rodriguez. St John's L Rev
48:104-24 (1973).
          The issue is appropriateness of use of the writ to
          scrutinize conditions of confinement or whether the
          Civil Rights Act of 1871 is preferable. The con-
          fusion results from the overlap of the two remedies.
          In the writ, exhaustion of state remedies is required.
          Author reviews the nature of both remedies; leading
          case Preiser, 411 US 475 (1973), is then analyzed
          as to issue and holdings. The dissension among the
          Supreme Court justices has further confused the
          issues, says the author.   4588

FOTH, J. R. and PALMER, A. E. Post conviction motions under the
Kansas Revised Code of Civil Procedure. Kan L Rev 12:493-505
(1964).
          Authors examine 60-1507 of Kansas Code of Civil Pro-
          dedure, providing in substance that a prisoner
          in custody under sentence must attack his conviction

or sentence by motion to vacate, set aside, or correct the sentence rather than resorting to habeas
corpus. Nature of the remedies, procedures, and
justifiable issues discussed. Authors conclude
that the remedy provided can be efficacious and
will permit the state to remedy its own errors if
construed as broadly as federal courts have construed similar statutes. Text of sec. 60-1507 given.
                                                    4589

FRIEDLAND, M. L. New trial after an appeal from conviction. L Q
Rev 84:48-63, 185-223 (1968).
          This two-part article deals with the power, or lack
          of power, of the British Court of Criminal Appeal
          to order a retrial; the possibility of retrial
          before the Court which was established in 1907; and
          other cases in which a form of rehearing occurs fol-
          lowing conviction.   4590

FRIENDLY, H. J. Is innocence irrelevant? Collateral attack on
criminal judgments. U of Chi L Rev 38:142-72 (1970).
          Federal appellate judge argues that as appeal gives
          convicted criminals one chance to litigate constitu-
          tional questions, without regard to innocence, col-
          lateral attack should be restricted to cases where
          there is a colorable claim of innocence.   4591

GALLIPOLI, M. Federal habeas corpus; the threat and the challenge.
Amer Crim L Q 4:211-29 (1966).
          Author discusses erosion of state power over criminal
          justice as a result of lack of final judgments. He
          analyzes the decisions in Fay v Noie and Townsend
          v Sain as the bases of his recommendations for re-
          turning control of the criminal system to the
          states.   4592

GOLD, G. and EMERLING, C. G. Federal habeas corpus for the state
prisoner: a new look. Ohio S L J 25:60-70 (1964).
          Lawyers briefly give history of the writ, then discuss
          the issues involved, referring to Reitz Study
          (Federal habeas corpus: post-conviction remedies for
          state prisoners, U Pa L Rev 108:461-532 (1960)) of
          thirty-five successful habeas corpus cases 1950-
          1960, where most successful claims were based on
          right to counsel. They explain federal requirements
          for use of the writ, with case examples, and the
          effects of certain district court decisions; authors
          predict dismal outlook for applicants for writ. 4593

HOLBROOK, J. R. Utah state prisoners and federal habeas corpus.
Utah B J 2:17-30 (Spring, 1974).

914   ADMINISTRATION OF CRIMINAL JUSTICE

How state prisoner allegations become federal habeas
corpus actions; the federal habeas corpus petition and
nature and scope of federal habeas corpus relief;
cases and statutes are examined. The article is ad-
dressed primarily to appointed attorneys; a checklist of frequent deficiencies in petitions for habeas
corpus is offered with reading and research suggestions.   4594

HOLMAN, R. M. Multiple post-trial litigation in criminal cases.
De Paul L Rev 19:490-5 (1970).
Present criminal post-trial litigation is repetitious
and wasteful, says Oregon supreme court justice, proposing that appeal and other post-trial litigation
go directly to federal court.   4595

HOPKINS, J. D. Federal habeas corpus: easing the tension between
state and federal courts. St John's L Rev 44:660-75 (1970).
New York intermediate appellate judge suggests procedural reforms by cooperation between federal and
state courts in habeas corpus cases, including:
state courts should give grounds for denial of relief, common data bank should be maintained, federal
courts should recognize the primary position of state
courts as finders of fact, and the retroactive
effect of new federal decisions should be limited.
                                                          4596

HUNTER, E. B. Post-conviction remedies. FRD 50:153-78 (1970).
Federal judge outlines federal statute and case law
requirements for post conviction review and the
attendant procedure in federal and state courts.
Provides a suggested program for federal state
courts to provide just and efficient remedies.   4597

KOPLOVITZ, J. N. An ABC of Federal Habeas Corpus. Crim L Bull
2:15-20 (1966).
Editor presents procedure for using federal habeas
corpus; explains need for federal constitutional
claim, exhaustion of state remedies, and petitioner
to be in custody; petition and memorandum of law at
the proceeding; and appeal of denial of petition.4598

LAY, D. P. Post-conviction remedies and the overburdened judiciary: solution ahead. Creighton L Rev 3:5-35 (1969).
U. S. Circuit Judge reviews history of habeas corpus
and various reforms attempting to alleviate the
confrontation between state and federal interests.
Discusses Brown v Allen, 344 US 443 (1953) which
held the state remedies were exhausted after the
constitutional issue had been presented to the state
court. Author discusses later developments and increasing number of habeas corpus petitions from

state prisoners, to provide an early adjudicated
record. The judge discusses: A. The Omnibus pretrial hearing; B. Post trial motions; C. Appellate
remand; D. State reform; and E. More imaginative
judges. App. A.: Order providing for omnibus hearing
(N. D. Mo). App. B: Missouri Supreme Court Rule 27.26
for post-conviction review.   4599

LIMITATIONS on federal habeas corpus by state prisoners: three
divergent views [position of the Standing Committee on Jurisprudence
and Law Reform, position of the Section of Criminal Law, position
of the Judicial Conference of the United States] Am Crim L Q 4:
36-55 (1966).
          Article presents views of two ABA groups regarding
          current proposals for federal legislation to cor-
          rect claimed abuses in the use of federal habeas cor-
          pus. Standing Committee supports H. R. 5958, which
          discourages repeated habeas corpus applications and
          requires that once writ is granted, the subsequent
          hearing shall be before a three judge panel. The
          Section of Criminal Law is opposed to this bill,
          suggesting that the problem can be overcome if states
          accept the burden of affording effective corrective
          processes. Also gives U.S. Judicial Conference view:
          approval of revised bill, eliminating all provisions
          regarding use of three judge courts. (Text included).
                                                     4600

LIPSIG, H. H. and SILVER, I. Civil remedies of prisoners released
on habeas corpus: a problem for the bar. NYSB J 37:502-09 (1965).
          Authors examine problems of civil redress for time
          spent in unwarranted incarceration through false
          imprisonment of malicious prosecution: difficulties
          an attorney presenting such a case will face includ-
          ing jurisdictional problems, problems of proof,
          statute of limitation, and termination of criminal
          proceedings against his client; and suggestions for
          legislative actions and alternative theories of
          suit which can cure these difficulties.   4601

LORENSON, W. D. The new scope of federal habeas corpus for state
prisoners. W Va L Rev 65:253-62 (1963).
          Discusses Faye v Noia and Townsend v Sain, which
          offer some help with problems facing a district
          court judge when application for the writ comes from
          a state prisoner.   4602

MACMILLAN, H. Jr. Trial court and prison perspectives on the collateral post conviction relief process in Florida. U Fla L Rev
21:503-15 (1969).
          Interview survey of prison officials and trial court
          judges indicates great dissatisfaction with what is

considered as a burdensome process and unsatisfactory
remedy, with most writs based on misconceptions of
law, and the entire process unregulated by the judiciary.   4603

MAYERS, L. Federal review of state convictions: some proposals for
change. Am Crim L Q 5:66-71(1967).
        Professor suggests federal statute to provide for
        uniform post-conviction proceeding in the state courts
        for the convict alleging a denial of federal rights,
        such proceeding to be separate and distinct from
        any proceeding instituted on state grounds. "Such fed-
        eral proceeding would be the exclusive state post-
        viction procedure for testing a claim of denial of
        federal rights allegedly not reflected in the record
        of the pre-conviction proceedings; and the perennially
        troublesome and frustrating question whether a fed-
        eral habeas corpus petitioner had exhausted his state
        remedies would disappear." Author discusses present
        weaknesses of state procedures calling for federal
        correction. He explains the machinery for federal
        review of a state conviction and appraises habeas
        appellate review. He suggests for final review the
        vesting of the function of federal review exclusively
        in a single federal multi-judge tribunal exercising
        both traditional appellate jurisdiction and habeas
        jurisdiction. This article appears to be a conden-
        sation of Mayers' Federal review of state convictions:
        the need for procedural reappraisal (item 4605). 4604

MAYERS, L. Federal review of state convictions: the need for procedural reappraisal. G W L Rev 34:615-65 (1966).
        Offers comprehensive procedural revision for state
        convictions, including Congressional standards for
        states to use in determination of federal rights, and
        a single nation-wide tribunal to handle the federal
        district courts' present habeas corpus and review
        functions.   4605

MAYERS, L. The habeas corpus act of 1867; the Supreme Court as
legal historian. U Chi L Rev 33:31-59 (1965).
        Law professor examines origin and purpose of the
        Habeas Corpus Act of 1867, exploring its relation-
        ship with the Reconstruction Acts, the Fourteenth
        Amendment, and scope of habeas corpus review. The
        Act is appended.   4606

MEADOR, D. J. Accommodating state criminal procedure and federal
post-conviction review. ABA L 50:928-31 (1964).
        To reduce the number of habeas corpus petitions in
        the federal district courts, the author proposes that
        the states alter their porcedures to meet the federal

standards, either by judicial construction or by
legislation; emphasizes the importance of fully recorded state post-conviction hearings; and recommends
the provision of legal counsel for prison inmates.
                                                    4607

MEADOR, D. J.   Habeas corpus and Magna Carta: dualism of power and
liberty. Charlottesville, U press of Va, 1966.
           Law professor traces the separate origins and the
           later union of the writ of habeas corpus and the
           charger, discussing the writ as a protection against
           executive detention, as a battleground of federalism,
           and as an instrument of constitutional transformation.
                                                    4608

MEADOR, D. J.   Habeas corpus and the "retroactivity" illusion. Va
L Rev 50:1115-20 (1964).
           Addressing the question of "retroactive" application
           of Mapp v Ohio, 367 US 643 (1961), professor finds
           the problem illusory, pointing out that the court's
           inquiry in a habeas corpus proceeding is limited
           to deciding the legality of present confinement, and
           not concerned with past detention.   4609

MEADOR, D. J.   Impact of federal habeas corpus on state trial procedures. Va L Rev 52:286-300 (1966).
           Argues that state trial judges must change trial
           procedure to catch possible federal Constitutional
           claims and ensure finality in the face of the ex-
           tension of the federal habeas corpus jurisdiction
           under which an independent inquiry into the facts
           and trial is undertaken by a federal court.   4610

MERRILL, A. J.   Federal habeas corpus and Maryland post-conviction
remedies. Md L Rev 24:46-66 (1964).
           Comment examines state remedies open to one convicted
           in Maryland which must normally be pursued before
           federal habeas corpus relief is available; direct
           remedies through motion for a new trial or direct
           appeal, limited collateral attacks, and the impact
           of Fay v Noia. Author concludes that the state's
           court should make greater use of post-conviction
           remedies by allowing the hearing of any allegation
           which raises federal constitutional grounds, whether
           or not brought out at trial.   4611

MISHKIN, P. J.   The high court and the great writ and the due process
of time and law. Harv L Rev 79:56-102 (1965).
           Examination of Linkletter v Walker in which the
           Supreme Court declared that Mapp has only prospective
           effect. Author posits that changes in Constitutional
           standards which do not affect the reliability of the
           guilt-determining process should not be retroactive.

See Schwartz, H. Retroactivity, reliability, due
process (item 4630).   4612

MITCHELL, J. N. Restoring the finality of justice. Ala Law
32:367-76 (1971); Judicature 55:203-06 (1971).
     In speech to Alabama State Bar, U.S. Attorney General
     discusses abuse of habeas corpus; suggests three
     alternatives for solving finality problem: limiting
     habeas corpus to claims demonstrating petitioner's
     innocence; limiting these claims to those concerning
     the reliability of the fact-finding process; and
     establishing a federal forum, other than the Supreme
     Court for direct review of state and federal convic-
     tions.   4613

MORAN, J. J. Legal services for the poor--the post-conviction
program. Mass L Q 49:327-33 (1964).
     Executive director of United Prison Association (UPA),
     a private organization carrying on a direct service
     program for Massachusetts inmates and parolees, dis-
     cusses the UPA program of legal services for indigent
     inmates now voluntarily being provided on an informal
     basis, and presents plans for the employment of a
     full time lawyer to coordinate activities of volun-
     teer ones. The new plan calls of inter-agency coop-
     eration and an efficient "follow-through" to meet
     the needs of the indigent inmate through the entire
     process of criminal justice after conviction and
     confinement.   4614

NEGRO defendants and Southern lawyers: review in federal habeas
corpus of systematic exclusion of negroes from juries. Yale L J
72:559-73 (1963).
     Federal courts, not to unduly interfere with the ad-
     ministration of state tribunals, should not disregard
     state dispositions based on local procedural rules.
     This note discusses the difference in relationship
     between the state and federal court systems in the
     habeas corpus context, as distinguished from direct
     review of court decisions by the Supreme Court.
     Cases dealing with jury exclusion are discussed. 4615

OAKS, D. Habeas Corpus in the states: 1776-1865. U Chi L Rev
32:243-88 (1965).
     Describes the early use of habeas corpus in civil
     and criminal cases; the interaction between slavery
     and habeas corpus; its role in child custody cases;
     and a comparison with the writ de homine replegiando.
                                                         4616

OLIVER, J. W. Postconviction applications viewed by a federal
judge. FRD 39:281-300 (1966).

Judge examines the recent developments in state
and federal habeas corpus proceedings: causes of additional habeas corpus applications; federal review
of state court decisions; similarities in state and
federal post-conviction proceedings and the impact
one has on the other; the need for more effective
post-conviction remedies and procedures in the state
courts; and how providing these state remedies would
both ease the burden on federal courts and lessen
federal "intrusion" in state decisions.   4617

OLIVER, J. W. Post-conviction applications viewed by a federal
judge - revisited. FRD 45:199-238 (1969).
Judge contrasts general increase since Noia in
petitions filed in federal district courts by state
prisoners with the decline in his district. He
discusses attitudes and procedures which foster
cooperation between federal and state courts, thus
minimizing need for appeals. Appendices include
Missouri Supreme Court Rule as example.   4618

PASCHAL, F. The Constitution and habeas corpus. Duke L J 1970:
605-651.
Historical and constitutional argument that habeas
corpus jurisdiction of the federal courts stems
not from a statute, but from the Constitution, and
cannot be restricted by Congress.   4619

POST-conviction relief from pleas of guilty: a diminishing right.
Brooklyn L Rev 38:182-210 (1971).
Note analyzes the increasing use of guilty pleas in
the overburdened criminal system, the diminishing
right to collateral appellate review, and the effect
on fundamental constitutional rights. Also examined
is Rule 11, F R Crim P, which sets forth guidelines
for the judge in accepting a guilty plea.   4620

POST-conviction relief in Pennsylvania. Dick L Rev 74:703-21 (1970).
Comment examines avenues of review open to defendant
after conviction and the operation and interpretation
of the Pennsylvania Post-Conviction Hearing Act; procedure in attacking a conviction on direct and collateral review, and under the Act, which replaces
all common law and statutory procedures for collateral
attack and is less arbitrary in nature. Author concludes that each petitioner should get at least one
review of the merits of his conviction as the Act's
many waivers of review has increased costly appeals.
                                                  4621

POST-conviction remedy procedures in Indiana. Notre Dame Law
48:435-45 (1972).

Note examines Indiana's attempt to resolve the
problem of inviting frivolous appeals by adopting a
variation of the Uniform Post-Conviction Procedures
Act, where all appeals are consolidated in one petition. Discussed are: constitutional background:
the impact of Noia; frivolous claims; and Indiana
Supreme Court; interpretation of the new Act. Author
feels that, with some additions, the Act can successfully provide for full, final, and fair state
adjudication.   4622

PROCEEDINGS of the Judicial Conference of the Eighth Judicial Circuit of the United States, August 26-28, 1970, held at Rapid City,
S.D.   FRD 50:427-48 (1971).
            Partial Contents: Knutson, O. R., State-federal re-
            lations in Minnesota--Finch, J. A., Jr., Post-
            conviction proceedings under Missouri Supreme Court
            rule 27.26.   4623

PROCESSING A MOTION attacking sentence.   U Pa L Rev 111:788-819
(1963).
            Note concentrates on the procedural problems of
            motions (habeas corpus) under 28 US Code sec. 2255,
            and attempts to determine optimum procedures which
            will reduce, through summary disposition, the judicial
            burden without sacrificing rights of the movant. Dis-
            cussed are: background and scope of sec. 2235;
            relevant Supreme Court cases; disposition without
            taking evidence; decision on the basis of files and
            records; and production of the prisoner at hearing.
                                                          4624

PROPOSED reformation of federal habeas corpus procedure: use of
federal magistrates.   Ia L Rev 54:1147-63 (1969).
            Shows that the use of magistrates to review habeas
            corpus petitions would neither sacrifice constitu-
            tional rights nor fail to reduce the number of cases
            which reach the district courts; enumerates defects
            apparent in other proposals to deal with the large
            number of petitions, and argues that implementation
            of magistrate use would be both easy and inexpensive.
                                                          4625

RAFALKO, W. A.   Indigent prisoner's new hope: the old writ of
habeas corpus and the right to counsel.   ND L Rev 42:168-84 (1966).
            Law professor investigates some of the habeas corpus
            problems presently faced by the courts: basic con-
            siderations, state and federal release procedures and
            how they differ, the indigent and the right to counsel
            guarantee, and the waiving of the constitutional right
            to counsel by accused. Author concludes that the
            Supreme Court is continuing its trend of incorpor-

ating the entire Bill of Rights into the 14th Amendment and discusses the tremendous responsibility
that Gideon places on the courts.   4626

RAPER, J. F.   Post-conviction remedies. Wyo L J 19:213-20 (1965).
Attorney general of Wyoming discusses Wyoming's Post-
Conviction Act, which consolidates the right to
habeas corpus review with all other post-conviction
remedies. The Act provides for: filing procedures,
appointed counsel for indigent prisoners, amendment
of improper petitions, reviewability. Author also
examines federal post-conviction relief law and the
conflict between state and federal courts in this
area. Author approves of the Act, concluding that
fewer cases will be appealed in the federal courts
if Wyoming courts provide proper review.   4627

SANDALOW, T.   Henry v Mississippi and the adequate state ground:
proposals for a revised doctrine. Sup Ct Rev 1965:187-239. (1965).
Law professor provides detailed analysis of Henry,
379 US 443 (1965); examines the significance of the
Court's intimation that it is prepared to redefine
the adequate state ground doctrine with a view toward
increased reviewability. Author discusses the doctrine of adequate state ground, including some mod-
ifications he feels are necessary.   4628

SCHAEFER, W. V.   Federalism and state criminal procedure. Harv
L Rev 70:1-26 (1956).
Reviews work of the Supreme Court in fixing standards
of procedure and reaction of the states to these
standards. Points out the occasional difficulty of
isolating procedural questions from the issue of
guilt. Identifies the habeas corpus jurisdiction
of the federal courts as the source of greatest
friction between the states and the federal system.
Criticizes proposed H.R. 5649 (limiting district
court jurisdiction of habeas corpus cases) and
recommends instead screening by three-judge panels.
          4629

SCHWARTZ, H.   Retroactivity, reliability and due process: a
reply to Professor Mishkin. U Chi L Rev 33:719-68 (1966).
Professor Schwartz discusses shortcomings in Mishkin's approach to the problem of retroactivity in
criminal cases as detailed in his article (see item
4612). Schwartz argues that all newly declared constitutional rights should be given retroactive
effect, because (1) the norms now being given federal
constitutional sanction are so basic to our kind of
democracy that convictions violative of them cannot
be allowed to stand; and (2) the disadvantages of
complete retroactivity have been exaggerated. In the

epilogue, the Court's decision in <u>Johnson v New
Jersey</u> is reviewed in terms of its impact on the
earlier discussion. Touched on is the reliability
test adopted by the court, the refusal to apply
<u>Escobedo</u> and <u>Miranda</u> to cases on direct review and
the relation of these cases to the theory of retroactivity.   4630

SHAPIRO, D. L. Federal habeas corpus: a study in Massachusetts.
Harv L Rev 57:321-72 (1973).
        Analyzes actions filed 1970, 1971, 1972. Professor
        examines merits of present habeas corpus jurisdiction;
        assesses impact of Supreme Court cases on habeas
        corpus; and suggests how process may be improved.
        Demonstrates that state prisoners fail to exhaust
        state remedies; examines activities of federal magis-
        trates in these proceedings; enumerates his own
        observations and conclusions. This is a statistical
        analysis of burdens imposed on federal courts through
        habeas corpus.   4631

SMITH, G. P. Title 28, Section 2255 of the United States Code -
motion to vacate, set aside or correct sentence: effective or ineffective aid to a federal prisoner. Notre Dame L Rev 40:171-90
(1965).
        Author discusses prisoner's right to move, vacate,
        set aside, or correct sentence which is subject to
        collateral attack. He describes the historical evo-
        lution of sec. 2255 and of the writ of habeas cor-
        pus, and traces the number of habeas corpus cases
        filed between 1941 and 1959, enumerating the reasons
        given for objecting to the sentence. Through an ex-
        amination of the cases arising under sec. 2255, the
        writer presents a critique of shortcomings of the
        courts in interpreting this section, pointing out,
        among other things, that the rule ensuring a petition-
        er's right to counsel in all criminal prosecutions
        laid down in <u>Johnson v Zerbst</u>, 304 US 458 (1938),
        was not applicable to parties seeking to have the sen-
        tences vacated and set aside in civil proceedings under
        this section. A request for counsel in such cases is
        within the discretion of the court. Author offers
        seven solutions to administrative problems arising
        under sec. 2255.   4632

SOKOL, R. P. Availability of transcripts for federal prisoners.
Am Crim L Q 2:63-74 (1964).
        Author discusses proposed legislation which will
        permit persons suing or appealing in forma pauperis
        to obtain free transcripts upon a finding of the
        trial or a circuit court judge that the transcript
        is necessary and the suit is not frivolous. Legis-
        lative history and possible interpretations of the
        statute are examined.   4633

SOKOL, R. P.   Federal habeas corpus.   Charlottesville, Va.,
Michie, 1969.   461 p.
>A practical handbook for practitioner and judge, set-
ting forth the pertinent statutory and case law on
federal habeas corpus. Includes a history of the writ,
an inquiry into the problems of suspension of the
writ, and, in the preface, suggested topics for
needed research. Appendices give statutes, rules,
forms, historical material, and a checklist of constitutional contentions often asserted in habeas
corpus proceedings. Bibliography.   4634

STATE criminal procedure and federal habeas corpus. Harv L Rev
80:422-38 (1966).
>Note examines recent increase in the use of habeas
corpus, the inadequacy of present state procedures in
providing means for the hearing of constitutional
claims, reform of state post-conviction remedies,
and the problem of waiver. Author concludes that the
states must take more responsibility in this area.
4635

STATE post-conviction remedies and federal habeas corpus. NYU L Rev
40:135-96 (1965).
>Part 1 discusses state post-conviction procedures in
light of Noia, with suggestions for meeting the
Noia standards. Part 2 discusses the requirements of
Townsend, emphasizing what various state courts have
done in the past and must do in the future. Part 3
considers the need for counsel, what various states
have provided for counsel and their effectiveness in
meeting the demands Townsend makes on the Federal
system.   4636

SWINDLER, W. F.   State post-conviction remedies and federal habeas
corpus; documentary supplement. W & M L Rev 12:147-234 (1970);
repr. as Documentary Supp.
>Study undertaken for the Federal Judicial Center by
law review editorial staff, directed by Prof. Swindler,
objective being to summarize present state post-
conviction processes and impact on adjudication in
federal courts; also statutory revision in states.
See Tent. Drafts No. 1, Nov. 1969; No. 2, May 1970
for state-by-state reports. Documentary Supplement
presents comments of authorities who reviewed the
tentative drafts; chart of state statutory references
indluded.   4637

SYMPOSIUM: Applications for writs of habeas corpus and post-conviction review of sentences in the United States Courts. FRD 33:363-
505 (1963).

Pope, W. L., Suggestions for lessening the burden of
frivolous applications.--Pope, W. L., Further developments in the field of frivolous applications: is
proliferation probable?--Breitenstein, J. S., Remarks
on recent post-conviction decisions.--Caffrey, A. A.,
The impact of the Townsend and Noia cases on federal
district judges.--Becker, W. H., Collateral and
post-conviction review of state and federal criminal
judgments on habeas corpus and on sec. 2255 motions-
view of a district judge.--O'Sullivan, C., Post-conviction remedies.   4638

SYMPOSIUM: Evolving post-conviction procedures. NYU L Rev 39:49-
192 (1964).
          Contents: Togman, L. S., the two-trial system in
          capital cases.--Sofaer, A. D., Federal habeas corpus
          for state prisoners: the isolation principle.--Abramo-
          witz, E., and Paget, D., Executive clemency in
          capital cases.   4639

SYMPOSIUM: Habeas corpus; proposals for reform. Utah L Rev 9:18-49
(1964).
          Hon. Charles Desmond, New York's Chief Judge and
          panelists, Professors Paul Freund, Walter Gellhorn and
          Edger Bodenheimer, discuss federal habeas corpus
          review of state court convictions, at dedication of
          University of Utah College of Law Building. Judge
          Desmond calls for reforms such as repealing the
          federal statutes pursuant to which state criminal
          convictions are in effect retried in the federal
          courts as to state-convicted prisoners, or setting
          a five-year statute of limitations for federal
          habeas corpus applications. He discusses the cases
          of Fay v Noia and People v Wade in which state con-
          victions were overturned and asks Congress or the
          Supreme Court to provide state courts with a set of
          implementing rules for due process. The professors
          address themselves to Judge Desmond's proposals and
          find fault with some of them.   4640

TUTTLE, E. P. Reflections on the law of habeas corpus. J Pub L
22:325-34 (1973).
          Fifth Circuit Judge emphasizes value of the writ by
          demonstrating its role in freeing unjustly condemned
          represented by him in three cases, before he became
          a judge. He warns against strong general criticism
          of the availability of the great writ of habeas
          corpus.   4641

TYSON, J. C. Whither: on habeas. Ala Law 24:271-83 (1963).
          Analysis of cases dealing with grounds for granting
          writ including adequacy of counsel, coerced confes-

sions, illegal search and seizure, knowing use of
perjured testimony, denial of witnesses, refers also
to coram nobis, the effect of <u>Gideon</u>.   4642

U. S. CONGRESS Senate Committee on the Judiciary. Enlargement of
jurisdiction of federal district courts with respect to petitions
for habeas corpus by persons in custody under judgments and sentences of state courts; report to accompany S.3576. Washington,
USGPO 1966. 11 p. (89th Cong., 2d sess., S Rep, 1502)
    The bill submitted by Sen. Tydings allows a person
    under judgment and sentence of state court to pet-
    ition for habeas corpus in federal district court of
    the district where he was convicted and sentenced.
    At present, a petitioner is limited to applying to
    the federal court in the district of his imprison-
    ment.   4643

WALTZ, J. R. Inadequacy of trial defense representation as a
ground for post-conviction relief in criminal cases. Nw U L Rev
59:289-342 (1964).
    Law professor examines the claim of inadequate rep-
    resentation: historical background of right to
    counsel; manner of asserting claim; effect of court-
    appointed counsel as compared with private counsel on
    claim; intrinsic and extrinsic causes and examples
    of ineffectiveness of counsel; and the possible bene-
    ficial impact that reviewing effectiveness of counsel
    would have on systems of counsel designation for the
    indigent and on trial lawyers in general.   4644

WEICK, P. C. Apportionment of the judicial resources in criminal
cases: should habeas corpus be eliminated? De Paul L Rev 21:740-
56 (1972).
    Judge calls for a curbing of the misuse of habeas
    corpus. Examined are the historical background of
    the expansion of federal habeas corpus and con-
    stitutional rights of the accused, the burden this
    expansion has placed on the federal courts, and
    possible means of alleviating this burden including
    presentation of all claims in the first habeas cor-
    pus application and time limits within which the
    prisoner must apply for habeas corpus.   4645

WHITE, W. S. Federal habeas corpus: the impact of the failure to
assert a constitutional claim at trial. Va L Rev 58:67-95 (1972).
    Professor White proposes two-step analysis Supreme
    Court should use to determine when a federal court
    may consider on habeas corpus a constitutional claim
    not appropriately presented to the state court. First
    the Court should allocate decision-making respon-
    sibility between the defendant and his attorney, and
    second, it should assess the validity of the choice
    to waive a constitutional claim. Recent Supreme

Court decisions are examined and criticized in
relation to both of these steps and the proposed
approaches are developed.   4646

WILLIAMS, P. H. Jr. Federal habeas corpus and the state courts.
Miss L J 36:520-26 (1965).
    Analyzes Harvey v Mississippi 340 F2d 263 (1965),
    to illustrate that federal courts have imposed mini-
    mum standards of procedure designed to guarantee due
    process to defendants charged with crimes in state
    courts, the violation of which will result in federal
    habeas corpus relief.   4647

WILLIAMSON, R. A. Federal habeas corpus: limitations on successive
applications from the same person. W & M L Rev 15:265-85 (1973).
    Law professor examines impact of Sanders v U. S.,
    373 US 1 (1963) on the treatment of successive fed-
    eral habeas corpus applications. His inquiry debates
    the conflicts arising between the objective to per-
    mit a full collateral determination of constitutional
    claims and the right to relitigate facts wherever a
    prior determination has been shown or can be shown
    to be inadequate or incomplete. He suggests modifi-
    cation of guidelines announced in Sanders, giving
    specifics.   4648

WRIGHT, J. S. and SOFAER, A. D. Federal habeas corpus for state
prisoners: the allocation of fact-finding responsibility. Yale
L J 75:895-985 (1966).
    Federal appellate judge and law clerk discuss guide-
    lines for federal courts fact-finding in habeas cor-
    pus cases of state prisoners which will effect
    smooth workings between the two systems, recognizing
    the state's primary fact-finding role.   4649

WULF, M. L. Limiting prisoner access to habeas corpus; assault on
the great writ. Brooklyn L Rev 40:253-75 (1973).
    Criticizes recent bill, S.567, which would restrict
    relief via 28 USC sec. 2254 to cases attacking the
    reliability of the fact-finding process, where the
    outcome would probably be different without the
    alleged illegality, and where the issue was not
    raised and determined at the state level. Bill pro-
    poses similar restrictions on sec. 2255. Author ar-
    gues that S.567 would foreclose completely federal
    review in some categories of cases and undermine
    constitutional rights. Compares "explosion" of
    habeas cases to similar increases in ICC and other
    cases, and concludes that it is dishonest to cur-
    tail constitutional rights on the ground that judges
    are overburdened.   4650

XI. Selected Organizations Working for Court Reform

> Items concerning a limited number of leading
> institutions and agencies which include data
> on annual reports or other descriptive mat-
> erials relating to their organization and
> activities. References to their studies, sur-
> veys, and other writings will be found in
> the Author Subject Index. References to these
> and other organizations are made also in Section
> XII, Selected Bibliographies, Guidebooks and
> Handbooks.

AMERICAN Bar Association. Report of the first-annual meeting of
the American Bar Association ... 1878- Baltimore, 1878-
> Title varies slightly.   4651

AMERICAN Bar Association. Oyez! Oyez! Bulletin of the Judicial
Administration Division. v.1- Nov. 1957- Chicago, 1957-   4652

AMERICAN Bar Association Criminal law section. Fifty-year
history (revised). Am Crim L Rev 10:229-62 (1971).   4653

AMERICAN Bar Foundation. Annual report, first- 1954/55- Chicago,
1955-
> American Bar Association's research arm; report
> includes organization, officers, committees,
> financial report, activities, library, work in
> progress and proposed, publications.   4654

AMERICAN Judicature Society. Judicature, v. 1- June, 1917-
Chicago, 1917-
> Title varies: v. 1-49: Journal of the American
> Judicature Society. Annual report of the executive
> director in some issues; issued separately other
> years.   4655

AMERICAN Law Institute. Annual meeting: proceedings. 1st-
1923- Philadelphia, 1924-   4656

AMERICAN Law Institute. Annual report ... Philadelphia.
> Report year ends May 1. In addition to the Director
> and the Treasurer's reports, pamphlets contain
> extensive bibliographies on subjects being studied
> by the Institute.   4657

BURKE, L. H. Recent milestones for effective justice. FRD
45:69-76 (1969).
> Justice Burke gives step-by-step report on organ-
> izations established in the recent program of
> improved judicial administration. He notes ABA
> Section of Judicial Administration, American Jud-

icature Society, Institute of Judicial Administration, and the Federal Judicial Center. He gives
details of development of judicial education and
the creation of various judges' conferences and
colleges, including the National College of State
Trial Judges, describing briefly the program of
each.   4658

CENTER for Criminal Justice, Harvard Law School. Annual report
for the year ending June 30, 1973. Cambridge, 1973. 66 p.
A report detailing the research program projects,
the Criminal Justice Fellowship Program, the
Internship Program, the staffing and finances of
the Center for Criminal Justice; appendix is
listing of Center publications and reports.   4659

CENTER for Judicial Education. Annual report, first- 1972-
Indianapolis, 1973-
Center is sponsored by consortium of Indiana law
schools, funded by Indiana Criminal Justice
Planning agency. Seminars and workshops for
judges described.   4660

CENTER for Studies in Criminal Justice, University of Chicago
Law School ... annual report [1st- 1966-] Chicago, 1966-
These reports describe the research and training
projects conducted by the Center to understand,
prevent, and treat crime and delinquency, and
list the publications written by persons associated with the Center.   4661

CENTER for the Administration of Criminal Justice, Univ. of
California School of Law, Davis. Annual report, 1968-
Seventh report, 1973/74, e.g., gives projects in
progress, cumulative list of publications.   4662

CLARK, T. C. The Federal Judicial Center. Judicature 53:99-103
(1969).
Director describes scientific research by the
Center respecting calendaring which resulted in
preference for individual calendaring; also Center's
investigation on use of data processing in particular courts, its weighted caseload study, and
its education and training programs.   4663

CLARK, T. C. The new Federal Judicial Center. ABA J 54:743-46
(1968).
Retired Supreme Court Justice Tom Clark, director,
describes the center and its future programs. He
relates some of the problem areas which federal
judges, in response to his inquiry, suggested
should be studies by the Center.   4664

CONFERENCE of Chief Justices. Annual meeting, 1st- 1949-
Chicago, Council of State Governments, 1949-
Title varies somewhat. Summaries of reports and
speeches; list of officers, text of resolutions. 4665

CONFERENCE of State Court Administrators. Summary of annual
meeting, 1st- 1955- Chicago, Council of State Governments
[1956-
1955-1971, called National Conference of Court
Administrative Officers. 4666

COUNCIL of State Governments. Serving the state since 1933: the
Council of State Governments. Lexington, Ky., 1973. 11 p. 4667
Descriptive brochure.

DEVITT, E. J. Statement ... before the Sub-committee on Improvement in Judicial Machinery of the Committee on the Judiciary
of the United States Senate, on S. 915, a bill to provide for
the establishment of a Federal Judicial Center. May 11, 1967.
Washington, 1967. 10 p.
Chief Judge, on the basis of findings by Special
Committee, proposes the establishment of a Federal
Judicial Center dedicated to the study of the best
methods of judicial administration. The report
outlines the organization and membership of the
proposed center. 4668

DUNHAM, A. A history of the National Conference of Commissioners
on Uniform State Laws. Law & Contemp Prob 30:233-249 (1965).
Article discusses the methods, policy objectives,
relation to federal action, and future of the
Conference; how it has worked to provide for
uniformity in such areas as the Uniform Commercial
Code, and how, although its role has been substantially changed since Congress has greater
legislative powers in these areas and special
interest organizations are drafting model legislation, the Conference still has an important
function. 4669

FEDERAL Judicial Center. Developments in judicial administration:
a five year summary. Washington, 1974. 10 p.
Report on procedural changes such as individual
calendar system, omnibus hearings, speedy trial
rules; also automated data processing. The internal
grievance procedure instituted by the Federal
Bureau of Prisons is commented on, as are the
changes in the old U. S. Commissioner system made
in 1968; gives statistics on case and appeal dispositions showing all-round improvement. 4670

FEDERAL Judicial Center. Report ... to Judicial Conference of the
United States. 1st- 1969- Washington, 1969. Periodicity varies.

Reports describe the Center's operations, activities
and programs.   4671

FORD Foundation ... and justice for all. New York, 1967. 47 p.
     Describes many areas of the Foundation's aid to
     legal research and clinical programs aimed at pro-
     viding more equal justice, including the National Of-
     fice for the Rights of the Indigent, the National De-
     fender Project, the Vera Institute of Justice and
     institutes at various law schools.   4672

HARRIS, A. ´ The Institute of Judicial Administration, with special
emphasis on its role in the administration of criminal justice;
address to Summer Workshop on Comparative Criminal Law and Administration, at NYU School of Law, Aug. 23, 1966. N.Y., 1966. 14 p.
     Author's lecture includes description of IJA's
     library, publications, judicial education program, and
     foreign visitor program. Recent projects mentioned
     cover minimum standards of criminal justice, bail and
     summons, Anglo-American criminal justice interchange,
     and survey of Rhode Island court system.   4673

HOWARD, J. C. Why we organize. J Pub L 20:381-83 (1971).
     Black judge gives reason behind formation of the
     National Bar Association's new Judicial Council:
     to work toward equal justice.   4674

INSTITUTE for Court Management. Annual report, first 1970/71-
Denver, 1971-   ,   4675

INSTITUTE for Court Management. Court Management Studies, fiscal
year 1971-72; background and purposes. Denver, 1971-72. 2 v.
     A review of work accomplished by the ICM.   4676

INSTITUTE for Court Management. Crime and the courts by H. Brownell,
Address to Appellate Judges Conference, Aug. 11, 1972. Denver, 1972.
18 p.
     Former United States Attorney General believes that
     well-financed courts and supportive agencies are
     a necessity and urges the establishment of state-
     wide planning and budget offices to allocate
     funds to the various units in the criminal justice
     system so that they may be properly balanced. He
     describes two programs for court administration
     improvement: the Institute for Court Management and
     a program in New York State for dealing with
     disruptive criminal trials by establishing rules
     and security arrangements.   4677

INSTITUTE for Court Management. Fellows and development program
yearbook, 1970-1971. Denver, 1971. 80 p.
     Background and history of ICM; program objectives,
     summary of development programs 1970, 1971; faculty,

speakers, judges, and panel of National Academy
of Public Administration; biographical sketches
of 1970-71 students, class rosters for 1970,
1971.   4678

INSTITUTE for Court Management. Justice system journal. v. 1-
Denver, 1974-
        Subtitle: A management review.   4679

INSTITUTE for the Study of Crime and Delinquency. Progress report.
Sacramento, 1969. 31 p.
        Surveys objectives, organization, and methods of
        the Institute. Included are summaries of major pro-
        jects, completed and in process.   4680

INSTITUTE of Government. Publications of the Institute of
Government, 1930-1962, by Palotai, O. G. 1963. 78 p.   4681

_____. 1963-65 Supplement. Chapel Hill, 1963-65. 2 v.

_____. Interim rev. ed. Mar 1975. 11 p.

INSTITUTE of Judicial Administration. [Brochure] 1960- New York,
1960-
            Cover title: Institute of Judicial Administration.
            Periodicity varies: 1960-66, biennial; 1968-
            annual. Includes Report of the director, 1973-. 4682

INSTITUTE of Judicial Administration. IJA publications, 1966-74.
N.Y., 1974. 5 p.   4683

INSTITUTE of Judicial Administration. Project effective justice;
an appraisal. N.Y., 1964. 140 p.
            Study reviews origin, organization, objectives,
            and accomplishments of the Joint Committee for
            the Effective Administration of Justice, dissolved
            12/31/64. Appendix contains evaluation of selected
            judicial seminars sponsored by the Joint Com-
            mittee.   4684

INSTITUTE of Judicial Administration. Report of the director.
1st- 1952/53- N.Y., 1953- annual.
            1972/73- combined with IJA brochure. 4685

JUDICIAL Conference of the United States. Memorandum from
Warren Olney III to Emanuel Celler, re H. R. 5385, H. R. 6111,
providing for the establishment of a Federal Judicial Center.
May 10, 1967. Washington, 1967. 8 p.
            This memorandum advises the Congressman that, where
            there is common assent to the creation of the Fed-
            eral Judicial Center, the Judicial Conference
            strongly urges that the membership be limited to

federal judges, except for the Director of the
Administrative Office.   4686

JUDICIAL Conference of the United States. Report of the ad hoc
Committee to study and report on the implementation of the act
of Congress establishing a Federal Judicial Center. Washington,
1968. 18 p.
          Recommendations are made regarding: functions and
          duties of the Center's Board; cooperation of judges
          and court personnel with Center; Center's role in
          research, education and training of judges, and in
          studying possible use of data systems in adminis-
          tration of courts.   4687

JUDICIAL Conference of the United States. Report of the Special
Committee on Continuing Education, Research, Training and Administration. Washington, 1967. 28 p.
          Proposed bill creating Federal Judicial Center is
          included with an estimate of its operating costs.4688

KAUFMAN, I. R. Courts in crisis: progress versus intransigence.
ABA J 52:1026-29 (1966).
          Judge suggests ways of reducing problems of con-
          gestion and delay, mainly through the help of law-
          yers. He recounts the work of the Institute of
          Judicial Administration, of which he was at the
          time president.   4689

KLEIN, F. J. The independent survey - new tool for court ad-
ministrators; the role of the Institute of Judicial Administration.
Address to the National Assn of Trial Court Administrators, Las
Vegas, Apr. 27, 1971. N.Y., 1971. 16 p.
          On court surveys, and how to present a proposal to
          LEAA by court administrators; mainly covers the
          work of IJA in court surveys.   4690

KLEIN, F. J. What's new at the Institute of Judicial Administration; address given at Fourth Annual Conference of National
Assn of Trial Court Administrators, Apr. 16-19, 1969, at Gaithers-
burg, Md. N.Y., 1969. 17 p.
          Describes the project on Minimum Standards for the
          Administration of Criminal Justice, surveys of
          Delaware criminal courts and Maine probate courts,
          the Academy for the Judiciary, and other present
          and future projects. Also, explains the fiscal
          structure, history, and staffing of the Institute.
                                                         4691

THE LAW Enforcement Assistance Administration: symposium on its
operation and impact. Colum Human Rights L Rev 5:1-214 (1973).
          Contents: Rogovin, C. The genesis of the LEAA: a
          personal account.--Gude, G., Mannina, G. J. Jr.
          The impact of crime of the LEAA in the District
          of Columbia.--Rector, M. G., Wolfe, J. The LEAA

in perspective.-- Peskoe, H. E. The 1968 Safe
Streets Act: Congressional response to the growing
crime problem.--An empirical analysis of the operation and impact of the LEAA in three states (Reid,
C. A., Philadelphia: city-state relations.--Gregware,
P. R. Massachusetts: experiments in crime prevention.--Purcell, J. North Carolina: corrections
and juvenile justice in a rural state).--
Conclusion.   4692

LOUSIANA State Law Institute. Biennial report. First- 1939/40-
These reports of this law revision, reform and
research agency list the officers and the members
of its governing body, and set forth the work and
current projects of the Institute, proposed legislation and programs of annual meetings.   4693

MCCLELLAN, J. L. Federal judicial center. Remarks in the Senate.
Cong. Rec. 113:2900-2902 (1967).
Mr. McClellan proposes the establishment of a
Center intended to enable the federal courts to
embark on a program of self analysis, research, and
planning; the Center is also to develop programs
of continuing education and training for personnel
in the judicial branch of government. Includes Text
of the Bill, S.915, and accompanying letter.   4694

MCCRAE, W. A., JR. The Federal Judicial Center. Judicature
53:8-13 (1969).
Founding, initial organization, officers, and
aims.   4695

NATIONAL Association of Trial Court Administrators. The Column.
v. 1- Oct. 1970-
Records items of interest to trial court administrators.   4696

NATIONAL Association of Trial Court Administrators. [Personnel,
methods, duties: tables] Chicago, 1970. 12 p.
(For annotation, see item 18).   4697

NATIONAL Association of Trial Court Administrators. Proceedings of
the [1st-4th] meeting, 1966-69. Reno, 1966-69.
First published by Institute of Judicial Administration, thereafter by National College of State
Trial Judges.   4698

NATIONAL Center for State Courts. Annual report, 1971/1973-
[First- [Washington, 1973-
Created June 1971, outgrowth of National Conference
on the Judiciary, Williamsburg, March 1971. First report covers first two years. 2d- reports published
in Denver.   4699

NATIONAL Center for State Courts. Court services package. Washington, 1973. 60 p. (Pub. W0002).
> History, purposes, organization, biographies of staff, budget, state funding, Board of Directors, Advisory Council, Council of State Representatives; includes description of divisions of Center to implement objectives.   4700

NATIONAL Center for State Courts. Master calendar. v. 1-
Jan. 1975- Denver, monthly.
> Contains notices of seminars, meetings, institutes and similar events of interest to the judiciary.4701

NATIONAL Center for State Courts. National judicial education programs, a report by J. W. Reed. July 8, 1972. Washington, 1972. 26 p.
> The operations and goals of the American Academy of Judicial Education, the Institute for Court Management, the Institute of Judicial Administration, the National College of Juvenile Justice, the National College of the State Judiciary and the ABA Traffic Court Program are described. After general observations on the programs of these organizations, the author presents findings and recommendations. He also comments on the role of the National Center for State Courts. (For more complete report see item 4704).   4702

NATIONAL Center for State Courts. Report (newsletter) v. 1-
Jan. 1974- monthly   4703

NATIONAL Center for State Courts. State judicial training profile, by B. A. Franklin. Denver, 1974. 142 p.
> (For annotation see item 1764)   4704

NATIONAL Conference of Commissioners on Uniform State Laws. Handbook ... and proceedings of the annual conference meeting in its 1st- year, 1891-   4705

NATIONAL Conference of State Trial Judges. Proceedings of the annual meeting, 2d-10th; 1959-1967. Chicago, 1959-1967.
> Proceedings of first meeting not published. 1968-meetings summarized in Judges' Journal.   4706

NATIONAL Conference on the Metropolitan Courts, 1970. National Conference of Metropolitan Courts, Bal Harbour, Fla., Oct. 21-23, 1970. Coral Gables, Univ. of Miami Law Center, 1970. 1 v., var. pag.
> Background material for the conference. Partial contents: a review of the Department of Transportation Auto Insurance and Compensation Study; Create university-trained court managers; Planning

function of the court administrator; Trial advocacy
at the crossroads; and Lawyers and their work. <u>4707</u>

NATIONAL Council of Juvenile Court Judges. Juvenile justice,
v. 1- 1950- quarterly.
Title varies: Juvenile Court Judges Journal through
1969, v. 20; Juvenile Court Journal, 1970-71, v. 21-
22; Juvenile Justice beginning with v. 23, 1972. <u>4708</u>

NATIONAL Council on Crime and Delinquency. Crime and delinquency,
v. 1- 1955- quarterly
Called National Probation and Parole Association
before 1960. <u>4709</u>

NATIONAL Council on Crime and Delinquency. Criminal justice
newsletter, v. 1- Sept. 14, 1970- biweekly.
"Published ... with the cooperation of the Institute of Judicial Administration which founded the
publication in 1970." <u>4710</u>

NATIONAL Council on Crime and Delinquency. Journal of research
in crime and delinquency. v. 1- Jan. 1964- semiannual. <u>4711</u>

NATIONAL Council on Crime and Delinquency. Advisory Council of
Judges. Proceedings [of] annual meeting. 1st- 1953- various
places.
First-7th as National Probation and Parole
Association [Agenda or minutes]. <u>4712</u>

NATIONAL District Attorneys Association. Prosecutor. v. 3 no. 4,
1967-
Contains NDAA, journal of the National District
Attorneys Assn., v. 1-v. 3, no. 3. <u>4713</u>

NEW YORK (City) Criminal Justice Coordinating Council. Reports,
1968- N. Y., Off. of the Mayor, 1968-
Title and periodicity vary; first report called
18-month report, covers Apr. 1, 1967-Nov. 1, 1968;
2d report called Two-year report, dated Apr. 1969;
reports thereafter called Criminal Justice Plan
for 1971, etc., issued annually. This is the city
planning agency that coordinates efforts of other
local criminal justice agencies and allocates LEAA
and local matching funds. Each report assesses
areas of greatest need, suggests types of projects
it would fund, reports on completed and current
projects, with some evaluation.

OLNEY, W. Statement ... before the Subcommittee on Improvements
in Judicial Machinery of the Committee on the Judiciary of the
United States Senate, on S.915, a bill to provide for the establishment of a Federal Judicial Center. May 4, 1967. Washington,
1967. 30 p.

Statement examines the problems of increase of judicial business and lack of fact-finding organizations which led to the development of the proposal for a Federal Judicial Center. The discussion
presents basic organizational ideas of the proposed
center including objectives, powers, membership,
and relationship with the Judicial Conference of
the United States.   4715

REARDON, P. S. The new National Center for State Courts: progress
and prospects. Judicature 55:66-69 (1971).
            Massachusetts appellate justice, who was acting
            director of the new Center gives background of
            formulation of Center at Williamsburg Conference;
            describes organization and current activities. 4716

SANDERS, J. L. The Institute of Government of the University of
North Carolina. Chapel Hill, Inst. of Gov., of N. C., 1963. 16 p.
            Creation, organization, operation, research.   4717

SNYDER, G. C. The conception, the labor, and the birth of the
National Center for State Courts. Judicature 56:17-23 (1972).
            The author, one of Center's incorporators, relates
            the process of its formation and of its articles
            of incorporation. He points out that the purposes
            of the Center are to improve the administration of
            justice in the state courts, to support research,
            and to assist and coordinate, but not supplant,
            organizations functioning in the field of judicial
            administration.   4718

SUTRO, J. A. Can the courts find improvement through science?
FRD 45:77-86 (1969).
            By science the author means "experimental research".
            He notes the establishment of the Federal Judicial
            Center and its potential for engaging in true
            scientific experimental research. He describes the
            structure, operation and various projects of the
            Center.   4719

TATE, A. JR. Judges help the legislature revise the law. Trial
Judges' J 5:9,27 (Apr. 1966).
            Louisiana judge relates the success of the Louisiana
            State Law Institute, a law reform commission
            established to receive law revision suggestions and
            to make recommendations to the legislature to
            improve statutory law.   4720

TATE, A. Jr. A ministry of justice in action: the Louisiana
State Law Institute. N J B J 9:1381,1399-1401 (1965).
            The presiding judge of the Louisiana Court of
            Appeal, 3d Cir., describes the purposes, operations
            and accomplishments of the Institute, which was
            created by the Legislature in 1938, as an official
            law revision and reform agency.   4721

U. S. ADVISORY Commission on Intergovernmental Relations. New
proposals for 1972: ACIR State legislative program. Washington,
USGPO, 1971. 98 p.   4722

U. S. ADVISORY Commission on Intergovernmental Relations. [Origin,
composition, functions, membership, etc.] Washington, 1962.
30 p.   4723

U. S. CONGRESS Senate Committee on the Judiciary. Crisis in the
federal courts; hearings before the Subcommittee on Improvements
in Judicial Machinery ... on the administration of justice in
the federal court system, and S.915 and H.R.6111, bills to establish a Federal Judicial Center, April 25-28, May 3, 4, 10, 11, and
September 8, 1967. Washington, USGPO, 1967. 466 p.   4724

U. S. CONGRESS Senate Committee on the Judiciary. Federal Judicial
Center, Nov. 15, 1967. Washington, USGPO, 1967. 32 p. (90th Cong.;
1st Sess., S. rep 781)
                    Text bill of establishing the Center, with legis-
                    lative history, background, and sectional analy-
                    sis.   4725

U. S. Law Enforcement Assistance Administration. Annual Report,
1969- Washington, 1969-
                    Summarizes internal activities, gives brief report
                    from each State Planning Agency; appendix compiles
                    financial data on all LEAA funding and other ex-
                    penditures, describing many projects as to purpose
                    and methodology, amount of grant, names of grantee,
                    sub-grantee, director.   4726

U. S. LAW Enforcement Assistance Administration. Safe streets ...
the LEAA program at work. Washington, 1971. 42 p.
                    Description of LEAA's organization and work, grant-
                    making, education, research, funding; sketches on
                    its activities in various areas including: "stren-
                    gthening police capabilities", modernizing courts,
                    reforming corrections, controlling organized crime,
                    prevention and control of civil disorders, control-
                    ling drug abuse, reducing juvenile delinquency, aid
                    to cities, and collection of statistics. Includes
                    instructions on applying for LEAA financial aid;
                    list of state planning agencies .   4727

U. S. NATIONAL Institute of Law Enforcement and Criminal Justice.
Publications. Washington, 1975. 47 p.   4727a

VERA Institute of Justice. Programs in criminal justice reform:
ten-year report 1961-1971. New York, 1972. 192 p.
                    Vera's many innovative experiments described: Man-
                    hattan Bail Project (release on recognizance) and
                    Summons Project (summons in lieu of arraignment)

from which grew Manhattan Court Employment Project
(charges dropped if defendant gets and holds job);
Bronx Sentencing Project and Neighborhood Youth
Diversion Program (for 12-15 year olds: neighborhood court with volunteer judges to arbitrate disputes, plus social services).   4728

WARREN, E. Address, American Law Institute, May 21, 1968, Washington. Washington, 1968. 30 p.
Chief Justice deplores the extensive backlog of
cases in the federal court system and stresses the
need for reform. He hails the newly established
Federal Judicial Center and traces its development,
names the members of the board and committees, and
describes its future activities.   4729

WRIGHT, E. L. An overview of the [American Bar] Association in
its 93rd year. ABA J 57:760-70 (1971).
ABA President relates recent projects and committees
in anticrime efforts, legal services, public service
activities, legal education, ethics, and the
judiciary.   4730

XII.   Selected Bibliographies, Guidebooks and Handbooks

A.   Selected Bibliographies

Bibliographies with short annotations on their
subject coverage. Arranged alphabetically by
author, these bibliographies cover subjects above
listed and related areas, not covered, such as
juvenile justice, penology, corrections.

ABRAHAM, H.J. [Four selected bibliographies] in his Judicial
process, 3d ed. N.Y., Oxford, 1975. p. 385-515

Contents: I. Classified general works--II. Bio-
graphies, autobiographies, and related works
of and by U.S. Supreme Court justices--III. Comparative law--IV. Classified works on civil
rights and civil liberties. Spanning a wide
horizon of constitutional law and legal philosophy, the bibliographies include entries on
court administration, judicial administration. <u>4731</u>

AMERICAN Association of Law Libraries. Current publications in
legal and related fields, 1966- South Hackensack, N.J., Rothman.
9 issues a year, with annual hardbound cumulation.

Includes annual Checklist of current state, federal and Canadian publications. (In Oct. issue,
1974) ‾Appeared in L Lib J through 1965 as
Current publications and bibliographies, ed. A.
Grech. 56:78-104, 155-62, 272-81 (1963);
57:84-92, 157-62, 253-59 (1964); 58:63-70,
174-81,302-08 (1965)   <u>4732</u>

AMERICAN Bar Association. Automated law research; a collection of presentations delivered at the First National Conference on Automated Law Research. Chicago, 1973. 191 p.

Articles show how to enlist the aid of computers in searching legal texts. A bibliography
is included.   <u>4733</u>

AMERICAN Bar Association Advisory Committee on Sentencing
and Review. Selected bibliography [on criminal appeals] in its
Standards relating to criminal appeals. N.Y., IJA, 1969.
p. 101-9.

Books, monographs, articles, and ALR annotations
covering every aspect, including appeal as of
right and by permission, speed, cost, appeals
by state, and more.   <u>4734</u>

AMERICAN Bar Association Special Committee on Youth Education
for Citizenship. Bibliography of law-related curriculum materials, annotated. Chicago, 1974. 80 p. (Working notes, no. 5)
> Books for use in elementary and high school, graded
> and classified, including sections on introduction
> to law, judicial process, U.S. Supreme Court,
> civil rights, aids for teachers. To be expanded
> and updated.   4735

AMERICAN Judicature Society. Annotated bibliography on appellate
procedure. Chicago, 1968. 8 p. (Rep 14)
> Covers problems involved, scope of appeal, mechanics
> of appeals, finality rule; criminal appeals; gen-
> eral reference works.   4736

AMERICAN Judicature Society. Bibliography on less-than-unanimous
verdicts and fewer than twelve persons. Chicago, 1963. 2 p.
(Information Sheet 21)   4737

AMERICAN Judicature Society. Annotated bibliography on the grand
jury, by J. Lubbers. Chicago, 1973. 19 p.
> (Previous edition, 1968, its Report no. 2.)   4738

AMERICAN Judicature Society. Bibliography [on procedural rule-
making in the United States] in its Study of the procedural rule-
making power in the United States, by J. A. Parness and C. A.
Korbakes. Chicago 1973. p. 68-75. (Rep 13)
> Covers published items since earliest days on
> rule-making power of the courts.   4739

AMERICAN Judicature Society. Citations and bibliography on
the unified bar in the United States; research report comp. by
J. A. Parness. Chicago, 1973. 32 p.
> Statutes, court rules, cases on establishment,
> responsibilities of unified bar associations,
> state-by-state listing and discussions pro and
> con on bar integration.   4740

AMERICAN Judicature Society. [Courthouses and courtrooms]
bibliography, in its Selected readings on courthouses and
courtrooms. Chicago, 1972. p. 81.   4741

AMERICAN Judicature Society. Judicial administration and
racial discrimination; fifteen years of literature. Chicago,
1970. 19 p. (Rep 19)   4742

AMERICAN Judicature Society. Judicial discipline and removal, by
W. Braithwaite. Chicago, 1969. (Rep 5) 47 p.   4743

AMERICAN Judicature Society. Judicial response to problems of
prison administration, by D. P. Flint. Chicago, 1971. 21 p.
(Rep 33)   4744

AMERICAN Judicature Society. The jury process; a bibliography.
Chicago, 1968. 15 p. (Rep 1)
          Classified: 1) General--2) Exemptions--3) Selec-
          tion--4) Challenges and voir dire--5) Instructions--
          6) Conduct--7) Challenging the verdict--8) Less
          than unanimous verdicts--9) Juries of less
          than twelve.   4745

AMERICAN Judicature Society. Lawyers speak the truth about
counsel-conducted voir dire; comment with bibliography. Chicago,
1970. 17 p. (Rep 22)
          Supersedes June 1967 and Aug. 1968 editions
          entitled Voir Dire.   4746

AMERICAN Judicature Society. Mass trials; courtroom disruptions
and the rights of defendants, by S. D. White. Chicago, 1971
5 p. (Rep 30)   4747

AMERICAN Judicature Society. News media and the administration
of justice, a bibliography, by D. Groose. Chicago, 1970.
33 p. (Rep 4)
          Bibliography: p. 16-33.   4748

AMERICAN Judicature Society. Probate courts; structure,
operation and procedure; a selected bibliography of recent
articles and materials. Chicago, 1962. 2 p. (Info. sheet
10)   4749

AMERICAN Judicature Society. Publications list. Chicago, 1973.
21 p.
          An updated list of books, research studies, bib-
          liographies, information reports, pamphlets and
          special Journal issues of the Society. Publications
          lists are updated periodically in the Society's
          Journal, Judicature.   4750

AMERICAN Judicature Society. Selected chronology and bibliography of court organization reform. Chicago, 1970. 37 p.
(Rep 12)
          State-by-state report, bibliographical notes
          throughout.   4751

AMERICAN Judicature Society. Sentencing patterns and problems;
an annotated bibliography, by W. S. Carr and V. J. Connelly.
Chicago, 1973. 97 p.   4752

ANDREWS, J. L. [and others] The law in the United States of
of America; a selective bibliographical guide. NYU Press, 1965. 100 p.

Aid to law libraries in selection of legal material
is divided into categories; includes law in general,
history, special legal systems, civil and commercial
private law, judicial system and civil procedure,
criminal law and procedure, public law, labor law
legal profession, air law, maritime law, and international law. Authors' recommendations are noted
and include quotations of prices. Annotated.   4753

APPELLATE Judges Seminar, New York University, 1963. Bibliography
and reading lists. N.Y., IJA, 1963. 1 v., var. pag. .   4754

ASSOCIATION of American Law Schools. Law books recommended for
libraries. No. 15: Criminal law and procedure, by J. Goldstein.
No. 18: Family law, by W. T. Dean. No. 22: Judicial administration, by F. J. Klein and K. Parkes. South Hackensack, N.J.,
Rothman, 1968-70.
        Includes pertinent treatises and reports, biblio-
        graphies, and periodicals.   4755

ASSOCIATION of the Bar of the City of New York Library. The
law in paperback; a bibliography. N.Y., 1963. 9 p.
        List of paperback titles on the law, including
        some legal classics otherwise out of print.   4756

ASSOCIATION of the Bar of the City of New York Library. The
press and the courts, by A. Grech. Record 19:166-170 (1964).
        Includes case notes and supplements bibliographies
        in Record 6:429-433 (1951) and Record 13:40-48
        (1958).   4757

ASSOCIATION of the Bar of the City of New York Library. Selected
bibliography on automobile insurance reform plans, by A. Grech.
Record 23:197-207 (1968).
        Subdivided by type of plan; 200 items.   4758

ASSOCIATION of the Bar of the City of New York Library. Selected
materials on the grand jury. Record 27:628-638 (1972).   4759

AUTOMATION in the public service, an annotated bibliography.
Chicago, Public Administration Service, 1966. 70 p.   4760

BASIC protection, a bibliography. Defense L J 17:149
(1968)   4761

BIBLIOGRAPHY of materials on the judge and his role in American
jurisprudence. Tulsa L J 2:166-79 (1965).
        This bibliography is limited to law reviews pub-
        lished by American law schools. Topics covered
        are biographical sketches; judicial independence;
        jurisdictional, administrative and legislative

powers; judicial responsibilities: administrative,
relations with bar and public, decision making
process; qualifications; immunity from prosecution
for judicial acts; limitations on service: dis-
qualification, tenure, retirement, removal for
cause, disbarment; salary and pension; selection
of judges; and judges in foreign jurisdictions. 4762

BIBLIOGRAPHY of the grand jury, Am Crim L Rev 10:867-878 (1972).
Books and articles covering arrest, disclosure,
history, immunity, membership, reports, right
to counsel, secrecy, wiretapping, and federal
statutes applicable to grand juries.   4763

BLAKE, M. E. Selected, annotated readings on group services
in the treatment and control of juvenile delinquency. Washington,
USGPO, 1960. 17 p.
          Contents: pt. I. Culture and hostile youth
          groups--Pt. 2. Reports and studies on adolescence
          --Pt. 3. Work with street clubs and youth gangs
          --Pt. 4. Use of group services in institutional
          treatment programs.   4764

CALIFORNIA State Library Law Library. Congestion and delay
in the courts, an annotated bibliography, 1967-71; comp. by
B. Jackson. Sacramento, 1971. 12 p.   4765

CALIFORNIA State Library Law Library. Fair trial and free
press; a bibliography. Sacramento, 1967. 10 p.   4766

CALIFORNIA State Library Law Library. Legal newsletters;
a listing, by C. W. Kenyon. Sacramento, 1968. 13 p.   4767

CALIFORNIA State Library Law Library. Legal services to the
poor, a selective bibliography. Sacramento, 1967. 12 p.   4768

CALIFORNIA State Library Law Library. The ombudsman, by
by C. A. Kenyon. Sacramento, 1966. 7 p.   4769

CANADA. Parliament. Library. Crime and criminal justice;
selected bibliography. Ottawa, 1967. 25 p.
          Canadian materials for the most part, concerning
          lawyers, police, crime and criminals.   4770

CHAMBLISS, W. J. and SEIDMAN, R. B. Sociology of the law; a
research bibliography. Berkeley, Cal., Glendessary Press,
1970. 113 p.
          Sections on criminal law, administration of
          justice and the legal profession are of inter-
          est.   4771

CHARTRAND, R. L. Improving judicial administration; the role
of systems technology. Oct. 5, 1972. Washington, Congressional
Research Service, Library of Congress, 1972. 9 p.
>   Bibliography of books and articles on court
>   administration and use of computers.   4772

CHICAGO Municipal Reference Library. Civil disturbance; a
selected bibliography. Chicago, 1967. 6 p.   4773

COMPREHENSIVE dissertation index, 1861-1972; law and political
science. Ann Arbor, Xerox univ. microfilms, 1974. (Its vol. 27)
>   Part of 37-volume work that identifies nearly
>   all doctoral dissertations honored by degree-
>   granting institutions in U.S.; subject arranged,
>   gives availability, including references to
>   Dissertation Abstracts International, American
>   Doctoral Dissertations, and L.C. listings. To
>   be supplemented. Available also in microfiche. 4774

COMUS, L. F. Use of computers and other automated processes by
the courts. Geneva, World Peace Through Law Center, 1967.
41 p.   4775

COUNCIL of State Governments. Suggested basic list of periodicals
useful for legislative reference and research. Chicago,
1967. 10 p.   4776

CRAY, E. Annotated bibliography on police review boards. L in
Trans Q 3:197-205 (Summer 1966).
>   Selected materials on police review boards,
>   proposed or in operation, in such areas as Los
>   Angeles, Massachusetts, New York City,
>   Philadelphia and Rochester; miscellaneous items
>   on boards in Detroit, Atlanta, Washington, D. C.
>   and Minnesota.   4777

CRIME and delinquency abstracts. Bethesda, Md., National
Clearinghouse for Mental Health Information, Jan. 1963-1972. 8 v.
>   Consists of abstracts of treatises and reports.
>   Ceased publication 1972. V. 1 prepared by the
>   National Council on Crime and Delinquency. Absorbed
>   Current projects in the prevention, control and
>   treatment of crime and delinquency in 1965.   4778

DAHL, R. C. and BOLDEN, C. E. The American judge, a bibliography.
Vienna, Va., Coiner, 1968. 330 p.
>   Includes 9105 books and articles, covers selected
>   items in English about the American judge, his
>   personality, selection, removal, functions,
>   performance, workload, politics and other aspects
>   of the office. Subject arrangement; not anno-
>   tated.   4779

DE SCHUTTER, B. Bibliography of international criminal law. Leiden, Netherlands, Sijthoff, 1972. 474 p.

Monographs, periodical articles, official documents classified, by country, under ten main headings: Extraterritorial jurisdiction, extradition, transmission of prosecutions, minor judicial assistance, status of foreign military forces, war crimes, other international crimes, humanitarian law, international criminal court, U.N. concern with international criminal law. To be supplemented. 4780

DORSEN, N. and FRIEDMAN, L. Selected bibliography on courtroom disorder. In their Disorder in the court. N.Y., Pantheon, 1973. p. 384-86.

Covers books and articles on judicial, prosecutorial, and other misconduct in courtroom; also general responsibilities of judge and counsel in criminal case. 4781

DUNN, D. J. The criminal justice reference library: a collection of informally published materials related to criminal law. Am J Crim L 1:351-57 (1972).

Supervising librarian describes the objectives of this U. of Texas Law School library and types of materials available: their characterization; selective dissemination of information through use of computer; services offered by library; staff; and funding. Appendix of library's publications. 4782

FISH, P. G. Bibliography on federal judicial administration. In Politics of federal judicial administration. Princeton, Princeton univ. press, 1973. p. 459-97

Includes published and unpublished manuscripts, books, articles and periodicals, public documents and Senate and House hearings regarding federal judicial administration. 4783

GANTT, P. H. Bibliography of the Court of Claims. Georgetown L J 55:647-55 (1967).

Organization, jurisdiction of U.S. Court of Claims; rules; period covered is 1859-1966. 4784

GORDON, R. I. and TEMERLIN, M. K. The behavioral scientist and the courtroom; a bibliography. Judicature 53:151-53 (1969).

Two psychologists have catalogued a series of publications on the relationship of law and the behavioral science and on the psychodynamics of courtroom behavior, with sections on procedure, evidence and testimony, insanity pleas, the judge, and the jury. 4785

946   ADMINISTRATION OF CRIMINAL JUSTICE

GROSSMAN, J. B. and LADINSKY, J. Law and society; a selected bibliography. Law and Soc Rev 2:291-339 (1968); 3:161-88 (1968); 4:123-55, 613-42 (1969-70); 5:417-54, 611-31 (1971); 6:443-68 (1972); 7:498-527 (1973).

> Annotated, these extensive bibliographies of books and articles by Wisconsin University professors include areas of interest. Examples are: response to judicial decisions, judicial administration, selection and education, judicial process and behavior, penology and crime prevention, police and criminal justice, juveniles and the law, and others.   4786

HALÉVY, B. J. A selective bibliography on state constitutional revision, 2d ed., compiled by B. J. Halevy with the assistance of L. H. Guth; supp comp by M. Fink. N.Y., National Municipal League, 1967. 203 p.   4787

HARVARD University Law School Library. Annual legal bibliography. Cambridge, 1960-.

> National and foreign writings appear monthly as Current Legal Bibliography. Annuals are subject divided: under Administration of Justice appear items respecting court administration and court costs, judges, and court officials; other pertinent subjects are police, criminal law, penology, criminology, juvenile delinquency, civil and criminal procedure, trials etc.   4788

INSTITUTE of Government, University of Georgia. Literature on parole, by F. K. Gibson, R. Payne and F. L. Bates. Athens, 1967. 95 p.

> A bibliography with abstracts: Origins and history; Research 1923-1967; Current literature (divided by subject).   4789

INSTITUTE of Governmental Research. Selected bibliography on state constitutional revision, prepared for the Florida Constitutional Revision Commission, by Albert L. Sturm... Tallahassee, 1966. 28 p.

> Bibliography is divided by subject: general works, materials on recent constitutional revision in other states, recent constitutional revision in Fla., and substantive areas of the constitutional system, including the judiciary.   4790

INSTITUTE of Judicial Administration. Law officer project in the Family Court of New York City; an evaluation N.Y., 1973. 103 p.

> Annotated entries include items regarding the roles of prosecutors and defense lawyers in juvenile courts. Model rules and recommendations of organi-

zations are included. Appendix A: Selected bibliography on prosecutors and lawyers and the juvenile
court, 3 p.   4791

INSTITUTE OF Judicial Administration. Selected bibliography on
news media and criminal justice, by F. J. Klein N.Y., 1964. 9 p.
     Includes bibliographies and articles; not
     annotated.   4792

INSTITUTE of Judicial Administration Juvenile Justice Standards
Project. Bibliography Draft 11/10/71. N.Y., IJA 66 p.
     Prepared for use of the Juvenile Justice Standards
     Project. Includes only material dealing specifically
     with children or families or juvenile and family
     courts; does not include causes and nature of
     juvenile delinquency or preventive detention.
     It is preliminary to a final draft.   4793

INSTITUTE of Judicial Administration Juvenile Justice Standards
Project. Child abuse and child abuse reporting; bibliography
N.Y., 1974. 46p.
     Books, reports, articles, and cases compiled by
     staff preparatory to drafting model child abuse
     reporting law.   4794

INSTITUTE of Judicial Administration Juvenile Justice Standards
Project. Child abuse reporting; a review of the literature, by
A. Sussman N.Y., 1974. 114 p.; Family L Q 8:245-313 (1974).
     Covers history and purpose of reporting laws,
     definitions of abuse and neglect, mandatory
     reporting, reporter's state of mind, the report,
     to whom, temporary emergency removal, immunity
     from prosecution, penalties for failure to report,
     waiver of privileged communications, central
     register, right to due process.   4795

INSTITUTE of Judicial Administration Minimum Standards for
Standards for Criminal Justice Project. Selected bibliography,
by F. J. Klein. N.Y., IJA, 1965. 87 p. Supplement, 1966. 21 p.
     Books and articles cover police functions, pre-
     trial proceedings, prosecution and defense func-
     tions, the criminal trial including speedy trial,
     sentencing review, free press-free trial.   4796

JACOBSTEIN, M. J. and PIMSLEUR, M. G. Law books in print. Dobbs
Ferry, N.Y., Glanville, 1971. 3 V.
     Supplemented by Pimsleur's Law books published
     (quarterly and cumulated annually). Subject listing
     includes subjects pertinent to administration
     of justice.   4797

KALVEN, H. and ZEISEL, H.   Project bibliography. In their The
American jury. Boston, Little, Brown, 1966. p. 712-34.
          Includes complete list of publications of the Jury
          Project of the University of Chicago; 62 items
          published up to 1966.   4798

KELLY J. Computerized management information systems. N.Y.,
Macmillan, 1970. p. 520-526.
          Books, articles, organizational publications,
          all about hardware and its uses in business;
          not annotated; for the sophisticated.   4799

Klein, F. J. Annotated bibliography [on administration of
justice] Williamsburg, Va., National Conference on the Judiciary
1971. 53 p; Justice in the states; addresses...of the Conference
(see item 81), p. 269-322.
          Prepared for the Conference, bibliography covers
          all phases of the discussions. I. The Courts
          (A. Court Systems B. Selected court surveys)
          --II. Court Administration--III. Judges--IV. Ad-
          ministration of Criminal Justice.   4800

KLEIN, F. J. Judicial administration and the legal profession;
a bibliography. Dobbs Ferry, N.Y., Oceana, 1963. 650 p.
          Includes 6654 annotated items giving books,
          articles and other items. Covers areas of judicial
          administration and the legal profession.   4801

KLEIN, F. J. Juries of less than twelve, an annotated bibliography. IJA Rep 4:3-4 (Jan. 1972).
          About 26 items of case, opinion, and legislation
          references regarding use of less than 12 member
          juries; 1956-71.   4802

KLEIN, F. J. The jury system in the federal courts; a bibliography. FRD 26:525-44 (1961).
          Covers methods of selection for the venire and
          for the panel; treatment of jurors; jurors hand-
          books; cost; the grand jury; and jury fees and
          juror compensation.   4803

KLEIN, F. J. Selected bibliography on Keeton-O'Connell basic
protection plan. In her Judicial administration, Ann Surv Am L
1967:667-8.
          Divided into: For the plan; For and against the
          plan; comparative laws in foreign juris-
          dictions.   4804

LOS ANGELES County Law Library. Jury selection: voir dire; a
selected bibliography. Los Angeles, 1970. 7 p.
          References are to articles and sections of
          books.   4805

LOS ANGELES County Law Library. Legal malpractice, a bibliography with California annotations, comp. by W. T. Ford. Apr. 1974.
Los Angeles, 1974. 12 p.
            Includes California practice materials and general
            books, ALR 2d and 3d annotations, and law review
            articles on lawyers' malpractice.   <u>4806</u>

LOS ANGELES County Law Library. Modern multi- and bilingual
legal dictionaries. 6th ed., 1968. Los Angeles, 1968. 9 p. <u>4807</u>

LOS ANGELES County Law Library. Scientific tests in the law;
selected bibliography. Los Angeles, 1963. 18 p.
            Divided by subject but not annotated; covers
            intoxication, paternity (blood tests), lie detector,
            truth serum, speed detection devices, and skid
            marks.   <u>4808</u>

MARU, O. Research on the legal profession; a review of work done.
Chicago, AB Found, 1972. 63 p.
            Historical studies, career development and patterns,
            regulating the profession, the organized bar, extra-
            professional activities, politics, among subjects
            covered. Bibliography: p. 51-63.   <u>4809</u>

MECKLENBURG Criminal Justice Pilot Project Annotated list of
publications, comp. by V. Rolett. Chapel Hill, Inst. of Gov't,
U of NC, 1973. 16 p.
            List of publications primarily on drug abuse,
            also covering aspects of crime and criminal justice
            problems, MCJPP progress reports, funding appli-
            cations for LEAA and various research instruments.
                                                         <u>4810</u>

MELTZER, M. F. The information imperative. N.Y., Am. Management
Assn, 1971. p. 194-203.
            Books, periodical articles, miscellaneous articles
            all dealing with systems technology. (Similar to
            item <u>4799</u>).   <u>4811</u>

MERSKY, R. M. Selected introductory materials on law and sociology.
Boulder, U of Colorado, Law Library, 1964. 3 p.   <u>4812</u>

MORELAND, C. C. Bibliography of reports published or adopted by
the Survey of the Legal Profession. L Lib J 63:249-56 (1970);
repr. Chicago, AB Found, 1970.   <u>4813</u>

MUELLER, G. O. W. Bibliography of local practice books on criminal
law and procedure. L Lib J 59:295-99 (1966).
            Listings for federal and many state jurisdictions
            were compiled on the basis of questionnaire
            responses from law librarians.   <u>4814</u>

NATIONAL Center for State Courts. Bibliography on grand juries.
Denver, 1974. 12 p.
> In three main sections: History and functions,
> Constitutional challenges, Alternatives; includes
> books, articles and statutes on state and federal
> applications, some British; items stem from earliest
> times to date.   4815

NATIONAL College of State Trial Judges. Bibliography, in its
Courts and the community, by D. R. Fretz. Reno, 1973. p. 147-54.
> Covers books and articles concerning public
> relations, relations between lawyers and judges,
> between courts, with court personnel, and judges'
> relations with law enforcement officers; also many
> other areas including fair trial, free press.   4816

NATIONAL College of the State Judiciary Court Studies Division.
Computers and courts; a selected and annotated bibliography.
Reno, 1972. 11 p.
> General discussions of computer capabilities,
> limitations, problems, as well as descriptions of
> applications such as jury management, calendaring,
> traffic summons processing, and accounting, in
> specific courts.   4817

NATIONAL College of the State Judiciary Court Studies Division.
Congestion and delay; a selected and annotated bibliography.
Reno, 1972. 7 p.
> General discussions, with analysis of problems and
> proposed solutions; some descriptions of remedies
> that have helped in specific courts.   4818

NATIONAL College of the State Judiciary Court Studies Division.
Court administration; a selected and annotated bibliography.
Reno, 1972. 12 p.
> From history and theory to selected problem areas,
> including articles by court administrators sharing
> their experiences on how they manage state or
> trial courts or solve certain problems.   4819

NATIONAL College of the State Judiciary Court Studies Division.
Operations research; a selected and annotated bibliography.
Reno, 1972. 10 p.
> Texts, discussions, and examples of theory and
> applications of operational research techniques
> such as game theory, queuing theory, decision
> theory, linear programming, and simulation, for
> problem solving and decision making in business
> and government.   4820

NATIONAL College of the State Judiciary Court Studies Division.
Organization development; a selected and annotated bibliography.
Reno, 1972. 11 p.
>Works on management theory and techniques generally;
not intended for, but of possible interest to,
court management.   4821

NATIONAL College of the State Judiciary Court Studies Division.
Systems analysis; a selected and annotated bibliography. Reno,
1972. 10 p.
>Books and articles on theory and applications of
analyzing, defining, and improving operations of
complex organizations and systems.   4822

NATIONAL Council of Juvenile Court Judges. Lawyers in juvenile
courts; a compilation of reference materials... Chicago, ABA,
1964. 105 p.
>A comprehensive bibliography with case annotations,
statutory excerpts, reading materials and survey
results on the status of legal representation in
selected juvenile courts.   4823

NATIONAL Council of Juvenile Court Judges. Reading materials
on judge-probation officer relations; a compilation of advance
readings, lecture materials and discussion summaries. Chicago,
ABA, 1963. 1 v., var. pag.
>Abstracts and quotations from articles; digests
of materials.   4824

NATIONAL Council on Crime and Delinquency. Selected reading list.
Hackensack, N.J., 1972. 30 p.
>NCDD books, standards, guides and model acts,
and other publications covering prevention,
criminology, juvenile delinquency, law enforcement
and the police, corrections, national directories
and published addresses.   4825

NEW YORK (State) Library. Legislative Reference Library. Bail
reform; a selective, annotated bibliography, comp. by R. Barth.
Albany, 1973. 24 p.
>Books, reports, articles, legislative hearings;
classified: Problems of bail system; Role of
bondsmen; Judicial role; Reform and preventive
detention; Experimental projects; Reform proposals
and legislation. 75 items.   4826

NEW YORK (State) Library. Legislative Reference Library. Campaign
financing; a selected annotated bibliography, comp. by M. Green
and M. Gehr. Albany, 1974. 35 p.   4827

NEW YORK (State) Library. Legislative Reference Library. Court
reform; a selected, annotated bibliography, comp. by G. Panton.

Albany, 1973.   55 p.
> Books, reports, hearings, legal periodical articles;
> classified: 1. General--2. Structure: federal,
> state, and local.--3. Administration: court managers,
> computers, other techniques.--4. Bibliographies.4828

NEW YORK (State) Library. Legislative Reference Library. Employment discrimination against ex-offenders; a selected annotated
bibliography, comp. by I. M. Hallowell. Albany, 1972. 25 p. 4829

NEW YORK (State) Library. Legislative Reference Library. Plea
bargaining; comp. by C. Campbell. Albany, 1973. 8 p.
> Annotated bibliography of 27 books, reports,
> articles from legal periodicals.   4830

NEW YORK (State) Library Legislative Research Service. Capital
punishment; philosophical and practical arguments; a selected,
annotated bibliography, comp. by C. Campbell. Albany, 1973. 9 p.
> Books, reports, articles (some foreign, all in
> English) giving pros, cons, statistics.   4831

NEW YORK (State) Library Legislative Research Service. Pretrial
intervention for adults: a selected annotated bibliography, by
I. M. Hallowell and M. Gehr. Albany, 1975. 34 p.

> Partially annotated bibliography of eighty items
> describing programs in operation which intervene
> to side-track the criminal justice offender from
> the criminal justice.   4832

NEW YORK (State) Library Legislative Research Service. The
rights of children and legal infants; a selected, annotated
bibliography, comp. by C. Campbell. Albany, 1973. 20 p.
> Covers infants' and students' rights   4833

NEW YORK (State) Library Legislative Research Service. Procedural aspects of juvenile justice; a selected, annotated
bibliography, comp. by G. Panton. Albany, 1973. 53 p.
> Texts, reports, articles; classified, including
> constitutional rights, statutory rights, detention,
> diversion, use of volunteers, proposed programs
> and legislation.   4834

NEW YORK (State) Library Legislative Reference Library. Selection
of judges; a bibliography. Albany, 1967. 15 p. (Convention
Series no. 4)
> ·· Annotated entries dealing with judicial selection
> in New York and in other states.   4835

_____. Judicial selection; an annotated selected bibliography,
Supp. to Selection of judges... comp. by I. M. Hallowell.
Albany, 1973. 14 p.   4835a

NEW YORK (State) Library Legislative Research Service. Sentencing; a selected, annotated bibliography, comp. by P. Massey and
I. M. Hallowell. Albany, 1974. 42 p.
> Books, reports, periodical literature; classified:
> general standards; probation and suspended sentence;
> appellate review of sentences; presentence reports;
> judicial education; model and proposed laws,
> standards, bibliographies. Some British and Euro-
> pean (in English). 135 items.   4836

NEW YORK University School of Law. Bibliography of materials on
legal education. N.Y., 1961-
> First ed. by F. C. Sullivan, 1961. 56 p.;
> 2d ed. by D. Y. Alspaugh, 1965. 107 p.; Supps.,
> 1966-69, by various authors; [3d] ed. D. Djonovich,
> called Legal education, a selective bibliography, 1970,
> 491 p., published as supp. to Ann Surv Am L, 1969/70,
> by Oceana (Dobbs Ferry, N.Y.); annual supps.
> thereafter in Ann Surv. Am L. .   4837

NO-FAULT, a bibliography. Suffolk U L Rev 6: 138-140 (1971).
> Arranged by leading articles, student comments,
> symposia.   4838

PENNSYLVANIA State Library. State constitutional revision;
a bibliography. Harrisburg, 1966. 10 p.   4839

[PRETRIAL] bibliography, appended to Fox, N. P., Settlement:
Helping the lawyers fulfill their responsibility. FRD 53:129, at
156-58.
> Covers mediation; settlement and pretrial,
> analysis, origin and methodology.   4840

RAND CORP. Privacy and security in databank systems; an annotated
bibliography, 1970-1973, prepared for the National Science
Foundation by M. K. Hunt and R. Turn. Santa Monica, 1974.
166 p. (R-1361-NSF)   4841

RANK, R. Criminal justice systems of the Latin-American nations:
a bibliography of the primary and secondary literature. So.
Hackensack, Rothman, 1974. 576 p.   4842

SAMAD, S. A. Bibliography on comparative legal education.
Foreign Exchange Bull 5:14 (Jul. 1963), 13-15 (Fall 1963). 4843

SCHUBERT, G. Bibliographical essay; behavioral research in
public law. Amer Pol Sci R 57:433-45 (1963).
> A narrative bibliographical account of research stu-
> dies in judicial behavior.   4844

SELECTED bibliography of the juvenile court. Hastings L J
19:263-65 (1967).
> 1) Criticism of--2) practice in--3) problems gener-
> ated--4) organization of juvenile courts.   4845

SILVERSTEIN, L. Representation of the indigent defendant and
related matters. Chicago, AB Found, 1963. 23 p. (Cromwell
Library. Bibliography ser 2)
> Covers: Field studies; books and pamphlets; legis-
> lative hearings, proposed statutes; articles and
> speeches, general; articles and speeches, by
> state.   4846

SMITH, C., ed. Ombudsman, citizen defender; a bibliography prepared for the Friends Committee on Legislation of California.
San Francisco, 1966. 10 p.   4847

SPECTOR, H. K. Juvenile delinquency, a bibliography. San
Quentin, Calif. State Prison, 1963. 109 p.
> Selected books, pamphlets, articles, proceedings,
> reports with notes and annotations; has analytical
> subject index   4848

TATE, A., Jr. and HEBERT, W. J. Treatises for judges; a selected
bibliography. Baton Rouge, L.S.U. Law School, Criminal Justice
Program, 1971. 55 p.
> Substantive and procedural subjects of interest
> to judges and lawyers, including criminal law and
> procedure, naming also periodicals and serials.
> Prepared for Appellate Judges Conference, ABA. 4849

TEXAS University School of Law Criminal Justice Reference Library
The adjudication and disposition phases in court handling of
juveniles; an annotated bibliography comp. by J. K. Maxwell and
B. Bridges. Austin 1972. 42 p.
> Includes material on court and corrections personnel
> functions as they relate to adjudication and
> disposition.   4850

TEXAS University School of Law Criminal Justice Reference
Library. Bibliography on juvenile delinquency in Texas ... pre-
pared for the Task Force on Juvenile Delinquency by Jane Olm.
Austin, 1970. 34 p.
> Eleven classifications: books and pamphlets;
> periodical articles; theses and dissertations;
> reports; statistics; statutes; cases; bibliographies;
> committee studies; handbooks and manuals; and
> other materials. Selectively annotated; location
> of most items is indicated.   4851

TEXAS University School of Law Criminal Justice Reference Library.
Criminal justice and related topics, a selected bibliography comp.
by J. G. Olm, J. K. Maxwell, Jr. and B. Alexander. Austin, 1971.
96 p.
> Covers all areas of the administration of criminal
> and juvenile justice, judicial administration
> generally, including judges. 4852

TEXAS University School of Law Criminal Justice Reference Library.
Organized crime; a selected bibliography, comp. by I. Hopkins,
J. K. Maxwell, and C. Mattson. Austin, 1973. 99 p. 4853

TEXAS University School of Law Criminal Justice Reference Library.
Police-public relations; a selected and annotated bibliography
comp. by J. Maxwell. Austin 1971. 34 p.
> Arranged by subtopic within the broad subject. 4854

TEXAS University School of Law Criminal Justice Reference Library.
Selected and annotated bibliography on regional correctional
facilities, comp. by J. G. Olm and J. Maxwell. Austin 1970.
10 p. 4855

TOMPKINS, D. C. Bail in the United States; a bibliography.
Berkeley, Univ of Calif, Inst. of Governmental Studies, 1964. 49 p.
> Entries cover history and theory of bail, the bail
> system as it operates in the states and the federal
> system; the role of the bondsman; use in traffic
> courts; in juvenile courts; covers bail jumping
> and no-bail programs. 4856

TOMPKINS, D. C. The confession issue from McNabb to Miranda; a
bibliography. Berkeley, U. of Calif, Inst of Governmental
Studies, 1968. 100 p.
> Writings respecting confession issue generally;
> specifically about McNabb v. U.S.; Mallory v U.S.,
> Escobedo v Ill., Miranda v Arizona and other
> decisions relating to confession. There is a
> separate section on materials relating to various
> aspects of confession. 4857

TOMPKINS, D. C. Court organization and administration, a
bibliography. Berkeley, U of Calif Inst of Governmental Studies,
1973. 200 p.
> Divided into Courts, Courts in the states, Federal
> courts, Appellate courts, Administration of courts.
> Includes lists of bibliographies, readings,
> conferences and meetings; sections subdivided by
> states. 4858

TOMPKINS, D. C. The offender; a bibliography. Berkeley, U of
Calif Inst of Governmental Studies, 1963. 268 p.
> Covers: types of offenders, factors involved in

Making offender, studies of the offender, including
predictive techniques. Partially annotated.   4859

TOMPKINS, D. C. The prison and the prisoner. Berkeley, U of Calif
Inst of Governmental Studies, 1972. 156 p.
    First in Public Policy Bibliographies Series,
    bibliography covers state and federal prisons
    and every aspect of their administration; types
    of prisoners- their impact; women prisoners,
    black offenders, proposals for reform.   4860

TOMPKINS, D. C. Probation since World War II; a bibliography.
Berkeley, U of Calif Inst of Governmental Studies, 1964. 311 p.
    Administration of probation systems; probation
    and various factors in the correction process,
    probation officers, probationers, statistics,
    associations and periodicals, bibliographies.   4861

TOMPKINS, D. C. Sentencing the offender; a bibliography.
Berkeley, U of Calif Inst of Governmental Studies, 1971. 102 p.
    Gives sentencing procedures, review of sentence,
    sentencing institutes for judges. Sentencing in
    state and federal courts; ABA and ALI Standards
    for Sentencing; Sentencing in other countries;
    list of cases; section on bibliographies.   4862

TOMPKINS, D. C. White collar crime; a bibliography. Berkeley,
U of Calif Inst of Governmental Studies, 1967. 85 p.
    Compiled for President's Commission on Law
    Enforcement and the Administration of Justice,
    the subjects include types of white collar crimes,
    illegal and sharp practices of legal profession
    and various business organizations; protection
    of the consumer.   4863

TOMPKINS, D. C. and BUSHER, W. H. Furlough from prison.
Berkeley, Inst of Governmental studies, Univ. of Calif, 1973.
68 p.
    Materials on work release collected by the
    American Justice Inst, augmented by Ms. Tompkins,
    including references to other types of leave or
    furlough from prison.   4864

TRANSPORTATION Center Library, Northwestern University. A
bibliography on police administration. Evanston, Traffic Inst.,
1968. 28 p.
    Covers police administration and personnel, traffic.
    Lists numerous bibliographies and periodicals
    dealing with police.   4865

U.S. CONGRESS Senate Committee on the Judiciary. Laws relating
to wiretapping and eavesdropping; submitted by the Subcommittee
on Administrative Practice and Procedure. Washington, USGPO,
1966. 63 p.
> Bibliographies p. 1-13; federal and state statutes
> p. 15-63.   4866

U. S. COURT of Military Appeals Law Library. Bibliography on
military justice and military law. Supp. II. Nov. 1, 1964.
[Washington, 1964] 24 p.   4867

U. S. DEPT. of Health, Education, and Welfare Children's Bureau.
Legal bibliography for juvenile and family courts, by W. H.
Sheridan and A. B. Freer. Washington, USGPO, 1966. 46 p.

_____. _____. Supp. 1, 1967. 34 p.

_____. _____. Supp. 2, 1969. 38 p.

U. S. Dept. of Health, Education, And Welfare. Office of Youth
Development. Legal bibliography for juvenile and family courts;
a supplement. Washington, USGPO, 1973. 18 p. [Supp 3]
> All are by Sheridan and Freer; all are classified,
> including case decisions, and articles in areas
> such as confessions, counsel, due process, parental
> liability, court administration, and many related
> topics, studies and reports.   4868

U. S. DEPT. of Health, Education, and Welfare Youth Development
and Delinquency Administration. Juvenile and family courts; a
legal bibliography. Washington, USGPO, 1973. 110 p.
> Reissue of Legal bibliography for juvenile and
> family courts, by W. H. Sheridan and A. B. Freer,
> published by Children's Bureau, 1966-1969. Includes
> supps through 1973. 110 p. [see item 4870].   4869

U. S. Law Enforcement Assistance Administration. Law enforcement
library book catalog, Apr. 17, 1972. Washington, 1972. 3 v.
> V. 1: Author index; v. 2: Subject index;
> v. 3: Title index   4870

U. S. LIBRARY of Congress. How can the administration of justice
be improved in the United States? Bibliography relating to the
high school debate topic 1971-72. Washington, USGPO, 1971. 122 p.
(92d Cong., 1st Sess., Sen. Doc. 10)   4871

U. S. NATIONAL Advisory Commission on Criminal Standards
and Goals. Courts. Washington, USGPO, 1973.
> Bibliography at p. 323-37: books, articles, cases
> on case screening, diversion, negotiated plea, the
> litigated case, sentencing, review of trial court
> proceedings, the judiciary, lower courts, court

administration, court-community relations, computers and the courts, prosecution, defense, juveniles, mass disorders.   4872

U. S. NATIONAL Criminal Justice Reference Service. Document
retrieval index, Sept 1973- Washington, U. S. Dept. of Justice,
LEAA, 1973- Semiannual, cumulative.
        Title-arranged list of books, reports, proceedings,
        similar materials in administration of criminal
        justice; gives source for each, very brief descrip-
        tion; subject index, but no author access.   4873

UNIVERSITY of Pennsylvania Biddle Law Library. Bibliography on
the appellate review of criminal sentences. In U. S. Congress
Senate Committee on the Judiciary. Appellate review of sentences;
hearings... Mar. 1-2, 1966. Washington, USGPO, 1966.
p. 146-49.   4874

VON PFEIL, H. P. Juvenile rights since 1967; an annotated,
indexed bibliography of selected articles and books. South
Hackensack, N.J., Rothman, 1974. 199 p.
        Arranged alphabetically and sometimes with state
        or country identification, this bibliography,
        briefly annotated, examines all aspects of juvenile
        rights, particularly as interpreted by the courts;
        consists of 1100 articles and 350 books.   4875

YALE Law Library. Bibliography: certiorari; selected writings,
comp. by S. C. Smith. Selected new acquisitions Pt. 2, 1-6
(Dec. 1970)
        Old and new books and periodical literature:
        includes courts and judicial administration.   4876

YALE Law Library. Bibliography: the contempt process; selected
writings, comp. by S. C. Smith. Selected new acquisitions, 40-46
(Mar. 1970).
        Covers all aspects of contempt, items go back to
        1924.   4877

YNGVESSON, B. and HENNESSEY, P. Small claims, complex disputes;
a review of the small claims literature. Law & Soc Rev 9:
219-74 (1975).
        Exhaustive discussion of articles, studies as
        follows (1) Early literature, 1906-50; (2) Empir-
        ical studies (from 1950 on), 14 of which are
        analyzed, with tables, as to court studied, data
        collection method, issues raised, types of
        plaintiffs and defendants, disposition of cases,
        use of attorney; (3) Problems in the small claims
        model; (4) Proposals for reform; (5) Conclusions.
        All works discussed are presented in bibliography
        at p. 271-74.   4877a

B. Selected Guidebooks and Handbooks

Arranged geographically under National, U.S.
and State, these selected references are to
directories, guidebooks, and handbooks prepared primarily for judges, court personnel,
and lawyers.

NATIONAL

AMERICAN Bar Association. Directory of state trial judges associations, 1974- Chicago, 1974-   <u>4878</u>

AMERICAN Bar Association. Preliminary bandbook on prepaid legal
services; papers and documents assembled by Special Committee on
Prepaid Legal Services. 1971. 290 p.
          Includes: general introduction to functions and
          history.--Checklist of basic considerations for
          developing a prepaid legal services ("open panel")
          program.--Comparative analysis of selected plans.--
          ABA Committee report on availability of legal
          services, and on eligibility for assistance and
          offer and waiver. ABA Standards for Defender System
          1960, 1964, 1966: sample eligibility questionnaires;
          Uniform Law Commissioners' Model Defense of
          Needy Persons Act.   <u>4879</u>

AMERICAN Bar Association and AMERICAN Correctional Association.
Legal responsibility and authority of correctional officers; a
handbook on courts, judicial decisions, and constitutional
requirements. Washington, 1974. 43 p.   <u>4880</u>

AMERICAN Bar Association Commission on Correctional Facilities
and Services. Directory of state and local bar association
correctional committees, compiled by Bar Association Program for
Correctional Reform. Washington, 1973. 46 p. (Coord Bill. 1, rev.
Mar. 1973).   <u>4881</u>

AMERICAN Bar Association Commission on Correctional Facilities and
Services. Sourcebook in pretrial criminal justice intervention
techniques and action programs. Washington, ABA National Pretrial
Intervention Service Center, 1974. 188 p.   <u>4882</u>

AMERICAN Bar Association Commission on Correctional Facilities and
Services. Survey and handbook on state standards and inspection
legislation for jails and juvenile detention facilities, by Statewide Jail Standards and Inspection Systems Project. Mar. 1973, 2d
ed. Washington, 1973. 60 p.   <u>4883</u>

AMERICAN Bar Association Section of Judicial Administration. Improvement of the administration of justice; a handbook. 5th ed.
Chicago, 1971. 175 p.
          Guide to court reform covering such areas as court
          structure, court administration, judicial conferences

and councils, judicial selection, conduct the jury
system, pretrial discovery, judicial education,
public relations, citizens committees. Each chapter
has a bibliograpny and the appendices include
reports of the Sections, ABA Model judicial articles,
and Act to provide for an Administrator of State
Courts.   4884

AMERICAN Bar Association Standing Committee on Judicial Selection,
Tenure, and Compensation. Handbook for members of judiciary
committees. Chicago, 1972. 12 p.   4885

AMERICAN Bar Association Standing Committee on Judicial Selection,
Tenure, and Compensation. Model by-laws for state and local bar
associations respecting appointment and election of judges, T.
Voorhees, Chair. Chicago, 1972. 15 p.   4886

AMERICAN Bar Association Standing Committee on Law and Technology.
Computers and the law; an introductory handbook ... R. P. Bigelow,
ed. 2d ed. New York, Commerce clearing house, 1969. 226 p.
          Has glossary and bibliography.   4887

AMERICAN Bar Foundation. Catalog of publications, 1960- 1st-
Chicago, 1961-   4888

AMERICAN Correctional Association. Guidelines for legal reference
service in correctional institutions; a tool for correctional
administrators. College Park, Md., Am Correctional Assn, 1973. 20 p.
          Recent federal court decisions make it obligatory
          for departments of correction to provide inmates
          with access of the courts, including legal counsel
          and law books. Recommendations are made; App. B in-
          cludes a state-by-state list of large law libraries
          that will give service to inmates: photocopying,
          inter-library loans, reference service, free or
          át small cost.   4889

AMERICAN Correctional Association. Juvenile and adult correctional institutions and agencies of the United States of America,
Canada, and Great Britain; Directory, 1973. College Park, Md.,
1973. 155 p.
          Based on questionnaire survey, U.S. and Canadian
          institutions listed by state or province, including
          addresses, telephone numbers, administrators, date
          started, limits as to capacity, type of inmate.
          Includes state and federal correctional agencies
          in addition to prisons, e.g.: Dept. of Justice,
          including LEAA regional offices, state parole and
          short-term institutions, military facilities. British
          section is discussion of prisons, borstals, deten-
          tion centers in England, Wales.   4890

AMERICAN Judicature Society. Judicial councils, conferences, and
organizations. Feb. 1968. Chicago, 1968. 13 p. (Rep 11).
    Lists, by state, judicial councils and conferences,
    and other state organizations studying the adminis-
    tration of justice.   4891

AMSTERDAM, A., SEGAL, B. & MILLER, M. Trial Manual for the
defense of criminal cases. Philadelphia, ALI-ABA Jt Cttee Cont
Legal Ed, 1967. 575 p.   4892
    (See also item 3750)

CAPE, W. H. A guide to federal grants and other types of assistance. 1966 rev. Lawrence, U of Kansas, Governmental Research
Center, 1966. 368 p.   4893

COURT Watching manuals. See items 4984, 4986, 4995, 5009, 5012,
5021.
    See also: Stecich, M. Keeping an eye on the courts:
    a survey of court observer programs. Judicature
    58:470-79 (1975).   4894

HANDBOOK for new juvenile court judges. Juvenile Court Judges J
23:1-31 (Winter 1972).   4895

HERMANN, M. G., and HAFT, M. G. Prisoners' rights sourcebook;
theory, litigation, practice. N.Y., Clark Boardman, 1973. 827 p.
    Comprehensive collection of articles by leading
    authorities active in prisoners' rights encompassing
    legal, historical, and sociological perspectives.
    Second section includes articles discussing sub-
    stantive and procedural aspects of litigating
    prisoners' suits with sample pleadings; includes
    also a comprehensive chapter summarizing new trends
    in prison and parole and alternatives to today's
    prisons. Sourcebook is aimed at lawyers, but it
    should be of interest to prisoners, concerned
    community groups, and prison administrators.   4896

INSTITUTE for Court Management. Court study process. Feb. 1975.
Denver, 1975. 330 p.
    Pt. 1: Guide to conducting court studies, consists
    of brief remarks on planning, selecting consultants,
    study techniques, computer use, etc. Pt. 2, Papers
    presented at the Conference on Court Studies (May
    1973): Friesen, E. C. Overview of the court study
    process.--Ebersole, J. L. Planning and organizing a
    court study.--Soloman, M. Conducting the court
    study.--Davey, J. F. Developing findings, con-
    clusions, recommendations in "change oriented" court
    studies.--Oberlin, B. L. Conducting a court study.--
    Gardner, N. Implementation: process of change.--
    Lawson, H. O. Commentary on the process of change.--
    Bohlin, E. Special features of studies involving

application of computer technology to court administration.--Short, E. H. Computers in the courts.--
Najelski, P. National standards and court studies.--
Corrigan, J. V. Court studies: the judicial perspective.--Rubin, T. Comparative court studies.   4897

INSTITUTE for Court Management. Courts and personnel systems; a
personnel administration handbook. Denver, 1973, 1 v., var. pag.
(For annotation see item 1874)   4898

INSTITUTE of Judicial Administration Juvenile Justice Standards
Project. Juvenile law litigation directory. N.Y., 1973. 1 v.,
unpaged.
     Agencies listed alphabetically by state, with addresses
     and administrators, dealing with all kinds of juvenile
     justice litigation. Courts are not included.   4899

INSTITUTE of Judicial Administration Juvenile Justice Standards
Project. Parallel table of model codes and recommendations concern-
ing juvenile and family justice systems, comp. by the staff of the
Juvenile Justice Standards Project for use by the Juvenile Justice
Standards Planning Committee. Nov. 1971. N.Y., 1971. 78 p. 4900

INTERNATIONAL Association of Chiefs of Police. Law enforcement
and criminal justice education directory, by R. W. Kobetz. Gaithers-
burg, Md., 1975. 766 p.
     Designed to provide assistance to students seeking
     information on colleges and universities offering
     law enforcement and criminal justice degree programs.
     Summaries of available programs listed by state
     giving degrees offered; useful also to counselors
     in planning for law enforcement careers; also to
     criminal justice personnel interested in academic
     training and advancement.   4901

KARLEN, D. Procedure before trial in a nutshell. St. Paul,
West, 1972. 258 p.
     Although compact volume summarizes in a down-to-earth
     and illustrative approach procedures preliminary to
     trial, covering pleadings (both plaintiff and defen-
     dant), challenges, summary judgment, amendments,
     discovery, pretrial conference and finally all
     elements of a law suit. Federal Rules of Civil Pro-
     cedure and code hearings of many states are illus-
     trated.   4902

LEONARD, R. F. Prosecutor's manual on screening and diversionary
programs. Chicago, Nat. Dist Attorneys Assn, 1972. 291 p.
     (For annotation, see item 4268)   4903

MCCREA. T. L. and GOTTFREDSON, D. M. Guide to improved handling
of misdemeanant offenders. Washington, USGPO, 1974. 122 p.
(National Inst. of Law Enforcement and Criminal Justice prescriptive package).

Handbook, based on research and experience drawn
from programs across the country, shows problem
areas and offers concrete suggestions for improving
misdemeanant correctional and lower court practices.
Topics examined include: court delay; pre-trial
detention; use of pre-sentencing reports, special
misdemeanant programs, alternatives to committal;
post-institutional period; and establishing reporting and evaluation mechanisms for the misdemeanant justice system. Appendices: review of
literature; descriptive reports on 11 existing
projects; and listing of other programs.   4904

MCDONOUGH, J. N., KING, D. B., and GARRETT, J. E. Juvenile court
handbook. South Hackensack, N. J., Rothman, 1970. 104 p.   4905

MANUAL on jail administration, a handbook designed to ease the
difficult task of the jail administrator. Washington, Nat
Sheriffs' Assn, 1970. 223 p.   4906

MURDY, R. G. Crime commission handbook. Baltimore, Criminal
Justice Cmssn, 1965. 119 p.
History of citizen crime fighter groups in the
United States, particularly such groups in New York
City and Baltimore. Proposals for federal crime
commissions are considered; Articles on conducting
state-wide surveys of criminal justice and on
forming a citizen crime commissions are presented;
appendices include Report of ABA Special Committee
on Commissions on Administration of Criminal
Justice and the by-laws of the Chicago Crime Commission.   4907

NATIONAL Association of Counties Research Foundation. Regional
criminal justice planning: a manual for local officials, by M. D.
Powell [and others] Part I: Regional Criminal Justice Planning
and Local Officials. Washington, USGPO, 1971. 1 v. unpaged.
Reviews structure of the criminal justice system,
discusses the Omnibus Crime Control and Safe Streets
Act of 1968 and its application to local government,
examines the need for regional planning and the
responsibilities and role of the local elected
officials in the system. Graphs; tables list state
courts and agencies.   4908

NATIONAL Center for State Courts. Court improvement programs:
a guidebook for planners. [Washington, 1972] 295 p.
How to set up project, including estimated costs,
personnel, whom to contact, methodology.Demonstration
projects concern: court administrators; systems and
technology; education and training; personnel; bail,
pretrial release, and diversion; community probation
services; volunteer programs; facilities, architecture,
and space utilization; appellate courts.   4909

NATIONAL Center for State Courts. Evaluation guidebook to
computer-aided transcription, by J. M. Greenwood and J. R. Toller,
Denver, 1975. 60 p.
> To assist courts in comparing computer-aided trans-
> cription with traditional stenotype methods, the
> Center has outlined 1) basic steps involved in
> computer-aided transcription process; 2) types of
> vendor services available; 3) evaluation of guidelines
> to be used to evaluate computer-aided transcription
> compared to traditional methods; 4) general guide-
> lines in selecting an approach to computer-aided
> transcription. Does not deal specifically with
> court use. (This advisory service may be obtained
> from Center).   4909a

NATIONAL Center for State Courts. Federal funding assistance for
state courts, by John C. Ruhnka [and others]. Denver, 1973.
1 v., var. pag.
> Lists funds available to the judiciary through
> Crime Control Act of 1973 (LEAA), Highway Safety Act
> of 1973; gives reports of judges on experience with
> LEAA funding, discusses pending legislation and pro-
> posals   4910

NATIONAL Center for State Courts. Guidebook of projects for
prosecution and defense planning, prepared by National College
of District Attorneys, National Association of Attorneys General,
National Legal Aid and Defender Association [and] Federal Defenders
of San Diego, Inc. [Washington, 1972] 201 p.
> Sample projects, studies and demonstrations.   4911

NATIONAL Center for State Courts. Guidelines for development of
computer training curricula for court personnel, by M. M.
Solomon. Denver, 1974. 136 p.
> (For annotation see item 2160)   4912

NATIONAL Center for State Courts. Implementation of Argersinger v.
Hamlin: a prescriptive program package. 1974. Denver, 1974. 78 p.
> (For annotation, see item 3873)   4913

NATIONAL College of State Trial Judges. Judicial seminar handbook. 2d ed., Jul. 1969, prepared for the exclusive use of the
National College of State Trial Judges. Reno, 1969. 43 p. 4914

NATIONAL College of the State Judiciary. Trial judges guide: objections to evidence, by E. G. Brownlee. Reno, 1974. 176 p.
> Geared specifically for magistrates, guidebook gives
> instructions helpful to all judges required to make
> evidentiary rulings; offers summary of law of
> evidence; discusses basic principles. Part 2 is a
> detailed study of evidence at a trial (based
> on Montana law, but generally applicable in other
> states).   4915

NATIONAL Conference of State Criminal Justice Planning Administrators. State of the states on crime and justice: an analysis
of state administration of the Safe Streets Act. Frankfort, Ky.
1973. 68 p.
>An examination of the 55 State Planning Agencies,
mandated by Congress in 1968, which are charged with
the responsibility of administering the national
crime reduction program. The report identifies
and explains by example and with tables, the general
strategies of the agencies, presents national
data on funding patterns, traces their capabilities,
provides a perspective on controversy, regarding
the Safe Streets Act, and suggests future action
and changes. Statistical data cover various funding
and expenditures. Appendix 6 is Minimum Standards
for State Planning Agencies, rev Feb., 1973.   4916

NATIONAL Conference of State Trial Judges. Bench book guide;
topical outline with citations and suggestions for writing and
financing state bench books ... Chicago, 1974. 21 p.   4917

NATIONAL Conference of State Trial Judges. State trial judge's
book. 2d ed. St. Paul, West, 1969. 407 p.
>(For annotation see item 2500)   4918

NATIONAL Council on Crime and Delinquency Advisory Council of
Judges. Guides for juvenile court judges on news media relations.
N.Y., 1965. 16 p.   4919

NATIONAL Council on Crime and Delinquency [Advisory] Council of
Judges. Guides to the judge in sentencing in racketeering cases.
Crime and Delin. 14:99-106 (1968); reprint by NCCD, N.Y., 1968. 16 p.
>To sentence effectively, a judge must have knowledge
about organized crime in his area, determine through
the presentence investigation whether the defendant
is involved in it, and be aware of the types of
dispositions most effective in dealing with members
of organized crime. Bibliography.   4920

NATIONAL Council on Crime and Delinquency Advisory Council of
Judges. Procedure and evidence in the juvenile court; a guidebook for judges. N.Y., 1962. 96 p.   4921

NATIONAL Council on Crime and Delinquency Advisory Council on
Parole. Guide for parole selection. N.Y., 1963. 96 p.   4922

NATIONAL Council of Juvenile Court Judges. Juvenile court judges
directory and manual. Chicago, 1963. 1 v. loose leaf.
>Kept up to date by added pages: 1970, 71, 1973-
74.   4923

NATIONAL directory of law enforcement administrators and correctional institutions, 1974. Milwaukee, Nat Police Chiefs and
Sheriffs Info Bur., 1974. 190 p.
    Directory lists, by county, sheriff and prosecution
    attorneys for each state, and chiefs of police by
    municipality, also several state agencies related
    to law enforcement with their directors, and
    federal law enforcement agencies and regional
    offices.   4924

NATIONAL District Attorneys Association. Managing case files
in the prosecutor's office. Chicago, 1973. 75 p.
    (For annotation see item 3730).   4925

NATIONAL District Attorneys Association. The prosecutor's deskbook,
ed by P. F. Healy and J. P. Manak. Chicago, 1971. 693 p.
    (For annotation see item 3731).   4926

NATIONAL Institute of Mental Health Center for Studies of Crime
and Delinquency. Crime and delinquency research in selected
European countries. Washington, USGPO, 1971. 21 p.   4927

NATIONAL Legal Aid and Defender Association. Directory of legal
aid and defender services, 1957- Chicago. annual.
    Called National Legal Aid Assn. before 1958. Dir-
    ectory issued by ABA in pamphlet along with its
    Directory of lawyer referral services ... ; also
    in Martindale-Hubbell Law Directory, (v. 6 p. 15B-
    44B, 1975 ed.)   4928

NATIONAL Legal Aid and Defenders Association. Handbook of standards for legal aid and defender offices. Chicago, 1965. 26 p.
    Includes standards for a defender system, sug-
    gestions for operating a defender service and a
    legal aid service together, instructions for
    setting up a public defender office.   4929

NATIONAL Legal Aid and Defenders Association. How to organize
a defender office: a handbook, 2d ed. Chicago, NLADA, 1967. 80 p.
    Scope of service, assessment of local needs, choice
    of system; administration, funding, staff. Appendices
    include abstract of four state statutes, Defender
    Association of Philadelphia charter and bylaws, N.Y.
    Legal Aid Society rules and regulations. Bib-
    liography, pp. 77-80.   4930

PIVEN, H. and ALCABES, A. Education and training for criminal
justice; directory of programs in universities and agencies
(1965-67). Washington, U.S. Dept. of Health, Education, and
Welfare, 1968. 126 p.
    Appendices present sources from which data was
    drawn for the directory.   4931

SINK, J. M. Political criminal trials, how to defend them. New
York, Clark Boardman, 1974. 693 p.
>Handbook for lawyers about to defend a political
criminal case for the first or second time, but
with some prior criminal experience. It spans from
preliminary advice on being retained and the necessary first steps through the final argument at the
close of the trial. Sample forms and sample jury
instructions, some from actual cases, are in-
cluded.   4932

UNITED Nations Social Defence Research Unit. A world directory
of criminological institutes, prep. by B. Kasme. Rome, 1974.
152 p.
>Directory, based on a questionnaire circulated
in 1972, lists institutes and agencies by coun-
try.   4933

U. S. LAW Enforcement Assistance Administration. Financial guide
for administration of planning and action grants, Title I, Omnibus
Crime Control and Safe Streets Act of 1968. Washington, D.C., 1970.
looseleaf, 1 v. Supplemented as needed.   4934

U. S. LAW Enforcement Assistance Administration. 1972 directory
of automated criminal justice information systems. Washington,
USGPO, 1972. 1 v., var. pag.
>(For annotation see item 2194).   4935

U. S. LAW Enforcement Assistance Administration Audio Visual Communications Div. Criminal justice audio visual materials directory.
Washington, 1974. 30 p.
>Films, film strips, slides, transparencies, video
tapes are classified as follows: prevention; police
techniques and training; courts; prisons, including
rehabilitation and corrections; public education.
Annotated, with rental and purchase information.
To be updated.   4936

U. S. NATIONAL Bureau of Standards. Directory of law enforcement
and criminal justice associations and research centers, by B. J.
Latka, Law Enforcement Standards Laboratory, National Bureau of
Standards. Washington, USGPO, 1973. 49 p. (N.B.S. Tech Note 752)
>Includes national, non-profit professional or vol-
unteer social action assns. and research centers,
in the U.S. or with substantial U.S. membership or
interest. Includes principal officer, membership,
aims and activities, publications, meetings.   4937

U. S. NATIONAL Institute of Law Enforcement and Criminal Justice.
Grant guide, March 12, 1970. Washington, Law Enforcement Assistance
Administration, 1970. 20 p.
>Provides rules for administering grants, includes other
administrative requirements.   4938

U. S. NATIONAL Institute of Law Enforcement and Criminal Justice.
Prosecution in the juvenile courts: guidelines for the future,
by M. M. Finkelstein [and others] Washington, USGPO,1974
109 p.   4938a

U. S. NATIONAL Instutite of Law Enforcement and Criminal Justice
Statistics Div. Criminal justice agencies in ... [individual
states] Washington, USGPO, 1972. 51 v. (Reps. no. SD-D-2 through
SD-D-52)
            Separate directory for each state, and the District
            of Columbia, (e.g. Criminal justice agencies in
            Alabama, 1971), lists official name and address of
            all courts, law enforcement agencies, correctional
            institutions, probation & parole, prosecutors, for
            states, counties, and municipalities of 1,000 pop.
            or over. Names offices, not people. 1974 supps
            issued by region rather than by states.   4939

U.S. NATIONAL Institute of Law Enforcement and Criminal Justice.
Statistics Div. Criminal justice agencies in the United States,
1970 (a statistical summary compiled from the 1970 National Criminal Justice Directory Survey). Washington, USGPO. 14 p.
(Rep. no. SD-D-1)   4940
            Totals nationwide, and for each state, numbers
            of following agencies: courts, law enforcement
            agencies, correctional institutions, probation &
            parole agencies, prosecutors, public defenders, all
            other criminal justice agencies.   4940

U. S. OFFICE of Economic Opportunity. Guidelines for legal
services programs. Washington, 1967. 14 p.
            (For annotation see item 3949)   4941

UNITED STATES lawyers reference directory. 1971-   Los Angeles,
Legal directories pub. co., 1971-   annual.
            Names most state, all federal judges; state legislators,
            some executives; county attorneys, sheriffs. 4942

                        UNITED STATES

FEDERAL Judicial Center. Benchbook for United States district
judges, prepared under the auspices of the Federal Judicial Center, after compilation by the staff of the Institute of Judicial
Administration under the supervision of a committee of United
States district judges. Washington, 1969. 1 v. looseleaf. 4943

FEDERAL Judicial Center. Guidelines for pre-recording testimony
on videotape prior to trial; a manual prepared by the Federal
Judicial Center. Nov. 1974. Washington, 1974. 60 p.
            Illustrated, with 2-p. bibliograpny. To be frequently
            revised.   4944

FEDERAL Judicial Center. Manual for complex litigation (with amendments to 1/1/73) prepared by the Board of Editors of the Federal Judicial Center, including Rules of Procedure of the Judicial Panel on Multidistrict Litigation. N.Y., Clark Boardman, 1973. 1 v., looseleaf.   4945

JUDICIAL Conference of the 7th Circuit.. Committee on Jury Instructions. Manual on jury instructions in federal criminal cases. W. J. La Buy, chair. FRD 36:457-679 (1965).   4946

JUDICIAL Conference of the United States. Handbook for effective pretrial procedure; a statement on pretrial procedure in the U. S. District Courts; adopted Sept. 1964. FRD 37:255-315 (1965).
          Statement discusses pretrial preparation, an effective pretrial conference, and the pretrial order. Appendices include relevant rules from the Southern District of New York, suggested local rules, and sample orders and notices.   4947

NORTH American Indian Court Judges Association. Criminal court procedures manual, a guide for American Indian court judges [by] S. Kalin. Washington, Arrow, Inc., for Nat. Amer. Indian Court Judges Assn., 1971. 90 p.

_____. Supplement: Research document in support of the criminal court procedure manual. Washington, 1971, 176 p.   4948

SOKOL, R. P. A handbook of federal habeas corpus. Charlottesville, Va., Michie, 1965. 277 p.
          Ready reference work for lawyers and judges, emphasizing practice rather than conceptual problems, with selective rather than exhaustive case authority. Broad classifications: General principles concerning availability of the writ; Limitations on the availability; Problems peculiar to the indigent. Forms, bibliograpny.   4949

U.S. ADMINISTRATIVE Office of the United States Courts. Guide to the administrative organization of the U.S. courts. Rev. ed. Washington, 1966. 1 v., looseleaf.
          Handbook for federal judges detailing administrative information on budget, communications, furniture, life insurance, law books, payroll staff, space, stationery, supplies and travel; sets forth statutory authorities.   4950

U. S. ADMINISTRATIVE Office of the United States Courts. Manual for the use of clerks of the U.S. District Courts. Washington, 1966. 1 v., looseleaf.   4951

U. S. ADMINISTRATIVE Office of the Courts. Div. of Probation. The presentence investigation report. Washington, 1965. 39 p. (Pub no. 103)

Developed to assist the Office in its administration
of the Federal Probation System, this monograph
serves as a guideline to probation officers in preparing presentence reports; should promote greater
uniformity in report writing to assist courts in
understanding the problems, needs, and concerns of
individual defendants; includes presentence report
outline and format.   4952

U. S. COURT of Appeals, Fifth Circuit. Manual. New Orleans,
1969. 3 v.
          V. 1: Court manual; standard operating procedures.--
          V. 2: Clerk's operations, functions, and procedures.--
          V. 3: Clerk's operations, functions, and procedures;
          forms, reports, etc.   4953

U. S. DEPT. of Health, Education and Welfare Office of Juvenile
Delinquency and Youth Development. Volunteer programs in court.
Washington, USGPO, 1969. 268.
          Manual presenting collected papers detailing major
          programs in utilizing local volunteers in the
          operation of probation programs; includes a
          description of court volunteer movement calling
          on local unpaid workers to supplement and amplify
          probation services for juveniles and young adult
          misdemeanants.   4954

U. S. DEPT. of Justice. Handbook on the law of search and seizure,
prep. by the Legislation and Special Projects Section, Criminal
Division. Rev. ed. Washington, USGPO, 1968. 80 p.   4955

U. S. DEPT. of Justice. A practical handbook of federal grand
jury procedure, prep. for use of attorneys in the criminal
division. Nov. 1968. Washington, 1968. 61 p.   4956

U. S. OFFICE of Economic Opportunity Community Action Program.
How to apply for a legal service program. Washington, 1966. 97 p.
          Manual gives ideas for programs from those already
          submitted, e.g. mobile, neighborhood, or prison
          offices; community education programs. Step-by-step
          instructions take applicant through preparing and
          submitting own program.   4957

                              ALASKA

ALASKA Administrative Office of the Courts. Alaska court system;
manual of electronic recording. Anchorage, 1972. 128 p.   4958

ALASKA Administrative Director of Courts. Alaska court system: manual of transcript procedures. Anchorage, 1971. 105 p.
          (For annotation see item 2206).   4959

ARIZONA

PIMA County Juvenile Court Center. New model of juvenile justice
system. Tucson, 1972. 69 p.
(For annotation see item 396).   4960

STATE Bar of Arizona. Arizona courtroom handbook by R. W.
Kaufman. Jul. 1967. Phoenix, Weekly Gazette, 1967. 1v.,
looseleaf.   4961

ARKANSAS

ARKANSAS Judicial Dept. Arkansas local court judges' manual;
for use by municipal courts, justice of the peace courts, city
courts (formerly mayors' courts) police courts; by S. Weems
and F. R. Rogers. Little Rock, 1971. 114 p.   4962

ARKANSAS. Supreme Court. Manual of rules and committees. Little
Rock, Judicial Dept., 1973. 52 p.   4963

PASVOGEL, G. E. and MURPHY, A. G., Jr. Juvenile court procedures
manual. Little Rock, Pulaski Co. Juvenile Court, 1973.
158 p.   4964

CALIFORNIA

ARNOLD, K. J. California courts and judges handbook. San
Francisco California law book co., 1968. 680 p.   4965

CALIFORNIA. Bureau of Criminal Identification and Investigation.
Modus operandi and crime reporting; manual for use in preparing
crime reports ... by staff of the Social Services Section; A. L.
Coffey, chief. Sacramento, 1964. 33 p.   4966

CALIFORNIA Controller's Dept. Manual of accounting for municipal
courts and justice courts of the state ... rev. ed. Sacramento,
1967. 1 v., looseleaf.   4967

CALIFORNIA justice court manual. San Francisco, Judicial Council,
1969. 1 v., looseleaf. Supps., 1971-
              Desk book covers justice's selection and tenure;
              facilities; records, accounts, and reports; juris-
              diction and venue; civil and criminal procedure,
              including appeals; small claims, traffic offenses and
              infractions; sentencing and probation; and evidence.
              Forms, table of cases, index.   4968

CONFERENCE of California Judges. California judicial retirement
handbook, by W. H. Levit and G. O. Farley. San Francisco, 1970.
1 v., looseleaf.
              (For annotation see item 1584).   4969

FRICKE, C. W., and KOLBRECK, L. M. California peace officers
manual by C. W. Fricke, rev. by M. Kolbreck. 11th ed. Los
Angeles, Legal book store, 1964. 219 p.   4970

GOCKE, B. W., and PAYTON, G. T. Police sergeant's manual. Los
Angeles, Legal book store, 1972. 366 p.   4971

HANDBOOK for expansion of pretrial release in the San Francisco
Bay Area, prepared by the Crime Prevention (adult) and Treatment
Steering Committee for the Regional Criminal Justice Advisory
Board. Berkely, Criminal Justice Planning Office, Association of
Bay Area Governments, 1971. 85 p.   4972

LOS ANGELES Daily Journal. Public relations manual for bench
and bar of California. Los Angeles, 1964. 96 p.   4973

LOS ANGELES (Co.) Dept. of County Clerk. Manual for Superior Court
clerks. 5th rev. ed. Los Angeles, 1969. 2 v., looseleaf.   4974

LOS ANGELES (Co.) Superior Court. Court reporters manual. Los
Angeles, 1975. 3 v., looseleaf.   4975

MCCOY, P. California civil discovery: the deposition officer; a
manual for the guidance of notaries public, certified shorthand
reporters, and attorneys in the taking and completion of depositions under the law of California. Los Angeles, Metropolitan
News, 1966. 27 p.   4976

WENCKE, R. A. Benchbooks and manuals of procedure: practical
guides for bench and bar. Neb L Rev 53:521-39 (1974).
                Writing specifically of the Los Angeles Superior
                Court publications, Judge first describes the
                differences between benchbooks for judges and
                manuals for lawyers - regarding procedures in the
                Court, to supplement statutes and rules. He describes
                Los Angeles Superior Court specific manuals and
                benchbooks and the benefits gained therefrom.
                Exhibits and appendices illustrate some practice
                guides; criminal benchbook included.   4977

YAGER, T. C. Guide book for effective judicial administration.
Los Angeles, author, 1968. 80 p.   4978

                            COLORADO

COLORADO. Judicial Dept. Judicial Administrator. Statistical
reporting instructions for all district courts and Denver Juvenile
[and] Superior Courts. Oct. 26, 1973. Denver, 1973. 1 v.,
var. pagings.   4979

COLORADO Office of the State Court Administrator. Municipal court manual; an operational guide for municipal judges and clerical personnel. Denver, 1970. 1 v., looseleaf.   4980

COLORADO Municipal League. Municipal court guide. Boulder, 1968. 1 v., var. pagings.   4981

DELAWARE

DELAWARE. Superior Court. Handbook for grand jurors serving in the Superior Court of Delaware. Rev. 1966. Wilmington, 1966. 28 p.
    Bound with Handbook for petit jurors.   4982

DISTRICT OF COLUMBIA

PRELIMINARY hearing in the District of Columbia; a manual for the defense attorney, by the E. Barrett Prettyman Fellows, 1965/66 of the Georgetown University Law Center Legal Internship Program. Washington, Lerner Law Book Co., 1967. 253 p.   4983

FLORIDA

COURT observer program. Dade County School Board, Div. of Elementary and Secondary Education. [Miami] 1974. 47 p.   4984

ILLINOIS

ADAMS, T. F. Training officers' handbook [police] Springfield, Ill., Thomas, 1964. 173 p.   4985

HOW to watch a court, by M. N. Borish and B. Fenoglio. Chicago, League of Women Voters of Illinois, Illinois Court Watching Project, 1974. 57 p.   4986

ILLINOIS. Administrative Office of the Courts. Manual on record-keeping. Springfield, 1972. 1 v., looseleaf.
            Result of extensive study, drafting, experimentation
            and redrafting by clerks, judges, lawyers to replace
            102 different, often archaic, county systems with one
            modern statewide system. Rules cover case records,
            financial records, statistical records, disposal,
            include forms, index. Further revision as needed
            planned.   4987

INDIANA

WURSTER, R. Court reporters manual. Indianapolis, Center for Judicial Education, 1973. 135 p.   4988

IOWA

IOWA Fifth Judicial Circuit Dept. of Court Services. A handbook
on community corrections in Des Moines, a coordinated approach to
the handling of adult offenders. Washington, USGPO, 1973. 145 p.
> A manual describing the coordinated programs of the
> Fifth Judicial District Department of Court Services;
> included are procedures governing pre-trial release,
> the department's approach to treatment, pre-trial
> supervision, probation, the Ft. Des Moines Men's
> Residential Facility, relations with law enforcement
> agencies and a summary of evaluation findings; ap-
> pendices are charts, forms and other materials used
> in the various programs of the Department of Court
> Services.   4989

MANUAL for Clerks, Iowa District Court. Des Moines, Office of
the Court Administrator, 1973. 1 v., looseleaf.   4990

KANSAS

KANSAS Municipal Court manual for handling traffic and municipal
ordinance violations, by the Judicial Council Advisory Committee
for a Municipal Court Manual. J. D. Waugh, chair. Topeka, 1974.
1 v., looseleaf.   4991

MAINE

ISAACSON, I. Manual for the arresting officer. 4th ed. Lewiston,
Me., Legal pubs. 1965 163 p.   4992

MICHIGAN

MANUAL for court reporters/recorders in the state of Michigan,
prep. at the direction of the Michigan Supreme Court. Detroit,
Center for the Administration of Justice, Wayne State U. Law
School, 1974. 64 p.
> Instructions, with examples, on preparing transcripts
> stenographically or electronically. Appended: Mich.
> uniform citations.   4993

MICHIGAN police law manual. 3d ed., rev. 1966. East Lansing,
Mich. Assn. of Chiefs of Police, 1966. 512 p.   4994

MISSOURI

COURT watcher's guide. St. Louis, Women's Crusade against Crime,
n. d. 16 p.   4995

NEW HAMPSHIRE

MANUAL of procedure for justices and clerks of district and
municipal courts, by R. Laraba. Concord, N.H., Administrative
Committee of the District and Municipal Courts, 1972. 169 p.
Presents the history and jurisdiction of New Hampshire district and municipal courts; details arraignments, practices and procedures in criminal and
civil cases, duties of the clerk, uniform criminal,
civil and juvenile forms, and the new criminal
code. 4996

NEW JERSEY

NEW JERSEY Administrative Office of the Courts. Administrative
regulations governing reporters in the New Jersey courts, April
10, 1972. Trenton, 1972. 64 p.
Description of rules and regulations on the reporters'
oath, duties generally and in specific types of
proceedings, supervision of reporters, transcripts,
salaries, retirement, sick leave and vacation. 4997

NEW JERSEY Administrative Office of the Courts. Manual for judges
hearing juvenile narcotic and drug abuse cases, by T. J. Savage.
Trenton, 1972. 61 p. 4998

NEW JERSEY Administrative Office of the Courts. Manual for
municipal court judges hearing narcotic and drug abuse cases, by
T. J. Savage. Trenton, 1972. 96 p. 4999

NEW JERSEY Administrative Office of the Courts. Manual on
presentence investigation and report. Trenton, 1965. 15 p. 5000

NEW JERSEY Administrative Office of the Courts. Manual on sound
recording in the New Jersey courts. Trenton, 1971. 57 p.
Manual to guide and instruct personnel of courts in
which electronic sound recording equipment is used.
Includes regulations for all courts on operation of
equipment and transcription and specified rules for
inferior courts such as juvenile courts. Includes
sample logs and continuation sheets. 5001

NEW JERSEY Administrative Office of the Courts. Manual on supervision of probationers. Trenton, 1965. 8 p.
Guide for probation officers, attitude to the job,
standards for parole revocation, counselling,
keeping informed about the activities of the
parolee. 5002

NEW JERSEY Administrative Office of the Courts. Manual on the
selection of grand and petit jurors. Trenton, 1973. 28 p. 5003

NEW JERSEY Administrative Office of the Courts. New Jersey
municipal court manual. Trenton, 1972. 123 p.
> Gives organization, jurisdiction and all procedural
> steps for cases in the Municipal courts of New
> Jersey.   5004

NEW JERSEY Administrative Office of the Courts. Regulations
pertaining to sound recording in the courts of New Jersey.
1969. 52 p.   5005

NEW JERSEY Administrative Office of the Courts. Sentencing
manual for judges. Trenton, 1971. 117 p.
> (For annotation see item 4401).   5006

NEW JERSEY Administrative Office of the Courts. Sentencing manual
for judges in narcotic and drug abuse cases, by Theodore J.
Savage. Trenton, 1972. 70 p.
> Primarily a listing of all available public and
> private drug programs in New Jersey current as of
> February 1, 1972, this booklet also discusses pro-
> visions of the law of narcotic and drug abuse in
> New Jersey.   5007

NEW JERSEY Administrative Office of the Courts. Summary of
administrative directives. April, 1965. Trenton, 1965. 1 v.,
various paging.
> Handbook for judges directing their attention to
> each specific rule and regulation governing
> their trial and other duties; travel regulations
> included.   5008

NEW YORK

DISTRICT Court action kit for court observers, by P. Rosenthal.
White Plains, N.Y., Westchester League of Women Voters of Westchester, 1971. 8 p.
> [151 Post Road, White Plains, 10601]   5009

ECONOMIC Development Council of New York City, Inc. Supreme Court,
Civil Branch, New York County; procedures manual by the EDC Supreme
Court Task Force. Jun. 1, 1973. N.Y., 1973. 1 v., var.
pagings.   5010

ECONOMIC Development Council of New York City, Inc. Supreme Court,
New York County: procedures manual for criminal term parts and
clerk's office [by] EDC Supreme Court Task Force. March 1973.
[New York, 1973] 1 v., var. paging.
> Richard F. Coyne, Chairman, Supreme Court Task
> Force.   5011

FUND for Modern Courts. Court monitor's handbook. N.Y., 1975.
27 p.   5012

GOODCHILD, L. C. Planning grant report ... for establishment of
an Office of Administrative Case Control in the Criminal Court of
the City of New York. Feb. 1, 1970. N.Y., New York City Criminal
Court, 1970. 1 v., var. pag.   5013

JUROR'S manual for New York City. N.Y., Departmental Committees
for Court Administration, 1973. 10 p.   5014

MILES, N. Manual for use of the small claims arbitrators of
the Civil Court of the City of New York; prep. under the sponsorship
of the Assn. of Small Claims Arbitrators of N.Y.C., by N. Miles,
chair., Bd. of Editors Committee. N.Y., 1972. 51 p.   5015

NEW YORK (City) Civil Court. Small claims part manual, by E. Thompson. N.Y., 1973. 19 p.
           Written for public, to acquaint potential litigants
           with procedures, purpose, history of court.   5016

NEW YORK (City) Transportation Administration, Parking Violations
Bureau. Manual for adjudication, ed. by A. H. Atlas and M. J.
Levine. N.Y., 1973. 1 v. looseleaf
           Based on 3 years experience with civil administrative
           processing of parking violations, handbook for the
           hearing examiners (lawyers on per diem) before whom
           defendants may plead not guilty in informal pro-
           ceedings: outlines history and intent of Bureau as well
           as suggestions for questioning, evaluation of evidence
           (less strict than court rules), dealing with unruly
           defendants, how to compute penalties, definitions of
           infractions.   5017

NEW YORK State Bar Association. Guidebook for grievance committees.
Albany, 1968. 1 v., looseleaf.   5018

NORTH CAROLINA

NORTH CAROLINA University Institute of Government. Manual for jury
commissioners, by C. E. Hinsdale. Chapel Hill, 1973. 14 p.   5019

OHIO

OHIO. Supreme Court. Rules of superintendence: Court of Common
Pleas, with implementation manual. Columbus, Ohio legal center
Inst., 1971. 72 p.
           The rules, designed to expedite the disposition of
           both criminal and civil cases in the trial courts are
           set forth together with an implementation manual which
           explains the application of the rules.   5020

PENNSYLVANIA

COURT action handbook; a manual on court monitoring and community action, by B. Leonard ... Media, Pa, Friends Suburban Project, 1974. 28 p.
[Box 54, Media, PA 19063]   5021

ELLENBOGEN, H. Space age electronics speed the wheels of justice; automated data processing manual. Pittsburgh, Court of Common Pleas of Allegheny County, 1964. 11 p.   5022

JUDICIAL orientation; a reference manual for Pennsylvania state trial judges, prep. by Pa. Conference of State Trial Judges and Pa. Bar Inst. Harrisburg, Pa. Bar Inst., 1968. 1 v., looseleaf.   5023

THIRD Pennsylvania judicial orientation seminar: a reference manual for Pa. state trial judges, prep. by Pa. Conference of State Trial Judges, and Office of the State Court Administrator ... Phila., Office of the State Court Administrator, 1972. 327 p. 5024

RHODE ISLAND

RHODE ISLAND Office of the State Court Administrator. Manual on sound recording. Providence, 1971. 30 p.   5025

TEXAS

TEXAS Civil Judicial Council. Manual for Texas Juvenile Court Judges. Austin, 1973. 1 v., looseleaf.   5026

VIRGINIA

ASSOCIATION of Justices of the Peace of Virginia. Handbook, 1964. Richmond, 1964. 17 p.   5027

ASSOCIATION of Justices of the Peace of Virginia and University of Virginia Inst. of Government. Virginia justices' of the peace manual, by W. R. Furr, II. Charlottesville, 1967. 134 p.   5028

HANDBOOK of standard procedures and model orders in certain cases for judges and clerks of courts of record; prep. for the information of judges and clerks of record of the commonwealth of Virginia by the Judicial Council for Virginia. Richmond, Supreme Court of Appeals, Off. of the Exec. Secretary, 1966. 93 p.   5029

WASHINGTON

JAILHOUSE Blues; way out information about the jailhouse, the legal system, and your rights, by A. Budd and S. Coffman. Seattle American Friends Service Committee, 197-. 68 p.
[814 NE 40th St, Seattle 98105]   5030

WASHINGTON (State) Superior Court. Handbook for bailiffs, prep.
by R. M. Ishakawa, Sept. 6, 1961; amended by L.L. Ogg, Feb. 16,
1967, and D. Ashbaugh, Feb. 1968. Seattle, 1968. 31 p.   5031

WASHINGTON (State) Superior Court, King County. The court system
of the State of Washington; a manual for high school students
supplementing lectures during visitation to the Superior Court of
the State of Washington for King County. 2d rev., Sept. 1964.
Seattle, 1964. 17 p.
> Report provided insight into court structure and court
> personnel. It examines the underlying principles of
> a unified court system, and court policies of ongoing
> studies leading to improvement through the use of
> Judiciary Committees, Councils, Conferences, and pro-
> fessional organizations. Included are tables contain-
> ing traffic information from Juvenile Court and max-
> imum/minimum sentences for selected crimes.   5032

WASHINGTON (State) Supreme Court. Judge's desk book for use with
Washington Pattern Jury Instructions. Olympia, 1967. 1 v.,
looseleaf.   5033

WASHINGTON State Magistrates' Association. Washington state
manual for justice courts. Olympia, 1971. 1 v., looseleaf. 5034

TABLE OF CASES

Brotherhood of Railroad Trainmen v. Virginia
    State Bar, 377 U.S. 1 (1964),   3930

Brown v. Allen, 344 U.S. 443 (1953),   219, 4569, 4585, 4599

Brown v. Board of Education, 347 U.S. 483
    (1954),   46, 1389

Bruton v. U.S., 391 U.S. 123 (1968),   4037

Bursey v. U.S., 466 F.2d 1059 (9th Cir.
    1972),   4038

Busik v. Levine, 63 N.J. 351, 307 A.2d
    571 (1973),   1804, 1807

California v. Stewart, 384 U.S. 436 (1966),   3082

Carroll v. Tate, 274 A.2d 193 (1971),   2327, 2347

Chandler v. Judicial Council of the Tenth
    Circuit, 398 U.S. 74 (1970),   1630, 2476, 3958

Chewning v. Cunningham, 368 U.S. 443 (1962), 3316

Coleman v. Alabama, 399 U.S. 1 (1970),   3420, 3459, 3462

Colgrove v. Battin, 456 F.2d 1379 (9th Cir.
    1972),   2685

Colgrove v. Green, 328 U.S. 549 (1946),   274

Colten v. Kentucky, 407 U.S. 104 (1971),   383, 4397

Commonwealth v. Evans, 434 Pa. 52 (1969),   3627

Davis v. Heyd, 479 F.2d 446 (5th Cir.
    1973),   3714

DeLuna v. U.S., 308 F.2d 140 (5th Cir.
    1962),   4039

Dennis v. U.S., 384 U.S. 855 (1966),   3485, 3492, 4011

Dorszynski v. U.S., 418 U.S. 424 (1974),   4514

U.S. v. McLeod, 385 F.2d 734 (5th Cir. 1967),   3862

U.S. v. Percevault, 61 F.R.D. 338 (N.Y.E.D. 1973),   3659

U.S. v. Rosenberg, 195 F.2d 583 (2d Cir. 1952),   4491, 4533

U.S. v. Wade, 388 U.S. 218 (1967),   3307, 3442

U.S. v. Wells, 163 F. 313 (D. Idaho 1908),   3480

U.S. v. Western, 448 F.2d 626 (9th Cir. 1971),   4480

U.S. v. Wiley, 278 F.2d 500 (7th Cir. 1960),   4522, 4536

U.S. v. Youngblood, 379 F.2d 365 (2d Cir. 1967),   3498

Vignera v. New York, 384 U.S. 436 (1966),   3082

Walker v. Caldwell, 476 F.2d 213 (5th Cir. 1973),   3760

Ward v. Village of Monroeville, 409 U.S. 345 (1972),   281
345 (
Ward v. Wakes, 258 A.2d 379 (N.J.App.Div. 1969),   2713

Wardius v. Oregon, 412 U.S. 470 (1973),   3665

Westover v. U.S., 384 U.S. 436 (1966),   3082

Williams v. Florida, 399 U.S. 78 (1970),   2671, 2676-2678, 2681, 2685

Williams v. Illinois, 399 U.S. 325 (1970),   4427

Witherspoon v. Illinois, 391 U.S. 510 (1968),   2528

Wood v. Ross, 434 F.2d 297 (4th Cir. 1970),   4501

Woosley v. U.S., 478 F.2d 139 (8th Cir. 1973),   4524

INDEX OF PERSONAL NAMES.

[See subject index for corporate and institutional names.]

ABBEY, G. M., 2291
ABEL-SMITH, B., 1-2
ABELL, J. P., 732a
ABRAHAM, H. J., 3, 128, 1301,
    1439, 4731
ABRAMOWITZ, E., 4639
ABRAMS, N., 3690
ACHESON, D. C., 2779
ACKROYD, G. G., 1099
ADAMANY, D. W., 1289, 1303
ADAMS, E., 105, 581, 2027,
    2097-2101, 2115, 2783, 3359
ADAMS, T. F., 4985
ADAMS, W. H., 2757h
ADKINS, W. H., II, 754
ADLOW, E., 789
AGATA, B. C., 3222, 4317, 4476
AGER, W. F., 2205
AIKMAN, A. B., 3200
AINSWORTH, R. A., Jr., 1601-
    1604, 1697, 4065
AKSEN, G., 3006
ALBRIGHT, D. J., 2374
ALBRIGHT, E., 3384
ALCABES, A., 4931
ALDISERT, R. J., 2780, 2783,
    3066
ALESSANDRONI, W. E., 108,
    2458, 2783
ALEXANDER, B., 4145, 4852
ALEXANDER, C. E., 3718
ALEXANDER, M. E., 4318, 4471
ALEXANDER, P., 3446
ALFINI, J. J., 357, 1450,
    1792, 2377, 3127
ALLAN, R., 131
ALLARD, R. E., 4, 591, 1285,
    1448, 1576
ALLEN, E. E., 3599
ALLEN, F. A., 3198, 3269a, 3589
ALLISON, J. L., 2738, 3411a,
    3783
ALMAND, B., 609
ALSHULER, A. W., 3600, 3691,
    3958
ALSPAUGH, D. Y., 4837
ALSUP, W. H., 132

ALTMAN, M. L., 2189
AMANDES, R. B., 2511
AMMERMAN, H. S., 137
AMOS, W. E., 1782
AMRAM, P. W., 14, 1097, 1140,
    2268
AMSTERDAM, A. G., 3750, 3751a,
    4892
ANCEL, L., 675
ANDALMAN, E., 3791
ANDERSEN, J. R., 1217
ANDERSON, A. S., 1647-1648
ANDERSON, B. B., 4075
ANDERSON, C. D., 4159
ANDERSON, G. L., 3419, 4565
ANDERSON, L. L., 138-139,
    1581, 1816, 3359, 3792
ANDERSON, R. P., 3901
ANDERSON, S. V., 3201
ANDREOLI, P. D., 3537, 4158
ANDREWS, J. L., 4753
ANGUS, W. H., 3201
ANOLIK, I., 3426
ANTELL, M. P., 3479
ANTHONY, D. V., 302
ARES, C. E., 3203k, 3348,
    3531, 3533-3534, 3572
ARMSTRONG, F. M., 15
ARMSTRONG, W. D., 1704
ARMSTRONG, W. P., 1611, 2788
ARN, E. F., 718
ARNOLD, K. J., 4965
ARNOLD, T., 3296
ARRAJ, A. A., 3348
ARTERBURN, N. F., 680
ARTHUR, L. G., 99, 810
ASH, M., 4030, 4199
ASHFORD, H. A., 3234
ASHMAN, A., 16, 357, 589, 738,
    1025, 1447, 1792, 2296,
    2516, 3127, 3693, 3749,
    3793
ASHMAN, C. R., 1612
ASPEN, M. E., 3130
ASPERK, T., 2209, 3693, 3749
ATKINS, B. M., 1291, 1303
ATKINSON, D. N., 1292

CALABRESI, G., 2911, 3009, 3013
CALDWELL, M. F., 1307
CALDWELL, T. D., Jr., 1099
CALKINS, R. M., 3485-3486, 3644
CALLAGHAN, T., 2894
CALVERT, R. W., 1190, 1196, 1202, 1207, 1212, 1610, 3038
CALVERT, W. M., 2424
CAMPBELL, C., 4830-4831, 4833
CAMPBELL, C. M., 1463
CAMPBELL, J. S., 3381d
CAMPBELL, R. V. D., 2074
CAMPBELL, W. J., 3362, 3488, 4165-66, 4472
CANNAVALE, F., Jr., 2090
CANNON, J. L., 3469
CANNON, M. W., 161, 1837a,1837b
CANNON, R. J., 1626
CANON, B. C., 1308, 1357, 1464, 3138, 3269b
CAPE, W. H., 4893
CAPLAN, G. M., 3259, 3386
CAPLAN, R. L., 26, 2217
CAPLOVITZ, D., 364
CARBINE, S. A., 3014
CARDOZO, B. N., 47
CARLIN, J. E., 2735, 3810, 3940
CARLSON, R. J., 2912
CARLSON, R. L., 4033
CARLTON, J. P., 1004
CARLTON, V. B., 590
CARMODY, D. W., 108, 2458
CARP, R. A., 1309, 1838, 3039
CARR, W. S., 4322, 4429, 4752
CARRIGAN, J. R., 1839, 1900, 2305, 3348
CARRINGTON, P. D., 162-163, 3025, 3097, 3124, 3126
CARSON, C. N., 2726b
CARSWELL, G. H., 1487
CARTER, O., 4473
CARTER, J. D., 4574
CARTER, J. M., 3657, 3696, 4331, 4464, 4472, 4575
CARTER, R. M., 4254
CARTWRIGHT, J. R., 4399
CARVER, M. H., 4412
CASAD, R. C., 2471
CASE, C. P., 4234
CASE, R., 768
CASEY, E. F., 2943
CASPER, G., 2706, 4167

CASPER, J. D., 3251-3252
CASSIBRY, F. J., 1781, 2472, 2805
CASSIDY, C. E., 1956
CAVE, J. M., 3697
CAVERS, D. F., 17
CAYWOOD, S., 2306
CECIL, H., 1310
CEDARQUIST, W. B., 4145
CELLER, E., 3942, 4466-67, 4472, 4528, 4686
CHADICK, T. C., 1191
CHADWICK, B., 2126
CHAFFEE, S. H., 4149
CHAMBERS, D. L., 3791
CHAMBLISS, W. J., 4771
CHANDLER, H. P., 675, 1840
CHANIN, L. F., 3040
CHANTRY, K. N., 81
CHAPIN, P., 1465
CHAPPELL, R. A., 4463, 4466-4467
CHARPENTIER, A. A., 3041
CHARTRAND, R. L., 2113, 4772
CHASE, H. W., 1466-1467
CHASE, S., 1701, 1711
CHAYES, A., 3953
CHEATHAM, E. E., 1704, 3812, 3940
CHERNICK, R., 1812, 2600
CHERRY, F., 1174
CHESLEY, S. M., 2806
CHEVIGNY, P., 3970
CHIKOTA, R., 3410
CHILTON, J. T., 164, 472, 3045
CHISUM, D. L., 3227
CHRIST, M. G., 2754
CHRISTENSEN, B. F., 3813-3814, 3940
CHRISTENSON, A. S., 3755
CHRISTENSON, G. A., 1775-1776
CHRISTIAN, W., 1212, 1232, 3025, 3042, 3097, 3124, 3139, 3331
CHRISTIE, G. C., 3253
CHROUST, A., 2737
CHUSED, R. H., 882
CLARK, C. E., 27, 122, 226, 1312-1313, 1388, 1795
CLARK, C. P., 3411a
CLARK, L. D., 3411a, 3490

CLARK, R., 3254, 3355, 3374, 3976
CLARK, R. X., 3357
CLARK, T. C., 28-32, 51, 82, 85, 97, 102, 119, 165-66, 1448, 1468, 1610, 1700, 2426-27, 2515, 2724, 2783, 2807, 3023, 3043, 3197, 3255-56, 3330-31, 3348, 3645, 4334, 4663-64
CLARK, T. P., 1793
CLARK, V. W., 3653
CLARKE, S., 1019
CLARKE, S. H., 3886, 4202
CLAVIR, J., 3971
CLAYTON, C. F., 4467
CLEAVINGER, H. C., 4144
CLIFF, J. W., 1204
CLIFTON, N. S., 2720
CLIFTON, R. R., 3866
CLOSE, G. R., 2533
COBURN, D., 4495
COFER, J. D., 4577
COFFEY, A. L., 4966
COFFMAN, S., 5030
COGAN, N. H., 3604
COGSWELL, D., 2473
COHEN, F., 4335, 4453
COHEN, H. B., 3433
COHEN, J., 3108, 3362
COHEN, M., 4168
COHEN, N. M., 3972
COHEN, N. P., 3973
COHEN, R., 2064
COHEN, S., 790
COHEN, S. E., 3542
COHN, A. W., 3257
COHN, M. E., 471
COHN, R. G., 649-650, 1610, 2382
COHN, S. L., 558
COLDSTREAM, G., 4084
COLE, C. D., 412
COLE, G. F., 3817, 3843
COLE, J., 4085
COLE, R. T., 1414
COLISTA, F. P., 3410
COLLINS, J. G., 3646
COLLINS, T. A., 3226
COLTRANE, G. A., 1024
COMAY, S. D., 1100
COMISKY, M., 1101, 1140, 4169

COMPTON, L. D., 3331
COMUS, L. F., Jr., 2116, 4775
CONARD, A. F., 2913-2915, 3009
CONFORD, M. B., 3044
CONNALLY, B. C., 4467
CONNELL, J. J., Jr., 1444
CONNELLY, M. J., 2647
CONNELLY, V. J., 1578, 4322, 4752
CONNER, L. L., 2474-2475, 3974
CONNICK, H. F., 3789
CONNOLLY, J. J., 3259
CONNOR, R. G., 4472
CONNORS, J. M., 2311
CONRAD, A. F., 35
CONRAD, J. P., 3200, 3260, 3269b, 3362
CONWAY, M. M., 329
COOGAN, R. A., 1145
COOK, B. B., 99, 473, 704, 708-709, 1314, 1469, 1630, 1698, 1846, 2476-2477, 4338, 4359
COOK, J. D., 965
COOK, J. G., 3262-3263
COOK, L., 965
COOK, V. G., 4256
COOKE, B., 3819
COOMBS, E. G., Jr., 3011
COOPER, A. M., 4542
COOPER, G., 2143
COOPER, G. B., 4147
COOPER, H. H. A., 3607, 4395
COPELAND, C. H., 1665
COPPOCK, R., 2672
CORBIN, S. N., 949-950, 3344
CORBOY, P. H., 2538, 2809, 3000
CORNELISON, R. G., 2189
CORNISH, W. R., 2539
CORNWELL, E. E., Jr., 1297
CORRIGAN, J. V., 4900
CORSI, J. R., 3410
COSTA, P. L., 1577
COSTIKYAN, E. N., 1452, 1470, 1532
COTSIRILOS, G. J., 3777
COTTON, W. D., 2428
COULSON, R., 2783, 4255
COUNTRYMAN, V., 101, 1315
COVELL, J. J., 2218
COWEN, W., 302

EDWARDS, G., 80, 1635, 3097,
3124, 3144, 3290, 3433, 3707
EDWARDS, J. L. J., 3322
EHRENZWEIG, A. A., 43, 3010
EICHMAN, C. J., 4351
EISENBERG, H. B., 4581
EISENDRATH, M. M., 653
EISENHOWER, D., 1335
EISENHOWER, M. S., 3381
ELDRIDGE, W. B., 1475, 2115,
2354, 3359, 4356
ELKIND, N. B., 2251
ELLENBOGEN, H., 2044, 2123-2124,
3359, 4175, 5022
ELLIOTT, S. D., 961
ELSEN, S. H., 3423
ELSON, A., 1704
ELSWORTH, J. R., 2045
ELY, J. H., 1352
EMERLING, C. G., 4593
EMPEY, L. T., 4261
ENGLAND, R. W., Jr., 3269
ENGLISH, R. E., 3145, 3470
ENGSTROM, R. L., 2431
ENKER, A. N., 3391, 3423
ENNIS, P. H., 3393
ENZER, S., 2927
EPSTEIN, J., 3984
EPTING, R. L., 3985
ERDMANN, M., 3869
ERICKSON, W. H., 514, 900, 3274,
3331, 3348, 3611, 3986, 4176
ERICKSTAD, R. J., 3146
ERLANGER, H. W., 2549
ERNST AND ERNST, 611
ERSKINE, H., 4311
ERVIN, R. M., 3330
ERVIN, R. W., 3331
ERVIN, S. J., Jr., 1566, 1700,
2639, 3549, 3580, 4151, 4177,
4231, 4237
ESCOVITZ, S., 1445
ESTES, J. E., 4467
EVANS, D. J., 2432
EVANS, W. N., 302
EVERSHED, F. R., 230
EVJEN, V. H., 4462
EXON, J. J., 44

FAGAN, O. R., 2550
FAHEY, R. P., 99
FAHRINGER, H. P., 3652, 4353

FAIR, D. R., 369, 3050
FAIRBANKS, P. M., 754, 900,
1232, 1729-1730
FAIRCHILD, T. E., 1290, 3024,
4582
FAIRLEY, W. B., 107, 2556
FALCO, J. E., 3989
FALL, J. G., 2803
FARBER, W. O., 1161
FARER, T. J., 3170
FARLEY, G. O., 1584, 4969
FARMER, J. E., 683
FARNSWORTH, E. A., 45
FARR, M. A. L., 2126
FARRIOR, R., Jr., 2757h
FATZER, H. R., 710-711b
FAY, P. T., 1782
FEATHERSTONE, M., 3219
FEELEY, M. M., 1303, 3276, 3576
FEENEY, F. F., 476, 984, 3424-
3425, 4249
FEERICK, J. D., 1637
FEIBELMAN, H. U., 1005
FEINBERG, W., 3122, 4475, 4503
FELLMAN, D., 3277
FELSHER, H., 4095
FELTS, S. L., Jr., 1732
FENDLER, O., 108, 449, 2458,
3826a
FENOGLIO, B., 4986
FENTON, W. B., 712, 857
FERELL, H. A., 4471
FERGUSON, W. J., 1781
FERREIRA, J., Jr., 3014
FEUILLAN, J., 3805
FICHENBERG, R., 4144
FIELD, J. S., 2433
FIELD, R. H., 136, 190-191,
352
FIGG, R. M., 352
FIGINSKI, M. A., 192
FINAN, T. B., 4587
FINCH, J. A., Jr., 832-832a,
3053, 4623
FINER, J. J., 3763
FINKELSTEIN, I., 4293
FINKELSTEIN, M. M., 790, 3278,
3698, 4938a
FINKELSTEIN, M. O., 2555-2556
FINLEY, R. C., 46-48, 98, 108,
1239, 1320, 2458, 3433,
3470, 4144
FINMAN, T., 3827

FRIENDLY, A., 4099
FRIENDLY, H. J., 131, 199-200,
  284, 300, 1327-1328, 1698,
  3279, 3397, 4591
FRIESEN, E. C., 98, 103, 591,
  919, 1735, 1858, 2115, 2131,
  2487, 2820, 3359, 4900
FRITZ, T. G., 2673
FROYD, P., 3798
FRYE, R. J., 414, 418
FUCHS, W. J., 52
FUCHSBERG, J. D., 3007, 3009,
  3433
FUERST, N. A., 1051
FULD, S. H., 102, 915-916,
  3148-3149, 3995, 4144
FULDA, C. H., 1052
FULLER, L., 1415
FULLER, L. L., 17
FULTON, E. D., 1696
FUNSTON, R., 1329
FURR, W. R., II, 5028

GABLE, R. W., 103, 1859
GABRIELSON, A. E., 1240, 1248
GAFFNEY, F. M., 99
GAFFNEY, G. H., 3426
GAINES, J. M., 429, 2091, 2867
GAINEY, J. A., 819-820
GALIANO, F. V., 2753
GALIN, M. P., 2075
GALLAGHER, O., 780, 3357
GALLAS, E. C., 103-104, 1858,
  1860-1861, 1871, 1911, 2870
GALLAS, N. M., 103, 1858
GALLATI, R. R. J., 2170, 3281
GALLIPOLI, M., 4592
GANGI, W., 3417
GANNON, E. J., 3269b
GANTT, P. H., 302, 4784
GARBER, J., 3709
GARDINER, J. A., 3199
GARDNER, N., 4900
GARFIELD, T. G., 108, 2435,
  2458
GARRATY, R. F., Jr., 3941
GARRETT, J. E., 4905
GARRIGAN, J. R., 98
GARRY, C. R., 3961, 3979, 4024
GARTLAND, R., 3410

GARWOOD, W. S. J., 591, 1112,
  1476
GASPERINI, E. L., 1647-1648
GATES, S. E., 3041
GATLIN, L., 789
GAUNT, W. W., 108
GAUS, W., 3540
GAUSEWITZ, R. L., 1736
GAZELL, J. A., 657, 1862-1869,
  4180
GEARY, T. C., 1169
GEBHARDT, L., 201
GEDDES, R. D., 3177
GEHR, M., 4287, 4827, 4832
GEILFUSS, J. G., 1276
GEIS, G., 4262
GELB, S., 3901
GELLEIN, H., 795
GELLHORN, W., 3201, 3280, 4640
GEMINGAMI, R. J., 4281
GENDELMAN, I., 202
GENTILE, C. L., 3613
GEORGE, B. J., Jr., 375, 3217,
  3331, 3433, 3707, 4506
GERALD, J. E., 4100
GERARD, J. B., 4545
GERMAN, C. E., 2931, 3009
GERMANN, A. C., 3281
GERSHENSON, A. H., 1649
GERSHONI, H., 2222
GERSTEIN, R. E., 3348
GETTY, L. M., 3845
GEWIN, W. P., 2557
GHIARDI, J. D., 2932-2936
GIBB, A. D., 1650
GIBBENS, D. G., 3203j, 3641
GIBBONS, J. J., 3331
GIBBONS, O. J., 2685
GIBSON, F. R., 203
GIBSON, W. W., Jr., 2757g
GIDLEY, R. S., 1254
GIESE, M. J., 675
GIGNOUX, E. T., 4472
GILES, M. W., 2431
GILL, D. R., 3317
GILLESPIE, J. R., 3331
GILLESPIE, W. M., 2937
GILLISPIE, J., 3348
GILLMOR, D. M., 3269,
  4101-4103
GILMORE, H. W., 3433, 4362

GRIFFEN, B., 3411a
GRIFFETH, R. E., 2189
GRIFFIN, H. C., 4147
GRIMES, W. A., 1766
GRISWOLD, E. N., 17, 106, 130,
    211-213, 1341, 3286
GROCE, J. H., 2822a
GROOMS, H. H., 4467
GROOSE, D., 4071, 4748
GROOT, R. D., 1006, 3151
GROSMAN, B. A., 3741
GROSS, M. P., 3834
GROSS, S. E., 4183
GROSSBLAT, M., 2726c
GROSSMAN, H., 2774
GROSSMAN, J. B., 99, 1333,
    1342-1344, 1413, 1415,
    1480-1484, 1689, 4786
GRUBB, K. P., 4466
GRUNBAUM, W. F., 99, 1344
GUDE, G., 4692
GUITTARD, C. A., 1195
GULLEY, R. O., 2822
GUNN, D., 833
GUNTHER, G., 1345
GURNEY, E. J., 1870, 2823
GURR, T. R., 3381a
GUSTAFSON, R. A., 478, 3152
GUTHRIE, D. S., 1109
GUTMAN, D., 1737-1738, 1747
GUTMAN, S. M., 2560
GUTTMACHER, W. S., 4462
GUZMAN, R., 3656, 4363
GWYN, W. B., 3201

HABERMANN, P. S., 1267
HADDAD, W. A., 1305
HADLOW, E. B., 2757h
HAEMMEL, W. G., 1007
HAFT, M. G., 4896
HAIMBAUGH, G. D., Jr., 4107
HAKMAN, N., 1344
HALE, F. D., 2437
HALEVY, B. J., 4787
HALL, C. F., 2413
HALL, D. J., 1655
HALL, H. A., 1485, 1545
HALL, J., 4364
HALL, J. C., 1654
HALL, J. H., Jr., 2127
HALL, L., 17, 4507

HALL, M., 1656
HALL, M. D., 811
HALL, R. H., 427, 619, 1798
HALLAUER, R. P., 3836-3837,
    3866
HALLORAN, N. A., 104, 2128,
    2130-2133, 2560a, 2783,
    2870, 3391
HALLOWELL, I. M., 4287, 4829,
    4832, 4835a-4836
HALLOWS, E. H., 1268-1270b,
    3057
HALNAN, P. J., 395
HALPER, T., 1486
HALPERIN, D. J., 424, 3174,
    4508-4509
HALPERN, J., 1739
HALPIN, J., 3153
HAMANN, C. M., 3358
HAMILTON, C. V., 1346
HAMILTON, W. A., 3362, 3488
HAMLETT, R. G., 3058
HAMLEY, F. G., 3020, 3066
HAMMOND, H., 758
HAMMOND, P. E., 2430
HANBURY, H. G., 57
HAND, J. R., 1592
HAND, L., 1347, 1412, 1531,
    3059
HAND, R. C., 4320, 4436
HANDLER, A. B., 2375
HANDLER, J., 3951
HANKIN, F. A., 2726
HANNAH, H. I., 2647
HANNAY, A. B., 4467
HANSBURY, T. S., 2413
HANSEN, C. T., 1740
HANSON, R. A., 1610, 1813
HARBINGER, R., 2377, 2394,
    2647
HARBRECHT, P. P., 3410
HARE, F. H., Jr., 2561
HARLAN, J. M., 1345, 3060
HARLEY, H., 2647
HARMEL, P. R., 302
HARNSBERGER, R., 2562
HARP, R. S., III, 123
HARPER, A. R., 3411a
HARRELL, M. A., 181
HARRIES, K. D., 4365
HARRINGTON, D. C., 2951
HARRIS, A., 69, 1348, 4673

HOLMES, O. W., Jr., 1306, 1317
HOLT, H. A., 1261
HOLT, I. L., Jr., 4369
HOLTZOFF, A., 3125
HOMAN, F. J., Jr., 4000
HOOD, J. T., Jr., 2564
HOOD, R., 4370
HOOPER, F. A., 2050
HOOPER, W., Jr., 1201
HOPKINS, I., 4853
HOPKINS, J. D., 1290, 3024,
   3044, 3061, 3157, 3537,
   4158, 4547, 4596
HOPKINS, P. M., 3215
HOPSON, D., Jr., 2745
HOROWITZ, A. R., 681
HORVATH, J., 2189
HORWITZ, J. J., 965
HOSNER, C. T., 4371
HOSTETLER, Z., 3259
HOTCHKISS, A., 3214
HOUGH, G., III, 4081, 4141
HOUSE, C. S., 540
HOUSTON, W. D., 2223
HOWARD, J., 3810, 3940
HOWARD, J. C., 4674
HOWARD, J. W., Jr., 1413
HRUSKA, R. L., 221, 311-312,
   321, 3360, 3560, 4510-4511,
   4529
HRYSJAM, R. L., 3348
HUBBARD, W. O., 729
HUDSON, E. A., 123, 3359
HUFF, R. M., 123
HUFSTEDLER, SETH M., 480-481,
   3157a, 3160
HUFSTEDLER, SHIRLEY M., 100,
   222-223, 481, 3062, 3158-
   3160, 3288
HUGHES, C. E., 1317, 1370
HUGHES, G., 88, 4001
HUIE, C. R., 3026
HUNT, M. K., 4841
HUNT, V. W., 2224
HUNTER, E. B., 1448, 1494-1496,
   4597
HUNTER, E. F., Jr., 4467
HUNTER, R. L. C., 4044
HUNTER, S. R., 1064
HUNTING, R. B., 908, 1452, 1497
HUNVALD, E. H., 3431
HURLBURT, W. H., 1696

HURLEY, J. E., 1825
HUTCHESON, J. C., Jr., 1351
HYDE, G. M., 4528
HYDE, L. M., 1448, 1744, 1758,
   3108
HYMAN, J. D., 965

I'ANSON, L. W., 1235
ILSLEY, J. L., 1404
IMLAY, C. H., 2565
INBAU, F. E., 3296, 3426,
   3436, 3470
IRVING, J. F., 3845
ISAACS, J. L., 965
ISAACSON, I., 4992
ISBELL, M., 2869
ISHAKAWA, R. M., 5031
ISRAEL, J. H., 3433
IVIE, C. C., 3788, 3828

J. F. BOYD ASSOCIATES, 1256
JACKSON, D. D., 1500
JACKSON, H. M., 4233
JACKSON, R. H., 1393
JACKSON, R. M., 63, 395,
   3292
JACOB, B. R., 3846
JACOB, C. M., 3170
JACOB, H., 64, 1344, 1354,
   1501-1502, 3293
JACOBS, J. E., 2915
JACOBS, L. W., 1056
JACOBSOHN, G. J., 1355
JACOBSTEIN, M. J., 4797
JACOBY, J. E., 3707a
JACOBY, S. B., 302
JAFFARY, S. K., 4373
JAFFE, I., 302
JAFFE, L. J., 4111
JAFFE, L. L., 1356
JAHNIGE, T. P., 207
JAMES, F., Jr., 3010
JAMES, H. J., 65, 381
JAMES, J. R., 714, 718
JAMES, R. B., 2144
JAMESON, F. L., 4281
JAMESON, W. J., 3203, 3294,
   3331, 4473
JAMIESON, D. D., 1135
JANATA, R., 2544, 2946

LERNER, R., 1412
LEROY, D. H., 3681
LERSCHEN, R. J., 2233
LESINSKI, T. J., 3025, 3066, 3165
LEUCHTENBURG, W. E., 243, 1517
LEVANTHAL, A., 705
LEVANTHAL, H., 2148
LEVI, E. H., 1367, 3306
LEVIN, A. L., 310-312
LEVIN, E. M., Jr., 675
LEVIN, G., 2071
LEVIN, M. A., 4381
LEVIN, T., 4382, 4467
LEVINE, F. J., 3307, 3442
LEVINE, H. I., 663, 2333, 2837
LEVINE, J. P., 244
LEVINE, M. J., 5017
LEVINE, M. L., 4025
LEVINSON, L. H., 605
LEVINTHAL, A., 385, 1285
LEVIT, W. H., 100, 1584, 2764-2766, 4969
LEVITT, W., 2600
LEVY, H. M., 4554
LEVY, M. R., 3524
LEVY, N., Jr., 541
LEVY, S. G., 3381e
LEVY, S. J., 245
LEWIN, L., 3428
LEWIN, N., 246
LEWINE, J. M., 4072, 4120
LEWIS, A., 3308-3309, 3767
LEWIS, L. L., 3080
LEWIS, O. C., 1058
LEWIS, O. R., 1775, 1776
LEWIS, P. H., 108
LI, P. M., 1555
LICHT, F., 1668, 2493
LIEBERMAN, J. B., 4313, 4383
LIEBERMAN, J. K., 3310
LIEBMANN, G. W., 247, 3360
LIGDA, P., 471
LILES, W. T., 3710
LILLY, G. C., 1230, 3165a, 3173
LINCOLN, J. H., 3408
LINDHEIMER, J. H., 4281
LINDQUIST, C. A., 248, 2601
LINDSAY, J. V., 927, 1448, 1518, 3411

LINDSLEY, B. F., 488
LIPPETT, G. L., 1759
LIPPMAN, D., 3713
LIPSIG, H. H., 4601
LITKE, W. W., 427, 1116
LITTLE, J. W., 1222, 2968
LITTLEJOHN, B., 2515, 4024
LITWIN, L., 4191
LIVERMORE, J. M., 3218
LLEWELLYN, K. N., 1404
LOBENTHAL, J. S., Jr., 88
LOCKE, H. G., 808, 3410
LOCKE, J. W., 581, 3593
LOCKHART, W. J., 1217
LOEB, L. S., 1368-1369
LOEVY, R. D., 776
LOFTON, J., 3269b, 4121
LOGAN, A. B., 75, 3311
LOGAN, W. B., 382
LOHMAN, J. D., 3395, 3443
LONG, J. M., 2767
LONGO, G. E., 1519, 2810
LOPER, M. W., 1370
LORD, H. R., 760
LORENSON, W. D., 4384, 4602
LOTH, D., 931
LOUISELL, D. W., 43, 3658-3659
LOVELL, R. E., II., 3862
LOW, P. W., 3203n, 3203r, 3331, 3348, 4319, 4478
LOWE, R. S., 76, 900, 1232, 1450, 1608
LOWER, E. W., 4147
LOWI, T. J., 3298
LUBBERS, J., 4738
LUBECK, S., 4411
LUCAS, J., 4012
LUCAS, J. D., 3171
LUCY, P. J., 1276
LUDWIG, F. J., 3411
LUGER, M., 3200
LUKOWSKY, R. O., 1765, 2494, 2769
LUMBARD, J. E., 98, 249, 1801, 2693, 2838, 3166, 3203, 3259, 3312, 3768, 3884, 3901
LUNDEN, W., 2065
LURA, R. P., 4365
LUVERA, P. N., Jr., 1244
LYBARGER, D. F., 2495
LYDAY, W., 3620a

LYLES, B., 2541
LYNCH, G. P., 3768a
LYNCH, J. M., 1802
LYNCH, T. C., 3433, 3707
LYNNE, S. H., 4467

MACANDREW, E., 4260
MCCAFFERTY, J. A., 2150
MCCART, S. W., 2604
MCCARTHY, C., 2961
MCCARTHY, D. J., 3567
MACCARTHY, T. F., 3661, 3777
MCCLEAN, J. D., 3313
MCCLELLAN, G. B., 3426
MCCLELLAN, J. L., 3360, 4694
MCCLURE, J. G., 2496
MCCOLLOUGH, R. C., II, 3224
MCCONNELL, E. B., 81, 883, 1829,
    1882-1885, 2151, 2839
MCCONNELL, J., 2516
MCCONNELL, J. P., 386
MCCONNELL, J. R., 2840
MCCORD, J. H., 2920, 2959
MCCORD, W. M., 4473
MACCORKLE, S. A., 3507
MCCORMACK, J. W., 1564
MCCOY, P., 4976
MCCOY, T. F., 908, 1001, 1112,
    1886, 1908
MCCRAE, W. A., Jr., 4695
MCCREA, T. L., 4904
MCCREE, W. H., Jr., 3543
MCCRYSTAL, J., 2235-2238, 2282
MCCULLOCH, W. M., 2152
MCCULLOUGH, D. H., 3543, 4122
MCCUNE, S. D., 1371, 1759
MCDERMOTT, E. A., 2398
MCDERMOTT, E. J., 250
MCDERMOTT, J. T., 251-252, 2202,
    2841
MCDERMOTT, R. A., 4258
MCDEVITT, J. J., III, 2072
MCDEVITT, R. E., 1140, 1670
MCDONALD, D. C., 1696
MCDONALD, D. P., 3348
MACDONALD, M., 2153
MACDONALD, M. E., 2189
MCDONALD, W. F., 3538
MCDONNELL, R. E., 2154
MCDONOUGH, J. N., 4905
MCELROY, P. R., 4385

MACFADEN, W. E., 387
MCGEE, R. A., 3200, 4386,
    4465
MCGINLEY, P. W., 1647-1648
MCGOWAN, C., 8, 77, 253, 900,
    3444
MCGRATH, W. H., 1894
MCGUIRK, R. H., 2605
MCGURK, H. L., 691
MCILVAINE, J. W., 3290, 4472
MCINTYRE, D. M., Jr., 791,
    3231, 3445, 3713
MCINTYRE, J., 3199
MACKAY, K. H., Jr., 2937
MCKAY, M. C., 2900
MCKAY, R. B., 80, 254, 947,
    1671, 1697, 1700, 2718,
    4123, 4146, 4387
MACKELL, T. J., 3411
MACKENZIE, J. P., 1672, 4124
MCKENZIE, S. P., 81, 2443
MCKESSON, W. B., 3942
MCKINNEY, L. C., 2335
MACKOFF, B. S., 2647, 3411a
MCKUSICK, V. L., 1112, 2606
MCLAIN, J. D., Jr., 1520
MCLAUGHLIN, G. T., 3863
MCLAUGHLIN, K. F., 1887
MCLAUGHLIN, W. H., 2074, 2076
MCLEAN, E. C., 3649, 3684
MACLEOD, I., 123
MCMANUS, J. E., Jr., 893
MACMILLAN, H., Jr., 4603
MCMURRAY, C. D., 1673
MCNAMARA, J. J., Jr., 928
MCNAMARA, M. B., 2320
MCNAMARA, R. M., Jr., 569
MCNAMEE, G. C., 4025
MCNAUGHTON, J., 3576
MCPEAK, M., (see also SOLOMON,
    M. MCP) 2155
MCRAE, W. A., Jr., 105
MCWHINNEY, E., 1414

MADDEN, T. J., 3377
MADDEN, W. M., 2225, 2239
MADDREA, T. G., 3008
MADSON, S. J., 2599
MAGIDSON, S. C., 3777
MAGNUSON, W. G., 3008, 3011
MAIDENBERG, H. J., 3009

MAIDMENT, R. A., 1372
MAIN, J., 2842
MAITLAND, G. H., 721
MAJOR, J. E., 1589
MALECH, A. M., 1888-1889
MALLARD, R. B., 1802a, 1890
MALTZ, M. D., 3314, 3385
MANAK, J. P., 3731, 4926
MANISCALCO, P. J., 664, 835
MANLY, P. T., 899-899a, 2337
MANN, C., 3543
MANN, G. E., 3009
MANNINA, G. J., Jr., 4692
MANNING, C. A., 2030
MANSON, P. C., 1231, 3865
MANY, M. H., 4467
MAR, P., 3508
MARCUS, B. H., 1934
MARCUS, M. M., 3209
MARDEN, H. C., 2497, 3081
MARDEN, O. S., 108, 2458,
    3888a-3888b, 3901, 3941
MARGOLIS, E., 4555
MARGOLIS, L. S., 255, 3315
MARGOLIS, P. M., 2399
MARINO, R. J., 4402
MARKEY, M. L., 1271
MARKLE, J. P., 3551
MARKS, F. R., 3866
MARLOW, R. A., 4196
MARQUIS, K. H., 4047
MARRYOTT, F. J., 2969-2971, 3009
MARSDEN, W. P., 492
MARSH, P. W., 795
MARSHALL, A. K., 2843
MARSHALL, JAMES, 3326, 4047
MARSHALL, JOHN, 1317
MARSHALL, P., 3326
MARSHALL, T., 1565-1566, 3035,
    3041
MARTEL, J. M., 2972
MARTIN, C., 2240
MARTIN, D. L., 2602
MARTIN, G., 2515a
MARTIN, J. A., 2603
MARTIN, J. C., 2278
MARTIN, J. M., 4313, 4383
MARTIN, P. L., 1521
MARTIN, R. A., 2444
MARTINEAU, R. J., 762, 1522,
    1674, 1697, 1892-1893
MARU, O., 2750, 4809

MASSEY, P., 4836
MATHENY, M. D., 3769
MATHER, L. M., 3621
MATHEWS, R. E., 1697
MATTICK, H. W., 3200
MATTINA, J. S., 4389
MATTIS, T., 3867
MATTSON, C., 4853
MAXWELL, J. K., 4850, 4852,
    4853-4855
MAXWELL, R. F., 2607
MAYERS, L., 78, 4556, 4604-06
MAYHUGH, S. L., 4281 ..
MAZETTI, J. P., 2075
MAZOR, L. J., 2751, 3203L,
    3786, 3868
MEADOR, D. J., 123, 256, 1775,
    3085, 3169, 3316, 3377,
    3378, 4515, 4557, 4607-10
MEAGHER, J. H., 2498
MEANY, G., 3008
MEDALIE, R. J., 3082, 3446,
    3770, 3758, 4269
MEDINA, H. R., 2499, 3083,
    4076-77
MEGARRY, R. E., 1696, 3117
MEHR, R. I., 3009
MEISENHOLDER, R., 2768
MELONE, A., 99
MELTSNER. M., 3568
MELTZER, M. F., 4811
MENDELSON, W., 1373
MENDES, R. G., 507
MENNINGER, K., 3319
MEREDITH, J. H., 1781
MERMIN, S., 1374, 2156
MERRILL, A. J., 4611
MERRILL, F., 2609-2610
MERRILL, M. H., 1072
MERRILL, P. J., 427
MERRILL, W. J., 3743
MERSKY, R. M., 1301, 4812
MERSON, A., 3411as
MESERVE, R. W., 2974
MESHBESHER, R. I., 3509
METH, T. S., 4390
METZGER, B., 2810
MEYER, B., 1895
MEYER, B. S., 2445, 2611,
    2647, 4125-4127, 4144
MICHAEL, J. H., Jr., 123
MICHELI, G. A., 2810

OLIVER, R. L., 2994
OLIVIERI, A., 4293
OLM, J. G., 4851-4852, 4855
OLNEY, W., III, 4472, 4686, 4715
OLSON, B. T., 3512
OLSON, D. G., 3014
O'NEAL, H. T., Jr., 3345
O'NEILL, W. I., 2088
ONION, J. F., 3331
OPALA, M., 1913
O'QUINN, J. N., 2515
ORFIELD, L. B., 2502, 3673-3674, 4050
ORGEL, L., 3121
ORLAND, L., 4403, 4468
OSKAMP, S., 4047
OSTHUS, M. O., 3127
O'SULLIVAN, C., 4566, 4638
OTIS, J. C., 1290, 3024
O'TOOLE, T. J., 3203f, 3959
OUGHTERSON, E. D., 965
OVERTON, B. F., 1382
OVERTON, E. E., 1177
OWENS, C. M., 1773

PABST, W. R., Jr., 2621-2623a, 2701-2702, 4199
PACKER, H. L., 3346, 3470
PADAWER-SINGER, A. M., 2624-2624a
PAGE, L., 395
PAGET, D., 4639
PALERMO, J. S., 3551
PALMER, A. E., 4589
PALMER, B. H., 2453
PALMER, K. T., 3892
PALMER, L. I., 4404
PALMER, O. T., Jr., 3093
PALMER, R. L., 2625
PALMORE, J. S., 4529
PALOTAI, O. G., 4681
PANETTA, L. E., 88
PANTON, G., 4828, 4834
PARKER, H. E., 4529
PARKER, J. J., 1483
PARKER, K. E., 2718
PARKES, K., 26, 4755
PARKHILL, B., 1446
PARLEY, L. I., 3675
PARMAS, R. I., 4294

PARNELL, A. W., 2626, 2755
PARNESS, J. A., 16, 1791, 2782, 2859, 4739-40
PARSONS, J. B., 4405, 4464
PARTRIDGE, A., 4356
PASCHAL, F., 4619
PASVOGEL, G. E., 4964
PATTERSON, J. C., 3710
PATTERSON, R. P., Jr., 4206
PATTERSON, W. A., 2211
PAUL, R., 301
PAULSEN, M. G., 959, 965, 3010, 3578, 3893-3894
PAYNE, M. L., 827
PAYNE, R., 4789
PAYTON, G. T., 4971
PEARSON, C., 3410
PEARSON, R. N., 3011
PEARTREE, F. T., 302
PEAT, MARWICK, MITCHELL & CO., 3347
PECK, C. J., 1383
PECK, R. C., 2344
PEDELISKI, T. B., 3795
PENDLETON, C. L., 1577
PENN, R. T., 581
PERLSWEIG, L., 474
PESKOE, H. E., 4692
PETERS, R. E., 3045
PETERSEN, T. K., 4295
PETERSON, D. J., 1303
PETERSON, D. L., 3676
PETERSON, R. W., 271-272, 3377, 3379
PETERSON, V. W., 3269a
PETERSON, W., 2413
PETRILLI, R. S., 734
PETROFF, D. D., 2629
PEVNA, J. D., 1857, 1899, 2434
PFAFF, R. A., 498
PHILLIPS, J. J., 4051
PHILIPPS, J. T., 3012
PHILLIPS, B. A., 1092
PHILLIPS, H., 3094
PHILLIPS, J. C., 2783
PHILLIPS, M. R., 2189
PHILLIPS, O. L., 4566
PHILLIPS, S. W., 2089, 3095
PICKERING, L. L., **2757h**
PIERCE, C. A., 1530
PIERSANTE, V. W., 3433
PIMSLEUR, M. G., 4797

ROSSMAN, D., 3798
ROSTOW, E. V., **226, 1325**
ROTHBLATT, H. B., 3681, 3751a, 4024
ROTHSTEIN, L. E., 3357, 3918
ROTHWAX, H. J., 3537, 4158, 4214
ROULSTON, R. E., 3426
ROWAT, D. C., 3201
ROWE, J., 2515
ROWLAND, H. H., 4024
ROYSTER, C. V., 4072
ROYLSTON, R. N., 4138
RUBEN, A. M., 3006
RUBIN, A. B., 1781
RUBIN, S., 390, 401, 4420-4424, 4465, 4470
RUBIN, T., 379, 1213, 4300, 4900
RUDOLPH, W. M., 2515
RUHNKA, J. C., 3327, 4910
RUNKLE, H., 1542
RUSH, P. E., 2232
RUSSELL, C. R., 86
RUSSELL, F. F., 3098
RUSSELL, T. B., 1779
RUTH, H. S., Jr., 3199
RUTHBERG, M. N., 2249, 2253
RYAN, J. M. F., Jr., 123
RYE, R. C., 2857

SAAIR, D. J., 573, 1919-1922, 2350, 2705
SAETA, P. M., 1700
SAHID, J. S., 3381d
SAIES, J. B., 1204
SALTIEL, E. P., 671
SAMAD, S. A., 4843
SAMMET, J. W., 2900
SAMUELS, A., 4049, 4057
SAMUELS, G., 1780
SAMUELS, R. L., 359
SANDALOW, T., 4628
SANDERS, F. P., 285
SANDERS, J. L., 4717
SANFORD, V., 1180
SANTARELLI, D. E., 3961
SANTO, H. E., 519
SARAT, A., 99
SARGANT, T., 3920
SARGENT, D. J., 3000, 3008
SARGENT, F. W., 4281

SARPY, L., 2864
SASTRI, D. S., 1413
SAVAGE, T. J., 4998-4999, 5007
SAWER, G., 90, 3297
SAYLOR, J. R., 286
SCALIA, A., 1230, 3165a
SCANLON, J. C., 965
SCARIANO, A., 3009
SCHABER, G. D., 2377, 2386, 2404
SCHACHTER, I. N., 2865
SCHACK, E. T., 961
SCHAEFER, R. C., 3463
SCHAEFER, W. V., 1391, 2512, 3303a, 3464-3465, 4157, 4629
SCHAFFER, S. A., 3585, 4313, 4383
SCHAFFER, T. L., 2640
SCHALL, W. J., 471
SCHALLER, J. P., 2757
SCHECTER, H., 3897
SCHEFLIN, A. W., 2637
SCHELL, O. H., 1615
SCHEMANSKE, F. G., 2377
SCHICK, M., 3099
SCHIER, C., 123
SCHILLER, S. A., 3212
SCHINDLER, P. M., 4216
SCHINITSKY, C., 962
SCHMERTZ, J. R., 2351
SCHMINHAUSER, J. R., 99, 1392, 1413-1414
SCHMIDT, A. M., 1282
SCHMIDT, J. R., 274
SCHMIDT, R. M., Jr., 4145
SCHNADER, W. A., 1112, 1118, 1121, 1136
SCHNEIDER, R., 144
SCHRAGE, L., 2609-2610
SCHRAM, G. N., 1543
SCHREIBER, A. M., 4425
SCHROEDER, R. A., 1285, 1544-1545
SCHUBERT, G. A., 1303, 1344, 1393-1398, 1413, 4844
SCHUCK, P. H., 1546
SCHULMAN, J., 2638, 2757a
SCHULMAN, S., 1097, 1140, 1808, 2268
SCHULTZ, J. L., 402, 3326
SCHULTZ, L. G., 3586
SCHUR, E. M., 403, 4301-03
SCHUTZ, R. S., 954
SCHWAB, H. M., 3177

SCHWARTZ, D., 302
SCHWARTZ, H., 4021, 4630
SCHWARTZ, H. E., 3516, 3523
SCHWARTZ, M. L., 3940
SCHWARTZ, R. A., 1344
SCHWARTZ, W., 104, 1668, 2493,
  2870, 3001
SCHWINDT, P., 26, 900
SCIGLIANO, R., 91
SCOTT, H., 123, 1448, 1547
SCRIPP, J., 4072, 4147
SCURLOCK, J., 3220, 3354-3354a
SEARLE, H. R., 3921
SEARS, D. W., 1704
SEEBURGER, R. H., 3466
SEEKAMP, L. M., 3939, 3944-3945
SEGAL, B. G., 92, 1466, 1548-1549,
  1690, 2394, 4892
SEGAL, B. L., 3750, 3751a
SEIDMAN, R. B., 4771
SEILER, D., 2597
SEILFR, M. G., 1550
SEITZINGER, E. F., 3002
SELIG, R. N., 1579
SELIKOFF, M., 2698
SELTZER, C. Z., 3518
SEMERAD, R. D., 3003
SENDROW, M., 3743
SENGSTOCK, M. C., 3410
SENTILLES, I. F. III, 2320
SESTRIC, A. J., 843
SETTLE, R. O., 4464
SEYMOUR, W. N., Jr., 70, 93,
  1697, 2405, 3041, 3884, 4139,
  4217, 4432-34
SHAFFER, T. L., 4147
SHAFROTH, W., 287-288, 315
SHAKMAN, M., 289
SHANKS, H., 1347
SHANNON, D. J., 520
SHAPIRA, H., 934
SHAPIRO, D. L., 136, 3203e,
  4631
SHAPIRO, E. D., 3433
SHAPIRO, L. J., 4466
SHAPIRO, M., 1303
SHAPIRO, R. A., 3127
SHARMA, K. M., 3846
SHARP, D., 3009
SHARP, L. J., 4466-67, 4472
SHEA, G. W., 2182, 2866

SHEEHY, J. W., 4472
SHELDON, C. H., 1399-1402, 1551
SHEPPARD, C. A., 2183
SHERAIN, H., 1691
SHERIDAN, M. F., 661
SHERIDAN, R. G., 1178
SHERIDAN, W. H., 408, 4868-69
SHERRILL, R., 3355
SHERRY, A. H., 3519
SHERRY, J. E. H., 963
SHIELDS, W. H., 2757b
SHIPLEY, C. L., 1700
SHOGAN, R., 1692
SHOOP, G. P., 1200, 2846
SHORT, E. H., 2249, 2251, 2253,
  4900
SHUCHMAN, P., 2352
SHUMAN, A. M., 4471
SHUTKIN, J. A., 2277
SIBLEY, J. A., 1435
SIEBERT, F. S., 4081, 4141
SIGLER, J. A., 1403, 3326
SIGMAN, H. C., 3045
SIGNORELLI, E. L., 4435
SIKES, B. H., 2726b, 2726c
SILBERMAN, J. J., 1303
SILBERT, E. J., 573
SILVER, A., 1512
SILVER, I., 4601
SILVER, M. T., 1003
SILVERSTEIN, L., 2353-2354,
  3391, 3543, 3587, 3924-3926,
  4846
SIMEONE, J. J., 3927
SIMON, C. K., 964, 2619
SIMON, R. J., 2641, 2990, 3326
SIMPSON, B., 4467
SIMPSON, F., III, 3940
SINCLAIR, T. C., 1491
SINGER, A., 2624a
SINGER, A. D., 4058
SINGER, L., 477
SINGER, L. R., 3361
SINGER, R., 2624a
SINGER, R. G., 3740, 4320, 4436
SINGER, S., 735, 3882
SINGLE, E., 364
SINK, J. M., 3776, 4932
SKOGAN, W. G., 99
SKOLER, D. L., 404, 1371, 1777,
  4437

SKOLNICK, J. H., 3381, 3467, 3928
SLESSER, H., 1404
SLIVKA, R. T., 2090
SMALL, B. J., 3213
SMITH, A. E., 1205, 1923
SMITH, C., 3798
SMITH, C. E., 4463, 4469
SMITH, C. H., 108, 591, 597, 1552, 2458, 2757h, 3938
SMITH, C. L., 4847
SMITH, E. L., 2757g
SMITH, F., 3227
SMITH, G. P., II, 2642-2643, 4525, 4632
SMITH, G. R., 3066, 3102
SMITH, J., 3410
SMITH, J. R., 2377
SMITH, L., 3410
SMITH, M. A., 4465
SMITH, R. H., 669, 2720
SMITH, R. L., 4281
SMITH, S., 730
SMITH, S. C., 1782, 4876-4877
SMITH, T., 290, 4438
SMITH, W. F., 4146, 4472
SMITH, W. H. T., 4147
SMITH, W. R., Jr., 4072
SNEAD, R. V., 1232
SNEED, E., 1076-1077
SNEED, J. T., 4235
SNODGRASS, J. D., 428-429, 2091, 2867
SNYDER, G. C., 108, 2644, 4718
SOBEL, N. R., 3468
SOBEL, W. H., 2377, 2406-2407, 2412
SOBELOFF, S. E., 1693, 3203n, 4319, 4478, 4526-4528, 4537, 4564
SOFAER, A. D., 4639, 4649
SOKOL, R. P., 4561, 4633-4634, 4949
SOLFISBURG, R. J., Jr., 673, 2355, 3023, 4218
SOLOMON, G. J., 4473
SOLOMON, H. E., 688, 741, 1406
SOLOMON, H. W., 3929
SOLOMON, K., 3410
SOLOMON, M. MCP. (see also MCPEAK, M.) 741, 2029, 2052, 2055, 2058, 2513, 4900, 4912
SORG, H. P., 1775, 1776
SOURIS, T., 3470

SOUTH, G. R., 4252
SPAETH, H. J., 1303
SPAIN, J., 3520
SPAK, M. I., 4085
SPALDING, E. O., 2721
SPANGENBERG, C., 3005, 3008, 3011
SPANGEBERG, R. L., 2185, 3543
SPANIOL, J. F., Jr., 316, 2186
SPARER, E. V., 3543, 3940
SPEAR, C. V., 643
SPEARS, A. A., 1781, 2686, 3331, 3348
SPECTER, A., 2072, 4146, 4304
SPECTOR, H. K., 4848
SPECTOR, P. L., 2356
SPEISER, L., 2456
SPERRY, F. B., 108, 2458
SPICER, G. W., 1407
SPIEGEL, F. C., 1573
SPITZER, J., 3971
SPIVACK, G. W., 1114
STAFFORD, C. F., 2457
STAKEL, W. J., 3426
STANG, D. P., 3381d
STANGA, J. R., 4142
STANLEY, E. M., 4474
STANLEY, T. P., 3939, 3944-45
STANTON, F., 4126, 4143
STANTON, N., 4439
STARKMAN, G. L., 3362, 4026
STARRS, J. E., 3742
STASON, E. B., 1448, 2720
STEADMAN, H. J., 4305
STEADMAN, J. M., 1137
STEBMEN, B. J., 2718
STECICH, M., 3180
STECKLER, W. E., 1775, 1776
STEELE, L. A., 2411
STEELE, W. A., 108, 2458
STEELE, W. W., 3522
STEFFENSON, J., 665
STEIGLER, M., 3879
STEIN, S. M., 204
STEINBERG, H., 3041, 3649, 3684
STEINBERG, R. A., 3360
STEPHENS, D. W., 1037
STEPHENS, O. H., Jr., 1408, 3469
STEPHENSON, D. G., Jr., 1409, 1924
STEPHENSON, R. C., 2187
STERN, G., 3403a

VANDERBILT, A. T., 71, 122, 1550, 1936
VANDERWICKEN, P., 2976
VANLANDINGHAM, K. E., 410
VANN, C. R., 4454
VANOSDOL, P., Jr., 427
VARCOE, J. R., 3797
VELDE, R. W., 81, 119
VENTERS, K. R., 608
VENTIERA, C. A., 2263
VESTAL, A. D., 2775
VETRI, D. R., 2738
VETTER, G., 2776
VINES, K. N., 53, 278, 333, 1303, 1344, 1354, 1428
VIRTUE, M. B., 124, 411, 2783
VOLPE, J. A., 3008, 3014
VOM BAUR, F. T., 2757L
VON PFEIL, H. P., 4875
VONN KANN, C. E., 586
VOORHEES, T., 108, 123, 2458
VORENBERG, E. W., 4314
VORENBERG, J., 3884, 3904, 4314

WADLINGTON, W., 123
WAGNER, R. C.,   2515, 2661
WAHL, A., 4473
WAHL, D., 2167
WAHL, J. J., 3567
WAITE, M. R., 1924
WALBERT, D. F., 2714
WALCK, R. E., 3226
WALD, P. M., 123, 3326, 3391, 3552, 3596-3597, 3953
WALD, R. L., 3953
WALDMAN, L., 2265
WALDRON, E., 855, 1429
WALKER, D. H., 1371
WALKER, O., 786
WALKER, R. L., 2878
WALLACE, J. A., 965
WALLACE, J. E., 2757g
WALLER, J. A., 3014
WALSH, J. T., 557
WALSH, L. E., 4472, 4528
WALTHER, D. L., 4241
WALTZ, J. R., 3780, 4644
WAMBACH, R. F., 324
WANG, J. C., 3322
WAREN, A. D., 2599

WARNER, V. O., 3359, 3792
WARREN, D., 803
WARREN, E., (see also Subject Index under "United States - Warren Court") 100, 149, 160, 171, 258, 268, 334-339, 1340, 1352, 1672, 1939-41, 2413, 2757n, 2870, 2879, 3398, 4272, 4729
WARREN, L. C., Jr., 1040
WARREN, M. Q., 3200, 4281
WASBY, S. L., 340, 1414, 1483-1484
WASSERSTROM, R. A., 1319
WATERMAN, S. R., 85, 1112
WATSON, A. S., 80, 1704
WATSON, R. A., 1448, 1570-1573
WATTS, L. P., 3477
WATTS, R. N., 2289
WAUGH, A. P., 1942, 2094
WAUGH, J. D., 4991
WAYBRIGHT, R. J., 2880
WEAVER, M. R., 1430
WEBER, M., 1413
WEBER, R. H., 4472
WECHSLER, H., 247, 341, 1431, 4342, 4528
WECKSTEIN, D. T., 1689, 1704, 2757g
WEESE, S. H., 3012
WEICK, P. C., 4645
WEIGEL, S. A., 4535
WEIL, F. B., 2726a
WEINGARTEN, K., 965
WEINGLASS, L. I., 3971
WEINSHIENK, Z. L., 81
WEINSTEIN, D., 4315
WEINSTEIN, J. B., 107, 932, 967-968, 1943
WEINSTEIN, N., 1448
WEINTRAUB, R. J., 100
WEIR, J. T., 86
WEIS, C. W., 4312
WEIS, J. F., Jr., 1782
WEISMAN, P., 3523
WEISS, E., 790
WEISTART, J. C., 1700
WEISZ, A. J., 506
WELLS, K. R., 3400
WELPTON, S. S., Jr., 2757p
WELSH, L. M., 471

A NOTE ON THE USE OF THIS INDEX

This index of general subject headings, political divisions,
associations and organizations, is in one alphabetical arrangement
with the following exception; where a hierarchy of political
divisions or a numerical arrangement seemed proper, such was used:
thus, APPELLATE COURTS, General, Federal, State, County, City, and
Foreign: and, UNITED STATES - Courts of Appeals - 1st, 2d, 3d,
etc.

Where information is sought on a specific federal court, find
that court as a subhead of UNITED STATES, i.e., Court of Claims,
Courts of Appeals, District Courts, Supreme Court, etc.

Where individual states are subdivisions of a general subject
heading, the District of Columbia and Puerto Rico have been entered
as if they were states.

New York City excepted, all cities are entered as a subdivision of the state of which they are a part.

INDEX

reports; judicial conferences
and councils.
ANTITRUST CASES, See also Protracted
Litigation, 301
APPELLATE BRIEFS, NON-PRINTED, 3182
APPELLATE COURTS, See also sub-
division "Courts" under individual
states.
(General)
75, 130, 145, 164, 217, 223,
230-232, 315, 384, 1360-61,
1364, 3088
Amicus curiae, 3082
Attorney pools for case
screening, 3085
Awards in personal injury
actions, 3093
Caseloads, 3025
Civil appeals, 3041, 3120
Compared, 3041
Criminal, 214
Criminal appeals, 3041
Delay in the courts, 3025,
3097, 3124, 3127-28, 3132,
3158, 3193
Criminal cases, 3125
English and American
compared, 3070, 3117
Errors, harmless and harmful,
3109a
Frivolous appeals, 3068
Internal operating procedures,
3020
Judicial innovation, 3076
Judicial statistics, 2186
Late docketing, 3027
Llewellyn, Karl N., 3108
Model system, 3158
Non-printed briefs on appeal,
3182
Oral argument, 3045, 3082
Predictability, 1419
Prehearing procedures, 3042,
3097, 3124
Process in criminal cases,
3082
Reckonability of appeals, 1404
Right of appeal, 3147, 3157
Sitting in divisions, 3053,
3132
Sitting in divisions (States),
3026

Staff research attorneys,
3169-74
Statistical reporting, 2103
Statistical standards, 3019
Torts, overruling outmoded
precedents, 3075
(Federal)
See also National Court of
Appeals, 284, 300-321,
326, 3041, 3134, 3195
Attorney pools for case
screening, 3085
Criminal cases, 300
Current problems, 3166
Delay in the courts, 3144,
3150
Differentiated case manage-
ment, 3191
Eighth circuit court of
appeals, 3039
Ninety-day rule for
opinions, 3131
Prospective overruling,
3047a
Revision of structure, 3088
Structure and procedure,
3111
(States, General)
Comparative data on supreme
courts, 3138
Oral argument, 3046
Workload, 3143
(States)
Alabama, 3058, 3123
Arizona, 3031
Arkansas, 3034
California, 472, 478, 480-
81, 503, 3037, 3062,
3068, 3084, 3805, 3137,
3152, 3156, 3157a, 3159-
60, 3164
Colorado, 3179
Florida, 1409, 3174
Illinois, 3085, 3130,
3145, 3171, 3175, 3182,
3184
Iowa, 3181
Kansas, 3054
Maine, 749b
Michigan, 3085, 3090,
3165, 3168
Minnesota, 821, 3085,
3162, 3194

Los Angeles, California, 2803
New York City, 2803
Philadelphia, Pennsylvania,
2803, 2877
San Francisco, California,
2803
ARCHITECTURE PLANNING RESEARCH
ASSOCIATES, 2379
ARDEN HOUSE CONFERENCE, 1965, See
American Assembly
ARIZONA
Administrative director of the
courts, 2297
Appellate review of sentences,
4484, 4500
Citizens' Association on Arizona
Courts, 1465
Contempt powers, 3975
Courts
Appellate, 435-437
Juvenile, 396
Limited Jurisdiction, 435-437
Modern Courts Amendment, 437
Supreme, 437
Judicial Conference, 1992
Judicial Conference of City
Magistrates, 1720
Phoenix
Calendaring system, 2027
University, 436
ARKANSAS
Bar Association, 438
Citizens' Advisory Conference
on the Arkansas Judicial
System, 517
Constitutional Commission, 448
Constitutional Convention, 439-
440
Constitutional Revision Study
Commission, 441-43
Judicial Branch Committee
Report, 443
Courts, 438-50
Corporation, 450
Court of Appeals, 440
Family, 438, 443, 445, 448
Judiciary, 443-445
Justice of the Peace, 438,
443, 448, 450
Mayors' Courts, 450
Municipal, 438, 443, 445, 448
Office of the Executive
Secretary, 447

Traffic, 444
Criminal Discovery Act, 3656
Criminal justice standards,
3208
Judicial Department, 1946,
3026
Judiciary Commission, 445-47,
449
Legal aid system, 3826a
Sheriff's Office, 1825
Speedy trial standards
compared with A.B.A., 4220
ARRAIGNMENT PROCEDURES
Los Angeles Municipal Court,
507
ARRAIGNMENTS
(State)
Ohio, 1060
Pennsylvania (Federal
Rule Compared), 1105
(Cities)
New York City, 971
Part 30, 978
Procedures during
civil disorders, 996
ARREST
Citation in lieu of, 3424
Citizen arrest, 3441
Decision process, 3438
Due process problems, 3364
Judges' procedures in
charging, 3445
Mass arrests during riots,
3411a
Night-arraignment procedures,
3452
Police
function, 3416
principles, 3437
role of, 3438
Pre-arraignment interrogation,
restrictions, 3429
Pre-arraignment procedure,
3418, 3419, 3420, 3422,
3426, 3476
Conflicting rights, 3455
Effect on conviction, 3458
Evidence and due process
requirements, 3454
Justices of the peace,
3478
Preliminary hearing, See
pre-arraignment procedure,
supra

New York, 950
Ohio, 1062
COURT ADMINISTRATIVE REPORTS,
See also Judicial Conferences
and Councils
(Federal)
Administrative Office of the
U. S. Courts, 1983-85
Judicial Conference of Senior
Circuit Judges, 1983
(State)
Alabama, 1944
Alaska, 1945
Arkansas, 1946
California, 1947
Colorado, 1948
Connecticut, 1949-50
Delaware, 1951
District of Columbia, 1952-53
Florida, 1954
Georgia, 1955
Hawaii, 1956
Idaho, 1957
Illinois, 1958-60
Iowa, 1961
Kansas, 1962
Maryland, 1964
Massachusetts, 1965
Michigan, 1966
Minnesota, 1967
New Jersey, 1968-70
New Mexico, 1971
North Carolina, 1972-73
Ohio, 1974
Oklahoma, 1975
Oregon, 1976
Pennsylvania, 1977-80
Puerto Rico, 1981
Tennessee, 1982
Vermont, 1986-87
Virginia, 1988
Washington, 1989
Wisconsin, 1990
(Counties)
Los Angeles County, 1963
COURT ADMINISTRATORS, See Courts,
Administrative Officers
COURT CASELOADS, See Caseloads
COURT COMMISSIONERS,
208, 215, 248, 262, 271
COURT CONGESTION, See Delay in
the Courts

COURT COSTS, See also Court
Financing; In forma pauperis;
Indigent Litigants, Civil
Cases; Judicare Systems.
(General)
2300, 2305, 2350
Appellate litigation, 3156
Attorney's fees, 2330, 2359
Direct costs, 2345
Economics of law enforcement
2348
Error costs, 2345
Fee shifting, 2366
LEAA and Census Bureau
Study, 2368
Losing party, 2332
Treble damage price-fixing
cases, 2335
Waiver by court for
indigents, 2292, 2353
(Federal), 2329
U. S. District Courts, 2344
(States)
Alaska, 2294
California, 2304
Colorado, 2306-10
Connecticut, 2352
Illinois, 2333, 2355, 2362
Kansas, 2328
Louisiana, 2363
Maine, 2336
Massachusetts, 2361
Michigan, 2365
Nevada, 871
New Hampshire, 2291
New Jersey, 1823
New York, 956, 2339-41
North Carolina, 1008, 1012-
1013
Oklahoma, 1079
Oregon, 1088
Texas, 2342, 2364
Washington, 1256
Wisconsin, 2372-73
(Cities)
Cleveland, Ohio, 2319
New York, 2312
New York (Criminal Court),
2299, 2343
(Foreign)
England, 2317, 2330, 2359-
60, 2795, 2821

Standards
  ABA, 3197
  Analyzed, 3274
  And Goals, 3328
  Appellate court
    implementation, 3300
  Compared, 3204, 3227
  Described, 3321
  For criminal trials, 3315
  History of project, 3244,
    3294
  Implementation, 3256
  Individually discussed,
    3331
  Project on, 3202
  Reforms in, 3272
  Report on, 3206
  Texts, 3330
  Training programs, 3257
  Weaknesses, 3242
Alternatives to imprisonment,
  4272
American system analyzed,
  3269-3269b
British and U. S. systems
  compared, 3192, 3304
Burger and Warren Courts
  compared, 1408
Citizen participation, 3280
Comparisons between English
  and American system, 3290,
  3297
Court costs and employment
  data, 2368
Criticism of system, 3248
Decentralizing and
  decriminalization, 4259
Defendant's view, 3251-3252
Deterrent effectiveness of
  sanctions, 4411
Dictionaries, 3235
Education programs develop-
  ment, 3363
Equality, 3245
Essays, 3296
Evaluation programs, 3384-
  3388
Hypocrisy and maladministration
  in, 3352
Individual rights, 3286
Information and statistics
  systems, 2143

LEAA Directory of
  Automated Information
  Systems, 2194
Law and order system,
  4394
Manpower requirements,
  3259
Minority communities,
  3351, 3361, 3398
Morality issues in,
  3296
National Advisory
  Commission on Criminal
  Justice Standards and
  Goals: Courts, 900
National policy,
  proposals for change,
  3258
Operations research,
  3350
Principles, 3281, 3362
Project crossroads,
  cost/benefit analysis,
  4273-4274
Public service
  responsibility, 3298
Purposes, 3247
Reform, 3239, 3246, 3276,
  3289, 3333, 3362, 3373
Removal of victimless
  crimes from system,
  4262, 4264, 4265
Roscoe Pound on, 3282
Scientific techniques
  in, 3336
Surveys, inventory, 3387
System analyzed, 3299
Systems planning, 3314,
  3317, 3347
Task Force Report on
  system, 3377
(Federal)
  Poverty and administratior
    of, 3946
  Pro se litigation, 3957
  Representation of
    indigent defendants
    at every stage, 3948
  Rights of accused,
    3262-3263
  U. S. Supreme Court,
    1353

(States)
  California, 4219
  North Carolina, 4210
(Counties)
  Cook County, Illinois,
    Efforts to stem backlog, 4180
  New York,
    Proposals for reducing, 4204
(Cities)
  New York, 4196, 4202, 4214
    Brooklyn plan for improve-
      ments, 4166
    "Instant" court reforms, 4197
    Steps to alleviate backlog,
      4205
  San Francisco, 4215
DELAY IN THE COURTS, See also
  Arbitration and award; Assignment
  of cases; Caseflow management;
  Caseloads, Weighted; Delay in
  criminal trials; Settlement;
  Trial calendars; subhead "Delay
  in the Courts" under individual
  states.
  (General)
    4, 31, 41, 49, 67, 93, 116,
    1864, 1868, 1927-28, 3332
    Attorney's lack of trial
      ability, 2891
    Attorney's negligence, 2885
    Civil and criminal, 2833
    Computer analysis, 2128
    Court caused, 2891
    Expansion of criminal
      defendants' rights as
      cause, 1321
    Gaming theory of advocacy,
      2879
    Insurance companies, 2783
    Measures to combat, 106
    Pettifoggery, 2884
    Remedies, 2810, 2836, 2860,
      2862-63, 2892, 3132, 3139,
      3144, 3189
    Split trials, 2809, 2893-94
    Summary of arguments, 2847
    Trial courts, 2778-2894
  (Federal)
    159, 222, 2779, 3133, 3150
    Split trials, 2837
  (States)
    See subdivision "Delay in
    the Courts" under individual
    states.

DELINQUENTS, See Juvenile
  Courts.
DENMARK
  Penal system compared with
    England, 3356
DERELICTS
  Arrest as unnecessary, 4291
DETENTION
  See arrest.
DETENTION CENTERS
  (Cities)
    New York, 1678
DETERRENCE
  Effect of corrections on,
    3200, 3242
DETROIT, See Michigan.
DEVIANT BEHAVIOR
  Decriminalization, 4262,
    4264, 4265, 4279
    Statistics, 4280
  Diversion from criminal
    process, 4301, 4303, 4316
DICTIONARIES
  Criminal justice glossary,
    3235
DISCIPLINE
  See Lawyers - Disciplinary
    Action.
DISCOVERY
  See Pretrial procedure -
    Discovery.
DISCRETION
  See Judicial Discretion.
DISCRETIONARY JUSTICE, 3271
  Police, 3472
DISCRETIONARY REVIEW
  Virginia, 1230
DISCRIMINATION, See also
  Racism.
  Bail availability, 3568
  Criminal justice system,
    3266
  Police exercise of, 3472
DISOBEDIENCE, See Riots.
DISRUPTION IN CRIMINAL TRIALS
  See Misconduct in criminal
    trials.
DISSENTING BEHAVIOR, See also
  Judicial Decision Making.
  North Dakota, 1405
DISTRICT ATTORNEYS
  Colorado
    Compensation, 3699

Montana
  Discretion in prosecutions,
    3700
New York, 967
DISTRICT COURTS, See United States
  - District Courts.
DISTRICT OF COLUMBIA
Agency for criminal law reform,
  572
Bail changes after King's
  assassination, 3405
Bail project, 3546-47, 3567,
  3571
Bail Reform Act, 3406, 3548-49,
  3590
Bar Association, 3547, 4090
Committee on the Administration
  of Justice under Emergency
  Conditions, 3405
Court Management Study, 564-567,
  581
Courts, 120
  Appellate, 571, 581
  Conciliation, 579
  Court of General Sessions
    Criminal Assignment Court,
      2040
  District Court, 560
  D. C. Court of Appeals,
    564, 566, 568, 571, 581
  Federal, 564-566, 581, 583
  Federal/Local Relationship,
    558
  General Sessions, 564-566,
    572, 579-581, 583
  Juvenile, 564-566, 573, 581
  Landlord and tenant, 569
  Nixon Plan, 559
  Reorganization Act, 558, 561-
    562, 568, 571, 573, 575-577,
    582, 584-585, 587, 1888
  Small Claims, 377, 391, 570,
    579
  Superior Court, 559, 586
Crime problems, 3389
Criminal clerk's office, 581
Criminal justice
  Custodial police interrogation,
    3446
  Pre-arraignment project, 3434
Criminal Procedure Act of 1970,
  561, 573, 575-577, 584-586

Delay in the Courts, 2779
Home Rule Act, 1458
Joint Committee on Judicial
  Administration, 1952
Judicial Council, 3406, 3548
Judicial Council Committee
  on the Administration of
  Justice, 564-566
Legal Aid Agency, 572, 577
Police handling of
  alcoholics, 4289
Pretrial detention problems,
  3561
Preventive detention
  practices, 3538, 3541
Prosecution and defense
  functions, minimum
  standards, 3735
Reorganization Act, See
  Courts, supra
Sentencing procedures, 4451
United States Attorney, 574
DISTRICT OF COLUMBIA COURT
REFORM AND CRIMINAL PROCEDURE
ACT, 3541
DISTRICT OF COLUMBIA CRIME
ACT, 3538
DIVERSION FROM CRIMINAL PROCESS
Addict treatment before
  conviction, 4244
Alcoholics, 4312
Alternative forms of
  prosecution, 4288
Derelicts in skid row
  areas, 4291
Deviant behavior and
  victimless crime offenders
  4250, 4301, 4303, 4316
Drug addicts, alcoholics,
  and others, 4278, 4299
Early diversion, pros and
  cons, 4314
Effect of Court Reform Act
  on D. C., 4451
Employment project for
  defendants, 4283, 4298
Family violence, 4294, 4296
In rural communities, 4252
Judicial discretion,
  innovations in, 4432
Juvenile delinquency
  prevention program, 4300

Criminal justice standards, 3211
Dade County
  Bar Association, 1715
  Criminal Justice Survey, 589
  Diversion from criminal process,
    4295
Defense pro se, nature of right,
  3823
Delay in the courts, 3174, 2880
Government study committee, 606
Government's informer privilege
  in criminal cases, 4041
Judges
  Voting behavior, 1305
Judicial council, 588, 597, 1995
Miami Police Department
  Videotaped confession, 2248
Post-conviction relief, 4603
Pre-trial conference in criminal
  cases, 3653
Rules of criminal procedure, 3598
Sentencing and recidivism, 4351
Sheriff's Office, 1825
Speedy trial, 4222
State Courts Administrator, 1954
University
  Public administration clearing
    service, 600-601
FORD FOUNDATION
Publications, 4672
FOURTEENTH AMENDMENT, See United
  States - Constitution -
  Amendments.
FRANCE
Courts, 3
  Administrative, 1052
Judicial conflict of interests,
  1699
Judicial selection, 1519, 1536,
  1547, 1554
Pre-trial procedures compared
  with American, 3669
Preventive detention practice,
  3579
Prosecutor's discretionary
  power, 3741
Trial in absentia, 3973
FRANKFURTER, JUSTICE F., 1303
FREE PRESS-FAIR TRIAL, See Fair
  Trial-Free Press
FREE SPEECH
  (States)
  Florida, 1409

FREEDOM OF INFORMATION
  Rights of researchers, 3338
FREUND REPORT, See National
  Court of Appeals
FREUND STUDY GROUP, See
  National Court of Appeals

GAMBLING
  As source of state revenues,
    4256
  Legalized, social and
    economic consequences,
    4315
  Public attitudes toward,
    3199
GEORGIA
  Administrative Office of the
    Courts, 1955
  Atlanta-Fulton County
    Citizens' Advisory
    Committee, 621
  Bar Association, 612
  Campaign Disclosure Act of
    1974, 1648a
  Chief Justice's Message,
    609, 618, 623
  Citizens' Conference on
    the Courts, 619
  Courts
    (General), 613
    Atlanta-Fulton Counties,
      621
    Bibb County,
      Civil Court and Court
      of Ordinary, 626
    Chatham County, 627
    City, 615
    City of Columbus, 625
    County, 615
    Court of Appeals
      (History), 622
    Justice of the Peace,
      617
    Juvenile, 379, 626
      (Fulton County), 620
    Macon County
      Municipal Courts, 626
    Muscogee County, 625
    State, 626
    Superior, 617, 626
    Supreme, 612, 624

ADMINISTRATION OF CRIMINAL JUSTICE

Royal Commission on Assizes and
Quarter Sessions, 55
GREATER SAN FRANCISCO CHAMBER OF
COMMERCE, See California.
GUIDE TO SMALL CLAIMS COURTS IN
THE UNITED STATES, See also
Small Claims Courts, 363.
GUILTY PLEAS, 3348
  Burger Court, 1408
  Charge reduction to obtain,
    3615
  Coercion to obtain, 3603
  Compromises by prosecutor to
    obtain, 3615
  Conflicting pleas, problems
    of, 3623
  Constitutional infirmities
    notwithstanding, 3602
  Constitutionality, 3605-06,
    3614
  Equivocal guilty pleas,
    acceptance of, 3610
  Finality, questions of, 3611
  Indigent defendant's waiver
    of counsel, 3598
  Lawyer's function following,
    3628
  Michigan
    Trial court procedure for
      acceptance, 3630
  Pre-sentence withdrawal in
    federal courts, 3629
  Review of convictions obtained
    by, 3602
  Right of appeal, 3632
  Role of defense counsel in
    decision, 3760
  Standards (ABA), 3601, 3613
  Standards relating to, 3203b
  Supreme Court's decisions,
    3633
  Understanding by defendant,
    3636
  Voluntariness
    and accuracy issues, 3609,
      3611
    Trial judge's acceptance,
      3636
  Waivers involved in, 3603
  Weakness, 3604
GUNS, See Firearms.

HABEAS CORPUS
  (General), 123, 147
    Civil remedies of
      prisoners released on,
      4601
    Civil Rights Act as more
      appropriate, 4588
    Defense of writ, 4641
    Duality of power and
      liberty, 4608
    Federal and state, 4579,
      4596, 4617, 4629
    Finality of state court
      decisions recommended,
      4613
    Grounds for grant of
      writ, 4642
    History, 4606
    Indigent prisoner's
      right, 4626
    Limitations, 4645, 4650
    Retroactivity illusion,
      4609, 4612
  (Federal)
    154, 214, 219, 277, 1781
    Applications, 4566, 4646
    Burdens on federal
      courts, 4631
    Constitutional origin,
      4619
    Erosion of state power
      over criminal justice,
      4592
    Exhaustion of state
      remedies, 4611, 4631
    Federal and state cases,
      4638
    Finality of state
      decisions, 4569
    Impact on state trial
      procedures, 4610
    Limitations on
      successive applications,
      4648
    Procedure and preliminary
      requirements, 4598
    Reforms, symposium, 4640
    Scope, 4583
    State convictions
      corrected by, 4567,
      4568

State criminal procedure,
4635, 4636, 4637
State fact-finding, treatment
of, 4585
State prisoners, 4567, 4569,
4572, 4574, 4584, 4586, 4593,
4600, 4602, 4639, 4649
Statutory and case law, 4634
Unjustified expansion of
litigation under, 4580
(State, General)
280, 4616
(States)
Minnesota, 236
New York, 951
Texas, 1190-91, 4577
Utah, 4594
Virginia, 1237
(Foreign)
European alternatives, 4573
HABEAS CORPUS ACT OF 1867, 4606
HANGING, See also Capital
Punishment; 3198
HARLEM, See New York (City)
HARMLESS ERROR
Misconduct by federal
prosecutors, 3740
Prosecutor's failure to
disclose as, 3710
HARVARD STUDENT DISTRICT ATTORNEY
PROJECT, 3704
HAWAII
Administrative Director of the
Courts, 629
Budget and Finance Commission
on Children and Youth, 632
Citizens' Conference, 630
Citizens' Conference on the
Administration of Justice,
628
Constitutional Convention
Studies, 631
Courts, 634
District court reorganization,
633
Family, 370, 632
Juvenile, 370, 635
Supreme, 634
Family Court Act, 629
Honolulu
Calendaring System, 2027
Council of Social Agencies,
635

Judges, 1295
Judicial Decision Making,
1398
Judiciary Department, 1956
Montana's constitution
compared, 848
Screening and diversionary
program, 4268
HEBREW BIBLE, See Pentateuch
HOLLAND
Penal system compared with
England, 3356
HOMOSEXUALITY, See Deviant
Behavior.
HOUSING AND ECONOMIC DEVELOP-
MENT LAW PROJECT, 3937

IDAHO
Bar Committee on Lower
Court Reform, 642
Citizens' Conference, 636
Constitutional Revision
Commission, 637
Courts, 639
Administrative Office,
639, 643
Limited Jurisdiction,
639-640, 642
Magistrate System, 640,
643
Small Claims, 643
Trial, 643
Two-level System, 643
Judicial Council, 639, 643
Law Enforcement Planning
Commission, 638
Legislative Council, 636,
639
Secretary of State, 641
Supreme Court
Administrative Assistant
1957
IDENTIFICATION
Line-ups, 3442, 3679
Pre-trial, 3457a, 3678
Psychological problems,
3307
ILLINOIS
Administrative Office of
the Court, 1958-59,
2225-27, 2322

JUDICIAL ADMINISTRATION
  (General)
    Demystification, 2429
    Training programs in
      educational institutions,
      1844
    (States)
      Georgia, 616
      Hawaii, 628
      New York, 950, 955
      Ohio, 1064
      Virginia, 1232
JUDICIAL ADMINISTRATORS, See
  Administrative Judges; Courts,
  Administrative Officers.
JUDICIAL ARTICLE, See
  Constitutions, State - Judicial
  Article.
JUDICIAL BEHAVIOR, See Behavioral
  Science; Judges - Decision
  Making: Voting Behavior of
  Judges.
JUDICIAL CAMPAIGNS, See Judicial
  Ethics.
JUDICIAL CODE OF 1911, 267
JUDICIAL CONFERENCE OF THE UNITED
  STATES, See also United States
  - Judicial Conference of Senior
  Circuit Judges.
  1603, 1681, 1713, 1840, 1855,
  1932, 1941, 1983, 1999, 2367,
  2396, 2573, 2763, 3067, 3657,
  4113-14
  Advisory Committee on Civil
    Rules, 2762
  Circuit Judicial Council,
    1601-02
  Committee on Court Administration,
    1602
  Judicial ethics, See Judicial
    ethics.
  Publications, 4686-4687
JUDICIAL CONFERENCE ON CRITICAL
  PROBLEMS OF THE LOWER COURT
  SYSTEM, 75, 382
JUDICIAL CONFERENCES AND COUNCILS,
  See also Court Administrative
  Reports.
  (General), 165
    Circuit Courts of Appeal
      First Circuit, 229

(Federal)
  Circuit Courts of Appeal
    Second Circuit, 3684
    Eighth Circuit, 4623
(States)
  Alabama, 412
  Alaska, 1991, 2294
  Arizona, 1992
  California, 110-111,
    458-463, 478, 485,
    1462, 1835-36, 1947,
    1993, 2031, 2034-37,
    2107, 2111-12, 2216,
    2760, 2801-03, 3036,
    3137
  Connecticut, 1994
  Florida, 588, 597, 1995
  Idaho, 639
  Illinois, 1996, 2395
  Indiana, 686
  Kansas, 1997
  Kentucky, 1998
  Louisiana, 740, 2000
  Massachusetts, 2001
  Michigan, 2002
  Minnesota, 817, 2003
  Missouri, 2004-05
  New Jersey, 883, 2007
  New Mexico, 896, 2008
  New York, 902, 911,
    1906-09, 2009-11,
    2085-86, 2264, 2340-
    2340a, 2402, 2754,
    2835a-b
  North Carolina, 1020,
    2012-13
  North Dakota, 2014
  Ohio, 1062, 2015-16
  Oregon, 1089, 2017
  Pennsylvania, 1895
  Rhode Island, 2018
  South Carolina, 1152-53
  Texas, 1203, 1207, 2019
  Utah, 1218
  Vermont, 1223, 2020
  Virginia, 1228, 2021-22,
    3189
  Washington, 1254, 2023
  West Virginia, 2024
  Wisconsin, 1270, 1272,
    1278, 1740, 2025-26

Judges, Conflicts of Interest;
Judicial Elections.
(General)
    80, 1605, 1610, 1629, 1671,
    1674, 1687-88, 1700, 1704,
    1707
    Brandeis, Justice Louis B.,
        1639
    Burger's (Chief Justice W.)
        Leadership, 1672
    Canons, See American Bar
        Association - Canons of
        Judicial Ethics
    Extra-judicial Activity,
        1664, 1703
    Extra-judicial Compensation,
        1601-02, 1703
    Federal Disqualification Act,
        1697
    Judicial Campaigns, 1614
        Dade County, Florida, 1715
    Judicial Qualification Act of
        1970, 2469, 2507
    Law school curriculums, 2884
    Rehnquist's (Justice W.)
        Comments, 1684
    Warren's (Chief Justice E.)
        Leadership, 1672
(Federal)
    1604, 1672, 1693
    Extra-judicial activity,
        1712-1713
    Financial disclosure, 1712-13
    Rehnquist (Justice) in Laird
        v. Tatum, 1662, 1672
(States, General)
    Canons, 1606
(States)
    Georgia
        Judicial Campaigns, 1648a
    Illinois, 1621, 1658
    Michigan, 1654
    South Carolina
        Stock Ownership, 1660
JUDICIAL INDEPENDENCE
    California, 1835
JUDICIAL LAW MAKING, 1356, 1360,
    1364, 1416
    England, 1386
JUDICIAL LEGISLATIVE PROGRAMS,
    2463

JUDICIAL MANAGEMENT, See
    Courts, Administration;
    Courts, Administrative
    Officers.
JUDICIAL MANPOWER
    (Federal)
        District Court Judge-
            ships, 2092
    (State)
        New York, 2085
    (Cities)
        Philadelphia,
            Pennsylvania, 2069,
            2072
JUDICIAL OPINIONS, See also
    Judges, Trial - Written
    Opinions; Judicial
    Opinions, Publications;
    3078-79
    Appellate, 3018, 3023,
        3077
    As historical source
        material, 3115
    As literature, 3121
    Definitive opinions, 3030
    Law clerk's primer, 3066
    Memorandum decisions, 3081
    Model rule, 3018
    Reduction in number and
        length, 3132
    Selectivity, 3098, 3101
    Style, 3029
    Unpublished appellate
        opinions, 3040, 3045,
        3069
    (Federal)
    Assignment practices of
        Chief Justice Warren,
        3110
    Ninety-day rule, 3131
    Second circuit court of
        appeals, 3083
    U. S. Courts of Appeals,
        3146a
    (States, General)
        Statistics, 3143
    (States)
        Arkansas, 3034, 3102
        California, 3101, 3106
        New York, 3032
        Ohio, 1912

Reform by diversion, 4261
Rehabilitation programs, 3384
Removal from criminal process, 4296
Royal Oak, Michigan
  Volunteer program, 4270
Task Force Report, 3390
(States)
Ohio, 1063
South Carolina, 1155-1156
(Cities)
Philadelphia, Pennsylvania, 1108
JUVENILE JUSTICE
Burger Court, 1408
Right to Treatment, 929
(Cities)
New York, 986
(State)
New York, 965
  (Children in Court and Institution), 960
Wisconsin, 1284

KANSAS
Bar Association of the State, 705
Chief Justice's Annual Report, 711-711b
Citizens' Committee on Constitutional Revision, 715
Citizens' Conference on Modernization of the Kansas Courts, 705
Courts
  Appellate, 718
  Courts of Appeals (History), 717
  District, 712, 720
  Justice of the Peace, 719
  Kansas City
    Court of Appeals (History), 721
    Police Court, 716
  Municipal, 707
  Small Claims, 373, 713
  Supreme, 714
    Judicial Conduct Code Adopted, 711b
  Trial, 718
Defense pro se, 3909

Delay in the courts, 2848, 2861
Judicial Council, 1997
Judicial Study Advisory Committee, 711b, 718, 1506
Legislative Council, 719
Office of Judicial Administrator, 1962
Plea bargaining case history 3622
Post-conviction remedies, 4589
Reception and Diagnostic Center, 4375
State protection of right to speedy trial, 4227
Ten court reform measures graphically displayed, 709
University
  School of Law Trial Judge Clerkship Program, 1774
Weighted Caseload System, 708
KEETON-O'CONNELL PLAN, See Automobile Accident Compensation.
KENT STATE UNIVERSITY, See Ohio.
KENTUCKY
Commission on Law Enforcement and Crime Prevention 723
Constitution Revision Assembly, 733
Courts, 722
  Circuit, 726-727
  Criminal, 735
  Family, 730, 734
  Fiscal, 732
  Justice, 729
  Justices of the Peace, 383, 731
  Juvenile, 730
  Quarterly, 729
Crime Commission, 724
Criminal Justice Standards 3215
Department of Law, 725
Legislative Research Commission, 726-733, 1587, 2831, 2962

Bar Association, 1112, 1119-1121
  Orphans' Court Referendum, 1119
  "Project Constitution", 1118,
    1121, 1136, 1142
  Special Committee on Project
    Constitution, 1118, 1121,
    1136
Bar Institute, 1748
Chief and Board of Magistrates,
  1096
Chief Justice's Addresses to
  State Bar Association, 1113-
  1113b
Citizens' Committee on the
  Modernization of Pennsylvania's
  Judicial System, 1112
Committee for Information on the
  Judicial Process, 1628
Conference of State Trial Judges,
  1748
Conference of Trial Court Judges,
  1785
Constitution of 1968, 1107
Constitutional Convention, 1967/68,
  1123-1126
  Preparatory Committee, 1124-1125
Courts
  Administrative Judge, 1125
  Allegheny County, 1138
    Common Pleas, 1095, 1811, 1915-
      1916, 1978-1979
    Family, 1107, 1141
  Appellate, 1097, 1111
  Appellate Court Jurisdiction
    Act of 1970, 1098
  Commonwealth, 1098, 1102, 1111
  Commonwealth Court Act and
    Rules, 1122
  Criminal, 1110
  "Depreciation of Precedent"
    Doctrine Discussed, 1143
  District Justice System
    Described, 1109, 1114
  Judicial Inquiry and Review
    Board, 1140
  Justice of the Peace, 1099,
    1109, 1133
  Magistrates', 1128
  Minor Court System Discussed,
    1112, 1116
  Orphans' Court, 1115, 1119
  Philadelphia, 1134
    Common Pleas, 1117, 1873, 2049

Magistrates' Courts,
  1118
Municipal Court Criminal
  Case Processing, 2060
Small Claims, 377, 392,
  1137
Traffic, 1096
Philadelphia and Allegheny
  Court Consolidation, 1130
Pittsburgh
  Common Pleas, 2123
  Housing Court, 1100
Prothonotaries' Offices,
  1111
Publication of Official
  Reports, 1111
Small Claims, 1099, 1133,
  1137
State Court Administrator,
  1125
Superior, 1098, 1111
Supreme, 1098, 1104, 1111,
  1133, 1139, 1143, 1332,
  1808
  Videotape Depositions,
    2268
Three-Tier Structure
  Discussed, 1143
Trial Court Administrator,
  1125
Crime Commission Comprehensive
  Plan, 1127
Delay in the Courts, 1110,
  2778, 2792, 2883
  Allegheny County, 2124
  Auto Accident Cases as
    Cause, 2814
  Philadelphia Common Pleas,
    2049
Department of Justice
  Attorney General's Report
    on Magisterial System,
    1128
  Bureau of Criminal Justice
    Statistics, 1129
District Attorney
  Annual Report (1969), 1110
District Criminal Justice
  System Described, 1105
Economy League, Inc., 1811
General Assembly
  Joint State Government
    Commission, 1130

REVENUE SHARING
(State)
  Texas, 1212
RHODE ISLAND
  Chief Justice, 1149
  Comprehensive Law Enforcement
    Plan (1970), 1150
  Constitutional Convention, 1147
  Courts (Generally), 1146
    Court Administrator, 1148
    District, 1145, 1149
    Family, 1145
    Probate, 1145, 1151-1151a
  Governor
    Committee on Crime, Delinquency
      and Criminal Administration,
      1150
  Judges (Generally), 1149
  Judicial Council, 2018
  Judicial System Discussed. 1145
  University
    Bureau of Government Research
      1151-1151a
  Workmen's Compensation Commission,
    1145
RIGHT TO COUNSEL
  (General)
    3279, 3296, 3308, 3316, 3326,
    3364, 3370
    Assigned counsel and defender
      systems explained, 3924-25
    At pretrial photographic
      display, 3914
    Civil commitment, survey and
      proposal, 3791
    Computer prediction of cases
      applied, 1366
    Constitutional justification
      and right to waive, 3823
    Constitutional right, scope,
      and systems, 3893
    Critique, 3423
    Determination of financial
      status of indigent criminal
      defendants, 3887
    Due process, effect on, 3832
    During police interrogation,
      3430
    During preliminary hearings,
      3431
    Failure of court to inform
      accused person, 3825

Grand jury proceedings,
  3509, 3522
Hughes Court, 1370
Implementation, lack of,
  3798
Indigent criminal
  defendants in federal
  district courts, 3907
Indigents in civil cases,
  1328, 2349
Ineffective use of
  Miranda, 3446
Methods of providing
  counsel, 3904
Misdemeanor cases, 3910
Preliminary hearing,
  3459, 3460, 3462
Pretrial rights, 3456
Right to waive, right to
  self-representation,
  3908-3909
Supreme Court's extension
  implementation by
  states and localities,
  3873
Symposium, 3942
(Federal), 948
(States)
  California, 3461
  Maine, 748
  Nebraska, 3301
  New York, 948, 951
  Ohio Traffic Offenses,
    1049
  Utah, 3868
RIGHT TO INTERPRETER, 3912
RIGHT TO TREATMENT
  Juveniles, 929
RIGHT OF ACCUSED PERSONS,
  See Defendant's Rights.
RIOTS
  See also Law and Order;
  Violence.
  Advisory Commission report,
    3412
  Causes and Effects, 3409-
    3410
  Civil rights related to,
    3403a, 3415
  Control by military, 3410
  Detroit, 3408
  Effect of firearms control,
    3411

(States)
  Alabama, 4378
  Alaska, 4477
  California, 4327-4330, 4386,
    4440
  Colorado, 4336-4337
  Florida, 4351
  Indiana, 4332
  Kansas, 4375
  Maryland, 4388
  Minnesota, 814
  New Jersey, 4401
  New York, 947, 4402, 4428
  Oklahoma, 1079
  Pennsylvania, 1135
  South Carolina, 1155
  Texas, 4443
  West Virginia, 4384
(Cities)
  District of Columbia, 4451
  New York, 4379, 4383
(Foreign)
  Australia, 4456
  Canada, 4373, 4399
  England, 1310, 4344, 4370,
    4441, 4444-4446, 4448, 4455
SENTENCING INSTITUTE FOR SUPERIOR
  COURT JUDGES, 4410
SENTENCING INSTITUTE, NEW YORK
  UNIVERSITY, 4428
SENTENCING INSTITUTE OF NINTH
  CIRCUIT, 4469
SENTENCING INSTITUTES
  Institute on Sentencing for
    United States District Judges,
    4462-4474
SERVICE OF PROCESS
  Connecticut, 2352
  In lieu of arrest, 3574
  New York City project in lieu
    of arrest, 3450
SETTLEMENT, See also Arbitration
  and Award; Delay in the Courts;
  subhead "Delay in the Courts"
  under individual states.
  (General)
    2785, 2788, 2840, 2881
    Insurance companies, 2806
    Judge's role, 2805
    Personal injury cases, 2788,
      2822a
    Techniques, 2820

(States)
  California, 2760, 2764-
    2765, 2774, 2802
  New Jersey, 2851
(Counties)
  Cook County, Illinois,
    2866
(Foreign)
  England, 2795
SEX CRIMES
  (States)
    California
      Indecent exposure,
      indeterminate
      sentences, 4345
SHERIFFS, SOUTHERN STATES,
  1825
SMALL CLAIMS COURTS
  (General)
    93, 363-364, 373-374,
    377, 391, 405
    Cost, 713
    Guide to United States
      Courts, 363
    State-by-State Table,
      713
  (States)
    California, 468, 470-471,
      474, 487, 497
    District of Columbia,
      391, 570, 579
    Idaho, 643
    Illinois, 671
      (Cook County), 665
    Indiana, 693
    Iowa, 698
    Kansas, 373, 713
    Michigan, 805
    Nebraska, 858-859
    North Carolina, 1007,
      1037
    Ohio, 1065
    Pennsylvania, 1099, 1133,
      1137
    Texas, 1206
    Vermont, 1223
    Washington, 1254
    Wisconsin, 1266
  (Cities)
    Chicago, Illinois, 669
    Denver, Colorado, 521
    New York, 975, 977, 989

STATE BAR ASSOCIATIONS, See as
  subdivision of individual states.
STATE COURT ADMINISTRATORS, See
  Courts, Administrative Officers.
STATE DEPARTMENT CORRECTION ACT,
  118
STATE-FEDERAL COUNCILS, 1853a
STATE-LOCAL RELATIONS
  Criminal justice matters, 3370
STATISTICAL REPORTING, See
  Statistics.
STATISTICS
  (General)
    2151
    Appellate Courts, 2186, 3019
    Cases docketed in United
      States, 3155
  (Federal)
    2198, 2204
  (States)
    Oklahoma, 1913
    Pennsylvania, 1895
  (Cities)
    Denver, Colorado, 2114
STATISTICS, APPELLATE COURTS
  ABA Standards, 2103
STATISTICS, CRIMINAL, See also
  Project SEARCH.
  (General)
    2121, 2139, 2150, 2172-2173,
    2175, 3382-3383a, 4173
    Developments in technology,
      4188
    Disparities in computation of
      sentencing laws and practices,
      4435
    FBI Uniform Crime Reports, 2118,
      2191, 2203
    Federal statistics, 2198, 2204
    International symposium, 2143
    National needs, 2192
    Uniform Criminal Statistics
      Act (1946), 2173
  (States)
    California, 1835, 2108, 2112,
      2181
  (Counties)
    Westchester County, New York,
      2200
  (Cities)
    Chicago, Illinois, 2197
    Detroit, Michigan, 2197
    Los Angeles, California, 2197

    New York, 1001, 2122,
      2197, 4174, 4202
    Philadelphia,
      Pennsylvania, 2197
    Pittsburgh, 3466
STATISTICS, STATE COURTS
  Publications, 2105
STATUTORY CONSTRUCTION
  (General)
    1324
STOP AND FRISK, 3245
STOP AND QUESTION, 3230
SUMMONS, See Process
  Service.
SUPERVISORY POWERS OF
  COURTS, See Courts,
  Supervisory Powers.
SUPERVISORY POWERS OF
  SUPREME COURT, See United
  States - Supreme Court -
  Supervisory Power.
SUPREME COURT, See United
  States - Supreme Court.
SURROGATE'S COURT, See
  Probate Court.
SWEDEN
  Penal system compared
    with England, 3356
SWITZERLAND
  Courts, 1344
SYMPOSIUM ON CRIME AND
  PUNISHMENT IN MINORITY
  COMMUNITIES, 3361

TABLES AND CHARTS
  Children in Court and
    Institutions in New
    York, 960
TANZANIA
  Judicial Selection, 1547
TASMANIA
  Electronic Court
    Reporting, 2272
TAX COURT BILL, 279
TAX COURT OF THE UNITED
  STATES, See United
  States - Tax Court.
TAX COURTS, See subdivision
  "Courts - Tax" under
  individual states;
  United States - Tax Court.